Obsessive-Compulsive Disorder

Contemporary Issues in Treatment

The LEA Series in Personality and Clinical Psychology
Irving B. Weiner, Editor

Obsessive-Compulsive Disorder

Contemporary Issues in Treatment

Edited by

Wayne K. Goodman
University of Florida

Matthew V. Rudorfer
National Institute of Mental Health

Jack D. Maser
University of California, San Diego

LEA

LAWRENCE ERLBAUM ASSOCIATES, PUBLISHERS

2000   Mahwah, New Jersey   London

Lawrence Erlbaum Associates, Inc., Publishers
10 Industrial Avenue
Mahwah, NJ 07430

Cover design by Kathryn Houghtaling Lacey

Library of Congress Cataloging-in-Publication Data

Obsessive-compulsive disorder : contemporary issues in
    treatment / edited by Wayne K. Goodman, Matthew V.
    Rudorfer, Jack D. Maser.
        p. cm.
Includes bibliographical references and index.
ISBN 0-8058-2837-0 (cloth : alk. paper)
1. Obsessive-compulsive disorder—Treatment.
    2. Phobias—Treatment. I. Goodman, W. K. (Wayne K.)
    II. Rudorfer, Matthew V. III. Maser, Jack D.
RC533.O267   1999
616.85′22706—dc21   98-56188
                                                      CIP

Books published by Lawrence Erlbaum Associates are printed
on acid-free paper, and their bindings are chosen for strength
and durability.

Printed in the United States of America
10 9 8 7 6 5 4 3 2 1

Contents

PART V. DRUG AND OTHER SOMATIC TREATMENTS

PART VI. COMBINED TREATMENT

PART VII. MECHANISMS OF ACTION

List of Contributors

Robert F. Ackermann, Department of Behavioral Neurobiology, University of Alabama at Birmingham

Lewis R. Baxter, Jr., Department of Psychiatry, University of Alabama at Birmingham, University of California, Los Angeles

Richard Bergeron, Department of Psychiatry, Harvard Medical School

Pierre Blier, Neurobiological Psychiatry Unit, McGill University

Arthur Brody, Department of Psychiatry and Behavioral Science, University of California, Los Angeles

Matthew J. Byerly, Department of Psychiatry, University of Texas, Southwestern Medical Center at Dallas

Dianne Chambless, Department of Psychology, University of North Carolina at Chapel Hill

Carlos Cuadros, Department of Psychiatry, Veteran's Administration Medical Center

Pinhas N. Dannon, Sheba Medical Center, Tel Aviv University

Joseph DeVeaugh-Geiss, Glaxo Wellcome Inc.

Paul M. G. Emmelkamp, Department of Clinical Psychology, University of Amsterdam

C. Neill Epperson, Yale University School of Medicine

Brian A. Fallon, The New York State Psychiatric Institute, Columbia University

Ulrike Feske, Anxiety Disorders Prevention Program, Western Psychiatric Institute and Clinic, University of Pittsburgh School of Medicine

Edna Foa, Department of Psychiatry, Allegheny University Hospitals

Elizabeth Forrester, Department of Psychiatry, Warneford Hospital, University of Oxford

Wayne K. Goodman, Department of Psychiatry, University of Florida

Jane Gregoritch, Department of Pediatrics, University of Alabama at Birmingham

Dorothy Grice, Center for Neurobiology and Behavior, University of Pennsylvania

Gregory L. Hanna, Department of Child Psychiatry, University of Michigan Medical Center

Nathan J. Henninger, School of Social Work, Boston University

William A. Hewlett, Vanderbuilt University School of Medicine

Eric Hollander, Department of Psychiatry, Mount Sinai School of Medicine

Iulian Iancu, Sheba Medical Center, Tel Aviv University

Michael A. Jenike, Massachusetts General Hospital, Harvard Medical School

Anita Kablinger, Department of Psychiatry, Louisiana State University

Richard Katz, Clinical Research and Development, Novartis Pharmaceuticals Corporation

Suck Won Kim, Department of Psychiatry, University of Minnesota Hospital and Clinic

Robert A. King, Yale Child Study Center, Yale University School of Medicine

Michael J. Kozak, Department of Psychiatry, Allegheny University Hospital

James F. Leckman, Yale Child Study Center, Yale University School of Medicine

Hichael Liebowitz, New York State Psychiatric Institute, Columbia University

Brett Liquori, Institute for Bio-Behavioral Therapy and Research, Great Neck, NY

Michal Lustig, Sheba Medical Center, Tel Aviv University

Mostafa El Mansari, Neurobiological Psychiatry Unit, McGill University

Jack D. Maser, Department of Psychiatry, University of California, San Diego

Christopher McDougle, Indiana University School of Medicine

Richard J. McNally, Department of Psychology, Harvard University

Tanya Murphy, Department of Psychiatry, University of Florida

Fugen A. Neziroglu, Institute for Bio-Behavioral Therapy and Research, Great Neck, NY

David Pauls, Yale Child Study Center, Yale University School of Medicine

Bradley Peterson, Yale Child Study Center, Yale University School of Medicine

Michael E. Phelps, Department of Molecular and Medical Pharmacology, University of California, Los Angeles

Katharine A. Phillips, Department of Psychiatry, Butler Hospital, Brown University School of Medicine

Teresa A. Pigott, Department of Psychiatry and Behavioral Sciences, University of Texas Medical Branch

Graciela Piñeyro, Neurobiological Psychiatry Unit, McGill University

C. Alec Pollard, Anxiety Disorders Center, St. Louis Behavioral Medicine Institute

Lawrence H. Price, Department of Psychiatry, Brown University School of Medicine

Stanley Rachman, Department of Psychology, University of British Columbia

Steven A. Rasmussen, Butler Hospital, Providence, RI

Scott L. Rauch, Massachusetts General Hospital, Harvard Medical School

Candida Richards, Department of Psychiatry, Warneford Hospital, University of Oxford

Matthew V. Rudorfer, Division of Services and Intervention Research, National Institute of Mental Health

Paul Salkovskis, Department of Psychiatry, Warneford Hospital, Oxford University

Yehuda Sasson, Sheba Medical Center, Tel Aviv University

Cary R. Savage, Department of Psychiatry, Harvard Medical School, Massachusetts General Hospital

Sanjaya Saxena, Department of Psychiatry and Behavioral Sciences, University of California, Los Angeles

Lawrence Scahill, Yale Child Study Center, Yale University School of Medicine

Jeffrey M. Schwartz, Department of Psychiatry and Behavioral Science, University of California, Los Angeles

Sheila Seay, Department of Psychiatry and Behavioral Science, University of Texas Medical Branch

Rosamund Shafran, Department of Psychiatry, Warneford Hospital, Oxford University

David Spiegel, Anxiety Clinic, Boston University

Gail S. Steketee, School of Social Work, Boston University

Kevin Stevens, Institute for Bio-Behavioral Therapy and Research

Paula Stoessel, Department of Psychiatry, University of California, Los Angeles

Neal R. Swerdlow, Department of Psychiatry, University of California, Los Angeles

Patricia van Oppen, Department of Psychiatry, Valeriuskliniek, Vrije Universiteit, The Netherlands

Herbert E. Ward, Department of Psychiatry, University of Florida

Cheryl Wong, Department of Psychiatry, Mount Sinai School of Medicine

Jose A. Yaryura-Tobias, Institute for Bio-Behavioral Therapy and Research

Joseph Zohar, Psychiatric Division, Sheba Medical Center, Tel Aviv University

Preface

Obsessive-compulsive disorder (OCD) is now recognized as a serious and chronic illness. It affects more than 2% of the population, making it more common than schizophrenia. Although in the last decade we have witnessed considerable advances on both the pharmacological and the behavioral fronts, fewer than 50% of cases benefit significantly from currently available treatments. Consequently, one of the questions most frequently discussed in the field today is how to manage OCD patients who do not respond to conventional therapeutic approaches. To address this question, we have included contributions from both theoretical and practical standpoints. Although etiology, diagnosis, assessment, and treatment of nonrefractory OCD are all covered, this volume emphasizes treatment-resistant illness.

We expect that it will appeal to mental health practitioners (e.g., psychiatrists, psychologists, and social workers) and some primary care physicians searching for better ways to help their patients. It will also be of considerable interest to educated consumers and to clinical researchers working in the field of OCD and related conditions. Many of the leading OCD clinical investigators are represented. From the beginning of the project we believed that it was essential to offer comprehensive accounts of the three leading modalities of treatment—cognitive behavioral, psychopharmacological, and combined. We also sought descriptions of novel or experimental approaches (e.g., neurosurgery or intravenous clomipramine) to treatment-refractory cases. The array of treatments targeted required a diverse set of authors. The resulting multidisciplinary nature of the volume should make it interesting to readers from a broad range of backgrounds and theoretical perspectives.

Although we strove to maintain stylistic consistency and accuracy, we made no attempt to homogenize the content. If the reader experiences "cognitive dissonance" in trying to reconcile the diverging viewpoints expressed herein, we intended it this way. At present, we are far from consensus when it comes to the treatment-refractory patient, and predictably so, as consensus can occur only when a treatment consistently ends the suffering of our patients and the treatment-resistant patient no longer exists. The best we can do at this point is to lay out the evidence and the arguments from leading thinkers. In doing so it is our hope that new ideas will emerge, new treatments will be tested, and we will perhaps find ourselves a little closer to agreement when a patient asks, "What are my (best) options?"

With support from the Obsessive-Compulsive Foundation (OCF) and the National Institute of Mental Health (NIMH), leaders from the OCD research, practice, and consumer communities have been discussing the present state of knowledge and gaps in our current understanding of this complex disorder since 1995. Written reviews of key areas, shaped by this interactive process, form the basis of this volume.

The book is divided into several parts. The first part, Clinical Subtypes and Spectrum, provides an overview of the diagnostic boundaries of OCD. Hollander and Wong introduce the concept of obsessive-compulsive (OC) spectrum disorders and discuss the implications of clinical subtyping for future research. Phillips examines the connection between body dysmorphic disorder and OCD in her scholarly review of the subject. Current knowledge concerning the distinction between tic-related and non-tic-related OCD is the subject of the chapter by Leckman, McDougle, Pauls, and their colleagues. In the final chapter of this section, Byerly, Goodman, and Cuadros deal with the treatment implications of OC symptoms that co-occur with schizophrenia.

The next part, Pathophysiology and Etiology, offers a sampling of theories from the vantage points of genetics research (Hanna), information-processing models (McNally), cognitive psychology (van Oppen & Emmelkamp), and functional neuroimaging (Rauch & Savage). These chapters set the stage for understanding the rationale of treatments discussed in greater detail late in the volume.

The part entitled Assessment includes two complementary contributions. Feske and Chambless survey and critically review the literature on assessment measures for OCD whereas Kim focuses on how the introduction of these rating scales has influenced how clinicians monitor the progress and outcome of treatment.

Four contributions compose the Cognitive-Behavioral Treatments part. In the field of OCD, *cognitive* and *behavioral* are not often linked terms. Salkovskis enunciates the problem of treatment-refractory illness and underscores the importance of applying cognitive theory (i.e., taking into account the person's appraisal or interpretation of the situation). Pollard examines the role of an indications for inpatient treatment of OCD. Neziroglu, Stevens, Liquori, and Yaryura-Tobias furnish a thorough review of the applications of behavioral treatment to selected OC spectrum disorders. Steketee, Henninger, and Pollard summarize the available evidence on the effects of comorbidity on treatment outcome, particularly in response to behavioral therapy, in OCD.

The length of the Drug and Other Somatic Treatments part is in keeping with the variety of interventions that have been tried in OCD, some with more scientific foundation than others. The first three chapters (Pigott & Seay; Iancu, Dannon, Lustig, Sasson & Zohar; and DeVeaugh-Geiss & Katz) provide a sound introduction to the experience and use of serotonin reuptake inhibitors (SRIs) in this condition. The chapter by Goodman, Ward, Kablinger, and Murphy can stand alone as a complete, up-to-date review of biological approaches to treatment-resistant OCD. The next series of chapters discuss in greater depth strategies mentioned in the previous overview chapter. McDougle, Epperson, and Price address the role of adjunctive neuroleptics; Fallon and Liebowitz take up intravenous clominpramine; Hewlett writes about benzodiazepines; Rudorfer surveys the use of electroconvulsive therapy in OCD; and Jenike handles the controversial topic of neurosurgery with skill and impartiality.

The part entitled Combined Treatment includes two chapters on concurrent treatment with SRIs and behavioral therapy (i.e., exposure and response treatment). Given the widely held belief that the most broadly effective treatment is this combination, it is surprising how meager the evidence is in its support. Spiegel provides a careful review of the early literature on combined modalities in both acute and long-term treatment. Kozak, Liebowitz, and Foa discuss the rationale for their NIMH-sponsored comparison trial and present an interim analysis.

The final part, Mechanisms of Action, is last because this topic is a stepping stone to the future. Understanding how our current treatments work may lead to better treatments. Rachman and Shafran consider the mechanisms responsible for the changes in OCD that are produced by behavioral therapy. One of the most consistent findings in OCD is the preferential efficacy of SRIs. Blier, Bergeron, Piñeyro, and El Manseri discuss the preclinical foundations of this observation and propose future neurochemical targets of treatment. Baxter et al., drawing heavily on neuroimaging findings, conclude the book with a chapter on brain mechanisms subserving treatment response to either medication or behavioral therapy.

Throughout this volume, starting with the first sentence of this Preface, you are reminded about the significance of the problem. You are quoted data from epidemiological studies, told of the number of nonresponders to standard treatment, and instructed on how a rating scale score of a typical patient translates into disability, distress, and time occupied by symptoms. Sometimes, however, nothing gives you more information than the story of one person battling the illness. We are indebted to Roger Sagalyn for his willingness to share his experience with OCD through a poem he wrote and permitted us to publish. This poignant poem conveys how the promise of a productive, happy life is destroyed by a brain-based mental illness.

Roger is now 37 years old. Born the son of two physicists, the accomplishments of his early years indicated he was on a similar trajectory. Nothing marked him as out of the ordinary except his extraordinary intellect.

Everything changed after his first hard bout of OCD at the age of 12. In high school, he set a record for tardiness and his grades collapsed. His obsessions have been with contamination, most usually fear of contact with "residues" and sticky substances. His compulsions involved elaborate self-cleansing rituals. In many ways, avoidance was worse than the rituals, and in the depths of his illenss he withdrew from all social and outside contact. When one of the editors (WKG) first met him, Roger was wearing yellow rubber gloves. Insight into the senselessness of his thoughts and the excessiveness of his actions has remained intact. He never seemed to worry about consequences of contamination, just recoiled at the notion of contact with substances on his trigger list. Depression has been a frequent complication, as evidenced by the handwritten note that precedes the poem.

Dear Dr Goodman,

I know that you're extremely busy, but if you could jot down your response to the poem and send it, I would be grateful. No rush.

I am not well, and I'm running out of treatment options. (Although 'TMS' is something I've never heard of.) More disturbingly, as the years creep by I feel increasingly distanced from my own interests, my health, my prospects, my future.

I cannot imagine how I might be redeemed in the time that may be left to me. I rebel against the rounds of appointments, new drug trials, behavioral programs. I'm just waiting it out, this ugly life.

I wish that I could have travelled more widely. And I wish that I could have stayed in touch with the small number of people I've really connected with, like yourself. I throw friendship away, I neglect it, I don't know why.—R

Souls' Diaspora

I

On Christmas Eve my father and I
sneak through doors unguarded
by holiday cheer, through soothing
Asian courtesies and empty tables
to pineapple chicken and beef satay
which is smuggled past tradition
like tools hidden in a prisoner's cake.
Toasting our ancestors I imagine
them descending into the vacant
spaces, exchanging convivial smiles,
looking rested and salacious and
all in love at last.
My father's Uncle Raphael, the labor organizer,
threatened by the police, and thus the first
to cross, says Kaddish for our Russians
who were never photographed.
Uncle Harry, whose dirty
and defiant jokes ricocheted
around his nursing home like
Hitchcock parrots in a Hopper café,
gives Aunt Louise a noodle for a ring.
Cousin Victor, the psychoanalyst, assures me
that the eternal therapy is guaranteed.
Blighted Lenore kisses her husband in the same
sweet way she kissed him the night he proposed.
Fanny, my grandmother, my lawless, druidical
sponsor, takes her first husband's hand in her
left hand and her second husband's hand
in her right, and soon they're thick with
conversation I'd have to be dead to understand.

II

My grandmother had a small vacation home
in upstate New York, the Delphian keep
of my childhood. A converted farmhouse
on the top of a hill, overlooking nothing
except the rural patina of pasture and
fences, woods and valleys and wildflowers,
endurance of insects, songbirds, deer, dairy cows.
She collected inexpensive things like depression glass,

broken watches and antique oil lamps
salvaged at auctions from farms which had
foundered on the end of the second world war.
In the kitchen there was a black iron stove
as huge and binding as an ocean liner's
anchor, ready to hold a family
fast against hungry weather.
How each generation saves not the hard
backbones of the last: the blackened
bricks, the sawdust that preserved a trove
of summer ice, the smell of blood offered
in childbirth, or in nature's melee;
rather a lamp dressed in easeful light,
a quilt, a doll, a brooch, a rocking chair
suggesting thoughtful indolence earned
through abundant labor.
On quilted Catskill summer nights
I was led to sleep under the influence
of my grandmother's sparse, tasteful
history. I listened to mice crowd behind
the old walls, portentousness of owls, the
compulsive bark of the auctioneers, the
mysterious detonations of deer hunters
abusing solitude. When I was older,
desirable girls emerged from trailers which
had started to crop up in a meadow below
the road, and I considered them, royally,
as befitted a boy living in the only real house
on Morton Hill. Grandmother commended me to sex.
She debunked obscenities.
"Don't be bothered by works," she would say ...

I went fishing with my father
on Tananah Lake, the worms' allure
preserved in the shade of the dashboard,
the disturbed shack of the boat renter
and his decrepit boats, coaxing the motor,
the quick duck of the bobber, the panicky
sweep of the line, lunge of the net,
suffocation, ceremony, cutting off their
heads on the flagstones for the cat, impatient.
Enthusiasm for the approved mess of guts.
The potency of the destroyer. Meanwhile

Fanny carried a torch for Stalin, ruthlessly
beat me a scrabble, and dutifully reared
every delirious ambition I conceived.
My parents murdered some of the mice.
I protested.

III
I was digging for night crawlers
after a storm, the sheath of wet
soil on my spade, the slick, unexpected
texture of the worms, their peculiar
toughness. The antique powers of knives, rakes
and shovels. Apprenticeship of the
hunter-gatherer. The lordly rummager.
To cast a weighted line into the
bestirred matters of the universe.
At twelve I still harvested the
secrets and the heaviness of storms.
And then the sickness
came slouching forward.
Anxiety. Obsession. A plague
of blue notions. Mysterious detonations
in the brain. A fortress dismayed by
treason, thoughts assaulting reason, arrows
shot from the inside, mental mud slides
shaking the foundations of my learning.
The Trojan darkness of an enemy undeclared.
The subtle stalking, thoughts sticking
and clotting, like pain, but with less meaning.

IV
The fabled and the true, pleasure and distress,
intermingle. As the flames of the candles
part and settle the spirits put on
their frivolous coats and hats,
a companionable pretense
of regard for the flesh.
A young woman sits alone in the restaurant,
eating and reading and drinking glasses of red wine
slowly. Aloof, defended, unconcerned. Not permitting
even this, this casual and incidental communion,
to touch her. Oblivious of jovial strangers.
I imagine her in a poor farmhouse

at the century's inception. She is using
grandmother's oil lamp to read
to a child from the Bible. She reads
slowly, sensing that her faith-steered
ship has been breached by chance and will
shortly go down. The oil will fall
and they'll be lost in antique darkness,
unmarked, a modest stock of relics for
someone else's fortune to collect.
I'm tempted to tap on the window
of her meticulous solitude,
invite her to taste the comforts of our table.
Would she be interested, amused or grateful?
Her shadowy flesh is made credible,
confirmed, by our attentive presence?
Or would she look up at me in astonishment?
The display of book and wine suspended,
a harder and more primitive face
instinctively raised in alarm.
The whole room suddenly grinding to a halt
like an underground train trapped between stations.
A fortress overthrown. Thoughts arrested.
The ambivalent pilgrim yielding to unknowns.
Foundering.

V
In the beginning there was a grand explosion,
and afterward the unwed ingredients of everything
embarked on a journey, Promethean seeds, scattered,
throughout time, to grow the cosmos,
compelled, charged, tyrannical, inflamed.
The souls' fires burn as the suns' fires burn,
questing, fated, unrepentant, ever-bursting,
driven to cultivate the energies they've
inherited, lit from the inside,
the way stars feed on, and engulf, themselves.
Such a vast and reckless consumption—we don't
have the means to dream about their deaths.
Fanny, the errant quests you favored,
the fuel consumed by your burning ambitions,
the illuminating stories we've conspired to save,
are safe in my collection. Their familial
gravity stops me from spinning

entire out of orbit.
I haven't dreamt of your death, grandmother,
scalding, remorseless star that I embraced.

I remain awake,
separating the salvage from the loss,
mixing my spirits with the moon,
not wanting to be cold sober
until my season is warm enough for sleeping.

—*Roger Raphael Sagalyn*

Roger has tried and complied with almost every reasonable treatment mentioned in this book. In 1987, he traveled to England to have a neurosurgical procedure called a limbic leukotomy. Since then he has had intravenous clomipramine as well as intensive trials of behavior therapy. He has been on the brink of suicide, but now is determined to live as normally as he can despite his OCD. He is trying to repair the fabric of his social and family life that has been torn by chronic illness. This book is dedicated to Roger Sagalyn and others like him who, despite years of suffering under the yoke of OCD, have not given up searching for effective treatment.

We have decided not to accept any royalties from sales of this book. Instead, all profits will be donated to the Research Fund of the OCF in Milford, Connecticut. These funds are earmarked for peer-reviewed grant proposals submitted by investigators conducting studies on OCD. The OCF is a nonprofit organization dedicated to the welfare of patients with OCD and their family members.

—*Wayne K. Goodman, MD*
Professor and Chairman of Psychiatry
University of Florida College of Medicine

—*Matthew V. Rudorfer, MD*
Acting Associate Director for Treatment Research
Division of Services and Intervention Research
National Institute of Mental Health

—*Jack D. Maser, PhD*
Professor of Psychiatry
University of California, San Diego

I

CLINICAL SUBTYPES
AND SPECTRUM

1

Spectrum, Boundary, and Subtyping Issues: Implications for Treatment-Refractory Obsessive-Compulsive Disorder

Eric Hollander
Cheryl M. Wong
Mount Sinai School of Medicine

Obsessive-compulsive disorder (OCD) and its relation to other related disorders has only recently become the focus of extensive investigations. Obsessive-compulsive (OC) spectrum disorders may conceivably affect up to 10% of the U.S. population (Hollander & Wong, 1995b). Our newly emerging knowledge raises many questions about research directions. In this chapter we define and elucidate the OCD spectrum, focus on the treatment-resistant population, and describe the future research initiatives that need to be undertaken.

DEFINITIONS OF THE OCD SPECTRUM

OC spectrum disorders share many features with OCD (Hollander, 1993a, 1993b; Hollander & Wong, 1995b). These include overlap in:

1. Symptom profile: characterized by intrusive obsessive thoughts or repetitive behaviors.
2. Associated features: demographics, family history, comorbidity, clinical course.
3. Neurobiology: assessed by pharmacological challenge studies, imaging, immune factors.

4. Response to selective antiobsessional behavioral therapies and pharmacotherapies.
5. Etiology: genetics, environmental factors.

OC-related disorders include many distinct psychiatric categories, which
are discussed later in this chapter.

It is important to note, however, that often these spectrum disorders
coexist in the same patient, thereby making accurate diagnoses even more
important. Many of these patients with comorbid spectrum disorders are
often labeled as *treatment-resistant* when they do not respond to conventional treatments that are targeted to a narrow diagnostic category. Therefore, knowledge of a broader spectrum of diagnostic entities that are often
associated and interrelated would lead to more tailored treatments, and
hopefully improved response rates.

Symptom Profile and Phenomenology

OCD is characterized by either *obsessions* (recurrent and persistent ideas,
thoughts, or images) or *compulsions* (repetitive behaviors performed according to certain rules or in a stereotyped fashion; American Psychiatric
Association, 1994). In addition, these obsessions or compulsions cause
marked distress or significantly interfere with the patient's function.
Symptomatically, both compulsivity and impulsivity have in common the
inability to inhibit or delay repetitive behaviors. The difference between
the two lies in the driving foci. In compulsivity, it is the need to decrease
the discomfort associated with rituals, and in impulsivity, it is the need
for the maximization of pleasure. It should also be noted, however, that
not all compulsions reduce anxiety. In more impulsive patients, there is
also an additional component of the rituals being pleasurable, albeit with
associated guilt after the behavior is carried out. In individuals with
OC-related disorders, features of both compulsivity and impulsivity may
be observed. Clearly, compulsivity and impulsivity are not mutually
exclusive, and individuals may have one set of behaviors driven by the
need to reduce anxiety, and another set of behaviors driven to obtain
pleasure. This could be due to differential dysregulation of serotonin
(5-HT) pathways in different brain areas in these patients, but more
research needs to investigate this possibility.

In the first subset or cluster of the OC spectrum disorders, there is a
marked preoccupation with bodily appearance or sensations, with associated behaviors performed to decrease anxiety brought on by these
preoccupations. Examples within this cluster include body dysmorphic
disorder (BDD), hypochondriasis (Hollander 1993a, 1993b), and eating
disorders such as anorexia nervosa (Thiel, Broocks, & Ohlmeier, 1995).

This group of patients may have a fixity of beliefs, contributing to the treatment resistance in BDD, hypochondriasis, and anorexia nervosa.

The second cluster of OC spectrum disorders includes impulsive-style disorders. These include impulse control disorders (McElroy, Harrison, Keck, & Hudson, 1995) such as pathological gambling (DeCaria & Hollander, 1993; Hollander & Wong, 1995a), compulsive buying (McElroy, Keck, & Phillips, 1995; McElroy, Keck, Pope, Smith, & Strakowski, 1994; Wong & Hollander, 1996), sexual compulsions (Anthony & Hollander, 1993; Coleman, 1987; Hollander & Wong, 1995a), trichotillomania (Stein et al., 1995; Winchel, 1992) and self-injurious behavior (Favazza, 1992). There is no clear functional significance of impulsive behavior with regard to anxiety regulation (either increased or decreased), but the functional impact of the behaviors centers on pleasure regulation. The largest obstacle to treating these patients often is keeping them engaged in therapy. Insufficient or inadequate treatment secondary to poor follow-up would often lead to a resurgence of symptoms and illness relapse.

The third large cluster of OC spectrum disorders includes neurological disorders with compulsive features. Patients with OCD have a higher incidence of tics and other neurological soft signs (Aronowitz et al., 1994; Baer, 1994; Denckla, 1989; Hollander, Schiffman, et al., 1990; Holzer et al., 1994; Nicolini, Wessbecker, Meija, & Sanchez de Carmona, 1993; Pauls, Alsobrook, Goodman, Rasmussen, & Leckman, 1995). The neurological cluster involves little obsessional content and mostly manifests motoric, repetitive symptomatology. It resembles the "just-so" symmetrical subtype discussed later. We found (Hollander, Schiffman, et al., 1990) that in our OCD participants compared to controls, all of whom were medication-free during the study period, soft signs correlated with severity of obsessions. There were was also a correlation between abnormality of visual memory and recognition on neuropsychological testing and total soft signs. We also found (Aronowitz et al., 1994) that OCD patients performed significantly more poorly than normal controls on visuospatial, visuoperceptual, and visual discrimination tasks, as well as set shifting, sequencing, and tracking tasks. These findings were especially prominant in male patients.

Disorders in this category include autism, which affects social, communicative, and imaginative development, with a compulsive core characterized by stereotypic movements, craving for sameness, and narrow repetitive interests (McDougle, Kresch, et al., 1995; Wong & Hollander, 1996); Asperger's disorder, which involves less severe speech disturbance than autism, but still affects social development with associated stereotypies and narrow repetitive interests (Hjort, 1994); Tourette's syndrome, which comprises multiple motor and vocal tics with associated obsessions and compulsions (Miguel et al., 1995; Swedo & Leonard, 1994); and

Sydenham's chorea, which occurs secondary to rheumatic fever and involves the basal ganglia with associated repetitive involuntary movements and anxiety (Swedo, Rapoport, et al., 1989; Swedo & Leonard, 1994). Swedo, Rapoport, et al. (1989) studied 23 children and adolescents with Sydenham's chorea and 14 with rheumatic fever but without chorea. They found that the Sydenham's patients had significantly more obsessive thoughts and compulsive behaviors and significantly greater interference from these behaviors. Three of these patients also met criteria for OCD. However, out of the initial 39 Sydenham's patients and 21 controls, 16 patients with Sydenham's and 7 control patients were lost to follow-up. The participants were asked to fill out a self-report questionnaire that they received by mail. If an individual reported more than 10 obsessional symptoms, he or she was interviewed by telephone with a structured diagnostic interview. Only a subgroup of low-scoring patients were interviewed by telephone. Therefore, given the high drop-out rate and lack of a comprehensive diagnostic and psychiatric evaluation, larger, well-controlled studies with better diagnostic procedures are needed.

Associated Features

Although OCD can start as early as age 2, there is also an increased incidence in the teenage and early adult years (American Psychiatric Association, 1994; A. Black, 1974). Likewise, the OC-related disorders tend to have an age of onset in adolescence or the early 20s (Hollander, 1993a, 1993b; Hollander & Wong, 1995b). There is a higher incidence of positive family history of OCD, other OC spectrum disorders, and mood disorders (Degonda, Wyss, & Angst, 1993; McElroy, Harrison, et al., 1995; Okasha, Saad, Khalil, Dawla, & Yehia, 1994; Pauls et al., 1995). Pauls et al. (1995) undertook an extensive and thorough study that looked at 100 probands with OCD and all available first-degree relatives. The participants were interviewed directly by structured interviews and the Yale Brown Obsessive Compulsive Scale (Goodman, Price, & Rasmussen, 1989), and best estimate diagnoses were assigned. The validities for OCD and Tourette's and chronic tics were excellent (kappas = 0.97 and 0.98, respectively). Comparison with first-degree relatives of 33 psychiatrically unaffected participants was also carried out. They found that the rate of OCD was significantly higher in probands with OCD (10.3%) than in comparison participants (1.9%). In addition, the rate of tics was also significantly greater among the family members of probands (4.6%) than among the comparison group (1.0%). The relatives of female probands with OCD were more likely to have tics, and the relatives of probands with early onset were at higher risk for both OCD and tics. There is also often comorbidity with other OC-related disorders. In kleptomania, McElroy et al. (1991) reported that all 20 kleptomaniac patients had a lifetime diagnoses of major mood disorders, 16 had a lifetime history of anxiety disorders, and 12 had lifetime diagnoses of eating disorders. A high morbid risk of major mood disorders was found in first-degree relatives. However, this study had a small sample size and larger future studies are needed. Ego-dystonic features are more common in the later onset OCD cases compared to earlier onset cases. There seems to be a chronic course in most of the cases. Although there is no reported male or female preponderance in adult OCD (A. Black, 1974), the spectrum disorders may differ with respect to gender. Women tend to be overrepresented in studies of BDD (Hollander & Wong, 1995a), compulsive buying (McElroy, Keck, & Phillips, 1995; McElroy et al., 1994), and kleptomania (McElroy et al., 1991). Men seem to predominate in pathological gambling (DeCaria & Hollander, 1993; Rosenthal, 1992) and hypochondriasis (Warwick, 1995). It is not clear whether the differences are due to endocrine, neuroanatomical, or social and cultural factors. It should also be noted that in the subtypes of childhood-onset and tic-related OCD, up to 75% of the cases are male (Hollingsworth, Tanguay, Grossman, & Pabst, 1980).

Neurobiology

Serotonin Function. Neurobiological models of OCD and related disorders stress the role of 5-HT in pathophysiological mechanisms. In some studies of OCD, pharmacological challenge with oral m-chlorophenyl-piperazine (m-CPP), a partial serotonergic agonist, produced increased severity of OC symptoms in a subgroup of OCD patients studied (Hollander, DeCaria, et al., 1992; Zohar, Muellar, Insel, Zohar-Kadouch, & Murphy, 1987). Hollander, DeCaria, et al. (1992) found that following m-CPP, but not after fenfluramine or placebo, 55% of OCD patients experienced an exacerbation of OC symptoms. Prolactin response was also blunted in OCD patients, and patients with greater behavioral response to m-CPP had smaller prolactin responses. These results were consistent with the findings reported by Zohar et al. (1987). To contrast with the impulsive end of the spectrum, borderline personality-disordered patients with impulsive features were also studied using m-CPP (Hollander, Stein, et al., 1994). Instead of obsessional symptoms, disinhibition or depersonalization—core symptoms of borderline personality disorder—were instead produced. In addition, male patients had higher cortisol levels and marginally blunted prolactin responses after receiving m-CPP. These are preliminary findings that have to be supported by future studies involving larger sample sizes.

Patients with OCD (Hollander, DeCaria, et al., 1992), Tourette's syndrome, and anorexia nervosa showed blunted prolactin response to m-

CPP challenge. On the other hand, impulsive disorders such as borderline personality disorder, pathological gambling, and trichotillomania showed normal or significantly increased neuroendocrine response to m-CPP (Hollander & Wong, 1995b). Platelet monoamine oxidase (MAO) activity, a peripheral marker of serotonin function, has also found to be lower in impulsive disorders such as pathological gambling (Carrasco, Saiz-Ruiz, Moreno, Hollander, & Lopez-Ibor, 1994).

Reduction of OC symptoms after treatment with clomipramine was associated with reduction of platelet serotonin levels (Flament et al., 1985) and cerebrospinal fluid 5-hydroxyindoleacetic acid (Thoren et al., 1980). These studies point to differential dysregulation in 5-HT pathways in more compulsive versus more impulsive disorders. This dysregulation is significant in that it may explain differences in response to serotonin reuptake inhibitor (SRI) treatment, such as lag of effective response and persistence of therapeutic response to SRIs. Further studies are needed to address these findings and elucidate the pathophysiology of the various OC spectrum disorders and treatment implications.

Neural Circuits. Another approach to OCD focuses on neurocircuits that may drive the symptoms. These include the orbitofrontal, basal ganglia, and limbic connections (Gray, 1992). Single photon emission computed tomography scans show increased activity in the orbitofrontal cortex, basal ganglia, and temporal regions (Machlin et al., 1991). Positron emission tomography (PET) scans have shown increased glucose metabolism in the orbitofrontal areas and cingulate gyrus, as well as in the caudate nucleus (Baxter et al., 1987; Baxter et al., 1992; Hoehn-Saric, Pearlson, Harris, Machlin, & Camargo, 1991; Swedo et al., 1992; Swedo, Schapiro, et al., 1989). Successful treatment with SRIs and behavioral therapy are associated with decreased hypermetabolism of the frontal region and caudate nucleus (Baxter et al., 1992; Swedo et al., 1992). Swedo et al. (1992) studied 13 adult patients with OCD at baseline and at 1-year follow-up (eight were taking clomipramine, two were taking fluoxetine, and three were on no medications). They found that as a group, the patients had a significant improvement in all OCD and anxiety ratings and PET revealed a significant decrease in normalized orbitofrontal regional cerebral glucose metabolism. In the treated patients, they found that the decrease in orbitofrontal metabolism was directly correlated with two measures of OCD improvement. However, the sample size for the study was small, there was no matched control group, the SRI used was not uniform in all patients, and there was a subgroup of patients who did not receive any treatment. Baxter et al. (1992) studied 18 patients: Nine of each received drug therapy (fluoxetine) and behavioral therapy at baseline and at 1-year follow-up. They found that after treatment with both drug and behavioral therapy, the head of the right caudate nucleus was decreased significantly compared with pretreatment values in the responders. They also found that percentage change in OCD ratings correlated significantly with the percentage of right caudate to ipsilateral hemisphere ratio with drug therapy. Although the samples for this study are also small, the comparison groups are matched and the study design much cleaner. Neurosurgical treatments that disconnect pathways from orbitofrontal to deeper limbic structures also seem to ameliorate OC symptoms in a subgroup of patients.

Treatment Response

OCD and spectrum disorders appear to be preferentially responsive to treatment with SRIs and behavioral therapy (Flament et al., 1985; Goodman et al., 1990). Goodman et al.'s (1990) important study compared fluvoxamine (an SRI) to desipramine (a norepinephrine reuptake inhibitor) in a double-blind, randomized fashion over 8 weeks in the treatment of OCD, and found that 11 of 21 patients on fluvoxamine compared to 2 of 19 patients on desipramine were treatment responders. One could argue that the treatment period of 8 weeks is too short and the lack of a placebo arm is questionable, but otherwise the study was well-designed and executed. Up to 60% of patients with OCD showed significant improvement during treatment with SRIs and this appears to be a selective efficacy to SRIs. Norepinephrine reuptake inhibitors, such as desipramine (Goodman et al., 1990) and nortriptyline (Thoren et al., 1980) are ineffective. Likewise, Thoren et al. (1980) found that clomipramine was superior to nortriptyline and placebo in the treatment of OCD, and that the effect was not clear cut until Week 5 of treatment in a double-blind, 5-week trial period. Once again, the study period of 5 weeks was too short. Response rates in some, but not all studies, have also been shown to increase to 80% to 90% with augmentation therapy with other serotonergic (buspirone [Pigott et al., 1992] and fenfluramine [Goodman, McDougle, & Price, 1992]), dopaminergic (haloperidol [Goodman et al., 1992], pimozide [Dominguez & Mestre, 1994], and risperidone [McDougle, Fleischman, & Epperson, 1995]), or gamma amino butyric acid (GABA)ergic (clonazepam [Leonard, Topol, & Bukstein, 1994]) agents. However, for the most part, double-blind controlled trials of augmentation treatments are lacking. In addition, OC spectrum disorders are often comorbid, and misdiagnosis is frequent, leading to poor treatment response, in addition to true treatment resistance.

Treatment studies for OC spectrum disorders are mostly open clinical trials and are less well-characterized than those for OCD. They have, however, shown preferential response to SRIs, including BDD (Hollander,

Cohen, Simeon, 1993; Hollander, Cohen, et al., 1994; Hollander, Liebowitz, Winchel, Klumker, & Klein, 1989), hypochondriasis (Fallon et al., 1993), depersonalization disorder (Hollander, Liebowitz, et al., 1990), anorexia nervosa (Gwirtsman, Guze, Yager, & Gainsley, 1990), pathological gambling (Hollander et al., 1998; Hollander, Frenkel, et al., 1992; Rosenthal, 1992), sexual compulsions and paraphilias (Emmanuel, Lydiard, & Ballenger, 1991; Kafka, 1991; Stein et al., 1992), self-injurious behavior (Favazza, 1992), and trichotillomania (Swedo, Leonard, et al., 1989).

Initial studies do indicate that there seem to be subtle differential responses between the impulsive and compulsive disorders with regard to dosage, response lag time, and maintenance of symptom remission (Hollander & Wong, 1995b). Patients with compulsive spectrum disorders, such as BDD and anorexia nervosa, have a significant lag time before response to SRIs, but once they respond, they tend to maintain their gains as long as they continue their treatment. Therefore, it is important to allow for an adequate trial at high enough doses before a patient is called a nonresponder or partial responder.

On the other hand, patients with impulsive disorders, such as binge eating disorder and compulsive buying, often have a quick response to SRIs that may diminish over time with treatment. Such a group of patients would therefore require addition of other augmentation strategies (e.g., a mood stabilizer) after initial stabilization given the diminishing response to SRI treatment over time.

Behavioral therapy is also a mainstay of treatment in OCD and OC spectrum disorders. A substantial number of patients benefit from prolonged exposure to feared situations (which is anxiety provoking) and response prevention (which blocks the rituals; Hollander, 1993b). Unfortunately, not all patients can tolerate behavioral therapy due to encompassing anxiety. Clearly, these behavioral approaches need to be altered in dealing with the impulsive end of the spectrum.

Etiology

In OCD, there has been converging evidence of the involvement of the basal ganglia and orbitofrontal regions of the brain. There have not been any etiologic factors ascertained in OC spectrum disorders. It is known that OC spectrum disorders are a heterogeneous group of disorders and probably multifactorial with regards to pathophysiology. Environmental factors (e.g., toxins and infections) and genetic factors have been cited as possible etiologic factors in this group of disorders. The production of OC symptoms associated with Sydenham's chorea raises the question of an immune component in the production of OCD. Recently, an association was found between OCD symptomatology and postviral or bacterial infections such as with beta-hemolytic Streptococcus A in a sample of children, mostly boys, who did not have any other symptoms compatible with Sydenham's chorea (Allen, Leonard, & Swedo, 1995). Data from Murphy et al. (1997) show that a cohort of patients with childhood-onset OCD or Tourette's syndrome show a significant increase in peripheral B cells expressing the monoclonal antibody, D8/17, which has been shown to be produced in response to streptococcal infection. D8/17 was found in 100% of patients who have been exposed to streptococcus as opposed to 11% of controls. This finding once again points to an immune-modulated component associated with childhood-onset OCD and Tourette's syndrome.

BOUNDARIES—MAY BE SECONDARY TO GOALS

Where we draw the boundaries and which disorders we include in the OC spectrum may relate to our long-term goals. For example, if we want to facilitate treatments that may be highly effective in a broad range of patients and diagnoses, we are justified in setting broader definitional boundaries. On the other hand, rigorously designed genetic studies may suggest the need for narrower boundaries. Hence, we may want to address the treatment goals and the prevention of illness in addressing boundary issues. Given the need to decrease symptomatology and improve quality of life in patients with OC spectrum disorders, we need to improve diagnostic tools and therapies for this group of patients and facilitate their implementation. Broader boundaries would hopefully lead to more effective dissemination of knowledge and exchange of ideas within a larger body of investigators.

DIAGNOSTIC CATEGORIES

As mentioned earlier, OC spectrum disorders overlap with many other distinct psychiatric diagnostic entities. One way of looking at the different categories is by dividing them into the following groups: somatoform disorders, neuropsychiatric disorders, impulse control disorders, eating disorders, delusional disorders, and stereotypic movement disorders (Hollander 1993a, 1993b; Hollander & Wong, 1995b).

Somatoform Disorders.   These disorders include hypochondriasis and BDD. Both are characterized by a preoccupation with bodily features. In hypochondriasis, persons are obsessed or preoccupied with having some kind of physical illness in the absence of confirmatory medical evidence (Fallon et al., 1993; Ford, 1995). In BDD (Andreasen & Bardach, 1977;

Braddock, 1982; Hollander et al., 1993; Phillips, 1991), there is a preoccupation with an imagined flaw in appearance in some part of the body.

Eating Disorders. The eating-disordered group of OC spectrum disorders includes anorexia nervosa, bulimia, and binge eating (Hsu, Kaye, & Weltzin, 1993; Theil et al., 1995). For example, persons with anorexia nervosa have an average of 10 OC concerns that are unrelated to their characteristic obsessions about body weight or image, or their typical compulsions concerning diet, exercise, or food preparation. Anorexic patients may become more obsessional when they are starving, but after they recover their weight, they continue to exhibit other OC traits. Eating-disordered patients often experience serious medical problems if their eating disorder is severe. Cotreatment of the patient with an internist is ideal in such a case to devise a comprehensive treatment plan to deal with treatment-refractory patients.

Neurological Cluster. This group may include Sydenham's chorea, autism, Asperger's disorder, and Tourette's syndrome. Basal ganglia involvement often gives rise to the development of stereotypic movements. These entities frequently have a compulsive core, but the nature of the obsessions and compulsions experienced by these patients are often qualitatively different from those experienced by patients with OCD per se. For example in autism, McDougle, Kresch, et al. (1995) found that there is less preoccupation with aggressiveness, counting, sexual and religious matter, symmetry, and somatic obsessions. There is however, a relative increase in repetition and ordering, hoarding, telling or asking, touching, tapping, and self-mutilatory behavior. In those with tic disorders, there seemed to be more prominent symptoms of touching, tapping, rubbing, blinking, and staring rituals, with less cleaning rituals (Holzer et al., 1994). In Tourette's syndrome, there are often sensory phenomena preceding intentional repetitive behaviors, whereas in OCD, there are usually preceding cognitions and autonomic anxiety instead (Miguel et al., 1995).

Impulse Control Disorders. This category of OC-related disorders includes pathological gambling, trichotillomania, kleptomania, compulsive buying, nail biting, sexual compulsions, and self-injurious behavior. Impulse control disorders are characterized by failure to resist impulses with harmful consequences; increasing tension or arousal; pleasure, gratification, or release during the act; and possible feelings of regret or guilt afterward (McElroy, Harrison, et al., 1995). These disorders are difficult to treat, as many patients favor the associated "high" that these behaviors give them. Some would look on these disorders as forms of addictions and would advocate that these patients also need additional motivational therapy to help engage and keep them in treatment, in addition to self-support groups such as Gamblers Anonymous.

Delusional Disorders. The *delusional cluster* of patients in the OC spectrum include those with somatic and jealous subtypes of delusional disorder with associated obsessions and compulsions related to their delusions (Wright, 1994). These patients generally have poorer treatment outcomes and tend to respond better to a combination of SRI and dopaminergic agent (McDougle, Goodman, & Price, 1994). In addition to OCD patients with delusional conviction, OCD patients with comorbid schizotypal personality and schizophrenic patients with comorbid OC symptoms may be included in this category.

Stereotypic Movement Disorders. These disorders fall within the OC spectrum and include head banging, onychophagia, and skin picking. These patients compulsively exhibit the associated movements, often resulting in some kind of trauma to their bodies. The dopaminergic (D1 and D2, in particular) and serotonergic systems have been shown to be involved in the production of stereotypies (Broderick, Gardner, & Van Praag, 1984; Yeshiayan & Kelley, 1995). The roles of the opiate system, other neuropeptides such as cholecystokinin and GABA, and the chloride and calcium channel systems have also been raised. A majority of patients with stereotypic movement disorders also have comorbid mental retardation (Lewis, Bodfish, Powell, & Golden, 1995) and they tend to be less responsive to therapy.

SUBTYPES

There have also been attempts to define distinct subtypes of OCD and related disorders. These may impact prognostic factors, treatment modalities, and outcome. Subtypes in OCD have been identified, but those for the spectrum disorders are still in the process of being studied and categorized. OCD subtypes may include:

1. A harm-avoidant, adult-onset, non-tic-related subtype.
2. A symmetry, childhood-onset, "just-so," tic-related subtype.
3. An obsessional slowness subtype.
4. An OC personality disorder subtype.
5. A poor insight subtype.

Family studies have found several subpopulations of OCD. Leckman et al. (1994a) described a group of OCD patients with higher oxytocin levels who did not have any family or personal history of tic disorder, and within these patients the level of oxytocin correlated with the severity of OCD. Pauls et al. (1995) described several different groups of OCD patients—those with a familial component, one subgroup associated with tic disorder, and the other not, and a group of OCD patients who did not have a family history of OCD or tics. Also in this study, it was noted that the relatives of female probands tended to have tics, and that the relatives of early-onset OCD patients tended to have both OCD and tic disorder. Holzer et al. (1994) described two groups of OCD patients—those with and without chronic tic disorder. McDougle, Goodman, and Leckman (1994) also described OCD patients with and without tics and reported that those with tics benefit from haloperidol augmentation. Baer (1994) described various symptom subtypes in OCD: those who had more symmetry or hoarding obsessions and behaviors, those with more obsessional and cleaning symptoms, and those with pure obsession. He found that the group preoccupied with symmetry and hoarding had first-degree relatives with a higher incidence of Tourette's syndrome or tics. The presence or absence of tics may be a prognostic factor, impacting the need for combination therapies and ultimate treatment response.

Obsessional slowness has also been described as a variant of OCD (Veale, 1993). Frost and Shaws (1993) used the Indecisiveness Scale to study indecisive individuals and found that they had problems with procrastination in a variety of life decisions and longer latencies on experimental decision-making tasks.

The relation between OC-related disorders and OC personality disorder has also been described. Findings have been mixed, however. Rosen and Tallis (1995) found that specific obsessive symptoms were only related to traits of OC personality disorder. On the other hand, D. W. Black, Noyes, Pfohl, Goldstein, and Blum (1993) and Thomsen and Mikkelson (1993) found that there was no significant association between OCD and OC personality disorder.

DIMENSIONAL APPROACHES

Compulsive-Impulsive Dimension

OCD can also be viewed along several dimensions. First, it could be seen along a continuum with risk avoidance and compulsively driven behaviors at one end, and underestimation of harm and impulsivity-driven behaviors on the other end (Hollander, 1993a, 1993b). This dimension may be defined within the biological framework of hyperfrontality and increased serotonergic sensitivity that may be involved in the compulsive disorders, and hypofrontality and low presynaptic serotonergic sensitivity within the impulsive group of disorders. Symptomatically, both compulsivity and impulsivity have in common the inability to inhibit or delay repetitive behaviors. The difference between the two, however, lies in the generator. In compulsivity, the driving force is the decrease of discomfort associated with the rituals. In impulsivity, the motivating or driving factor is the maximization of pleasure (Hollander & Wong, 1995b). However, individuals may possess both compulsive and impulsive features simultaneously. This most certainly impacts the individual's treatment response, given the differential response to SRIs in compulsive versus impulsive symptomatology discussed earlier. Hence, more studies are needed to further delineate the components of compulsivity and impulsivity with respect to treatment outcome.

Motoric and Obsessional Dimension

Another dimensional view is a continuum between motoric ritualistic behavior and obsessiveness. About 25% of patients with OCD have purely obsessional symptoms. On the other end lie patients with more stereotypic behaviors with little or no precedent obsessive thought. Obsessional slowness without many associated compulsions can be seen to lie closer to the obsessional end of the dimension, whereas involuntary movement disorders with associated ritualistic behaviors and few if any obsessions would lie more toward the motoric end. As mentioned before, early-onset, tic-related OCD and the neurological cluster of OC spectrum disorders tend to be more motoric. Once again, there may be differential response rates between motoric behaviors and obsessions, impacting again on treatment outcome.

Insight Dimension

A third dimension along which to view the OC spectrum disorders is poor versus intact insight. As OC-related disorders are studied, it has become evident that a subpopulation of these patients have poor insight into their illness, which may be a major barrier to successful treatment outcomes. Okasha et al. (1994) found that 9% of patients had no insight into their OC behaviors. The change from the *Diagnostic and Statistical Manual of Mental Disorders* (3rd ed., rev. [*DSM–III–R*]; American Psychiatric Association, 1987) to the *Diagnostic and Statistical Manual of Mental Disorders* (4th ed. [*DSM–IV*]; American Psychiatric Association, 1994) now includes the qualifier of OCD with poor insight. In BDD, up to 48% of patients are mostly or completely certain that their defect really exists. This therefore blurs the boundary between BDD and delusional disorder, somatic type, with fixity of beliefs lying along a continuum of severity. Surprisingly, Rotter and Goodman (1995) found that the expression of volitional control was not significantly related to the level of insight into the irrationality of behavior.

RECOMMENDATIONS: AREAS FOR STUDY

It is evident that there are still many key questions that remain unresolved in the field of OCD and related disorders. Before we are able to success-fully treat all individuals affected with these disorders, more needs to be known. The following areas are recommended for further study:

1. Developmental determinants: What is normal development with respect to obsessional symptoms? Are there critical phases of develop-ment? What factors may interact with these developmental aspects?

2. More precise definition and categorization of the disorders would be helpful for diagnosis and treatment.

3. Assessment: Scales for diagnosis, severity, and assessing change to further delineate diagnosis and treatment response, such as the develop-ment of screening instruments, Structured Clinical Interview for DSM–IV Axis I Disorders (SCID) modules, and Schedule for Affective Disorders & Schizophrenia (SADS) questionnaires that specifically assess these spectrum disorders and comorbid OC-related disorders. This will facilitate prevalence, association, and outcome studies, and ultimately benefit the treatment-resistant patient.

4. Genetic factors: Given the recent growth and collaboration between the fields of genetics and psychiatry, this would be a fertile area to spearhead efforts to investigate the genetic etiology of OCD and its related disorders, which could possibly lead to gene therapy.

5. New and innovative treatment modalities need to be pursued and developed, as well as further characterizing and studying the currently available therapies.

6. Animal models of OCD and specific spectrum disorders need to be developed to allow more thorough and specific investigations to be done in the area of neurobiology and OCD and spectrum disorders. As of yet, no acceptable animal model exists. In other areas where such models do exist, gains in knowledge are made more rapidly as there are no human matters that could constrain the questions posed in research protocols.

7. Postmortem studies: Utilizing available resources, we should con-centrate on expanding and pursuing postmortem studies and developing a national OCD brain bank. This resource would provide tissue for multiple areas of study and facilitate collaboration with various basic science special-

ists in genetics, molecular biology, neuroendocrinology, and neuroanatomy. Also, the development of an OCD national brain bank facilitated by the Obsessive-Compulsive Foundation would be an invaluable resource.

8. The role of oxytocin: Central oxytocin affects cognition, grooming, affiliative, sexual, and reproductive behaviors, and early studies suggest that some forms of OCD are related to oxytocin dysfunction (Leckman, Goodman, North, Chapell, Price, Pauls, Anderson, Riddle, McDougle, et al., 1994). The study of oxytocin could provide invaluable information into the pathophysiology and treatment of OC spectrum disorders.

9. Cultural, ethnic, and gender issues should also be investigated to provide new approaches to treatment, further define OC subgroups that impact on treatment selection, and further understand the basis of OC-related disorders.

10. Striatal disorders could also be investigated given their known neurological basis, and this may open up another means to study OC spectrum disorders in the neurological cluster and hopefully lead to more effective tools for treatment.

11. Comparison of the relative occurrences of OC spectrum disorders and family studies could provide important clues to further characterize subtypes. This in turn could lead to more specific treatment methods being developed to target each subtype identified.

FUTURE RESEARCH NEEDS

Information that research can provide would positively impact on the treatment of the spectrum of treatment-resistant OCD and related disorders. As such, increased awareness of the extent of the problem, as well as continued and increased levels of support for research funding, would be paramount in furthering efforts in this area. In addition, separate review committees to address problems specific to this area would be important. It would also be advantageous to quantify and qualify steps needed to facilitate multifaceted collaborative efforts with other areas in psychiatry and medicine. As such, much work has been accomplished, and much more work needs to be pursued before we can fully understand and apply our knowledge to the often hard-to-treat individuals affected by OC spectrum disorders.

REFERENCES

Allen, A. J., Leonard, H. L., & Swedo, S. E. (1995). Case study: A new infection-triggered, autoimmune subtype of pediatric obsessive-compulsive disorder and Tourette's syndrome. *Journal of the American Academy of Child and Adolescent Psychiatry, 34*(3), 307–311.

American Psychiatric Association. (1994). *Diagnostic and statistical manual of mental disorders* (4th ed.). Washington, DC: Author.

Andreasen, N. C., & Bardach, J. (1977). Dysmorphophobia: Symptom or disease. *American Journal of Psychiatry, 134,* 673–676.

Anthony, D. T., & Hollander, E. (1993). Sexual compulsions. In E. Hollander (Ed.), *Obsessive compulsive related disorders* (pp. 139–150). Washington, DC: American Psychiatric Press.

Aronowitz, B. A., Hollander, E., DeCaria, C. M., Cohen, L., Saoud, J. B., Stein, D. J., Liebowitz, M. R., & Rosen, W. G. (1994). Neuropsychology of obsessive-compulsive disorder. *Neuropsychiatry, Neuropsychology, and Behavioral Neurology, 7,* 81–86.

Baer, L. (1994). Factor analysis of symptom subtype of OCD and their relation to personality and tic disorders. *Journal of Clinical Psychiatry, 55*(Suppl.), 18–23.

Baxter, L. R., Phelps, M. E., Mazziotta, J. C., Guze, B. H., Schwartz, J. M., & Selin, C. E. (1987). Local cerebral glucose metabolic rates in obsessive-compulsive disorder: A comparison with rates in unipolar depression and in normal controls. *Archives of General Psychiatry, 44,* 211–218.

Baxter, L. R., Schwartz, J. M., Bergman, K. S., Szuba, M. P., Guze, B. H., Mazziotta, J. C., Alazraki, A., Selin, C. E., Ferngh, I. C., & Munford, P. (1992). Caudate glucose metabolic rate changes with both drug and behavioral therapies for obsessive-compulsive disorder. *Archives of General Psychiatry, 49,* 681–689.

Black, A. (1974). The natural history of obsessional neurosis. In H. K. Beech (Ed.), *Obsessional states* (pp. 1–23). London: Methuen.

Black, D. W., Noyes, R., Jr., Pfohl, B., Goldstein, R. B., & Blum, N. (1993). Personality disorders in OCD volunteers, well-comparison subjects, and their first degree relatives. *American Journal of Psychiatry, 150*(8), 1226–1232.

Braddock, L. E. (1982). Dysmorphophobia in adolescence: A case report. *British Journal of Psychiatry, 140,* 199–201.

Broderick, P. A., Gardner, E. L., & Van Praag, H. M. (1984). In vivo electrochemical and behavioral evidence for specific neural substrates modified differentially by the encephalon in rat stimulant stereotypy and locomotion. *Biological Psychiatry, 19,* 45–54.

Carrasco, J. L., Saiz-Ruiz, J., Moreno, I., Hollander, E., & Lopez-Ibor, J. J. (1994). Low platelet monoamine oxidase activity in pathological gambling. *Acta Psychiatrica Scandinavica, 90,* 427–431.

Coleman, E. (1987). Sexual compulsivity: Definition, etiology, and treatment considerations. In E. Coleman (Ed.), *Chemical dependency and intimacy dysfunction* (pp. 189–204). New York: Hawarth.

DeCaria, C. M., & Hollander, E. (1993). Pathological gambling. In E. Hollander (Ed.), *Obsessive compulsive related disorders* (pp. 151–178). Washington, DC: American Psychiatric Press.

Degonda, M., Wyss, M., & Angst, J. (1993). The Zurich Study XVIII: Obsessive-compulsive disorder and syndromes in the general population. *European Archives of Psychiatry and Clinical Neuroscience, 243*(1), 16–22.

Denckla, M. B. (1989). Neurological examination. In J. L. Rapoport (Ed.), *Obsessive-compulsive disorder in children and adolescents* (pp. 107–115). Washington, DC: American Psychiatric Press.

Dominguez, R. A., & Mestre, C. M. (1994). Management of treatment-resistant obsessive-compulsive patients. *Journal of Clinical Psychiatry, 55*(Suppl.), 86–92.

Emmanuel, N. P., Lydiard, R. B., & Ballenger J. C. (1991). Fluoxetine treatment of voyeurism [letter]. *American Journal of Psychiatry, 148,* 950.

Fallon, E., Liebowitz, M. R., Salmon, E., Schneier F. R., Jusino, C., Hollander, E., & Klein, D. F. (1993). Fluoxetine for hypochondriacal patients without major depression. *Journal of Clinical Psychopharmacology, 13,* 438–441.

Favazza, A. R. (1992). Repetitive self-mutilation. *Psychiatric Annals, 22*(2), 60–63.

Flament, M. F., Rapoport, J. L., Berg, C. L., Sceery, W., Kitts, C., Mellstrom, B., & Linnoila, M. (1985). Clomipramine treatment of childhood obsessive-compulsive disorder: A double-blind controlled study. *Archives of General Psychiatry, 42*, 977–986.

Ford, C. V. (1995). Dimensions of somatization and hypochondriasis. *Neurology Clinics, 13*(2), 241–253.

Frost, R. O., & Shaws, D. L. (1993). The nature and measurement of compulsive indecisiveness. *Behavioral Research and Therapeutics, 31*(7), 683–692.

Goodman, W. K., McDougle, C. J., & Price, J. H. (1992). Pharmacotherapy of obsessive-compulsive disorder. *Journal of Clinical Psychiatry, 53*(Suppl.), 29–37.

Goodman, W. K., Price, L. H., Delgado, P. L., Palumbo, J., Krystal, J. H., Nagy, L. M., Rasmussen, J. A., Heninger, G. R., & Charney, D. J. (1990). Specificity of serotonergic reuptake inhibitors in the treatment of obsessive-compulsive disorders: A comparison of fluvoxamine and desipramine. *Archives of General Psychiatry, 47*, 577–585.

Goodman, W. K., Price, L. H., Rasmussen, S. A., Mazure, C., Fleischmann, R. L., Hill, C. L., Heninger, G. R., & Charney, D. S. (1989). The Yale Brown Obsessive Compulsive Scale. I. Development, use and reliability. *Archives of General Psychiatry, 46*, 1006–1011.

Gray, J. A. (1992). *The neuropsychology of anxiety.* New York: Oxford University Press.

Gwirtsman, H. E., Guze, B. H., Yager, J., & Gainsley, B. (1990). Fluoxetine treatment of anorexia nervosa: An open clinical trial. *Journal of Clinical Psychiatry, 51*, 378–382.

Hjort, C. (1994). Asperger's syndrome: A new diagnosis in the international classification of diseases. *Ugeskr Laeger, 156*(18), 2729–2734.

Hoehn-Saric, R., Pearlson, G. D., Harris, G. J., Machlin, S. R., & Camargo, E. E. (1991). Effects of fluoxetine on regional cerebral blood flow in obsessive-compulsive patients. *American Journal of Psychiatry, 148*(9), 1243–1245.

Hollander, E. (1993a). *Obsessive-compulsive related disorders.* Washington, DC: American Psychiatric Press.

Hollander, E. (1993b). Obsessive-compulsive spectrum disorders: An overview. *Psychiatric Annals, 23*(7), 355–358.

Hollander, E., Cohen, L., & Simeon, D. (1993). Body dysmorphic disorder. *Psychiatric Annals, 23*(7), 359–364.

Hollander, E., Cohen, L., Simeon, D., Rosen, J., DeCaria, C. M., & Stein, D. J. (1994). Fluvoxamine treatment of body dysmorphic disorder [letter]. *Journal of Clinical Psychopharmacology, 14*, 75–77.

Hollander, E., DeCaria, C., Mari, E., Wong, C., Mosovich, S., Grossman, R., & Begaz, T. (1998). Short-term single-blind fluvoxamine treatment of pathological gambling. *American Journal of Psychiatry, 155*, 1781–1783.

Hollander, E., DeCaria, C. M., Nitescu, A., Gulley, R., Suckow, R. F., Cooper, T. B., Gorman, J. G., Klein, D. F., & Liebowitz, M. R. (1992). Serotonergic function in obsessive-compulsive disorder: Behavioral and neuroendocrine responses to oral m-chlorophenyl-piperazine and fenfluramine in patients and healthy volunteers. *Archives of General Psychiatry, 49*, 21–28.

Hollander, E., Frenkel, M., DeCaria, C. M., Trungold, S., & Klein, D. F. (1992). Treatment of pathological gambling with clomipramine [letter]. *American Journal of Psychiatry, 149*, 710–711.

Hollander, E., Liebowitz, M. R., Fallon, B., Fairbanks, J., DeCaria, C. M., & Klein, D. F. (1990). Treatment of depersonalization disorder with serotonin reuptake inhibitors. *Journal of Clinical Psychopharmacology, 10*, 200–203.

Hollander, E., Liebowitz, M. R., Winchel, R. W., Klumker, A., & Klein, D. F. (1989). Treatment of body dysmorphic disorder with serotonin reuptake blockers. *American Journal of Psychiatry, 146*, 768–770.

Hollander, E., Schiffman, E., Cohen, B., Rivera-Stein, M. A., Rosen, W., Gorman, J. M., Fryer, A. J., Papp, L., & Liebowitz, M. R. (1990). Signs of central nervous system dysfunction in obsessive-compulsive disorder. *Archives of General Psychiatry, 47*, 27–32.

Hollander, E., Stein, D. J., DeCaria, C. M., Cohen, L. J., Saoud, J. B., Skodol, A. E., Kellman, D., Rosnick, L., & Oldham, J. (1994). Serotonergic sensitivity in borderline personality disorder: Preliminary findings. *American Journal of Psychiatry, 151*, 277–280.

Hollander, E., & Wong, C. M. (1995a). Body dysmorphic disorder, pathological gambling, and sexual compulsions. *Journal of Clinical Psychiatry, 56*(Suppl. 4), 7–12.

Hollander, E., & Wong, C. M. (1995b). Introduction: Obsessive-compulsive spectrum disorder. *Journal of Clinical Psychiatry, 56*(Suppl. 4), 3–6.

Hollingsworth, C., Tanguay, P., Grossman, L., & Pabst, P. (1980). Longterm outcome of obsessive-compulsive disorder in childhood. *Journal of the American Academy of Child Psychiatry, 19*, 134–144.

Holzer, J. C., Goodman, W. K., McDougle, C. J., Baer, L., Boyarsky, B. K., Leckman, J. F., & Price L. H. (1994). Obsessive-compulsive disorder with and without chronic tic disorder: A compilation of symptoms in 70 patients. *British Journal of Psychiatry, 164*(4), 469–473.

Hsu, L. K., Kaye, W., & Weltzin, T. (1993). Are the eating disorders related to obsessive-compulsive disorder? *International Journal of Eating Disorders, 14*(3), 305–318.

Kafka, M. P. (1991). Successful treatment of paraphilic coercive disorder (a rapist) with fluoxetine hydrochloride. *British Journal of Psychiatry, 158*, 844–847.

Leckman, J. F., Goodman, W. K., North, W. G., Chapell, P. B., Price, L. H., Pauls, D. L., Anderson, G. M., Riddle, M. A., McDougle, D. J., & Baer, L. C. (1994). The role of central oxytocin in obsessive-compulsive disorder and relative normal behavior. *Psychoneuroendocrinology, 19*(8), 723–749.

Leonard, H. L., Topol, D., & Bukstein, O. (1994). Clonazepam as an augmentation agent in the treatment of childhood-onset obsessive-compulsive disorder. *Journal of the American Academy of Child and Adolescent Psychiatry, 33*(6), 792–794.

Lewis, M. H., Bodfish, J. W., Powell, S. B., & Golden, R. N. (1995). Clomipramine treatment for stereotypy and related repetitive movement disorder associated with mental retardation. *American Journal of Mental Retardation, 100*(3), 299–312.

Machlin, S. R., Harris, G. J., Pearlson, G. D., Hoehn-Saric, R., Jeffrey, P., & Camargo, E. E. (1991). Elevated medical frontal cerebral glucose blood flow in obsessive-compulsive patients: A SPECT study. *American Journal of Psychiatry, 148*(9), 1240–1242.

McDougle, C. J., Fleischman, R. L., & Epperson, C. N. (1995). Risperidone addition in fluvoxamine-refractory obsessive-compulsive disorder: 3 cases. *Journal of Clinical Psychiatry, 56*(11), 526–528.

McDougle, C. J., Goodman, W. K., & Leckman, J. F. (1994). Haloperidol addition in fluvoxamine-refractory obsessive-compulsive disorder: A double-blind placebo-controlled study in patients with and without tics. *Archives of General Psychiatry, 51*(4), 302–308.

McDougle, C. J., Goodman, W. K., & Price, L. A. (1994). Dopamine antagonists in tic-related and psychotic spectrum obsessive-compulsive disorder. *Journal of Clinical Psychiatry, 55*(Suppl.), 24–31.

McDougle, C. J., Kresch, L. E., Goodman, W. K., Naylor, S. T., Volkmar, F. R., Cohen, D. J., & Price, L. H. (1995). A case-controlled study of repetitive thoughts and behaviors in adults with autistic disorder and obsessive-compulsive disorder. *American Journal of Psychiatry, 152*(5), 772–777.

McElroy, S. L., Harrison, G. P., Keck, P. E., & Hudson, J. I. (1995). Disorders of impulse control. In E. Hollander & D. J. Stein (Eds.), *Impulsivity and aggression* (pp. 109–136). London: Wiley.

McElroy, S. L., Hudson, J. I., Pope, H. G., Hudson, J. I., Keck, P. E., & White, K. L. (1991). Kleptomania: A report of 20 cases. *American Journal of Psychiatry, 148*, 652–657.

McElroy, S. L., Keck, P. E., & Phillips, K. A. (1995). Kleptomania, compulsive buying, and binge-eating disorder. *Journal of Clinical Psychiatry, 56*(Suppl. 4), 14–26.

McElroy, S. L., Keck, P. E., Pope, H. G., Smith, J. M., & Strakowski, S. M. (1994). Compulsive buying: A report of 20 cases. *Journal of Clinical Psychiatry, 55*(5), 242–248.

Miguel, E. C., Coffey, B. I., Baer, L., Savage, C. R., Rauch, S. L., & Jenike, M. A. (1995). Phenomenology of intentional repetitive behaviors in obsessive-compulsive disorder and Tourette's disorder. *Journal of Clinical Psychiatry, 56*(6), 246–255.

Murphy, T. K., Goodman, W. K., Fudge, M. W., Williams, R. C., Jr., Ayoub, E. M., Dalal, M., Lewis, M. H., & Zabriskie, J. B. (1997). B Lymphocyte antigen D8/17: A peripheral marker for childhood onset obsessive-compulsive disorder and Tourette's syndrome? *American Journal of Psychiatry, 154*(3), 402–407.

Nicolini, H., Wessbecker, K., Mejia, J. M., & Sanchez de Carmona, M. (1993). Family study of obsessive-compulsive disorder in a Mexican population. *Archives of Medical Research, 24*(2), 193–198.

Okasha, A., Saad, A., Khalil, A. H., Dawla, A. S., & Yehia, N. (1994). Phenomenology of obsessive-compulsive disorder: A transcultural study. *Comprehensive Psychiatry, 35*(3), 191–197.

Pauls, D. L., Alsobrook, J. P., Goodman, W. K., Rasmussen, S., & Leckman, J. F. (1995). A family study of obsessive-compulsive disorder. *American Journal of Psychiatry, 152*(1), 76–84.

Phillips, K. A. (1991). Body dysmorphic disorder: The distress of imagined ugliness. *American Journal of Psychiatry, 148*, 1138–1149.

Pigott, T. A., L'Heureux, F., Hill, J. L., Bjhari, K., Bernstein, S. E., & Murphy, D. L. (1992). A double-blind study of adjuvant buspirone hydrochloride in clomipramine-treated patients with obsessive-compulsive disorder. *Journal of Clinical Psychopharmacology, 12*(1), 11–18.

Rosen, K. V., & Tallis, F. (1995). Investigation into the relationship between personal traits and obsessive-compulsive disorder. *Behavioral Research and Therapy, 33*(4), 445–450.

Rosenthal, R. J. (1992). Pathological gambling. *Psychiatric Annals, 22*(2), 72–78.

Rotter, M., & Goodman, W. K. (1995). The relationship between insight and control in obsessive-compulsive disorder: Implications for the insanity defense. *Bulletin of the American Academy of Psychiatry and the Law, 21*(2), 245–252.

Stein, D. J., Hollander, E., Anthony, D. T., Scneier, F. R., Fallon, B. A., Liebowitz, M. R., & Klein, D. F. (1992). Serotonergic medications for sexual obsessions, sexual addictions, and paraphilias. *Journal of Clinical Psychiatry, 53*, 267–271.

Stein, D. J., Mullen, L., Islam, M. N., Cohen, L., DeCaria, C. M., & Hollander, E. (1995). Compulsive and impulsive symptoms in trichotillomania. *Psychopathology, 28*(4), 208–213.

Swedo, S. E., & Leonard, H. L. (1994). Childhood movement disorder and obsessive-compulsive disorder. *Journal of Clinical Psychiatry, 55*(Suppl.), 32–37.

Swedo, S. E., Leonard, H. L., Rapoport, J. L., Lenane, M. C., Goldberger, E. L., & Cheslow, D. L. (1989). A double-blind comparison of clomipramine and desipramine in the treatment of trichotillomania (hair-pulling). *New England Journal of Medicine, 321*, 491–501.

Swedo, S. E., Peitrini, P., Leonard, H. L., Schapiro, M. B., Rettew, D. C., Goldberger, E. L., Rapoport, S. I., Rapoport, J. L., & Grady, C. L. (1992). Cerebral glucose metabolism in childhood-onset obsessive-compulsive disorder: Revisualization during psychopharmacology. *Archives of General Psychiatry, 49*(9), 690–694.

Swedo, S. E., Rapoport, J. L., Cheslow, D. L., Leonard, H. L., Ayoub, E. M., Hosier, D. M., & Wald, E. R. (1989). High prevalence of obsessive-compulsive symptoms in patients with Sydenham's chorea. *American Journal of Psychiatry, 146*, 246–249.

Swedo, S. E., Schapiro, M. B., Grady, C. L., Cheslow, D. L., Leonard, H. L., Kumar, A., Freidlan, J. R., Rapoport, S. I., & Rapoport, J. L. (1989). Cerebral glucose metabolism in childhood-onset obsessive-compulsive disorder. *Archives of General Psychiatry, 46*, 518–523.

Theil, A., Broocks, A., & Ohlmeier, M. (1995). Obsessive-compulsive disorder among patients with anorexia nervosa and bulimia nervosa. *American Journal of Psychiatry, 152*(1), 72–75.

Thomsen, P. H., & Mikkelsen, H. U. (1993). Development of personality disorders in children and adolescents in obsessive-compulsive disorder: A 6 to 22 year follow-up study. *Acta Psychiatrica Scandinavica, 87*(6), 456–462.

Thoren, P., Asberg, M., Bertilsson, L., Mellstrom, B., Syoquist, F., & Traskman, L. (1980). Clomipramine treatment of obsessive-compulsive disorder: II. Biological aspects. *Archives of General Psychiatry, 37*, 1281–1289.

Veale, D. (1993). Classification and treatment of obsessive slowness. *British Journal of Psychiatry, 162*, 198–203.

Warwick, H. M. (1995). Assessment of hypochondriasis. *Behavioral Research and Therapy, 33*(7), 845–853.

Winchel, R. M. (1992). Trichotillomania: Presentation and treatment. *Psychiatric Annals, 22*(2), 84–89.

Wong, C. M., & Hollander, E. (1996, March). New dimensions in the OCD spectrum: Autism, pathological gambling, and compulsive buying. *Primary Psychiatry, 3*(3), 20–34.

Wright, S. (1994). Familial obsessive-compulsive disorder presenting as pathological jealousy successfully treated with fluoxetine [letter]. *Archives of General Psychiatry, 51*(5), 430–431.

Yeshiayan, S. K., & Kelley, A. E. (1995). Serotonergic stimulation of ventrolateral striatum causes orofacial stereotypy. *Pharmacology, Biochemistry, and Behavior, 52*(3), 493–501.

Zohar, J., Mueller, E. A., Insel, T. R., Zohar-Kadouch, R. C., & Murphy, D. L. (1987). Serotonergic responsivity in obsessive-compulsive disorder: Comparison of patients and healthy controls. *Archives of General Psychiatry, 44*, 946–951.

2

Connection Between Obsessive-Compulsive Disorder and Body Dysmorphic Disorder

Katharine A. Phillips
Butler Hospital, Providence, RI
Brown University School of Medicine

> *The dysmorphophobic patient is really miserable; in the middle of his daily routines, talks, while reading, during meals, everywhere and at any time, he is caught by the doubt of deformity. . . .*
> —Enriqo Morselli, 1891 (quoted in Fava, 1992, p. 117)

Written more than a century ago, this description captures the doubt and obsessional preoccupation, as well as the suffering, that characterize body dysmorphic disorder (BDD; Fava, 1992; Morselli, 1891). Morselli was one of several early psychopathologists who considered BDD to be related to obsessive-compulsive disorder (OCD). Another was Janet (1903), who referred to BDD as *obsession de la honte du corps*, or obsession with shame of the body, and classified it within a group of syndromes related to OCD.

More recently, a number of investigators have similarly conceptualized BDD as an OCD-spectrum disorder—that is, a disorder with similarities to OCD in a variety of domains (Hollander, 1993; Hollander & Wong, chap. 1, this volume). A reflection of this hypothesis, BDD is included in the Symptom Checklist of the Yale–Brown Obsessive Compulsive Scale (Y–BOCS; Goodman, Price, Rasmussen, Mazure, Delgado, et al., 1989; Goodman, Price, Rasmussen, Mazure, Fleischman, et al., 1989) as a disorder that may be related to BDD. In addition, consideration was given to transferring BDD from the somatoform to the anxiety disorder section of the *Diagnostic and Statistical Manual of Mental Disorders* (4th ed. [*DSM–IV*]; American Psychiatric Association, 1994; Phillips & Hollander, 1996). Reflecting their similarities, some patients diagnosed with OCD, including treatment-refractory OCD, actually have BDD (K. A. Phillips, unpublished observations; Vitiello & deLeon, 1990).

The hypothesis that BDD is related to OCD is controversial, however. Some early authors considered BDD a form of schizophrenia (e.g., Zaidens, 1950). In Japan, BDD is considered a member of a larger group of disorders, *Taijin Kyofushu*, that closely resembles *DSM–IV*'s social phobia (Kasahara, 1987). In *DSM–IV* and in the International Classification of Diseases (10th ed. [ICD–10]; World Health Organization, 1992), BDD is classified as a somatoform disorder—as a separate disorder in *DSM–IV* and as a type of hypochondriasis in ICD–10.

BDD is defined as a preoccupation with an imagined or slight defect in appearance that causes clinically significant distress or impairment in functioning. The following is the *DSM–IV* definition of BDD:

1. Preoccupation with some imagined defect in appearance. If a slight physical anomaly is present, the person's concern is markedly excessive.
2. The preoccupation causes clinically significant distress or impairment in social, occupational, or other important areas of functioning.
3. The preoccupation is not better accounted for by another mental disorder (e.g., dissatisfaction with body shape and size in Anorexia Nervosa). (American Psychiatric Association, 1994, p.)

It has been described for more than 100 years and reported around the world under such rubrics as dysmorphophobia, beauty hypochondria, dermatologic hypochondriasis, and *Hässlichkeitskümmerer* ("one who is worried about being ugly"; Phillips, 1991). Although BDD has been little investigated, research on this relatively common but often secret and underrecognized disorder is rapidly increasing.

The following case illustrates many of BDD's clinical features, including some of its similarities to and differences from OCD:

> Mr. A., a 31-year-old carpenter, had been excessively preoccupied since age 16 with pores on his nose, which he was convinced were too large, making him look "as ugly as the Elephant Man." He thought about the pores for hours a day and covered them with makeup and a baseball hat pulled down over his nose. He frequently checked mirrors, sought reassurance, and thought others took special notice of and laughed at the "grotesque holes." He felt comfortable only on Halloween, when he could cover them with a mask.
>
> Mr. A. described his concern as "extremely painful," stating that he would rather have cancer. Because his preoccupation made him self-conscious and interfered with his concentration, Mr. A. missed work and was eventually fired. He also missed many social events, causing his girlfriend

to leave him. Because he thought the pores made him unworthy, unlovable, and rejected by others, Mr. A. had made more than 15 suicide attempts. During his numerous hospitalizations, he kept his appearance concerns a secret because of his shame and fear that he would not be taken seriously.

Mr. A. received fluoxetine, up to 80 mg/day, which after 8 weeks notably diminished his preoccupation, distress, and BDD-related behaviors. These symptoms further improved with addition of buspirone 60 mg/day. Clonazepam 1.5 mg/day did not diminish his BDD symptoms but lessened his anxiety. Mr. A. was much improved for the next 2 years, resuming work and starting a new relationship. However, after decreasing the fluoxetine to 60 mg/day, his BDD symptoms significantly worsened, leading to a serious suicide attempt. Mr. A.'s medications were increased again, and for the past 2 years his symptoms have been in near remission on fluoxetine 120 mg/day, buspirone 70 mg/day, and clonazepam 1.5 mg/day.

A HISTORICAL PERSPECTIVE

Early descriptions of BDD emphasized the great anxiety that patients experience as well as BDD's similarities to OCD (Janet, 1903; Morselli, 1891). Morselli, who in the 1800s saw numerous patients with BDD, noted the obsessive nature of the "idea of deformity" and the compulsive checking (such as mirror checking) that accompanies the obsessional worry (Fava, 1992; Morselli, 1891). These OCD-like characteristics are evident in the following description of the Wolf Man (Brunswick, 1928), who appears to have had BDD:

> The Wolf Man neglected his daily life and work because he was engrossed, to the exclusion of all else, in the state of his nose (its supposed scars, holes, and swelling). His life was centered on the little mirror in his pocket, and his fate depended on what it revealed or was about to reveal. (p. 265)

Stekel (1949) also underscored the similarities between BDD and OCD when he described BDD as

> The peculiar group of compulsive ideas which concern the body. There are people who occupy themselves continuously with a specific part of the body. In one case it is the nose, in another it is the bald head; in a third case the ear, the eyes, or (in women) the bosom, the genitalia, etc. These obsessive thoughts are very tormenting. (p. 131)

However, other theories have been proposed. Zaidens (1950), for example, considered "dermatologic hypochondriasis" (excessive preoccupation with minor defects of the skin or hair) a form of schizophrenia. Anderson (1964) similarly noted that many individuals with BDD probably had mild schizophrenia, and more recently, Connolly and Gipson

(1978) described BDD as an "ominous symptom" that was often a precursor of schizophrenia.

IS BDD AN OCD-SPECTRUM DISORDER?

Current hypotheses postulate that BDD is more closely related to OCD
than to schizophrenia (Phillips, in press). A number of investigators
conceptualize BDD as an OCD-spectrum disorder; that is, a disorder that
shares features with OCD (Brady, Austin, & Lydiard, 1990; Hollander &
Phillips, 1993; McElroy, Phillips, & Keck, 1994; Phillips, McElroy, Hudson,
& Pope, 1995). Some of the other disorders included in this hypothesized
spectrum are Tourette's disorder, hypochondriasis, trichotillomania, and
kleptomania (Hollander, 1993). Disorders are posited to have spectrum
membership on the basis of their similarities with OCD in domains such
as symptoms, sex ratio, age of onset, course, comorbidity, joint familial
loading, treatment response, premorbid personality characteristics, and
presumed etiology (Klein, 1993). Presumed etiology is inferred from such
characteristics as neurologic deficits, psychological test performance,
response to biological challenges, biochemical indexes, brain imaging
patterns (functional and anatomical), and epidemiologic risk factors.

The following analysis assesses similarities and differences between
BDD and OCD in the preceding domains for which data are available
(see Table 2.1). This analysis is limited by the small number of studies
and preliminary nature of research on BDD, a near absence of data on
BDD in certain domains (e.g., presumed etiology), and a paucity of direct
comparison studies of BDD and OCD. In addition, the OCD-spectrum
concept is not operationally defined—for example, how similar must BDD
be to OCD in these domains and in how many domains must similarities
exist to demonstrate that BDD is related to, or a form of, OCD? Ultimately,
to determine whether these disorders are related, their etiology and pathophysiology must be understood.

The following discussion, although limited in these ways, suggests that
BDD and OCD have many similarities but also some differences. Thus,
at this time, BDD and OCD appear to be closely related but probably
distinct disorders.

EVIDENCE FOR A CONNECTION
BETWEEN BDD AND OCD

Phenomenology

Phenomenology is an important starting point for an analysis of the
similarities and differences between BDD and OCD. As has been noted
for the past century, the core symptoms of BDD structurally resemble

TABLE 2.1
Some Similarities and Differences Between
BDD and OCD in Selected Domains

Domain	Similarities	Differences
Phenomenology	Obsessional preoccupations	Content of concern
	Repetitive, compulsive behaviors in a similar percentage of patients	Insight generally good in OCD; often poor or absent in BDD
	Content of concern similar in some cases (symmetry, perfection, "not right" concern)	Referential thinking common in BDD but not OCD
	Behaviors similar (e.g., checking, reassurance seeking, skin picking)	Lower self-esteem and more shame and rejection sensitivity in BDD?
	Degree of resistance and control	Rituals more likely to increase anxiety in BDD?
Demographics	Sex ratio	Fewer with BDD ever married
	Educational level	
Course	Age at onset	
	Course of illness (often chronic)	
Comorbidity	BDD and OCD often comorbid	Higher rate of major depression and social phobia in BDD
	Comorbidity patterns generally similar	Earlier age of onset of major depression in BDD
Family history	Relatively high rate of OCD in relatives of BDD probands	Higher rate of substance use disorder in relatives of BDD probands
	Family history patterns generally similar	
Treatment response	Possible preferential response to SRIs in BDD; similar time to response, dose required, rate of relapse with discontinuation?	More important role for neuroleptics in delusional BDD than delusional OCD?
	Possible similar response to pharmacologic augmentation strategies	Poorer response of delusional BDD to cognitive-behavioral therapy?
	Possibly a better response to exposure and response prevention than to supportive and insight-oriented therapies in BDD	
Presumed etiology	Possible important role for serotonin and dopamine in BDD	
	Similar findings on neuropsychological testing	
Other domains	Illness severity	Higher rate of suicidal ideation and attempts in BDD

Note. Information in this table should be considered preliminary, given the relative paucity and preliminary nature of research on BDD, a near absence of data on BDD in certain domains (e.g., presumed etiology), and a paucity of direct comparison studies of BDD and OCD.

OCD obsessions and compulsions. BDD preoccupations—which focus on perceived defects of the skin, hair, nose, or other body parts—are distressing, anxiety-producing, persistent, recurrent thoughts that are difficult to resist or control (Phillips, McElroy, Keck, Pope, & Hudson, 1993). Patients may describe their appearance preoccupation as an obsession, and BDD symptoms are not infrequently misdiagnosed as OCD.

In addition, more than 90% of patients with BDD engage in repetitive and often time-consuming behaviors similar to OCD compulsions (Phillips et al., 1993). The behaviors, generally aimed at examining, hiding, improving, or obtaining reassurance about the perceived defect, are often described as compulsive, or difficult to resist or control. They include checking the perceived defect in mirrors and other reflecting surfaces, excessive grooming (e.g., hair styling, shaving), skin picking, comparing the body part with that of other people, hiding or covering the perceived defect, and seeking reassurance. A substantial number of individuals— referred to as "polysurgery addicts" (Fukuda, 1977)—repeatedly request surgery for their nonexistent or minimal deformity.

In addition to these similarities in symptom form, some BDD and OCD symptoms have nearly identical content. These include preoccupations with symmetry, a need for perfection, and a sense that something "isn't right," focusing on appearance in BDD and other concerns in OCD. Behaviors such as repetitive checking, seeking reassurance, and skin picking are also remarkably similar in the two disorders. In addition, in some cases BDD and OCD symptoms are so interwoven that it is difficult to differentiate the disorders. One patient, for example, performed time-consuming OCD-like rituals to prevent worsening of his minimal acne. He repeatedly walked through his dining room until he avoided all "spots" on the floor that symbolized his acne, repeatedly sat down until he felt no acnelike "bumps" on the chair, and repeatedly lifted his glass until he saw no "spots" (i.e., anything small, red, and round) in his environment. To prevent an "acne breakout," he forbade his family members to move the radio. Subsequently, over time, this patient performed these rituals not to improve his skin but to prevent general harm.

In support of these clinical observations on the similarities of BDD and OCD symptoms, Hay (1970) found that patients with dysmorphophobia were more "obsessoid" than a control group, and Hardy and Cotterill (1982) found that patients with dysmorphophobia ($N = 12$) and controls with psoriasis both scored higher on the Leyton Obsessional Inventory (Cooper, 1970) than healthy controls. In addition, my colleagues and I found that on the Y–BOCS (using the first 10 items of a slightly modified version for BDD, the BDD–Y–BOCS; Phillips et al., 1997), total and individual-item scores of 53 patients with BDD were nearly identical to those of 53 patients with OCD (Phillips, Gunderson, Mallya, McElroy, & Carter, 1998).

However, there are some apparent phenomenologic differences between BDD and OCD. The most evident is the content of the preoccupations, which focus on appearance in BDD and other concerns in OCD. In addition, BDD preoccupations appear to more often be associated with shame, rejection sensitivity, and low self-esteem, and BDD behaviors (such as mirror checking) appear to often increase rather than decrease anxiety. These clinical observations require empirical validation.

Another apparent difference involves insight. The beliefs that underlie BDD preoccupations appear to more often be delusional, or characterized by poor insight or overvalued ideation, than those underlying OCD obsessions (Eisen, Phillips, Rasmussen, & Luce, 1997; Simeon, Hollander, Stein, Cohen, & Aronowitz, 1995; Vitiello & deLeon, 1990). In one study, more than half of 100 patients with BDD were delusional for a significant period of time, a percentage far higher than that reported for patients with OCD (Eisen & Rasmussen, 1993; Phillips, McElroy, Keck, Pope, & Hudson, 1994). In addition, BDD appears to be accompanied more often by ideas or delusions of reference (Eisen, Phillips, Rasmussen, & Luce, 1997). In a series of 100 patients with BDD, two thirds thought that others took special notice of, talked about, or mocked the supposed defect (Phillips, McElroy, et al., 1994).

On balance, clinical observations and available empirical evidence suggest that BDD symptoms have many striking similarities to those of OCD, especially in the obsessional preoccupation and ritualistic behaviors characteristic of both disorders. However, there also appear to be some differences. These apparent similarities and differences require further investigation in direct comparison studies of the two disorders.

Demographic Features, Age at Onset, and Course of Illness

There appear to be more similarities than differences between BDD and OCD in demographic features, age at onset, and course of illness. A comparison study of *DSM–IV* BDD ($n = 53$) and OCD ($n = 53$) found a similar sex ratio (approximately 1:1; Phillips, Gunderson, et al., 1998). In the largest known series of individuals with *DSM–IV*-defined BDD, the ratio of men to women was 1:1 (Phillips & Diaz, 1997), although several smaller BDD series have found either a preponderance of women (Rosen, Reiter, & Orosan, 1995; Veale, Boocock, et al., 1996) or of men (Fukuda, 1977; Hollander, Cohen, & Simeon, 1993).

In the BDD–OCD comparison study, the two groups were also similar in educational level, an often-chronic course of illness, and age at onset. Like OCD, a sizable percentage of cases of BDD appear to have onset during childhood. However, in the comparison study, individuals with

BDD were significantly less likely to have ever been married (13% vs. 39%).

Comorbidity

Supporting the hypothesis that BDD is related to OCD, the two disorders appear to be highly comorbid with each other and with similar other psychiatric disorders. In one series, which based diagnosis on the Structured Clinical Interview for the *Diagnostic and Statistical Manual of Mental Disorders* (3rd ed., rev. [*DSM–III–R*]; American Psychiatric Association, 1987; Spitzer, Williams, Gibbon, & First, 1992), 34% of 100 patients with BDD had lifetime OCD (Phillips, McElroy, et al., 1994). Conversely, rates of BDD among patients with OCD, although variable, are also fairly high. Studies have reported rates of 8% (4 of 53; Brawman-Mintzer et al., 1995), 12% (51 of 442; Simeon et al., 1995), 15% (9 of 62; Phillips, Gunderson, et al., 1998), and 37% (Hollander et al., 1993). In addition, BDD and OCD are both associated with high rates of major depression and other anxiety disorders. In the previously mentioned BDD–OCD comparison study, comorbidity patterns were generally similar for the two disorders (Phillips, Gunderson, et al., 1998). However, several differences were found in that study: Individuals with BDD had a significantly higher rate of comorbid social phobia and major depression and an earlier age of onset of major depression.

Studies that have used structured instruments to assess the rate of comorbid *DSM–III–R* personality disorders in patients with BDD have found somewhat higher rates (72% of 50 participants [Veale, Boocock, et al., 1996], 100% of 17 patients [Neziroglu, McKay, Todaro, & Yaryura-Tobias, 1996], and 57% of 74 patients [Phillips & McElroy, 1993]) than have generally been reported for OCD (Baer, Jenike, Black, et al., 1992; Baer, Jenike, Ricciardi, et al., 1990). In these studies, avoidant and paranoid personality disorders were most common and were present at notably higher rates than in studies of OCD.

Family History

Hollander et al. (1993) found that OCD was the most common disorder in relatives of 50 patients with BDD. Although the presence of comorbid OCD in a high percentage of probands (78%) could account for this finding, it may also indicate that BDD and OCD are related disorders. Our group found that 4% of first-degree relatives of BDD probands had OCD, a rate approximately twice that in the general population (McElroy, Phillips, Keck, Hudson, & Pope, 1993). The family history method used in this study, in which probands rather than relatives were interviewed, probably underestimated the rate of OCD in relatives.

Family history data from the previously mentioned BDD–OCD comparison study (obtained using the family history method with a structured instrument by a rater blind to proband diagnosis) found that BDD and OCD probands had a similar family history except for a higher rate of alcohol or drug abuse or dependence in first-degree relatives of BDD probands (Phillips, Gunderson, et al., 1998).

Treatment Response

The majority of patients with BDD (72% in one series; Phillips, 1996a) seek often costly nonpsychiatric medical treatment, most often from surgeons (Fukuda, 1977) and dermatologists (Cotterill, 1981). A wide variety of practitioners may be seen—for example, ophthalmologists to evaluate "cross-eyed" eyes, endocrinologists to evaluate "excessive" body hair, or urologists to evaluate "small" genitals. Such treatments usually do not improve, and may even worsen, BDD symptoms. In some cases, concern with the treated body part improves but only temporarily, or preoccupation with another body part develops. Some patients receive multiple procedures in their quest for a surgical solution to a psychiatric problem. Rarely, dissatisfied patients are violent toward the treating physician (Phillips, McElroy, & Lion, 1992).

Preliminary data suggest that psychiatric treatment is more promising. Findings from uncontrolled studies suggest that BDD may, like OCD, respond preferentially to serotonin reuptake inhibitors (SRIs) and perhaps also to exposure and response prevention. Early case reports produced mixed findings and little consensus on the pharmacologic treatment of choice for BDD (Phillips, 1991). Successful outcomes were reported in a small number of cases with a variety of psychotropic agents, such as tricyclic antidepressants, monoamine oxidase (MAO) inhibitors, and antipsychotics. However, most reported outcomes with these and other medications and with electroconvulsive therapy (ECT) have been negative.

More recent data suggest that SRIs are often effective for BDD, whereas other medications are usually ineffective. Hollander and colleagues first reported that five patients who had failed to respond to a variety of psychotropic agents responded to fluoxetine and clomipramine (Hollander, Liebowitz, Winchel, Klumker, & Klein, 1989), and Brady et al. (1990) reported that three patients with BDD responded to fluoxetine. Phillips et al. (1993) then reported that among 30 patients with BDD (who were treated by the authors in an open fashion or whose treatment response was assessed retrospectively), 58% of SRI treatment trials significantly decreased symptoms compared to only 5% with a variety of other medications.

Our expanded series of 100 and 130 patients yielded similar results (Phillips, 1996a; Phillips, McElroy, et al., 1994). Of 316 retrospectively assessed treatment trials in 130 patients, 42% of 65 SRI trials (fluoxetine, clomipramine, paroxetine, sertraline, or fluvoxamine) resulted in clinically significant improvement, in contrast to 30% of 23 trials with MAO inhibitors, 15% of 48 trials with non-SRI tricyclics, 3% with neuroleptics, and 6% with other medications (such as benzodiazepines and mood stabilizers). In 45 patients from this series who were treated in an open fashion by the authors, 70% (43 of 61) of SRI trials resulted in clinically significant improvement. (The higher response rate in the authors' series was probably due to the use of higher SRI doses and longer treatment trials.) In a retrospective study of 50 patients, 35 SRI trials resulted in a mean improvement on the Clinical Global Impression Scale (Guy, 1976) of 1.9 (much improved), whereas 18 non-SRI tricyclic trials resulted in no overall improvement in BDD symptoms (Hollander et al., 1993; Hollander et al., 1994).

A systematic open-label study of BDD confirms these earlier reports (Phillips, Dwight, & McElroy, 1998). Of the 30 participants, 19 (63.3%) were responders (much or very much improved on the Clinical Global Impression Scale and 30% or greater improvement on the BDD–Y–BOCS). Obsessional preoccupation, distress, functioning, ritualistic behaviors, and insight all significantly improved. Another open-label study of fluvoxamine in BDD ($n = 15$) yielded similar improvement rates (Perugi et al., 1996). A crossover study of desipramine and clomipramine in BDD found a significantly higher rate of response to clomipramine than to desipramine (Hollander et al., in press).

Of note, our data suggest that delusional BDD (delusional disorder, somatic type) is as likely to respond to SRIs as nondelusional BDD (Phillips, McElroy, et al., 1994; Phillips, Dwight, & McElroy, 1998). Decrease in BDD–Y–BOCS scores is similar in the two groups, and insight often improves (Phillips & McElroy, 1993). An earlier report on the efficacy of pimozide in delusional disorder, somatic type (Munro & Chmara, 1982) also raises the question of whether this medication is effective for delusional BDD.

Although available data are still very preliminary, response of BDD to SRIs appears similar to that of OCD in a number of ways. For example, in the open-label fluvoxamine study, which used a fairly rapid titration schedule, mean time to response was 6.1 weeks ($SD = 3.7$), with a range of 2 to 16 weeks. Although fixed-dose studies have not been done, doses higher than those typically effective for major depression appear to often be necessary for BDD, as some studies suggest is the case for OCD (Pato, Eisen, & Phillips, 1996). In addition, in both disorders, response to SRIs is often partial, rather than complete. Although formal medication discontinuation studies have not been done, clinical experience suggests that the majority of patients with BDD relapse with discontinuation and that long-term treatment is often needed.

Several augmentation strategies that are sometimes effective for OCD appear promising for treatment-refractory BDD. In an open study ($n = 13$), buspirone was added to fluoxetine or clomipramine after reaching the highest dose tolerated or recommended by the manufacturer (fluoxetine dose $M = 84.4$ mg/day, $SD = 29.6$; clomipramine dose $M = 230.0$ mg/day, $SD = 47.7$) and at least 10 weeks of treatment ($M = 34.7$ weeks, $SD = 46.0$; Phillips, 1996b). Six participants (46%) were considered much or very much improved with buspirone augmentation (buspirone dose $M = 48.3$ mg/day, $SD = 14.7$; response time $M = 6.4$ weeks). Three responders decreased or discontinued buspirone, which was followed by increased symptom severity in all three individuals; symptoms again improved in the one responder who resumed the previous dose.

Of interest, response rate was higher in those who had a partial response to the SRI (56%, $n = 5$) than in those who had no response to the SRI (25%, $n = 1$). Although buspirone has been noted to effectively augment SRIs in few patients with OCD (Grady et al., 1993), an examination of the OCD literature reveals a similar pattern. Of those reports of buspirone augmentation in OCD that note degree of response to the SRI alone, 8 of 18 (44%) cases with a partial response to the SRI alone versus 3 of 25 (12%) cases with minimal or no response to the SRI alone responded to buspirone augmentation.

Neuroleptic augmentation of SRIs, another approach effective for certain patients with treatment-refractory OCD (McDougle et al., 1990), also holds promise for BDD. In 9 of 15 (60%) patients with BDD treated in a clinical practice, neuroleptic augmentation of SRIs resulted in improved insight or decreased delusions of reference (E. Hollander, personal communication; K. A. Phillips, unpublished data). Whether this approach is more often effective for BDD with comorbid tics or skin picking (or whether it is effective for OCD with poor insight or delusional thinking) is not known.

Another strategy for treatment-refractory BDD, which some data suggest may be effective for OCD (Jenike, Surman, Cassem, Zusky, & Anderson, 1983), is use of an MAO inhibitor. Retrospective data from one series found a response rate of 30% (7 of 23 trials; Phillips et al., 1994b). In some refractory cases, combining clomipramine with a selective SRI appears more effective than an adequate trial with either medication alone (K. A. Phillips, unpublished data; although clomipramine blood levels should be monitored). Finally, patients who fail one adequate SRI trial may respond to another SRI, and several trials may be needed before an effective medication is found.

Data on the efficacy of cognitive-behavioral strategies are also preliminary but promising. Case reports have noted both unsuccessful and successful outcomes, the latter with systematic desensitization (Munjack, 1978)
and exposure therapy (Marks & Mishan, 1988). A more recent report of five
patients with BDD described a successful outcome using techniques similar
to those effective for OCD (Neziroglu & Yaryura-Tobias, 1993). These
consisted of exposure (e.g., exposing the defect in avoided social situations),
response prevention (e.g., resistance of mirror checking), and cognitive
techniques.

Another study found that exposure and response prevention plus
cognitive techniques were effective in 77% of 27 patients who received
this treatment in eight weekly 2-hour sessions in a group format (Rosen
et al., 1995). Exposure (e.g., exposure to social situations and avoiding
camouflage), response prevention (e.g., resisting body-checking behaviors), and cognitive techniques (e.g., changing negative self-statements
about appearance) were used. Individuals in the treatment group improved more than those in a no-treatment waiting-list control group.
These results are promising, although the participants appeared to have
relatively mild BDD, and many seemed to be in a diagnostic "gray zone"
between BDD and eating disorders. In a third study of 19 patients with
BDD, similar cognitive-behavioral techniques were more effective than a
waiting-list group (Veale, Gournay, et al., 1996).

Although adequate data are lacking, it appears that, like OCD, BDD
symptoms are unlikely to diminish with supportive and insight-oriented
psychotherapy alone, although these approaches may have a useful adjunctive role (Phillips et al., 1993). Taken together, available treatment
data suggest that BDD's treatment response is similar to that of OCD and
they give strong support to the hypothesis that BDD is related to OCD.
However, these data are very preliminary, requiring confirmation in controlled treatment trials currently in progress.

Presumed Etiology: Neurobiology and Psychological Antecedents

The etiology of BDD is unknown at this time, although it is most likely
multifactorial, with contributions from neurobiological, psychological,
and sociocultural factors. Several clues point toward possible involvement
of serotonin. Available treatment response data, although providing only
indirect evidence about etiology and pathophysiology, suggest a possible
role for serotonin. In addition, a case report indicated worsening of BDD
in association with abuse of cyproheptadine, a serotonin antagonist (Craven & Rodin, 1987). Another case report of acute tryptophan depletion
in a patient with BDD, OCD, and depression noted dramatic exacerbation

of BDD and depressive symptoms but not OCD symptoms (Barr, Goodman, & Price, 1992).

These findings seem to implicate the importance of serotonin in the pathophysiology of BDD, although the tryptophan depletion report suggests that BDD and OCD may have a somewhat different underlying pathophysiology. It is likely that, as in OCD (Goodman et al., 1990), dopamine plays an important role in BDD. This hypothesis may be particularly applicable to the delusional form of BDD, as a number of investigators have hypothesized that the dopamine system is involved in the formation of positive psychotic symptoms, such as delusions (Fricchione, Carbone, & Bennett, 1995).

Possible neuroanatomical abnormalities in BDD are currently being investigated. Two neuropsychological studies found impaired executive function in BDD (Hanes, 1998; Deckersbach et al., unpublished data), implicating frontal-striatal dysfunction. In one of these studies (Hanes, 1998), BDD and OCD patients were directly compared, with overall performance similar in the two groups. It is important to determine in future studies if abnormalities are present, and, if so, whether they are similar to those implicated in OCD (Baxter, 1992) or in neurological disorders of disturbed body image, which may involve the parietal, occipital, and temporal lobes (Tranel, 1992). Given the importance of the temporal and occipital lobes in processing facial images (Perrett, Hietanen, Oram, & Benson, 1992; Tranel, 1992), it is important to investigate these areas for possible abnormalities.

Regarding the possible role of psychological antecedents, one study (Phillips, Steketee, & Shapiro, 1996) examined similarities and differences between BDD and OCD using the Parental Bonding Instrument, a validated and widely used measure of parental care and overprotection up to age 16 (Parker, Tupling, & Brown, 1979). BDD ($n = 40$) and OCD ($n = 43$) participants had similar scores, although parental care scores in both groups were notably lower than normative means. However, the group with comorbid BDD and OCD ($n = 18$) reported significantly poorer parenting than the OCD group.

Additional Domains

In the previously mentioned BDD–OCD comparison study (Phillips, Gunderson, et al., 1998), illness severity was similar in the two disorders, with a mean total score of 23.7 ($SD = 6.6$) for BDD on the first 10 items of the BDD–Y–BOCS and 23.1 ($SD = 7.4$) for OCD on the Y–BOCS. Individual item scores were also nearly identical in the two groups. However, BDD participants had a significantly higher rate of suicidal ideation (70% vs. 47%) and history of suicide attempts (22% vs. 8%) attributed to the disorder.

CONCLUSIONS

On balance, available data suggest that BDD and OCD have more simi-larities than differences and are probably closely related. It is reasonable to conceptualize BDD as an OCD-spectrum disorder. Indeed, it is likely that BDD will be shown to be more closely related to OCD than will many of the disorders included in this putative spectrum. Their apparent differences, however, suggest that they are not identical disorders.

Reflecting some of the more notable differences between BDD and OCD, BDD could be conceptualized as a more psychotic, depressed, and socially phobic variant of OCD. Indeed, BDD may also be related to other disorders, such as social phobia, with which it has notable similarities, and mood disorder (Phillips, in press). It is also likely that BDD is a heterogeneous disorder, with some forms more closely related to OCD or social phobia, and others more closely related to other disorders, such as the eating disorders.

BDD seems more similar to OCD than the somatoform disorders with which it is classified (an exception being the OCD-like variant of hypo-chondriasis). The somatoform disorders are classified together largely on the basis of their frequent presentation in a consultation-liaison setting and the somatic content of the core symptoms. However, if form (i.e., prominent obsessional thinking and compulsive behaviors) rather than content of symptoms is considered, BDD seems more similar to OCD than to the other somatoform disorders. As previously noted, however, the content of BDD preoccupations and behaviors is also sometimes strikingly similar to that of OCD. Direct comparison studies of BDD and the soma-toform disorders, as well as other research, is needed to inform the question of whether BDD should be classified alongside OCD, rather than the somatoform disorders, in future editions of the *DSM*.

It is also worth noting that delusional BDD, a type of delusional dis-order, somatic type, is probably more closely related to OCD than to the psychotic disorders with which it is classified. Available data suggest that BDD and its delusional disorder variant may be the same disorder, with insight spanning a spectrum from good to absent (Phillips & McElroy, 1993). In *DSM–IV*, in recognition of this possibility, delusional BDD may be double coded as delusional disorder and BDD. OCD also appears to span a spectrum of insight (Insel & Akiskal, 1986), with the delusional variant classified as delusional disorder or psychotic disorder not other-wise specified. It seems likely that delusional disorder is a heterogeneous construct, with some forms (e.g., the paranoid type) more closely related to schizophrenia and other forms (e.g., the somatic type) more closely related to OCD.

BDD's relation to OCD has clinical implications. For example, prelimi-nary data suggest that delusional BDD may respond better to SRIs than to neuroleptics. In addition, given their relatively high comorbidity, it is important that clinicians inquire about BDD in patients with OCD and vice versa. BDD should also be looked for in family members of individuals with OCD and vice versa. Because BDD concerns are often not revealed because of embarrassment and shame, the diagnosis may be missed unless it is specifically inquired about.

However, given that BDD and OCD have not been shown to be identical, they should be differentiated in clinical settings for a number of reasons. First, available data suggest that when BDD and OCD co-occur, they do not always resolve concurrently with treatment; one of these disorders, but not the other, may improve (Phillips, Dwight, & McElroy, 1998). In addition, it is possible that BDD—in particular, delusional BDD—may not respond as well to behavior therapy as OCD does, given the high rate of depression, poor insight, and referential thinking present in BDD. Thus, clinicians should be aware that both diagnoses are present and not assume that because OCD has improved, BDD symptoms have also improved, or vice versa. In addition, patients with BDD should be carefully assessed for major depression, social phobia, and suicidality, as these clinical features appear to be more common among patients with BDD.

BDD and OCD should also be differentiated in research settings. For example, OCD treatment studies—especially studies of treatment-refractory OCD—should exclude patients who have BDD but not OCD. It would also be desirable for BDD and OCD treatment studies to account for the presence of the other disorder to determine the influence of comorbidity, if any, on treatment outcome. BDD should also be identified in neurobiological and other OCD studies to assure adequate homogeneity of study populations.

Despite BDD's long historical tradition, research on this underrecognized disorder is still in its infancy, and the conclusions in this chapter are preliminary. Further research on BDD and direct comparison studies with OCD in multiple domains are needed. Ultimately, to answer the question of whether BDD and OCD are the same or closely related disorders, studies comparing their neurobiology are needed. As more is learned about BDD, and its etiology and pathophysiology are better understood, its relation to OCD will become clearer. Such understanding will increase the accuracy of its classification and will have important implications for clinical practice.

REFERENCES

American Psychiatric Association. (1987). *Diagnostic and statistical manual of mental disorders* (3rd ed., rev.). Washington, DC: Author.

American Psychiatric Association. (1994). *Diagnostic and statistical manual of mental disorders* (4th ed.). Washington, DC: Author.

Anderson, E. W. (1964). *Psychiatry.* London: Bailliere, Tindall, & Cox.

Baer, L., Jenike, M. A., Black, D. W., Treece, C., Rosenfeld, R., & Greist, J. (1992). Effect of Axis II diagnosis on treatment outcome with clomipramine in 55 patients with obsessive-compulsive disorder. *Archives of General Psychiatry, 49,* 862–866.

Baer, L., Jenike, M. A., Ricciardi, J. N., Holland, A. D., Seymour, R. J., Minichiello, W. E., & Buttolph, M. L. (1990). Standardized assessment of personality disorders in obsessive-compulsive disorder. *Archives of General Psychiatry, 47,* 826–830.

Barr, L. C., Goodman, W. K., & Price, L. H. (1992). Acute exacerbation of body dysmorphic disorder during tryptophan depletion [Letter to the editor]. *American Journal of Psychiatry, 149,* 1406–1407.

Baxter, L. R. (1992). Neuroimaging studies of obsessive compulsive disorder. *Psychiatric Clinics of North America, 15,* 871–884.

Brady, K. T., Austin, L., & Lydiard, R. B. (1990). Body dysmorphic disorder: The relationship to obsessive-compulsive disorder. *Journal of Nervous and Mental Disease, 178,* 538–540.

Brawman-Mintzer, O., Lydiard, R. B., Phillips, K. A., Morton, A., Czepowicz, V., Emmanuel, N., Villareal, G., Johnson, M., & Ballenger, J. C. (1995). Body dysmorphic disorder in patients with anxiety disorders and major depression: A comorbidity study. *American Journal of Psychiatry, 152,* 1665–1667.

Brunswick, R. M. (1928). A supplement to Freud's "History of an Infantile Neurosis." *International Journal of Psychoanalysis, 9,* 439–476.

Connolly, P. H., & Gipson, M. (1978). Dysmorphophobia—A long-term study. *British Journal of Psychiatry, 132,* 568–570.

Cooper, J. (1970). The Leyton Obsessional Inventory. *Psychological Medicine, i,* 48–64.

Cotterill, J. A. (1981). Dermatological non-disease: A common and potentially fatal disturbance of cutaneous body image. *British Journal of Dermatology, 104,* 611–619.

Craven, J. L., & Rodin, G. M. (1987). Cyproheptadine dependence associated with atypical somatoform disorder. *Canadian Journal of Psychiatry, 32,* 143–145.

Eisen, J. L., Phillips, K. A., Rasmussen, S. A., & Luce, D. (1997). Insight in body dysmorphic disorder versus OCD. *New Research Program & Abstracts,* APA 150th Annual Meeting, San Diego, p. 199.

Eisen, J. L., & Rasmussen, S. A. (1993). Obsessive compulsive disorder with psychotic features. *Journal of Clinical Psychiatry, 54,* 373–379.

Fava, G. A. (1992). Morselli's legacy: Dysmorphophobia. *Psychotherapy and Psychosomatics, 58,* 117–118.

Fricchione, G. L., Carbone, L., & Bennett, W. I. (1995). Psychotic disorder caused by a general medical condition, with delusions. In M. J. Sedler (Ed.), *Delusional disorders: The psychiatric clinics of North America* (pp. 363–378). Philadelphia: Saunders.

Fukuda, O. (1977). Statistical analysis of dysmorphophobia in out-patient clinic. *Japanese Journal of Plastic and Reconstructive Surgery, 20,* 569–577.

Goodman, W. K., McDougle, C. J., Price, L. H., Riddle, M. A., Pauls, D. L., & Leckman, J. F. (1990). Beyond the serotonin hypothesis: A role for dopamine in some forms of obsessive compulsive disorder? *Journal of Clinical Psychiatry, 51*(Suppl.), 36–43.

Goodman, W. K., Price, L. H., Rasmussen, S. A., Mazure, C., Delgado, P., Heninger, G. R., & Charney, D. S. (1989). The Yale–Brown Obsessive Compulsive Scale (Y–BOCS): Part II. Validity. *Archives of General Psychiatry, 46,* 1012–1016.

Goodman, W. K., Price, L. H., Rasmussen, S. A., Mazure, C., Fleischman, R. L., Hill, C. L., Heninger, G. R., & Charney, D. S. (1989). The Yale–Brown Obsessive Compulsive Scale (Y–BOCS): Part 1. Development, use, and reliability. *Archives of General Psychiatry, 46,* 1006–1011.

Grady, T. A., Pigott, T. A., L'Heureux, F., Hill, J. L., Bernstein, S. E., & Murphy, D. L. (1993). Double-blind study of adjuvant buspirone for fluoxetine-treated patients with obsessive-compulsive disorder. *American Journal of Psychiatry 150*, 819–821.

Guy, W. (Ed.). (1976). *ECDEU assessment manual for psychopharmacology* (rev., DHEW Pub. No. (ADM) 76–338). Rockville, MD: National Institute of Mental Health.

Hanes, K. R. (1998). Neuropsychological performance in body dysmorphic disorder. *Journal of the International Neuropsychological Society, 4*, 167–171.

Hardy, G. E., & Cotterill, J. A. (1982). A study of depression and obsessionality in dysmorphophobic and psoriatic patients. *British Journal of Psychiatry, 140*, 19–22.

Hay, G. G. (1970). Dysmorphophobia. *British Journal of Psychiatry, 116*, 399–406.

Hollander, E. (1993). Introduction. In E. Hollander (Ed.), *Obsessive-compulsive related disorders* (pp. 1–16). Washington, DC: American Psychiatric Press.

Hollander, E., Allen, A., Aronowitz, B., Kwon, J., Mosovich, S., Schmeidler, J., & Wong, C. (in press). Clomipramine/desipramine cross-over trial in body dysmorphic disorder: Selective efficacy of serotonin reuptake inhibitors in an obsessive-compulsive spectrum disorder.

Hollander, E., Cohen, L. J., & Simeon, D. (1993). Body dysmorphic disorder. *Psychiatric Annals, 23*, 359–364.

Hollander, E., Cohen, L., Simeon, D., Rosen, J., DeCaria, C., & Stein, D. J. (1994). Fluvoxamine treatment of body dysmorphic disorder [Letter to the editor]. *Journal of Clinical Psychopharmacology, 14*, 75–77.

Hollander, E., Liebowitz, M. R., Winchel, R., Klumker, A., & Klein, D. F. (1989). Treatment of body-dysmorphic disorder with serotonin reuptake blockers. *American Journal of Psychiatry, 146*, 768–770.

Hollander, E., & Phillips, K. A. (1993). Body image and experience disorders: Body dysmorphic and depersonalization disorders. In E. Hollander (Ed.), *Obsessive-compulsive related disorders* (pp. 1–16). Washington, DC: American Psychiatric Press.

Insel, T. R., & Akiskal, H. S. (1986). Obsessive-compulsive disorder with psychotic features: A phenomenologic analysis. *American Journal of Psychiatry, 143*, 1527–1533.

Janet, P. (1903). *Les obsessions et la psychasthenie* [Obsessions and psychaesthenia]. Paris: Felix Alcan.

Jenike, M. A., Surman, O. S., Cassem, N. H., Zusky, P., & Anderson, W. H. (1983). Monoamine oxidase inhibitors in obsessive compulsive disorder. *Journal of Clinical Psychiatry, 44*, 131–132.

Kasahara, Y. (1987). Social phobia in Japan. In *Social phobia in Japan and Korea: Proceedings of the first cultural psychiatry symposium between Japan and Korea* (pp. 3–14). Seoul, South Korea: Academy of Cultural Psychiatry.

Klein, D. F. (1993). Foreword. In E. Hollander (Ed.), *Obsessive-compulsive related disorders* (pp. xi–xvii). Washington, DC: American Psychiatric Press.

Marks, I., & Mishan, J. (1988). Dysmorphophobic avoidance with disturbed bodily perception: A pilot study of exposure therapy. *British Journal of Psychiatry, 152*, 674–678.

McDougle, C. J., Goodman, W. K., Price, L. H., Delgado, P. L., Krystal, J. H., Charney, D. S., & Heninger, G. R. (1990). Neuroleptic addition in fluvoxamine-refractory obsessive-compulsive disorder. *American Journal of Psychiatry, 147*, 652–654.

McElroy, S. L., Phillips, K. A., & Keck, P. E., Jr. (1994). Obsessive-compulsive spectrum disorders. *Journal of Clinical Psychiatry, 55*(Suppl.), 33–51.

McEiroy, S. L., Phillips, K. A., Keck, P. E., Jr., Hudson, J. I., Pope, H. G., Jr. (1993). Body dysmorphic disorder: Does it have a psychotic subtype? *Journal of Clinical Psychiatry, 54*, 389–395.

Morselli, E. (1891). Sulla dismorfofobia e sulla tafefobia [ ]. *Bolletinno della R accademia di Genova, 6*, 110–119.

Munjack, D. J. (1978). The behavioral treatment of dysmorphophobia. *Journal of Behavior Therapy and Experimental Psychiatry, 9,* 53–56.

Munro, A., & Chmara, J. (1982). Monosymptomatic hypochondriacal psychosis: A diagnostic checklist based on 50 cases of the disorder. *Canadian Journal of Psychiatry, 27,* 374–376.

Neziroglu, F., McKay, D., Todaro, J., & Yaryura-Tobias, J. A. (1996). Effect of cognitive behavior therapy on persons with body dysmorphic disorder and comorbid Axis II diagnoses. *Behavioral Therapy, 27,* 67–77.

Neziroglu, F. A., & Yaryura-Tobias, J. A. (1993). Exposure, response prevention, and cognitive therapy in the treatment of body dysmorphic disorder. *Behavioral Therapy, 24,* 431–438.

Parker, G., Tupling, H., & Brown, L. B. (1979). A parental bonding instrument. *British Journal of Medical Psychology, 52,* 1–10.

Pato, M. T., Eisen, J. L., & Phillips, K. A. (1996). Obsessive compulsive disorders. In A. Tasman, J. Kay, & J. A. Lieberman (Eds.), *Psychiatry* (pp. 1060–1084). Philadelphia: Saunders.

Perrett, D. I., Hietanen, J. K., Oram, M. W., & Benson, P. J. (1992). Organization and functions of cells responsive to faces in the temporal cortex. *Philosophical Transactions of the Royal Society of London, 335,* 23–30.

Perugi, G., Giannotti, D., Di Vaio, S., Frare, F., Saettoni, M., & Cassano, G. B. (1996). Fluvoxamine in the treatment of body dysmorphic disorder (dysmorphophobia). *International Clinical Psychopharmacology, 11,* 247–254.

Phillips, K. A. (1991). Body dysmorphic disorder: The distress of imagined ugliness. *American Journal of Psychiatry, 148,* 1138–1149.

Phillips, K. A. (1996a). Body dysmorphic disorder: Diagnosis and treatment of imagined ugliness. *Journal of Clinical Psychiatry 57*(Suppl.), 61–64.

Phillips, K. A. (1996b). An open study of buspirone augmentation of serotonin-reuptake inhibitors in body dysmorphic disorder. *Psychopharmacology Bulletin, 32,* 175–180.

Phillips, K. A. (in press). The nosologic boundaries of body dysmorphic disorder. In E. Hollander & L. Sanchez-Planell (Eds.), *Controversies in dysmorphophobia.* Washington, DC: American Psychiatric Press.

Phillips, K. A., & Diaz, S. F. (1997). Gender differences in body dysmorphic disorder. *Journal of Nervous and Mental Disease, 185,* 570–577.

Phillips, K. A., Dwight, M., & McElroy, S. L. (1998). Efficacy and safety of fluvoxamine in body dysmorphic disorder. *Journal of Clinical Psychiatry, 59,* 165–171.

Phillips, K. A., Gunderson, C. G., Mallya, G., McElroy, S. L., & Carter, W. (1998). A comparison study of body dysmorphic disorder and obsessive compulsive disorder. *Journal of Clinical Psychiatry, 59,* 568–575.

Phillips, K. A., & Hollander, E. (1996). Body dysmorphic disorder. In T. A. Widiger, A. J. Frances, H. A. Pincus, R. Ross, M. B. First, & W. W. Davis (Eds.), *DSM–IV sourcebook* (Vol. 2, pp. 17–48). Washington, DC: American Psychiatric Association.

Phillips, K. A., Hollander, E., Rasmussen, S. A., Aronowitz, B. R., DeCaria, C., & Goodman, W. K. (1997). A severity rating scale for body dysmorphic disorder: Development, reliability, and validity of a modified version of the Yale–Brown Obsessive Compulsive Scale. *Psychopharmacology Bulletin, 33,* 17–22.

Phillips, K. A., & McElroy, S. L. (1993). Insight, overvalued ideation, and delusional thinking in body dysmorphic disorder: Theoretical and treatment implications. *Journal of Nervous and Mental Disease, 181,* 699–702.

Phillips, K. A., McElroy, S. L., Hudson, J. I., & Pope, H. G., Jr. (1995). Body dysmorphic disorder: An obsessive compulsive spectrum disorder, a form of affective spectrum disorder, or both? *Journal of Clinical Psychiatry, 56*(Suppl.), 41–51.

Phillips, K. A., McElroy, S. L., Keck, P. E., Jr., Pope, H. G., Jr., & Hudson, J. I. (1993). Body dysmorphic disorder: 30 cases of imagined ugliness. *American Journal of Psychiatry, 150,* 302–308.

Phillips, K. A., McElroy, S. L., Keck, P. E., Jr., Pope, H. G., Jr., & Hudson, J. I. (1994). A comparison of delusional and nondelusional body dysmorphic disorder in 100 cases. *Psychopharmacology Bulletin, 30,* 179–186.

Phillips, K. A., McElroy, S. L., & Lion, J. R. (1992). Body dysmorphic disorder in cosmetic surgery patients [Letter to the editor]. *Journal of Plastic and Reconstructive Surgery, 90,* 333–334.

Phillips, K. A., Steketee, G., & Shapiro, L. (1996, May). *Parental bonding in OCD and body dysmorphic disorder. New Research Program & Abstracts* (p. 261). APA 149th Annual Meeting, New York.

Rosen, J. C., Reiter, J., & Orosan, P. (1995). Cognitive-behavioral body image therapy for body dysmorphic disorder. *Journal of Consulting and Clinical Psychology, 63,* 263–269.

Simeon, D., Hollander, E., Stein, D. J., Cohen, L., & Aronowitz, B. (1995). Body dysmorphic disorder in the DSM–IV field trial for obsessive compulsive disorder. *American Journal of Psychiatry, 152,* 1207–1209.

Spitzer, R. L., Williams, J. B. W., Gibbon, M., & First, M. B. (1992). The Structured Clinical Interview for DSM–III–R (SCID)): I. History, rationale, and description. *Archives of General Psychiatry, 49,* 624–629.

Stekel, W. (1949). *Compulsion and doubt.* (G. A. Gutheil, Trans.). New York: Liverwright.

Tranel, D. (1992). Functional neuroanatomy: Neuropsychological correlates of cortical and subcortical damage. In S. C. Yudofsky & R. E. Hales (Eds.), *Neuropsychiatry* (pp. 57–88). Washington, DC: American Psychiatric Press.

Veale, D., Boocock, A., Gournay, K., Dryden, W., Shah, F., Willson, R., & Walburn, J. (1996). Body dysmorphic disorder: A survey of fifty cases. *British Journal of Psychiatry, 169,* 196–201.

Veale, D., Gournay, K., Dryden, W., Boocock, A., Shah, F., Willson, R., & Walburn, J. (1996). Body dysmorphic disorder: A cognitive behavioural model and pilot randomized controlled trial. *Behaviour Research and Therapy, 34,* 717–729.

Vitiello, B., & deLeon, J. (1990). Dysmorphophobia misdiagnosed as obsessive-compulsive disorder. *Psychosomatics, 31,* 220–222.

World Health Organization. (1992). *Classification of mental and behavioural disorders—Clinical descriptions and diagnostic guidelines* (10th ed). Geneva: World Health Organization.

Zaidens, S. H. (1950). Dermatologic hypochondriasis: A form of schizophrenia. *Psychosomatic Medicine, 12,* 250–253.

Tic-Related Versus Non-Tic-Related Obsessive-Compulsive Disorder

James F. Leckman
Christopher J. McDougle
David L. Pauls
Bradley S. Peterson
Dorothy E. Grice
Robert A. King
Lawrence Scahill
Lawrence H. Price
Yale University School of Medicine

Steven A. Rasmussen
Butler Hospital, Providence, RI

Obsessive-compulsive disorder (OCD) is characterized by sudden, recurrent, upsetting thoughts or images that intrude into consciousness (obsessions) and/or rule-governed acts that the person feels driven to perform (compulsions; American Psychiatric Association, 1994). OCD is a prevalent life-long condition that frequently is associated with marked impairment and disability. Historically, a vast array of treatments have been tried in OCD with variable success. Although clinical care has improved, a significant number of patients fail to respond adequately to either cognitive-behavioral or pharmacological treatments or they experience troublesome side effects. A long-term objective of many research programs is the safe and effective treatment of OCD and related disorders. However, the effectiveness of these interventions depends largely on the extent and quality of our knowledge base. It is essential that we understand the natural history of these disorders over the course of development (from childhood onset through adolescence and into adulthood) and the pathophysiological mechanisms that mediate symptom expression in vulnerable individuals. We expect that this information will extend to an understanding at the molecular level of how specific genetic factors confer vulnerability, as well as how developmental changes in the hormonal and neurochemical microenvironment influence the course of these disorders.

The cause of OCD is unknown. As reviewed later, we anticipate that a thorough understanding of the pathogenesis of OCD will reveal multiple overlapping forms of this disorder. This chapter emphasizes the putative distinction between tic-related and non-tic-related OCD and considers this distinction in light of a growing body of empirical data concerning possible differences in the clinical phenotype and natural history, genetic vulnerability, risk and protective factors, neurobiological substrates, and treatment response.

Historically, the distinction between tic-related and non-tic-related OCD was initially based on family genetic data that indicated OCD was likely to be an etiologically heterogenous set of conditions. Some forms of OCD are familial and may be associated with a specific genetic vulnerability (Pauls, Alsobrook, Goodman, Rasmussen, & Leckman, 1995; Rasmussen, 1994). Others present as sporadic cases. Among the familial cases, a portion appeared to be etiologically related to Tourette's syndrome (TS) and other tic disorders (Pauls & Leckman, 1986; Pauls, Raymond, Leckman, & Stevenson, 1991).

This chapter reviews our current knowledge concerning the distinction between tic-related and non-tic-related OCD. We begin with a review of our overall model of the pathogenesis of OCD and then consider each of the components of this general model (clinical phenotype and natural history, genetic factors, other risk and protective factors, neurobiological substrates, and treatment response) before offering a few predictions and summarizing future prospects for this area of research.

A WORKING MODEL OF OCD PATHOGENESIS

A schematic presentation of the general model of pathogenesis is presented in Fig. 3.1. Our model for OCD involves the reciprocal interaction of genes and environment. The normal copies of these specific vulnerability genes are presumed to be turned on and off at specific points in development. Abnormal copies of these genes alter the course of development by changing the timing or degree of expression of specific gene products. A number of other risk and protective factors are also likely to be involved, some of which may influence gene expression directly. In other cases, gene expression may be affected indirectly when aspects of the macroenvironment of the individual alter the microenvironment of particular neural systems through a variety of signal transduction and second messenger systems. Conversely, these vulnerability genes directly influence their microenvironment by facilitating or repressing the production of specific proteins. This general model also presumes that these vulnerability genes, acting in

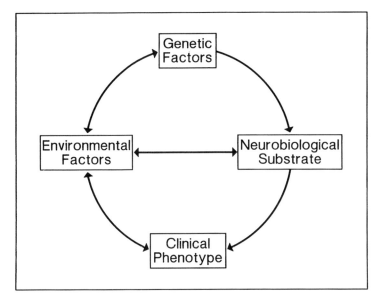

FIG. 3.1.   A working model of OCD pathogenesis. This figure depicts the interactions among genetic factors, neurobiological substrates, and environmental factors in the production of the clinical phenotypes. The genetic vulnerability factor(s) that underlie OCD undoubtedly influence the structure and function of the brain, which in turn produces clinical symptoms. Available evidence also indicates that a range of epigenetic or environmental factors are also critically involved in the pathogenesis of OCD. In addition, symptoms of the disorder can affect and alter aspects of the microenvironment of the brain, which in turn may alter the expression of the genetic factor(s).

concert with specific environmental factors, play a crucial role in the formation and activity of specific neural circuits that provide the neurobiological substrate for symptoms associated with these disorders. Finally, this general model depicts the potentially vicious cycle that can sometimes be seen in which increasing tic or obsessive-compulsive (OC) symptoms create secondary problems in peer and family relationships that then indirectly lead to a further exacerbation of tic or OC symptoms.

We next turn to a consideration of the phenomenology and natural history of OCD in light of the putative distinction between tic-related and non-tic-related OCD.

CLINICAL PHENOTYPE AND NATURAL HISTORY

Several empirical studies involving more than 300 OCD patients have recently appeared specifically addressing the question of possible differences between tic-related and non-tic-related OCD (Table 3.1). All of the

TABLE 3.1

Clinical Phenotype and Natural History: Tic-Related Versus Non-Tic-Related Obsessive-Compulsive Disorder

Study	N	Sex[a]	OCD Onset (Years)	OCD Severity (Y–BOCS)[b]	Distinctive OC Symptoms[c]
George et al. (1993)					
Tic-related OCD	15	26%	NA	24.8 ± 4.9	Touching, symmetry, sexual and violent obsessions, blinking/staring rituals
Non-tic-related OCD	10	60%	NA	22.2 ± 6.8	Contamination fears and cleaning compulsions
Holzer et al. (1994)					
Tic-related OCD	35	23%	13.2 ± 6.2	27.1 ± 5.4	Touching, tapping, repeating, blinking/staring rituals
Non-tic-related OCD	35	23%	16.1 ± 8.6	25.8 ± 4.7	Cleaning compulsions
Leckman et al. (1995)					
Tic-related OCD	56	41%	13.4 ± 8.9	17.8 ± 9.0	Touching, sexual, violent, and religious obsessions, checking, counting, hoarding, intrusive images or sounds
Non-tic-related OCD	121	61%	15.9 ± 10.2	17.3 ± 8.7	None
de Groot et al. (1995)					
Tic-related OCD	21	24%	NA	16.6 ± 6.4	Somatic obsessions, intrusive images or sounds
Non-tic-related OCD	37	65%	21.3 ± 9.8	29.7 ± 5.4	Contamination fears and cleaning compulsions, checking

Note. OCD = obsessive-compulsive disorder; Y-BOCS = Yale-Brown Obsessive Compulsive Scale; OC = obsessive-compulsive; NA = not available. [a]Percentage female. [b]Y-BOCS Total score (Goodman, Price, Rasmussen, Mazure, Delgado, et al., 1989; Goodman, Price, Rasmussen, Mazure, Fleischmann, et al., 1989). [c]Symptoms listed were reported more frequently ($p < .05$) in the tic-related versus the non-tic-related groups.

participants in these studies were drawn from clinic samples and assessed using versions of the Yale–Brown Obsessive Compulsive Scale (Y–BOCS; Goodman, Price, Rasmussen, Mazure, Delgado, et al., 1989; Goodman, Price, Rasmussen, Mazure, Fleischmann, et al., 1989). In other respects the methods differed between studies. For example, the study by de Groot, Bornstein, Janus, and Mavissakalian (1995) included some TS patients with OC symptoms who failed to meet criteria for OCD. Each of the other samples only included patients with OCD. All but one of the studies assessed patients using direct interview methods with the severity ratings being completed by an experienced clinician. The remaining study (Leckman et al., 1995) relied on self-report information collected by questionnaire.

The picture that emerges across these studies is remarkably consistent. Tic-related OCD tends to have an earlier age of onset and to affect males predominantly. The one study that had equal numbers of male and female participants intentionally matched their samples on this variable (Holzer et al., 1994). This finding is consistent with the reports of other investigators. For example, Leonard et al. (1992) reported 54 cases of childhood-onset OCD. In their series, 32 patients had a lifetime history of tics or TS and 22 did not. The tic-related group included fewer females than did the non-tic-related group (25% vs. 45%, respectively). The tic-related group also had a slightly earlier age of onset (9.2 years old vs. 10.8 years old).

The current severity of OC symptoms does not appear to be a useful discriminator. The one study that reported a significant difference between tic-related and non-tic-related groups included TS patients who did not meet full criteria for OCD (de Groot et al., 1995).

The number and nature of the OCD symptoms, however, do emerge as important discriminators. Although none of the symptoms are pathognomonic, the need to touch, tap, or rub was present in 70% to 80% of the OCD patients with comorbid TS (George, Trimble, Ring, Sallee, & Robertson, 1993; Leckman, Walker, Goodman, Pauls, & Cohen, 1994) and in 20% to 40% of the OCD patients with chronic comorbid tics (Holzer et al., 1994; Leckman et al., 1995) compared to 5% to 25% of the non-tic-related OCD group (Holzer et al., 1994; Leckman et al., 1995). Although there is considerable overlap, each of the studies reports a higher percentage of tic-related OCD patients having intrusive violent or aggressive thoughts and images and worries about symmetry and exactness (de Groot et al., 1995; George et al., 1993; Holzer et al., 1994; Leckman et al., 1995). Where reported, blinking and staring rituals and intrusive images, sounds, words, or music were also more common in the tic-related group. In contrast, the only symptoms that were consistently found in non-tic-related OCD patients were contamination worries and cleaning compulsions (de Groot et al., 1995; George et al., 1993; Holzer et al., 1994; Leckman et al., 1995).

A similar picture emerges from a study by Baer (1994), who performed a factor analysis of the symptom checklist of the Y–BOCS. Three factors emerged. One factor, encompassing symmetry and saving obsessions and ordering, repeating, counting, and hoarding compulsions, was associated with having a comorbid tic disorder. Indeed, individuals scoring high on this factor had a relative risk for a comorbid tic disorder that was more than eight times higher than for those individuals with OCD who scored low on this factor. Scores on this factor were also significantly correlated with touching compulsions. Consistent with the other reports, Baer's study also reported a second factor comprised of contamination worries and cleaning and checking compulsions that was statistically independent of the individual's tic status. Unfortunately, Baer did not report the proportion of the 107 cases with a comorbid tic disorder, the age at OCD onset, or the sex ratio for the tic-related versus the non-tic-related groups. As a result, this study is not included in Table 3.1.

As in most areas of science, our ability to discern meaningful patterns depends in large part on the instruments used to study the phenomena. The reduction of the rich complexity of OC symptoms to particular content categories may obscure more salient themes. For example, intrusive thoughts of something terrible happening to one's mother might be placed in the aggressive or sexual domain on scales like the Y–BOCS, but it may be more appropriate to emphasize the separation worries that frequently accompany these obsessions. Alternatively, inquiries directed at the degree to which particular obsessions reflect an inflated sense of personal responsibility might prove to be a promising approach (Rachman, 1993).

Other clinical features also appear to distinguish tic-related from non-tic-related OCD. In particular, investigators have indicated that patients with non-tic-related OCD report that their compulsions and rituals are frequently preceded by obsessive worries and feelings of anxiety, compared to patients with tic-related OCD (George et al. 1993; Miguel et al., 1995).

In contrast, patients with tic-related OCD frequently report that a range of "just right" perceptions frequently precede or accompany the exacting performance of their compulsive rituals (Leckman et al., 1995; Leckman, Walker, et al., 1994). In cases of primary TS comorbid with OCD, fully 81% of participants reported needing to perform compulsions until they were "just right" (Leckman, Walker, et al., 1994). Among patients with primary OCD, with or without comorbid tics, the rate of endorsement of "just right" perceptions was 73% (Leckman et al., 1995). Although classical descriptions of OCD contain detailed accounts of mental states associated with compulsive urges, the precisely determined form of particular rituals, and the heightened and idiosyncratic standards of rightness applied, they tend not to focus on the importance of perceptual cues, nor do they distinguish between patients with or without a personal history of tics (Jaspers, 1923/1963; Kräupl Taylor, 1979; Slater & Roth, 1969). One intriguing feature of the "just right" story is the relative importance of things needing to "look" just right as opposed to "feeling" or "sounding" just right (Leckman et al., 1995). In most instances, individuals will either report the need for things to "look" just right or the need for things to both "look and feel" just right. The minority of patients reporting the need for things at times to "sound" just right will also have the need for things to "look and feel" just right. Other combinations, such as "looks and sounds" or "feels and sounds" just right were rare (Leckman et al., 1995; Leckman, Walker, et al., 1994). These "just right" phenomena, which typically involve aspects of the home environment, closely parallel behavioral features that are commonly seen in children between the ages of 18 and 36 months (Evans et al., 1997). They also figure in emerging evolutionary perspectives on OCD (Leckman & Mayes, 1998).

Janet and Raymond (1903/1976) linked tic symptoms with obsessions and compulsions arising from the continual torment of *psychasthenia*—an inner sense of incompleteness, imperfection, and insufficiency. In our clinical experience, Janet's formulation aptly describes a subset of OCD patients with tics. However, in the one attempt to study this phenomenon no differences were observed between the tic-related and non-tic-related samples of OCD patients (Leckman et al., 1995). The relation between these psychasthenic feelings and the "just right" perceptions has not been clearly delineated and awaits further study. Indeed, even among the authors of this chapter there are differing views on this point, with some of us considering the need for things to look, feel, or sound just right to be just another way of describing what Janet meant by psychasthenia, as opposed to the view that these phrases actually describe two different phenomena.

In sum, although the natural history and clinical presentation of OCD is quite variable, the available phenomenological and natural history data support the distinction between tic-related and non-tic-related OCD. The most salient features of the tic-related form of illness are its prepubertal onset; male predominance; and a mix of aggressive and sexual obsessions, concerns of symmetry and exactness, and ticlike compulsions. In contrast, the more frequently encountered non-tic-related OCD is characterized by a peri- or postpubertal onset, sex-equivalent vulnerability, and prominent contamination worries and cleaning compulsions. With few exceptions (see later discussion of treatment response), other features of the natural history of OCD—comorbid depression and anxiety disorders and long-term outcome—have not been systematically evaluated with regard to the predictive power of whether a patient does or does not have a tic-related form of OCD. Careful documentation of these phenotypic features may be useful in designing early intervention, treatment, and outcome studies.

GENETIC FACTORS

Tic-related OCD first gained wider currency in the context of family genetic studies of TS, where a high rate of OCD was observed within first-degree family members (Pauls & Leckman, 1986; Pauls et al., 1991). The hypothesis that some forms of OCD are alternate expressions of the same genetic factors that conferred TS vulnerability arose from the observation that the increased rate of OCD in family members was present whether or not the TS proband had comorbid OCD. In particular, it was the presence of family members, usually women, with OCD and without a personal history of tics, that prompted us to coin the term tic-related OCD (Fig. 3.2). These findings have subsequently been replicated and extended by a number of investigators (Comings & Comings, 1987; Eapen, Pauls, & Robertson, 1993; van de Wetering, 1993).

The familial nature of OCD, tic-related or not, has been observed since the 1930s and twin studies have provided limited evidence for the im-

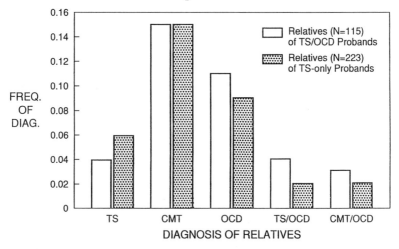

FIG. 3.2. Distribution by diagnosis of first-degree family members of TS probands with or without a personal history of OCD. These data are taken from the study of Pauls et al. (1991). This figure depicts the recurrence of OCD, TS, and chronic tic disorders among the first-degree relatives of probands with TS divided according to the OCD status of the proband. No significant differences were observed between the two groups, suggesting that an increased risk of OCD is present among the first-degree relatives of TS probands regardless of the presence of comorbid OCD in the TS proband.

portance of genetic factors in the manifestation of this disorder (Pauls, 1992; Rasmussen, 1994). In several twin studies, the concordance rates ranged from 53% to 87% for monozygotic twins and from 22% to 47% for dizygotic twins depending on the sample and the diagnostic criteria (Carey & Gottesman, 1981; Rasmussen & Tsuang, 1986). However, in two recent twin studies (Andrews, Stewart, Allen, & Henderson, 1990; Torgerson, 1983) the findings have tended to emphasize the overlap between OCD and other anxiety disorders.

Although a number of family studies on OCD have been completed since the 1930s, the degree to which genetic factors influence an individual's susceptibility to OCD remains controversial. Some studies report rates as high as 35% among first-degree relatives (Lenane et al., 1990) and others report no increase (McKeon & Murray, 1987). Many of these studies are difficult to interpret because of differences in diagnostic criteria and assessment methodologies. Some of the shortcomings of earlier research were addressed in seven recent studies of OCD (Bellodi, Sciuto, Diaferia, Ronchi, & Smeraldi, 1992; Black, Noyes, Goldstein, & Blum, 1992; Lenane et al., 1990; Leonard et al., 1992; Nicolini, Weissbecker, Mejia, & de Carmona, 1993; Pauls et al., 1995; Riddle et al., 1990). Findings from these studies provide further support for the hypothesis that familial factors, genetic factors, or both contribute to expression of OCD. Three of the studies focused on families of children and four investigated families of adults, making them potentially valuable sources of information concerning early-onset, tic-related OCD. Lenane et al. (1990) studied families of 46 children and adolescents and found that 25% of fathers and 9% of mothers had OCD. When subthreshold OCD was included, the age-corrected morbid risk for all first-degree relatives was 35%. In this study, OCD cases with comorbid TS were excluded and no current case of TS was found among the first-degree relatives. However, of the 18 families who were specifically questioned about the presence of a lifetime history of tics, 44% had a positive history (Lenane et al., 1990). In a subsequent follow-up study involving many of the same families, Leonard et al. (1992) found that 13% of all first-degree relatives met criteria for OCD. Although probands with OCD and comorbid TS were again excluded, three cases (1.8%) of TS among the first-degree relatives were identified (one father and two brothers). An additional 21 cases of chronic tic disorder were also identified so that the overall recurrence risk for chronic tics was 14% among the 171 relatives. The presence or absence of a chronic tic disorder in the proband did not make much difference with regard to the recurrence risk for either OCD or chronic tics.

A third study of 21 childhood OCD families found that 9.5% of parents received a diagnosis of OCD and another 26.2% met criteria for subthreshold OCD (Riddle et al., 1990). This study also specifically excluded OCD probands with comorbid TS. Again no cases of TS were observed among the first-degree relatives, but two probands were found to have chronic tics and both had at least one parent with a chronic tic disorder.

Results from the four family studies of adult OCD probands were mixed. Bellodi et al. (1992) reported that only 3.4% of the relatives in 92 families had OCD. However, when probands were separated on the basis of age at onset, the morbid risk for OCD among relatives of early-onset (age 14 or earlier) probands was 8.8% compared to 2.2% or less among the relatives of later onset probands. Unfortunately, although tics were assessed in this study, the data were not included in the initial report. Black et al. (1992) studied families of 32 adult OCD probands and found no evidence that OCD was familial. However, the risk of a more broadly defined OCD (i.e., subthreshold OCD) was increased among the parents of OCD probands. In addition, rates of anxiety disorders were significantly increased among relatives of obsessional probands. Although TS and chronic tics were assessed in the relatives, no information was provided concerning whether or not any of the probands had a lifetime history of tics. Further, the rates of tics did not differentiate the relatives of probands (4.3% recurrence) compared to the relatives of controls (7.0% recurrence).

Nicolini et al. (1993) reported on the psychiatric diagnoses of 268 first-degree relatives, and 4.9% were found to meet criteria for OCD. No controls were ascertained and subsyndromic forms of OCD were not evaluated. Eight of the 27 probands were found to have a positive family history of OCD, and four of these families also had a positive family history for a chronic tic disorder.

Finally, in our own family study of adult OCD probands (Pauls et al., 1995), rates of OCD (10.9%) and subthreshold OCD (7.9%) were significantly increased among relatives of OCD probands compared to control participants. Furthermore, the relatives of early-onset (before age 12) probands were at highest risk for OCD. Eighteen of the 373 (5.0%) first-degree relatives of the early-onset OCD probands were diagnosed with a chronic tic disorder compared to 1 of 113 first-degree relatives (0.9%) of the control probands. The 86 relatives of OCD probands with comorbid tics compared to the 380 relatives of the OCD probands without comorbid tics were at increased risk for tics (10.6% vs. 3.2%) but not OCD (17.7% vs. 18.3%).

These studies provide additional evidence that some forms of OCD are familial. Family studies alone cannot demonstrate that genetic factors are necessary for the manifestation of the illness, but the data can be used to examine specific genetic hypotheses. If segregation analysis reveals that the patterns within families are consistent with a fairly simple mode of inheritance, the results can be taken as indirect evidence for the importance of genes in the etiology of the disorder. Nicolini et al. (1991) performed segregation analyses on data collected from 24 OCD families to examine whether transmission patterns were consistent with simple Mendelian models of inheritance. These investigators were unable to distinguish between an autosomal dominant or recessive model; however the dominant model was statistically more likely and most compatible with the observed patterns. In all likelihood there is not a single gene that is responsible for either tic-related or non-tic-related OCD.

In sum, the genetic vulnerability factors associated with TS also appear to place individuals at risk for OCD. If tic-related forms of OCD represent a valid subtype of OCD, the genetic factors that confer vulnerability may also be distinctive. Indeed, it seems likely that success in detecting the genes responsible for TS vulnerability will be directly relevant to our understanding of tic-related OCD. Future studies may also confirm that the form of OCD segregating in these families has the distinctive clinical phenotype and natural history previously described.

The identification of even partially homogenous subtypes should also add to our ability to identify the vulnerability genes associated with non-tic-related OCD by reducing the complexity of the task. Future studies using affected sibling pairs and other nonrestrictive designs should lead to the identification of chromosomal regions of interest associated with OCD vulnerability for both forms of the disorder. Subsequent characterization of these genetic factors should illuminate the neurobiological substrates and developmental trajectories associated with OCD and contribute to the development of valid animal models for the disorder. Specifically, with the identification of particular vulnerability genes it will be possible to examine when and where in the developing brain these genes are expressed and what the normal physiological role their products have in brain function. In addition, using molecular genetic techniques (e.g., homologous recombination), it will be possible to insert the human OCD vulnerability genes directly into mice strains, thus creating an etiologically valid animal model for OCD for a whole range of neurobiological and behavioral studies. Progress on this front will also set the stage for a deeper appreciation of the role of nongenetic factors in the pathogenesis of OCD and point the way to early interventions designed to limit the expression of the individual's genetic vulnerability.

OTHER RISK AND PROTECTIVE FACTORS

Our model of OCD pathogenesis emphasizes the importance of the interaction between genes and epigenetic or environmental factors over the course of central nervous system (CNS) development. The twin data already cited, indicating that genetically identical individuals do not necessarily have the same clinical phenotype, provide the most compelling evidence that nongenetic factors play a crucial role in the pathogenesis of OCD. In contrast to the relatively slow progress in identifying specific vulnerability genes, efforts to identify risk and protective factors that mediate the expression of TS and OCD have been more successful (Leckman & Peterson, 1993).

Events during the perinatal period have been consistently implicated in TS and tic-related OCD (Hyde, Aaronson, Randolph, Rickler, & Weinberger, 1992; Pasamanick & Kawi, 1956; Santangelo et al., 1994). We hypothesize that perinatal risk and protective factors influence the development and function of specific brain circuits that, in turn, influence the natural history of TS and tic-related OCD (Leckman & Peterson, 1993). In the most relevant study, we found that several perinatal factors were associated with the emergence of tic-related OCD including maternal coffee use (more than 2 cups per day), cigarette smoking (more than 10 per day), and alcohol consumption (more than 2 drinks per day; odds ratio [OR] = 6.1, 95% confidence interval [CI] = 1.3 to 19.4, $p < .05$), as was forceps delivery (OR = 7.9, 95% CI = 3.2 to 19.5, $p < .015$; Santangelo et al., 1994).

Other putative nutritional and hormonal factors active during early CNS development may also play some role in the development of tic-related or non-tic-related OCD. Indeed as suggested by Hyde et al. (1992), it may be useful to consider these as high-risk pregnancies, warranting an extra measure of caution. The data are less consistent with regard to non-tic-related OCD, with some studies suggesting a role for perinatal influences (Capstick & Seldrup, 1977) and others reporting no such association (Douglass, Moffitt, Dar, McGee, & Silva, 1995).

A second set of environmental risk and protective factors concerns the role of accidents of nature (infections, trauma, toxins, and drugs). For example, during the epidemic of encephalitis lethargica (1916–1926), tic, OC, and attentional problems were commonplace. Various basal ganglia ischemic lesions have also been associated with OCD-like behaviors (Bhatia & Marsden, 1994; Laplane et al., 1989). As reviewed in detail by Swedo, Allen, and others (Allen, Leonard, & Swedo, 1995; Swedo, Leonard, & Kiessling, 1994), recent attention has focused on the role of poststreptococcal autoimmune phenomena in the development of Sydenham's chorea, tics, and tic-related OCD. We hypothesize that infectious agents and autoimmune phenomena can influence the development and function of specific brain circuits and that these effects result in a range of phenotypic outcomes with regard to OC and tic symptoms. Measurement of a variety of titers of various strep-related antibodies found in serum, and possibly in cerebrospinal fluid (CSF), should allow for the examination the role of these environmental factors in greater detail.

A third and potentially crucial set of nongenetic risk factors are an individual's developmental history and level of adaptive functioning. No direct evidence supports this assertion at present, but the level of enmeshment and overinvolvement in daily living skills seen in many families of OCD patients (Calvocoressi et al., 1993; Riddle et al., 1990) may speak to both the current desperation of the family and an earlier history of difficulties with separation and attachment.

A fourth set of nongenetic risk factors includes aspects of the interpersonal and social environment. TS and OCD are to some extent stress-sensitive conditions so that events experienced as stressful by the individual (exciting holidays, marital discord, punitive parenting styles, and limited peer and family acceptance) may contribute to a worsening of the syndrome (Bornstein, Stefl, & Hammond, 1990; Silva, Munoz, Barickman, & Friedhoff, 1995). The effects of supportive family, peer, and social environments have not been systematically evaluated.

In sum, nongenetic risk and protective factors must play a crucial role in the development of OCD. This remains an understudied area that has great potential to provide insights into the psychological and neurobiological processes at work in OCD and leads for the development of early intervention programs.

NEUROBIOLOGICAL SUBSTRATES

Based on available neuroanatomical and neurobiological data, there is convincing evidence for the involvement of specific cortico-striato-thalamo-cortical (CSTC) circuits in the expression of OCD. These circuits contain multiple modular units distributed according to highly ordered repetitive patterns. These anatomic arrangements are well suited to convey cortical information in a highly specific manner throughout the basal ganglia and to modulate precisely the neuronal activity of several functional brain systems that are intimately related to the control (initiation and monitoring vs. inhibition) of different aspects of psychomotor behavior (Alexander, DeLong, & Strick, 1986; Parent & Hazrati, 1995a, 1995b).

One CSTC circuit, labeled *lateral orbitofrontal* (LOF) by Alexander et al. (1986), includes projections from the lateral orbital frontal, cingulate, and temporal cortices to portions of the head of the caudate nucleus. Striatal neurons, in turn, project to portions of the internal segment of the globus pallidus, the pars reticulata of the substantia nigra, and the ventral pallidum. These output neurons then project to portions of the ventral anterior and medial dorsal nuclei in the thalamus that in turn project back to the cortex. We hypothesize that the development and functional activity of this circuit and its commissural connections are critically involved in the pathobiology of OCD (Baxter et al., 1992; Insel, 1992a, 1992b). This reasoning is largely based on the results of in vivo neuroimaging studies that have demonstrated increased glucose metabolism in the LOF and in ventral striatum (see Baxter et al., chap. 28, this volume, for a complete discussion of these data).

We presume that the LOF circuits are to some degree functionally distinct from the remaining other *association* circuits described by Parent and Hazrati (1995a, 1995b). These association circuits include projections from various association cortices in the frontal, temporal, and parietal lobes to striatum (most of the caudate and portions of the putamen). These striatal neurons then project to portions of the internal segment of the globus pallidus and the pars reticulata of the substantia nigra. These output neurons then project to portions of the parvicellular areas of the ventral anterior and medial dorsal nuclei in the thalamus that, in turn, project to cortex. We hypothesize that the development and functional activity of these circuits and their commissural connections are critically involved in compensatory cognitive efforts to regulate or inhibit maladaptive psychomotor behaviors such as OC symptoms and tics.

A third CSTC circuit, labeled *limbic* by Parent and Hazrati (1995a, 1995b) includes projections from anterior cingulate, hippocampal, entorhinal, and temporal cortices and amygdala to the ventral striatum (ventralmost putamen and caudate nuclei, nucleus accumbens, and portions of the olfactory tubercle). These ventral striatal neurons project to the ventral pallidum and to portions of the internal segment of the globus pallidus and the pars reticulata of the substantia nigra. Output neurons then project to portions of the parvicellular areas of the ventral medial dorsal nuclei in the thalamus that, in turn, project back to various cortical regions. This circuit is thought to process emotionally laden limbic information. There is evidence for the involvement of this circuit in OCD and other anxiety disorders (Baxter et al., 1992; Rauch et al., 1994) and it may also provide part of the neurobiological substrate for TS as well (Leckman et al., 1997).

Despite the rapid advances in in vivo neuroimaging and the exciting findings concerning blood flow and treatment response in OCD in general (Baxter et al., 1992; Schwartz, Stoessel, Baxter, Martin, & Phelps, 1996), there is a paucity of data regarding tic-related versus non-tic-related OCD using these measures. Anecdotally, few differences have been observed when individuals with tic-related OCD are compared with non-tic-related OCD on measures of cerebral metabolic activity (L. Baxter, personal communication, 1995). Nevertheless, we would expect that individuals with tic-related OCD would have a distinctive neuropathology and profile on functional indexes as measured using in vivo neuroimaging techniques and that those distinctive features would be evident in brain structures closely related to those found to be abnormal in TS. For example, if one of the distinctive features of TS is a hyperinnervation of putamen as reflected by increased numbers of dopamine transporters in the putamen

(Malison et al., 1995; Singer, Hahn, & Moran, 1991), then we would predict that tic-related OCD would be characterized by a similar hyperinnervation of the equivalent structures in the LOF and limbic CSTC circuits (i.e., in the head of the caudate, the nucleus accumbens, and other portions of the ventral striatum).

Limited data suggest that gonadal steroids and hypothalamic neuro-hormones, oxytocin and arginine vasopressin (AVP), may play a role in TS and OCD. The results of genetic studies that have shown that TS is transmitted within families as an autosomal dominant trait suggest that males and females should be at equal risk. However, males are several-fold more frequently affected with TS than females (see Shapiro, Shapiro, Young, & Feinberg, 1988, for a review). This observation has led us to hypothesize that androgenic steroids may be involved in determining the phenotypic expression of the TS gene and in exacerbating tic-related symptoms (Peterson et al., 1992). Although some TS patients respond favorably to antiandrogens, this is not a universal response, nor is it long lasting (Peterson et al., 1994).

Based on the cognitive and behavioral effects of AVP and oxytocin and their neuroanatomic distributions, recent interest has focused on their role in the pathobiology of OCD (Altemus et al., 1992; Ansseau et al., 1987; Swedo et al., 1992). Hypothesized relations have emphasized the role of AVP in promoting repetitive grooming behaviors, possibly analogous to hand washing and cleaning compulsions, and maintaining conditioned responses to aversive stimuli in experimental animals (see de Wied, Diamant, & Fodor, 1993; Leckman, Goodman, North, Chappell, Price, Pauls, Anderson, Riddle, McDougle, et al., 1994, for reviews). Elevated levels of CSF AVP in OCD patients (Altemus et al., 1992) and anecdotal clinical reports of OCD among patients with diabetes insipidus, in which central AVP levels are increased (Barton, 1987), are also consistent with this hypothesis. However, we have been unable to replicate the finding of elevated CSF AVP in OCD patients (Leckman, Goodman, North, Chap-pell, Price, Pauls, Anderson, Riddle, McSwiggan-Hardin, et al., 1994). The empirical evidence indicating a role for oxytocin in the pathogenesis of OCD rests mostly on our recent finding of a marked elevation of CSF oxytocin levels in non-tic-related OCD patients (Leckman, Goodman, North, Chappell, Price, Pauls, Anderson, Riddle, McDougle, et al., 1994; Leckman, Goodman, North, Chappell, Price, Pauls, Anderson, Riddle, McSwiggan-Hardin, et al., 1994).

In this study, CSF was collected by lumbar puncture at noontime from patients with non-tic-related OCD, patients with tic-related OCD, TS patients without OCD, and normal controls (Leckman, Goodman, North, Chappell, Price, Pauls, Anderson, Riddle, McSwiggan-Hardin, et al., 1994). CSF levels of oxytocin clearly distinguished the tic-related and non-tic-related OCD groups, with the tic-related OCD patients having a mean CSF oxytocin level (6.2 ± 5.5 fmol/ml) similar to both the TS patients (4.6 ± 2.2 fmol/ml) and the normal controls (5.0 ± 2.7 fmol/ml) but markedly less than the remaining OCD cases (10.8 ± 8.7 fmol/ml; Fig. 3.3). Within the non-tic-related group, a significant correlation between the total score on the Y–BOCS and CSF oxytocin was observed ($r = 0.47$, $N = 19$, $p < .05$). This relation was not seen in the tic-related OCD group.

The first step is to replicate these CSF oxytocin findings in an independent sample of OCD patients. A review of the behavioral effects of centrally administered oxytocin to animals has led to the hypothesis that some cases of non-tic-related OCD are directly influenced by oxytocin and related systems. Indeed, the range of symptomatology seen in some forms of OCD is highly congruent with the range of behavioral effects seen after the central administration of oxytocin in animal studies (Leckman, Goodman, North, Chappell, Price, Pauls, Anderson, Riddle, McDougle, et al., 1994). A list of specific predictions concerning oxytocin-related OCD is offered in the next section.

In addition to the CSF oxytocin findings, Hanna, McCracken, and Cantwell (1991) reported that basal (nonfasting) afternoon levels of plasma prolactin are lower in non-tic-related OCD compared to tic-related OCD in a small number of patients (non-tic-related OCD, $N = 13$, 10.7 ± 4.7 ng/ml vs. tic-related OCD, $N = 5$, 16.2 ± 3.5 ng/ml; $p < .05$). This peripheral measure may reflect differences in both the central oxytocin and dopaminergic systems.

In sum, the past decade has seen remarkable advances in our understanding of the organization of neural systems and concomitant advances in the field of functional neuroimaging. Application of this knowledge to OCD has generated some of the most exciting data and has focused attention on LOF and limbic CSTC circuits in OCD. Thus far, the distinction between tic-related and non-tic-related OCD has not been an important distinction for understanding the growing body of structural and functional neuroimaging studies. Studies of neurohormones, particularly oxytocin and prolactin, in contrast, have suggested that there are neurobiological differences between these two putative subtypes of OCD. Both findings require replication. If the CSF oxytocin is replicated, it may open a number of new approaches to treatment and a more complete understanding of OCD within the context of brain development and evolution.

TREATMENT RESPONSE

As reviewed in detail elsewhere in this volume, major advances in the treatment of OCD have occurred over the past decade, including the development and refinement of cognitive-behavioral, neuropsychophar-

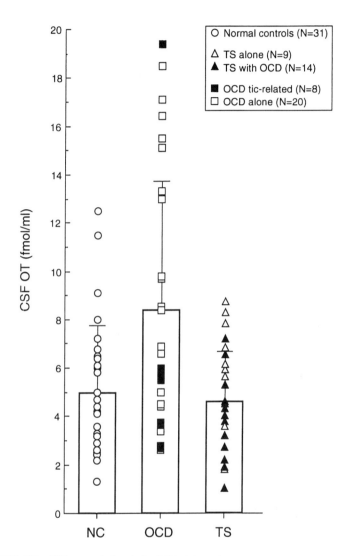

FIG. 3.3. CSF oxytocin levels in OCD, TS, and normal controls. Cerebro-spinal fluid (CSF) oxytocin levels in patients with OCD, patients with TS, and normal controls (Leckman, Walker, et al., 1994). The OCD patients had significantly higher CSF levels of oxytocin ($p < .01$) than either of the comparison groups. Note that elevation of CSF oxytocin was confined to those OCD patients without a personal or family history of a chronic tic disorder.

macological, and neurosurgical approaches (see Kozak, Liebowitz, & Foa, chap. 25, and McDougle, Epperson, & Price, chap. 19, this volume, for reviews of this field). With the exception of pharmacotherapy, the putative distinction between tic-related OCD and non-tic related OCD has not been addressed. Specifically, McDougle and colleagues (McDougle et al., 1995; McDougle, Goodman, Leckman, Barr, et al., 1993; McDougle et al., 1994; McDougle, Goodman, Leckman, & Price, 1993) performed a series of pharmacological studies that indicated that tic-related OCD patients tend to respond less well to potent and selective serotonin reuptake inhibitors, and that this partial response is improved with either the addition of dopamine D_2 receptor antagonists such as haloperidol or atypical neuroleptics such as risperidone that has mixed D_2 and 5-HT_2 antagonism.

Similar studies using other treatment paradigms are needed to evaluate the potential importance of the distinction between tic-related and non-tic-related OCD. Anecdotally, our impression is that OCD patients with tic-related forms of illness tend to fair less well with cognitive-behavioral approaches. Rigorously conducted clinical trials are needed to confirm or refute this impression.

The implications for treatment-refractory OCD are clear. OCD is a phenotypically heterogeneous disorder, and evidence is emerging that this heterogeneity at a descriptive level is also reflected at the levels of etiology and biological vulnerability. If so, then it is no surprise that successful treatments for one form of OCD may not be successful for other forms. Close attention to the phenotypic characteristics and natural history of individuals with OCD may eventually guide clinicians to specific treatments known to be effective for particular forms of this disorder. Additional research is needed to clarify these distinctions.

RECOMMENDATIONS, FUTURE PROSPECTS, AND PREDICTIONS

Given the emerging evidence concerning phenotypic differences between tic-related and non-tic-related OCD and supporting genetic, neurobiological, and pharmacological data, it may be appropriate to subtype OCD patients participating in clinical trials according to this distinction. This distinction is best drawn using family-genetic data by which someone is considered to have tic-related OCD only if they or a first-degree family member has TS or another chronic tic disorder. Eventually, specific trials may be limited to specific subtypes so that there is sufficient power to detect clinically meaningful differences.

Identification of biologically homogenous subtypes of OCD may facilitate advances along a number of fronts including the development of early detection and intervention programs and the development of more specific forms of treatment. It will also set the stage for advances in genetics, studies of risk and protective factors, and neurobiology.

Thus far, at least three putative forms of OCD can be discerned: familial tic-related OCD, familial non-tic-related OCD (possibly involving altera-tions in activity of the central oxytocin pathways), and sporadic, nonfa-milial (or not) OCD (possibly involving a range of traumatic, infectious, autoimmune injuries to specific brain regions participating in the LOF and limbic CSTC circuits). Although overlapping, we anticipate that these forms of OCD will have distinctive phenotypic, genetic, environmental, and neurobiological features. Above all, these forms of OCD may show unique or distinctive patterns of treatment response.

Given our existing knowledge, and in the spirit of scientific discourse a number of specific predictions are offered.

Clinical Phenotype, Natural History, and Treatment Response

In tic-related OCD, male patients with a personal history of chronic tics and female patients, often without a personal history of tics, will report prepubertal onsets and be more likely to present with a broad range of OC symptoms (as described earlier). The course of illness may show a waxing and waning course and be less responsive to standard psycho-pharmacologic or cognitive-behavioral approaches.

In non-tic-related (oxytocin-related) OCD, many of the OC symptoms are experienced in the service of harm avoidance as opposed to needing something to look or feel "just right." If the association with the oxytocin system is confirmed, based on what is known concerning centrally ad-ministered oxytocin's ability to initiate pair bonding and maternal behav-ior, as well as stimulate anogenital grooming, we also predict that in this form of OCD the predominant obsessions would involve separation wor-ries and contamination fears (e.g., urine, feces, and semen; Leckman & Mayes, 1998). Oxytocin-related OCD is predicted to have a later age of onset, with most cases beginning during the peripubertal period, given the need for steroid priming of the oxytocin system. Males and females with a vulnerability to OCD would be at greater risk during courtship periods. Females with a vulnerability to this form of illness would also be at greater risk of onset or exacerbation during pregnancy and the immediate postpartum period. Patients with oxytocin-related OCD may be more responsive to serotonin reuptake inhibitors than patients with tic-related OCD. A recent case series, describing 15 cases of postpartum onset of OCD, provides circumstantial support for this hypothesis, as virtually all of the patients responded well to serotonin reuptake inhibitors

(Sichel, Cohen, Dimmock, & Rosenbaum, 1993). Patients with oxytocin-related OCD might also be expected to benefit from treatments that influence the status of oxytocin receptors or that alter oxytocin release. Cognitive-behavioral treatments may be included in this category. Changes in clinical severity in response to successful behavioral or pharmacological treatment should also be reflected in changes in the dynamics or pattern of oxytocin release in the CNS.

In sporadic, nonfamilial (or not) OCD, we predict that the OCD phenotype might have atypical features including sudden onsets or exacerbations involving the precipitous loss of a preexisting response to medication or other treatments. Supportive interventions and those directed at etiological mechanisms, including antibiotic therapy and plasmapheresis, may be beneficial in some cases where a Sydenham's-like autoimmunity is suspected (Allen et al., 1995). Caution is warranted, however, with regard to plasmapheresis, the administration of pooled immunoglobulins, and other experimental therapeutic interventions given the paucity of data concerning their efficacy.

Genetic Factors

Tic-related OCD is frequently a familial condition. The genetic vulnerability genes are likely to be the same or similar to those involved in TS. We predict that some of the genes will normally be involved in the development and regulation of the basal ganglia and the LOF and limbic CSTC circuits.

Some forms of non-tic-related OCD appear to be familial, so it may be worth performing segregation analyses just within the oxytocin-related OCD families. We would predict that genes that regulate the activity of the oxytocin system including thé genes that control the expression of the oxytocin receptor during the course of development would be particularly important in the pathogenesis of this form of non-tic-related OCD.

In the remaining forms of sporadic or atypical OCD, genetic susceptibility may also play a role. This is perhaps most likely in autoimmune forms of illness where inherited immune elements may predispose to the emergence of an autoimmune response.

Nongenetic Risk and Protective Factors

Many of the risk and protective factors may be nonspecific. For example, a perinatal insult that alters the development of the LOF and limbic circuits may predispose to more severe forms of OCD, be it tic-related or not.

In the case of oxytocin-related OCD, given the hypothesized importance of interpersonal attachment and bonding in this form of OCD, we would predict that the individual's early life experience in the formation of the mother–infant dyad might be an important nongenetic risk or protective factor for the later development of this form of OCD (Leckman & Mayes, 1998).

Neurobiology and Neuroimaging

Recent progress in neuroanatomy, systems neuroscience, and functional neuroimaging also sets the stage for a major advance in our understanding of these disorders and the neurobiological substrates that underlie them. Success in this area will lead to the targeting of specific brain circuits for more intensive study. Diagnostic and prognostic advances can also be anticipated; for example, which circuits are involved and to what degree? How does that degree of involvement likely affect outcome?

As in the case of the CSF study (Leckman, Goodman, North, Chappell, Price, Pauls, Anderson, Riddle, McSwiggan-Hardin, et al., 1994), separation of existing neurochemical and neuroimaging data sets into subgroups of OCD patients (tic-related OCD vs. oxytocin-related OCD vs. other) may prove to be of value.

Neuropathological studies need to be undertaken to help identify more precisely the neuroanatomic sites involved in the various subtypes of OCD. Given the large number of individuals affected with this disorder and the degree of disability frequently associated with this condition, it should not be too daunting a task.

If the abnormalities in central oxytocin pathways systems are confirmed in some cases of non-tic-related OCD, it would be anticipated that the rates of glucose utilization would be elevated in the paraventricular nucleus and other hypothalamic and extrahypothalamic structures receiving projections from the paraventricular nucleus. In sporadic cases of OCD, serial neuroimaging studies may be particularly useful, as they might detect instances of swelling and inflammation in the basal ganglia (Tucker et al., 1996).

This is an ideal time to advance our knowledge of OCD. Recent advances in the fields of genetics and the developmental neurosciences have led to optimism that the vulnerability genes that underlie these conditions can be characterized and their role in normal development understood. Advances in this area will improve the accuracy of diagnoses and permit the identification of vulnerable individuals prior to the onset of disease. A number of other nongenetic risk and protective factors have already been identified that appear to mediate the course and outcome of these diseases in vulnerable individuals. A more complete understanding of these factors should lead the way to the development of successful preventive interventions. Given this potential, OCD can be considered a model disorder in which to study the interplay of genetic, neurobiological, and environmental factors during development. It is likely that the research paradigms developed in these studies, and many of the empirical findings resulting from them, will be relevant to other disorders of childhood onset and our understanding of normal development.

Finally, the study and care of children and adults with OCD remains a challenge. We have found that much of what is learned from patients and their families in the broad biopsychosocial context of these competing models of pathogenesis can be returned to their improved treatment. It is our earnest hope that aspects of these models and their predictions will not only guide future research but also illuminate the path to improved understanding and care.

ACKNOWLEDGMENTS

The research reported here was supported by Grants MH-49351, MH-44843, MH-30929, HD-03008, and RR-06022 from the National Institutes of Health, Bethesda, MD. We thank Drs. Wayne K. Goodman, Thomas R. Insel, Paul Lombroso, Jack Maser, Daniel Tucker, and Yanki Yazgan; Ms. Sharon I. Ort; Ms. Kimberly Lynch; Ms. Amy Vitale; and Mr. Colin Bondi for their assistance and comments on an earlier draft of this chapter.

REFERENCES

Alexander, G. E., DeLong, M. R., & Strick, P. L. (1986). Parallel organization of functionally segregated circuits linking basal ganglia and cortex. *Annual Review of Neuroscience, 9,* 307–311.

Allen, J. A., Leonard, H. L., & Swedo, S. E. (1995). Infection-triggered, autoimmune, subtype of pediatric OCD and Tourette's syndrome. *Journal of the American Academy of Child and Adolescent Psychiatry, 34,* 307–311.

Altemus, M., Pigott, T., Kalogeras, K. T., Demitrack, M., Dubbert, B., Murphy, D. L., & Gold, P. W. (1992). Abnormalities in the regulation of vasopressin and corticotropin releasing factor secretion in obsessive-compulsive disorder. *Archives of General Psychiatry, 49,* 9–20.

American Psychiatric Association. (1994). *Diagnostic and statistical manual of mental disorders* (4th ed.). Washington, DC: Author.

Andrews, G., Stewart, G., Allen, R., & Henderson, A. S. (1990). The genetics of six neurotic disorders: A twin study. *Journal of Affective Disorders, 19,* 23–29.

Ansseau, M., Legros, J. J., Mormont, C., Cerfontaine, J., Papart, P., Geenen, V., Adam, F., & Franck, G. (1987). Intranasal oxytocin in obsessive-compulsive disorder. *Psychoneuroendocrinology, 12,* 231–236.

Baer, L. (1994). Factor analysis of symptom subtypes of obsessive compulsive disorder and their relation to personality and tics. *Journal of Clinical Psychiatry, 55*(Suppl. 3), 18–23.

Barton, R. (1987). Diabetes insipudus and obsessional neurosis. *Advances in Biochemical Psychopharmacology, 43,* 347–349.

Baxter, L. R., Schwartz, J. M., Bregman, K., Szuba, M., Guze, B., Mazziotta, J., Alazraki, A., Selin, C., Ferng, H.-K., Minford, P., & Phelps, M. (1992). Caudate glucose metabolic rate changes with both drug and behavior therapy for obsessive-compulsive disorder. *Archives of General Psychiatry, 49,* 681–689.

Bellodi, L., Sciuto, G., Diaferia, G., Ronchi, P., & Smeraldi, E. (1992). Psychiatric disorders in the families of patients with obsessive-compulsive disorder. *Psychiatry Research, 42,* 111–120.

Bhatia, K., & Marsden, C. (1994). The behavioral and motor consequences of focal lesions of the basal ganglia in man. *Brain, 117,* 859–876.

Black, D. W., Noyes, R., Jr., Goldstein, R. B., & Blum, N. (1992). A family study of obsessive-compulsive disorder. *Archives of General Psychiatry, 49,* 362–368.

Bornstein, R. A., Stefl, M. E., & Hammond, L. (1990). A survey of Tourette syndrome patients and their families: The 1987 Ohio Tourette survey. *Journal of Neuropsychiatry, 2,* 275–281.

Calvocoressi, L., McDougle, C. J., Wasylink, S., Goodman, W. K., Trufan, S. J., & Price, L. H. (1993). Hospital treatment of patients with severe obsessive compulsive disorder. *Hospital and Community Psychiatry, 44,* 1150–1154.

Capstick, N., & Seldrup, J. (1977). Obsessional states: A study in the relationship between abnormalities occurring at the time of birth and the subsequent development of obsessional symptoms. *Acta Psychiatrica Scandinavica, 56,* 427–431.

Carey, G., & Gottesman, I. I. (1981). Twin and family studies of anxiety, phobic and obsessive disorders. In D. F. Klein & J. Rabkin (Eds.), *Anxiety: New research and changing concepts* (pp. 117–136). New York: Raven.

Comings, D. E., & Comings, B. G. (1987). A controlled study of Tourette syndrome: IV. Obsessions, compulsions, and schizoid behaviors. *American Journal of Human Genetics, 41,* 782–803.

de Groot, C. M., Bornstein, R. A., Janus, M.-D., & Mavissakalian, M. R. (1995). Patterns of obsessive compulsive symptoms in Tourette subjects are independent of severity. *Anxiety, 1,* 268–274.

de Wied, D., Diamant, M., & Fodor, M. (1993). Central nervous system effects of neurohypohyseal hormones and related peptides. *Frontiers in Neuroendocrinology, 14,* 251–302.

Douglass, H. M., Moffitt, T. E., Dar, R., McGee, R., & Silva, P. (1995). Obsessive-compulsive disorder in a birth cohort of 18-year-olds: Prevalence and predictors. *Journal of the American Academy of Child and Adolescent Psychiatry, 34,* 1424–1431.

Eapen, V., Pauls, D. L., & Robertson, M. M. (1993). Evidence for autosomal dominant transmission in Tourette's syndrome—United Kingdom cohort study. *British Journal of Psychiatry, 162,* 593–596.

Evans, D. W., Leckman, J. F., Carter, A., Reznick, J. S., Henshaw, D., & Pauls, D. L. (1997). Ritual, habit, and perfectionism: The prevalence and development of compulsive-like behavior in normal young children. *Child Development, 68,* 58–68.

George, M. S., Trimble, M. R., Ring, H. A., Sallee, F. R., & Robertson, M. M. (1993). Obsessions in obsessive-compulsive disorder with and without Gilles de la Tourette's syndrome. *American Journal of Psychiatry, 150,* 93–97.

Goodman, W. K., Price, L. H., Rasmussen, S. A., Mazure, C., Delgado, P., Heninger, G. R., & Charney, D. S. (1989). The Yale–Brown Obsessive Compulsive Scale: Part II. Validity. *Archives of General Psychiatry, 46,* 1012–1016.

Goodman, W. K., Price, L. H., Rasmussen, S. A., Mazure, C., Fleischmann, R. L., Hill, C. L., Heninger, G. R., & Charney, D. S. (1989). The Yale–Brown Obsessive Compulsive Scale: Part I. Development, use and reliability. *Archives of General Psychiatry, 46,* 1006–1011.

Hanna, G. L., McCracken, J. T., & Cantwell, D. P. (1991). Prolactin in childhood obsessive-compulsive disorder: Clinical correlates and response to clomipramine. *Journal of the American Academy of Child and Adolescent Psychiatry, 30,* 173–178.

Holzer, J., Goodman, W. K., Price, L. H., Bear, L., Leckman, J. F., & Heninger, G. R. (1994). Obsessive compulsive disorder with and without a chronic tic disorder: A comparison of symptoms in 70 patients. *British Journal of Psychiatry, 164,* 469–473.

Hyde, T., Aaronson, B., Randolph, C., Rickler, K., & Weinberger, D. (1992). Relationship of birth weight to the phenotypic expression of Gilles de la Tourette's syndrome in monozygotic twins. *Neurology, 42,* 652–658.

Insel, T. (1992a). Oxytocin: A neuropeptide for affiliation. *Psychoneuroendocrinology, 17,* 1–35.

Insel, T. (1992b). Towards a neuroanatomy of obsessive compulsive disorder. *Archives of General Psychiatry, 49,* 739–744.

Janet, P., & Raymond, F. (1976). *Les obsessions et la psychasthéniae* [Obsessions and psychasthenia]. New York: Arno. (Original work published 1903)

Jaspers, K. (1963). *Allgemeine Psychopathologie* [General Psychopathology]. Chicago: University of Chicago Press. (Original work published 1923)

Kräupl Taylor, F. (1979). *Psychopathology—Its causes and symptoms.* Baltimore: Johns Hopkins University Press.

LaPlane, D., Levasseur, M., Pillon, B., DuBois, B., Baulac, M., Sette, G., Danze, F., & Baron, J. C. (1989). Obsessive-compulsive and other behavioral changes with bilateral basal ganglia lesions. *Brain, 112,* 699–723.

Leckman, J. F., Goodman, W. K., North, W. G., Chappell, P. B., Price, L. H., Pauls, D. L., Anderson, G. M., Riddle, M. A., McDougle, C. J., Barr, L. C., & Cohen, D. J. (1994). The role of oxytocin in obsessive compulsive disorder and related normal behavior. *Psychoneuroendocrinology, 19,* 742–758.

Leckman, J. F., Goodman, W. K., North, W. G., Chappell, P. B., Price, L. H., Pauls, D. L., Anderson, G. M., Riddle, M. A., McSwiggan-Hardin, M. T., McDougle, C. J., Barr, L. C., & Cohen D. J. (1994). Elevated levels of CSF oxytocin in obsessive compulsive disorder: Comparison with Tourette's syndrome and healthy controls. *Archives of General Psychiatry, 51,* 782–783.

Leckman, J. F., Grice, D. E., Barr, L. C., deVries, A. L. C., Martin, C., Cohen, D. J., Goodman, W. K., & Rasmussen, S. A. (1995). Tic-related vs. non-tic related obsessive compulsive disorder. *Anxiety, 1,* 208–215.

Leckman, J. F., & Mayes, L. C. (1998). Maladies of love: An evolutinary perspective on some forms of obsessive-compulsive disorder. In D. M. Hann, L. C. Huffman, I. I. Lederhendler, & D. L. Meinecke (Eds.), *Advancing research in developmental plasticity: Integrating the behavioral science and neuroscience of mental health* (pp. 134–152). Rockville, MD: National Institute of Mental Health, U.S. Department of Health and Human Services.

Leckman, J. F., & Peterson, B. S. (1993). The pathogenesis of Tourette's syndrome: Role of epigenetic factors active in early CNS development. *Biological Psychiatry, 34,* 425–427.

Leckman, J. F., Peterson, B. S., Anderson, G. M., Arnsten, A. F. T., Pauls, D. L., & Cohen, D. J. (1997). Pathogenesis of Tourette's syndrome. *Journal of Child Psychology and Psychiatry, 38,* 119–142.

Leckman, J. F., Walker, W. K., Goodman, W. K., Pauls, D. L., & Cohen, D. J. (1994). "Just right" perceptions associated with compulsive behaviors in Tourette's syndrome. *American Journal of Psychiatry, 151,* 675–680.

Lenane, M. C., Swedo, S. E., Leonard, H., Pauls, D. L., Sceery, W., & Rapoport, J. (1990). Psychiatric disorders in first degree relatives of children and adolescents with obsessive-compulsive disorder. *Journal of the American Academy of Child and Adolescent Psychiatry, 29,* 407–412.

Leonard, H. L., Lenane, M. C., Swedo, S. E., Rettew, D. C., Gershon, E. S., & Rapoport, J. L. (1992). Tics and Tourette's disorder: A 2- to 7-year follow-up of 54 obsessive-compulsive children. *American Journal of Psychiatry, 149,* 1244–1251.

Malison, R. T., McDougle, C. J., van Dyck, C. H., Scahill, L., Baldwin, R. M., Seibyl, J. P., Price, L. H., Leckman, J. F., & Innis, R. B. (1995). [^{123}I]β-CIT SPECT imaging of striatal dopamine transporter binding in Tourette's disorder. *American Journal of Psychiatry, 152,* 1359–1361.

McDougle, C. J., Fleischmann, R. L., Epperson, C. N., Wasylink, S., Leckman, J. F., & Price, L. H. (1995). Risperidone addition in fluvoxamine-refractory obsessive compulsive disorder: A case series. *Journal of Clinical Psychiatry, 56,* 526–528.

McDougle, C. J., Goodman, W. K., Leckman, J. F., Barr, L. C., Heninger, G. R., & Price, L. H. (1993). The efficacy of fluvoxamine in obsessive compulsive disorder: Effects of comorbid chronic tic disorder. *Journal of Clinical Psychopharmacology, 13,* 354–358.

McDougle, C. J., Goodman, W. K., Leckman, J. F., Lee, N. C., Heninger, G. R., & Price, L. H. (1994). Haloperidol addition in fluvoxamine-refractory obsessive compulsive disorder: A double blind placebo-controlled study in patients with and without tics. *Archives of General Psychiatry, 51,* 302–308.

McDougle, C. J., Goodman, W. K., Leckman, J. F., & Price, L. H. (1993). The psychopharmacology of obsessive compulsive disorder: Implications for treatment for pathogenesis. *Psychiatric Clinics of North America, 16,* 749–766.

McKeon, P., & Murray, R. (1987). Familial aspects of obsessive-compulsive neurosis. *British Journal of Psychiatry, 151,* 528–534.

Miguel, E. C., Coffey, B. J., Baer, L., Savage, C. R., Rauch, S. L., & Jenike, M. A. (1995). Phenomenology of intentional repetitive behaviors in obsessive-compulsive disorder and Tourette's disorder. *Journal of Clinical Psychiatry, 56,* 246–255.

Nicolini, H., Hanna, G., Baxter, L., Schwartz, J., Weissbacker, K., & Spence, M. A. (1991). Segregation analysis of obsessive compulsive and associated disorders. Preliminary results. *Ursus Med, 1,* 25–28.

Nicolini, H., Weissbecker, K., Mejia, J. M., & de Carmona, M. S. (1993). Family study of obsessive-compulsive disorder in a Mexican population. *Archives of Medical Research, 24,* 193–198.

Parent, A., & Hazrati, L.-N. (1995a). Functional anatomy of the basal ganglia: I. The cortico-basal ganglia-thalamo-cortical loop. *Brain Research Reviews, 20,* 91–127.

Parent, A., & Hazrati, L.-N. (1995b). Functional anatomy of the basal ganglia: II. The place of the subthalamic nucleus and the external pallidum in basal ganglia circuitry. *Brain Research Review, 20,* 128–154.

Pasamanick, B., & Kawi, A. (1956). A study of the association of prenatal and paranatal factors in the development of tics in children. *Pediatrics, 48,* 596–601.

Pauls, D. L. (1992). The genetics of obsessive compulsive disorder and Gilles de la Tourette's syndrome. In M. A. Jenike (Ed.), *Psychiatric Clinics of North America* (pp. 759–766). Philadelphia: Saunders.

Pauls, D. L., Alsobrook, J. P., II, Goodman, W., Rasmussen, S., & Leckman, J. F. (1995). A family study of obsessive compulsive disorder. *American Journal of Psychiatry, 152,* 76–84.

Pauls, D. L., & Leckman, J. F. (1986). The inheritance of Gilles de la Tourette's syndrome and associated behaviors: Evidence for autosomal dominant transmission. *New England Journal of Medicine, 315,* 993–997.

Pauls, D. L., Raymond, C. L., Leckman, J. F., & Stevenson, J. M. (1991). A family study of Tourette's syndrome. *American Journal of Human Genetics, 48,* 154–163.

Peterson, B. S., Leckman, J. F., Scahill, L., Naftolin, F., Keefe, D., Charest, N. J., & Cohen, D. J. (1992). Hypothesis: Steroid hormones and sexual dimorphisms modulate symptom expression in Tourette's syndrome. *Psychoneuroendocrinology, 17,* 553–563.

Peterson, B. S., Leckman, J. F., Scahill, L., Naftolin, F., Keefe, D., Charest, N. J., & Cohen, D. J. (1994). Steroid hormones and Tourette's syndrome: Early experience with antiandrogen therapy. *Journal of Clinical Psychopharmacology, 14,* 131–135.

Rachman, S. (1993). Obsessions, responsibility and guilt. *Behavior Research and Therapy, 31,* 149–154.

Rasmussen, S. A. (1994). Genetic studies of obsessive compulsive disorder. In E. Hollander, J. Zohar, D. Marazziti, & B. Olivier (Eds.), *Current insights in obsessive compulsive disorder* (pp. 105–114). New York: Wiley.

Rasmussen, S. A., & Tsuang, M. T. (1986). Clinical characteristics and family history in DSM–III obsessive compulsive disorder. *American Journal of Psychiatry, 143,* 317–322.

Rauch, S. L., Jenike, M. A., Alpert, N. M., Baer, L., Breiter, H. C. R., Savage, C. R., & Fischman, A. J. (1994). Regional cerebral blood flow measured during symptom provocation in obsessive-compulsive disorder using oxygen 15-labeled carbon dioxide and positron emission tomography. *Archives of General Psychiatry, 51,* 62–70.

Riddle, M. A., Scahill, L., King, R., Hardin, M. T., Towbin, K. E., Ort, S. I., Leckman, J. F., & Cohen, D. J. (1990). Obsessive compulsive disorder in children and adolescents: Phenomenology and family history. *Journal of the American Academy of Child and Adolescent Psychiatry, 29,* 766–772.

Santangelo, S. L., Pauls, D. L., Goldstein, J., Faraone, S. V., Tsuang, M. T., & Leckman, J. F. (1994). Tourette's syndrome: What are the influences of gender and comorbid obsessive-compulsive disorder? *Journal of the American Academy of Child and Adolescent Psychiatry, 33,* 795–804.

Schwartz, J. M., Stoessel, P. W., Baxter, L. R., Martin, K. M., & Phelps, M. E. (1996). Systematic cerebral glucose metabolic rate changes after successful behavior modification treatment of obsessive-compulsive disorder. *Archives of General Psychiatry, 53,* 109–116.

Shapiro, A. K., Shapiro, E. S., Young, J. G., & Feinberg, T. E. (1988). *Gilles de la Tourette syndrome* (2nd ed.). New York: Raven.

Sichel, D. A., Cohen, L. S., Dimmock, J. A., & Rosenbaum, J. F. (1993). Postpartum obsessive compulsive disorder: A case series. *Journal of Clinical Psychiatry, 54,* 156–159.

Silva, R. R., Munoz, D. M., Barickman, J., & Friedhoff, A. J. (1995). Environmental factors and related fluctuation of symptoms in children with Tourette's disorder. *Journal of Child Psychology and Psychiatry, 36,* 305–312.

Singer, H., Hahn, I., & Moran, T. (1991). Tourette's syndrome: Abnormal dopamine uptake sites in postmortem striatum from patients with Tourette's syndrome. *Annals of Neurology, 30,* 558–562.

Slater, E., & Roth, M. (1969). *Clinical psychiatry.* London: Bailliere, Tindall & Cassell.

Swedo, S. E., Leonard, H. L., & Kiessling, L. S. (1994). Speculations on antineuronal antibody mediated neuropsychiatric disorders of children. *Pediatrics, 93,* 323–326.

Swedo, S. E., Leonard, H. L., Kruesi, M. J. P., Rettew, D. C., Listwak, S. J., Berrettini, W., Stipec, M., Hamburger, S., Gold, P. W., Potter, W. Z., & Rapoport, J. L. (1992). Cerebrospinal fluid neurochemistry in children and adolescents with obsessive-compulsive disorder. *Archives of General Psychiatry, 49,* 29–36.

Torgerson, S. (1983). Genetic factors in anxiety disorder. *Archives of General Psychiatry, 40,* 1085–1089.

Tucker, D. M., Leckman, J. F., Scahill, L., Epstein, G., LaCamera, R., Cardona, L., Cohen, P., Heidmann, S., Goldstein, J., Judge, J., Snyder, E., Bult, A., Peterson, B. S., & Lombroso, P. (1996). A putative post-streptococcal case of obsessive-compulsive disorder with chronic tic disorder, not otherwise specified. *Journal of the American Academy of Child and Adolescent Psychiatry, 35,* 1684–1691.

van de Wetering, B. J. M. (1993). *The Gilles de la Tourette syndrome: A psychiatric-genetic study.* Unpublished doctoral dissertation, Erasmus University, Rotterdam, The Netherlands.

4

Comorbid Schizophrenia: Implications for Treatment of Obsessive-Compulsive Disorder

Matthew J. Byerly
University of Texas Southwestern Medical Center at Dallas

Wayne K. Goodman
Carlos Cuadros
University of Florida College of Medicine

The relation between obsessive-compulsive (OC) symptoms and schizophrenia has interested researchers for more than a century. Westphal (1878) and Bleuler (1919) described OC phenomena as a variant or prodrome to schizophrenia. A. Lewis (1936) supported a link between psychotic and OC symptoms by suggesting that insight is often lost in patients with obsessive-compulsive disorder (OCD). Nine years later, Stengel (1945) argued that OC symptoms may serve an important integrating influence in patients with schizophrenia, hypothesizing that schizophrenia patients with comorbid OC symptoms would experience a more benign course.

Insel and Akiskal (1986) differentiated OCD patients with impaired insight (those with OC psychosis) from patients with schizophrenia. Patients with OC psychosis were described as having an "extreme extension of previous obsessional symptoms" (p. 1532). Insel and Akiskal further suggested that patients with OC psychosis differed from those with schizophrenia by a lack of hallucinations, an episodic course of psychosis, and the potential for responding to antidepressant treatments.

The following review focuses on the treatment implications of OC symptoms that occur in a comorbid state with schizophrenia. Patients with OC psychosis are not the focus of this review as they do not necessarily meet criteria for schizophrenia. For a review of the concept of OC psychosis, the reader may refer to Insel and Akiskal (1986).

EPIDEMIOLOGY

Early study of schizophrenia patients found low rates of OC symptom comorbidity. In a retrospective chart review of 1,000 schizophrenia patients, Jahrreiss (1926) found significant OC symptoms in only 1.1%. Rosen (1957) performed a similar chart review of 848 schizophrenia patients and reported that 30 (3.5%) had prominent obsessions, compulsions, or both. Several methodologic limitations of these early studies, including lack of prospective evaluation and standardized diagnostic criteria for schizophrenia (possibly including patients with other psychoses), may have led to an underestimation of comorbid OC symptom rates. In a more rigorously designed retrospective study, Fenton and McGlashan (1986) reported that 21 of 163 patients (13%) meeting *Diagnostic and Statistical Manual of Mental Disorders* (3rd ed. [*DSM–III*]; American Psychiatric Association, 1980) criteria for schizophrenia also had OC symptoms.

Using diagnoses generated by the Diagnostic Interview Schedule (DIS), the Epidemiologic Catchment Area Study found a comorbid OCD rate of 12.2% among those with schizophrenia (Karno, Golding, Sorenson, & Burnam, 1988). The DIS was used in a second epidemiologic study that found 20% of schizophrenia patients (66 of 288) exhibited OC symptoms (Samuel et al., 1993). The sensitivity of the DIS in screening for OC symptoms has been questioned, however. Only two DIS screening questions relate to obsessions and three to compulsions. Insufficient numbers of screening questions could result in underreporting. Alternatively, general screening questions may capture individuals with only subclinical OCD. Two studies comparing clinician and DIS-based diagnoses further highlight concerns about the validity of DIS-generated diagnoses of OCD. Both studies found that diagnostic agreement between clinicians and the DIS was only slightly greater than chance (Anthony et al., 1985; Helzer et al., 1985).

In a recent study, Berman, Kalinowski, Berman, Lengua, and Green (1995) examined the occurrence of OC symptoms in 102 patients diagnosed with chronic schizophrenia as defined by the *Diagnostic and Statistical Manual of Mental Disorders* (3rd ed., rev. [*DSM–III–R*]; American Psychiatric Association, 1987). Patients were not evaluated directly; instead diagnoses were based on chart review and a semistructured interview with the patient's treating clinician. Therapists were asked to report on OC symptoms described by the patient or observed during the course of treatment. The semistructured interview of therapists included the eight symptom categories used by Fenton and McGlashan (1986) supplemented by four categories obtained from the Yale–Brown Obsessive Compulsive Scale (Y–BOCS; Goodman et al., 1989). A relatively liberal definition of obsessions and compulsions was applied. Clearly psychotic symptoms (e.g., paranoid delusions) were excluded, but OC symptoms that bordered psychosis were included. In this paradigm, 25% of schizophrenia patients

(27 of 102) were found to have significant OC symptoms at the time of assessment.

Estimates of the frequency with which OC symptoms occur in schizophrenia have varied depending on the means of assessment. Early studies utilizing retrospective chart evaluations resulted in low reported rates of comorbid schizophrenia and OC symptoms. This may be explained by the retrospective nature of these studies, requiring that patients complain of and clinicians record the reported OC symptoms. Additionally, evidence suggests that patients who experience obsessions and compulsions may not readily report these symptoms. Rasmussen and Tsuang (1986), for example, found that 7.5 years lapsed between the onset of OCD and first psychiatric treatment. The identification of OC symptoms in those with schizophrenia may be even more difficult due to the masking of these symptoms by psychosis. Because of potential difficulties in identifying OC symptoms in schizophrenia, a systematic, prospective study that directly examines schizophrenia patients could provide valuable information about rates of comorbid OC symptoms and improve methods of screening for OC symptoms in this population.

PROGNOSTIC SIGNIFICANCE

The effect OC symptoms may have on the prognosis of schizophrenia has been examined by several investigators. Based on psychoanalytic theory and a case series of seven patients, Stengel (1945) suggested that the presence of OC symptoms would play a protective role against symptom progression in psychotic disorder patients. In his series, Stengel noted a marked tendency to remission in schizophrenia patients who exhibited OC symptoms. Likewise, an early chart survey conducted by Rosen (1957) evaluated the outcome of 30 schizophrenia patients with comorbid OC symptoms, again describing favorable outcomes. However, the lack of standardized diagnostic criteria for schizophrenia in the studies of Rosen and Stengel may have led to the inclusion of patients with affective psychosis, thus resulting in a bias toward good outcome.

In contrast to these early reports, three studies have reported that the presence of OC symptoms predicted a poor outcome in schizophrenia patients. Fenton and McGlashan (1986) retrospectively examined the relation of OC symptoms to schizophrenia in the Chestnut Lodge Follow-up Study. The long-term outcome of 21 schizophrenia patients with comorbid OC symptoms was significantly poorer on measures of social relations, employment, psychopathology, and global functioning than in schizophrenia patients without OC symptoms.

Two prospective studies evaluated the effect of OC symptoms on the outcome of schizophrenia patients. In a preliminary report, Merson et al.

(1995) described results of psychopathologic (assessed by the Positive and Negative Syndrome Scale [PANSS] of Kay, Fiszbein, & Opler, 1987) and cognitive measures in 20 schizophrenia patients with and without OC symptoms. Patients with OC symptoms scored significantly higher on the PANSS general psychophathology subscale than those without OC symptoms. This PANSS subscale includes symptoms such as anxiety, depression, and somatic preoccupation. Patient groups did not differ on PANSS positive or negative symptom subscales. No between-group differences were found for cognitive measures, but there was a significant inverse relation between the severity of OC symptoms and performance on visual memory tests. Although this preliminary finding suggests that OC symptoms do not appear to differentiate OC and non-OC groups on cognitive measures, OC symptoms may predict greater impairment on some specific cognitive measures within a group of schizophrenia patients affected by OC symptoms. If replicated, such findings might indicate discrete neurocognitive abnormalities in patients with schizophrenia and OC symptoms, and may assist in identifying localized regions of brain dysfunction that result in the co-occurrence of these conditions.

In a second prospective study, Berman, Kalinowski, et al. (1995) compared the level of functioning and course of illness in 27 schizophrenia patients with OC symptoms to that of 75 non-OC schizophrenia patients. Results obtained from indirect interview with patients' treating clinicians showed that the OC group experienced a worse outcome compared to patients without OC symptoms. Patients with OC symptoms had an earlier age of onset of schizophrenia, and were significantly more impaired on measures of duration of hospitalization in the past 5 years and a 5-point scale of overall functioning. The OC group was also less likely to be living with a spouse, stay married, and be employed at the time of assessment.

The understanding of the effect that OC symptoms have on the outcome of patients with schizophrenia has changed with data collected from recent, more rigorously designed studies. Whereas early reports suggested that the presence of OC symptoms were predictive of a favorable prognosis in schizophrenia patients, recent retrospective and prospective studies now indicate that comorbid OC symptoms are associated with a worse outcome in those with schizophrenia.

Theories explaining the relation between poor prognosis and associated OC symptoms in schizophrenia have been proposed previously by Fenton and McGlashan (1986). One hypothesis suggests that schizophrenia with comorbid OC features may constitute a distinct subtype of schizophrenia with a more virulent clinical course. A second possibility is that more severe impairment may be due to additive or multiplicative effects of the two combined conditions. Yet another explanation is based on the finding that premorbid functioning is predictive of outcome in schizophrenia patients (Lee, Lieh, Yu, & Spinks, 1993; Werry, McClellan, Andrews, & Ham,

1994). Patients who develop OC symptoms prior to the onset of schizophrenia may experience more impaired premorbid functioning, and, in turn, a greater degree of disability during their subsequent schizophrenic illness. Merson et al.'s (1995) finding that the more severe psychopathology of patients with schizophrenia and OC symptoms is limited to nonpsychotic, general psychopathologic symptoms is consistent with the latter two hypotheses. Regardless of the cause of poor outcome in schizophrenia patients with comorbid OC symptoms, successful treatment of OC symptoms should reduce functional impairment that is the direct result of OC symptomatology.

ETIOLOGY OF OC SYMPTOMS IN SCHIZOPHRENIA

The model of brain system mediation of OCD described by Baxter et al. (chap. 28, this volume; Fig. 4.1) seems to fit well with clinical evidence of high rates of OC symptoms in patients with schizophrenia. It should be acknowledged that the following adaptation of Baxter's model, which attempts to explain a diathesis for OC symptoms in schizophrenia, is hypothetical in nature and its relation to treatment is currently unclear. The verification of anatomic structures related to Baxter's model in OCD, however, is supported by human (Baxter et al., 1992; Schwartz, Stoessel, Baxter, Martin, & Phelps, 1996) and monkey (Baxter et al., 1996) positron emission tomography (PET) and rat ^{14}C-2-deoxyglucose autoradiographic studies (Baxter et al., chap. 28, this volume).

In the model proposed by Baxter et al. (chap. 28, this volume), the cortical-basal ganglionic-thalamic-cortical circuit (a circuit implicated in the pathophysiology of OCD) is further refined to include two pathways that provide basal ganglia outflow to the thalamus. The direct pathway consists of cortical input from the orbital prefrontal cortex, which projects to ventral regions of the striatum. The effect of striatal efferents passing from the direct pathway to the thalamus is to disinhibit the related thalamic regions. Thalamic disinhibition, in turn, stimulates orbital prefrontal cortex and produces a sustained activation of the direct pathway, potentially leading to the initiation and continuation of OC symptoms. The indirect pathway, comprising lateral prefrontal cortical (LPFC) afferents to the dorsolateral striatum, acts in an opposing manner by providing efferents that largely moderate thalamic activity. In this model, overactivity of orbital prefrontal cortex (relative to that of the LPFC) could lead to a predominance of direct striatal pathway tone and OC symptoms (Fig. 4.2).

Baxter et al. (chap. 28, this volume) further suggested that, likewise, hypofunctioning of the LPFC, relative to orbital frontal cortex, may also produce a shifting of substriatal tone to favor the direct pathway, with a resulting increase in OC phenomena. Evidence supporting a role of hypofunctioning LPFC in mediating OC symptoms is supported by the

Brain Mediation of OC Symptoms: Normals

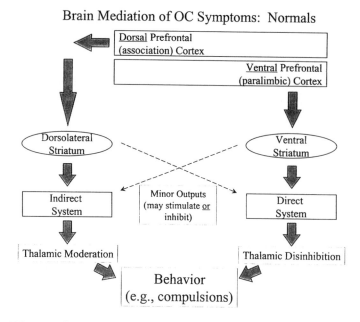

FIG. 4.1. Effects of dorsal and ventral prefrontal cortical activity on direct and indirect basal ganglionic systems, with resultant behavior. This represents Baxter et al.'s proposed model of relative contributions of direct and indirect basal ganglia systems to behavior. In this model, the cortical-basal ganglionic-thalamic-cortical circuit is further refined to emphasize two pathways that provide basal ganglia outflow to the thalamus. The effect of striatal efferents passing from the direct pathway is to disinhibit the thalamus, and thereby enable actions. The indirect pathway acts in an opposing manner by providing efferents that moderate thalamic activity. Recent evidence suggests that orbital prefrontal cortex (which projects to ventral striatum) drives the direct pathway more than the indirect, whereas LPFC (projecting to dorsal striatum) has an indirect → direct path bias. The equal size of arrows in both direct and indirect striatal pathways represents a balance of activity between these systems in normals. (Adapted from Baxter et al., chap. 28, this volume, with permission.)

finding that LPFC activity is decreased in patients with major depression superimposed on OCD (Baxter et al., 1989).

Hypofunctioning of frontal cortical regions has been a consistent finding in patients with schizophrenia (Andreasen et al., 1992; Buchsbaum et al., 1982; Ingvar & Franzen, 1974; Weinberger, Berman, & Zec, 1986). Decreased metabolic activity of the dorsolateral prefrontal cortex (DLPFC), in particular, has been demonstrated by several studies utilizing PET (Buchsbaum et al., 1982; Weinberger, Berman, & Illowsky, 1988; Weinberger et al., 1986; Wolkin et al., 1992). An examination of the relation between symptomatology and DLPFC function in schizophrenia has found a close and inverse relation between DLPFC activity (measured by

Brain Mediation of OC Symptoms: OCD

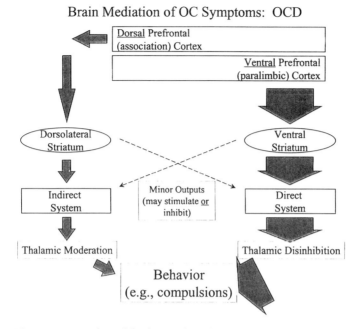

FIG. 4.2. Proposed model of ventral prefrontal cortical overactivity in patients with OCD. Overactivity of orbital prefrontal cortex relative to that of the LPFC could lead to a predominance of direct striatal pathway tone (indicated by larger arrows of the direct pathway), increasing the likelihood of OC symptoms. (Adapted from Baxter et al., chap. 28, this volume, with permission.)

PET) and negative symptoms (Wolkin et al., 1992). A second study reported that neuropsychological performance was inversely related to DLPFC area measured by magnetic resonance imaging (Seidman et al., 1994). Relevant to the model described by Baxter et al. (chap. 28, this volume), negative symptoms and abnormalities on neurocognitive measures were not related to disturbances in measures of the orbital frontal cortex (Seidman et al., 1994; Wolkin et al., 1992). We hypothesize that hypofunctioning of DLPFC (a region associated with activity of the indirect pathway) in patients with schizophrenia may shift the balance of substriatal systems to favor activity of the direct pathway, thus increasing the likelihood that schizophrenia patients will experience OC symptoms (Fig. 4.3). We are not aware of such data, but this theory would be supported by findings suggesting a positive relation between OC and negative or frontal neurocognitive symptoms in schizophrenia.

Several alternative etiologic factors may be equally important in explaining the frequent occurrence of OC symptoms in schizophrenia. Among these are the interaction of serotonin and dopamine brain systems in OCD and schizophrenia (Goodman et al., 1990; Meltzer, 1989), changes

Brain Mediation of OC Symptoms in Schizophrenia

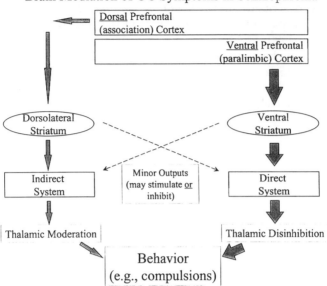

FIG. 4.3. Relative overactivity of ventral versus dorsal prefrontal cortical activity in schizophrenia, and resulting OC symptoms. Hypofunctioning of the LPFC in schizophrenia relative to orbital frontal cortex (indicated by smaller arrows of the indirect vs. direct pathways) may produce shifting of substriatal tone to favor activity of the direct striatal pathway with resulting OC phenomena.

in basal ganglionic structures in schizophrenia patients treated chronically with D2 antagonists (Bilder et al., 1994; inducing disturbances in the cortical-basal ganglionic-thalamic-cortical circuit), or a shared genetic risk for schizophrenia and OCD (S. W. Lewis, Chitkara, & Reveley, 1991) with related or unrelated pathophysiologic abnormalities.

TREATMENT OF OC SYMPTOMS OCCURRING IN SCHIZOPHRENIA

Even though the efficacy of potent serotonin reuptake inhibitors (SRIs)[1] in treating OC symptoms associated with OCD has been demonstrated in many double-blind, placebo-controlled trials, there are few data de-

---

[1]SRI is used to denote drugs that are potent inhibitors of serotonin reuptake sites. Under this definition, SRIs would include drugs that are nonselective (e.g., clomipramine) and selective (e.g., fluvoxamine, sertraline, paroxetine, and fluoxetine) SRIs. SSRI refers to drugs that are selective serotonin reuptake inhibitors (e.g., fluvoxamine, sertraline, paroxetine, and fluoxetine), and, therefore, would not include clomipramine.

scribing the use of these agents in schizophrenia. Of the reports published, most have described improvement in general psychopathology when schizophrenia patients are treated with SRIs (Goff, Brotman, Waites, & McCormick, 1990; Goldman & Janecek, 1990; Silver & Nassar, 1992). However, some have reported a worsening of symptoms, including agitation and increased psychosis (Bacher & Ruskin, 1991; Rocco & De Leo, 1992).

Worsening psychotic symptoms have also been reported in schizophrenia patients receiving SRIs for the treatment of comorbid obsessions and compulsions. Lindenmayer, Vakharia, and Kanofsky (1990) reported on two patients with comorbid schizophrenia and OC symptoms who received the selective serotonin reuptake inhibitor (SSRI) fluoxetine added to ongoing neuroleptic therapy. Both experienced a worsening of psychosis and no meaningful improvement in OC symptoms. Baker (1992) described a similar case of a schizophrenia patient with obsessive thinking who became more psychotic after the addition of fluoxetine. Sewell, Lopez, Paulsen, and Gilbert (1994) published two cases of fluoxetine added to the neuroleptic regimen of patients with OC symptoms and schizophrenia. One patient showed a marked reduction in OC symptoms without worsening of psychosis. The other exhibited a worsening of psychosis and no change in OC symptoms.

The SRI clomipramine has been associated with similar cases of psychotic exacerbation when added to stable neuroleptic therapy in schizophrenia patients. Bark and Lindenmayer (1992) reported a single case of this phenomenon in a schizophrenia patient with OC symptoms. Table 4.1 includes a summary of studies reporting the incidence of psychotic exacerbation occurring during open-label clomipramine treatment of OC symptoms in schizophrenia. Of 37 patients from four studies, 7 (19%) experienced psychotic exacerbation (Kindlar, Kaplan, & Zohar, 1993; Pul-

TABLE 4.1
Studies Examining Clomipramine Treatment
of OC Symptoms in Schizophrenia

Authors	Patients Exhibiting Anti-OC Response		Patients Experiencing an Exacerbation of Psychosis	
	N	%	N	%
Stroebel & Szarek (1984)	7/17	41	4[a]/21	19
Pulman et al. (1984)	4/6	67	1/6	17
Kindlar et al. (1993)	5/5	100	1/5	20
Zohar et al. (1993)	5/5[b]	100	1/5	20
Total	21/33	64	7/37	19

[a]Excluded from analysis of responders. [b]2 of 5 diagnosed with schizoaffective disorder.

man, Yassa, & Ananth, 1984; Stroebel & Szarek, 1984; Zohar, Kaplan, & Benjamin, 1993). These reports suggest that SRIs have the potential to worsen psychotic symptoms when added to the neuroleptic regimens of some patients with schizophrenia, including those who are being treated for comorbid obsessions and compulsions.

In contrast to the negative outcomes reported in these case reports, case series, and small open trials, there is preliminary evidence that supports the safety and efficacy of SRIs in treating OC symptoms occurring in the context of schizophrenia. Four case reports of SSRI addition—two utilizing fluoxetine (Hwang, Martin, Lindenmayer, Stein, & Hollander, 1993; Tajera, Mayerhoff, Safferman, & Ramos-Lorenzi, 1994) and two paroxetine (Scholl, Kasper, Danos, Hoflich, & Moller, 1994)—to regimens of traditional antipsychotics in schizophrenia patients have described marked reductions in OC symptoms without worsening psychosis. The case report by Hwang et al. (1993) included on–off–on periods of fluoxetine coadministration. Supporting the anti-OC efficacy of fluoxetine added to a regimen of a typical neuroleptic, the patient reported by Hwang et al. experienced exacerbation of OC symptoms when her fluoxetine dose was lowered from 40 mg/day to 20 mg/day, and again exhibited significant symptom improvement when this agent was increased to a dose of 60 mg/day.

The cause of SSRI-related improvement in patients with comorbid schizophrenia and OCD may be related to both pharmacodynamic and pharmacokinetic mechanisms. Through serotonergic reuptake inhibition, these agents likely exert anti-OC effects in a manner similar to that seen in patients with OCD alone. Potential pharmacokinetic interactions of some SSRIs, causing increased plasma levels of coadministered antipsychotic medications (Goff, Midha, Brotman, Waites, & Baldessarini, 1991), may also account for certain cases of improvement, particularly those characterized by decreases in psychotic symptoms.

Table 4.1 also summarizes results from four separate, open trials that have evaluated the efficacy of clomipramine in a total of 31 schizophrenia patients (and 2 with schizoaffective disorder) with OC symptoms (Kindlar et al., 1993; Pulman et al., 1984; Stroebel & Szarek, 1984; Zohar et al., 1993). Twenty-one (64%) of these patients exhibited improvement in OC symptoms. Employing an on–off–on design, Zohar et al. (1993) reported that 5 of 5 patients who initially demonstrated substantial reductions of OC symptoms during clomipramine addition relapsed on clomipramine discontinuation. In the 3 patients in whom clomipramine treatment was reinstituted, an improvement in OC symptoms was seen again. Kindlar et al. (1993) also reported OC symptom relapse in 5 of 5 schizophrenia patients when previously effective clomipramine was withdrawn. Open trials of the anti-OC efficacy of clomipramine in patients with schizophrenia indicate that approximately two in three patients will have a meaningful reduction of OC symptoms, but that as many as one in five patients will experience an exacerbation of psychotic symptoms with the addition of clomipramine to ongoing antipsychotic treatment.

In the only controlled trial to date, Berman, Sapers, et al. (1995) investigated the tolerability and efficacy of clomipramine added to the stable antipsychotic regimens of 6 patients with schizophrenia and comorbid OC symptoms. Patients received 6 weeks of treatment with clomipramine versus placebo (12-week study duration) in a double-blind crossover design. Patients on low-potency neuroleptics were excluded because the side effects of such agents could potentially be additive to those of clomipramine. The combination of clomipramine plus traditional antipsychotics was tolerated fairly well. One patient experienced dry mouth prohibiting clomipramine doses above 100 mg/day. Another experienced orthostatic hypotension, but remained asymptomatic and tolerated a clomipramine dose of 200 mg/day. No patients experienced exacerbation of psychotic symptoms. The efficacy of clomipramine coadministration was measured by the Y–BOCS and PANSS for OC and psychotic symptoms, respectively. Compared to placebo, clomipramine demonstrated superior efficacy in reducing both OC and psychotic symptoms. Although medication plasma levels were not reported, one possible explanation for the observation of clomipramine-related improvement in symptoms, particularly psychotic symptoms, is a potential drug–drug interaction resulting in increased plasma antipsychotic levels. This double-blind trial revealed that clomipramine was superior to placebo in treating the OC symptoms of patients with schizophrenia. The small number of patients entered, however, limits the generalizability of this data, particularly regarding issues of tolerability and safety.

Several case reports suggest that SRIs may also be effective in treating OC symptoms that emerge or worsen during treatment with serotonin$_2$/dopamine$_2$ (S2/D2) antagonists such as clozapine and risperidone. Although questions remain about the frequency with which S2/D2 antagonists induce or worsen OC symptoms in schizophrenia patients (Baker, Ames, Umbricht, Chengappa, & Schooler, 1995; Ghaemi, Zarate, Popli, Pillay, & Cole, 1995), case reports with on–off–on designs appear to support the validity of this finding (Eales & Layeni, 1994; Levkovitch, Kronnenberg, & Gaoni, 1995). Five of six reported cases involving SSRI treatment of clozapine-induced OC symptoms in schizophrenia described marked reductions in obsessions and compulsions (Allen & Tejera, 1994; Cassady & Thaker, 1992; Patel & Tandon, 1993; Steingard, Chengappa, Baker, & Schooler, 1993). Clomipramine was also effective in decreasing OC symptom severity in one case of clozapine-related OC symptoms (Steingard et al., 1993). Kopala and Honer (1994) reported one case of risperidone-induced OC symptoms that responded favorably to the addition of fluvoxamine. The successful treatment of OC symptoms arising during treatment with S2/D2 antagonists has not been limited to pharmacologic approaches. Behavior therapy was successful in reducing OC symptoms that began after the initiation of the S2/D2 antagonist clothiapine in one case of childhood-onset schizophrenia (Toren et al., 1995). In aggregate, these reports suggest that OC symptoms may begin or worsen after the introduction of S2/D2 antagonists, but that these symptoms are generally responsive to the addition of an SRI.

In summary, OC symptoms may be difficult to detect in schizophrenia unless specific screening for obsessions and compulsions is performed. Recent studies, utilizing more systematic screening procedures, indicate that clinically meaningful OC symptoms are experienced by approximately one in five of those with schizophrenia. The outcome of schizophrenia patients with OC symptoms appears to be worse than that of non-OC patients. Finally, results from case reports, case series, open trials, and one small double-blind study suggest that SRIs may be effective in reducing OC symptoms occurring in schizophrenia. These agents should be used with caution in patients with schizophrenia, however, as some patients may experience an exacerbation of psychotic symptoms. A double-blind trial of the safety and efficacy of an SRI has yet to be performed in adequate numbers of patients with schizophrenia and OC symptoms, and is needed.

ACKNOWLEDGMENTS

This research was supported, in part, by grants from the National Alliance for Research on Schizophrenia and Depression and the University of Florida College of Medicine.

REFERENCES

Allen, L., & Tejera, C. (1994). Treatment of clozapine-induced obsessive-compulsive symptoms with sertraline. *American Journal of Psychiatry, 151*, 1096–1097.

American Psychiatric Association. (1980). *Diagnostic and statistical manual of mental disorders* (3rd ed.). Washington, DC: Author.

American Psychiatric Association. (1987). *Diagnostic and statistical manual of mental disorders* (3rd ed., rev.). Washington, DC: Author.

Andreasen, N. C., Rezai, K., Alliger, R., Swayze, V. W., Flaum, M., Kirchner, P., Cohen, G., & O'Leary, D. S. (1992). Hypofrontality in neuroleptic-naive patients and in patients with chronic schizophrenia: Assessment with xenon 133 single-photon emission computed tomography and the Tower of London. *Archives of General Psychiatry, 49*, 943–958.

Anthony, J. C., Folstein, M., Romanski, A. J., Von Korff, M. R., Nesdadt, G. R., Chahal, R., Merchant, A., Brown, C. H., Shapiro, S., Kramer, M., & Gruenberg, E. M. (1985). Comparison of the lay Diagnostic Interview Schedule and a standardized psychiatric diagnosis. *Archives of General Psychiatry, 42,* 667–675.

Bacher, N. M., & Ruskin, P. (1991). Addition of fluoxetine to treatment of schizophrenic patients. *American Journal of Psychiatry, 148,* 274–275.

Baker, R. (1992). Fluoxetine and schizophrenia in a patient with obsessional thinking. *Journal of Neuropsychiatry and Clinical Neurosciences, 4,* 232–233.

Baker, R., Ames, D., Umbricht, D., Chengappa, K. N. R., & Schooler, N. (1995). *Olanzapine's impact on depressive and obsessive-compulsive symptoms in schizophrenia* [Abstract]. Poster presented at 35th Annual NCDEU Meeting, Orlando, FL.

Bark, N., & Lindenmayer, J. P. (1992). Ineffectiveness of clomipramine for obsessive-compulsive symptoms in a patient with schizophrenia. *American Journal of Psychiatry, 149,* 136–137.

Baxter, L. R., Saxena, S., Brody, A. L., Ackermann, R. F., Colgan, M., Schwartz, J. M., Allen-Martinez, Z., Fuster, J. M., & Phelps, M. E. (1996). Brain mediation of obsessive-compulsive disorder symptoms: Evidence from functional brain imaging studies in the human and non-human primate. *Seminars in Clinical Neuropsychiatry 1,* 32–47.

Baxter, L. R., Schwartz, J. M., Berman, K. S., Szuba, M. P., Guze, B. H., Mazziotta, J. C., Alazraki, A., Selin, C. E., Ferng, H. K., Munford, P., & Phelps, M. E. (1992). Caudate glucose metabolic rate changes with both drug and behavior therapy for obsessive-compulsive disorder. *Archives of General Psychiatry, 49,* 681–689.

Baxter, L. R., Schwartz, J. M., Phelps, M. E., Mazziotta, J. C., Guze, B. H., Selin, C. E., Gerner, R. H., & Sumida, R. M. (1989). Reduction of prefrontal cortex glucose metabolism common to three types of depression. *Archives of General Psychiatry, 46,* 243–250.

Berman, I., Kalinowski, A., Berman, S. M., Lengua, J., & Green, A. I. (1995). Obsessive and compulsive symptoms in chronic schizophrenia. *Comprehensive Psychiatry, 36,* 6–10.

Berman, I., Sapers, B. L., Chang, H. H. J., Losonczy, M. F., Schmilder, J., & Green, A. I. (1995). Treatment of obsessive-compulsive symptoms in schizophrenic patients with clomipramine. *Journal of Clinical Psychopharmacology, 15,* 206–210.

Bilder, R. M., Houwei, W., Chakos, M. H., Bogerts, B., Pollack, S., Aronowitz, J., Ashtari, M., Degreef, G., Kane, J. M., & Lieberman, J. A. (1994). Cerebral morphometry and clozapine treatment in schizophrenia. *Journal of Clinical Psychiatry, 55*(Suppl. B), 53–56.

Bleuler, E. (1919). *Dementia praecox and paraphrenia.* Edinburgh, Scotland: Livingstone.

Buchsbaum, M. S., Ingvar, D. H., Kessler, R., Waters, R. N., Cappelletti, J., van Kammen, D. P., King, A. C., Johnson, J. L., Manning, R. G., Flynn, R. W., Mann, L. S., Bunney, W. E., & Sokoloff, L. (1982). Cerebral glucography with positron tomography. *Archives of General Psychiatry, 39,* 251–259.

Cassady, S. L., & Thaker, G. K. (1992). Addition of fluoxetine to clozapine. *American Journal of Psychiatry, 149,* 1274.

Eales, M. J., & Layeni, A. O. (1994). Exacerbation of obsessive-compulsive symptoms associated with clozapine. *British Journal of Psychiatry, 164,* 687–688.

Fenton, W. S., & McGlashan, T. H. (1986). The prognostic significance of obsessive-compulsive symptoms in schizophrenia. *American Journal of Psychiatry, 143,* 437–441.

Ghaemi, S. N., Zarate, C. A., Popli, A. P., Pillay, S. S., & Cole, J. O. (1995). Is there a relationship between clozapine and obsessive-compulsive symptoms. *Comprehensive Psychiatry, 36,* 267–270.

Goff, D. C., Brotman, A. W., Waites, M., & McCormick, S. (1990). Trial of fluoxetine added to neuroleptics for treatment-resistant schizophrenic patients. *American Journal of Psychiatry, 147,* 492–494.

Goff, D. C., Midha, K. K., Brotman, A. W., Waites, M., & Baldessarini, R. J. (1991). Elevation of plasma concentrations of haloperidol after the addition of fluoxetine. *American Journal of Psychiatry, 148,* 790–792.

Goldman, M. B., & Janecek, H. M. (1990). Adjunctive fluoxetine improves global function in chronic schizophrenia. *Journal of Neuropsychiatry and Clinical Neurosciences, 2*, 429–431.

Goodman, W., McDougle, C., Price, L., Riddle, M., Pauls, D., & Leckman, J. (1990). Beyond the serotonin hypothesis: A role for dopamine in some forms of obsessive compulsive disorder? *Journal of Clinical Psychiatry, 51*, 36–43.

Goodman, W. K., Rasmussen, S. A., Price, L. H., Mazure, C., Heninger, G. R., & Charney, D. S. (1989). Yale–Brown Obsessive Compulsive Scale: Development, use, reliability. *Archives of General Psychiatry, 46*, 1006–1016.

Helzer, J. E., Robins, L. N., McEvoy, L. T., Spitznagel, E. L., Stoltzman, R. K., Farmer, A., & Brockington, I. F. (1985). A comparison of clinical and Diagnostic Interview Schedule diagnoses. *Archives of General Psychiatry, 42*, 657–666.

Hwang, M. Y., Martin, A. M., Lindenmayer, J. P., Stein, D., & Hollander, E. (1993). Treatment of schizophrenia with obsessive-compulsive features with serotonin reuptake inhibitors. *American Journal of Psychiatry, 150*, 1127.

Ingvar, D. H., & Franzen, G. (1974). Abnormalities of cerebral blood flow distribution in patients with chronic schizophrenia. *Acta Psychiatrica Scandinavica, 50*, 425–462.

Insel, T. R., & Akiskal, H. S. (1986). Obsessive-compulsive disorder with psychotic features: A phenomenologic analysis. *American Journal of Psychiatry, 143*, 1527–1533.

Jahrreiss, W. (1926). Obsessions during schizophrenia. *Archives of Psychiatry, 77*, 740–788.

Karno, M., Golding, J. M., Sorenson, S. B., & Burnam, M. A. (1988). The epidemiology of obsessive-compulsive disorder in five U.S. communities. *Archives of General Psychiatry, 45*, 1094–1099.

Kay, S. R., Fiszbein, A., & Opler, L. S. (1987). The Positive and Negative Syndrome Scale (PANSS) for schizophrenia. *Schizophrenia Bulletin, 13*, 261–276.

Kindlar, S., Kaplan, Z., & Zohar, J. (1993). Obsessive-compulsive symptoms in schizophrenia. In E. Hollander (Ed.), *Obsessive-compulsive related disorders* (pp. 203–214). Washington, DC: American Psychiatric Press.

Kopala, L., & Honer, W. G. (1994). Risperidone, serotonergic mechanisms, and obsessive-compulsive symptoms in schizophrenia. *American Journal of Psychiatry, 151*, 1714–1715.

Lee, P. W., Lieh, M. F., Yu, K. K., & Spinks, J. A. (1993). Coping strategies of patients and their relationship to outcome. *British Journal of Psychiatry, 163*, 177–182.

Levkovitch, Y., Kronnenberg, Y., & Gaoni, B. (1995). Can clozapine trigger OCD? *Journal of the American Academy of Child and Adolescent Psychiatry, 34*, 263.

Lewis, A. (1936). Problems of obsessional illness. *Proceedings of the Royal Society of Medicine, 29*, 325–336.

Lewis, S. W., Chitkara, B., & Reveley, A. M. (1991). Obsessive-compulsive disorder and schizophrenia in three identical twin pairs. *Psychological Medicine, 21*, 135–141.

Lindenmayer, J. P., Vakharia, M., & Kanofsky, D. (1990). Fluoxetine in chronic schizophrenia. *Journal of Clinical Psychopharmacology, 10*, 76.

Meltzer, H. Y. (1989). Clinical studies on the mechanism of action of clozapine: The dopamine-serotonin hypothesis of schizophrenia. *Psychopharmacology, 99*, S18–S27.

Merson, A., Viegener, B., Allan, E. R., Parker, L., Losonczy, M. F., & Berman, I. (1995, May). *Relationship between schizophrenic and obsessive compulsive symptoms.* Paper presented at the 148th Annual Meeting of the American Psychiatric Association, Miami, FL.

Patel, B., & Tandon, R. (1993). Development of obsessive-compulsive symptoms during clozapine treatment. *American Journal of Psychiatry, 150*, 836.

Pulman, J., Yassa, R., & Ananth, J. (1984). Clomipramine treatment of repetitive behavior. *Canadian Journal of Psychiatry, 29*, 254–255.

Rasmussen, S. A., & Tsuang, M. T. (1986). Epidemiolgy and clincial features of obsessive-compulsive disorder. In M. A. Jenike, L. Baer, & W. E. Minichiello (Eds.), *Obsessive compulsive disorders* (pp. 23–44). Littleton, MA: PSG Publishing.

Rocco, P. L., & De Leo, D. (1992). Fluvoxamine-induced acute exacerbation in residual schizophrenia. *Pharmacopsychiatry, 25,* 245.

Rosen, I. (1957). The clinical significance of obsessions in schizophrenia. *Journal of Mental Science, 103,* 778–785.

Samuel, J., Nesdadt, G., Walyniec, P., Adler, L., Liong, K. Y., & Pulver, A. E. (1993). Obsessive-compulsive symptoms in schizophrenia. *Schizophrenia Research, 9,* 139.

Scholl, H. P., Kasper, S., Danos, P., Hoflich, G., & Moller, H. J. (1994). Selective serotonin reuptake inhibitors in treatment of compulsive symptoms within the scope of schizophrenia. *Nervenarzt (Neurology), 65,* 478–481.

Schwartz, J. M., Stoessel, P. W., Baxter, L. R., Martin, K. M., & Phelps, M. E. (1996). Systematic changes in cerebral glucose metabolic rate after successful behavior modification treatment of obsessive-compulsive disorder. *Archives of General Psychiatry, 53,* 109–113.

Seidman, L. J., Yurgelun, T. D., Kremen, W. S., Woods, B. T., Goldstein, J. M., Faraone, S. V., & Tsuang, M. T. (1994). Relationship of prefrontal and temporal lobe MRI measures to neuropsychological performance in chronic schizophrenia. *Biological Psychiatry, 35,* 235–246.

Sewell, D. D., Lopez, W. M., Paulsen, J., & Gilbert, P. (1994). Treatment of obsessive-compulsive symptoms in schizophrenia with a neuroleptic-selective serotonin reuptake inhibitor combination: Two case reports. *Journal of Nervous and Mental Disorders, 182,* 725–727.

Silver, H., & Nassar, A. (1992). Fluvoxamine improves negative symptoms in treated chronic schizophrenia: An add-on double-blind, placebo-controlled study. *Biological Psychiatry, 31,* 698–704.

Steingard, S., Chengappa, K. N. R., Baker, R. W., & Schooler, N. R. (1993). Clozapine, obsessive symptoms, and serotonergic mechanisms. *American Journal of Psychiatry, 150,* 1435.

Stengel, E. (1945). A study on some clinical aspects of the relationship between obsessional neurosis and psychotic reaction types. *Journal of Mental Science, 91,* 166–187.

Stroebel, C. F., & Szarek, B. L. (1984). Use of clomipramine in treatment of obsessive-compulsive symptomatology. *Journal of Clinical Psychopharmacology, 4,* 98–100.

Tajera, C. A., Mayerhoff, D. J., Safferman, A. Z., & Ramos-Lorenzi, J. R. (1994). Fluoxetine for obsessional symptoms in schizophrenia. *American Journal of Psychiatry, 151,* 149–150.

Toren, P., Samuel, E., Weizman, R., Golomb, A., Eldar, S., & Laor, N. (1995). Case study: Emergence of transient compulsive symptoms during treatment with clothiapine. *Journal of the American Academy of Child and Adolescent Psychiatry, 34,* 1469–1472.

Weinberger, D. R., Berman, K. F., & Illowsky, B. P. (1988). Physiological dysfunction of dorsolateral prefrontal cortex in schizophrenia: III. A new cohort and evidence for a monoaminergic mechanism. *Archives of General Psychiatry, 45,* 609–615.

Weinberger, D. R., Berman, K. F., & Zec, R. F. (1986). Physiologic dysfunction of dorsolateral prefrontal cortex in schizophrenia: I. Regional cerebral blood flow evidence. *Archives of General Psychiatry, 43,* 114–124.

Werry, J. S., McClellan, J. M., Andrews, L. K., & Ham, M. (1994). Clinical features and outcome of child and adolescent schizophrenia. *Schizophrenia Bulletin, 20,* 619–630.

Westphal, K. (1878). Ueber Zwangsvorstellungen [About obsession]. *Archives for Psychiatry and Neurology, 8,* 734–750.

Wolkin, A., Sanfilipo, M., Wolf, A. P., Angrist, B., Brodie, J. D., & Rotrosen, J. (1992). Negative symptoms and hypofrontaltiy in chronic schizophrenia. *Archives of General Psychiatry, 49,* 959–965.

Zohar, J., Kaplan, Z., & Benjamin, J. (1993). Clomipramine treatment of obsessive compulsive symptomatology in schizophrenic patients. *Journal of Clinical Psychiatry, 54,* 385–388.

II

*PATHOPHYSIOLOGY
AND ETIOLOGY*

5

Clinical and Family-Genetic Studies of Childhood Obsessive-Compulsive Disorder

Gregory L. Hanna
University of Michigan Medical Center

Obsessive-compulsive disorder (OCD) is characterized by recurrent and persistent thoughts that are experienced as intrusive and inappropriate and that cause marked distress, and by repetitive behaviors or mental acts that are aimed at reducing distress or preventing a dreaded event (American Psychiatric Association, 1994). The phenomenologic description of OCD has remained stable over the past century. The case descriptions of Janet (1908) and others seem remarkably consistent with the clinical picture seen today (Pitman, 1987). Furthermore, its presentation appears similar across cultures (Honjo et al., 1989; Thomsen, 1991). In contrast to other forms of severe psychopathology, the symptoms of OCD are virtually identical in children and adults (Fischer, Himle, & Hanna, 1997; Hanna, 1995a). Although a majority of OCD patients respond to treatment, most of those who improve significantly are left with residual symptoms and about 30% are treatment refractory (Rasmussen, 1996). More effective treatments may result from current studies of genetic and environmental factors in the etiology of OCD.

This chapter reviews the epidemiologic and clinical studies of OCD in children and adolescents. Comparisons are made with the literature on OCD in adults. Gender differences in age at onset, symptom severity, and comorbidity are described. Twin, family, and molecular genetic studies of OCD are also reviewed and the methodologic problems in genetic linkage studies of OCD are discussed, along with the rationale for family-genetic studies of early-onset OCD. Several points are illustrated by data collected at the UCLA Neuropsychiatric Institute.

PREVALENCE AND SEX RATIO

OCD is a common anxiety disorder with a lifetime prevalence of 2% to 3% (D. W. Black, 1996). It is the fourth most common psychiatric disorder, more common than schizophrenia, bipolar disorder, and panic disorder (Karno, Golding, Sorenson, & Burnam, 1988). The Epidemiologic Catchment Area (ECA) survey found a 6-month prevalence of 1.6% and a lifetime prevalence of 2.5% in five U.S. communities (Karno et al., 1988). Comparable rates were found in five other countries (Bland, Newman, & Orn, 1988; Canino et al., 1987; Lee et al., 1990; Wittchen, Essau, Von Zerssen, Krieg, & Zaudig, 1992). Those studies showed a female-to-male ratio between 1.2 and 2.3, with the exception of the Canadian study, in which the ratio was 1.0 (Bland et al., 1988).

In three epidemiologic studies of adolescents, the point prevalence of OCD ranged from 1.0% to 3.6% (Flament et al., 1988; Valleni-Basile et al., 1994; Zohar et al., 1992). Prevalences were similar in boys and girls. There have been no community surveys of prepubertal OCD. In contrast to the slight preponderance of women in virtually all studies of OCD in adults, most studies of referred children and adolescents have found that OCD is more common in boys than in girls (Adams, 1973; Apter, Bernhout, & Tyano, 1984; Bolton, Collins, & Steinberg, 1983; Despert, 1955; DeVeaugh-Geiss, Moraz, & Biederman, 1992; Geller, Biederman, Griffin, Jones, & Lefkowitz, 1996; Hanna, 1995a; Hollingsworth, Tanguay, Grossman, & Pabst, 1980; Last & Strauss, 1989; Swedo et al., 1989; Thomsen, 1991; Toro, Cervera, Osejo, & Salamero, 1992). However, the sex ratio in clinical studies may be influenced by clinical severity and comorbidity, as well as an earlier onset in male patients, described later (Hanna, 1995a). Thus, the disorder is thought to be equally common in males and females taken across all ages (American Psychiatric Association, 1994).

AGE AT ONSET

Community and clinical studies of adults with OCD have established an average onset age in early adulthood, with men having an earlier onset than women (Burke, Burke, & Regier, 1990; Minichiello, Baer, Jenike, & Holland, 1990; Noshirvani, Kasvikis, Marks, Tsakiris, & Monteiro, 1991; Rasmussen & Eisen, 1992). The median age at onset for OCD in the ECA study was 23 years (Burke et al., 1990). About one third of cases begin by age 15 (A. Black, 1974), with fewer than 15% of cases developing after age 35 (Rasmussen & Eisen, 1992). The average age at onset for OCD in referred children and adolescents is about 10 years (Geller et al., 1996; Hanna, 1995a; Last & Strauss, 1989; Riddle et al., 1990; Swedo et al., 1989;

Thomsen, 1991; Toro et al., 1992). Rapoport (1989) described cases with an onset as early as age 2.

The age at onset for OCD is, in general, between 6 and 15 years for male patients and between ages 20 and 29 years for female patients (American Psychiatric Association, 1994). Divergent peaks in the maximal incidence of OCD may be indicative of genotypic as well as phenotypic heterogeneity. Family studies of OCD comparing child and adult onset probands may be useful in resolving this issue, especially because logistic models have been extended recently to incorporate data on age at onset, age at examination, and other covariates in the analysis of family data (Elston & George, 1989).

SYMPTOM SEVERITY

The effect of gender and age at onset on symptom severity was examined in 31 children and adolescents with OCD evaluated prospectively as outpatients at UCLA (Hanna, 1995a). The demographic characteristics of the participants are summarized in Table 5.1. Rating scale characteristics are summarized in Table 5.2. Symptom severity was assessed with the child and adolescent version of the Yale–Brown Obsessive Compulsive Scale (CY–BOCS; Goodman, Price, Rasmussen, Mazure, Delgado, et al., 1989; Goodman, Price, Rasmussen, Mazure, Fleischmann, et al., 1989; Scahill et al., 1997) and the National Institute of Mental Health Global

TABLE 5.1
Demographic Characteristics of 31 Children and Adolescents With OCD

Item	N	%
Sex		
Male	19	61
Female	12	39
Age at onset		
7 years or less	9	29
8–12 years	16	52
13 years or more	6	19
Race		
White	30	97
Asian	1	3
Social status		
I (High)	13	42
II	6	19
III	8	26
IV	2	6
V (Low)	2	6

TABLE 5.2
Rating Scale Characteristics of Children and Adolescents With OCD

Rating Scale	M	SD	Range
CY–BOCS score	24.4	6.4	13–36
NIMH GOCS score	9.2	1.7	6–12
CBCL Total Problem T score	66.2	8.4	51–83
CBCL Internalizing T score	69.6	7.7	54–86
CBCL Externalizing T score	54.8	10.6	40–80
CBCL Withdrawn T score	64.7	10.6	50–88
CBCL Somatic Complaints T score	62.1	9.7	50–83
CBCL Anxious/Depressed T score	72.1	10.0	50–95
CBCL Social Problems T score	60.7	11.4	50–87
CBCL Thought Problems T score	77.1	7.2	63–88
CBCL Attention Problems T score	64.6	12.4	50–95
CBCL Delinquent Behavior T score	54.8	7.3	50–78
CBCL Aggressive Behavior T score	57.9	9.7	50–83
CBCL Total Competence T score	40.6	11.0	20–60
CBCL Activities Competence T score	43.2	8.8	22–55
CBCL Social Competence T score	39.6	10.9	23–55
CBCL School Competence T score	44.7	8.4	30–55

Note. CY–BOCS = Children's Yale–Brown Obsessive-Compulsive Scale; NIMH GOCS = National Institutes of Mental Health Global Obsessive-Compulsive Scale; CBCL = Child Behavior Checklist.

Obsessive-Compulsive Scale (NIMH GOCS; Insel et al., 1983). The Child Behavior Checklist (CBCL) was completed by the parents of 24 children (Achenbach, 1991). Social status was determined for each family with the two-factor index of social position (Hollingshead, 1965).

The sample consisted of 19 boys and 12 girls who ranged in age from 7.7 years to 18.0 years. Mean ages at onset and intake were 10.0 (SD = 3.0) and 13.5 (SD = 2.8) years, respectively. There were no significant differences between the boys and girls in age at onset (M = 10.5, SD = 3.3 vs. M = 9.5, SD = 2.4 years), age at intake (M = 14.1, SD = 2.6 vs. M = 12.5, SD = 2.8 years), or duration of illness (M = 3.7, SD = 2.7 vs. M = 3.1, SD = 2.3 years).

The interaction between gender and age at onset dichotomized as before or after 10 years of age had a significant effect on the CY–BOCS, $F(1, 27) = 4.291$, $p < .05$ and NIMH GOCS scores, $F(1, 27) = 6.711$, $p < .02$. The interaction between gender and age at onset analyzed as a continuous variable had a more pronounced effect on the CY–BOCS, $F(1, 28) = 14.892$, $p < .001$, and NIMH GOCS scores, $F(1, 28) = 14.210$, $p < .001$. The results indicate that symptom severity is influenced by an interaction between gender and age at onset, with the illness tending to be more severe in boys with an onset before 10 years of age and girls with an onset after 10 years of age. Neither age at intake nor duration of illness appear to be involved in an interactive effect with gender on symptom severity. This interaction may account partially for the preponderance of boys in most clinical studies of OCD in children and adolescents.

SOCIAL STATUS

Social status in the UCLA series correlated significantly with the CY–BOCS, $r(29) = .40$, $p < .05$, and NIMH GOCS scores, $r(29) = .45$, $p < .02$. However, the CY–BOCS, NIMH GOCS, and social status had no significant correlations with age at onset, age at intake, or duration of illness. The significant positive correlation between social status and the severity ratings of obsessive-compulsive (OC) symptoms in this study requires replication. It is possible that lower social status exacerbates OC symptoms or that patients with milder symptoms and lower social status do not receive clinical referral.

The preponderance of White patients in this sample from intact, middle-class to upper middle-class families is consistent with three series described previously (Adams, 1973; Last, Perrin, Hersen, & Kazdin, 1992; Riddle et al., 1990). The series reported by Last and Strauss (1989), in contrast, had social strata ratings that were more evenly distributed, suggesting that there may have been less of an ascertainment bias in that sample. In the ECA study of adults in five communities, OCD was less common among Black than among non-Hispanic White respondents (Karno et al., 1988).

SYMPTOMATOLOGY

The frequency of lifetime OC symptom categories in the UCLA series is depicted in Table 5.3. All participants had both obsessions and compulsions with most reporting many different symptoms that spanned several symptom categories. Obsessions without compulsions did not occur. All but one participant reported obsessions from more than one category, and all reported more than one type of compulsion. Eighteen participants (58%) reported a history of washing and checking compulsions. Twelve (39%) reported a history of washing, checking, and repeating rituals. Only four (13%) reported a history of washing rituals without either checking or repeating rituals.

The pattern of obsessions and compulsions in this series is similar to that seen in recent clinical (Geller et al., 1996; Last & Strauss, 1989; Rettew, Swedo, Leonard, Lenane, & Rapoport, 1992; Riddle et al., 1990; Swedo et al., 1989; Toro et al., 1992) and epidemiologic studies (Flament et al., 1988;

TABLE 5.3
Lifetime Symptom Categories in 31 Children and Adolescents With OCD

Symptom Categories	N	%
Obsessions		
Contamination (e.g., dirt, germs, illness)	27	87
Aggressive (e.g., harm to self or others)	25	81
Symmetry/exactness	20	64
Hoarding/saving	11	36
Magical (e.g., special numbers, colors)	8	26
Sexual	8	26
Religious (scrupulosity)	7	23
Somatic	3	10
Miscellaneous (e.g., nonaggressive images)	17	55
Compulsions		
Washing, cleaning	26	84
Checking	20	64
Repeating	20	64
Ordering/arranging/straightening	19	61
Touching	18	58
Counting	13	42
Hoarding/saving/collecting	13	42
Miscellaneous (e.g., needing to ask)	12	39
Associated behaviors		
Avoidance	25	81
Slowness	21	68
Indecisiveness	12	39
Doubt	11	36
Overvalued sense of responsibility	10	32
Rituals involving other people	9	29

Valleni-Basile et al., 1994). The high lifetime rates for the various symptom categories probably reflect the severity of the disorder in this sample. Most participants had multiple obsessions and compulsions that had changed over time in their content and severity. This suggests that in most clinical settings it would be difficult to classify children and adolescents with OCD according to a single type of compulsion, such as cleaning or checking compulsions.

No relation between age and the number of symptom categories was found, which is consistent with one previous study (Thomsen, 1991). No gender differences in the frequency of various symptom categories were detected. However, some studies of adults with OCD have found that cleaning rituals are more common among women (Minichiello et al., 1990; Noshirvani et al., 1991; Rachman & Hodgson, 1980).

The CBCL ratings indicated a high level of behavioral problems for most of the children and adolescents in the UCLA sample (see Table 5.2).

The mean internalizing T score (69.6) was almost 2 SDs above the norm. The internalizing T scores were significantly higher than the externalizing T scores, $t(23) = 8.022$, $p < .001$. The mean T scores for the anxious/depressed and thought problems scales were more than 2 SDs above the norm. Boys had significantly higher T scores than did girls on the withdrawn, $t(22) = 2.252$, $p < .05$, and anxious/depressed scales, $t(22) = 2.156$, $p < .05$.

The mean T score for social competence was approximately 1 SD below the norm. Furthermore, the social competence T scores were significantly lower than the school competence T scores, $t(22) = 2.073$, $p = .05$, indicating that the children were perceived by their parents as more impaired socially than academically. Boys had significantly lower T scores than did girls on the total competence scale, $t(21) = 2.819$, $p = .01$; social competence scale, $t(21) = 2.314$, $p < .05$; and school competence scale, $t(21) = 2.292$, $p < .05$. None of the CBCL T scores had significant correlations with the CY–BOCS or NIMH GOCS scores or with age at onset, age at intake, or duration of illness.

ASSOCIATED PSYCHOPATHOLOGY

Twenty-six participants (84%) in the UCLA sample had other lifetime psychiatric diagnoses that are summarized in Table 5.4. Sixteen participants (52%) received two or more additional diagnoses. The lifetime rates of depressive, anxiety, disruptive behavior, and tic disorders ranged from 26% to 32%. The series provides further evidence that severe OCD in children and adolescents is usually associated with other psychiatric disorders (Geller et al., 1996; Swedo et al., 1989; Toro et al., 1992). However, it should be noted that the assessment of a disorder within a clinical setting results in an overestimate of the comorbidity with related disorders (Berkson, 1946; Zohar et al., 1992).

Sixteen of the 19 boys (84%) and 10 of the 12 girls (83%) received at least one additional diagnosis. There were no statistically significant gender differences in the frequency of comorbid depressive, anxiety, disruptive behavior, or tic disorders. However, the sample size may have been too small to detect some important gender differences in comorbidity.

Other studies have found that tic-related OCD occurs more often in males than in females (Leckman et al., 1995) and has an earlier age at onset than non-tic-related OCD (Leonard et al., 1992). The distinction between tic-related and non-tic-related OCD has also been validated by differences in phenomenology (Leckman et al., 1995), natural history (Leonard et al., 1992), neuroendocrine function (Hanna, McCracken, & Cantwell, 1991), familial aggregation (Pauls, Alsobrook, Goodman, Rasmussen, & Leckman, 1995) and treatment response (McDougle et al., 1994).

TABLE 5.4
Associated Lifetime Psychopathology in
31 Children and Adolescents With OCD

	No. (%) of Patients[a]		
	Boys (n = 19)	Girls (n = 12)	Total (n = 31)
Major depression	4	0	4 (13)
Dysthymia	2	1	3 (10)
Adjustment disorder with depressed mood	1	2	3 (10)
Depressive disorder, NOS	0	1	1 (3)
Separation anxiety disorder	0	2	2 (6)
Overanxious disorder	1	3	4 (13)
Simple phobia	2	0	2 (6)
Avoidant disorder	0	1	1 (3)
Attention-deficit hyperactivity disorder	4	1	5 (16)
Oppositional-defiant disorder	4	1	5 (16)
Conduct disorder	1	0	1 (3)
Alcohol abuse	1	0	1 (3)
Substance abuse	1	0	1 (3)
Tourette's disorder	2	2	4 (13)
Transient tic disorder	2	2	4 (13)
Trichotillomania	1	0	1 (3)
Enuresis	2	0	2 (6)
Specific developmental disorder	5	2	7 (23)
Pervasive developmental disorder	1	0	1 (3)

Note. NOS = not otherwise specified.
[a]Multiple diagnoses were given to some children.

In the UCLA series, whole blood serotonin content was significantly lower in OCD participants with a disruptive behavior disorder than in those without a disruptive behavior disorder (Hanna, Yuwiler, & Coates, 1995). Furthermore, blood serotonin levels had significant negative correlations with the total score, externalizing score, and aggressive behavior score of the CBCL. Previous reports have commented that the rate of depressive disorders is lower in children and adolescents with OCD than in adults with OCD (Last & Strauss, 1989; Last et al., 1992; Rapoport, 1986; Welner, Reich, & Robins, 1976).

TWIN STUDIES

Twin studies have provided limited evidence for the heritability of OCD. In two of the larger studies, the concordance rates ranged from 80% to 87% for monozygotic twins and from 25% to 47% for dizygotic twins, depending on the sample and diagnostic criteria (Carey & Gottesman,

1981; Inouye, 1965). Multivariate analyses gave a heritability estimate of 47% for obsessional symptoms (Clifford, Murray, & Fulker, 1984). However, findings from two twin registries indicated that there is a genetic contribution to neuroticism or anxiety disorders in general, but not to OCD or other specific disorders (Andrews, Stewart, Allen, & Henderson, 1990; Andrews, Stewart, Morris-Yates, Holt, & Henderson, 1990; Torgerson, 1983). Those studies suggested that genetic factors may contribute to the development of OCD only to the extent that it is a part of a general neurotic syndrome. There have been no adoption studies of OCD.

FAMILY STUDIES

Family studies of OCD over the past 60 years have tended to indicate that the disorder is familial (D. W. Black, 1996; Rasmussen, 1993). However, the findings in the studies using adult probands are inconsistent, and methodologic differences probably contributed to those inconsistencies. Of the first six published studies, only one had a control group (Brown, 1942) and none of them used structured interviews, diagnostic criteria, or blinding to proband status (Kringlen, 1965; Lewis, 1936; Lo, 1967; Luxenburger, 1930; Rosenberg, 1967; Rudin, 1953). Of the seven more recent studies, the rate of OCD in the first-degree relatives ranged from 0% to 10.3% (Bellodi, Sciuto, Diaferia, Ronchi, & Smeraldi, 1992; D. W. Black, Noyes, Goldstein, & Blum, 1992; McKeon & Murray, 1987; Pauls et al., 1995; Rasmussen & Tsuang, 1986; Sciuto, Pasquale, & Bellodi, 1995).

Phenotype definition and age at onset appear to influence the familiality of OCD. The study by D. W. Black et al. (1992), although showing no increase in OCD among relatives of patients with OCD, found an increase in subsyndromal cases (generally the presence of obsessions and compulsions in the absence of impairment). Furthermore, the rates of anxiety disorders were significantly greater among the relatives of the OCD probands than among the relatives of the control participants. Similarly, the study by Pauls et al. (1995) reported that 8% of relatives had subthreshold OCD, compared with 2% of a control group. Two of the larger recent studies demonstrated that the relatives of probands with early onset were at higher risk for OCD (Bellodi et al., 1992; Pauls et al., 1995). Early age at onset has been associated with increased familial risk in a range of psychiatric disorders, including major depression (Weissman, Warner, Wickramaratne, & Prusoff, 1988), bipolar disorder (Pauls, Morton, & Egeland, 1992), schizophrenia (Pulver et al., 1990), and panic disorder (Goldstein, Wickramaratne, Horwath, & Weissman, 1997).

OCD family studies using child and adolescent probands have provided more consistent evidence for the familiality of the disorder. The rate of OCD in the first-degree relatives in those studies ranged from 7.7%

to 17% (Last, Hersen, Kazdin, Orvaschel, & Perrin, 1991; Last & Strauss, 1989; Lenane et al., 1990; Leonard et al., 1992; Riddle et al., 1990). In one of the larger studies, the age-corrected rate of OCD and subclinical OCD in the first-degree relatives was 35% (Lenane et al., 1990). Furthermore, in a family study of several anxiety disorders, there was a trend for OCD to be more prevalent among relatives of children with OCD than among relatives of children with other anxiety disorders, suggesting that the risk was specific for OCD (Last et al., 1991). Panic disorder was the only other anxiety disorder that appeared to show a similar specific relation between children and their relatives. Controlled family studies of early-onset OCD may be able to delineate a more familial form of the illness.

Segregation analysis of data from 24 families with early-onset OCD by our group at UCLA provided substantial evidence for a major gene (Nicolini et al., 1991). The analyses were unable to discriminate between autosomal dominant and recessive models. However, the dominant model was statistically more likely and compatible with the observed patterns. Thus, at least in some families studied previously by our group, the transmission of OCD could be explained by simple genetic models. The results from this study provide further evidence that early-onset OCD may be a more strongly genetic form of the illness.

Twin and family studies of Tourette's syndrome (TS) have provided further support for the hypothesis that genetic factors are important in the transmission and expression of some forms of OCD (Hanna, 1995b). TS is a familial disorder that appears to have a substantial genetic basis (LaBuda & Pauls, 1993). Several studies have demonstrated that the rate of OCD is higher in the first-degree relatives of probands with TS than in the relatives of controls (Eapen, Pauls, & Robertson, 1993; Pauls & Leckman, 1986; Pauls, Raymond, Stevenson, & Leckman, 1991; Pauls, Towbin, Leckman, Zahner, & Cohen, 1986). OCD occurs equally frequently among relatives of probands with TS regardless of whether the probands themselves have OCD. Conversely, studies have shown that the rates of TS and chronic tics are elevated among the relatives of probands with OCD (Leonard et al., 1992; Pauls et al., 1995). The data indicate that OCD is a heterogeneous condition and that some forms of OCD may be related genetically to TS. However, not all forms of OCD are related to TS, as the rate of tics is higher in the relatives of OCD probands with tics than in the relatives of OCD probands without tics (Pauls et al., 1995).

MOLECULAR GENETIC STUDIES

Although molecular genetic techniques have been applied successfully to a variety of medical disorders (Lander & Schork, 1994), an extensive effort has not been made to map and clone genes for OCD. Nonetheless, some recent candidate gene studies have yielded promising results. A common functional allele of the gene for catechol-O-methyltransferase (COMT) was found in a case-control study to be associated in a recessive manner with susceptibility to OCD, particularly in males (Karayiorgou et al., 1997). There was a trend for an increased frequency of comorbid tic disorders among males homozygous for the low-activity allele. Close linkage with a nearby susceptibility locus could not be excluded. Moreover, the finding could be the result of population stratification so that the transmission of the COMT alleles in OCD patients needs to be tested within families.

A case-control study showed a trend for a similar association between an allele for the dopamine D2 receptor gene and tic-related OCD (Nicolini et al., 1996). However, another case-control study found no association between the dopamine D2 receptor gene and any form of OCD (Novelli, Nobile, Diaferia, Sciuto, & Catalano, 1994). Case-control studies have also found no evidence for the involvement of the dopamine D3 and serotonin 2A receptor loci in OCD (Catalano et al., 1994; Nicolini et al., 1996).

The selective response of OCD to serotonin reuptake inhibitors has led to the hypothesis that a serotonergic dysfunction may be involved in the disorder (Hanna, Yuwiler, & Cantwell, 1993; Murphy et al., 1989). Serotonergic genes are, therefore, plausible candidate loci for OCD. Two studies detected no mutations in the serotonin transporter (HTT) gene in adults with OCD using single stranded conformational polymorphism gel electrophoresis (Altemus, Murphy, Greenberg, & Lesch, 1996; Wright, Hanna, Vander Weele, Leventhal, & Cook, 1994). However, a polymorphism in the regulatory region of the HTT may be preferentially transmitted in OCD (McDougle, Epperson, Price, & Gelernter, 1998). Ongoing studies are examining the role of serotonergic genes in OCD using the transmission disequilibrium test (Spielman & Ewens, 1996; Spielman, McGinnis, & Ewens, 1993). This technique is particularly useful for detecting genes with modest effects (Risch & Merikangas, 1996). Genetic linkage studies may also implicate susceptibility loci that have not been previously considered in the etiology of OCD.

SUMMARY OF DESCRIPTIVE AND FAMILY-GENETIC STUDIES

OCD is a common, heterogeneous illness of unknown etiology (D. W. Black, 1996). It has a distinctive phenomenology, neurobiology, and psychopharmacology (Hanna, 1995a; Hanna et al., 1991; Hanna et al., 1993; Murphy et al., 1989; Rasmussen & Eisen, 1992). Although some forms of OCD are familial, the genetics of this disorder is probably complex. Genetic linkage studies of OCD are likely to be complicated by genetic (or locus) heterogeneity; variable expressivity, reduced penetrance, and phenocopy; bilateral transmission and assortative mating; misspecification of the mode of inheritance parameters; and gene–gene and gene–environment interactions (Lander & Schork, 1994).

By ascertaining probands with an early onset of the disorder, families may be identified for linkage studies with an extensive aggregation of the disorder and limited etiologic heterogeneity. This strategy has been used successfully in molecular genetic studies of other complex diseases including breast cancer (Hall et al., 1990) and Alzheimer's disease (St. George-Hyslop et al., 1987). Family studies have demonstrated that relatives are at higher risk for OCD when they are ascertained through pediatric or early-onset probands. Because of the variability in the findings from the twin and family studies, genetic studies of OCD will need to examine the diagnostic specificity of any susceptibility loci implicated in OCD to determine whether they are involved with OCD and subthreshold OCD specifically or with a spectrum of tic or anxiety disorders.

REFERENCES

Achenbach, T. M. (1991). *Manual of the Child Behavior Checklist/4–18 and 1991 Profile*. Burlington: University of Vermont, Department of Psychiatry.

Adams, P. L. (1973). *Obsessive children*. New York: Brunner/Mazel.

Altemus, M., Murphy, D. L., Greenberg, B., & Lesch, K. P. (1996). Intact coding region of the serotonin transporter gene in obsessive-compulsive disorder. *American Journal of Medical Genetics, 67*, 409–411.

American Psychiatric Association. (1994). *Diagnostic and statistical manual of mental disorders* (4th ed.). Washington, DC: Author.

Andrews, G., Stewart, G., Allen, R., & Henderson, A. S. (1990). The genetics of six neurotic disorders: A twin study. *Journal of Affective Disorders, 19*, 23–39.

Andrews, G., Stewart, G., Morris-Yates, A., Holt, P., & Henderson, A. S. (1990). Evidence for a general neurotic syndrome. *British Journal of Psychiatry, 157*, 6–12.

Apter, R., Bernhout, E., & Tyano, S. (1984). Severe obsessive compulsive disorder in adolescence: A report of eight cases. *Journal of Adolescence, 7*, 349–358.

Bellodi, L., Sciuto, G., Diaferia, G., Ronchi, P., & Smeraldi, E. (1992). Psychiatric disorders in the families of patients with obsessive-compulsive disorder. *Psychiatry Research, 42*, 111–120.

Berkson, J. (1946). Limitations of the fourfold table analysis in hospital data. *Biometrics Bulletin, 2*, 47–53.

Black, A. (1974). The natural history of obsessional neurosis. In H. R. Beech (Ed.), *Obsessional states* (p. 38). London: Methuen.

Black, D. W. (1996). Epidemiology and genetics of OCD: A review and discussion of future directions for research. *CNS Spectrums, 1*, 10–16.

Black, D. W., Noyes, R., Jr., Goldstein, R. B., & Blum, N. (1992). A family study of obsessive-compulsive disorder. *Archives of General Psychiatry, 49*, 362–368.

Bland, R. C., Newman, S. C., & Orn, H. (1988). Lifetime prevalence of psychiatric disorders in Edmonton. *Acta Psychiatrica Scandinavica, 77*(Suppl. 338), 24–32.

Bolton, D., Collins, S., & Steinberg, D. (1983). The treatment of obsessive-compulsive disorder in adolescence: A report of fifteen cases. *British Journal of Psychiatry, 142*, 456–464.

Brown, F. W. (1942). Heredity in the psychoneuroses. *Proceedings of the Royal Society of Medicine, 35*, 785–790.

Burke, K. C., Burke, J. D., & Regier, D. A. (1990). Age at onset of selected mental disorders in five community populations. *Archives of General Psychiatry, 47*, 511–518.

Canino, G. J., Bird, H. R., Shrout, P. E., Rubio-Stipec, M., Bravo, M., Martinez, R., Sesman, M., & Guevara, L. M. (1987). The prevalence of specific psychiatric disorders in Puerto Rico. *Archives of General Psychiatry, 44*, 727–735.

Carey, G., & Gottesman, I. (1981). Twin and family studies of anxiety, phobic and obsessive disorders. In D. F. Klein & J. Rabkin (Eds.), *Anxiety: New research and changing concepts* (pp. 117–136). New York: Raven.

Catalano, M., Sciuto, G., Di Bella, D., Novelli, E., Nobile, M., & Bellodi, L. (1994). Lack of association between obsessive-compulsive disorder and the dopamine D3 receptor gene: Some preliminary considerations. *American Journal of Medical Genetics, 54*, 253–255.

Clifford, C. A., Murray, R. M., & Fulker, D. W. (1984). Genetic and environmental influences on obsessional traits and symptoms. *Psychological Medicine, 14*, 791–800.

Despert, L. (1955). Differential diagnosis between obsessive-compulsive neurosis and schizophrenia in children. In P. H. Hoch & J. Zubin (Eds.), *Psychopathology of childhood* (pp. 240–253). New York: Grune & Stratton.

DeVeaugh-Geiss, J., Moroz, G., & Biederman, J. (1992). Clomipramine hydrochloride in childhood and adolescent obsessive-compulsive disorder: A multicenter trial. *Journal of the American Academy of Child and Adolescent Psychiatry, 31*, 45–49.

Eapen, V., Pauls, D. L., & Robertson, M. M. (1993). Evidence for autosomal dominant transmission in Tourette's syndrome—United Kingdom cohort study. *British Journal of Psychiatry, 162*, 593–596.

Elston, R. C., & George, V. T. (1989). Age of onset, age at examination, and other covariates in the analysis of family data. *Genetic Epidemiology, 6*, 217–220.

Fischer, D. J., Himle, J. A., & Hanna, G. L. (1997). Age and gender effects on obsessive-compulsive symptoms in children and adults. *Depression and Anxiety, 4*, 237–239.

Flament, M. F., Whitaker, A., Rapoport, J. L., Davies, M., Berg, C. Z., Kalikow, K., Sceery, W., & Shaffer, D. (1988). Obsessive-compulsive disorder in adolescence: An epidemiological study. *Journal of the American Academy of Child and Adolescent Psychiatry, 27*, 764–771.

Geller, D. A., Biederman, J., Griffin, S., Jones, J., & Lefkowitz, T. R. (1996). Comorbidity of juvenile obsessive-compulsive disorder with disruptive behavior disorders. *Journal of the American Academy of Child and Adolescent Psychiatry, 35*, 1637–1646.

Goldstein, R. B., Wickramaratne, P. J., Horwath, E., & Weissman, M. (1997). Familial aggregation and phenomenology of "early"-onset (at or before age 20 years) panic disorder. *Archives of General Psychiatry, 54*, 271–278.

Goodman, W. K., Price, L. H., Rasmussen, S. A., Mazure, C., Delgado, P., Heninger, G. R., & Charney, D. S. (1989). The Yale–Brown Obsessive Compulsive Scale II: Validity. *Archives of General Psychiatry, 46*, 1012–1018.

Goodman, W. K., Price, L. H., Rasmussen, S. A., Mazure, C., Fleischmann, R. L., Hill, C. L., Heninger, G. R., & Charney, D. S. (1989). The Yale–Brown Obsessive Compulsive Scale I: Development, use, and reliability. *Archives of General Psychiatry, 46*, 1006–1011.

Hall, J. M., Lee, M. K., Newman, B., Morrow, J. E., Anderson, L. E., Huey, B., & King, M.-C. (1990). Linkage of early-onset familial breast cancer to chromosome 17q21. *Science, 250*, 1684–1689.

Hanna, G. L. (1995a). Demographic and clinical features of obsessive-compulsive disorder in children and adolescents. *Journal of the American Academy of Child and Adolescent Psychiatry, 34*, 19–27.

Hanna, G. L. (1995b). Tic disorders. In H. I. Kaplan & B. J. Sadock (Eds.), *Comprehensive textbook of psychiatry* (Vol. 6, pp. 2325–2336). Baltimore: Williams & Wilkins.

Hanna, G. L., McCracken, J. T., & Cantwell, D. P. (1991). Prolactin in childhood obsessive-compulsive disorder: Clinical correlates and response to clomipramine. *Journal of the American Academy of Child and Adolescent Psychiatry, 30,* 173–178.

Hanna, G. L., Yuwiler, A., & Cantwell, D. P. (1993). Whole blood serotonin during clomipramine treatment of juvenile obsessive-compulsive disorder. *Journal of Child and Adolescent Psychopharmacology, 3,* 223–229.

Hanna, G. L., Yuwiler, A., & Coates, J. K. (1995). Whole blood serotonin and disruptive behaviors in juvenile obsessive-compulsive disorder. *Journal of the American Academy of Child and Adolescent Psychiatry, 34,* 28–35.

Hollingshead, A. B. (1965). *Two factor index of social position.* New Haven, CT: Yale University, Department of Sociology.

Hollingsworth, C. E., Tanguay, P. E., Grossman, L., & Pabst, P. (1980). Long-term outcome of obsessive-compulsive disorder in children. *Journal of the American Academy of Child Psychiatry, 19,* 134–144.

Honjo, S., Hirano, C., Murase, S., Kaneko, T., Sugiyama, T., Ohtaka, K., Aoyama, T., Takei, Y., Inoko, K., & Wakabayashi, S. (1989). Obsessive-compulsive symptoms in childhood and adolescence. *Acta Psychiatrica Scandinavica, 80,* 83–91.

Inouye, E. (1965). Similar and dissimilar manifestations of obsessive-compulsive neurosis in monozygotic twins. *American Journal of Psychiatry, 21,* 1171–1175.

Insel, T. R., Murphy, D. L., Cohen, R. M., Alterman, I., Kilts, C., & Linnoila, M. (1983). Obsessive-compulsive disorder: A double-blind trial of clomipramine and clorgyline. *Archives of General Psychiatry, 40,* 605–612.

Janet, P. (1908). *Les obsessions et al psychasthenie, ed. 2* [Obsessions and psychasthenia, 2nd ed.]. Paris: Bailliere.

Karayiorgou, M., Altemus, M., Galke, B., Goldman, D., Murphy, D. L., Ott, J., & Gogos, J. A. (1997). Genotype determining low catechol-O-methyltransferase activity as a risk for obsessive-compulsive disorder. *Proceedings of the National Academy of Sciences, 94,* 4572–4575.

Karno, M., Golding, J. M., Sorenson, S. B., & Burnam, M. A. (1988). The epidemiology of obsessive-compulsive disorder in five U.S. communities. *Archives of General Psychiatry, 45,* 1094–1099.

Kringlen, E. (1965). Obsessional neurotics: A long-term follow-up. *British Journal of Psychiatry, 111,* 700–722.

LaBuda, M. C., & Pauls, D. L. (1993). Gilles de la Tourette syndrome. In P. M. Conneally (Ed.), *Molecular basis of neurology* (pp. 199–214). Boston: Blackwell Scientific.

Lander, E. S., & Schork, N. J. (1994). Genetic dissection of complex traits. *Science, 265,* 2037–2048.

Last, C. G., Hersen, M., Kazdin, A., Orvaschel, H., & Perrin, S. (1991). Anxiety disorders in children and their families. *Archives of General Psychiatry, 48,* 928–934.

Last, C. G., Perrin, S., Hersen, M., & Kazdin, A. E. (1992). DSM–III–R anxiety disorders in children: Sociodemographic and clinical characteristics. *Journal of the American Academy of Child and Adolescent Psychiatry, 31,* 1070–1076.

Last, C. G., & Strauss, C. C. (1989). Obsessive-compulsive disorder in childhood. *Journal of Anxiety Disorders, 3,* 295–302.

Leckman, J. F., Grice, D. E., Barr, L. C., de Vries, A. L. C., Martin, C., Cohen, D. J., McDougle, C. J., Goodman, W. K., & Rasmussen, S. A. (1995). Tic-related vs non-tic-related obsessive compulsive disorder. *Anxiety, 1,* 208–215.

Lee, C. K., Kwak, Y. S., Yamamoto, J., Rhee, H., Kin, Y. S., Han, J. H., Choi, J. O., & Lee, Y. H. (1990). Psychiatric epidemiology in Korea. *Journal of Nervous and Mental Disorders, 178,* 242–252.

Lenane, M., Swedo, S., Leonard, H., Pauls, D., Sceery, W., & Rapoport, J. (1990). Psychiatric disorders in first degree relatives of children and adolescents with obsessive compulsive disorder. *Journal of the American Academy of Child and Adolescent Psychiatry, 29*, 407–412.

Leonard, H. L., Lenane, M. C., Swedo, S. E., Rettew, D. C., Gerson, E. S., & Rapoport, J. L. (1992). Tics and Tourette's disorder: A 2- to 7-year follow-up of 54 obsessive-compulsive children. *American Journal of Psychiatry, 149*, 1244–1251.

Lewis, A. J. (1936). Problems of obsessional illness. *Proceedings of the Royal Society of Medicine, 29*, 325–336.

Lo, W. H. (1967). A follow-up study of obsessional neurotics in Hong Kong Chinese. *British Journal of Psychiatry, 113*, 823–832.

Luxenburger, H. (1930). Hereditat und Familientypus der Zwangsneurotiker [Heredity and family type of obsessional neurosis]. *Archiv für Psychiatrie, 91*, 590–594.

McDougle, C. J., Epperson, C. N., Price, L. H., & Gelernter, J. (1998). Evidence for linkage disequilibrium between serotonin transporter protein gene (SLC6A4) and obsessive compulsive disorder. *Molecular Psychiatry, 3*, 270–273.

McDougle, C. J., Goodman, W. K., Leckman, J. F., Lee, N. C., Heninger, G. R., & Price, L. H. (1994). Haloperidol addition in fluvoxamine-refractory obsessive-compulsive disorder: A double-blind, placebo-controlled study in patients with and without tics. *Archives of General Psychiatry, 51*, 302–308.

McKeon, P., & Murray, R. (1987). Familial aspects of obsessive-compulsive neurosis. *British Journal of Psychiatry, 151*, 528–534.

Minichiello, W. E., Baer, L., Jenike, M. A., & Holland, A. (1990). Age of onset of major subtypes of obsessive-compulsive disorder. *Journal of Anxiety Disorders, 4*, 147–150.

Murphy, D. L., Zohar, J., Benkelfat, C., Pato, M. T., Pigott, T. A., & Insel, T. R. (1989). Obsessive-compulsive disorder as a 5-HT subsystem-related behavioural disorder. *British Journal of Psychiatry, 155*, 15–24.

Nicolini, H., Cruz, C., Camarena, B., Orozco, B., Kennedy, J. L., King, N., Weissbacker, K., de la Fuente, J. R., & Sidenberg, D. (1996). DRD2, DRD3, and 5HT2A receptor genes polymorphisms in obsessive-compulsive disorder. *Molecular Psychiatry, 1*, 461–465.

Nicolini, H., Hanna, G., Baxter, L., Schwartz, J., Weissbacker, K., & Spence, M. A. (1991). Segregation analysis of obsessive-compulsive and associated disorders: Preliminary results. *Ursus Medicus, 1*, 25–28.

Noshirvani, H. A., Kasvikis, Y., Marks, I. A., Tsakiris, F., & Monteiro, W. O. (1991). Gender-divergent aetiological factors in obsessive-compulsive disorder. *British Journal of Psychiatry, 148*, 260–263.

Novelli, E., Nobile, M., Diaferia, G., Sciuto, G., & Catalano, M. (1994). A molecular investigation suggests no relationship between obsessive-compulsive disorder and the dopamine D2 receptor. *Neuropsychobiology, 29*, 61–63.

Pauls, D. L., Alsobrook, J. P., Goodman, W., Rasmussen, S., & Leckman, J. F. (1995). A family study of obsessive-compulsive disorder. *American Journal of Psychiatry, 152*, 76–84.

Pauls, D. L., & Leckman, J. F. (1986). The inheritance of Gilles de la Tourette's syndrome and associated behaviors: Evidence for autosomal dominant transmission. *New England Journal of Medicine, 315*, 993–997.

Pauls, D. L., Morton, L. A., & Egeland, J. A. (1992). Risks of affective illness among first-degree relatives of bipolar I Old-Order Amish probands. *Archives of General Psychiatry, 49*, 703–708.

Pauls, D. L., Raymond, C. L., Stevenson, J. M., & Leckman, J. F. (1991). A family study of Tourette's syndrome. *American Journal of Human Genetics, 48*, 154–163.

Pauls, D. L., Towbin, K. E., Leckman, J. F., Zahner, G. E. P., & Cohen, D. J. (1986). Gilles de la Tourette's syndrome and obsessive-compulsive disorder: Evidence supporting a genetic relationship. *Archives of General Psychiatry, 43*, 1180–1182.

Pitman, R. (1987). Pierre Janet on obsessive-compulsive disorder. *Archives of General Psychiatry, 44,* 226–232.

Pulver, A. E., Brown, C. H., Wolyniec, P., McGrath, J., Tam, D., Adler, L., Carpenter, T., & Childs, B. (1990). Schizophrenia: Age at onset, gender, and familial risk. *Acta Psychiatrica Scandinavica, 82,* 344–351.

Rachman, S. J., & Hodgson, R. J. (1980). *Obsessions and compulsions.* Englewood Cliffs, NJ: Prentice-Hall.

Rapoport, J. L. (1986). Annotation: Childhood obsessive compulsive disorder. *Journal of Child Psychology and Psychiatry, 27,* 289–295.

Rapoport, J. L. (1989). *The boy who couldn't stop washing.* New York: Dutton.

Rasmussen, S. A. (1993). Genetic studies of obsessive-compulsive disorder. *Annals of Clinical Psychiatry, 5,* 241–248.

Rasmussen, S. A. (1996). The meta-analytic saga of serotonin reuptake inhibitors in an obsessional world. *CNS Spectrums, 1,* 9.

Rasmussen, S. A., & Eisen, J. L. (1992). The epidemiology and clinical features of obsessive-compulsive disorder. *Psychiatric Clinics of North America, 15,* 743–758.

Rasmussen, S. A., & Tsuang, M. T. (1986). Clinical characteristics and family history in DSM–III obsessive compulsive disorder. *American Journal of Psychiatry, 143,* 317–322.

Rettew, D. C., Swedo, S. E., Leonard, H. L., Lenane, M. C., & Rapoport, J. L. (1992). Obsessions and compulsions across time in 79 children and adolescents with obsessive-compulsive disorder. *Journal of the American Academy of Child and Adolescent Psychiatry, 31,* 1050–1056.

Riddle, M. A., Scahill, L., King, R., Hardin, M. T., Towbin, K. E., Ort, S. I., Leckman, J. F., & Cohen, D. J. (1990). Obsessive-compulsive disorder in children and adolescents: Phenomenology and family history. *Journal of the American Academy of Child and Adolescent Psychiatry, 29,* 766–772.

Risch, N., & Merikangas, K. (1996). The future of genetic studies of complex human diseases. *Science, 273,* 1516–1517.

Rosenberg, C. M. (1967). Familial aspects of obsessional neurosis. *British Journal of Psychiatry, 113,* 405–413.

Rudin, E. (1953). Ein Beitrag zur Frage der Zwangskrankheit insebesondere ihrere hereditaren Beziehungen [A contribution to the question of the obsessive-compulsive disorder especially of its hereditary relations]. *Archiv für Psychiatrie und Zeitschrift fur Neurologie, 191,* 14–54.

Scahill, L., Riddle, M. A., McSwiggan-Hardin, M., Ort, S. I., King, R. A., Goodman, W. K., Cicchetti, D., & Leckman, J. F. (1997). Children Yale–Brown Obsessive Compulsive Scale: Reliability and validity. *Journal of the American Academy of Child and Adolescent Psychiatry, 36,* 844–852.

Sciuto, G., Pasquale, L., & Bellodi, L. (1995). Obsessive-compulsive disorder and mood disorders: A family study. *American Journal of Medical Genetics, 60,* 475–479.

Spielman, R., & Ewens, W. J. (1996). The TDT and other family-based tests for linkage disequilibrium and association. *American Journal of Human Genetics, 59,* 983–989.

Spielman, R., McGinnis, R. E., & Ewens, W. J. (1993). Transmission test for linkage disequilibrium: The insulin gene region and insulin-dependent diabetes mellitus (IDDM). *American Journal of Human Genetics, 52,* 506–516.

St. George-Hyslop, P. H., Tanzi, R. E., Polinsky, R. J., Haines, J. L., Nee, L., Watkins, P. C., Myers, R. H., Feldman, R. G., Pollen, D., & Drachman, D. (1987). The genetic defect causing familial Alzheimer's disease maps on chromosome 21. *Science, 235,* 885–890.

Swedo, S. E., Rapoport, J. L., Leonard, H., Lenane, M., & Cheslow, D. (1989). Obsessive-compulsive disorder in children and adolescents. *Archives of General Psychiatry, 46,* 335–341.

Thomsen, P. H. (1991). Obsessive-compulsive symptoms in children and adolescents: A phenomenological analysis of 61 Danish cases. *Psychopathology, 24,* 12–18.

Torgerson, S. (1983). Genetic factors in anxiety disorders. *Archives of General Psychiatry, 40,* 1085–1089.

Toro, J., Cervera, M., Osejo, E., & Salamero, M. (1992). Obsessive-compulsive disorder in childhood and adolescence: A clinical study. *Journal of Child Psychology and Psychiatry, 33,* 1025–1037.

Valleni-Basile, L. A., Garrison, C. Z., Jackson, K. L., Waller, J. L., McKeown, R. E., Addy, C. L., & Cuffe, S. P. (1994). Frequency of obsessive-compulsive disorder in a community sample of young adolescents. *Journal of the American Academy of Child and Adolescent Psychiatry, 33,* 782–791.

Weissman, M. M., Warner, V., Wickramaratne, P., & Prusoff, B. (1988). Early-onset major depression in parents and their children. *Journal of Affective Disorders, 15,* 269–277.

Welner, A., Reich, T., & Robins, L. (1976). Obsessive compulsive neurosis: Record follow-up and family studies: I. Inpatient record study. *Comprehensive Psychiatry, 17,* 527–539.

Wittchen, H. U., Essau, C. A., Von Zerssen, D., Krieg, J. C., & Zaudig, M. (1992). Lifetime and 6-month prevalence of mental disorders in the Munich follow-up study. *European Archives of Psychiatry and Clinical Neuroscience, 241,* 247–258.

Wright, K., Hanna, G. L., Vander Weele, J. M., Leventhal, B. L., & Cook, E. H. (1994, October). *Mutation screening of the serotonin transporter gene in children and adolescents with obsessive-compulsive disorder.* Paper presented at the Annual Meeting of the American Academy of Child and Adolescent Psychiatry, New York.

Zohar, A. H., Ratzoni, G., Pauls, D. L., Apter, A., Bleich, A., Kron, S., Rappaport, M., Weizman, A., & Cohen, D. J. (1992). An epidemiological study of obsessive-compulsive disorder and related disorders in Israeli adolescents. *Journal of the American Academy of Child and Adolescent Psychiatry, 31,* 1057–1061.

6

Information-Processing Abnormalities in Obsessive-Compulsive Disorder

Richard J. McNally
Harvard University

Psychopathologists have increasingly applied the concepts and methods of cognitive experimental psychology to identify information-processing abnormalities that may cause the signs and symptoms of anxiety disorders (for reviews, see Eysenck, 1992; Mathews & MacLeod, 1994; McNally, 1994, 1996; Williams, Watts, MacLeod, & Mathews, 1997). Several assumptions undergird this approach. First, introspection provides an insufficient basis for investigating cognition. Phenomenological self-report is crucial for diagnosis and for identifying abnormal beliefs, but fails to disclose the information-processing biases that underlie symptoms.

Second, cognitive biases have consequences. Dysfunctions at the information-processing level of analysis are not mere epiphenomenal sequelae of disorders, but rather constitute the pathogenic mechanisms themselves.

Third, psychologists characterize cognitive biases functionally, not neurobiologically. Although disturbances in attention, memory, and so forth are instantiated in the brain, generalizations about them are not readily reduced to concepts at the neurobiological level of analysis. Likewise, neurobiological generalizations are not readily expressed in terms of the underlying quantum mechanics. Dissimilarities between brains and digital computers notwithstanding, cognitive biases are analogous to defects in a computer's software rather than its hardware. The cognitive approach to psychopathology, however, by no means precludes derangement in the hardware as well.

Fourth, functional characterization of cognitive biases nevertheless must be compatible with neurobiology. Indeed, data at the neurobiological level can usefully constrain theorizing at the functional level and vice versa.

Fifth, anxiety researchers distinguish between *content-dependent* and *content-independent* cognitive biases. Some abnormalities emerge only when patients process information having certain content (e.g., related to threat), whereas others emerge irrespective of the content of the information processed.

Sixth, some biases occur across all anxiety disorder diagnostic categories, and therefore may partly explain pathological anxiety in general. Other biases are specific to certain disorders, and therefore may partly explain why a person has one anxiety disorder rather than another. Some researchers emphasize commonalities across nosological entities (e.g., Mathews & MacLeod, 1994), whereas others seek to identify the impairments specific to certain disorders (e.g., Foa, 1991).

The purpose of this chapter is to provide a review of research on information-processing abnormalities in obsessive-compulsive disorder (OCD). In contrast to generalized anxiety disorder (Mathews & MacLeod, 1994), panic disorder (McNally, 1994), and posttraumatic stress disorder (PTSD; McNally, 1995), OCD has been understudied from the cognitive-experimental perspective. Nevertheless, progress has occurred; abnormalities have been identified in some cognitive functions and ruled out in others. Ultimately, elucidation of cognitive derangements will clarify the origins of obsessional phenomena, and will increase the likelihood of improved treatments for treatment-refractory OCD.

ATTENTIONAL BIAS

People can attend only to a limited amount of information at any given time. Therefore, given the capacity limitations of the human information-processing system, biases favoring the encoding of threat stimuli should foster persistent anxiety. If OCD patients are acutely sensitive to any stimuli potentially related to harm (e.g., possible contaminants), they ought to be especially prone to chronic anxiety. Anxiety, in turn, may exacerbate hypervigilance for threat. Alternatively, people with OCD may engage in attentional avoidance of threat, perhaps thereby inadvertently missing opportunities for exposure to therapeutically corrective information (Foa & Kozak, 1986).

Experiments testing hypotheses about hypervigilance for threat have involved processing of visual and auditory verbal stimuli. Researchers have assumed that verbal representations of threat engage the same cognitive mechanisms as do veridical threat cues. For example, if patients selectively attend to mere verbal representations of threat (e.g., the word *feces*), they should exhibit at least as great a processing bias when encountering the referent of the representation (e.g., feces itself).

Data from different paradigms indicate that OCD is characterized by selective processing of obsession-relevant cues. In an early study, Foa and McNally (1986) tested whether OCD patients exhibit attentional vigilance for threat, and whether detection of threat cues is accompanied by physiological arousal indicative of fear. They administered a dichotic listening procedure to OCD patients both before and after behavior therapy. For each patient, they selected an idiographic threat word or phrase (e.g., *cancer, mouse feces*) and randomly inserted it 10 times out of context in a standardized prose passage in one dichotic passage, and 10 times in another dichotic passage presented to the other ear. For the neutral dichotic tape, the target word *pick* occurred out of context 10 times in another prose passage in one ear, and 10 times out of context in a different prose passage presented to the other ear. For both threat and neutral tapes, patients were told to shadow (repeat aloud) the passage presented to the right ear, and to push a button whenever they heard the target occur in either ear. Skin conductance responses (SCRs) to targets were measured.

Both behavioral (button press) and physiological (SCR) measures revealed that threat targets were detected more often than neutral targets on the unattended channel before but not after treatment. These findings imply that enhanced detection of threat was linked to fear rather than to mere familiarity. After receiving intensive behavior therapy, patients no longer exhibited attentional and physiologic responsivity to their threat cues.

Data from emotional Stroop experiments further indicate that OCD is characterized by selective processing of obsession-relevant cues. In this paradigm, individuals are shown words of varying emotional significance and are asked to ignore the meanings of the words and to name the colors in which the words are printed as quickly as possible (Williams, Mathews, & MacLeod, 1996). Color naming is delayed when the meaning of the word captures the individual's attention despite his or her effort to attend to its color.

All anxiety-disordered groups exhibit delayed color naming (Stroop interference) for words related to their current concerns (McNally, 1996; Williams et al., 1996), and OCD is no exception (Foa, Ilai, McCarthy, Shoyer, & Murdock, 1993; Lavy, van Oppen, & van den Hout, 1994). Foa et al. (1993) tested OCD washers, OCD nonwashers, and control participants. Participants saw a series of words presented one at time on a computer screen, and their color-naming latencies were recorded in response to each word. The results revealed that washers exhibited more interference for contamination words (e.g., *poison*) than for neutral words (e.g., *peach*), whereas control participants exhibited the opposite pattern of interference. Washers exhibited nonsignificantly more interference to contamination words than did OCD nonwashers, and the latter exhibited more interference to general threat words (e.g., *death*) than to neutral words. Likewise, Lavy et al. (1994) found that OCD patients exhibited interference for negative obsession-relevant words (e.g., *disease*), but not for positive obsession-relevant words 180 degrees conceptually removed from threat (e.g., *healthy*).

OCD patients usually do not exhibit Stroop interference for threat words unrelated to their primary concerns. In one study they failed to do so for words that provoked interference for patients with panic disorder (e.g., *suffocate*; McNally et al., 1994), and in another study they failed to do so for words that provoked interference for Vietnam veterans with combat-related PTSD (e.g., *bodybags*; McNally, Kaspi, Riemann, & Zeitlin, 1990). Perhaps because of the atypical focus of their obsessions (e.g., cat dander, WD40 motor oil, LSD), OCD patients in the second study also failed to exhibit interference for words related to typical contaminants (e.g., *feces, urine*).

REDUCED COGNITIVE INHIBITION

Attention may be dysfunctional in at least two ways. OCD patients may selectively attend to threat cues, as suggested by dichotic listening and emotional Stroop research (i.e., a content-dependent bias), but they may also exhibit difficulties inhibiting irrelevant information in general (i.e., a content-independent bias; Enright & Beech, 1990, 1993a, 1993b).

Enright and Beech applied negative priming methods to investigate whether OCD is characterized by deficits in preconscious mechanisms for inhibiting irrelevant cues (Tipper, 1992). In a typical negative priming experiment, participants are simultaneously shown two stimuli (e.g., two words, two line drawings), one red, and the other green. The participant is told to name the red stimulus (the target) and to ignore the green one (the distractor). If the distractor on one trial becomes the target on the next, participants exhibit delays in naming the target on this second trial (i.e., they exhibit negative priming). Because of active inhibition of the distractor on the first trial, participants are normally delayed in naming the next target if it had just appeared as the distractor on the previous trial.

In a typical semantic negative priming task, participants receive control trials where they simultaneously view, say, the target word *dog* in red letters and the distractor word *chair* in green letters, and are told to classify a probe semantically unrelated to the distractor (e.g., the word *foot* in red letters) into one of five categories: music, body, tools, furniture, or animal. On ignored semantic trials, participants are simultaneously shown *chair* in red letters and *dog* in green letters, and are told to classify a probe semantically related to the distractor (e.g., the word *cat* in red letters). Because they normally inhibit processing of the distractor, participants do not exhibit facilitation of probe classification when the probe is semantically associated with the previous distractor. However, participants who cannot inhibit processing of the distractor exhibit especially fast reaction times when the distractor semantically primes classification of the probe.

In an elegant series of experiments, Enright and Beech (1990, 1993a, 1993b) demonstrated that OCD, unlike other anxiety disorders, is characterized by deficits in the ability to inhibit processing of distracting information. In standard negative priming tasks, OCD patients exhibited markedly reduced negative priming effects, whereas patients with other anxiety disorders responded like normal control participants. On a semantic negative priming task, OCD patients exhibited enhanced probe classification times when the distractor on one trial was semantically linked to the probe on the next. In contrast, patients with other anxiety disorders, like normal control participants, did not exhibit this facilitation effect. Taken together, these data indicate that OCD is characterized by a preconscious deficit in the ability to inhibit processing of irrelevant information. As Simon and Beech emphasized, breakdown in the automatic ability to gate out irrelevant input may lead to strategic attempts at thought suppression. However, active attempts to suppress thoughts, especially negative ones (McNally & Ricciardi, 1996; Salkovskis & Westbrook, 1989), may trigger an increase in their frequency (Wegner, 1994). Therefore, Simon and Beech may have identified an important cognitive dysfunction perhaps at the root of recurrent obsessions.

REALITY MONITORING

OCD patients are often uncertain whether they have performed an action or merely imagined having performed it. Such uncertainty may develop into obsessional doubts that motivate repetitive checking of locks, doors, and so forth.

There are several cognitive explanations for compulsive checking. Compulsive checkers may fail either to encode or to retrieve memory traces of actions they have performed; that is, they may have poor memory for motor behavior. Consistent with this possibility, college students (Rubenstein, Peynircioglu, Chambless, & Pigott, 1993; Sher, Mann, & Frost, 1984) and non-OCD psychiatric patients (Sher, Frost, Kushner, Crews, & Alexander, 1989) who score high on the Checking subscale of the Maudsley Obsessional-Compulsive Inventory (MOCI; Hodgson &

Rachman, 1977) remember fewer experimental tasks performed than do individuals with low MOCI checking scores.

Another possibility is that checkers may have a deficit in *reality monitoring*, the process whereby one determines whether a memory originated from perception or imagination (Johnson & Raye, 1981). Although they may have no difficulty either encoding or accessing a memory trace, they may have difficulty determining whether the trace is attributable to a performed action or to an imagined action. That is, compulsive checking may arise because patients cannot readily distinguish between memories of doing from memories of imagined doing.

Finally, compulsive checkers may lack confidence in their reality monitoring abilities; that is, their memory may be just as good as everyone else's, but they may not think so. Sher et al. (1984) reported data consistent with this possibility in an experiment involving college students with elevated MOCI checking scores. Participants viewed either complete (e.g., *hot:cold*) or incomplete (e.g., *north:s___*) antonym pairs on a computer screen, and read the second word from complete pairs (e.g., *cold*) and imagined the implied word from incomplete pairs (e.g., *south*). Recognition tests detected no differences between checkers and noncheckers in the ability to distinguish between words that had been read and words that had been imagined. Checkers, however, reported less confidence in their memories than did noncheckers.

Studying patients rather than college students, McNally and Kohlbeck (1993) investigated reality monitoring in OCD checkers, OCD noncheckers (e.g., washers), and normal control participants. Participants traced with a capped pen, imagined tracing, or merely looked at a series of cards on which were written words or line drawings of common objects. They were subsequently shown each line drawing and each word, and asked whether they had traced it, imagined tracing it, or merely looked at it, and to rate their confidence in each decision. If OCD checkers are characterized by reality monitoring deficits, they should encounter difficulties distinguishing between memories of doing (tracing) and memories of imagined doing (imagined tracing). The results revealed no evidence of reality monitoring deficits in either group of OCD patients relative to normal control participants; the memory performance of patients was no worse than that of control participants, but trends indicated that patients expressed less confidence in their memories than did control participants. That is, OCD is characterized by a deficit in memory confidence, not in memory performance.

Other researchers have also failed to detect reality monitoring deficits in OCD (Brown, Kosslyn, Breiter, Baer, & Jenike, 1994; Brown et al., 1997; Constans, Foa, Franklin, & Mathews, 1995). Constans et al. (1995) had OCD checkers and normal control participants perform or imagine performing tasks that were either potentially distressful (e.g., plugging and unplugging an iron) or not (e.g., opening and closing a book). Participants were later asked whether they had performed or imagined performing each task. They also provided ratings of memory confidence, memory vividness, and desired memory vividness. Finally, their recall of details regarding the status of objects manipulated in the tasks was assessed (e.g., was the iron left unplugged).

Results revealed that OCD checkers and control participants did not differ in their ability to distinguish between memories of actions and memories of imagined actions, regardless of whether the action was potentially distressful. Moreover, OCD checkers were more accurate than control participants in recalling the status of manipulated objects, but only when the task was distressing. Patients and control participants did not differ in either memory vividness or confidence, but patients expressed a much higher level of desired memory vividness than did control participants. That is, OCD checkers are plagued by a marked disparity between their level of memory vividness and the level they desire to feel comfortable about having performed important actions.

Using words unrelated to OCD (e.g., *bike*), Brown and her colleagues investigated several explanations for why people might engage in compulsive checking (Brown et al., 1994; Brown et al., 1997). They endeavored to determine why checkers, for example, might have difficulty deciding whether their memories of locking a door originated from having watched themselves locking it (i.e., perception) or from having imagined themselves locking it (i.e., imagery). First, OCD patients might be characterized by diminished sensitivity to the difference between memories of visual percepts and memories of self-generated visual images, either because of dim percepts or vivid imagery. In signal detection terms, they may have a low d prime. Second, OCD patients may be especially conservative about judging that a memory arose from a percept rather than from an image; that is, their ability to discriminate memories of percepts from memories of images may not be impaired, but repetitive checking may arise because they have an extremely high beta (criterion or response bias). Third, they may experience difficulty tagging information during encoding as arising either from perception or encoding.

In their first experiment, Brown et al. (1994) asked participants to make orthographic judgments about words presented either visually or auditorially. Judgments about the latter required formation of a visual image of the word. Participants subsequently were shown all words and asked to identify which ones had been seen rather than imagined. The results revealed that OCD patients were better than control participants at discriminating between memories of percepts and memories of images; OCD patients had a higher d prime than did control participants. There was no difference in beta. Moreover, the results did not markedly change when the task was repeated after the experimenter explicitly instructed participants to attend to the context of the word (i.e., perception vs. imagery). Brown et al. concluded that OCD is associated with enhanced ability to discriminate between perception and imagery relative to control participants, and with no differences in either response bias or in difficulty encoding context.

In subsequent research, Brown et al. (1997) tested unmedicated as well as medicated OCD patients and rigorously screened control participants for possible psychopathology. The results revealed that patients and control participants did not differ in their ability to discriminate memories of percepts from memories of images. Scrutiny of the data from both experiments led Brown et al. (1997) to conclude that control participants in the first experiment (Brown et al., 1994) had inexplicably low *d* prime values; OCD patients performed similarly in both experiments. Taken together, Brown et al.'s investigations clearly indicate, however, that OCD is not associated with impairment in the ability to discriminate memories of percepts from memories of images.

DIRECTED FORGETTING

OCD patients experience unbidden, recurrent obsessions, and their efforts to suppress them may increase their frequency (Salkovskis & Westbrook, 1989). It is unclear whether problems dispelling obsessional thoughts arise because of dysfunction in mechanisms of forgetting or because of elaborative encoding of threatening information.

To address these issues, Wilhelm, McNally, Baer, and Florin (1996) used a *directed forgetting* procedure. During the encoding phase of the experiment, OCD patients and healthy control participants viewed a series of threat words (e.g., *disease*), positive words (e.g., *cheerful*), and neutral words (e.g., *paneling*) on a computer screen. Each word appeared for 2 seconds, and immediately thereafter participants were told either to forget or to remember the word. After the encoding phase, participants were given free recall, cued recall, and recognition tests for all words, regardless of initial instructions to remember or forget.

Results revealed that OCD patients were relatively unable to forget threat words in contrast to positive and neutral words, whereas control participants had no such problem. Further analyses indicated that superior memory for threat words in the OCD group was best attributable to enhanced processing during the encoding phase. That is, OCD patients may allocate disproportionate attentional resources to threat words, thereby enhancing their subsequent memorability. Alternatively, they may experience special difficulty inhibiting further processing of threat words that they have been told to forget.

Enhanced memory for threat words receiving forget instructions seems specific for threat material. Not only did OCD patients forget positive and neutral material receiving forget instructions at rates comparable to those of control participants, but Maki, O'Neill, and O'Neill (1994) reported no deficits in mechanisms of directed forgetting for nonthreat words in college students with high MOCI checking scores.

AUTOBIOGRAPHICAL MEMORY

While studying mood-congruent memory in depressed people and suicide attempters, Williams and his colleagues noted that these patients had great difficulty retrieving specific personal memories in response to cue words (e.g., *happy*; for a review, see Williams, 1996). When asked to retrieve a specific autobiographical memory, they instead tended to retrieve overgeneral memories that referenced no specific episode. Although control participants readily retrieved specific memories, say, to *happy* (e.g., that reminds me of the day my first child was born), depressed patients tended to retrieve a general category rather than a specific event (e.g., that reminds me of times when I was playing tennis). The inability to retrieve specific autobiographical memories is strongly related to interpersonal problem-solving deficits and strongly predicts failure to recover from depressive episodes (Williams, 1996).

Given that overgeneral memory occurs in PTSD as well as in major depressive disorder (e.g., McNally, Lasko, Macklin, & Pitman, 1995), Wilhelm, McNally, Baer, and Florin (1997) wondered whether it might characterize any psychiatric condition associated with intrusive thoughts, such as OCD. However, using positive and negative cue words, they found that only those OCD patients who currently had comorbid depression exhibited this autobiographical memory deficit. OCD patients, including those on medication, did not exhibit overgeneral memory. These results indicate that this dysfunction is unrelated to OCD per se.

CONCLUSIONS

The purpose of cognitive experimental psychopathology is to locate disturbances in the information-processing system and to elucidate how such dysfunctions give rise to the signs and symptoms of emotional disorder. Although still relatively scarce, research on OCD has begun to accomplish these objectives. Patients with OCD exhibit both content-dependent and content-independent abnormalities in attentional processing. They are more distracted by threat cues related to their obsessional concerns than by disturbing material unrelated to these concerns. Extant studies, however, are confined to dichotic listening and emotional Stroop tasks, and convergent confirmation arising from other attentional paradigms is needed. OCD patients also exhibit a general inability to inhibit processing of irrelevant information. This deficit may give rise to strategic attempts to suppress intrusive information that, if negatively valent, may foster recurrent obsessions. Researchers have yet to test whether this inability is exacerbated when the content of the irrelevant information is obsession relevant.

Studies have repeatedly shown that OCD is not characterized by reality monitoring deficits. People with OCD are certainly no worse than healthy people when it comes to discriminating memories of percepts and actions from memories of imagined stimuli and actions. Whatever dysfunctions lead to repetitive checking, it does not seem linked to deficits in reality monitoring. Some evidence, however, points to deficits in the confidence of OCD patients in their memories, despite objective evidence that their memories are fine.

Other memory studies show that OCD patients are not characterized by an inability to access specific autobiographical episodes unless they also have current comorbid depression. However, directed forgetting data indicate that OCD patients, unlike healthy control individuals, are characterized by an inability to forget information when it is tagged to be forgotten. This disturbance seems to arise because patients cannot inhibit further processing of threat stimuli despite instructions to do so.

In summary, recurrent obsessions may arise partly because OCD patients preferentially attend to threatening input and fail to inhibit processing of this input automatically. Why certain stimuli become functionally linked to threat is yet to be resolved. Moreover, insights gleaned from cognitive experimental research have yet to be translated into new strategies for helping the treatment-resistant patient.

REFERENCES

Brown, H. D., Kosslyn, S. M., Breiter, H. C., Baer, L., & Jenike, M. A. (1994). Can patients with obsessive-compulsive disorder discriminate between percepts and mental images? A signal detection analysis. *Journal of Abnormal Psychology, 103,* 445–454.

Brown, H. D., Kosslyn, S. M., Wilhelm, S., Savage, C., Moretti, C., Reid, N., & Jenike, M. A. (1997). *Can patients with obsessive-compulsive disorder discriminate between percepts and mental images? Replication and further investigations.* Manuscript in preparation, Department of Psychology, Harvard University, Cambridge, MA.

Constans, J. I., Foa, E. B., Franklin, M. E., & Mathews, A. (1995). Memory for actual and imagined events in OC checkers. *Behaviour Research and Therapy, 33,* 665–671.

Enright, S. J., & Beech, A. R. (1990). Obsessional states: Anxiety disorders or schizotypes? An information processing and personality assessment. *Psychological Medicine, 20*, 621–627.

Enright, S. J., & Beech, A. R. (1993a). Further evidence of reduced cognitive inhibition in obsessive-compulsive disorder. *Personality and Individual Differences, 14*, 387–395.

Enright, S. J., & Beech, A. R. (1993b). Reduced cognitive inhibition in obsessive-compulsive disorder. *British Journal of Clinical Psychology, 32*, 67–74.

Eysenck, M. W. (1992). *Anxiety: The cognitive perspective.* Hillsdale, NJ: Lawrence Erlbaum Associates.

Foa, E. B. (1991, November). *Pathological anxiety and its treatment: What we know and what we don't know.* Invited address delivered at the meeting of the Association for Advancement of Behavior Therapy, New York.

Foa, E. B., Ilai, D., McCarthy, P. R., Shoyer, B., & Murdock, T. (1993). Information processing in obsessive-compulsive disorder. *Cognitive Therapy and Research, 17*, 173–189.

Foa, E. B., & Kozak, M. J. (1986). Emotional processing of fear: Exposure to corrective information. *Psychological Bulletin, 99*, 20–35.

Foa, E. B., & McNally, R. J. (1986). Sensitivity to feared stimuli in obsessive-compulsives: A dichotic listening analysis. *Cognitive Therapy and Research, 10*, 477–485.

Hodgson, R. J., & Rachman, S. (1977). Obsessional-compulsive complaints. *Behaviour Research and Therapy, 15*, 389–395.

Johnson, M. K., & Raye, C. L. (1981). Reality monitoring. *Psychological Review, 88*, 67–85.

Lavy, E., van Oppen, P., & van den Hout, M. (1994). Selective processing of emotional information in obsessive compulsive disorder. *Behaviour Research and Therapy, 32*, 243–246.

Maki, W. S., O'Neill, H. K., & O'Neill, G. W. (1994). Do nonclinical checkers exhibit deficits in cognitive control? Tests of an inhibitory control hypothesis. *Behaviour Research and Therapy, 32*, 183–192.

Mathews, A., & MacLeod, C. (1994). Cognitive approaches to emotion and emotional disorders. *Annual Review of Psychology, 45*, 25–50.

McNally, R. J. (1994). *Panic disorder: A critical analysis.* New York: Guilford.

McNally, R. J. (1995). Cognitive processing of trauma-relevant information in PTSD. *PTSD Research Quarterly, 6*(2), 1–7.

McNally, R. J. (1996). Cognitive bias in the anxiety disorders. *Nebraska Symposium on Motivation, 43*, 211–250.

McNally, R. J., Amir, N., Louro, C. E., Lukach, B. M., Riemann, B. C., & Calamari, J. E. (1994). Cognitive processing of idiographic emotional information in panic disorder. *Behaviour Research and Therapy, 32*, 119–122.

McNally, R. J., Kaspi, S. P., Riemann, B. C., & Zeitlin, S. B. (1990). Selective processing of threat cues in posttraumatic stress disorder. *Journal of Abnormal Psychology, 99*, 407–412.

McNally, R. J., & Kohlbeck, P. A. (1993). Reality monitoring in obsessive-compulsive disorder. *Behaviour Research and Therapy, 31*, 249–253.

McNally, R. J., Lasko, N. B., Macklin, M. L., & Pitman, R. K. (1995). Autobiographical memory disturbance in combat-related posttraumatic stress disorder. *Behaviour Research and Therapy, 33*, 619–630.

McNally, R. J., & Ricciardi, J. N. (1996). Suppression of negative and neutral thoughts. *Behavioural and Cognitive Psychotherapy, 24*, 17–25.

Rubenstein, C. S., Peynircioglu, Z. F., Chambless, D. F., & Pigott, T. A. (1993). Memory in sub-clinical obsessive-compulsive checkers. *Behaviour Research and Therapy, 8*, 759–765.

Salkovskis, P. M., & Westbrook, D. (1989). Behaviour therapy and obsessional ruminations: Can failure be turned into success? *Behaviour Research and Therapy, 27*, 149–160.

Sher, K. J., Frost, R. O., Kushner, M., Crews, T. M., & Alexander, J. E. (1989). Memory deficits in compulsive checkers: Replication and extension in a clinical sample. *Behaviour Research and Therapy, 27*, 65–69.

Sher, K. J., Mann, B., & Frost, R. O. (1984). Cognitive dysfunction in compulsive checkers: Further explorations. *Behaviour Research and Therapy, 22*, 493–502.

Tipper, S. P. (1992). Selection for action: The role of inhibitory mechanisms. *Current Directions in Psychological Science, 1*, 105–109.

Wegner, D. M. (1994). Ironic processes of mental control. *Psychological Review, 101*, 34–52.

Wilhelm, S., McNally, R. J., Baer, L., & Florin, I. (1996). Directed forgetting in obsessive-compulsive disorder. *Behaviour Research and Therapy, 34*, 633–641.

Wilhelm, S., McNally, R. J., Baer, L., & Florin, I. (1997). Autobiographical memory in obsessive-compulsive disorder. *British Journal of Clinical Psychology, 36*, 21–31.

Williams, J. M. G. (1996). Depression and the specificity of autobiographical memory. In D. C. Rubin (Ed.), *Remembering our past: Studies in autobiographical memory* (pp. 271–296). Cambridge, UK: Cambridge University Press.

Williams, J. M. G., Mathews, A., & MacLeod, C. (1996). The emotional Stroop task and psychopathology. *Psychological Bulletin, 120*, 3–24.

Williams, J. M. G., Watts, F. N., MacLeod, C., & Mathews, A. (1997). *Cognitive psychology and emotional disorders* (2nd ed.). Chichester, UK: Wiley.

7

Issues in Cognitive Treatment of Obsessive-Compulsive Disorder

Patricia van Oppen
Vrije Universiteit

Paul M. G. Emmelkamp
University of Amsterdam

The effects of behavior therapy (i.e., exposure in vivo and response prevention) with obsessive-compulsive (OC) patients have been well established (Marks, 1987; Steketee, 1993; van Balkom et al., 1994). Improvements of exposure in vivo and response prevention have been found to be maintained at up to 3.5 years follow-up (Visser, Hoekstra, & Emmelkamp, 1990). However, there are still a number of OC patients who cannot be treated or who are inadequately treated by behavioral methods only (Foa et al., 1983; Rachman, 1983; Steketee, 1993). Although for some patients treatment effects of behavior therapy may be enhanced by adding drugs like clomipramine or fluvoxamine, there is little evidence that the effects of a combined behavioral and drug treatment are superior to those of behavior therapy on its own (e.g., Kasvikis & Marks, 1988; Marshall & Segal, 1990; Mawson, Marks, & Ramm, 1982; van Balkom, de Haan, van Oppen, Spinhoven, Hoogduin, & van Dyck, 1998; van Balkom et al., 1994). Given the fact that most OC behavior is evoked by thoughts, in recent years some authors have suggested that the role of cognitive factors must be considered (McFall & Wollersheim, 1979; Salkovskis, 1985, 1989).

COGNITIVE MODEL

A first attempt to conceptualize obsessive-compulsive disorder (OCD) in cognitive terms was made by Carr (1974), who emphasized unrealistic threat appraisals. This threat appraisal is an individual's evaluation of a situation in terms of its harmful implications. He assumed that OC patients experience a high degree of threat because they overestimate both the probability and the cost of the occurrence of undesired outcomes. His model was based on the finding that OCD patients have an abnormally high subjective estimate of the probability of an unfavorable outcome. This idea was supported by findings that OCD patients were more cautious of getting involved in risk-taking activities than other groups of psychiatric patients (Steiner, 1972). Carr (1974) assumed that threat is some multiplicative function of the subjective cost of an event and its subjective probability. Because of the high subjective estimate of the probability of the undesired outcome, a number of situations will lead to a high level of anxiety, and OC rituals are developed to lower the subjective probability of the unfavorable outcome. Consequently these activities are threat reducing. This strategy is reinforced by anxiety reduction and in averting the unfavorable outcome, which never did have a high probability of actually occurring.

McFall and Wollersheim (1979) proposed that cognitions have a mediating role in the performance of compulsions. Their model emphasizes factors that influence the unrealistic subjective estimates of catastrophic outcomes. According to McFall and Wollersheim, the threat is generated by an immediate cognitive primary appraisal process whereby the individual estimates the danger of an event relative to the perceived resources to cope with it. After a primary appraisal of threat, anxiety is heightened and OC behavior is initiated on the basis of the person's secondary appraisal of the likely consequence of his or her efforts to cope with the threat. The unreasonable beliefs that are considered to influence the primary appraisal process of the OCD patient are: (a) one should be perfect, (b) making mistakes results in punishment or condemnation, (c) one is powerful enough to initiate or prevent the occurrence of disastrous outcomes, and (d) certain thoughts and feelings are unacceptable and could lead to a catastrophe. McFall and Wollersheim (1979) further formulated a number of unreasonable beliefs that negatively influence secondary appraisals including the following: (a) if something is or may be dangerous, one should be terribly upset by it; (b) magical rituals or obsessive ruminating will circumvent feared outcomes; (c) it is easier and more effective to carry out a magical ritual or to obsess than it is to confront one's feelings or thoughts directly; and (d) feelings of uncertainty and loss of control are intolerable, should make one afraid, and something must be done about them. As a result of these beliefs, people with OCD experience themselves as helpless in coping with perceived threat, except through the performance of rituals to prevent the foreseeable catastrophic outcomes. Although obsessions and compulsions are themselves distressing, patients prefer these over the distress associated with the unfavorable outcomes that might occur if the rituals are not performed. Patients perceive these rituals as being more tolerable than the guilt feelings related to the unacceptable impulses (see also Rosen, 1975).

A third cognitive model for OCD was proposed by Salkovskis (1985, 1989) based on the same model of emotions as that used in the cognitive models of Beck for depression and anxiety (Beck, 1976; Beck, Emery, & Greenberg, 1985). The central theme is the idea that not an event, but rather the individual's interpretation of an event, leads to a specific emotional response. The response to particular stimuli (thoughts, situations, or events) occurs as a result of negative automatic thoughts. Salkovskis emphasized the difference between intrusions and automatic thoughts. Negative automatic thoughts are relatively autonomous, idiosyncratic, and experienced as reasonable and egosyntonic, as opposed to the obsessions, which are intrusive thoughts that evoke negative automatic thoughts leading to neutralizing by the obsessional. As a consequence of this neutralizing activity, intrusive thoughts become more salient and frequent, and they evoke more discomfort, so that the probability of further neutralizing increases (Salkovskis, 1985). Although intrusions also occur frequently in normal individuals (Edwards & Dickerson, 1987), they do not lead to anxiety or tenseness despite their contents, which are virtually identical to those of the intrusions experienced by OCD patients. Attempts to neutralize intrusions cause greater anxiety and increase the frequency of their occurrence (Rachman, Shafran, Mitchell, Trant, & Teachman, 1996; Salkovskis, 1989). Salkovskis (1989) supposed that the negative automatic thoughts of OCD patients are related to ideas of personal responsibility. Several experiments (Lopatka & Rachman, 1995; Rachman & Hodgson, 1980; Röper & Rachman, 1976; Röper, Rachman, & Hodgson, 1973) showed the significance of the sense of responsibility in determining compulsive checking.

In all recent formulations of OCD just discussed, the importance of cognitive processes has been stressed. The following account of the development of compulsions is a comprehensive summary of these various contributions. In OCD it is assumed that the pathological cognitive processes involve evaluative processes linking the intrusion and the compulsion. Two such evaluative processes are assumed to take place: the perception of danger and the appraisal of personal responsibility. When an intrusion occurs, it is hypothesized to lead to a perception of danger. Further, it is important whether or not the individual perceives personal responsibility. When the person believes that he or she should do something to prevent or reduce the danger or the perceived personal responsibility the result is a compulsion (van Oppen & Arntz, 1994). van Oppen and Arntz (1994) hypothesized that phobias and other anxiety disorders are defined by the expectations of a catastrophe in the future, but the individual perceives little responsibility for the event. Both OCD and other anxiety disorders involve ruminations about future catastrophic events; however, OCD differs from the other anxiety disorders in perceived responsibility. Furthermore, OCD resembles depression with respect to the personal responsibility for the catastrophic event, but differs from depression on a time dimension. Depression is defined by the combination of perceived high responsibility for an event that took place in the past evaluated as very catastrophic. OCD can be described as a condition in which the patient tries to avoid the depressive position of being guilty, being worthless, or having failed by performing rituals. In this model OCD is defined by perceived high responsibility for a future catastrophe (van Oppen & Arntz, 1994).

Over the last few years, increasing attention has been paid to the cognitive mechanisms of anxiety disorders. Cognitive experimental research has shown that, as opposed to the behavior of normal individuals, patients with anxiety disorders pay more attention to anxiety-relevant threatening stimuli than to neutral or positive stimuli (Williams, Watts, MacLeod, & Mathews, 1988). This selective attention in anxiety patients was studied three times in OCD patients, twice by means of a modified Stroop task and once by means of a modified dichotic listening task (Foa, Ilai, McCarthy, Shoyer, & Murdock, 1993; Foa & McNally, 1986; Lavy, van Oppen, & Van den Hout, 1994). These three studies found that OCD patients did indeed pay more attention to anxiety-related threatening stimuli than to neutral words. However, this attentional bias disappeared after behavior therapy (Foa & McNally, 1986). In the Lavy et al. (1994) study, three possible explanations for attentional bias effects in OCD participants were tested: (a) the threat-relatedness hypothesis (selective bias for threatening stimuli), (b) the emotionality hypothesis (selective bias for emotional stimuli, thus also for positive stimuli), and (c) the concern-relatedness hypothesis (selective bias for disorder-related stimuli; positive and negative stimuli). An experiment was carried out with 33 OCD patients and 29 normal control participants. Both groups color named a Stroop card with five word sets: neutral words and four emotional word sets (related OCD words, unrelated OCD words, positive emotional words, and negative emotional words). In this study evidence was found only for the threat-relatedness hypothesis. The OCD patients selectively attended to threatening OCD-related words and did not show an attentional bias for positive OCD-related words and for OCD-unrelated emotional words. It is, as yet, unclear whether selective attention causes OC complaints or whether it results from the OC complaints. Patients suffering from anxiety appear to interpret ambiguous events as more threatening than do normal individuals and they estimate the subjective cost of these threatening events to be higher (Butler & Mathews, 1983).

Arntz, van Eck, and Heijmans (1990) and van Hout and Emmelkamp (1994) found that anxiety patients expect to experience more anxiety (overestimation) than they actually did and need more experiences to arrive at a more accurate assessment of their anxiety. So far no experimental studies have been conducted in OCD patients on overestimation of the chances of being confronted with unpleasant situations and of the seriousness of those situations.

COGNITIVE THERAPY

Compared to other anxiety disorders, for which numerous studies have evaluated the effectiveness of cognitive therapy (e.g., Hollon & Beck, 1994), little research on cognitive treatment with OCD has been undertaken. This discrepancy is remarkable because OCD is characterized by several forms of cognitive dysfunction. Common cognitive dysfunctions are overestimation of the chance of danger, overestimation of the extent or the consequence of the danger, overestimation of responsibility, and overestimation of the perceived consequence of having been responsible (van Oppen & Arntz, 1994). Cognitions seem to play an important role in the triggering of compulsions. For example, during the execution of washing rituals, cognitions about possible contamination play a prominent role and control rituals seem to be provoked by ideas concerning harming others or oneself (Emmelkamp, 1987). Three different forms of cognitive therapy have been evaluated with OCD patients: self-instructional training, rational emotive therapy (RET), and cognitive therapy along the lines of Beck (1976) and Salkovskis (1985). These studies are discussed in some detail.

Self-Instructional Training

A first attempt to investigate the clinical utility of a cognitive approach on OCD was made by Emmelkamp, van der Helm, van Zanten, and Plochg (1980). They investigated whether a modification of cognitions (Meichenbaum, 1975) could enhance the effectiveness of exposure in vivo and response prevention. The cognitive component of the treatment consisted of self-instructional training, at that time a quite popular cognitive method. Patients were trained to emit more productive self-statements. After a short relaxation period, patients cognitively rehearsed self-instructional means of handling anxiety by an imagination procedure. The therapist asked the patient to imagine situations described by the therapist as vividly as possible. The patient was then instructed to determine how anxious he or she felt, to become conscious of his or her negative self-statements, and then to replace them by productive self-statements and relaxation. Situations that were cognitively rehearsed were items from the hierarchy of anxiety- and discomfort-arousing situations that triggered OC rituals. Preparing, confronting, coping, and reinforcing self-statements were practiced (Meichenbaum, 1975). After half an hour of self-instructional training, exposure in vivo followed in each session: Now the patient had to practice in vivo the items of the hierarchy that had been cognitively rehearsed. The patients were instructed to use their productive self-statements during practice in vivo. Half of the patients were treated with self-instructional training plus exposure in vivo in the presence of the therapist, and the other half of the patients were treated with exposure in vivo in the presence of the therapist only. In both conditions all items in the hierarchy had to be practiced in vivo, starting with the easiest. More difficult tasks were given only if tasks lower in the hierarchy were performed successfully. The speed at which the patient worked through the hierarchy was determined by the patient himself or herself, although some pressure was exerted to induce the patient to continue practicing. For clinical guidelines the reader is referred to Emmelkamp, Bouman, and Scholing (1992).

To control for the self-instructional part in each session, exposure-only participants received relaxation before actual exposure started, effects of which are negligible with OCD patients. Results indicated that self-instructional training did not enhance the effectiveness of exposure in vivo. If anything, there was a trend that the exposure in vivo condition was superior. Presumably, time devoted to self-instructional practice during the exposure in vivo phase had slowed down the tempo at which exposure in vivo had been carried out. Several patients questioned the usefulness of the self-instructional training, as they did not experience that their positive self-statements were helpful during exposure in vivo. In spite of their attempts at controlling their anxiety, they became as anxious as before.

It is questionable whether self-instructional training is the most appropriate cognitive technique to deal with OCD patients who are already engaging in excessive self-talk, ruminations, and doubting. With self-instructional training, cognitions are dealt with rather superficially; only peripheral structures are changed. The deeper cognitive structures are left untouched. Treatment that focuses on the irrational beliefs of OCD patients (McFall & Wollersheim, 1979) might be more appropriate for these patients.

RET

The critical elements of this treatment involve determining the (irrational) thoughts that mediate the negative feeling (e.g., anxiety, discomfort, tension), and comforting and modifying them so that undue feelings of anxiety or discomfort are no longer experienced, so compulsive rituals are no longer necessary to reduce these negative feelings.

In studies into RET with OCD patients (Emmelkamp & Beens, 1991; Emmelkamp, Visser, & Hoekstra, 1988), Ellis's (1962) ABC framework was used. *A* refers to an *activating* event or experience, *B* to the person's *belief* about the activating event, and *C* to the emotional or behavioral *consequence*, assumed to result from the beliefs.

The first stage of therapy was directed to training patients to observe and record their cognitions. By using precoded ABC homework sheets, patients learned to discriminate between the actual event and their own thoughts. The next stage of therapy involved rationally disputing the irrational cognitions. The therapist challenged the irrational beliefs in a Socratic fashion and the patients were instructed to do this on their own as a homework assignment. Patients had to practice analyzing their problems by using the precoded ABC homework sheets. In the following therapy sessions, problems encountered during the homework tasks were discussed and irrational beliefs were analyzed together with the therapist, with a special emphasis on the beliefs associated with the primary and secondary appraisal process (McFall & Wollersheim, 1979). Patients were not instructed to expose themselves to fear-provoking situations. As homework assignments patients had to analyze their irrational beliefs 6 days a week for 30 minutes on precoded ABC sheets.

In the first study (Emmelkamp et al., 1988) RET along the lines of Ellis (1962) and McFall and Wollersheim (1979) was compared with treatment consisting of exposure in vivo and response prevention. Exposure was self-controlled and applied by means of homework assignments. Treatment in both conditions consisted of 10 sessions. On the OC targets (Maudsley Obsessional-Compulsive Inventory [MOCI] and anxiety and discomfort scale) the results of cognitive therapy were about equally effective as self-controlled exposure in vivo (Emmelkamp et al., 1988). Both treatments were found to lead to a reduction of social anxiety. On depression (Self-Rating Depression Scale [SDS]; Zung, 1965) cognitive therapy led to significant improvement, whereas self-controlled exposure did not.

The primary aim of the Emmelkamp and Beens (1991) study was to investigate whether a combined package (cognitive therapy followed by exposure in vivo) would enhance the effects of exposure in vivo and response prevention. Patients were randomly assigned to two conditions: (a) self-controlled exposure, and (b) cognitive therapy. After two sessions devoted to assessment (Assessment I) and preparation for the treatment, a 4-week waiting period followed. After another assessment session (Assessment II), six treatment sessions followed. Half of the patients received cognitive therapy and the other half received exposure. After the experimental treatment, which lasted 4 weeks, another assessment (Assessment

III) was held, and patients were reassessed (Assessment IV) 4 weeks later. No treatment was provided during this period. After Assessment IV the patients in the exposure condition received another six sessions of exposure; for patients in the cognitive therapy condition exposure was now added to cognitive therapy. After this second treatment phase, which lasted 4 weeks, another assessment (Assessment V) was held, followed by a 4-week no-treatment period; then patients were reassessed (Follow-Up I). With two thirds of the patients treatment was continued after Follow-Up I. Six months after the posttest, Follow-Up II was held.

In the second phase of treatment (after Assessment IV) exposure exercises were added to the cognitive treatment. A hierarchy was constructed and the patient was given tasks that he or she had to perform by himself or herself at home. In the sessions the emphasis was on analyzing the irrational beliefs associated with the exposure tasks.

A significant time effect during the first and second treatment blocks was found on all OC measures (e.g., MOCI and anxiety and discomfort). Further, the first treatment block led to a significant reduction in depressed mood (SDS; Zung, 1965). During the three waiting periods before, in between, and after the treatment blocks, hardly any changes occurred. A differential treatment effect was not found on any of the measures: At the intermediate test after the first treatment block and at the posttest after the second treatment block, both treatments were found to be equally effective.

The results of this study again demonstrated that cognitive therapy is effective with OCD. On none of the OC measures was there a significant difference between cognitive therapy and exposure in vivo, thus replicating the findings of the Emmelkamp et al. (1988) study in which cognitive therapy also was found to be as effective as exposure in vivo. There is, however, no evidence that the effects of a treatment package in which cognitive therapy and exposure in vivo are combined is more effective than exposure in vivo alone.

Cognitive Therapy Along the Lines of Beck (1976) and Salkovskis (1985)

Cognitive therapy for OCD is primarily based on the cognitive model of emotional and anxiety disorders (Beck, 1976; Beck et al., 1985). This treatment focuses on a short-term, structured, and problem-oriented treatment. The general strategies are (a) to consider the intrusions as stimuli, (b) to identify the distressing thoughts (negative automatic thoughts), (c) to challenge these automatic thoughts, and (d) to change the distressing thoughts into nondistressing thoughts. It is important to the credibility of the treatment that the therapist is confident about the principles of the cognitive model. An important condition for successful cooperation between patient and therapist is a good therapeutic relationship.

Before different phases of cognitive therapy are discussed, it is important to emphasize the Socratic attitude of the therapist. This implies that the therapist will patiently keep asking emphatically, for the patient to come to another insight by himself or herself. The cognitive therapeutic style is distinguished by respect for the patient's ideas and by frequent use of communicative skills, such as summing up, reflection, and encouraging further exploration. In every session homework assignments are given, taking approximately half an hour daily.

It is important at the beginning of treatment to extensively linger over the rationale of the therapy. In this phase the therapist teaches the patient to discriminate between thoughts and feelings and it is made clear that there is a link among events, thoughts, feelings, and behavior. Moreover, patients are shown that different interpretations of one event are possible. During the whole treatment patients were instructed to monitor and challenge automatic thoughts in diaries as homework assignments. In the therapy sessions problems with the diary were discussed and worked out, and in each session at least one automatic thought was challenged. During the treatment, behavioral experiments are introduced and used to test the empirical basis of the dysfunctional cognitions and assumptions.

To date, only one controlled study (van Oppen, de Haan, et al., 1995) has been reported in which cognitive therapy along the lines of Beck et al. (1985) and Salkovskis (1985) has been evaluated. This form of cognitive therapy was compared with self-controlled exposure in vivo with response prevention. A pretreatment OC assessment consisted of the Padua Inventory–Revised (Sanavio, 1988; van Oppen, Emmelkamp, van Balkom, & van Dyck, 1995), the Yale–Brown Obsessive Compulsive Scale (Goodman, Price, Rasmussen, Mazure, Delgado, et al., 1989; Goodman, Price, Rasmussen, Mazure, Fleischmann, et al., 1989; van Oppen, Hoekstra, & Emmelkamp, 1995c), and the Anxiety Discomfort Scale. A pretreatment generalized assessment consisted of the Symptom Checklist–Revised (SCL–90–R; Derogatis, 1977), the Beck Depression Inventory (Beck, Ward, Mendelson, Mock, & Erbaugh, 1961), and the Irrational Belief Inventory (IBI; Koopmans, Sanderman, Timmerman, & Emmelkamp, 1994). The same measurements were used for the midtest and posttest. After six sessions an intermediate test (midtest) took place, and after 16 sessions (16 weeks) a posttest was held. Only after Session 6 were behavioral experiments introduced.

Both cognitive therapy and self-controlled exposure in vivo plus response prevention led to statistically and clinically significant improvement. Patients treated with cognitive therapy improved on all variables, and patients treated with exposure in vivo improved on almost all variables, except on the SCL–90–R and on the IBI (Koopmans et al., 1994).

In the van Oppen, de Haan, et al. (1995) study multivariate significant interaction effects on the OC measures and on the generalized measures suggested a greater efficacy of cognitive therapy in comparison to exposure in vivo. However, these differences did not stand up in separate univariate analyses of variances in which initial differences between conditions were taken into account. The differences in effect size and in the percentage of recovered patients suggest that cognitive therapy might be superior to exposure in vivo. Significantly more patients were rated as reliably changed or as recovered in the cognitive therapy.

In contrast, Emmelkamp et al. (1988) and Emmelkamp and Beens (1991) did not find significant differences between cognitive therapy and exposure in vivo on the OC measures. As the effects obtained for exposure in vivo are comparable to those found in other studies, these findings cannot be explained by a smaller effect of exposure in vivo. In a meta-analysis of van Balkom et al. (1994) the mean effect size for exposure was 1.47, which is roughly comparable to the effect sizes in the van Oppen, de Haan, et al. (1995) study. Another explanation might be the large ns in both conditions in the van Oppen, de Haan, et al. (1995) study. Large ns solve the power problem that has frequently plagued outcome studies in OCD. Finally, the differences in outcome between the van Oppen et al. (1995) study and those by Emmelkamp and his colleagues might be related to the particular form of cognitive therapy used in this study. Van Oppen, de Haan, et al. (1995) used cognitive therapy along the lines of Beck and Salkovskis, which also included behavioral experiments, whereas Emmelkamp and his colleagues used RET (Ellis, 1962) and excluded all behavioral exercises. Further, the cognitive therapy used in the van Oppen, de Haan, et al. (1995) study was specifically developed for OCD and focused mainly on estimation of catastrophes and estimation of personal responsibility (van Oppen & Arntz, 1994).

One might expect that cognitive therapy would be more effective than exposure in vivo in checkers, given the presumed role of responsibility in checking behavior (e.g., Lopatka & Rachman, 1995). Post hoc comparisons in the van Oppen et al. (1995) study, however, did not reveal any significant difference between cognitive therapy and exposure in vivo for the subgroup checkers. This may be due to the small ns for each subgroup per condition (7 vs. 10). Further, even though the overestimation of responsibility was an important focus of the cognitive therapy, other issues were also addressed, such as the estimation of the chance of a catastrophe (van Oppen & Arntz, 1994). The cognitive treatment was adapted to the individual patient. Further research is needed to test whether cognitive therapy that only aims at modifying the inflated sense of responsibility is more effective than self-controlled exposure in vivo for the subgroup checkers.

Although some (e.g., Kendall, 1983; Reed, 1985) have proposed that cognitive therapy may be inappropriate for treating individuals with OCD, because these patients already overemphasize their thoughts, the results here indicate that this does not necessarily have to be the case. Although self-instructional training was not found to enhance the effects of exposure in vivo, cognitive therapy along the lines of Ellis and MacFall and Wollersheim was found to be as effective as exposure in vivo, and cognitive therapy along the lines of Beck and Salkovskis might even be superior. One of the main limitations of the studies into RET is the relatively small sample sizes in each group (in the Emmelkamp et al. [1988] study: cognitive $n = 9$, exposure $n = 9$; in the Emmelkamp & Beens [1991] study: cognitive $n = 10$, exposure $n = 11$). It could be argued that these studies probably do not have sufficient power to detect a small difference in treatment effectiveness. However, in both studies there was no sign of a difference in treatment effectiveness, which makes it very unlikely that with a large sample size in each group, statistically significant between-group differences would have emerged.

Another limitation of the three studies (Emmelkamp et al., 1988; Emmelkamp & Beens, 1991; van Oppen, de Haan, et al., 1995) could be that exposure was self-directed rather than therapist-directed. However, self-controlled exposure has been found to be as effective as therapist-guided exposure (e.g., Emmelkamp, van Linden van den Heuvel, Rüphan, & Sanderman, 1989). Also, improvement on the main outcome measures in these studies is comparable to that found in other studies using therapist-guided exposure (Emmelkamp, 1982). Nevertheless, a study directly comparing cognitive therapy and therapist-guided exposure seems worthwhile.

It is possible that the effects of cognitive therapy on OC behavior are mediated by its effect on depressed mood. Cognitive therapy in all three studies resulted in improvement of depressed mood. Whether improvement of depressed mood enabled patients to resist their compulsive urges is a question for further study.

Further studies are needed to examine which type cognitive therapy is helpful for which OCD patients and for which type of patients treatment can better focus on deemphasizing the thoughts and reducing the attention paid to it. Further, there is a clear need to establish the long-term effects of cognitive therapy with OCD patients.

Although we found some evidence that cognitive therapy resulted in changes in irrational beliefs as assessed with the Irrational Beliefs Test (IBT; Jones, 1968) and the IBI (Koopmans et al., 1994), it is questionable whether a change in irrational beliefs alone would be sufficient for patients with OCD to stop their rituals. As a result of their rational analyses, patients who did improve with cognitive therapy started to expose themselves to distressing situations and attempted not to give in to their compulsive urges, although they were not instructed by the therapist to do so. It is possible that RET operates largely by exerting pressure on patients to not behave irrationally; that is, to engage in exposure rather than OC rituals. In the cognitive therapy of van Oppen and Arntz (1994), behavioral experiments were prescribed with all patients.

Further, it is questionable whether scores on the IBT and IBI reflect irrational beliefs or alternatively reflect mood states. The relative primacy of cognition and affect is an important issue in contemporary cognitive theories on emotional disorders. Changes on irrational belief question-naires may represent epiphenomena of changes in mood states rather than changes in deeper cognitive structures.

The issue has been raised whether it is possible to measure deeper cognitive structures by means of self-report. Kendall (1983), for example, questioned the validity of self-report measures of irrational beliefs to assess treatment outcome: Changes in scores on such questionnaires would not accurately reflect the timing and degree of changes in beliefs.

An area in need of research is the assessment of the cognitive processes of obsessional patients. At the time the outcome studies into cognitive therapy were conducted, only very crude measures were available: the IBT and IBI. However, it is questionable whether such questionnaires are the most appropriate measure to assess the cognitive processes of OCD patients. Themes that are characteristic of the specific thought content of obsessional patients are absent or underrepresented in this questionnaire. Such themes include the beliefs associated with primary and secondary appraisal processes, as previously discussed. Until now, the assessment of specific dysfunctional beliefs of OCD patients are still in the develop-mental stage (Clark & Purdon, 1995; Obsessive Compulsive Cognitions Working Group, 1997). For clinical purposes, other assessment proce-dures, such as thought listing, may be more useful than questionnaires. One could ask patients at various points each day to list the thoughts that have just run through their minds. More adequate assessment of the cognitions of OCD patients may lead to a better understanding of these disorders and more detailed evaluation of the specific effects of treatment on the thought disorders of these patients.

It has been noted in the literature that cognitive therapy may be effec-tive in dealing with obsessions (Emmelkamp, 1987; Rachman, 1993; Sal-kovskis & Warwick, 1985; Salkovskis & Westbrook, 1989). In the van Oppen, de Haan, et al. (1995) study no difference was found in the efficacy of cognitive therapy and exposure in vivo on obsessions on the one hand and compulsions on the other as assessed by the subscale obsessions and compulsions of the Y–BOCS. However, it must be noted that patients with obsessions only were excluded from this study. Obviously, another valuable area of research is the evaluation of the efficacy of cognitive therapy for patients with obsessions only.

One final question should be addressed: Do we need cognitive therapy for OCD patients, given the success of exposure in vivo and response prevention? There are at least three groups of OCD patients in which cognitive therapy may be of value: (a) patients who do not improve with exposure and response prevention; (b) about 30% of the patients who are suitable for behavioral treatment but refuse to participate or are dropouts from exposure and response prevention treatment (Foa et al., 1983); and (c) patients with only obsessions. Until now the treatment of pure obsessions can be summarized as difficult and often unsuccessful. Rachman (1983) argued that this may be due to the cognitive nature of obsessions. For these three groups of OCD patients, cognitive therapy may be an alternative treatment to exposure in vivo with response prevention. Future studies should investigate whether these subgroups of OCD patients are indeed better helped with cognitive therapy than with exposure in vivo and response prevention.

REFERENCES

Arntz, A., van Eck, M., & Heijmans, M. (1990). Predictions of dental pain: The fear of any expected evil is worse than the evil itself. *Behaviour Research and Therapy, 28,* 29–41.

Beck, A. T. (1976). *Cognitive therapy and the emotional disorder.* New York: International Universities Press.

Beck, A. T., Emery, G., & Greenberg, R. L. (1985). *Anxiety disorders and phobias: A cognitive perspective.* New York: Basic Books.

Beck, A. T., Ward, C. H., Mendelson, M., Mock, J. E., & Erbaugh, J. K. (1961). An inventory for measuring depression. *Archives of General Psychiatry, 4,* 561–571.

Butler, G., & Mathews, A. (1983). Cognitive processes in anxiety. *Advances Behaviour Research and Therapy, 5,* 51–62.

Carr, A. T. (1974). Compulsive neuroses: A review of the literature. *Psychological Bulletin, 81,* 311–318.

Clark, D. A., & Purdon, C. L. (1995). The assessment of unwanted intrusive thoughts: A review and critique of the literature. *Behaviour Research and Therapy, 33,* 967–976.

Derogatis, L. R. (1977). *SCL–90: Administration, scoring and procedures manual-I for the revised version.* Baltimore: Johns Hopkins University School of Medicine, Clinical Psychometrics Research Unit.

Edwards, S., & Dickerson, M. (1987). On the similarity of positive and negative intrusions. *Behaviour Research and Therapy, 25,* 207–211.

Ellis, A. (1962). *Reason and emotion in psychotherapy.* New York: Lyle-Stuart.

Emmelkamp, P. M. G. (1982). *Phobic and obsessive-compulsive disorders: Theory, research and practice.* New York: Plenum.

Emmelkamp, P. M. G. (1987). Obsessive-compulsive disorders. In L. Michelson & L. M. Ascher (Eds.), *Anxiety and stress disorders, cognitive behavioral assessment and treatment* (pp. 310–331). New York: Guilford.

Emmelkamp, P. M. G., & Beens, H. (1991). Cognitive therapy with obsessive-compulsive patients: A comparative evaluation. *Behaviour Research and Therapy, 29,* 293–300.

Emmelkamp, P. M. G., Bouman, T. K., & Scholing, A. (1992). *Anxiety disorders: A practitioner's guide.* Chichester, UK: Wiley.

Emmelkamp, P. M. G., Kraaijkamp, M. J. M., & van den Hout, M. A. (in press). The Maudsley Obsessional-Compulsive Inventory: Reliability and validity. *Behavior Modification.*

Emmelkamp, P. M. G., van der Helm, M., van Zanten, B., & Plochg, I. (1980). Contributions of self-instructional training to the effectiveness of exposure in vivo: A comparison with obsessive-compulsive patients. *Behaviour Research and Therapy, 18,* 61–66.

Emmelkamp, P. M. G., van Linden van den Heuvell, G., Rüphan, M., & Sanderman, R. (1989). Home-based treatment of obsessive-compulsive patients: Intersession interval and therapist involvement. *Behaviour Research and Therapy, 27,* 89–93.

Emmelkamp, P. M. G., Visser, S., & Hoekstra, R. J. (1988). Cognitive therapy vs exposure in vivo in the treatment of obsessive-compulsives. *Cognitive Therapy and Research, 12,* 103–144.

Foa, E. B., Ilai, D., McCarthy, P. R., Shoyer, B., & Murdock, T. (1993). Information processing in obsessive-compulsive disorder. *Cognitive Therapy and Research, 17,* 173–189.

Foa, E. B., & McNally, R. J. (1986). Sensitivity to feared stimuli in obsessive-compulsives: A dichotic listening analysis. *Cognitive Therapy and Research, 10,* 477–485.

Foa, E. B., Grayson, J. B., Steketee, G., Doppelt, H. G., Turner, R. M., & Latimer, P. R. (1983). Success and failure in the behavioral treatment of obsessive-compulsives. *Journal of Consulting and Clinical Psychology, 51,* 287–297.

Goodman, W. K., Price, L. H., Rasmussen, S. A., Mazure, C., Delgado, P., Heninger, G. R., & Charney, D. S. (1989). The Yale–Brown Obsessive Compulsive Scale: II. Validity. *Archives of General Psychiatry, 46,* 1012–1016.

Goodman, W. K., Price, L. H., Rasmussen, S. A., Mazure, C., Fleischmann, R., Hill, C. L., Henninger, G. R., & Charney, D. S. (1989). The Yale–Brown Obsessive Compulsive Scale: I. Development, use, and reliability. *Archives of General Psychiatry, 46,* 1006–1011.

Hollon, S. D., & Beck, A. T. (1994). Cognitive and cognitive behavioral therapies. In A. E. Bergin & S. L. Garfield (Eds.), *Handbook of psychotherapy and behaviour change* (4th ed., pp. 428–466). New York: Wiley.

Jones, R. (1968). *A factored measure of Ellis' irrational beliefs system with personality and maladjustment correlated.* Unpublished doctoral dissertation, Texas Technological University, Austin.

Kasvikis, Y., & Marks, I. M. (1988). Clomipramine, self-exposure, and therapist-accompanied exposure in obsessive-compulsive ritualizers: Two-year follow-up. *Journal of Anxiety Disorders, 2,* 291–298.

Kendall, P. C. (1983). Methodology and cognitive-behavioral assessment. *Behavioral Psychotherapy, 11,* 285–301.

Koopmans, P. C., Sanderman, R., Timmerman, I., & Emmelkamp, P. M. G. (1994). The Irrational Beliefs Inventory: Development and psychometric evaluation. *European Journal of Psychological Assessment, 10,* 15–27.

Lavy, E., van Oppen, P., & van den Hout, M. A. (1994). Selective processing of emotional information in obsessive compulsive disorder. *Behaviour Research and Therapy, 32,* 243–246.

Lopatka, C., & Rachman, S. (1995). Perceived responsibility and compulsive checking: An experimental analysis. *Behaviour Research and Therapy, 33,* 673–684.

Marks, I. M. (1987). *Fears, phobias and rituals: Panic, anxiety and their disorders.* New York: Oxford University Press.

Marshall, W. L., & Segal, Z. V. (1990). Drugs combined with behavioral psychotherapy. In A. S. Bellack, M. Hersen, & A. E. Kazdin (Eds.), *International handbook of behavior modification and therapy* (pp. 267–279). New York: Plenum.

Mawson, D., Marks, I. M., & Ramm, E. (1982). Clomipramine and exposure for chronic OC rituals: III. Two year follow-up. *British Journal of Psychiatry, 140*, 11–18.

McFall, M. E., & Wollersheim, J. P. (1979). Obsessive-compulsive neurosis: A cognitive-behavioral formulation and approach to treatment. *Cognitive Therapy and Research, 3*, 333–348.

Meichenbaum, D. H. (1975). Self-instructional methods. In F. H. Kanver & A. P. Goldstein (Eds.), *Helping people change* (pp. 242–265). New York: Pergamon.

Obsessive Compulsive Cognitions Working Group. (1997). Cognitive assessment of obsessive compulsive disorder. *Behaviour Research and Therapy, 35*, 667–681.

Rachman, S. (1983). Obstacles to the successful treatment of obsessions. In E. B. Foa & P. M. G. Emmelkamp (Eds.), *Failures in behavior therapy* (pp. 35–57). New York: Wiley.

Rachman, S. (1993). Obsessions, responsibility and guilt. *Behaviour Research and Therapy, 31*, 149–154.

Rachman, S., & Hodgson, R. J. (1980). *Obsessions and compulsions.* Englewood Cliffs, NJ: Prentice-Hall.

Rachman, S., Shafran, R., Mitchell, D., Trant, J., & Teachman, B. (1996). How to remain neutral: An experimental analysis of neutralization. *Behaviour Research and Therapy, 35*, 889–898.

Reed, G. F. (1985). *Obsessional experience and compulsive behavior: A cognitive structural approach.* Orlando, FL: Academic Press.

Röper, G., & Rachman, S. (1976). Obsessional compulsive checking: Experimental replication and development. *Behaviour Research and Therapy, 14*, 23–32.

Röper, G., Rachman, S., & Hodgson, R. (1973). An experiment on obsessional checking. *Behaviour Research and Therapy, 11*, 271–277.

Rosen, M. (1975). A dual model of obsessional neurosis. *Journal of Consulting and Clinical Psychology, 43*, 453–459.

Salkovskis, P. M. (1985). Obsessional-compulsive problems: A cognitive-behavioral analysis. *Behaviour Research and Therapy, 23*, 571–583.

Salkovskis, P. M. (1989). Cognitive-behavioural factors and the persistence of intrusive thoughts in obsessional problems. *Behaviour Research and Therapy, 27*, 677–682.

Salkovskis, P. M., & Warwick, H. M. C. (1985). Cognitive therapy of obsessive-compulsive disorder: Treating treatment failures. *Behavioral Psychotherapy, 13*, 243–255.

Salkovskis, P. M., & Westbrook, D. (1989). Behaviour therapy and obsessional ruminations: Can failure be turned into success? *Behaviour Research and Therapy, 27*, 149–160.

Sanavio, E. (1988). Obsessions and compulsions: The Padua Inventory. *Behaviour Research and Therapy, 26*, 167–177.

Steiner, J. (1972). A questionnaire study of risk-taking in psychiatric patients. *British Journal of Medical Psychology, 45*, 365–374.

Steketee, G. S. (1993). *Treatment of obsessive-compulsive disorder.* New York: Guilford.

van Balkom, A. J. L. M., de Haan, E., van Oppen, P., Spinhoven, P., Hoogduin, C. A. L., & van Dyck, R. (1998). Fluvoxamine versus cognitive-behavior therapy in obsessive compulsive disorder. *Journal of Nervous and Mental Disease, 186*, 492–499.

van Balkom, A. J. L. M., van Oppen, P., Vermeulen, A. W. A., Nauta, M. M. C., Vorst, H. C. M., & van Dyck, R. (1994). A meta-analysis on the treatment of obsessive compulsive disorder: A comparison of antidepressants, behaviour and cognitive therapy. *Clinical Psychology Review, 14*, 359–381.

van Hout, W. J. P. J., & Emmelkamp, P. M. G. (1994). Overprediction of fear in panic disorder patients with agoraphobia: Does the (mis)match model generalize to exposure in vivo therapy? *Behaviour Research and Therapy, 32*, 723–734.

van Oppen, P., & Arntz, A. (1994). Cognitive therapy for obsessive compulsive disorder. *Behaviour Research and Therapy, 32*, 79–87.

van Oppen, P., de Haan, E., van Balkom, A. J. L. M., Spinhoven, P., Hoogduin, C. A. L., & van Dyck, R. (1995). Cognitive therapy and exposure in vivo in the treatment of obsessive compulsive disorder. *Behaviour Research and Therapy, 33,* 379–390.

van Oppen, P., Emmelkamp, P. M. G., van Balkom, A. J. L. M., & van Dyck, R. (1995). The sensitivity to change of measures for obsessive compulsive disorder. *Journal of Anxiety Disorders, 9,* 241–248.

van Oppen, P., Hoekstra, R. J., & Emmelkamp, P. M. G. (1995). The structure of obsessive compulsive symptoms. *Behaviour Research and Therapy, 33,* 15–23.

Visser, S., Hoekstra, R. J., & Emmelkamp, P. M. G. (1990). Follow-up study on behavioral treatment of obsessive-compulsive disorders. In A. Ehlers, W. Fiegenbaum, I. Florin, & J. Margraf (Eds.), *Perspectives and promises of clinical psychology* (pp. 157–170). New York: Plenum.

Williams, J. M. G., Watts, F. N., MacLeod, C., & Mathews, A. (1988). *Cognitive psychology and emotional disorders.* Chichester, UK: Wiley.

Zung, W. W. K. (1965). A self rating depression scale. *Archives of General Psychiatry, 12,* 63–70.

Investigating Cortico-Striatal Pathophysiology in Obsessive-Compulsive Disorders: Procedural Learning and Imaging Probes

Scott L. Rauch
Cary R. Savage
Massachusetts General Hospital and Harvard Medical School

Obsessive-compulsive disorder (OCD) is a common condition afflicting up to 1% to 3% of the population worldwide (Rasmussen & Eisen, 1994). Its hallmark signs and symptoms include repetitive cognitive intrusions (i.e., obsessions) and repetitive behaviors (i.e., compulsions), as well as affective accompaniments (i.e., anxiety; American Psychiatric Association, 1994). Although the current diagnostic scheme classifies OCD as an anxiety disorder, many investigators are inclined to focus on a so-called OC spectrum of disorders that share the commonality of repetitive symptoms (Hollander, 1993; McElroy, Phillips, & Keck, 1994). A medical model dictates that the classification of psychiatric disorders should reflect their respective underlying pathophysiologies. Unfortunately, contemporary psychiatric neuroscience data cannot yet fully support such an approach. OCDs are no exception in this regard, as the neural mechanisms underlying OCDs remain incompletely understood. Delineating pathophysiology represents a critical step toward improving diagnosis and treatment of psychiatric disease. Toward that end, there is great value in developing testable hypotheses regarding the pathophysiology of psychiatric diseases and proceeding to test them.

In this chapter, we review evolving models regarding the pathophysiology of OCD and purportedly related disorders. Moreover, we introduce strategies for testing these hypotheses that entail neuropsychological and brain imaging methods. In conjunction with the proposed experimental strategy, a heuristic explanation of OCDs as disorders of procedural learning is offered.

THE CORTICO-STRIATO-THALAMO-CORTICAL (CSTC) LOOP MODEL OF OCD

The historical evolution of neurocircuitry-based models of OCD can be traced through the literature. Many different investigators and theoreticians contributed to the process whereby the CSTC loop became implicated in the pathophysiology of OCD (Baxter, Schwartz, Guze, Bergman, & Szuba, 1990; Baxter, Schwartz, Bergman, et al., 1992; Insel, 1992; Modell, Mountz, Curtis, & Greden, 1989; Rapoport & Wise, 1988; Rauch & Jenike, 1993, 1997). Briefly, this model suggests that the mutually excitatory communication between frontal cortex and thalamus can reverberate out of control if unchecked by the negative feedback collateral projections from cortex via striatum to the corresponding thalamic territory. By this model, reentrant frontal hyperactivity represents the neural substrate for the repetitive cognitive intrusions of OCD.

THE STRIATAL TOPOGRAPHY HYPOTHESIS AND OCDs

By 1990, it was established that OCD and Tourette's syndrome (TS) might be linked genetically or pathophysiologically (Pauls et al., 1995; Pauls & Leckman, 1986; Pauls et al., 1990; Pauls, Towbin, Leckman, Zahner, & Cohen, 1986). To our knowledge, however, Baxter et al. (1990) were the first to clearly articulate a neuroanatomy-based explanation for how OCD and TS might be related pathophysiologically. Specifically, they proposed that OCD and TS both resulted from striatal dysfunction. Moreover, they suggested that the clinical spectrum associated with OCD and TS reflected the topographic distribution of pathology within the striatum. To elaborate, whereas caudate and accumbens involvement were hypothesized to mediate OCD symptoms, putamen involvement was hypothesized to mediate tics. By extension, intermediate distributions of striatal dysfunction could explain the full spectrum of different OCD and TS signs and symptoms. This conceptualization benefitted from contemporaneous basic neuroscience advances in the understanding of cortico-striatal organization (Alexander, Crutcher, & DeLong, 1990; Alexander, DeLong, & Strick, 1986).

A more thorough review of cortico-striatal systems is necessary to fully appreciate the intricacies of the striatal topography model. Alexander and colleagues (Alexander, 1994; Alexander et al., 1990; Alexander et al., 1986) published a series of reviews that describe anatomically and functionally segregated basal ganglia–thalamocortical circuits. Alexander et al. (1986) outlined four separate pathways, identified as motor, oculomotor, prefrontal, and limbic, each consisting of unique cortical, striatal, and thalamic territories of innervation. In each case, projections are topographically organized, and pass from cortex to striatum, and then through parallel pathways via the globus pallidus to thalamic nuclei, from which feedback projections close the circuit by returning to the cortical territories of origin (Albin, Young, & Penney, 1989; Alexander et al., 1990).

For the purposes of this chapter, we initially focus on the cortical and striatal components of the relevant circuits and the functions that each is purported to mediate. The motor circuit entails projections from motor and somatosensory cortex as well as the supplementary motor area to the putamen, mediating motor movements, preparation for motor movements, and somatosensory capacities. The prefrontal circuit entails projections from dorsolateral prefrontal and lateral orbitofrontal cortex to the head of the caudate, mediating behavioral and cognitive abilities including spatial memory, maintaining or switching set, and behavioral inhibition (see Fig. 8.1). The limbic circuit entails projections from medial orbitofron-

MOTOR SYSTEM

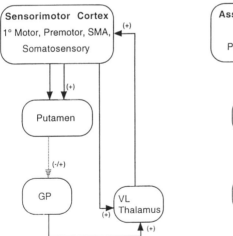

PREFRONTAL SYSTEM

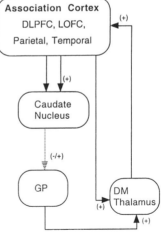

FIG. 8.1. Schematic diagram illustrating the parallel organization of motor and prefrontal cortico-striatal systems, after data from Alexander et al. (1990). Abbreviations: SMA = supplementary motor area; GP = globus pallidus; VL = ventrolateral nucleus; DLPFC = dorsolateral prefrontal cortex; LOFC = lateral orbitofrontal cortex; DM = dorsomedial nucleus; + = excitatory influence; – = inhibitory influence.

tal cortex and anterior cingulate cortex to the nucleus accumbens and related structures, together termed the ventral or limbic striatum, mediating emotional and motivational functions. It is noteworthy that although Alexander et al. made the prefrontal versus limbic distinction within orbitofrontal cortex along lateral versus medial lines (Alexander et al., 1990; Alexander et al., 1986), Mesulam and others (see Mesulam, 1985) subdivide the orbitofrontal cortex into posterior (limbic) and anterior (prefrontal) portions. Zald and Kim (1996) recently published a scholarly review that helps to clarify the complexity of the orbitofrontal cortex and its functional subdivisions.

With this knowledge of neuroanatomy in mind, the striatal topography model of OCDs can be elaborated. For the model to serve an explanatory function, it must resonate with the phenomenology observed in the clinical setting. For the model to be accepted as neurobiologically sound, it must not only be consistent with this neuroanatomy, but also find empirical support from neuroscientific investigations of pathophysiology.

PHENOMENOLOGY AND FACE VALIDITY

As noted, OCD is fundamentally a disorder of cognitive intrusions, with accompanying anxiety and repetitive behaviors. Although the tics of TS were formerly viewed as spontaneous motor events, recent observations have clarified that tics are typically preceded by premonitory symptoms (Leckman, Walker, & Cohen, 1993; Miguel, Coffey, et al., 1995). In this way, the cognitive intrusions that precede compulsions may be viewed as analogous and parallel to sensory intrusions that precede the motor and vocal repetitive behaviors classified as tics. In fact, although the distinction between tics and compulsions is usually straightforward, there are some repetitive movements for which classification is more difficult. For instance, behaviors such as rubbing, tapping, and touching can be classified as either compulsions or complex tics.

Recently, Miguel, Coffey, et al. (1995) proposed that intentional repetitive behaviors (i.e., compulsions and tics) be classified based on their accompaniments of cognitions, sensations, or anxiety symptoms. As predicted, patients with TS primarily reported sensory intrusions, with rare cognitions or anxiety symptoms associated with their repetitive behaviors, whereas patients with OCD reported frequent cognitions and anxiety symptoms but rare sensory phenomena (Miguel, Coffey, et al., 1995). It is appealing to note that each of these dimensions was conceived as corresponding to one of the parallel cortico-striatal circuits outlined earlier. That is, cognitive intrusions can be conceptualized as being mediated by the prefrontal circuit via the caudate; somatosensory phenomena (as well as spontaneous tics) can be conceptualized as being mediated by the motor and somatosensory circuit via the putamen; and, affective symptoms, such as anxiety, might be mediated by the limbic circuit via the ventral striatum (i.e., nucleus accumbens).

Analogous phenomenologic and comorbidity data have yet to be formally presented regarding other OCDs; however, such studies are ongoing in conjunction with the Massachusetts General Hospital Obsessive Compulsive Disorders Unit. For example, the phenomenology of trichotillomania is, anecdotally, characterized by compulsive hair pulling in response to sensory phenomena rather than cognitions (R. L. O'Sullivan, personal communication, 1995). In keeping with the model, pilot comorbidity studies suggest that trichotillomania may be more closely associated with TS than with OCD (O'Sullivan et al., 1997). In contrast, clinical features of body dysmorphic disorder include prominent cognitive and affective components, arguably more akin to OCD, or perhaps most reminiscent of major depression rather than OCDs at all (Phillips, McElroy, Hudson, & Pope, 1995). Extending this scheme to other purported OCDs is one excellent way to expand and test the model empirically.

STRUCTURAL IMAGING FINDINGS

Several early structural imaging studies of OCD yielded positive findings, but somewhat inconsistent results. Investigations employing computed tomographic methods revealed increased ventricular:brain ratios or decreased caudate size (Behar et al., 1984; Luxenberg et al., 1988) and an initial magnetic resonance imaging (MRI) study measuring caudate cross-sectional area (rather than volume) found no significant difference between patients with OCD and controls (Kellner et al., 1991). Modern volumetric MRI studies of OCD have yielded convergent findings with respect to the presence of abnormalities within the caudate (Jenike et al., 1996; Robinson et al., 1995; Scarone et al., 1992; see Table 8.1). Imperfect replication as to the laterality of findings and the direction of change might be a result of differences in technique or study population. For instance, the gender breakdown differed between studies, and the protocol for segmenting the caudate with respect to its ventromedial boundary, which interfaces with the ventral striatum, is not uniform across research teams. It is also possible, however, that the apparent subtle differences in findings reflect uncertainties about the optimal parameters to be compared. For instance, it could be that the laterality quotient (i.e., a ratio of left to right caudate volume) is a more salient factor in identifying the neural substrate of OCDs than absolute volumes per se (see Jenike et al., 1996; Peterson et al., 1993; Singer et al., 1993). Nonetheless, extant struc-

TABLE 8.1
Striatal Findings in Recent Volumetric MRI
Studies of OCD and Related Disorders

Study	Groups Compared	Striatal Findings
Scarone et al. (1992)	OCD vs. normal controls	Increased caudate (R)
Robinson et al. (1995)	OCD vs. normal controls	Decreased caudate (B)
Jenike et al. (1996)	OCD vs. normal controls	Decreased or reversed caudate laterality (toward R > L)
Peterson et al. (1993)	TS vs. normal controls	Decreased lenticulate (L); Decreased or reversed lenticulate laterality (toward R > L)
Singer et al. (1993)	TS vs. normal controls	Decreased or reversed putamen and lenticulate laterality (toward R > L)
O'Sullivan et al. (1997)	TTM vs. normal controls	Decreased lenticulate (L), putamen (L)

Note. MRI = magnetic resonance imaging; OCD = obsessive-compulsive disorder; TS = Tourette's syndrome; TTM = trichotillomania; R = right; L = left; B = bilateral.

tural imaging data clearly converge to suggest some structural abnormality involving the caudate nucleus in OCD.

It is impressive that analogous findings have been observed and replicated in studies of TS (Peterson et al., 1993; Singer et al., 1993; Witelson, 1993). Specifically, patients with TS appear to exhibit some structural abnormality localized to the putamen or lenticulate (the term *lenticulate* refers to the putamen plus the globus pallidus) that is reliably characterized as a reduction or reversal of the left greater than right asymmetry found in normal controls. Furthermore, in light of the clinical characteristics of trichotillomania, it is striking that one preliminary study has detected reductions in left putamen and lenticulate volumes in trichotillomania versus controls, very closely paralleling the previously mentioned findings in TS (O'Sullivan et al., 1997).

Taken together, these structural findings represent the strongest support for the striatal topography model of OCDs. Caudate abnormalities in OCD and putamen or lenticulate differences in TS and trichotillomania precisely correspond to the features of clinical presentation and the prevailing understanding of normal cortico-striatal functions involving these territories. Still, the functional consequences, etiogenesis, and specificity of these anatomical findings remain to be established. With respect to specificity, it should be noted that studies of both OCD and TS have found widespread abnormalities in white matter volumes (Breiter et al., 1994; Jenike et al., 1996; Peterson, Leckman, & Duncan, 1994), and that volumetric studies of other psychiatric disorders, such as attention deficit hyperactivity disorder, have found regional abnormalities in the striatum as well (e.g., Castellanos et al., 1994; Hynd et al., 1993).

FUNCTIONAL IMAGING FINDINGS

Over the past decade numerous functional imaging studies of OCD and TS have been conducted (for reviews, see Hoehn-Saric & Benkelfat, 1995; Insel, 1992). In the current review, we focus on studies employing the high-resolution technique of positron emission tomography (PET), and limit our discussion to studies with eight or more participants, employing methodologies that account for issues of medication effects and comorbidities. With these constraints, relevant studies to date can be categorized into three types of paradigms: (a) neutral state, (b) pre- and posttreatment, and (c) symptom provocation (see Table 8.2). Taken together, PET studies of OCD converge to implicate orbitofrontal cortex, caudate nucleus, and thalamus, as well as anterior cingulate cortex, in the pathophysiology of OCD.

Whereas neutral state paradigms have been consistently sensitive to orbitofrontal hyperactivity, only treatment and symptom provocation

TABLE 8.2
Findings in Recent PET Studies of OCD

	Neutral State Paradigms (FDG)	
Study	*Groups Compared*	*Normalized Glucose Metabolic Findings*
Baxter et al. (1988)	OCD vs. controls	Increased OFC (B)
Nordahl et al. (1989)	OCD vs. controls	Increased OFC (B)
Swedo et al. (1989)	OCD vs. controls	Increased OFC (R), anterior cingulate (L)

	Pre & Post-Treatment Paradigms (FDG)	
Study	*Treatment*	*Findings Associated With Successful Treatment*
Benkelfat et al. (1990)	Clomipramine	Decreased activity in caudate (L), OFC (R)
Baxter et al. (1992)	Fluoxetine	Decreased activity in caudate (R), cingulate (R), thalamus (L)
	Behavioral therapy	Decreased activity in caudate (R)
Swedo et al. (1992)	Clomipramine or fluoxetine	Decreased activity in OFC (B)
Perani et al. (1995)	Clomipramine or fluoxetine or fluvoxamine	Decreased activity in cingulate (B)

	Symptom Provocation Paradigm (^{15}O)
Study	*Findings Associated With the Symptomatic State*
Rauch et al. (1994)	Increased activity in caudate (R), OFC (B), anterior cingulate (L), thalamus (L)

Note. PET = positron emission tomography; OCD = obsessive-compulsive disorder; FDG = fluorodeoxyglucose; OFC = orbitofrontal cortex; R = right; L = left; B = bilateral; ^{15}O = oxygen-15.

studies have implicated caudate involvement. Imperfect replications in this regard could be attributed to differences in methods or study populations. Given the sample sizes and techniques employed, Type II error at the observed rate is plausible. This may also explain why single photon emission computed tomography (SPECT) studies of OCD have likewise often found medial frontal hyperactivity, but failed to detect differences in the striatum (see Harris, Hoehn-Saric, Lewis, Pearlson, & Streeter, 1994). Most SPECT studies of OCD have been of the neutral state variety, and SPECT is likely less sensitive for detecting activation in small subcortical structures.

Current OCD PET data do not paint a clear picture with regard to laterality, although right-sided orbitofrontal and caudate involvement predominate. There are several plausible explanations, both for the inconsistency and the tendency toward right-sided findings. First, the inconsistency could be a consequence of Type II error. In the case of small structures, such as the head of the caudate (i.e., about 1–2 cc), whose volume approaches the PET methods' limits of resolution (about 6–12 mm in these studies), structural volume can influence the magnitude of signal, and hence the statistical power for detecting differences. This point may be particularly germane given the shift in volumetric findings toward the right in OCD, and it may explain greater protection against Type II error with respect to the right caudate versus the left. Second, such differences between studies could be an artifact of the laterality of attentional bias introduced by the experimental conditions. To elaborate, the PET-fluorodeoxyglucose studies performed at the University of California at Los Angeles and National Institute of Mental Health have generally produced lateralized findings contralateral to the side of vascular access (L. R. Baxter, personal communication, 1993); similarly, Rauch and colleagues' (1994) symptom provocation study yielded right caudate activation in the context of left-sided provocative stimulus presentation. Third, it may be that the pathophysiology of OCD preferentially involves the right hemisphere.

Stoetter et al. (1992) employed a PET neutral state paradigm and a sophisticated correlational data analytic approach to study TS. They found a reversed correlation between sensorimotor cortex and ventral striatum in TS versus controls.

Therefore, the functional neuroimaging data for OCD and TS provide strong support for the striatal topography model of OCDs. Together with structural imaging data these findings give weight to a clear topographic dichotomy: OCD is associated with paralimbic, prefrontal, and caudate abnormalities, whereas TS is associated with sensorimotor cortical and putamen abnormalities.

The role of the limbic striatum in these disorders is less obvious. Whereas Baxter et al. (1990) cast the accumbens squarely within an obsession-mediating role, the limbic quality of urges preceding tics, and Stoetter et al.'s (1992) findings suggestive of ventral striatal involvement in TS raise questions about this aspect of the model. Similarly, although Miguel, Coffey, et al. (1995) conceptualized the anxiety symptoms of OCD as a product of the limbic cortico-striatal pathway, and the urges of TS as a manifestation of the sensorimotor pathway, an alternative perspective might frame both anxiety and urges as limbic equivalents. Moreover, it could be that the very same limbic signal translates into anxiety or urges depending on its expression through cognitive or sensorimotor channels in concert with corresponding paralimbic cortical zones. Thus, in addition to the proposed dichotomy in striatal topography, there may also be considerable topographic overlap in ventral striatum between various OCDs.

EXPERIMENTAL STRATEGIES FOR PROBING CORTICO-STRIATAL FUNCTIONAL INTEGRITY

New experimental strategies are needed to directly test cortico-striatal based models of OCDs. The hypothesized normal functional anatomy of cortico-striatal systems can be studied directly in human participants, using PET activation paradigms designed to selectively activate each circuit. Furthermore, specific hypotheses pertaining to cortico-striatal pathophysiology in model disorders, such as TS, OCD, and trichotillomania, can be tested empirically by studying the performance of individuals on cognitive-behavioral tasks as well as individuals' PET activation profiles while performing the tasks online.

In the case of OCD, anterior cingulate cortex, orbitofrontal cortex, and the caudate have been implicated in the pathophysiology of the disorder; for TS, motor and somatosensory cortex along with putamen and ventral striatum have been implicated. Therefore, the prefrontal, motor, and limbic circuits should all be systematically explored. To develop selective cognitive-behavioral probes for these cortico-striatal systems, we must next consider what functions each mediates, and what types of tasks might selectively recruit them.

STRIATAL FUNCTION AND PROCEDURAL LEARNING

The basal ganglia have been implicated in the pathophysiology of a broad range of neuropsychiatric disorders, including Huntington's disease, Parkinson's disease, schizophrenia, and major depression, as well as OCDs. Moreover, a wealth of normal sensorimotor, cognitive, behavioral, and affective functions are mediated via cortico-striatal pathways. Much of the current understanding of cortico-striatal anatomy and physiology, however, has been inferred from nonhuman data (see Alexander et al., 1986, for review).

Popular theories suggest that brain systems involving the striatum mediate habitual behaviors (Mishkin, Malamut, & Bachevalier, 1984; Mishkin & Petri, 1984), as well as sequential, overlearned, or automatic behaviors (see Roland, 1993). A burgeoning literature supports the notion that the striatum allows organisms to recognize patterns of stimuli and associations, corresponding to unique patterns of activity in cortico-striatal projections, and facilitate behavior that has historically resulted in reward or inhibit behavior that has historically resulted in nonreward or aversive outcomes (Houk, Davis, & Beiser, 1995). In fact, neuroanatomically and physiologically, cortico-striatal systems, and specifically the type of information processing that occurs at the level of spiny neurons within striatum, are ideally suited for certain types of learning (Houk et al., 1995). Neuropsychological studies with clinical populations as well as imaging studies in normal point to the role of the striatum in a particular nonconscious form of learning called *procedural learning*. Therefore, candidate probes of cortico-striatal functional integrity include tasks that entail procedural learning.

Contemporary learning theory acknowledges the existence of different kinds of memory and dissociable neuranatomic substrates of different learning and memory functions (see Squire, 1986, for review). Procedural learning, also called *skill learning*, refers to a subtype of implicit learning, characterized by nonconscious acquisition of skills as a consequence of practice. In contrast, *explicit* (also called declarative) *learning* or memory is associated with the conscious retrieval of information. Explicit memory is believed to be mediated via prefrontal cortex and medial temporal structures, including the hippocampus. Procedural memory is purportedly mediated via cortico-striatal circuits. Compelling evidence for the distinct functional neuroanatomy underlying these two types of memory comes both from animal studies (Packard, Hirsch, & White, 1989) and studies of humans with known distributions of brain dysfunction (e.g., Martone, Butters, & Payne, 1984). *Double dissociation* refers to the fact that individuals with hippocampal lesions exhibit impaired explicit memory and preserved procedural memory, whereas individuals with striatal lesions (e.g., early Huntington's disease) exhibit preserved explicit memory, but impaired procedural memory.

A range of tasks have been developed that assess procedural learning capacities, each validated, in part, via the demonstration of double dissociation. Procedural learning tasks can be conceptualized along a motor to cognitive continuum (Saint-Cyr & Taylor, 1992). Tasks such as rotary pursuit (Heindel, Butters, & Salmon, 1988; Heindel, Salmon, Shults, Walicke, & Butters, 1989) are largely dependent on primary sensorimotor systems, whereas tasks such as mirror reading (Martone et al., 1984) and the Tower of Toronto (Saint-Cyr, Taylor, & Lang, 1988) are largely dependent on visuospatial and cognitive capacities. The models of cortico-striatal functional anatomy proposed by Alexander et al. (1990), cited earlier, would predict that the prefrontal basal ganglia–thalamocortical circuit via the caudate would mediate cognitive procedural learning, whereas the motor basal ganglia–thalamocortical pathway via the putamen would mediate motor procedural learning. Combined motor and visuosptial tasks, such as Nissen and Bullemer's (1987) serial reaction time task (SRT; Knopman & Nissen, 1991) may be intermediate within, or span, this proposed continuum of cognitive-motor procedural learning.

Grafton et al. (1992) were the first to study procedural learning with PET. They utilized a pursuit rotor paradigm, and demonstrated changes in regional cerebral activity in motor and supplementary motor cortex, as well as lesser activation of the putamen associated with early motor procedural learning. Subsequently, several teams of investigators have shown striatal activation with other procedural learning paradigms (Doyon, Owen, Petrides, Sziklas, & Evans, 1996; Grafton, Hazeltine, & Ivry, 1995; Krebs et al., 1996; Rauch, Savage, Brown, et al., 1995). Interestingly, several research groups have also observed that these procedural learning tasks seem to activate prefrontal cortex and a ventral territory within striatum, preferentially on the right side (Doyon et al., 1996; Krebs et al., 1996; Rauch, Savage, Brown, et al., 1995). It is intriguing to consider that this may represent an ideal probe for studying OCDs, given its activation of striatum and apparent right-sided lateralization.

We are currently conducting PET and functional MRI (Rauch, Whalen, et al., 1997) studies employing the SRT and other procedural learning paradigms in hopes of developing sensitive probes of cortico-striatal functional integrity. As previously noted, such tasks have already been validated in normal control cohorts. Studies of patients with OCD and patients with TS along with well-matched controls are now underway (see Rauch, Savage, et al., 1997). Such an approach has the distinct advantage of utilizing a standardized, well-controlled series of task conditions that can be applied across the full spectrum of OCDs. This strategy will allow investigators to compare and contrast the behavioral and imaging profiles from across the different study populations.

UPDATING NEUROBIOLOGICAL MODELS OF CORTICO-STRIATAL CIRCUITRY AND OCDS

The Direct and Indirect Pathways

In the initial rendition of the striatal topography model, the striato-pal-lido-thalamic route of transmission was treated as a unitary entity (Baxter et al., 1990). Other neuroscientists had already developed more detailed models of cortico-striatal functional anatomy and chemistry that reflected the presence of dual pathways within each cortico-striatal circuit (Albin et al., 1989; Alexander et al., 1990): the direct cortico-pallido-thalamic pathway (via the globus pallidus interna) and an indirect pathway (via the globus pallidus externa). This point is critical in that these two pathways, present in each of the parallel cortico-striatal circuits previously described, provide opposing and presumably balanced influences on the thalamic target nuclei (see Fig. 8.2). Therefore, the proposed hyperactivity of the cortico-striato-thalamo-frontal loop central to models of TS and OCD pathophysiology (Baxter et al., 1992; Baxter et al., 1990; Leckman et al., 1992) could be a consequence of imbalance between the direct and indirect pathways in one or more corresponding cortico-striatal circuits (Rauch & Jenike, 1997; Rauch & Savage, 1994).

Of further interest is the observation that although neurotransmission along the direct and indirect pathways is mediated by many of the same neurotransmitters, the neuropeptide transmitter substance P is prominent only in the direct pathway, whereas enkephalin is prominent only in the

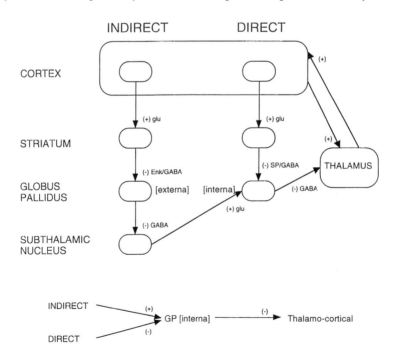

FIG. 8.2. Schematic diagram illustrating the pathways and neurotransmitters of the direct and indirect cortico-striatal pathways, after data from Albin et al. (1989) and Rauch and Jenike (1997). Abbreviations: glu = glutamate; Enk = enkaphalin; SP = substance P; + = excitatory influence; − = inhibitory influence.

indirect pathway. Moreover, dopamine is hypothesized to play a fundamental role in modulating the balance between the two systems. This neurochemical information is critical in that it points to some as yet unexploited possibilities for developing new and specific treatments for OCDs. For instance, these models suggest that a substance P antagonist might be an effective treatment for OCDs (Rauch & Jenike, 1997).

The Patch-Matrix Compartmental Organization of the Striatum

Yet another level of complexity in cortico-striatal functional anatomy must be considered. Whereas a literal application of the topographic model assigns the limbic role to ventral striatum, this is not necessarily the source of urges and anxiety symptoms in OCDs. The striatal domain of each parallel circuit is characterized by different regional subdivisions based on subtle aspects of neurochemistry as well as the targets of their descending efferent projections. These regions are termed *striosomes* (or patches) and *matrisomes* (or matrix; see Gerfen, 1992; Graybiel, 1990; Graybiel & Kimura, 1995; Houk et al., 1995). The spiny neurons within striosomes project to the dopamine-containing neurons of the ventral tegmental area and substantia nigra pars compacta, the ascending projections of which in turn are thought to play a critical role in reward. Moreover, even in striatal territories that receive predominantly prefrontal or motor inputs (i.e., the caudate and putamen, respectively), there are descending projections from paralimbic cortex to these striosomes. Consequently, within each parallel, segregated, cortico-striatal circuit, there is a striosomal compartment that serves as an embedded limbic component (see Fig. 8.3). Thus, it is conceivable that pathology within the caudate or putamen alone could produce both segregated cortico-striatal-circuit-specific and limbic symptoms. This elaboration serves as one example of how, as our understanding of brain mechanisms becomes more sophisticated, our models can evolve.

THE HEURISTIC OF OCDS AS DISORDERS OF PROCEDURAL LEARNING

One of the challenges in constructing a model of OCD is to account for the broad range of different symptoms characterizing the disease. How could a unitary brain lesion cause intrusive thoughts of sex or violence, doubting and checking, counting, repeating, organizing and ordering, or washing and cleaning in response to fears of contamination? How could premonitory somatosensory symptoms and tics result from some related

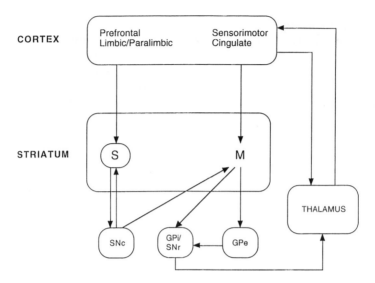

FIG. 8.3. Schematic diagram illustrating cortico-striatal pathways projecting through striosome and matrix compartments in the striatum, after data
from Graybiel (1990). Abbreviations: S = striosome; M = matrix; SNc =
substantia nigra, pars compacta; SNr = substantia nigra, pars reticulata;
GPi = globus pallidus, interna; GPe = globus pallidus, externa.

lesion? We propose that the varied clinical manifestations of OCD, as well
as the spectrum of OCDs, could reflect a fundamental impairment in the
neural mechanisms that underlie procedural learning. Although we readily acknowledge the speculative nature of this model, an elaboration of
the concept follows. In addition, we are hopeful that empirical data from
relevant ongoing studies will be forthcoming.

We suggest that in the normal condition, the priority or importance
assigned to any constellation of temporally related cortical events is gov-
erned via the limbic system, by the ventral striatum, and ascending
dopaminergic reward systems, essentially as a phenomenon of learning.
Attention and conscious processing are then allocated, in part, as a consequence of gating at the level of the thalamus, via cortico-striatal feedback.
Jackson and Houghton (1995) proposed a critical role for cortico-striatal
processing in this function of attentional allocation. Specifically, the direct
pathway focuses and amplifies attention toward salient stimuli; the indirect
pathway helps to inhibit distraction from nonsalient cues. Thus, in the
normal condition, familiar or innocuous inputs from the cortex (both those
originating via primary sensory systems and those that arise from association with other cortical territories) are recognized as not mandating conscious attention. Recognition of such familiar, innocuous, constellations of
inputs occurs at the level of the striatal spiny neurons, and leads to efficient

processing nonconsciously via the cortico-striatal system, by virtue of shifting the balance in favor of the indirect pathway. Conversely, novel or threatening stimuli shift the balance within cortico-striatal circuits to the direct pathway, opening the thalamic gate, and thereby facilitating attention to and conscious processing of those cortical events.

These neural mechanisms, centered around the striatal spiny neurons, that recognize patterns of cortical input and modify behavior, without recruiting (in fact, suppressing) attentional focus or conscious processing, are fundamental to procedural learning. They also play a critical role in maintaining the normal balance between what is processed consciously and what is "put to rest" without conscious awareness.

We know from experience that familiarity and innocuous repetition have a generally soothing effect on limbic tone. In this sense, simple repetitive behaviors help to redirect attentional allocation and appropriate focus, also helping to filter out both extraneous stimuli and disruptive paralimbic accompaniments (such as affect-laden cognitions or sensorimotor drives). This may explain the common phenomenon of finger tapping, leg bouncing, pencil flipping, and hair stroking observable among normal students in any classroom, and the way in which the frequency of such behaviors increases on exam days or other times of high stress. We propose that these are examples of normal, adaptive, repetitive behaviors that hone arousal to optimal levels and help to focus attention appropriately.

Conversely, the threshold or bias for conscious versus nonconscious processing is modulated by the general level of arousal. For example, in the highly aroused, hypervigilant, or anxious state, attention and conscious processing are more likely to be allocated to incoming stimuli than in the case of low-level arousal (i.e., in a relaxed state). Again, this makes sense from an adaptive standpoint; in the setting of threat, high risk, or high potential for reward, the full capability of conscious processes must be more readily available for allocation.

With this background, OCDs can be understood as the consequence of impaired nonconscious processing (paralleling impaired procedural learning). The result is that innocuous stimuli and associations that normally would be processed nonconsciously (i.e., outside of conscious awareness) are instead processed consciously and inefficiently, further exacerbated by misallocation of attention and limbic misprioritization. If this impairment exists within the sensorimotor cortico-striatal circuit, the result is sensorimotor intrusions (e.g., spontaneous tics or premonitory sensations). If the impairment is within the prefrontal cortico-striatal circuit, the result is cognitive intrusions (i.e., obsessions).

We propose that repetitive behaviors are then performed because they are limbically driven, and represent an attempt to homeostatically reduce levels of arousal. Such repetitive behaviors are, in a sense, designed to enhance the cortico-striatal gating mechanism, in hopes of ultimately facilitating a compensatory shift toward appropriate nonconscious processing and appropriate attentional allocation (i.e., a shift from the direct to the indirect pathway). Phenomenologically, tics occur in response to limbic urges and sensory premonitions in TS, just as compulsions are performed in response to anxiety and obsessions in OCD, until the limbic drive subsides.

Furthermore, it should be appreciated that this heuristic model suggests a final common pathway or phenotype of cortico-striatal functional impairment that could result from disparate etiologies and pathophysiologies. Primary striatal pathology is only one example. This model would suggest that such striatal pathology could be genetic in origin or acquired. Moreover, phenocopies could also be produced via cortical abnormalities or impaired cortico-striatal connectivity. For instance, impaired frontal capacities could result in inefficient organization or transmission of cortical stimuli to the striatum, resulting in inefficient nonconscious processing, misallocation of attention, emergent conscious intrusions, and limbically driven repetitive behaviors (see Savage et al., 1995). This may explain how diffuse white matter abnormalities can contribute to clinical presentations of OCD (Jenike et al., 1996; Miguel, Stein, et al., 1995).

SUMMARY, CONCLUSIONS, AND FUTURE DIRECTIONS

Mounting evidence points to the role of cortico-striatal systems in the pathophysiology of OCDs. The striatal topography model suggests that various disorders within the OC spectrum reflect differential distributions of dysfunction across striatal subterritories. Phenomenology as well as structural and functional brain imaging data in support of the model have, thus far, primarily focused on OCD and TS. The scope of future phenomenology, neuropsychology, and imaging research should be expanded to cover the full spectrum of purported OCDs. Identifying neural substrates that form the basis for a diagnostic classification scheme would represent a tremendous advance in psychiatry.

As the anatomy, physiology, biochemistry, and computational function of the basal ganglia become better understood, neuroscientists will be better equipped to test and modify neurobiological models of OCDs. Currently, cortico-striatal pathways have been implicated in procedural learning and attention, as well as many other normal functions. Therefore, we have proposed that procedural learning paradigms might represent an excellent probe for studying the functional integrity of cortico-striatal systems in OCDs, and have initiated a program of research along these lines. In parallel, we have proposed an initial heuristic scheme that considers the possibility that OCDs fundamentally represent an impairment in the neural mechanisms underlying procedural learning.

It should be apparent that mechanisms central to the pathophysiologic models of OCDs span a range of scales, from the lobar or molar level, to the cellular level, to the molecular level, and back. In fact, neural network models, for example, must simultaneously consider brain behavior at the molecular level of signal processing or computation and at the level of large neuronal populations as well as translobar connections. Consequently, no single experimental approach will be sufficient to unravel the mysteries of OCDs and their pathophysiology. The phenomenologic studies to which we have alluded, as well as the imaging and neuropsychological approaches that we have proposed, cannot address some of the fundamental questions, the answers to which lie at a finer level of spatial resolution. Still, in vivo receptor activation studies, imaging studies combined with pharmacologic probes, and neural network analysis of imaging data all represent new techniques that can reach beyond the depths previously assayed with conventional neuroimaging methods (e.g., Gonzalez-Lima & Macintosh, 1994; Morris, Fisher, Alpert, Rauch, & Fischman, 1995). Such modes of inquiry should be integrated with the full range of other contemporary approaches to face the scientific and clinical challenges that OCDs present.

ACKNOWLEDGMENTS

We are supported in part via grants from the National Institute of Mental Health (MH01215 & MH01230) and the Tourette Syndrome Association. The research carried out in conjunction with the Obsessive Compulsive Disorders Clinic and Research Unit at Massachusetts General Hospital is also funded in part by the David Judah Research Fund. Finally, we wish to express our thanks to Dr. Michael Jenike and Dr. Lee Baer for their dependable supervison and mentorship, as well as the profound influence that they have had on our thinking regarding OCD.

REFERENCES

Albin, R. L., Young, A. B., & Penney, J. B. (1989). The functional anatomy of basal ganglia disorders. *Trends in Neuroscience, 12,* 366–375.

Alexander, G. E. (1994). Basal ganglia-thalamocortical circuits: Their role in control of movements. *Journal of Clinical Neurophysiology, 11,* 420–431.

Alexander, G. E., Crutcher, M. D., & DeLong, M. R. (1990). Basal ganglia-thalamocortical circuits: Parallel substrates for motor, oculomotor, "prefrontal" and "limbic" functions. *Progress in Brain Research, 85,* 119–146.

Alexander, G. E., DeLong, M. R., & Strick, P. L. (1986). Parallel organization of functionally segregated circuits linking basal ganglia and cortex. *Annual Review of Neuroscience, 9,* 357–381.

American Psychiatric Association. (1994). *Diagnostic and statistical manual of mental disorders* (4th ed.). Washington, DC: Author.

Baxter, L. R., Jr., Schwartz, J. M., Bergman, K. S., Szuba, M. P., Guze, B. H., Mazziotta, J. C., Alazraki, A., Selin, C. E., Ferng, H., Munford, P., & Phelps, M. E. (1992). Caudate glucose metabolic rate changes with both drug and behavior therapy for obsessive-compulsive disorder. *Archives of General Psychiatry, 49,* 681–689.

Baxter, L. R., Schwartz, J. M., Guze, B. H., Bergman, K., & Szuba, M. P. (1990). Neuroimaging in obsessive-compulsive disorder: Seeking the mediating neuroanatomy. In M. A. Jenike, L. Baer, & W. E. Minichiello (Eds.), *Obsessive compulsive disorder: Theory and management* (2nd ed., pp. 167–188). Chicago: Year Book Medical.

Baxter, L., Schwartz, J., Mazziotta, J., Phelps, M. E., Pahl, J. J., Buze, B. E., & Fairbanks, L. (1988). Cerebral glucose metabolic rates in nondepressed patients with obsessive-compulsive disorder. *American Journal of Psychiatry, 145,* 1560–1563.

Behar, D., Rapoport, J. L., Berg, C. J., Denckla, M. B., Mann, L., Cox, C., Fedio, P., Zahn, T., & Wolfman, M. G. (1984). Computerized tomography and neuropsychological test measures in adolescents with obsessive-compulsive disorder. *American Journal of Psychiatry, 141,* 363–368.

Benkelfat, C., Nordahl, T. E., Semple, W. E., King, A. C., Murphy, D. L., & Cohen, R. M. (1990). Local cerebral glucose metabolic rates in obsessive-compulsive disorder: Patients treated with clomipramine. *Archives of General Psychiatry, 47,* 840–848.

Breiter, H. C., Filipek, P. A., Kennedy, D. N., Baer, L., Pitcher, D. A., Olivares, M. J., Renshaw, P. F., & Caviness, V. S., Jr. (1994). Retrocallosal white matter abnormalities in patients with obsessive compulsive disorder. *Archives of General Psychiatry, 51,* 663–664.

Castellanos, F. X., Giedd, J. N., Eckburg, P., Marsh, W. L., Vaituzis, A. C., Kaysen, D., Hamburger, S. D., & Rapoport, J. L. (1994). Quantitative morphology of the caudate nucleus in attention deficit hyperactivity disorder. *American Journal of Psychiatry, 151,* 1791–1796.

Doyon, J., Owen, A. M., Petrides, M., Sziklas, V., & Evans, A. C. (1996). Functional anatomy of visuomotor skill learning in human subjects examined with positron emission tomography. *European Journal of Neuroscience, 8,* 637–648.

Gerfen, C. R. (1992). The neostriatal mosaic: Multiple levels of compartmental organization in the basal ganglia. *Annual Review of Neuroscience, 15,* 285–320.

Gonzalez-Lima, F., & Macintosh, A. R. (Eds.). (1994). Computational approaches to network analysis in functional imaging. *Human Brain Mapping, 2,* 1–122.

Grafton, S. T., Hazeltine, E., & Ivry, R. (1995). Functional mapping of sequence learning in normal humans. *Journal of Cognitive Neuroscience, 7,* 497–510.

Grafton, S. T., Mazziotta, J. C., Presty, S., Friston, K. J., Frackowiak, R. S. J., & Phelps, M. E. (1992). Functional anatomy of human procedural learning determined with regional cerebral blood flow and PET. *Journal of Neuroscience, 12,* 2542–2548.

Graybiel, A. M. (1990). Neurotransmitters and neuromodulators in the basal ganglia. *Trends in Neuroscience, 13,* 244–253.

Graybiel, A. M., & Kimura, M. (1995). Adaptive neural networks in the basal ganglia. In J. C. Houk, J. L. Davis, & D. G. Beiser (Eds.), *Models of information processing in the basal ganglia* (pp. 103–116). Cambridge, MA: MIT Press.

Harris, G. J., Hoehn-Saric, R., Lewis, R., Pearlson, G. D., & Streeter, C. (1994). Mapping of SPECT regional cerebral perfusion abnormalities in obsessive-compulsive disorder. *Human Brain Mapping, 1,* 237–248.

Heindel, W. C., Butters, N., & Salmon, D. P. (1988). Impaired learning of a motor skill in patients with Huntington's disease. *Behavioral Neuroscience, 102,* 141–147.

Heindel, W. C., Salmon, D. P., Shults, C. W., Walicke, P. A., & Butters, N. (1989). Neuropsychological evidence for multiple implicit memory systems: A comparison of Alzheimer's, Huntington's, and Parkinson's disease patients. *Journal of Neuroscience, 9,* 582–587.

Hoehn-Saric, R., & Benkelfat, C. (1995). Structural and functional brain imaging in obsessive compulsive disorder. In E. Hollander, J. Zohar, D. Marazziti, & B. Olivier (Eds.), *Current insights in obsessive compulsive disorder* (pp. 183–214). New York: Wiley.

Hollander, E. (Ed.). (1993). Obsessive-compulsive spectrum disorders. *Psychiatric Annals, 23,* 355–407.

Houk, J. C., Davis, J. L., & Beiser, D. G. (Eds.). (1995). *Models of information processing in the basal ganglia.* Cambridge, MA: MIT Press.

Hynd, G. W., Hern, K. L., Novey, E. S., Eliopulos, D., Marshall, R., Gonzalez, J. J., & Voeller, K. K. (1993). Attention deficit-hyperactivity disorder and asymmetry of the caudate nucleus. *Journal of Child Neurology, 8,* 339–347.

Insel, T. R. (1992). Toward a neuroanatomy of obsessive-compulsive disorder. *Archives of General Psychiatry, 49,* 739–744.

Jackson, S., & Houghton, G. (1995). Sensorimotor selection and the basal ganglia. In J. C. Houk, J. L. Davis, & D. G. Beiser (Eds.), *Models of information processing in the basal ganglia* (pp. 337–367). Cambridge, MA: MIT Press.

Jenike, M. A., Breiter, H. C., Baer, L., Kennedy, D. N., Savage, C. R., Olivares, M. J., O'Sullivan, R. L., Shera, D. M., Rauch, S. L., Keuthen, N., Caviness, V. S., & Filipek, P. A. (1996). Cerebral structural abnormalities in obsessive-compulsive disorder: A quantitative morphometric magnetic resonance imaging study. *Archives of General Psychiatry, 53,* 625–632.

Kellner, C. H., Jolley, R. R., Holgate, R. C., Austin, L., Lydiard, R. B., Laraia, M., & Ballenger, J. C. (1991). Brain MRI in obsessive-compulsive disorder. *Psychiatry Research, 36,* 45–49.

Knopman, D., & Nissen, M. J. (1991). Procedural learning is impaired in Huntington's disease: Evidence from the serial reaction time task. *Neuropsychologia, 29,* 245–254.

Krebs, H. I., Brashers-Krug, T., Rauch, S. L., Savage, C. R., Hogan, N., Rubin, R. H., Fischman, A. J., & Alpert, N. M. (1996). Integration of robotic technology with functional imaging [Abstract]: Proceedings of the 2nd International Conference on Functional Mapping of the Human Brain. *Neuroimage, 3,* S394.

Leckman, J. F., Pauls, D. L., Peterson, B. S., Riddle, M. A., Anderson, G. M., & Cohen, D. J. (1992). Pathogenesis of Tourette syndrome: Clues from the clinical phenotype and natural history. *Advances in Neurology, 58,* 15–24.

Leckman, J. F., Walker, D. E., & Cohen, D. J. (1993). Premonitory urges in Tourette's syndrome. *American Journal of Psychiatry, 150,* 98–102.

Luxenberg, J. S., Swedo, S. E., Flament, M. F., Friedland, R. P., Rapoport, J., & Rapoport, S. I. (1988). Neuroanatomical abnormalities in obsessive-compulsive disorder determined with quantitative x-ray computed tomography. *American Journal of Psychiatry, 145,* 1089–1093.

Martone, M., Butters, N., & Payne, P. (1984). Dissociations between skill learning and verbal recognition in amnesia and dementia. *Archives of Neurology, 41,* 965–970.

McElroy, S. L., Phillips, K. A., & Keck, P. E. (1994). Obsessive compulsive spectrum disorder. *Journal of Clinical Psychiatry, 55*(Suppl.), 15–32.

Mesulam, M.-M. (1985). Patterns in behavioral neuroanatomy: Association areas, the limbic system, and hemispheric specialization. In M.-M. Mesulam (Ed.), *Principles of behavioral neurology* (pp. 1–70). Philadelphia: Davis.

Miguel, E. C., Coffey, B. J., Baer, L., Savage, C. R., Rauch, S. L., & Jenike, M. A. (1995). Phenomenology of intentional repetitive behaviors in obsessive-compulsive disorder and Tourette's syndrome. *Journal of Clinical Psychiatry, 56,* 246–255.

Miguel, E. C., Stein, M. C., Rauch, S. L., O'Sullivan, R. L., Stern, T. A., & Jenike, M. A. (1995). Obsessive-compulsive disorder in patients with multiple sclerosis. *Journal of Neuropsychiatry and Clinical Neurosciences, 7,* 507–510.

Mishkin, M., Malamut, B., & Bachevalier, J. (1984). Memories and habits: Two neural systems. In G. Lynch, J. L. McGaugh, & N. M. Weinberger (Eds.), *Neurobiology of learning and memory* (pp. 65–77). New York: Guilford.

Mishkin, N., & Petri, H. L. (1984). Memory and habits: Some implications for the analysis of learning and retention. In L. R. Squire & N. Butters (Eds.), *Neuropsychology of memory* (pp. 287–296). New York: Guilford.

Modell, J., Mountz, J., Curtis, G., & Greden, J. F. (1989). Neurophysiologic dyfunction in basal ganglia/limbic striatal and thalamocortical circuits as a pathogenetic mechanism of obsessive-compulsive disorder. *Journal of Neuropsychiatry and Clinical Neurosciences, 1,* 27–36.

Morris, E. D., Fisher, R. E., Alpert, N. M., Rauch, S. L., & Fischman, A. J. (1995). In vivo imaging of neuromodulation using positron emission tomography: Optimal ligand characteristics and task length for detection of activation. *Human Brain Mapping, 3,* 35–55.

Nissen, M. J., & Bullemer, P. (1987). Attentional requirements of learning: Evidence from performance measures. *Cognitive Psychology, 19,* 1–32.

Nordahl, T. E., Benkelfat, C., Semple, W., Gross, M., King, A. C., & Cohen, R. M. (1989). Cerebral glucose metabolic rates in obsessive-compulsive disorder. *Neuropsychopharmacology, 2,* 23–28.

O'Sullivan, R., Rauch, S. L., Breiter, H. C., Grachev, I., Baer, L., Kennedy, D., Keuthen, N., Savage, C. R., Caviness, V., & Jenike, M. A. (1997). Reduced basal ganglia volumes in trichotillomania by morphometric MRI. *Biological Psychiatry, 42,* 39–45.

Packard, M. G., Hirsch, R., & White, N. M. (1989). Differential effects of fornix and caudate nucleus lesions on two radial arm maze tasks: Evidence for multiple memory systems. *Journal of Neuroscience, 9,* 1465–1472.

Pauls, D. L., Alsobrook, J. P., Goodman, W., Rasmussen, S., & Leckman, J. F. (1995). A family study of obsessive-compulsive disorder. *American Journal of Psychiatry, 152,* 76–84.

Pauls, D. L., & Leckman, J. F. (1986). The inheritance of Gilles de la Tourette's syndrome and associated behaviors: Evidence for autosomal dominant transmission. *New England Journal of Medicine, 315,* 993–997.

Pauls, D. L., Pakstis, A. J., Kurlan, R., Kidd, K. K., Leckman, J. F., Cohen, D. J., Kidd, J. R., Como, P., & Sparkes, R. (1990). Segregation and linkage analysis of Tourette's syndrome and related disorders. *Journal of the American Academy of Child and Adolescent Psychiatry, 29,* 195–203.

Pauls, D. L., Towbin, K. E., Leckman, J. F., Zahner, G. E. P., & Cohen, D. J. (1986). Gilles de la Tourette syndrome and obsessive-compulsive disorder: Evidence supporting a genetic relationship. *Archives of General Psychiatry, 43,* 1180–1182.

Perani, D., Colombo, C., Bressi, S., Bonfanti, A., Grassi, F., Scarone, S., Bellodi, L., Smeraldi, E., & Fazio, F. (1995). FDG PET study in obsessive-compulsive disorder: A clinical metabolic correlation study after treatment. *British Journal of Psychiatry, 166,* 244–250.

Peterson, B. S., Leckman, J. F., & Duncan, J. S. (1994). Corpus callosum morphology from magnetic resonance images of Tourette's syndrome. *Psychiatry Research, 55,* 85–99.

Peterson, B., Riddle, M. A., Cohen, D. J., Katz, L. D., Smith, J. C., Hardin, M. T., & Leckman, J. F. (1993). Reduced basal ganglia volumes in Tourette's syndrome using three-dimensional reconstruction techniques from magnetic resonance images. *Neurology, 43,* 941–949.

Phillips, K. A., McElroy, S. L., Hudson, J. I., & Pope, H. G. (1995). Body dysmorphic disorder: An obsessive-compulsive spectrum disorder, a form of affective spectrum disorder, or both? *Journal of Clinical Psychiatry, 56*(Suppl. 4), 41–51.

Rapoport, J. L., & Wise, S. P. (1988). Obsessive-compulsive disorder: Is it a basal ganglia dysfunction. *Psychopharmacology Bulletin, 24,* 380–384.

Rasmussen, S. A., & Eisen, J. L. (1994). The epidemiology and differential diagnosis of obsessive compulsive disorder. *Journal of Clinical Psychiatry, 55*(Suppl.), 5–14.

Rauch, S. L., & Jenike, M. A. (1993). Neurobiological models of obsessive-compulsive disorder. *Psychosomatics, 34*, 20–32.

Rauch, S. L., & Jenike, M. A. (1997). Neural mechanisms of obsessive-compulsive disorder. *Current Review of Mood & Anxiety Disorders, 1*, 84–94.

Rauch, S. L., Jenike, M. A., Alpert, N. M., Baer, L., Breiter, H. C., Savage, C. R., & Fischman, A. J. (1994). Regional cerebral blood flow measured during symptom provocation in obsessive-compulsive disorder using 15O-labeled CO2 and positron emission tomography. *Archives of General Psychiatry, 51*, 62–70.

Rauch, S. L., & Savage, C. R. (1994). Functional neuroimaging of obsessive compulsive disorders: New paradigms and new models. *Chinese Mental Health Journal, 8*, 181–185.

Rauch, S. L., Savage, C. R., Alpert, N. M., Dougherty, D., Kendrick, A., Curran, T., Brown, H. D., Manzo, P., Fischman, A. J., & Jenike, M. A. (1997). Probing striatal function in obsessive compulsive disorder: A PET study of implicit sequence learning. *Journal of Neuropsychiatry and Clinical Neurosciences, 9*, 568–573.

Rauch, S. L., Savage, C. R., Brown, H. D., Curran, T., Alpert, N. M., Kendrick, A., Fischman, A. J., & Kosslyn, S. M. (1995). A PET investigation of implicit and explicit sequence learning. *Human Brain Mapping, 3*, 271–286.

Rauch, S. L., Whalen, P. J., Savage, C. R., Curran, T., Kendrick, A., Bush, G., Breiter, H. C., Brown, H. D., & Rosen, B. R. (1997). Striatal recruitment during an implicit sequence learning task as measured by functional magnetic resonance imaging. *Human Brain Mapping, 5*, 124–132.

Robinson, D., Wu, H., Munne, R. A., Ashtari, M., Alvir, J. M. J., Lerner, G., Koreem, A., Cole, K., & Bogerts, B. (1995). Reduced caudate nucleus volume in obsessive-compulsive disorder. *Archives of General Psychiatry, 52*, 393–398.

Roland, P. E. (1993). *Brain activation.* New York: Wiley-Liss.

Saint-Cyr, J. A., & Taylor, A. E. (1992). The mobilization of procedural learning: The "key signature" of the basal ganglia. In L. Squire & N. Butters (Eds.), *Neuropsychology of memory* (2nd ed., pp. 188–202). New York: Guilford.

Saint-Cyr, J. A., Taylor, A. E., & Lang, A. E. (1988). Procedural learning and neostriatal dysfunction in man. *Brain, 111*, 941–959.

Savage, C. R., Baer, L., Keuthen, N. J., Brown, H. D., Jenike, M. A., Rauch, S. L., Kendrick, A. D., Manzo, P., & Albert, M. S. (1995). Organizational strategies and nonverbal memory in obsessive-compulsive disorder [Abstract]. *The Clinical Neuropsychologist, 9*, 293–294.

Scarone, S., Colombo, C., Livian, S., Abbruzzese, M., Ronchi, P., Locatelli, M., Scotti, G., & Smeraldi, E. (1992). Increased right caudate nucleus size in obsessive compulsive disorder: Detection with magnetic resonance imaging. *Psychiatry Research: Neuroimaging, 45*, 115–121.

Singer, H. S., Reiss, A. L., Brown, J. E., Aylward, E. H., Shih, B., Chee, E., Harris, E. L., Reader, M. J., Chase, G. A., Bryan, R. N., & Denckla, M. B. (1993). Volumetric MRI changes in basal ganglia of children with Tourette's syndrome. *Neurology, 43*, 950–956.

Squire, L. R. (1986). Mechanisms of memory. *Science, 232*, 1612–1619.

Stoetter, B., Braun, A. R., Randolph, C., Gernert, J., Carson, R. E., Herscovitch, P., & Chase, T. N. (1992). Functional neuroanatomy of Tourette syndrome: Limbic-motor interactions studied with PET FDG. *Advances in Neurology, 58*, 213–226.

Swedo, S. E., Pietrini, P., Leonard, H. L., Schapiro, M. B., Rettew, D. C., Goldberger, E. L., Rapoport, S. I., Rapoport, J. L., & Grady, C. L. (1992). Cerebral glucose metabolism in childhood-onset obsessive-compulsive disorder: Revisualization during pharmacotherapy. *Archives of General Psychiatry, 49*, 690–694.

Swedo, S. E., Schapiro, M. B., Grady, C. L., Cheslow, D. L., Leonard, H. L., Kumar, A., Friedland, R., Rapoport, S. I., & Rapoport, J. L. (1989). Cerebral glucose metabolism in childhood-onset obsessive-compulsive disorder. *Archives of General Psychiatry, 46,* 518–523.

Witelson, S. F. (1993). Clinical neurology as data for basic neuroscience: Tourette's syndrome and the human motor system. *Neurology, 43,* 859–861.

Zald, D. H., & Kim, S. W. (1996). Anatomy and function of the orbital frontal cortex: II. Function and relevance to obsessive-compulsive disorder. *Journal of Neuropsychiatry and Clinical Neurosciences, 8,* 249–261.

III

ASSESSMENT

9

A Review of Assessment Measures for Obsessive-Compulsive Disorder

Ulrike Feske
Western Psychiatric Institute and Clinic
University of Pittsburgh Medical Center

Dianne L. Chambless
University of North Carolina at Chapel Hill

Although effective psychosocial and pharmacological treatments for obsessive-compulsive disorder (OCD) have been developed (see reviews by Abel, 1993; Cox, Swinson, Morrison, & Lee, 1993; Taylor, 1995; van Balkom et al., 1994), there is still much room for improvement in the treatment of this recalcitrant disorder. The development of more powerful treatments requires the use of psychometrically sound instruments for the assessment of treatment outcome and the standardization of assessment procedures across studies testing different treatments. In this brief review, we therefore examine the reliability and validity of the most widely used measures for OCD. Based on our findings, we make recommendations about assessment strategies for treatment outcome research on OCD.

We begin by making explicit our criteria for interpreting psychometric data. For the evaluation of internal consistency and test–retest reliability, we follow Nunnally's (1978) recommendations of defining coefficients of ≥ .70 and ≥ .80 as acceptable and good, respectively. With regard to interrater reliability, we suggest that Kappas of ≥ .65 and correlation coefficients of ≥ .70 are needed for adequate agreement.

A measure of obsessive-compulsive (OC) symptoms has good content validity if it assesses the symptom parameters it is intended to assess as defined by the current criteria of the *Diagnostic and Statistical Manual of Mental Disorders* (4th ed. [*DSM–IV*]; American Psychiatric Association, 1994) for OCD. Evaluation of convergent and discriminant validity is more complex. Good convergent validity requires a strong association with measures assessing the same construct, but good convergence is only meaningful if the comparison measures are themselves psychometrically sound. Moreover, the strength of associations between measures of the same construct is dependent, in part, on the modality of assessment. Same-modality measures (e.g., interviews) tend to be more strongly related than nonmatched modality measures (e.g., self-report, behavioral observation). Consistent with the size of correlations typically found in monotrait and heteromethod psychometric research, we suggest that correlations ranging from .30 to .50 indicate acceptable convergence between heteromethod measures of OC symptoms. Acceptable convergent validity will be defined by correlations ≥ .50 between same-modality measures. Because OCD is frequently associated with depression and general anxiety, it is likely that any measure of OC symptoms will also be substantially related to dissimilar measures of depression and anxiety. Nonetheless, adequate discriminant validity requires stronger correlations with measures of OC symptoms than with measures of different constructs.

To determine criterion-related validity, investigators have typically examined whether OC measures reliably distinguish between different diagnostic groups. Thus, persons with OCD should score higher on measures of OC symptoms than persons without OCD. Very few of the studies we reviewed included adequate diagnostic procedures, however. Findings about criterion-related validity should therefore be interpreted with caution, unless otherwise noted.

DIAGNOSTIC INTERVIEWS

The most widely used standardized diagnostic interviews developed to diagnose OCD according to *DSM* criteria are the Anxiety Disorders Interview Schedule (ADIS; DiNardo, Brown, & Barlow, 1994) and the Structured Clinical Interview for *DSM* Axis I (SCID–I; First, Spitzer, Gibbon, & Williams, 1995). The Composite International Diagnostic Interview (CIDI; World Health Organization [WHO], 1990) is a comprehensive standardized interview designed for the assessment of major diagnostic categories, including OCD, according to the criteria of both the International Classification of Diseases, 10th revision (ICD–10; WHO, 1992) and the *Diagnostic and Statistical Manual of Mental Disorders* (3rd ed., rev. [*DSM–III–R*]; American Psychiatric Association, 1987).

The ADIS is a semistructured interview devised specifically to diagnose *DSM* anxiety disorders, including OCD, and disorders frequently associated with anxiety disorders, such as major depression and dysthymia. Revisions of the ADIS for DSM–III (DiNardo, O'Brien, Barlow, Waddell, & Blanchard, 1983) prompted the introduction of the ADIS–Revised for

DSM–III–R (ADIS–R; DiNardo & Barlow, 1988) and the ADIS for *DSM–IV* (*ADIS–IV*; DiNardo et al., 1994).

The ADIS and ADIS–R have demonstrated excellent reliability. Barlow (1987) had two diagnosticians conduct independent interviews using the ADIS and found high agreement for the diagnosis of current OCD (Kappa = .82). Employing a similar methodology, DiNardo, Moras, Barlow, Rapee, and Brown (1993) observed excellent Kappas (.80 and .75) for current OCD based on the ADIS–R as well. To our knowledge, reliability of the ADIS–IV has yet to be examined.

The SCID is a semistructured interview developed to diagnose the most frequent *DSM–III–R* Axis I disorders (Spitzer, Williams, Gibbon, & First, 1990). The most current edition of the SCID–I is adapted for *DSM–IV* (First et al., 1995).

Reliability of the SCID–I for *DSM–III–R* was examined by Williams et al. (1992) in a large-scale multisite study including five patient and two nonpatient samples. Two clinicians independently interviewed and evaluated the same individual. Kappa for the combined sample was rather low for a diagnosis of current (.59) and lifetime (.67) OCD. Using the SCID–I for *DSM–III–R*, Steketee, Chambless, Tran, Worden, and Gillis (1996) observed excellent interrater agreement (Kappa = 1.0) for current OCD in a small reliability sample of 11 OCD patients. Reliability data for the SCID–I for *DSM–IV* have not yet been published.

The CIDI is a highly structured instrument developed for use by trained lay interviewers and in epidemiological studies of mental disorders in general populations. CIDI computer programs allow users to enter and score the results yielded by the interview. The most recent version of the CIDI is the Core Version 1.1. (WHO, 1993); a version of the CIDI that will incorporate *DSM–IV* is in preparation.

In a large-scale, multicenter, cross-cultural study examining the interrater reliability of a predecessor of the CIDI Core Version 1.1., the CIDI, Wittchen et al. (1991) found excellent agreement (Kappa = .94) between interviewer and observer ratings of the same interview for a diagnosis of current OCD. Using a more stringent test–retest design, Semler et al. (1987) reported excellent reliability (Kappa > .80) for a CIDI diagnosis of OCD obtained by two different interviewers who examined the same individual within a 3-day period. Reliability data on the most recent versions of the CIDI are not yet available.

The ADIS, SCID–I, and CIDI adhere closely to *DSM* criteria for OCD, and the CIDI also shows high concordance with the ICD, indicating good content validity. Adequate tests for convergent, discriminant, and criterion-related validity are lacking. Of course, it is difficult to conceive how these tests might be conducted, given that the *DSM* and ICD criteria are themselves the standard against which diagnostic validity is measured.

Informal comparison of data suggests that the ADIS is more reliable than the SCID; however, these findings may be due, in part, to the varying methodologies that researchers have applied. For example, reliability of the ADIS was tested at an anxiety disorders specialty clinic, using a relatively homogeneous population presenting with anxiety symptoms and interviewers who were probably exceptionally well-trained in diagnosing anxiety disorders (Barlow, 1987; DiNardo et al., 1993). In contrast, the main reliability study on the SCID (Williams et al., 1992) was conducted using individuals who presented with a wide variety of disorders and interviewers who did not specialize in anxiety. Nonetheless, these findings emphasize the importance of employing well-trained assessors for the administration of diagnostic interviews. Note that the ADIS provides information beyond what is needed for establishing a diagnosis of OCD, especially regarding severity of OC fears, insight into OC symptoms, resistance, and avoidance. This valuable information is nevertheless redundant when researchers employ the ADIS in conjunction with the Yale–Brown Obsessive Compulsive Scale (Y–BOCS; Goodman, Price, Rasmussen, Mazure, Delgado, et al., 1989; Goodman, Price, Rasmussen, Mazure, Fleischmann, et al., 1989), an instrument designed specifically to assess the severity of OC symptoms.

We strongly recommend that treatment outcome studies for OCD at the very least include a standardized diagnostic interview for the initial assessment of OC symptoms.

CLINICAL INTERVIEWS

Y–BOCS

This semistructured 10-item interview was introduced by Goodman and colleagues (Goodman, Price, Rasmussen, Mazure, Delgado, et al., 1989; Goodman, Price, Rasmussen, Mazure, Fleischmann, et al., 1989) to assess the severity of OCD independent of symptom content. Using a 64-item checklist, the interviewer first identifies the most prominent OC symptoms. The main obsessions and compulsions are then rated separately for five different symptom parameters: duration, interference, distress, resistance, and perceived control. The Y–BOCS provides one total and two subscale scores. The construct validity of the Y–BOCS was confirmed in a study by McKay, Danyko, Neziroglu, and Yaryura-Tobias (1995), who found distinct factors for obsessions and compulsions.

The Y–BOCS total score has demonstrated excellent interrater reliability with intraclass correlations ranging from .80 to .99 (Goodman, Price, Rasmussen, Mazure, Fleischmann, et al., 1989; Jenike et al., 1990; Price,

Goodman, Charney, Rasmussen, & Heninger, 1987; Woody, Steketee, & Chambless, 1995a). However, these estimates are based on two independent evaluators' ratings of the same interview. Agreement between independently administered interviews would most likely be lower (cf. Taylor, 1995).

The Y–BOCS has acceptable internal consistency with coefficient alphas ranging from .69 to .91 for the total scale and from .51 to .85 for the two subscales (Frost, Steketee, Krause, & Trepanier, 1995; Goodman, Price, Rasmussen, Mazure, Fleischmann, et al., 1989; Richter, Cox, & Direnfeld, 1994; Steketee, Frost, & Bogart, 1995; Woody et al., 1995a). Test–retest reliability of the Y–BOCS has proved somewhat variable across studies. Using the same rater and a 1-week test–retest interval, Kim and colleagues observed excellent stability with intraclass correlations ranging from .81 to .97 (Kim, Dysken, & Kuskowski, 1990, 1992; Kim, Dysken, Kuskowski, & Hoover, 1993). In Woody et al.'s (1995a) study, intraclass correlations ranged from .56 to .64, probably because researchers used a larger retest interval ($M = 49$ days) and two different raters.

The Y–BOCS total scale and its subscales have demonstrated good convergence (*Mdn r* = .54) with questionnaire measures of OC symptoms, including the Maudsley Obsessional Compulsive Inventory (MOCI; Hodgson & Rachman, 1977), Compulsive Activity Checklist (CAC; Philpott, 1975), and the symptom scale of the Leyton Obsessional Inventory (LOI; Cooper, 1970; Frost et al., 1995; Goodman, Price, Rasmussen, Mazure, Delgado, et al., 1989; Kim et al., 1990; Richter et al., 1994; Woody et al., 1995a). Correlations with behavioral avoidance tests (*Mdn r* = .34) and target ratings of OC symptoms (*Mdn r* = .31) were lower (Woody et al., 1995a), as would be expected for heteromethod coefficients. Findings for discriminant validity are problematic due to relatively strong associations with anxiety (*Mdn r* = .35) and especially depression (*Mdn r* = .48; Goodman, Price, Rasmussen, Mazure, Delgado, et al., 1989; Hewlett, Vinogradov, & Agras, 1992; Richter et al., 1994; Woody et al., 1995a). In two studies, the Y–BOCS was more strongly related to measures of depression and anxiety than to measures of OC symptoms (Goodman, Price, Rasmussen, Mazure, Delgado, et al., 1989; Woody et al., 1995a).

Few studies have examined the criterion-related validity of the Y–BOCS. Rosenfeld, Dar, Anderson, Kobak, and Greist (1992) showed that the total score distinguishes between persons with OCD and persons with other anxiety disorders and normals. Similarly, Steketee et al. (1995) found that the total and both subscale scores differentiated OCD patients from those with other disorders.

Inspection of the Y–BOCS checklist and interview items suggests that the measure has excellent content validity. Although not exhaustive, the symptom checklist captures a wider spectrum of *DSM* OC symptoms than any other available measure. In addition, the Y–BOCS interview is the only instrument that assesses the various parameters (e.g., duration, distress) of OC symptoms as defined by the *DSM–IV* diagnostic criteria for OCD.

The Y–BOCS is a psychometrically sound and exceptionally comprehensive measure, and has, therefore, become the gold standard for assessment of OC symptoms. It does not perform well with respect to discriminant validity vis-à-vis depression, but this weakness is common to OCD measures. Low item–remainder correlations and poor test–retest reliability have been reported for the resistance items (Steketee et al., 1995; Woody et al., 1995a), suggesting the need for further exploration of these items. Given that persons with OCD commonly avoid threatening situations to reduce their distress, additional research is needed to determine whether inclusion of the investigational avoidance items in the Y–BOCS proper enhances the validity of the instrument (Woody et al., 1995a). Persons who present with either obsessions or compulsions may obtain spuriously low scores on the Y–BOCS total scale, despite severe symptoms (cf. Kim, Dysken, & Katz, 1989). Use of the subscale scores instead of the total score circumvents this problem and is therefore preferable. We conclude that the Y–BOCS is essential to the assessment of OC symptoms.

CAC

This 62-item interview was developed by Hallam to assess the degree to which OC symptoms interfere with everyday activities (Philpott, 1975). The rarely used original CAC has been replaced by more popular versions, including the 39-item interview and self-report CAC (Marks, Hallam, Connolly, & Philpott, 1977), 38-item interview CAC (Freund, Steketee, & Foa, 1987), 37-item and 18-item self-report CAC (Cottraux, Bouvard, Defayolle, & Messy, 1988), and 28-item self-report CAC (Steketee & Freund, 1993). The total scores of the interview and self-report versions are highly correlated (rs = .94 and .83; Freund et al., 1987; Marks, Stern, Mawson, Cobb, & McDonald, 1980). A factor analytic study with OCD clients revealed two subscales, washing and checking (Freund et al., 1987).

Recent versions of the CAC have demonstrated good internal consistency. Coefficient alphas for the 28-item, 37-item, and 38-item self-report CAC range from .78 to .95 for the total scale (Cottraux et al., 1988; Frost et al., 1995; Steketee & Freund, 1993; Sternberger & Burns, 1990a). Using the 38-item interview, Freund et al. (1987) reported good homogeneity for the total scale (alpha = .91) and its washing (alpha = .93) and checking (alpha = .89) subscales. Tests for interrater and test–retest reliability are sparse and have yielded variable results. Interrater agreement for two independent raters in separate interviews was excellent (r = .95) for the

39-item CAC (Marks et al., 1980) but notably lower ($r = .62$) for the 38-item CAC (Freund et al., 1987). Two studies yielded marginal results for the 1-month test–retest reliability of the 37-item self-report CAC ($r = .62$; Cottraux et al., 1988) and the 37-day test–retest reliability of the 38-item interview CAC ($r = .68$; Freund et al., 1987). Sternberger and Burns (1990a), on the other hand, observed adequate 6- to 7-month test–retest stability for the 38-item self-report CAC ($r = .74$).

Convergence of the CAC total scale with other measures of OC symptoms is adequate. The self-report CAC revealed a strong association ($r = .55$) with the assessor-rated Y–BOCS (Frost et al., 1995), whereas correlations with the same-modality MOCI were more variable across studies ($rs = .58$ and $.29$; Steketee & Freund, 1993; Sternberger & Burns, 1990a). The interview CAC has shown moderate associations with the MOCI ($rs = .33–.70$) and with target ratings of OC symptoms ($Mdn\ r = .31$; Freund & Foa, 1988a). As would be expected, the CAC is weakly related to dissimilar measures of anxiety ($Mdn\ r = .19$) as well as extraversion and introversion, general distress, and social desirability ($Mdn\ |r| = .15$; Freund et al., 1987; Steketee & Freund, 1993). However, correlations with depression are nearly as large ($Mdn\ r = .34$) as those with measures of OC symptoms (Foa, Steketee, Kozak, & Dugger, 1987; Freund et al., 1987), thereby failing to support the discriminant validity of the CAC total scale. Findings on the convergent and discriminant validity of the CAC subscales are also mixed. Although the washing and checking scales were more strongly related to the corresponding than to the noncorresponding MOCI scales in OCD patients (Freund et al., 1987), this did not prove to be the case in nonclinical students (Sternberger & Burns, 1990a).

Some evidence exists for the criterion-related validity of the CAC. Cottraux et al. (1988) found that the total score of the 37-item self-report CAC differentiated persons with OCD from those with panic disorder or social phobia and from normals. Using the 38-item questionnaire CAC, Steketee and Freund (1993) reported that all but nine items discriminated persons with OCD from those with other anxiety disorders and from normals. Freund et al. (1987) observed satisfactory agreement between the CAC washing and checking subscales and therapist ratings of respective symptoms.

With respect to content validity, it seems that the CAC adequately measures the interference of certain OC symptoms with daily activities, although it does not address interference with social relationships, nor does it reflect other symptom parameters such as duration and distress. The CAC also fails to assess covert rituals (e.g., counting) and obsessions.

Like the MOCI, the CAC primarily measures cleaning and checking rituals. Because the former has generally shown stronger psychometric properties, there is presently little reason to recommend the CAC over the MOCI. Two possible advantages of the CAC over the MOCI should be noted, however: (a) The CAC uses a 4-point rather than a dichotomous rating scale, and (b) the CAC assesses highly specific compulsive behaviors that can be readily quantified. Nonetheless, given the weaknesses of the CAC, the instrument should only be used in conjunction with other measures of OC symptoms (e.g., Y–BOCS, Padua Inventory [PI; Sanavio, 1988]).

Comprehensive Psychopathological Rating Scale–Obsessive Compulsive (CPRS–OC) Subscale

The CPRS (Asberg, Montgomery, Perris, Schalling, & Sedvall, 1978) is an interview measure of various psychopathological symptoms that also contains eight items intended to measure OC symptoms (Thoren, Asberg, Cronholm, Jörnestedt, & Träskman, 1980). Insel et al. (1983) modified the CPRS–OC by deleting three of the original items that do not capture specific OC symptoms.

Information on the psychometric properties of the CPRS–OC is scarce. Initial evidence suggests that the eight-item CPRS–OC total score has good interrater reliability ($r = .97$; Thoren et al., 1980), but data on test–retest reliability and convergent, discriminant, and criterion-related validity are lacking.

Of particular concern is the poor content validity of the CPRS–OC. As noted by Taylor (1995), the majority of items reflect nonspecific features of depressed and anxious mood (inner tension, concentration difficulties, worrying over trifles, sadness, lassitude, and indecision), leaving only two items that specifically address OC symptoms (rituals and compulsive thoughts). These drawbacks clearly argue against the use of the CPRS–OC as a measure of OC symptoms.

SELF-REPORT INSTRUMENTS

Padua Inventory (PI)

The 60-item PI is a self-report questionnaire developed by Sanavio (1988) to measure the degree of distress caused by obsessions and compulsions. Factor analytic studies on nonclinical samples yielded four factors: contamination, checking, impaired control of mental activities, and urges or worries of losing control over motor behaviors (Sanavio, 1988; Sternberger & Burns, 1990b; van Oppen, 1992). The PI thus provides one total and four subscale scores. The only factor analytic study including clinical participants revealed a five-factor solution, prompting development of the 41-item revised PI (PI–R; van Oppen, Hoekstra, & Emmelkamp, 1995). One drawback of the PI is its relative lack of differentiation between symptoms of obsession and worry (Freeston et al., 1994). To rectify this weakness, Burns, Keortge, Formea, and Sternberger (1996) organized 39 of the 60 PI items into five categories of obsessions and compulsions (based on the content of items), excluding those items they judged to reflect both worry and obsessions. The five content analytically derived dimensions were replicated in factor-analytic studies on a very large sample of nonclinical individuals, prompting introduction of the 39-item PI–R (Burns et al., 1996).

The PI and PI–R have demonstrated good-to-excellent internal consistency with coefficient alphas ranging from .89 to .94 for the total scale and alphas generally exceeding .80 for the subscales (Burns et al., 1996; Kyrios, Bhar, & Wade, 1996; Sanavio, 1988; Sternberger & Burns, 1990b; van Oppen, 1992; van Oppen, Hoekstra, & Emmelkamp, 1995). The PI total scale has shown satisfactory test–retest reliability (rs = .78–.83) for intervals of 1 and 2 months (Kyrios et al., 1996; Sanavio, 1988; van Oppen, 1992). Van Oppen (1992) and Kyrios et al. (1996) observed adequate 2-month test–retest stability (rs = .71–.83) for the PI subscales as well. Using intervals of 6 to 7 months, Burns et al. (1996) found adequate retest stability for the 39-item PI–R total scale (r = .76) and its five subscales (rs = .61–.79).

Tests for convergent and discriminant validity have yielded mixed results. Although the PI and 41-item PI–R total scores show good convergence ($Mdn\ r$ = .73) with other self-report measures of OCD, the MOCI and LOI symptom scale, they do not relate well to the interview Y–BOCS (rs = .17 and .36) or target ratings of OC symptoms (rs = .27 and .51; Kyrios et al., 1996; Sanavio, 1988; Sternberger & Burns, 1990b; van Oppen, 1992; van Oppen, Emmelkamp, van Balkom, & van Dyck, 1995; van Oppen, Hoekstra, & Emmelkamp, 1995). Where discriminant reliability is concerned, the total scale shows low correlations with social desirability ($Mdn\ |r|$ = .08), extraversion ($Mdn\ |r|$ = .19), and psychoticism ($Mdn\ |r|$ = .14), but large correlations with anxiety ($Mdn\ r$ = .54), depression ($Mdn\ r$ = .55), and neuroticism ($Mdn\ r$ = .60; Kyrios et al., 1996; Sanavio, 1988; Sternberger & Burns, 1990b; van Oppen, 1992; van Oppen, Hoekstra, & Emmelkamp, 1995). The 39-item PI–R total scale has demonstrated good discriminant validity vis-à-vis worry and has proven to be more independent of worry than the PI (Burns et al., 1996). Overall, the PI and PI–R total scales appear to be more strongly related to OC symptoms than to dissimilar symptoms, although their substantial association with anxiety and depression is disconcerting.

The PI and 41-item PI–R contamination and checking subscales have good convergent and discriminant validity (Sternberger & Burns, 1990b; van Oppen, 1992; van Oppen, Hoekstra, & Emmelkamp, 1995). Furthermore, all five subscales of the 39-item PI–R proved to be largely independent of worry (Burns et al., 1996). However, discriminant validity of the two PI obsessional subscales (impaired mental control and urges and worries) is problematic, as both scales were found to correlate more highly with depression and general anxiety than with OC symptoms (Kyrios et al., 1996; van Oppen, 1992).

Two studies lend support for the criterion-related validity of the PI. Sanavio (1988) found that the PI total score distinguished between OCD patients and a mixed group of patients with other disorders. Van Oppen, Hoekstra, and Emmelkamp (1995) observed that the 41-item PI–R total, washing, checking, rumination, and precision scales discriminated persons with OCD from those with panic disorder or social phobia and from normals. The impulses subscale differentiated between OCD patients and normals, but not between OCD patients and those with panic disorder or social phobia.

Inspection of items suggests that the PI and PI–R assess the main types of compulsions and obsessions delineated by the *DSM–IV* criteria, indicating good content validity. Nonetheless, relatively few of the items address mental rituals and sexual imagery. Although the PI and PI–R measure the distress associated with OC symptoms, they do not provide information on other features of OC symptoms, such as duration or resistance. Burns et al. (1996) pointed out that a number of PI items lack content specificity because they reflect both worry and obsessions (e.g., I invent doubts and problems about most of the things that I do). Indeed, elimination of these items in the 39-item PI–R was successful in reducing the overlap between these two symptom domains. Some items of the PI urges and worries subscale (e.g., the impulse to jump from high places) also appear to lack content specificity because they may reflect behaviors associated with depression (cf. Kyrios et al., 1996) or fear of loss of control in anxiety disorders other than OCD.

We conclude that the PI and PI–R and their respective subscales are psychometrically sound instruments, although validity of the obsessional subscales begs further improvement. The majority of studies tested the utility of the PI and PI–R in nonclinical participants so that exploration of these measures for use with OCD populations is sorely needed. However, at least the 41-item PI–R has been found to be sensitive to change with treatment and to produce large effect sizes that were in the same range as those yielded by the interview Y–BOCS (van Oppen, Emmelkamp, et al., 1995). Apart from the Y–BOCS, the PI and PI–R are the most promising of the measures that specifically assess obsessions and compulsions.

Because the PI and PI–R include items reflecting ruminations and impulses that are not included in the majority of other OC measures (e.g., MOCI, CAC, LOI), we strongly encourage their use.

Y–BOCS

The Y–BOCS was originally developed as a clinician-rated interview to assess the severity of OC symptoms (Goodman, Price, Rasmussen, Mazure, Delgado, et al., 1989; Goodman, Price, Rasmussen, Mazure, Fleischmann, et al., 1989). Although the Y–BOCS interview is a promising instrument, it has the disadvantage of being a time-consuming, and, therefore, costly measure to employ. To address this problem, researchers have recently devised self-report paper-and-pencil and computer-administered versions of the Y–BOCS (Baer, Brown-Beasley, Sorce, & Henriques, 1993; Rosenfeld et al., 1992; Steketee et al., 1995; Warren, Zgourides, & Monto, 1993).

Several studies have shown good agreement between interview and self-report formats. Correlations of the Y–BOCS total scales and the obsession and compulsion subscales for the two versions ranged from .73 to .99 among persons with OCD (Baer et al., 1993; Rosenfeld et al., 1992; Steketee et al., 1995). Using nonclinical participants, Rosenfeld et al. (1992) found poor agreement ($rs = -.02-.03$) due to severe restriction of range, whereas Steketee et al. (1995) observed adequate correlations ($rs = .65-.75$). Tests for internal consistency have yielded positive results, with coefficient alphas ranging from .55 to .91 for the total and subscale scores (Steketee et al., 1995; Warren et al., 1993). Steketee et al. (1995) obtained excellent 1-week test–retest reliability ($rs = .82-.88$) for the three Y–BOCS scores. The self-report Y–BOCS reliably distinguished between OCD and non-OCD patients (Rosenfeld et al., 1992; Steketee et al., 1995), suggesting good criterion-related validity. (Note that Rosenfeld et al., 1992, used a computer-administered self-report version.)

In sum, initial findings regarding the utility of the self-report Y–BOCS are positive, although additional data are clearly needed for more definitive conclusions. Given the good psychometric properties of the interview Y–BOCS and the strong convergence between the self-report and interview formats, there is reason to believe that the self-report Y–BOCS will prove to be a valuable instrument for the assessment of OC symptoms.

Consistent with a heteromethod approach to the assessment of OC symptoms, we suggest that researchers administer the self-report Y–BOCS in addition to the interview Y–BOCS.

MOCI

This 30-item true–false self-report questionnaire was developed by Hodgson and Rachman (1977) to assess obsessions and compulsions associated with overt rituals. The MOCI consists of four factor analytically derived subscales: checking, washing, slowness, and doubting. It provides one total and four subscale scores. Factor analytic studies have replicated the washing, checking, and doubting factors, but not the slowness factor (Chan, 1990; Rachman & Hodgson, 1980; Sanavio & Vidotto, 1985; Sternberger & Burns, 1990a).

Studies on clinical samples have demonstrated acceptable internal consistency (coefficient alphas) for the MOCI total (range = .85–.89), checking (range = .63–.79), washing (range = .67–.87), and doubting (range = .70–.86) scales, but poor internal consistency for the slowness scale (range = .26–.70; Hodgson & Rachman, 1977; Kraaijkamp, Emmelkamp, & van den Hout, 1986; Richter et al., 1994). Studies on nonclinical samples have yielded lower homogeneity (Chan, 1990; Sanavio & Vidotto, 1985; Sternberger & Burns, 1990a), possibly due to the restriction of the range of scores. The MOCI total scale has acceptable stability with coefficients ranging from .69 to .84 for test–retest intervals of 1 to 7 months, whereas test–retest reliability of the subscales is largely unknown (Freund & Foa, 1988b; Hodgson & Rachman, 1977; Kraaijkamp et al., 1986; Sternberger & Burns, 1990a).

The MOCI total scale shows good convergence (Mdn r = .69) with self-report measures of OCD, the LOI symptom scale, PI, and the paper-and-pencil version of the CAC (Hodgson & Rachman, 1977; Richter et al., 1994; Sanavio, 1988; Steketee & Freund, 1993; Sternberger & Burns, 1990a, 1990b; van Oppen, 1992; van Oppen, Hoekstra, & Emmelkamp, 1995). Correlations with the assessor-rated Y–BOCS and CAC are somewhat lower (Mdn r = .54; Freund & Foa, 1988a; Frost et al., 1995; Goodman et al., 1989b; Richter et al., 1994; Woody et al., 1995a). As is typical for measures of OC symptoms, the total score shows substantial correlations with depression (rs = .41 and .54; Chan, 1990; Richter et al., 1994) and general distress (Mdn r = .33; Sternberger & Burns, 1990a). Nevertheless, the MOCI total score is more strongly related to measures of OC symptoms than to measures of dissimilar symptoms, thereby lending support for its discriminant validity.

Several studies attest to the convergent and discriminant validity of the MOCI washing and checking subscales. The washing scale is strongly associated with the PI contamination subscale (rs = .53–.87), but not with the PI checking subscale (rs = –.05–.33; Sternberger & Burns, 1990b; van Oppen, 1992; van Oppen, Hoekstra, & Emmelkamp, 1995). Similar results have been obtained for the MOCI checking subscale vis-à-vis the PI checking subscale (rs = .62–.84) and the PI contamination subscale (rs = .24–.50; Sternberger & Burns, 1990b; van Oppen, 1992; van Oppen, Hoekstra, & Emmelkamp, 1995). Correlations between the MOCI washing and checking subscales and depression tend to be lower (Mdn r = .33; Chan, 1990; Richter et al., 1994) than the convergent validity correlations, thereby supporting the discriminant validity of these two subscales. Convergent and discriminant validity of the doubting and slowness subscales have yet to be examined in detail.

Tests of criterion-related validity have generally yielded positive results. The MOCI total score distinguished persons with OCD from those with non-OC anxiety disorders and anorexia nervosa, and from normals (Hodgson, Rankin, & Stockwell, 1980, cited in Emmelkamp, 1988; Kraaijkamp et al., 1986). In Kraaijkamp et al.'s (1986) study, the MOCI subscales also differentiated between persons with OCD and persons with mixed psychiatric diagnoses. The washing, checking, and doubting subscales, but not the slowness subscale, distinguished persons with OCD from normals. Two studies yielded satisfactory concordance between the MOCI washing and checking subscales and evaluator ratings of respective symptoms (Hodgson & Rachman, 1977; Kraaijkamp et al., 1986).

Several limitations should be considered with respect to the content validity of the MOCI. Although the MOCI assesses two of the most common compulsions, washing and checking, it does not assess other important overt compulsions such as ordering (American Psychiatric Association, 1994), nor does it reflect covert compulsions such as praying. The MOCI does not sufficiently measure obsessions associated with cleaning and checking (cf. Taylor, 1995) and fails to assess aggressive and sexual impulses (cf. Sanavio, 1988). The MOCI also fails to reflect important content-free features of OC symptoms: duration, interference, distress, or resistance. Although the MOCI has shown good sensitivity to drug treatment and behavior therapy (cf. Taylor, 1995), it may not provide optimal information on the severity of symptoms or their change with treatment due to its dichotomous response format (cf. Kim et al., 1993). To rectify this problem, Dominguez, Jacobson, Gandara, Goldstein, and Steinbook (1989) revised the MOCI to include a polychotomous response format, but few psychometric data are yet available on this version.

We recommend that the MOCI be used in conjunction with other measures of OCD (e.g., Y–BOCS, PI) that capture the symptoms and symptom dimensions the MOCI fails to assess. The psychometric properties of the MOCI doubting subscale have not yet been adequately examined. Given the rare occurrence of symptoms reflecting obsessional slowness (Khanna, Kaliaperumal, & Channabasavanna, 1990; Rachman, 1974), it is not surprising that psychometric studies have failed to support the usefulness of the MOCI slowness scale. We strongly discourage the use of the MOCI doubting or slowness subscales.

LOI

This 69-item true–false inventory was developed by Cooper (1970) as a card-sort procedure to assess OC symptoms and personality traits. The LOI yields four subscale scores reflecting the number of OC symptoms and personality traits, as well as the degree to which the person resists

OC behaviors and the degree of interference caused by OC behaviors. The LOI total score is rarely used. The card-sort procedure was simplified with the introduction of a self-report version (Kazarian, Evans, & Lefave, 1977; Snowdon, 1980) that correlated reasonably well ($rs = .73-.77$) with the original LOI (Snowdon, 1980).

Studies on clinical samples have demonstrated acceptable-to-good internal consistency for the symptom, trait, interference, and resistance scales, with coefficient alphas ranging from .75 to .93 (Richter et al., 1994; Stanley et al., 1993). In addition, the four subscales have shown adequate retest reliability over periods of 1 and 2 weeks, with intraclass correlations ranging from .79 to .89 (Kim et al., 1989; Kim et al., 1990).

Evidence for convergent validity is good. The LOI subscales show very large correlations (*Mdn r* = .70) with other self-report measures of OC symptoms, the MOCI and PI (Hodgson & Rachman, 1977; Richter et al., 1994; Sanavio, 1988). Associations with the assessor-rated Y–BOCS are somewhat weaker (*Mdn r* = .54; Kim et al., 1990; Richter et al., 1994), as would be expected for heteromethod coefficients. The LOI subscales show medium-size correlations with depression (*Mdn r* = .44), neuroticism (*Mdn r* = .37), and social desirability (*Mdn |r|* = .30), but low correlations with extraversion (*Mdn |r|* = .13) and general distress (*Mdn |r|* = .22; Kendell & DiScipio, 1970; Richter et al., 1994; Stanley et al., 1993). Overall, the LOI subscales are more strongly related to measures of OC symptoms than to measures of dissimilar symptoms, thereby supporting their discriminant validity.

In three studies testing the criterion-related validity of the LOI, each of the four subscales discriminated between OCD patients and normals (Cooper, 1970; Millar, 1980; Murray, Cooper, & Smith, 1979). Millar (1983) observed that the interference and resistance scales, but not the symptom and trait scales, differentiated OCD patients from depressed patients. Stanley et al. (1993) were the only researchers who used a standardized and reliable interview to diagnose their participants. Of the four subscales, only the trait scale failed to distinguish patients with OCD from those with other anxiety disorders. Thus, the LOI symptom, interference, and resistance scales have demonstrated adequate criterion-related validity. This does not hold true for the trait scale.

A number of problems have to be noted with respect to the content validity of the LOI, however. The majority of items comprising the symptom, interference, and resistance scales reflect compulsive behaviors concerning household cleanliness and personal hygiene. Items assessing other common compulsions (e.g., checking) and items pertaining to obsessions are largely lacking. Moreover, the LOI resistance scale is conceptualized such that greater resistance reflects more severe OC pathology. In contrast, several authors have argued that greater resistance is more often associated with less severe OC symptoms (Goodman, Price, Rasmussen, Mazure, Fleischmann, et al., 1989; Taylor, 1995). The LOI trait scale has unacceptable content validity by virtue of failing to include items that specifically reflect OC symptoms (American Psychiatric Association, 1987, 1994).

The LOI symptom, interference, and resistance scales generally have acceptable psychometric properties, although less than desirable content validity. Because they are highly correlated with one another ($rs = .70-.91$; Richter et al., 1994; Stanley et al., 1993), use of all three subscales seems redundant. In addition, the three subscales only capture a very restricted range of OC symptoms. Thus, persons with checking or obsessional symptoms may not score in the pathological range on the LOI, despite incapacitating symptoms. Given the availability of instruments assessing a much broader spectrum of OC symptoms (e.g., Y–BOCS, PI), there is little reason to recommend the use of the LOI. We particularly discourage the use of the LOI trait scale due to its lack of both criterion-related and content validity.

Symptom Checklist–90–Revised (SCL–90–R) OC Scales and Predecessors

The Hopkins Symptom Checklist (HSCL; Derogatis, Lipman, Rickels, Uhlenhuth, & Covi, 1974) is a self-report questionnaire of various dimensions of psychopathology that also contains eight items intended to measure the number and severity of OC symptoms. Revisions of the HSCL led to the introduction of the SCL–90 (Derogatis, Lipman, & Covi, 1973) and SCL–90–R (Derogatis, 1977), both of which include 10 OC items.

Good internal consistency has been reported for the three OC scales with coefficient alphas ranging from .86 to .91 (Derogatis, 1977; Derogatis et al., 1974; Shutty, DeGood, & Schwartz, 1986; Woody, Steketee, & Chambless, 1995b). Studies examining the test–retest reliability of the HSCL OC scale yielded variable results. Derogatis et al. (1974) found good stability ($r = .84$) over a 7-day interval, whereas Steketee and Doppelt (1986) observed unacceptable intraclass correlations (.56) over a mean period of 24 days. Using the SCL–90, Kim and colleagues (Kim et al., 1989; Kim et al., 1992) found intraclass correlations of .74 and .79 over an interval of 7 and 14 days, respectively. Thus, at least the SCL–90 OC scale has acceptable stability over time.

The SCL–90–R OC scale and its predecessors have shown large correlations ($Mdn\ r = .51$) with other self-report measures of OC symptoms and somewhat lower correlations ($Mdn\ r = .43$) with the assessor-rated Y–BOCS (Kim et al., 1992; Stanley et al., 1993; Steketee & Doppelt, 1986; Sternberger & Burns, 1990a, 1990b; van Oppen, 1992; van Oppen, Hoekstra, & Emmelkamp, 1995; Woody et al., 1995b). However, the HSCL and SCL OC scales are strongly associated with depression (*Mdn r* = .51) and anxiety (*Mdn r* = .56; Clark & Friedman, 1983; Derogatis, Rickels, & Rock, 1976; Dinning & Evans, 1977; Steketee & Doppelt, 1986; Woody et al., 1995b). In two studies with OCD patients, the OC scales were more strongly related to measures of depression than to measures of OCD (Steketee & Doppelt, 1986; Woody et al., 1995b). The pattern of correlations with convergent and divergent measures of OCD indicates that the HSCL and SCL OC scales have moderate convergent but unacceptable discriminant validity.

Evidence for the criterion-related validity of the HSCL and SCL OC scales is mixed. Steketee and Doppelt (1986) found that the HSCL OC scale distinguished between OCD patients and a mixed group of non-OCD patients. Woody et al. (1995b) observed that the SCL–90–R OC scale discriminated between patients with OCD and their relatives, but not between patients with OCD and agoraphobia.

Taylor (1995) rightly called attention to the poor content validity of the SCL–90–R OC scale and its predecessors. Indeed, at least half of the HSCL and SCL OC items reflect general distress associated with depression and anxiety (e.g., trouble remembering, difficulty making decisions, mind going blank, trouble concentrating), rather than specific OC symptoms.

Given that the HSCL and SCL–90 OC scales appear to reflect general distress rather than OC symptoms, we strongly discourage their use for the assessment of OC symptoms.

LIKERT SCALES

Likert scaling refers to a method of assessment that measures a subject's responses on a continuous dimension with numerical anchor points, which typically correspond to a written descriptor (e.g., 0 = no anxiety, 1 = mild anxiety, 2 = moderate anxiety, 3 = considerable anxiety, 4 = extreme anxiety). Intervals between anchor points are generally presumed to be equal, although researchers have rarely investigated this assumption.

Target Rating Scales

These single-item 9-point Likert scales are rated by assessors, therapists, and clients to measure the severity of the most distressing obsessions, compulsions, and avoidance behaviors (e.g., van Oppen, de Haan, et al., 1995). Target symptoms are usually selected jointly by patient and assessor. They may reflect different aspects of OCD, such as the degree of anxiety elicited by feared situations, duration of rituals, or degree of avoidance.

Initial evidence suggests that target rating scales have good interrater reliability. Cottraux et al. (1990) found large correlations (*rs* = .74–.95) between client and assessor ratings of two types of target symptoms (duration of rituals and anxiety associated with compulsions). Foa et al. (1987) obtained acceptable agreement (rs = .65–.83) between client, assessor, and therapist ratings of anxiety associated with feared objects or situations. Tests of the scales' stability over time are less encouraging. Freund and Foa (1988b) reported good test–retest reliability over intervals of 37 to 60 days for self-rated avoidance (rs = .72–.87), but not for self-rated fear (rs = .35–.59). Test–retest stability was below acceptable standards (rs = .16–.70) for assessor ratings of both fear and avoidance. Finally, Steketee and Chambless (1994) observed adequate 2-week test–retest coefficients for client ratings of fear and avoidance (rs = .68), but not for rituals (rs = .46). However, stability data are difficult to interpret, because clients in both studies received some type of intervention during the retest interval.

Convergence with measures of OC symptoms tends to be moderate. Clients' target ratings have shown medium-size correlations ($Mdn\ r$ = .30) with interview and questionnaire measures, including the CAC, MOCI, PI–R, and Y–BOCS (Freund & Foa, 1988a; van Oppen, Emmelkamp, et al., 1995; Woody et al., 1995a). Moderate correlations ($Mdn\ |r|$ = .29) also emerged between observer ratings of target symptoms and other measures of OCD, the CAC and MOCI (Freund & Foa, 1988a). Uniformly high ratings on target symptom scales at pretest may have contributed to the low correlations, as convergence was usually better at posttest when restriction of range was not a problem. Given that target ratings merely assess the most disturbing symptoms, whereas other measures of OCD capture a much broader spectrum of symptomatology, moderate convergence between these measures seems acceptable. Adequate tests of discriminant and criterion-related validity are lacking, but content validity appears satisfactory.

In summary, target rating scales are a valuable assessment tool by virtue of measuring idiosyncratic and highly specific OC symptoms. Because they reflect the client's main fears that are the target of behavioral and cognitive interventions during therapy, they are highly sensitive to change with psychosocial treatment (Taylor, 1995; van Oppen, Emmelkamp, et al., 1995). Indeed, perhaps due to their high specificity, target ratings have been shown to yield larger effect sizes than broader measures of OC symptoms (van Oppen, Emmelkamp, et al., 1995) and thus may introduce a measurement bias when aggregating across the scores of these different types of instruments. Disadvantages include poor stability over time and lack of information regarding the scales' validity.

Due to their limited range of assessment, target ratings should only be employed in conjunction with more comprehensive measures of OC symptoms (e.g., Y–BOCS, MOCI, PI). Because single-item scales cannot be expected to show good reliability, researchers are advised to obtain target ratings of three or five main symptoms and use the average score derived from these ratings. To further enhance reliability, we strongly recommend that assessors use the average score of at least two repeated measurements obtained during baseline (cf. de Beurs, 1993). Finally, we caution that target rating scores are not evidently comparable across patients and studies (cf. Steketee, Freund, & Foa, 1988). Standardized instructions for identifying target symptoms and defining response choices may increase the accuracy of target ratings.

NIMH–GOCS

This single-item Likert-type scale is a clinician-rated measure of the overall severity of OC symptoms (Insel et al., 1983). The NIMH–GOCS provides a global severity score ranging from 1 (*minimal symptoms*) to 15 (*very severe OC behavior*). Few studies have examined its reliability and validity. Kim and colleagues (Kim et al., 1992; Kim et al., 1993) observed excellent 1-week test–retest intraclass correlations of .87 and .98. The NIMH–GOCS has shown good convergence with the assessor-rated Y–BOCS (*Mdn r* = .68; Black, Kelly, Myers, & Noyes, 1990; Goodman, Price, Rasmussen, Mazure, Delgado, et al., 1989; Kim et al., 1992; Kim et al., 1993), although correlations may have been spuriously inflated because both instruments were usually administered by the same rater (cf. Taylor, 1995).

Thus, little is known about the psychometric properties of the NIMH–GOCS. The scale does provide written descriptions of five different symptom clusters, but these tend to be very general. For example, Taylor (1995) noted that scores from 10 to 12 indicate severe OC symptoms, described as "symptoms that are crippling to the patient, interfering so that daily activity is an 'active struggle'. Patient may spend full time resisting symptoms. Requires much help from others to function" (p. 277). The scale does not include structured guidelines for the identification of specific OC symptoms. Its reliability and validity may, therefore, vary considerably, depending on the quality of the interview.

Lack of specificity and largely unknown psychometric properties strongly argue against the use of the NIMH–GOCS as a measure of OC symptoms.

BEHAVIORAL OBSERVATION

Behavioral Avoidance Test (BAT)

BATs are designed to assess observable avoidance behavior and self-reported anxiety that occur while the client is attempting to carry out anxiety-evoking tasks in vivo. BATs of varying methodology and complexity have been employed to assess OC symptoms. Foa and colleagues (e.g., Foa, Steketee, Grayson, Turner, & Latimer, 1984; Foa, Steketee, & Milby, 1980) measured subjective levels of discomfort while clients approached their most feared contaminant. Rachman et al. (1979) asked participants to attempt five different tasks prone to elicit ritualistic behavior and assessed the degree of avoidance and the level of discomfort during each task. The most ambitious effort to assess OC symptoms in vivo was conducted by Steketee et al. (1996). Therapists in this study selected three tasks that were difficult or impossible for clients to perform without significant anxiety or rituals. Each task was broken down into three to seven steps intended to provoke increasing levels of anxiety. Dependent variables included the percentage of steps completed, subjective levels of discomfort, degree of avoidance, and degree of ritualizing.

Because of the difficulty of adapting BATs to the wide variety of OC fears, this approach has rarely been used to assess OC symptoms. Thus, little is known about the psychometric properties of BATs. Based on data from Foa and colleagues' research, Freund (1986) found mixed support for convergent validity. The BAT correlated well with the interview CAC (rs = .37 and .62), but correlations with the self-report MOCI were more variable (rs = .04 and .62). Steketee et al. (1996), on the other hand, observed adequate convergent and discriminant validity. Associations with the assessor-rated Y–BOCS (Mdn $|r|$ = .33) and self-report MOCI (Mdn $|r|$ = .30) were moderately strong and within the range typically obtained for heteromethod coefficients. The BAT bore little relation to target ratings of fear and avoidance and rituals (Mdn $|r|$ = .21), but correlations were probably attenuated by the low reliability of target ratings. Overall, correlations with depression (Mdn r = .20) and $DSM–III–R$ criteria for OC personality disorder (Mdn $|r|$ = .06) were lower than the convergent validity correlations, thereby lending support for the discriminant validity of the BAT. Moreover, the BAT has demonstrated treatment sensitivity (e.g., Freund, 1986; Rachman et al., 1979; Steketee et al., 1996). Despite these positive findings there are a number of drawbacks to BATs: They are costly to administer, patients often object to their time-consuming nature, and the idiosyncratic nature of fear cues and the safety of the assessor may make it difficult to reliably replicate BATs for persons with OCD.

In light of these disadvantages, we do not endorse the BAT as an essential measure for the assessment of treatment outcome. Nonetheless, because behavioral change reflects a unique component of treatment response, we strongly encourage further exploration of the BAT for use with an OCD population. To increase reliability, we recommend that BATs be administered following a standardized protocol. This should include specific instructions aimed at reducing demand characteristics (cf. Taylor, 1995). Moreover, researchers are advised to combine individual

BAT variables into composite scores because appropriately constructed composites are likely to improve reliability (Steketee et al., 1996).

Behavioral Monitoring

Self-monitoring of the frequency and duration of obsessions and compulsions offers valuable clinical information about the daily fluctuation and situational triggers of symptoms (Steketee, 1993). In addition, continuous monitoring promises to yield more accurate information than questionnaire and interview measures that may be distorted by retrospective recall. It is surprising that diary methods have rarely been employed in treatment outcome research on OCD (for an exception see Foa et al., 1980) and that their psychometric properties have not yet been examined. The development of self-monitoring instruments for the assessment of OC symptoms is highly desirable.

CONCLUSIONS AND RECOMMENDATIONS

The data reviewed in this chapter clearly demonstrate that reliable and valid instruments for the assessment of OCD have been developed, although discriminant validity vis à vis depression is problematic for most measures. Heteromethod assessment procedures may reflect different features of OCD and are essential to its comprehensive assessment. Employing meta-analytic procedures, both Taylor (1995) and van Balkom et al. (1994) obtained significantly larger effect sizes for assessor-rated than for self-rated measures of OC symptoms. Pooling the data of two separate treatment outcome studies, van Oppen, Emmelkamp, et al. (1995) found target ratings of OC symptoms to be more sensitive to change with treatment than the Y–BOCS and the 41-item PI–R. These findings, along with the results of convergent validity analyses across methods of measurement, suggest that different assessment instruments are likely to yield different outcomes. Because this measurement factor makes the comparison of treatment effects difficult, it is important that researchers employ similar assessment procedures across sites to facilitate the synthesis of research results. To address these issues, we recommend the following minimum set of assessment procedures as essential to any treatment outcome study on OCD. We emphasize the use of a heteromethod assessment approach to increase the reliability and validity of outcome assessment.

To establish an initial diagnosis, researchers are strongly advised to employ a structured diagnostic interview for *DSM–IV* or ICD–10 OCD, such as the most recent editions of the ADIS (DiNardo et al., 1994), SCID–I

(First et al., 1995), or CIDI (WHO, 1993). We recommend that researchers use the following instruments to assess treatment outcome: both the interview (Goodman, Price, Rasmussen, Mazure, Delgado, et al., 1989; Goodman, Price, Rasmussen, Mazure, Fleischmann, et al., 1989) and questionnaire (Baer et al., 1993) version of the Y–BOCS, the PI (Sanavio, 1988) or PI–R (Burns et al., 1996; van Oppen, Hoekstra, & Emmelkamp, 1995), the MOCI (Dominguez et al., 1989; Hodgson & Rachman, 1977), and target ratings of clients' idiosyncratic symptoms. The majority of these treatment outcome measures have demonstrated sensitivity to change with psychological and pharmacological treatment as determined by statistical group comparisons conducted to evaluate treatment efficacy, but a few of the newer measures (self-report Y–BOCS, PI, 39-item PI–R) have not yet been used in treatment outcome studies. Because only three studies provide data on the comparative sensitivity to treatment-induced change across different measures of OC symptoms (Taylor, 1995; van Balkom et al., 1994; van Oppen, Emmelkamp, et al., 1995), additional data on this issue are highly desirable.

Most recent efforts are focused on identifying the cognitive features associated with OCD. A growing body of data suggests that dysfunctional beliefs such as an increased sense of responsibility, lack of insight into the senselessness of OC fears, perceived danger, and overprediction of harm may play an important role in the development and maintenance of OCD. A large number of instruments assessing cognitive distortions are currently being developed and require further testing. When reliable and valid cognitive measures are devised, they will be integral to any comprehensive assessment.

REFERENCES

Abel, J. L. (1993). Exposure with response prevention and serotonergic antidepressants in the treatment of obsessive compulsive disorder: A review and implications for interdisciplinary treatment. *Behaviour Research and Therapy, 31*, 463–478.

American Psychiatric Association. (1987). *Diagnostic and statistical manual of mental disorders* (3rd ed., rev.). Washington, DC: Author.

American Psychiatric Association. (1994). *Diagnostic and statistical manual of mental disorders* (4th ed.). Washington, DC: Author.

Asberg, M., Montgomery, S. A., Perris, C., Schalling, D., & Sedvall, G. (1978). The Comprehensive Psychopathological Rating Scale. *Acta Psychiatrica Scandinavica, 271*(Suppl.), 5–27.

Baer, L., Brown-Beasley, M. W., Sorce, J., & Henriques, A. I. (1993). Computer-assisted telephone administration of a structured interview for obsessive-compulsive disorder. *American Journal of Psychiatry, 150*, 1737–1738.

Barlow, D. H. (1987). The classification of anxiety disorders. In G. L. Tischler (Ed.), *Diagnosis and classification in psychiatry: A critical appraisal of DSM–III*. Cambridge, UK: Cambridge University Press.

Black, D. W., Kelly, M., Myers, C., & Noyes, R., Jr. (1990). Tritiated imipramine binding in obsessive-compulsive volunteers and psychiatrically normal controls. *Biological Psychiatry, 27,* 319–327.

Burns, L. G., Keortge, S. G., Formea, G. M., & Sternberger, L. G. (1996). Revision of the Padua Inventory of obsessive compulsive disorder symptoms: Distinctions between worry, obsessions, and compulsions. *Behaviour Research and Therapy, 34,* 163–173.

Chan, D. W. (1990). The Maudsley Obsessional-Compulsive Inventory: A psychometric investigation on Chinese normal subjects. *Behaviour Research and Therapy, 28,* 413–420.

Clark, A., & Friedman, M. J. (1983). Factor structure and discriminant validity of the SCL–90 in a veteran psychiatric population. *Journal of Personality Assessment, 47,* 396–404.

Cooper, J. (1970). The Leyton Obsessional Inventory. *Psychological Medicine, 1,* 48–64.

Cottraux, J., Bouvard, M., Defayolle, M., & Messy, P. (1988). Validity and factorial structure study of the Compulsive Activity Checklist. *Behavior Therapy, 19,* 45–53.

Cottraux, J., Mollard, E., Bouvard, M., Marks, I., Sluys, M., Nury, A. M., Douge, R., & Cialdella, P. (1990). A controlled study of fluvoxamine and exposure in obsessive-compulsive disorder. *International Clinical Psychopharmacology, 5,* 17–30.

Cox, B. J., Swinson, R. P., Morrison, B., & Lee, P. S. (1993). Clomipramine, fluoxetine, and behavior therapy in the treatment of obsessive-compulsive disorder: A meta-analysis. *Journal of Behavior Therapy and Experimental Psychiatry, 24,* 149–153.

de Beurs, E. (1993). *The assessment and treatment of panic disorder and agoraphobia.* Amsterdam: Thesis.

Derogatis, L. R. (1977). *SCL–90–R: Administration, scoring and procedures manual I.* Baltimore: Clinical Psychometrics Research.

Derogatis, L. R., Lipman, R. S., & Covi, L. (1973). SCL–90: An outpatient psychiatric rating scale—Preliminary report. *Psychopharmacology Bulletin, 9,* 13–17.

Derogatis, L. R., Lipman, R. S., Rickels, K., Uhlenhuth, E. H., & Covi, L. (1974). The Hopkins Symptom Checklist (HSCL): A self-report symptom inventory. *Behavioral Science, 19,* 1–15.

Derogatis, L. R., Rickels, K., & Rock, A. F. (1976). The SCL–90 and the MMPI: A step in the validation of a new self-report scale. *British Journal of Psychiatry, 128,* 280–289.

DiNardo, P. A., & Barlow, D. H. (1988). *Anxiety Disorders Interview Schedule, Revised (ADIS–R).* Albany: Phobia and Anxiety Disorders Clinic, State University of New York.

DiNardo, P. A., Brown, T. A., & Barlow, D. H. (1994). *Anxiety Disorders Interview Schedule for DSM–IV (ADIS–IV).* Albany, NY: Graywind.

DiNardo, P. A., Moras, K., Barlow, D. H., Rapee, R. M., & Brown, T. A. (1993). Reliability of DSM–III–R anxiety disorder categories: Using the Anxiety Disorders Interview Schedule–Revised (ADIS–R). *Archives of General Psychiatry, 50,* 251–256.

DiNardo, P. A., O'Brien, G. T., Barlow, D. H., Waddell, M. T., & Blanchard, E. B. (1983). Reliability of DSM–III anxiety disorder categories using a new structured interview. *Archives of General Psychiatry, 40,* 1070–1074.

Dinning, D. W., & Evans, R. G. (1977). Discriminant and convergent validity of the SCL–90 in psychiatric inpatients. *Journal of Personality Assessment, 41,* 304–310.

Dominguez, R. A., Jacobson, A. F., Gandara, J., Goldstein, B. J., & Steinbook, R. M. (1989). Drug response assessed by the modified Maudsley Obsessive-Compulsive Inventory. *Psychopharmacology Bulletin, 25,* 215–218.

Emmelkamp, P. M. G. (1988). The Maudsley Obsessional-Compulsive Inventory. In M. Hersen & A. S. Bellack (Eds.), *Dictionary of behavioral assessment techniques* (pp. 294–296). New York: Pergamon Press.

First, M. B., Spitzer, R. L., Gibbon, M., & Williams, J. B. W. (1995). *Structured Clinical Interview for DSM–IV axis I disorders.* New York: Biometrics Research Department.

Foa, E. B., Steketee, G. S., Grayson, J. B., Turner, R. M., & Latimer, P. R. (1984). Deliberate exposure and blocking of obsessive-compulsive rituals: Immediate and long-term effects. *Behavior Therapy, 15,* 450–472.

Foa, E. B., Steketee, G. S., Kozak, M. J., & Dugger, D. (1987). Effects of imipramine on depression and obsessive-compulsive symptoms. *Psychiatry Research, 21,* 123–136.

Foa, E. B., Steketee, G. S., & Milby, J. B. (1980). Differential effects of exposure and response prevention in obsessive-compulsive washers. *Journal of Consulting and Clinical Psychology, 48,* 71–79.

Freeston, M. H., Ladouceur, R., Rheaume, J., Letarte, H., Gagnon, F., & Thibodeau, N. (1994). Self-report of obsessions and worry. *Behaviour Research and Therapy, 32,* 29–36.

Freund, B. (1986). *Comparison of measures of obsessive-compulsive symptomatology.* Unpublished doctoral dissertation, Southern Illinois University at Carbondale.

Freund, B., & Foa, E. B. (1988a, September). *Obsessive-compulsive measures: Validity studies.* Poster session presented at the Behavior Therapy World Congress, Edinburgh, Scotland.

Freund, B., & Foa, E. B. (1988b, November). *Reliability of symptomatology and mood state measures in the assessment of obsessive-compulsive disorder.* Poster session presented at the annual meeting of the Association for Advancement of Behavior Therapy, New York.

Freund, B., Steketee, G. S., & Foa, E. B. (1987). Compulsive Activity Checklist (CAC): Psychometric analysis with obsessive-compulsive disorder. *Behavioral Assessment, 9,* 67–79.

Frost, R. O., Steketee, G. S., Krause, M. S., & Trepanier, K. L. (1995). The relationship of the Yale–Brown Obsessive Compulsive Scale (YBOCS) to other measures of obsessive compulsive symptoms in a nonclinical population. *Journal of Personality Assessment, 65,* 158–168.

Goodman, W. K., Price, L. H., Rasmussen, S. A., Mazure, C., Delgado, P., Heninger, G. R., & Charney, D. S. (1989). The Yale–Brown Obsessive Compulsive Scale: II. Validity. *Archives of General Psychiatry, 46,* 1012–1016.

Goodman, W. K., Price, L. H., Rasmussen, S. A., Mazure, C., Fleischmann, R. L., Hill, C. L., Heninger, G. R., & Charney, D. S. (1989). The Yale–Brown Obsessive Compulsive Scale: I. Development, use, and reliability. *Archives of General Psychiatry, 46,* 1006–1011.

Hewlett, W. A., Vinogradov, S., & Agras, W. S. (1992). Clomipramine, clonazepam, and clonidine treatment of obsessive-compulsive disorder. *Journal of Clinical Psychopharmacology, 12,* 420–429.

Hodgson, R. J., & Rachman, S. (1977). Obsessional-compulsive complaints. *Behaviour Research and Therapy, 15,* 389–395.

Insel, T. R., Murphy, D. L., Cohen, R. M., Alterman, I., Kilts, C., & Linnoila, M. (1983). Obsessive compulsive-disorder: A double-blind trial of clomipramine and clorgyline. *Archives of General Psychiatry, 40,* 605–612.

Jenike, M. A., Hyman, S., Baer, L., Holland, A., Minichiello, W. E., Buttolph, L., Summergrad, P., Seymour, R., & Ricciardi, J. (1990). A controlled trial of fluvoxamine in obsessive-compulsive disorder: Implications for a serotonergic theory. *American Journal of Psychiatry, 147,* 1209–1215.

Kazarian, S. S., Evans, D. R., & Lefave, K. (1977). Modification and factorial analysis of the Leyton Obsessional Inventory. *Journal of Clinical Psychology, 33,* 422–425.

Kendell, R. E., & DiScipio, W. J. (1970). Obsessional symptoms and obsessional personality traits in patients with depressive illness. *Psychological Medicine, 1,* 65–72.

Khanna, S., Kaliaperumal, V. G., & Channabasavanna, S. M. (1990). Clusters of obsessive-compulsive phenomena in obsessive-compulsive disorder. *British Journal of Psychiatry, 156,* 51–54.

Kim, S. W., Dysken, M. W., & Katz, R. (1989). Rating scales for obsessive compulsive disorder. *Psychiatric Annals, 19,* 74–79.

Kim, S. W., Dysken, M. W., & Kuskowski, M. (1990). The Yale–Brown Obsessive-Compulsive Scale: A reliability and validity study. *Psychiatry Research, 34,* 99–106.

Kim, S. W., Dysken, M. W., & Kuskowski, M. (1992). The Symptom Checklist–90: Obsessive-compulsive subscale: A reliability and validity study. *Psychiatry Research, 41,* 37–44.

Kim, S. W., Dysken, M. W., Kuskowski, M., & Hoover, K. M. (1993). The Yale–Brown Obsessive Compulsive Scale (Y–BOCS) and the NIMH Global Obsessive Compulsive Scale (NIMH–GOCS): A reliability and validity study. *International Journal of Methods in Psychiatric Research, 3*, 37–44.

Kraaijkamp, H. J. M., Emmelkamp, P. M. G., & van den Hout, M. A. (1986). *The Maudsley Obsessional-Compulsive Inventory: Reliability and validity.* Unpublished manuscript, University of Groningen, The Netherlands.

Kyrios, M., Bhar, S., & Wade, D. (1996). The assessment of obsessive-compulsive phenomena: Psychometric and normative data on the Padua Inventory from an Australian non-clinical student sample. *Behaviour Research and Therapy, 34*, 85–95.

Marks, I. M., Hallam, R. S., Connolly, J., & Philpott, R. (1977). *Nursing in behavioural psychotherapy.* London: Royal College of Nursing of the United Kingdom.

Marks, I. M., Stern, R. S., Mawson, D., Cobb, J., & McDonald, R. (1980). Clomipramine and exposure for obsessive-compulsive rituals: I. *British Journal of Psychiatry, 136*, 1–25.

McKay, D. R., Danyko, S. J., Neziroglu, F. A., & Yaryura-Tobias, J. A. (1995). Factor structure of the Yale–Brown Obsessive Compulsive Scale: A two-dimensional measure. *Behaviour Research and Therapy, 33*, 865–869.

Millar, D. G. (1980). A repertory grid study of obsessionality: Distinctive cognitive structure or distinctive cognitive content? *British Journal of Medical Psychology, 53*, 59–66.

Millar, D. G. (1983). Hostile emotion and obsessional neurosis. *Psychological Medicine, 13*, 813–819.

Murray, R. M., Cooper, J. E., & Smith, A. (1979). The Leyton Obsessional Inventory: An analysis of the responses of 73 obsessional patients. *Psychological Medicine, 9*, 305–311.

Nunnally, J. C. (1978). *Psychometric theory* (2nd ed.). New York: McGraw-Hill.

Philpott, R. (1975). Recent advances in the behavioural measurement of obsessional illness: Difficulties common to these and other instruments. *Scottish Medical Journal, 20*, 33–40.

Price, L. H., Goodman, W. K., Charney, D. S., Rasmussen, S. A., & Heninger, G. R. (1987). Treatment of severe obsessive-compulsive disorder with fluvoxamine. *American Journal of Psychiatry, 144*, 1059–1061.

Rachman, S. (1974). Primary obsessional slowness. *Behaviour Research and Therapy, 12*, 9–18.

Rachman, S., Cobb, J., Grey, S., McDonald, B., Mawson, D., Sartory, G., Stern, R. (1979). The behavioural treatment of obsessional-compulsive disorders, with and without clomipramine. *Behaviour Research and Therapy, 17*, 467–478.

Richter, M. A., Cox, B. J., & Direnfeld, D. M. (1994). A comparison of three assessment instruments for obsessive-compulsive symptoms. *Journal of Behavior Therapy and Experimental Psychiatry, 25*, 143–147.

Rosenfeld, R., Dar, R., Anderson, D., Kobak, K. A., & Greist, J. H. (1992). A computer-administered version of the Yale–Brown Obsessive Compulsive Scale. *Psychological Assessment, 4*, 329–332.

Sanavio, E. (1988). Obsessions and compulsions: The Padua Inventory. *Behaviour Research and Therapy, 26*, 169–177.

Sanavio, E., & Vidotto, G. (1985). The components of the Maudsley Obsessional-Compulsive Questionnaire. *Behaviour Research and Therapy, 23*, 659–662.

Semler, G., Wittchen, H.-U., Joschke, K., Zaudig, M., von Geiso, T., Kaiser, S., von Cranach, M., & Pfister, H. (1987). Test–retest reliability of a standardized psychiatric interview (DIS/CIDI) for DSM–III diagnoses. *European Archives of Psychiatric Neurological Science, 236*, 214–222.

Shutty, M. S., DeGood, D. E., & Schwartz, D. P. (1986). Psychological dimensions of distress in chronic pain patients: A factor analytic study of Symptom Checklist–90 responses. *Journal of Consulting and Clinical Psychology, 54*, 836–842.

Snowdon, J. (1980). A comparison of written and postbox forms of the Leyton Obsessional Inventory. *Psychological Medicine, 10*, 165–170.

Spitzer, R. L., Williams, J. B. W., Gibbon, M., & First, M. B. (1990). *Structured Clinical Interview for DSM–III–R*. Washington, DC: American Psychiatric Press.

Stanley, M. A., Prather, R. C., Beck, G. J., Brown, T. C., Wagner, A. L., & Davis, M. L. (1993). Psychometric analyses of the Leyton Obsessional Inventory in patients with obsessive-compulsive and other anxiety disorders. *Psychological Assessment, 5*, 187–192.

Steketee, G. S. (1993). *Treatment of obsessive compulsive disorder*. New York: Guilford.

Steketee, G. S., & Chambless, D. L. (1994). *Reliability of target ratings data for obsessive-compulsive disorder* [Unpublished data]. Boston: School of Social Work, Boston University.

Steketee, G. S., Chambless, D. L., Tran, G. Q., Worden, H., & Gillis, M. M. (1996). Behavioral Avoidance Test for obsessive compulsive disorder. *Behaviour Research and Therapy, 34*, 73–83.

Steketee, G. S., & Doppelt, H. (1986). Measurement of obsessive-compulsive symptomatology: Utility of the Hopkins Symptom Checklist. *Psychiatry Research, 19*, 135–145.

Steketee, G. S., & Freund, B. (1993). Compulsive Activity Checklist (CAC): Further psychometric analyses and revision. *Behavioural Psychotherapy, 21*, 13–25.

Steketee, G. S., Freund, B., & Foa, E. B. (1988). Likert scaling. In M. Hersen & A. S. Bellack (Eds.), *Dictionary of behavioral assessment techniques* (pp. 289–291). New York: Pergamon.

Steketee, G. S., Frost, R., & Bogart, K. (1995). *The Yale–Brown Obsessive Compulsive Scale: Interview versus self-report*. Manuscript under review.

Sternberger, L. G., & Burns, G. L. (1990a). Compulsive Activity Checklist and the Maudsley Obsessional-Compulsive Inventory: Psychometric properties of two measures of obsessive-compulsive disorder. *Behavior Therapy, 21*, 117–127.

Sternberger, L. G., & Burns, G. L. (1990b). Obsessions and compulsions: Psychometric properties of the Padua Inventory with an American college population. *Behaviour Research and Therapy, 28*, 341–345.

Taylor, S. (1995). Assessment of obsessions and compulsions: Reliability, validity, and sensitivity to treatment effects. *Clinical Psychology Review, 15*, 261–296.

Thoren, P., Asberg, M., Cronholm, B., Jörnestedt, L., & Träskman, L. (1980). Clomipramine treatment of obsessive-compulsive disorder: A controlled clinical trial. *Archives of General Psychiatry, 37*, 1281–1285.

van Balkom, A. J. L. M., van Oppen, P., Vermeulen, A. W. A., van Dyck, R., Nauta, M. C. E., & Vorst, H. C. M. (1994). A meta-analysis on the treatment of obsessive compulsive disorder: A comparison of antidepressants, behavior, and cognitive therapy. *Clinical Psychology Review, 14*, 359–381.

van Oppen, P. (1992). Obsessions and compulsions: Dimensional structure, reliability, convergent and divergent validity of the Padua Inventory. *Behaviour Research and Therapy, 30*, 631–637.

van Oppen, P., de Haan, E., van Balkom, A. J. L. M., Spinhoven, P., Hoogduin, K., & van Dyck, R. (1995). Cognitive therapy and exposure in vivo in the treatment of obsessive compulsive disorder. *Behaviour Research and Therapy, 33*, 379–390.

van Oppen, P., Emmelkamp, P. M. G., van Balkom, A. J. L., & van Dyck, R. (1995). The sensitivity to change of measures for obsessive-compulsive disorder. *Journal of Anxiety Disorders, 9*, 241–248.

van Oppen, P., Hoekstra, R. J., & Emmelkamp, P. M. G. (1995). The structure of obsessive-compulsive symptoms. *Behaviour Research and Therapy, 33*, 15–23.

Warren, R., Zgourides, G., & Monto, M. (1993). Self-report versions of the Yale–Brown Obsessive-Compulsive Scale: An assessment of a sample of normals. *Psychological Reports, 73*, 574.

Williams, J. B. W., Gibbon, M., First, M. B., Spitzer, R. L., Davies, M., Borus, J., Howes, M. J., Kane, J., Pope, H. G., Jr., Rounsaville, B., & Wittchen, H.-U. (1992). The Structured Clinical Interview for DSM–III–R (SCID). II. Multisite test–retest reliability. *Archives of General Psychiatry, 49*, 630–636.

Wittchen, H.-U., Robins, L. N., Cottler, L. B., Sartorius, N., Burke, J. D., & Regier, D. (1991). Cross-cultural feasibility, reliability and sources of variance of the Composite International Diagnostic Interview (CIDI). *British Journal of Psychiatry, 159,* 645–653.

Woody, S. R., Steketee, G. S., & Chambless, D. L. (1995a). Reliability and validity of the Yale–Brown Obsessive-Compulsive Scale. *Behaviour Research and Therapy, 33,* 597–605.

Woody, S. R., Steketee, G. S., & Chambless, D. L. (1995b). The usefulness of the obsessive-compulsive scale of the Symptom Checklist–90–Revised. *Behaviour Research and Therapy, 33,* 607–611.

World Health Organization. (1990). *The Composite International Diagnostic Interview (CIDI).* Geneva: World Health Organization.

World Health Organization. (1992). *International statistical classification of diseases and related health problems, tenth revision (ICD–10).* Geneva: Author.

World Health Organization. (1993). *The Composite International Diagnostic Interview, core version 1.1.* Washington, DC: American Psychiatric Press.

10

Measuring Outcome in Drug Trials of Obsessive-Compulsive Disorder

Suck Won Kim
University of Minnesota Medical School

The purpose of this chapter is to summarize how the application of assessment measures for obsessive-compulsive disorder (OCD) has affected treatment, especially drug treatment, and outcomes and to provide suggestions for the future development of improved assessment scales. An assessment of comorbid symptoms such as anxiety and depression and their significance in the management of treatment-refractory OCD cases is also discussed.

Prior to the introduction of the Yale–Brown Obsessive Compulsive Scale (Y–BOCS) investigators involved in OCD research did not have widely accepted reliable and valid instruments to assess symptom change for their treatment studies (Goodman, Price, Rasmussen, Mazure, Delgado, et al., 1989). Insel et al. (1983) expressed their concerns when undertaking a comprehensive OCD drug treatment study. In their published report they stated, "The design of sensitive and valid assessment scales for obsessional symptoms has been one of the most challenging aspects of research in this area. There is no widely accepted rating scale for measuring change in patients with OCD" (p. 607). Montgomery and Montgomery (1980) also said, "Measuring change in obsessional illness is extremely difficult. The absence of any published trials demonstrating superiority of one pharmacological treatment over another can be partly attributed to the difficulty in rating the symptoms of these disorders" (p. 51).

These concerns were expressed when investigators began to apply rigorous study designs to evaluate efficacy of various antidepressants, including clomipramine, in the treatment of OCD. Investigators involved in clomipramine treatment studies in the 1970s still did not have established OCD rating scales for use in their studies (Allen & Rack, 1975; Ananth, 1977; Schulz, 1986; Singh, Sexena, & Gent, 1977; Waxman, 1975, 1977; Wyndowe, Solyom, & Ananth, 1975; Yaryura-Tobias & Neziroglu, 1975; Yaryura-Tobias, Neziroglu, & Bergman, 1976). Cooper (1970) developed a comprehensive OCD rating scale, the Leyton Obsessional Inventory (LOI), in 1970. A number of investigators have used the LOI in their studies, but further work has shown that the scale has limitations (Insel et al., 1983; Kim, Dysken, & Kuskowski, 1990; Thoren, Asberg, Cronholm, Jornestedt, & Traskman, 1980). The LOI interference subscale, however, has been found to be sensitive to clinical change (Flament et al., 1985; Insel et al., 1983; Kim et al., 1990; Prasad, 1984; Thoren et al., 1980). Allen and Rack (1975) applied the LOI in their clomipramine study in OCD and presented data showing the superiority of the interference subscale of the LOI in comparison to other subscales such as the symptom inventory subscale or resistance subscale. They reported that the interference subscale of the LOI is the most relevant and sensitive in measuring symptom severity or change during treatments.

Other OCD assessment scales that investigators used in the 1970s, such as the Obsessive Compulsive Rating Scale (Beaumont, 1975, 1977) or the Psychiatric Questionnaire for Obsessive Compulsive Disorder (Wyndowe et al., 1975), were not as comprehensive as the LOI. Even through the mid-1980s, there were no satisfactory rating scales for assessment of OCD symptom change. Rapoport, Elkins, and Mikkelsen (1980) used the modified LOI in their clomipramine and desipramine comparison study. In the same year, Thoren and his colleagues used the Comprehensive Psychiatric Rating Scale, Obsessive Compulsive Subscale (CPRS–OCS; Asberg, Montgomery, Perris, Schalling, & Sedvall, 1978), LOI, and Individual Self-Rating Scale (Thoren et al., 1980) in their clomipramine treatment study in OCD. The LOI used in this study failed to demonstrate efficacy of clomipramine in the treatment of OCD except in the interference subscale. Other scales they used are limited in scope and are no longer used widely. Insel et al. (1983) used the modified LOI and found the scale insensitive in assessing obsessive compulsive (OC) symptom change. Again, the interference subscale of the LOI was more sensitive than the rest of its subscales. The interference subscale of the LOI, however, is not as sensitive in assessing OC symptoms as the Y–BOCS (Kim et al., 1990).

The array of rating scales the investigators assembled for their studies is a measure of the depth of the problems they faced in accurately assessing changing symptoms during treatment. A brief summary described in Table 10.1 depicts the plights the investigators faced in assessing OC symptom change through the mid-1980s.

TABLE 10.1

OCD Rating Scales Used for Clinical Treatment Studies Prior to the Development of the Yale–Brown Obsessive Compulsive Scale

Authors	Year	Rating Scales Used	References
Kahn, Westenberg, & Jolles	1984	Obsessive Compulsive Rating	Beaumont (1975)
Prasad	1984, 1985, 1986	Leyton Obsessional Inventory	Cooper (1970)
Turner, Jacob, Beidel, & Himmelhoch	1985	Maudsley Obsessive Compulsive	Rachman & Hodgson (1980)
		Clinical Global Impression	Guy (1976)
		Symptom Checklist-58–OC	Derogatis, Lipman, Rickels, Uhlenhuth, & Covi (1974)
Fontaine & Chouinard	1986	Comprehensive Rating Scale–OC Subscale	Asberg et al. (1978)
		Clinical Global Impression	Guy (1976)
		Symptom Checklist-58–OC	Derogatis et al. (1974)
Flament et al.	1985	Leyton Obsessional Inventory	Berg, Rapoport, & Flament (1986)
		Obsessive Compulsive Rating	Rapoport et al. (1980)
		Comprehensive Rating Scale–OC Subscale	Asberg et al. (1978)
		NIMH-Global Obsessive Scale	Murphy, Picker, & Alterman (1982)
Mavissakalian et al.	1985	Obsessive Compulsive Neurotic	Mavissakalian et al. (1985)
		Obsessive Compulsive Scale	
Perse et al.	1987	Obsessive Compulsive Checklist	Rachman & Hodgson (1980)
		Maudsley Obsessive Compulsive	
		Symptom Checklist-90–OCS	Derogatis, Lipman, & Covi (1973)
		General Rating Scale	Perse et al. (1987)

Most of the rating scales listed in Table 10.1 were not systematically studied or validated. The majority of these OCD rating scales were designed and introduced without extensive field trials.

The problem was more acute for OCD treatment studies because effect size is often not as pronounced. In the original multicenter clomipramine treatment studies in OCD (two separate protocols) the Y–BOCS scores decreased 38% and 44% each for the clomipramine-treated patients and 3% and 5% for the placebo-treated patients when compared to baseline scores (The Clomipramine Collaborative Study Group, 1991). A meta-analysis by Greist, Jefferson, Kobak, Katzelnick, and Serlin (1995) showed that newer drugs such as fluoxetine, fluvoxamine, and sertraline were not even as effective as clomipramine. There have not been large-scale head-to-head comparison studies to confirm this finding. One of the most frequently asked questions from OCD patients and their families is the efficacy ranking of the available drugs. There are now five drugs that have been shown to be effective in the treatment of OCD (The Clomipramine Collaborative Study Group, 1991; Goodman, Price, Rasmussen, Delgado, et al., 1989; Greist, Chouinard, et al., 1995; Perse, Greist, Jefferson, Rosenfeld, & Dar, 1987; Price, Goodman, Charney, Rasmussen, & Heninger, 1987; Tollefson et al., 1994; Wheadon, Bushnell, & Steiner, 1993). A highly sensitive, reliable, and valid rating scale may detect even a small difference in efficacy size if the sample size is large enough.

Investigators involved in the development of the Y–BOCS had significant experience with OCD patients and were aware of the limitations of existing rating scales. Studies have shown that the Y–BOCS is reliable and valid (Goodman, Price, Rasmussen, Mazure, Delgado, et al., 1989; Goodman, Price, Rasmussen, Mazure, Fleischmann, et al., 1989; Kim et al., 1990; Woody, Steketee, & Chambless, 1995a), as well as more sensitive than existing OCD rating scales. Inventory-driven rating scales can pose a risk because if a patient has OC symptoms that are not listed in the inventory, the result may not correctly reflect the nature and intensity of underlying symptoms. In addition, patients who have multiple OC symptoms are often assessed as having more severe OCD even if these symptoms are mild, whereas patients who have few symptoms are assessed as having mild OCD although these symptoms are severe. These problems can be corrected by a change in design, but there is no existing inventory-driven OCD rating scale that has taken these factors into account. Price et al. (1987) used the Y–BOCS in their fluvoxamine study in the treatment of OCD in the mid-1980s. From then on, the Y–BOCS quickly became the standard OCD rating scale, and very few other existing scales have been used in OCD research studies since.

The Y–BOCS is a clinician-administered OCD rating scale, not a diagnostic instrument. It was designed to measure symptom severity or change in patients who have prediagnosed OCD. Systematic collection of symptom inventory is necessary before the scale can be applied properly. Patients are then asked to average all obsessions or compulsions for the past 7 days. This aspect of the Y–BOCS is perhaps one of the reasons the Y–BOCS has been shown to be more sensitive in assessing OC symptom change in comparison to other existing OCD rating scales. Without symptom averaging, short-term symptom fluctuation can adversely affect assessment outcome. Assessment of collective symptom severity is advantageous because it is not influenced by the number of OC symptoms as much as the severity of overall OC symptoms.

The LOI was designed to remedy the shortcomings of the existing inventory-driven OCD rating scales. It not only includes a number of OC symptoms, but the inventory items a patient selects as present are assessed later for their severity. Two severity measures are included in the LOI. The resistance subscale assesses a degree of resistance against an OC symptom and later computes the total score, which becomes the resistance score. *Resistance* is defined as a volitional effort from OCD patients to defeat underlying OC symptoms. For example, a patient who has an urge to wash hands resists against the urge and refrains from doing so. In the LOI, higher resistance scores are interpreted as more severe symptoms. By comparison, on the Y–BOCS, higher resistance scores are designed to reflect milder OC symptoms. Validation studies suggest that the Y–BOCS resistance subscale is more sensitive in assessing OC symptom changes than the LOI resistance subscale (Kim et al., 1990; Kim, Dysken, Pheley, & Hoover, 1994). Investigators involved in the design of the Y–BOCS were aware of the difficulties involved in the design of the resistance subscale. We found that resistance subscales are generally not as sensitive as other subscales on the LOI or Y–BOCS in assessing symptom change during treatment (Kim et al., 1990; Kim et al., 1994).

In designing a new OCD rating scale, these aspects need to be taken into account. Inventory-driven scales, such as the LOI, Maudsley Obsessional-Compulsive Inventory (MOCI; Rachman & Hodgson, 1980), CPRS–OCS, and Symptom Checklist–90–OCS (SCL–90–OCS; Derogatis, Lipman, & Covi, 1973), present such risks even though some of these rating scales have symptom severity measurement features. For some OCD scales, such as the LOI, SCL–58–OCS, and SCL–90–OCS, extensive studies were carried out prior to the introduction of the scales but recent studies demonstrated either a decreased sensitivity (LOI; Kim et al., 1990) or poor outcome in validation studies (SCL–58–OCS and SCL–90–OCS; Kim, Dysken, & Kuskowski, 1992; Steketee & Doppelt, 1986; Woody, Steketee, & Chambless, 1995b).

Although uncommon, some OCD patients have difficulty assessing total time occupied with obsessions and this problem can affect the assessment outcome for the first item of the Y–BOCS. If a patient has only obsessions or compulsions, total Y–BOCS scores may be low and may not correctly reflect underlying symptom severity. We also have found that in rare cases when symptoms are severe, patients remain in their bedrooms and refuse to come out. The reason for this restriction in mobility is that patients want to avoid triggering stimuli that provoke OC symptoms. As long as they stay in their rooms they seem to have few OC symptoms and report little or no distress coming from symptoms. We know that these patients have perhaps the most severe OC symptoms, yet if they are assessed concretely the Y–BOCS scores may be low. To remedy some of these shortcomings the scale has been modified recently.

The Y–BOCS was not designed to examine individual OC symptoms or to assess subclinical OC symptoms that do not pose significant subjective distress. For these reasons the scale is not suitable for a large-scale population study. An inventory-driven scale would be more appropriate for such purposes. The Y–BOCS total scores, obsession and compulsion subscale scores, and individual item scores within obsession or compulsions subscales (see Feske & Chambless, chap. 9, this volume) have provided an important source of information in analyzing treatment outcome data. The Y–BOCS also requires initial gathering of symptom inventory. Baer (1994) used such data for a factor analysis study. The factor analytic data not only provided three cohesive subgroups of OC symptoms, but correlation data among three groups of symptoms as well. Another important and interesting fact that emerged from the study was that one of the three factors in OCD and one of the two factors in obsessive-compulsive personality disorder (OCPD) showed statistically significant correlations ($p < .01$). OC symptoms that cohere within this factor include preoccupation with details, indecision, inability to throw things away, perfectionism, and restricted affection. Factor 2 (overconscientiousness, devotion to work, insistence that others comply, and lack of generosity) within OCPD seems to correlate poorly with all three factors of OCD. In a comparison among medical students, law students, and controls, we used a log linear model for testing associations between categorical OC symptom variables. When we fitted three groups of OC symptoms and three groups of OC traits and goodness-of-fit statistics were computed, future medical doctors were found to have more Factor 2 traits and future lawyers had primarily Factor 1 traits. It would be interesting to find out if the OCPD patients who have primarily Factor 1 symptoms develop OCD more often than OCPD patients who have Factor 2 symptoms. These factorial data may become an important source of information for the future OCD–OCPD comparison and other OCD research studies.

Because the Y–BOCS assesses only collective symptom severity, it is difficult to extrapolate individual symptom information from the outcome data. For example, if the individual inventory symptoms are assessed on a weekly basis during treatment, a response pattern for various OC symptoms could be analyzed at a later time. Differential treatment response patterns for individual OC symptoms or subgroups of OC symptoms have not been studied extensively. For example, we still do not understand if hoarding, order, or symmetry symptoms respond as well as other OC symptoms during an OCD treatment study.

The Y–BOCS was first applied in a large-scale multicenter OCD treatment study in 1986 to evaluate the efficacy of clomipramine in OCD (The Clomipramine Collaborative Study Group, 1991). Since then the Y–BOCS has been used in all major multicenter drug treatment studies. The scale played a pivotal role in advancing new knowledge in the OCD field in recent years and made a major contribution in the development and introduction of newer pharmacological agents in the management of OCD. The Y–BOCS is now considered a standard scale in OCD research.

The Y–BOCS is likely to remain the standard assessment scale in OCD research because a majority of investigators involved in OCD research agree that it is easy to administer in clinical and research settings. Greist and his colleagues have developed a computerized Y–BOCS (Rosenfeld, Dar, Anderson, Kobak, & Greist, 1992). Scores obtained with this computerized Y–BOCS correlate highly ($\gamma = .88$) with clinician administered Y–BOCS scores (Rosenfeld et al., 1992). Goodman (unpublished data) recently introduced a Screening Test of OCD. This instrument was adapted from the Y–BOCS. Each questionnaire in the Screening Test asks about the presence or absence of a group of OCD symptoms rather than individual OC symptoms. The questionnaires then inquire about intensity and duration of symptoms and levels of subjective distress and interference in daily function.

RATING SCALES AND THE TREATMENT-REFRACTORY PATIENT

Although significant progress has been made and OCD rating scales have contributed in the process, there are a number of OCD patients who are refractory to drug or behavior treatments or improve only minimally. Application of rating scales and their implications in managing treatment-refractory cases are discussed in the following sections.

Assessment of Anxiety Symptoms in OCD and Its Implications in Treatment Outcome

How the presence, absence, or severity of anxiety symptoms in OCD affects treatment outcome has not been studied extensively. Subgroups of OCD patients may have different levels of anxiety symptoms. For example, some OCD patients who have symmetry, precision, ordering, and repeating obsessions have been described as having less anxiety. There are also OCD patients who have symmetry, precision, and perfectionism obsessions and severe fear. They are often extremely afraid of initiating any act. This type of fear and the fear that is evoked when an OCD patient is exposed to a feared object may be qualitatively different from anxiety symptoms provoked when an OCD patient resists against obsessions or compulsions. The strongest anxiety symptoms are often provoked when one resists against one's compulsions. This area has not been studied extensively. Systematic documentation of different anxiety symptoms in OCD by using appropriate rating scales may provide diagnostic and therapeutic clues.

If an OCD rating scale has individual OC symptom inventory items and an anxiety symptom measurement subscale (or an independent anxiety scale is used along with an OCD rating scale), it can be applied in large-scale treatment studies. Data from such studies can be analyzed to examine the relations between anxiety symptoms and certain OC symptoms. The same data can be analyzed to assess prognostic implications of anxiety symptoms in OCD. Existing OCD rating scales do not have built-in subscales that measure anxiety symptoms; thus, anxiety symptoms need to be assessed independently. It is not difficult to understand that improvement of OC symptoms would accompany improvement in anxiety symptoms. What is still unclear is what subtypes of OC symptom groups are associated with anxiety symptoms and to what degree. We also do not know how the different levels of anxiety symptoms in OCD are affecting overall behavior and drug treatment outcomes.

In a drug treatment study, Insel et al. (1983) assessed not only change in OC symptoms, but anxiety symptoms as well. Most, if not all, recent multicenter drug treatment studies did not include anxiety rating scales in their study protocols even though OCD is diagnosed as an anxiety disorder in the *Diagnostic and Statistical Manual of Mental Disorders* (4th ed. [*DSM–IV*]; American Psychiatric Association, 1994). Thus, we are unable to extrapolate from these data the role of anxiety in the overall treatment outcome. Because anxiety symptoms are a significant component of overall OC symptom manifestation it seems reasonable to assess these symptoms simultaneously. Anxiety symptoms in OCD appear to have more than one component. Those that result from provoking stimuli appear to be different from anxiety symptoms that are evoked when patients resist against their obsessions or compulsions. Anxiety symptoms provoked by a triggering stimulus appear to correlate strongly with underlying obsessions but anxiety symptoms triggered by resistance symptoms do not seem to correlate with underlying obsessions or OCD treatment outcome (Kim et al., 1994). Anxiety symptoms that occur in anticipation of future obsessions may be qualitatively different from the fear that is provoked from exposure to a feared object. OCD patients may also have ongoing anxiety symptoms not directly linked to specific anticipatory events. Anxiety symptoms and their relation with other psychiatric disorders have been reviewed recently (Maser & Cloninger, 1990). Study results have demonstrated that OC symptom improvement is independent of underlying depressive symptoms. The same may be true for anxiety symptoms, but this area has not been examined as carefully. Further studies may provide insights that may eventually lead to improved understanding for treatment-resistant cases.

Assessment of Depressive Symptoms in OCD and Its Implications in the Treatment Outcome

In the 1960s, European investigators began to notice change in obsessive symptoms while they were evaluating efficacy of clomipramine in clinical trials, especially in depressive disorders (De Voxvrie, 1968; Fernandez & Lopes-Ibor, 1967; Guyotat, Favre-Tissot, & Marie-Gardine, 1968; Lopes-Ibor, 1966). This has led to the belief that improvement in obsessive symptoms in OCD is secondary to improvement in depressive symptoms. Subsequent studies have shown evidence that obsessive symptom improvement in OCD by clomipramine is independent of improvement in underlying depressive symptoms (The Clomipramine Collaborative Study Group, 1991; Flament et al., 1985; Insel et al., 1983; Mavissakalian, Turner, Michelson, & Jacob, 1985; Thoren et al., 1980; Volavka, Neziroglu, & Yaryura-Tobias, 1985).

Depressive symptoms are perhaps the most common comorbid symptoms in OCD. Drugs that are effective in the treatment of OCD are also effective in reducing depressive symptoms. Three groups of commonly prescribed psychotropic drugs for depressive and anxiety disorders are benzodiazepines, tricyclic antidepressants, and selective serotonin reuptake inhibitors (SSRIs). These three classes of drugs have different efficacy spectrums for depressive and anxiety disorders. Benzodiazepines are usually effective in the treatment of anxiety disorders only. Tricyclic antidepressants are generally effective for both anxiety and depressive disorders. SSRIs are effective in anxiety, depressive disorders, and OCD. Thus, it is generally understood that depressive symptoms that occur in OCD patients are secondary to underlying OC symptoms. If depressive symptoms are primary, treatment by one of the traditional antidepressants should be sufficient to bring OC symptoms under control.

When a patient is refractory to treatments, correct assessment of affective symptoms becomes more important. Although in most cases depressive symptoms decrease during drug treatment, there are patients who develop depressive symptoms while they are receiving clomipramine or other SSRI treatments. Some OCD patients show shifting symptom patterns in which predominantly obsessive symptoms will appear at one time and depressive symptoms at another. This can also be true in the case of either concurrent or shifting bipolar disorder. The pattern of symptom shifting or symptom mixture varies significantly from patient to patient. Although lithium augmentation has been shown to be ineffective (McDougle, Price, Goodman, Charney, & Heninger, 1991; Pigott et al., 1991), some of these patients respond better when lithium is added to the therapeutic regimen. In a few patients who fail to respond to every other known treatment mode, lithium as an adjunctive medicine can be an important addition. A diagnostic instrument or rating scale sometimes can detect comorbid psychiatric symptoms that are missed in a busy clinic. In practice, it would be inconvenient to administer depression rating scales to all OCD patients. Such scales should perhaps be reserved for those patients whose clinical progress is in doubt. Most of the recent drug treatment studies, especially the large-scale multicenter studies, did not evaluate depressive symptoms closely except during the baseline period. For this reason we still do not have a valid large-scale database to analyze the therapeutic and prognostic implications of the concurrent or past depressive symptoms in OCD patients. In this regard, administration of a depression rating scale or scales during a large OCD drug treatment study would provide clinically relevant information, especially for those patients who are refractory to conventional treatments.

Assessment of Resistance Symptoms in OCD and Its Implications in Treatment Outcome

Resistance is one of the major symptoms of OCD. A number of OCD rating scales have a resistance subscale, because patients who have mild OC symptoms generally have mild resistance against their obsessions or compulsions and patients who have more serious symptoms tend to resist more. Phenomenology of resistance in a given OCD patient, however, is unpredictable. Sometimes resistance symptoms increase commensurate with escalating OC symptoms. When symptoms become very severe or extreme, however, patients are unable to resist and tend to give in to their obsessions or compulsions. Some OCD patients resist more during the early phase of symptom improvement. Patients who have had OCD for a long time also tend to resist less. Thus, an assessment of resistance symptoms alone usually does not provide guidance as to the nature or progress of the underlying illness. Resistance symptoms, however, may provide important clinical clues during the course of behavior or drug treatments. Systematic studies in this area may provide important information about how baseline levels of resistance and resistance during treatment affect overall treatment outcome. Resistance against obsessions and compulsions brings about anxiety symptoms. How these anxiety symptoms participate and contribute during the therapeutic process has not been studied systematically for their effect on pharmacotherapeutics or cognitive-behavior therapy.

Assessment of Subgroup of OCD Symptoms and Their Implications in Treatment Outcome

We do not have a highly sensitive, comprehensive, and valid rating scale that can correctly assess presence, absence, or change in individual OC symptoms and their severity. It is desirable to have such a scale because it would allow a detailed analysis of individual OC symptom change during treatments. Baer (1994) demonstrated a pattern of related OC symptom aggregation such as symmetry, saving, hoarding, ordering, repeating, and counting symptoms. These symptoms have been known to occur not only in OCD patients, but in Tourette's syndrome patients as well. McDougle and his colleagues reported that patients who have these symptoms show enhanced treatment outcome when a neuroleptic is added to traditional OCD drugs (McDougle et al., 1993; McDougle et al., 1994; McDougle et al., 1990). These findings suggest that some OC symptoms respond better to drug treatment than others. There have not been systematic studies, other than what was described earlier, in this area. An inventory-driven rating scale will allow this type of analysis and provide potentially important data that have implications for treatment outcome, especially for treatment-resistant patients. Given a large database, one would be able to study treatment response rate of various OC symptoms such as slowness and hoarding. In population, twin, or family studies, inventory-driven rating scales would provide even more important data, especially if there are changes in symptom severity during an observation period.

Assessment of Personality Disorders in OCD and Its Implications in Treatment Outcome

Studies have shown that OCD patients often have concurrent personality disorders when assessed by standardized diagnostic instruments such as the Structured Interview for the DSM–III Personality Disorders (SID–P; Baer et al., 1990; Black, Noyes, Pfohl, Goldstein, & Blum, 1993) or the Millon Clinical Multiaxial Inventory Personality Scales (Millon, 1981). OCD patients who have Cluster A personality disorder have more severe OC symptoms at baseline, and OCD patients who have more severe symptoms have an increased number of personality disorders (Baer et al., 1992). In the same study, authors reported that OCD patients who have schizotypal, borderline, or avoidant personality disorders responded poorly to drug treatment. OCD patients who have a higher number of total personality disorders also responded poorly. Presence of Cluster A personality disorder was a predictor of poorer treatment outcome. Earlier, Jenike and his colleagues reported evidence of poorer treatment outcome in OCD patients with schizotypal personality disorder (Jenike, Baer, Minichiello, Schwartz, & Carey, 1986). Ricciardi et al. (1992) found improvement or resolution of underlying personality disorders in patients who responded to OCD drug or behavior treatments. They also found that OCD patients who did not improve continued to have pretreatment personality disorders, suggesting that some concurrent Axis II diagnoses may be, in part, a product of underlying OCD. Baer and Jenike (1992) reviewed studies involving OCD patients and their personality disorders in detail. Administration of the SID–P (Stangl, Pfohl, Zimmerman, Bowers, & Corethal, 1985) is time consuming and the administrator is required to go through a training period. The administrator also must contact a family member. For these reasons it is difficult to administer this instrument routinely. However, if a patient is refractory to treatment, an assessment of possible underlying personality disorders becomes more important. The Auto SCID–II (Structured Clinical Interview for DSM–II) computerized version for DSM–III–R personality disorders (Spitzer, Williams, Gibbon, & First, 1990) is now available, but a revised version for DSM–IV personality disorders has not yet been introduced.

CONCLUDING REMARKS

Historically, disease concepts evolve over time from phenomenology to pathophysiology and eventually to etiology. The temporal sequence of development of these three stages coincides with the development of scientific knowledge required for the understanding for each stage. Traditionally, phenomenology of a disease is investigated before pathophysiological investigations can be launched. The cause or causes of the disease are usually the last to be investigated or known. In each of the three steps, a spectrum of possible differential diagnoses decreases in number as the understanding of the disease moves forward. When an etiology is known for a disease, diagnostic assessment becomes easier and clinicians disagree less frequently. To understand the psychopathologies or study pathophysiologies of a disease, one requires patients with a homogeneous group of symptoms and signs. Reliable and valid diagnostic and symptom assessment instruments are also essential for this purpose.

Aside from using the standardized diagnostic instruments for screening purposes (Feske & Chambless, chap. 9, this volume), other areas that need to be addressed involve anxiety symptoms and avoidance. Level of functioning in OCD is another important area that has not received much attention. In this regard, a recently published paper by Koran, Thienemann, and Davenport (1996) on the subject of functioning among OCD patients is a welcome addition. The paper details role limitations due to emotional problems and significantly decreased social functioning among OCD patients. The authors also stated, "The respondents reported that the greatest effect of obsessive compulsive disorder on their lives was disruption of their careers and of their relationships with family and friends" (p. 786). The findings also suggest that the disability caused by OCD is greater than the disability caused by Type II diabetes. Although many people in the general public believe that mental illnesses are not as disabling as physical illnesses, facts usually do not support such perception.

REFERENCES

Allen, J. J., & Rack, P. H. (1975). Changes in obsessive/compulsive patients as measured by the Leyton Inventory before and after treatment with clomipramine. *Scottish Medical Journal, 20*, 41–44.

American Psychiatric Association. (1994). *Diagnostic and statistical manual of mental disorders* (4th ed.). Washington, DC: Author.

Ananth, J. (1977). Treatment of obsessive-compulsive neurosis with clomipramine (Anafranil). *Journal of International Medical Research, 5*(Suppl.), 38–41.

Asberg, M., Montgomery, S. A., Perris, C., Schalling, D., & Sedvall, G. (1978). A comprehensive psychopathological rating scale. *Acta Psychiatrica Scandinavica, 271*(Suppl.), 5–25.

Baer, L. (1994). Factor analysis of symptom subtypes of obsessive compulsive disorder and their relation to personality and tic disorders. *Journal of Clinical Psychiatry, 55*(Suppl.), 18–23.

Baer, L., & Jenike, M. A. (1992). Personality disorders in obsessive compulsive disorder [Review]. *Psychiatric Clinics of North America, 15*, 803–812.

Baer, L., Jenike, M. A., Black, D. W., Treece, C., Rosenfeld, R., & Greist, J. (1992). Effect of axis II diagnoses on treatment outcome with clomipramine in 55 patients with obsessive-compulsive disorder. *Archives of General Psychiatry, 49*, 862–866.

Baer, L., Jenike, M. A., Ricciardi, J. N., Holland, A. D., Seymour, R. J., Minichiello, W. E., & Buttolph, M. L. (1990). Standardized assessment of personality disorders in obsessive-compulsive disorder. *Archives of General Psychiatry, 47*, 826–830.

Beaumont, G. (1975). A new rating scale for obsessional and phobic states. *Scottish Medical Journal, 20*, 25–32.

Beaumont, G. (1977). Some aspects of the measurement of phobias and obsessions. *Journal of International Medical Research, 5*(Suppl.), 8–11.

Berg, C. J., Rapoport, J. L., & Flament, M. (1986). The Leyton Obsessional Inventory–Child version. *Journal of the American Academy of Child Psychiatry, 25*, 84–91.

Black, D. W., Noyes, R., Jr., Pfohl, B., Goldstein, R. B., & Blum, N. (1993). Personality disorder in obsessive-compulsive volunteers, well comparison subjects, and their first-degree relatives. *American Journal of Psychiatry, 150,* 1226–1232.

The Clomipramine Collaborative Study Group. (1991). Clomipramine in the treatment of patients with obsessive-compulsive disorder. *Archives of General Psychiatry, 48,* 730–738.

Cooper, J. (1970). The Leyton Obsessional Inventory. *Psychological Medicine, 1,* 48–64.

Derogatis, L. R., Lipman, R. S., & Covi, L. (1973). SCL–90: An outpatient psychiatric rating scale: Preliminary report. *Psychopharmacology Bulletin, 9,* 13–28.

Derogatis, L. R., Lipman, R. S., Rickels, K., Uhlenhuth, E. H., & Covi, L. (1974). The Hopkins Symptom Checklist (HSCL): A measure of primary symptom dimensions. In P. Pichot & R. Olivier-Martin (Eds.), *Psychological measurements in psychopharmacology: Modern problems in pharmacopsychiatry* (Vol. 7, pp.). Basel, Switzerland: Karger.

De Voxvrie, G. V. (1968). Anafranil (G34586) in obsessive neurosis. *Acta Neurologica Belgica, 68,* 787–792.

Fernandez, C. E., & Lopes-Ibor, J. J. (1967). Monochlorimipramine in the treatment of psychiatric patients resistant to other therapies. *Actas Luso Espanolas de Neurologia Psiquiatria y Ciencias Afines, 26,* 119–147.

Flament, M. F., Rapoport, J. L., Berg, C. J., Sceery, W., Kilts, C., Mellstrom, B., & Linnoila, M. (1985). Clomipramine treatment of childhood obsessive-compulsive disorder: A double-blind controlled study. *Archives of General Psychiatry, 42,* 977–983.

Fontaine, R., & Chouinard, G. (1986). An open clinical trial of fluoxetine in the treatment of obsessive-compulsive disorder. *Journal of Clinical Psychopharmacology, 6,* 98–101.

Goodman, W. K., Price, L. H., Rasmussen, S. A., Delgado, P. L., Heninger, G. R., & Charney, D. S. (1989). Efficacy of fluvoxamine in obsessive-compulsive disorder: A double-blind comparison with placebo. *Archives of General Psychiatry, 46,* 36–44.

Goodman, W. K., Price, L. H., Rasmussen, S. A., Mazure, C., Delgado, P., Heninger, G. R., & Charney, D. S. (1989). The Yale–Brown Obsessive Compulsive Scale: II. Validity. *Archives of General Psychiatry, 46,* 1012–1016.

Goodman, W. K., Price, L. H., Rasmussen, S. A., Mazure, C., Fleischmann, R. L., Hill, C. L., Heninger, G. R., & Charney, D. S. (1989). The Yale–Brown Obsessive Compulsive Scale: I. Development, use, and reliability. *Archives of General Psychiatry, 46,* 1006–1011.

Greist, J., Chouinard, G., DuBoff, E., Halaris, A., Kim, S. W., Koran, L., Liebowitz, M., Lydiard, B., Rasmussen, S., White, K., & Sikes, C. (1995). Double-blind parallel comparison of three dosages of sertraline and placebo in outpatients with obsessive-compulsive disorder. *Archives of General Psychiatry, 52,* 289–295.

Greist, J. H., Jefferson, J. W., Kobak, K. A., Katzelnick, D. J., & Serlin, R. C. (1995). Efficacy and tolerability of serotonin transport inhibitors in obsessive-compulsive disorder. A meta-analysis. *Archives of General Psychiatry, 52,* 53–60.

Guy, W. (1976). *ECDEU assessment manual for psychopharmacology.* Washington, DC: U.S. Department of Health, Education, and Welfare.

Guyotat, J., Favre-Tissot, M., & Marie-Gardine, M. (1967). A clinical trial with a new antidepressant G34586. In P. Warot (Ed.), *Comptes Rendus: Congres de psychiatrie et de neurologie de langue francais, Dijon* (pp. 717–772). Paris: Masson.

Insel, T. R., Murphy, D. L., Cohen, R. M., Alterman, I., Kilts, C., & Linnoila, M. (1983). Obsessive-compulsive disorder: A double-blind trial of clomipramine and clorgyline. *Archives of General Psychiatry, 40,* 605–612.

Jenike, M. A., Baer, L., Minichiello, W. E., Schwartz, C. E., & Carey, R. J., Jr. (1986). Concomitant obsessive-compulsive disorder and schizotypal personality disorder. *American Journal of Psychiatry, 143,* 530–532.

Kahn, R. S., Westenberg, H. G., & Jolles, J. (1984). Zimeldine treatment of obsessive-compulsive disorder. Biological and neuropsychological aspects. *Acta Psychiatrica Scandinavica, 69,* 259–261.

Kim, S. W., Dysken, M. W., & Kuskowski, M. (1990). The Yale–Brown Obsessive-Compulsive Scale: A reliability and validity study. *Psychiatry Research, 34,* 99–106.

Kim, S. W., Dysken, M. W., & Kuskowski, M. (1992). The Symptom Checklist–90: Obsessive-Compulsive Subscale: A reliability and validity study. *Psychiatry Research, 41,* 37–44.

Kim, S. W., Dysken, M. W., Pheley, A. M., & Hoover, K. M. (1994). The Yale–Brown Obsessive-Compulsive Scale: Measures of internal consistency. *Psychiatry Research, 51,* 203–211.

Koran, L. M., Thienemann, M. L., & Davenport, R. (1996). Quality of life for patients with obsessive compulsive disorder. *American Journal of Psychiatry, 153,* 783–788.

Lopes-Ibor, J. J. (1966, September). *Ensayo Clinico de la monochlorimipramina* [Clinical trial of monochlorimipramine]. Paper presented at the Fourth World Congress of Psychiatry, Madrid, Spain.

Maser, J. D., & Cloninger, C. R. (Eds.). (1990). *Comorbidity of mood and anxiety disorders.* Washington, DC: American Psychiatric Press.

Mavissakalian, M., Turner, S. M., Michelson, L., & Jacob, R. (1985). Tricyclic antidepressants in obsessive-compulsive disorder: Antiobsessional or antidepressant agents? II. *American Journal of Psychiatry, 142,* 572–576.

McDougle, C. J., Goodman, W. K., Leckman, J. F., Barr, L. C., Heninger, G. R., & Price, L. H. (1993). The efficacy of fluvoxamine in obsessive-compulsive disorder: Effects of comorbid chronic tic disorder. *Journal of Clinical Psychopharmacology, 13,* 354–358.

McDougle, C. J., Goodman, W. K., Leckman, J. F., Lee, N. C., Heninger, G. R., & Price, L. H. (1994). Haloperidol addition in fluvoxamine-refractory obsessive-compulsive disorder: A double-blind, placebo-controlled study in patients with and without tics. *Archives of General Psychiatry, 51,* 302–308.

McDougle, C. J., Goodman, W. K., Price, L. H., Delgado, P. L., Krystal, J. H., Charney, D. S., & Heninger, G. R. (1990). Neuroleptic addition in fluvoxamine-refractory obsessive-compulsive disorder. *American Journal of Psychiatry, 147,* 652–654.

McDougle, C. J., Price, L. H., Goodman, W. K., Charney, D. S., & Heninger, G. R. (1991). A controlled trial of lithium augmentation in fluvoxamine-refractory obsessive-compulsive disorder: Lack of efficacy. *Journal of Clinical Psychopharmacology, 11,* 175–184.

Millon, T. (1981). *Disorder of personality, Axis II.* New York: Wiley.

Montgomery, S. A., & Montgomery, D. B. (1980). Measurement of change in psychiatric illness: New obsessional, schizophrenia and depression scales. *Postgraduate Medical Journal, 56*(Suppl. 1), 50–52.

Murphy, D. L., Picker, D., & Alterman, I. S. (1982). Method for the quantitative assessment of depressive and manic behavior. In E. I. Burdock, A. Sudilovsky, & S. Gershon (Eds.), *The behavior of psychiatric patients* (pp. 355–392). New York: Marcel Dekker.

Perse, T. L., Greist, J. H., Jefferson, J. W., Rosenfeld, R., & Dar, R. (1987). Fluvoxamine treatment of obsessive-compulsive disorder. *American Journal of Psychiatry, 144,* 1543–1548.

Pigott, T. A., Pato, M. T., L'Heureux, F., Hill, J. L., Grover, G. N., Bernstein, S. E., & Murphy, D. L. (1991). A controlled comparison of adjuvant lithium carbonate or thyroid hormone in clomipramine-treated patients with obsessive-compulsive disorder. *Journal of Clinical Psychopharmacology, 11,* 242–248.

Prasad, A. (1984). A double blind study of imipramine versus zimelidine in treatment of obsessive compulsive neurosis. *Pharmacopsychiatry, 17,* 61–62.

Prasad, A. (1985). Efficacy of trazodone as an anti obsessional agent. *Pharmacology, Biochemistry and Behavior, 22,* 347–348.

Prasad, A. (1986). Efficacy of trazodone as an anti-obsessional agent. *Neuropsychobiology, 15*(Suppl. 1), 19–21.

Price, L. H., Goodman, W. K., Charney, D. S., Rasmussen, S. A., & Heninger, G. R. (1987). Treatment of severe obsessive-compulsive disorder with fluvoxamine. *American Journal of Psychiatry, 144,* 1059–1061.

Rachman, S. J., & Hodgson, R. J. (1980). *Obsessions and compulsions* (pp. 406–409). Englewood Cliffs, NJ: Prentice-Hall.

Rapoport, J., Elkins, R., & Mikkelsen, E. (1980). Clinical controlled trial of chlorimipramine in adolescents with obsessive-compulsive disorder. *Psychopharmacology Bulletin, 16,* 61–63.

Ricciardi, J. N., Baer, L., Jenike, M. A., Fischer, S. C., Sholtz, D., & Buttolph, M. L. (1992). Changes in DSM–III–R Axis II diagnoses following treatment of obsessive-compulsive disorder. *American Journal of Psychiatry, 149,* 829–831.

Rosenfeld, R., Dar, R., Anderson, D., Kobak, K. A., & Greist, J. H. (1992). A computer-administered version of the Yale–Brown Obsessive-Compulsive Scale. *Psychological Assessment, 4,* 329–332.

Schulz, S. C. (1986). The use of low-dose neuroleptics in the treatment of "schizo-obsessive" patients [Letter]. *American Journal of Psychiatry, 143,* 1318–1319.

Singh, A. N., Sexena, B., & Gent, M. (1977). Clomipramine (Anafranil) in depressive patients with obsessive neurosis. *Journal of International Medical Research, 5*(Suppl.), 25–32.

Spitzer, R. L., Williams, J. B. W., Gibbon, M., & First, M. (1990). Structured Clinical Interview for DSM–III–R—Non-patient edition (SCID–NP, Version 1.0). Washington, DC: American Psychiatric Press.

Stangl, D., Pfohl, B., Zimmerman, M., Bowers, W., & Corethal, C. (1985). A structured interview for the DSM–III personality disorders. *Archives of General Psychiatry, 42,* 591–596.

Steketee, G., & Doppelt, H. (1986). Measurement of obsessive-compulsive symptomatology: Utility of the Hopkins Symptom Checklist. *Psychiatry Research, 19,* 135–145.

Thoren, P., Asberg, M., Cronholm, B., Jornestedt, L., & Traskman, L. (1980). Clomipramine treatment of obsessive-compulsive disorder: I. A controlled clinical trial. *Archives of General Psychiatry, 37,* 1281–1285.

Tollefson, G. D., Rampey, A. H., Jr., Potvin, J. H., Jenike, M. A., Rush, A. J., Dominguez, R. A., Koran, L. M., Shear, M. K., Goodman, W., & Genduso, L. A. (1994). A multicenter investigation of fixed-dose fluoxetine in the treatment of obsessive-compulsive disorder. *Archives of General Psychiatry, 51,* 559–567.

Turner, S. M., Jacob, R. G., Beidel, D. C., & Himmelhoch, J. (1985). Fluoxetine treatment of obsessive-compulsive disorder. *Journal of Clinical Psychopharmacology, 5,* 207–212.

Volavka, J., Neziroglu, F., & Yaryura-Tobias, J. A. (1985). Clomipramine and imipramine in obsessive-compulsive disorder. *Psychiatry Research, 14,* 85–93.

Waxman, D. (1975). An investigation into the use of anafranil in phobic and obsessional disorders. *Scottish Medical Journal, 20,* 61–66.

Waxman, D. (1977). A clinical trial of clomipramine and diazepam in the treatment of phobic and obsessional illness. *Journal of International Medical Research, 5*(Suppl.), 99–110.

Wheadon, D. E., Bushnell, W. D., & Steiner, M. (1993, December). *A fixed dose comparison of 20, 40, or 60 mg Paroxetine to placebo in the treatment of obsessive-compulsive disorder.* Paper presented at the 32nd Annual Meeting of the ACNP, Honolulu, HI.

Woody, S. R., Steketee, G. S., & Chambless, D. L. (1995a). Reliability and validity of the Yale–Brown Obsessive-Compulsive Scale. *Behavior Research and Therapy, 33,* 597–605.

Woody, S. R., Steketee, G. S., & Chambless, D. L. (1995b). The usefulness of the obsessive compulsive scale of the Symptom Checklist–90–Revised. *Behavior Research and Therapy, 33,* 607–611.

Wyndowe, J., Solyom, L., & Ananth, J. (1975). Anafranil in obsessive compulsive neurosis. *Current Therapeutic Research, Clinical and Experimental, 18,* 611–617.

Yaryura-Tobias, J. A., & Neziroglu, F. (1975). The action of chlorimipramine in obsessive-compulsive neurosis: A pilot study. *Current Therapeutic Research, Clinical and Experimental, 17,* 111–116.

Yaryura-Tobias, J. A., Neziroglu, F., & Bergman, L. (1976). Chlorimipramine, for obsessive-compulsive neurosis: An organic approach. *Current Therapeutic Research, 20,* 541–548.

IV

*COGNITIVE-BEHAVIORAL
TREATMENTS*

11

Psychological Treatment of Refractory Obsessive-Compulsive Disorder and Related Problems

Paul M. Salkovskis
Candida Richards
Elizabeth Forrester
University of Oxford
Warneford Hospital

Behavioral treatment of obsessive-compulsive disorder (OCD) has long been recognized as a highly effective approach to a previously intractable disorder. This type of psychological therapy has been found to be at least as effective as clomipramine, a selective serotonin reuptake inhibitor (SSRI) in the short term and is considerably better than this medication once medication is withdrawn (Kozak, Liebowitz, & Foa, chap. 25, this volume). Typically, cognitive-behavioral treatment programs report success rates of 75% or better (Abel, 1993; Abramowitz, 1996; Christensen, Hadzi-Pavlovic, Andrews, & Mattick, 1987; Stanley & Turner, 1995). Recent developments in drug treatment of OCD have resulted in newer, more selective SSRIs; however, the data may suggest that the more selective medication is to serotonin the less effective it is. Contrary to predictions from the reduced side-effect profile of the newer SSRIs, the data suggest that they do not decrease the dropout rate. Thus, even if the best interpretation is made of recent findings, development of pharmacological treatment of OCD has not resulted in an appreciable increase in treatment effectiveness. This is not to say that it is not useful to find better ways of blocking serotonin reuptake.

These observations make the further development of psychological treatments, particularly for those patients not currently helped (or incompletely helped) by existing treatments, all the more important. If the intention is to find ways of helping patients who do not respond to currently available treatments, this cannot be accomplished merely by developing different ways of delivering the same treatment, such as exposure. The most likely effect of such efforts is a gradual dilution of treatment effectiveness to reduce the financial cost of therapeutic interventions.

DEALING WITH TREATMENT REFRACTORINESS: THE PROBLEM

Success in the treatment of OCD, whether psychological or pharmacological, usually means the patients are much improved or at least improved; the proportion of patients fully relieved of their obsessional problem is considerably less. Treatment refusal and early dropouts are common, reducing the proportion obtaining actual benefit to a modest 50% or less of those suitable for inclusion and seeking treatment in clinical trials. Clearly, the proportion of patients who are completely rid of their problems is still smaller. The significant residual levels of social and occupational impairment at the end of treatment persist to longer term follow-up, with little sign of further improvement (e.g., Kasvikis & Marks, 1988). Thus, despite use of behavioral and pharmacological therapies to their fullest extent (in the form of maximal exposure and 24-hour response prevention; Foa & Goldstein, 1978), there is considerable room for improvement both in the response rate for those offered treatment and the extent to which patients are completely better at the end of treatment.

Obsessional thinking in the absence of obvious behavioral ritualizing (often referred to as *obsessional ruminations*) has been a further issue. No behavioral treatment has previously been shown in controlled trials to be effective in the treatment of patients whose predominant problem is ruminations. Only 46% of patients treated in previous studies experienced at least a 50% reduction in rumination frequency, and only 12% experienced a 50% reduction in distress (reviewed in detail in Salkovskis & Westbrook, 1989).

Thus, the limitations of presently available treatments make it particularly appropriate and important to consider new developments in the psychological treatment of OCD to evaluate whether advances have been or could be made in that area, and whether psychological treatment may help people suffering from OCD with problems previously described as intractable. In this chapter, the present basis of behavioral treatment of obsessions where clear compulsive behaviors are present is described briefly, and the limitations of this approach are considered. Extension of psychological treatment to obsessional thinking where there are no obvious overt compulsive behaviors is outlined. The addition of cognitive elements to the theory provides a further extension that opens up a range of possibilities for new therapeutic strategies. The view that hypochondriasis is related to OCD as part of the so-called OCD spectrum is critically evaluated and psychological developments of this area are outlined.

CLINICAL FOUNDATIONS OF THE PSYCHOLOGICAL APPROACH: BASIC PHENOMENOLOGY OF OCD

The core features of obsessional problems that are crucial to cognitive-behavioral theory and its application to therapy are:

1. Avoidance of objects or situations that trigger obsessions.
2. Intrusive cognitions (obsessional thoughts, images, or impulses).
3. Appraisals of the occurrence and content of intrusive cognitions as indicating inflated responsibility.
4. Neutralizing (compulsive behaviors and thought rituals; attempts to suppress unwanted cognitions).
5. Discomfort (anxiety, depression, or some mixture).

Patients attempt to avoid obsessions by keeping away from situations or objects that trigger them. Many patients limit their activities and environment to minimize contact with their obsessional stimuli, such as the checker who moved to a house with only one door, and only left the house if someone else locked the door and kept the key for her. When, despite avoidance, obsessions occur, neutralizing behavior (most commonly rituals) usually results if the patients interpret the occurrence or content of the intrusion as a sign of personal responsibility for harm to themselves or to others. Neutralizing behaviors are generally more recognizable as characteristic obsessional behaviors, particularly when they are repetitive and associated with temporary anxiety relief or the expectation that, without ritualizing, anxiety would have worsened or some other negative or catastrophic consequence occurred. As the obsessions persist and rituals become extensive, patients can present with ritualistic behavior apparently independent of the obsessions. This occurs because, when confronted with an obsessional trigger, the patient neutralizes before the obsession occurs, and thereby prevents its occurrence. This person will thus describe the occurrence of obsessional ritualizing, but not obsessional thinking. Another important type of behavior is *thought suppression*, in which the patient tries to exclude intrusive cognitions from his or her mind with counterproductive results. Thus, the person who is afraid that he or she assaults children tries to stop having any intrusive thoughts or impulses; when the person does so, he or she experiences more frequent obsessional thoughts. Such

paradoxical thought suppression effects are well documented with negative intrusive thoughts (Trinder & Salkovskis, 1994; Wegner, 1989).

THE DEVELOPMENT OF BEHAVIORAL MODELS

According to two-process conditioning theory, OCD is best regarded as
a problem acquired through learning. It is hypothesized that the initial
fear of specific stimuli and situations is acquired through classical conditioning involving the pairing of intrinsically aversive events with the
situations that subsequently come to evoke anxiety (i.e., triggering stimuli
and actual intrusive thoughts or images). Distress and compulsive behavior are then maintained by operant conditioning processes because the
person learns to reduce aversive stimuli initially by escaping and later
by avoiding the fear-associated conditioned stimuli. Solomon and Wynne
(1960) found in animal experiments that if stimuli had become classically
conditioned by previous association with strongly aversive events (e.g.,
electric shocks), then avoidance responses to the conditioned stimuli were
extremely resistant to extinction; that is, escape and avoidance responses
continued unabated long after any pairing of conditioned stimuli with
aversive consequences had ceased. The avoidance behavior observed under these circumstances became stereotyped in a way similar to the
behavior of obsessional patients. Only when the avoidance behavior was
blocked did high levels of anxiety reappear; these animals would persistently attempt to continue the avoidance and escape behavior for a considerable time after the behavior was blocked, although these efforts
eventually ceased.[1]

Rachman and associates (see Rachman & Hodgson, 1980, for a detailed
review) conducted a series of key experimental studies with obsessional
patients to examine the applicability of this model to people suffering
from OCD. As predicted by their adaptation of the two-process theory
to obsessional problems, they found that: (a) elicitation of the obsession
was associated with increased anxiety and discomfort; (b) if the patient
was then allowed to ritualize, anxiety and discomfort almost immediately
decreased; and (c) if the ritualizing was delayed, anxiety and discomfort
decreased ("spontaneously decayed") over a somewhat longer period (up
to 1 hour). This work was the experimental foundation for the treatment

---

[1]This is the best established animal model of compulsive behavior. It models all key
features of obsessional behavior, and can be readily linked to the development and treatment
of OCD. For some reason, this existing model has been almost entirely ignored by biological
researchers in favor of more recently developed models such as the rat pup ultrasonic
squeak and canine acral lick dermatitis, which appear to be harder to justify.

that came to be known as exposure with response prevention (ERP), following the earlier work of Meyer (1966).

In summary, behavioral treatment of OCD is directly based on the hypothesis that obsessional thoughts have been associated, through conditioning, with anxiety that has subsequently failed to extinguish. Sufferers have developed escape and avoidance behaviors (such as obsessional checking and washing) that prevent extinction of the anxiety (Rachman & Hodgson, 1980). ERP arises directly from this theory. Treatment requires identification of exposure to stimuli that provoke the obsessional response combined with the prevention of any avoidance and escape (compulsive) responses (see Salkovskis & Kirk, 1989; Salkovskis, 1999, Steketee & Foa, 1985, for further details of treatment). In practice, this means helping patients to expose themselves to feared stimuli and encouraging them to block any behaviors that prevent or terminate this exposure. In more recent versions of this approach, reappraisal of the fears is encouraged so that patients discover that the things they fear do not actually happen. This more general cognitive-behavioral approach requires some specific modification when it is applied to the treatment of obsessional problems (Salkovskis, 1996b; Salkovskis, Richards, & Forrester, 1995). A fuller integration of cognitive and behavioral approaches requires the application of a more specific and focused cognitive-behavioral approach.

COGNITIVE APPROACHES

Two principal types of cognitive approach have been suggested, with the second of these having important implications for treatment. These are (a) obsessional patients have generalized deficits (in memory, decision making, or some other key cognitive function), or (b) obsessional patients have a tendency to interpret the occurrence and content of intrusive thoughts as a sign of inflated personal "responsibility," resulting in a range of responses, including excessive attempts to control their own thinking.

Cognitive Deficit Theories

General deficit models are difficult to reconcile with the clinical phenomenology of OCD; for example, obsessional patients report difficulty remembering locking the front door, but not when accompanied by a trusted person who watches them lock it; there are also no problems remembering locking a cupboard. One of the more plausible deficit theories has focused on the possibility that obsessional patients confuse having seen something with imagining seeing it. Two studies found that obsessional patients were, if anything, rather better than nonclinical controls at making this distinction. This was true both for percepts in signal detection analysis (Brown, Kosslyn, Breiter, Baer, & Jenike, 1994) and in memory for actions or imagined actions (McNally & Kohlbeck, 1993). The notion of a deficit in basic information processing in OCD patients receives little or no support (Salkovskis, 1996c).

The Cognitive-Behavioral Hypothesis

Like the behavioral theory, the cognitive-behavioral hypothesis suggests that intrusive cognitions are a normal phenomenon, and that the content of clinical obsessions is not distinguishable from such normal intrusions (Rachman & de Silva, 1978; Salkovskis & Harrison, 1984). The clinical problem occurs when patients interpret the occurrence and content of intrusions in a particularly threatening way; that is, as an indication that they might be responsible for harm to themselves or others unless they take action to prevent it. This interpretation results in attempts to both suppress and neutralize the thought, image, or impulse. Neutralizing is defined as voluntarily initiated activity intended to reduce the perceived responsibility and can be overt or covert (compulsive behavior such as washing or checking or thought rituals such as praying). As a consequence of neutralizing activity, intrusive cognitions become more salient and frequent, they evoke more discomfort, and the probability of further neutralizing increases. By the same token, attempts to suppress the thought increase the likelihood of recurrence.

For example, an obsessional patient may believe that the occurrence of a thought such as "I will kill my baby" means that there is a risk that she will succumb to the action unless she does something to prevent it, such as avoiding being left alone with her child or seeking reassurance from people around her, by trying to think positive thoughts to balance the negative ones, and so on. Thus, the interpretation of obsessional thoughts as indicating increased responsibility has a number of important effects in people suffering from OCD: (a) increased discomfort, anxiety, and depression; (b) greater accessibility of the original thought and other related ideas; and (c) behavioral neutralizing responses that constitute attempts to escape or avoid responsibility. These may include compulsive behavior, avoidance of situations related to the obsessional thought, seeking reassurance (thus diluting or sharing responsibility) and attempts to get rid of or exclude the thought from one's mind. Each of these effects contributes not only to the prevention of extinction of anxiety but also to a worsening spiral of intrusive thoughts leading to maladaptive affective, cognitive, and behavioral reactions.

•

The cognitive–behavioral theory therefore suggests that the problem in obsessions is not poor mental control. Instead, it is hypothesized that obsessional patients tend to misinterpret aspects of their own mental functioning, including memory for actions and intrusive (obsessional) thoughts and doubts, and as a result they then try too hard to exert control. The discomfort experienced is due to the patient's appraisal of the content and occurrence of intrusive thoughts. The increased frequency of intrusions relative to nonobsessional behavior is largely due to the behaviors (overt and covert) motivated by the appraisal made. These appraisals in obsessional patients center on distorted beliefs about responsibility. The distorted sense of responsibility sufferers attach to their activities (including intrusive thoughts and memories and overt behavior) leads them to attempt a pattern of mental effort characterized by both overcontrol and preoccupation.

Responsibility here means that the person believes that he or she may be, or come to be, the cause of harm (to self or others) unless he or she takes some preventative or restorative action. A group of researchers working on obsessions recently defined the responsibility appraisals of obsessionals as:

> The belief that one has power which is pivotal to bring about or prevent subjectively crucial negative outcomes. These outcomes are perceived as essential to prevent. They may be actual, that is, having consequences in the real world, and/or at a moral level. (Salkovskis et al., 1996)

The appraisal that intrusive thoughts have implications for responsibility for harm to self or others is important because appraisal links the intrusive thought with both distress and the occurrence of neutralizing behavior. If the appraisal solely concerns harm or danger without an element of responsibility, then the effect is more likely to be anxiety or depression, which may become part of a mood appraisal spiral (Teasdale, 1983), but would not result in clinical obsessions without the additional component of the responsibility-neutralizing link. Hearing someone else making blasphemous statements or talking about harming one's children might not be upsetting in itself. This is not to say that, if one perceives what is said as personally significant (e.g., "Perhaps this person wants to harm my children"), some emotional response (anxiety or anger) would not be expected. However, without the specific appraisal of responsibility, an obsessional episode would not result. Some of the symptoms of generalized anxiety disorder (in terms of worrisome intrusions) might be regarded as similar to those of OCD, but the key element of responsibility appraisal is central only to OCD.

An obsessional pattern would be particularly likely in vulnerable individuals when intrusions are regarded as self-initiated (e.g., resulting in appraisals such as "these thoughts might mean I want to harm the children; I
must guard against losing control"). The useful comparison here is between
the effects of asking an obsessional checker to lock the door or to watch
someone else lock the same door. This responsibility effect is clearly
demonstrated by the experiments conducted by Rachman, de Silva, and Roper
(1976), Roper and Rachman (1975), and Roper, Rachman, and Hodgson
(1973). In these important experiments, situations that usually provoked
checking rituals in obsessional patients (e.g., locking the door) produced
little or no discomfort or checking when the therapist was present, in sharp
contrast to the effects of such situations when alone (see Rachman, 1993, for
a detailed description of responsibility and checking links).

The core of the cognitive formulation is therefore found in the occurrence of neutralizing behavior elicited by the appraisal of responsibility.
Neutralizing and other mechanisms serve to maintain both the person's
beliefs about responsibility and, as a consequence, specific responsibility
appraisals of the occurrence and content of intrusive thoughts. Note that
part of this appraisal is linked to the occurrence of the intrusion itself;
this is likely to be linked with beliefs about thoughts such as those
described by Salkovskis (1985); for example, "not neutralising when an
intrusion has occurred is similar or equivalent to seeking or wanting the
harm involved in the intrusion to happen" (p. 579) or "thinking something
is as bad as doing it" (p. 579). Under these circumstances, appraisal will
then tend to be of the form "My thinking this thought means . . . ." In
this way, an appraisal is regarded as sensible based on a thought that is
itself regarded as senseless. It is, of course, quite common to be told by
anxious patients, "I must be crazy because I have crazy thoughts, and I
know that they are crazy thoughts . . . ." The counterproductive effects
of neutralizing were demonstrated by Salkovskis, Westbrook, Davis, Jeavons, and Gledhill (1997). In this study, subclinical obsessives were selected from a larger sample of normal individuals. All participants listened
to a tape recording of a personally relevant, naturally occurring intrusive
thought; half were required to use their usual neutralizing response (i.e.,
covert ritual). The results of this study indicated, first, that engaging in
neutralizing resulted in a considerably greater tendency to neutralize
during a subsequent exposure series, and second, that neutralizing was
associated with greater discomfort during the second presentation of the
intrusive thoughts. The results of this study are consistent with the hypothesis that neutralizing is associated with increased long-term discomfort as a response to intrusion and an increased tendency to engage in
further neutralizing.

The cognitive-behavioral hypothesis thus differs in major ways from general cognitive deficit theories. Rather than having a general failure of mental control, memory, or decision making, patients are hypothesized to be especially concerned about these areas; as a consequence, they try too hard to exert control over mental processes and activity in a variety of counterproductive and therefore anxiety-provoking ways. Efforts at overcontrol increase distress because (a) direct and deliberate attention to mental activity can modify the contents of consciousness; (b) efforts to deliberately control a range of mental activities apparently and actually meet with failure and even opposite effects; (c) attempts to prevent harm and responsibility for harm increase the salience and accessibility of the patients' concerns with harm; and (d) neutralizing directed at preventing harm also prevents disconfirmation (i.e., prevents the patient from discovering that the things he or she is afraid of will not occur); this means that exaggerated beliefs about responsibility and harm do not decline.

Clinically this is important because, by definition, obsessional patients attempt to ignore, suppress, or neutralize their intrusive thoughts. Several studies have demonstrated that if normal individuals are asked to suppress personally relevant, negative, intrusive thoughts, such thoughts increase in frequency both in the short term (Salkovskis & Campbell, 1994) and over periods of up to 4 days (Trinder & Salkovskis, 1994). The cognitive theory has recently been extended by the proposal that the occurrence of intrusive thoughts about possible negative consequences increases perceived responsibility in situations where, prior to the occurrence of the intrusion, no action was considered appropriate (Salkovskis, 1996c; Salkovskis et al., 1995). However, once negative consequences have intruded, an active decision (to prevent the harm or to ignore the thought) becomes necessary. In this way, situations where no danger appears to be involved except by unknown omissions become the subject of active decision making about risks others would not perceive. For example, it is easier to ignore a piece of glass on the pavement than to decide not to pick up a sharp fragment after you vividly pictured a child falling and being blinded by it. Intrusive thoughts thus prompt compulsive and neutralizing behaviors. Active attempts to suppress intrusive thoughts will increase intrusions and therefore perceived responsibility in precisely the situations in which the obsessional person most wishes to be free of "risky" decisions. Thus, having locked the door, the person tries not to think that it could be open, experiences the thought again, and is therefore constrained to act or risk being responsible through choosing not to check. The motivation to suppress will increase, but it is very difficult to suppress a thought that is directly connected to an action just completed, so the action serves as a further cue for intrusion or suppression, and so on. It is in precisely this nightmarish way that obsessionals find themselves being tortured.

TREATMENT IMPLICATIONS OF THE
COGNITIVE-BEHAVIORAL THEORY

Given the success of ERP, cognitive approaches were initially used in identifying and modifying the thoughts and beliefs that prevent the patient from engaging in or benefitting from exposure treatment (Salkovskis & Warwick, 1985) and in the modification of anxious or depressed mood concurrent with the obsessions (Salkovskis & Warwick, 1988).

More recently, treatment has been more focused on modification of the key appraisals indicated by the cognitive conceptualization (Freeston, Rheaume, & Ladouceur, 1996; Salkovskis, 1989b, 1989c; Salkovskis & Warwick, 1985, 1988; van Oppen et al., 1995). Cognitive–behavioral theory predicts that successful treatment requires modification of beliefs involved in and leading to the misinterpretation of intrusive thoughts as indicating heightened responsibility and of the associated responses involved in the maintenance of these beliefs. Given that neutralizing behavior arises directly from responsibility appraisals, achievement of the first aim will usually facilitate (and sometimes accomplish) the second.

Prior to treatment, obsessional patients are distressed because they have a particularly threatening perception of their obsessional experience; for example, that their thoughts mean that they are a child molester, or that they are in constant danger of passing disease to other people, and so on.[2] The crucial focus in treatment is helping the sufferer to construct and test a new, less threatening model of his or her experience, emphasizing the normalization of worrying intrusive thoughts. Obsessional washers are helped to shift their view of their problem away from the idea that they might be contaminated and must ensure that they do not pass this on to someone else or come to harm themself onto the idea that they have a specific problem that concerns their fears of contamination. That is, patients are helped to understand their problem as one of thinking and deciding rather than the real-world risks they fear. A subsidiary goal may be to help the person directly disconfirm his or her fears; however, this is often not possible given that the obsessional patient usually believes that the feared consequence will occur at a more distant future point (e.g., the patient troubled by blasphemous thoughts may fear being punished

---

[2]This is similar to the treatment of a panic patient who believes that his palpitations mean that he is dying. Therapy is intended to help him form and test a psychological model of his problem as arising from his misinterpretation.

after death; see Salkovskis, 1996b). Furthermore, great care needs to be taken to ensure that any therapeutic strategies that help the patient actively disconfirm his or her negative beliefs do not get bogged down in discussion of probabilities and become the mere provision of reassurance that the feared consequence is, in the opinion of the clinician, unlikely to occur if the patient were to refrain from rituals. Reassurance tends to involve the clinician implicitly or explicitly assuming some responsibility for the action that the patient takes on the clinician's advice or authorization.

Cognitive–behavioral theory predicts that successful treatment requires modification of both beliefs leading to the misinterpretation of intrusive thoughts as indicating heightened responsibility and the associated behaviors involved in the maintenance of these beliefs. The cognitive material is particularly easily evoked and dealt with in the course of exposure, when the key beliefs are activated. The main elements of treatment are as follows.

1. Working with the patient to develop and agree on a comprehensive and personalized cognitive-behavioral explanation of the maintenance of that person's obsessional problems. This involves the identification of key distorted beliefs and the collaborative construction of a nonthreatening alternative account of obsessional experience to allow the patient to explicitly test beliefs about responsibility.

2. Detailed identification and self-monitoring of obsessional thoughts and patient's appraisal of these thoughts combined with exercises designed to help the patient to identify and modify his or her responsibility beliefs (e.g., by using the daily record of dysfunctional thoughts). Care is taken to ensure that the patient seeks to challenge the way in which he or she interprets intrusive thought rather than the intrusions themselves. It is also important to ensure that answering thoughts does not become a neutralizing behavior in itself; the key is to help the person challenge the beliefs that generate negative appraisals rather than to modify every appraisal as it occurs. It is important that therapist and patient agree that the goal is to change the significance the sufferer attaches to intrusive cognitions rather than to prevent intrusions from occurring. The occurrence of intrusions is regarded as a normal and functional part of psychological life.

3. Discussion techniques for challenging appraisals and basic assumptions on which these appraisals are based are used. Again, the aim is modification of the patient's negative beliefs about the extent of his or her own personal responsibility (e.g., having the patient describe all contributing factors for a feared outcome and then dividing the contribution in a pie chart).

4. Behavioral experiments are used to directly test appraisals, assumptions, and processes hypothesized to be involved in the patient's obsessional problems (e.g., demonstrating that attempts to suppress a thought lead to an increase in the frequency with which it occurs, or showing that beliefs such as "If I think it I therefore want it to happen" are incorrect). Each behavioral experiment is idiosyncratically devised to help the patient test his or her previous (threatening) explanation of his or her experience against the new (nonthreatening) explanation worked out with the therapist.

5. Patients are helped to identify and modify underlying general assumptions (e.g., "not trying to prevent harm is as bad as making it happen deliberately") that give rise to their misinterpretation of their own mental activity. For example, some patients believe that, if one imagines performing an act (e.g., stabbing one's children), this increases the probability that one will carry out the action. The patients would be encouraged to test that belief by finding out directly whether thinking about things really can make them happen. The same patient might later be encouraged to actively bring about the feared consequence by adopting particular thinking patterns to fully demonstrate the limits of his or her responsibility. This type of sequence is designed to help the patient reappraise his or her obsessional problem as being an understandable result of trying too hard to control mental activity, rather than as one of being dangerously out of control and liable to act on these thoughts and therefore cause harm.

In cognitive therapy, patients are thus helped to understand and test the way their beliefs and related efforts to prevent harm are not only unnecessary, but also create the problems they experience. The aim is to allow them to see the problem as one of thinking rather than one of actual danger of harm, and to see that worrying thoughts are both normal and, by definition, concern the things one most fears.

This style of therapy is particularly powerful in patients who are afraid of fully committing themselves to ERP because the cognitive elements target the beliefs that produce distress and initiate and motivate compulsive behavior. Rather than simply asking patients to stop carrying out their compulsive behavior, cognitive–behavioral therapy seeks to identify and challenge the misinterpretations that lead the patient to ritualize, so that stopping compulsive behavior is perceived by the patient as less dangerous and therefore irrelevant. The early development of cognitive therapy was in fact carried out with patients refusing and failing to respond to ERP (Salkovskis & Warwick, 1985). Direct modification of the misinterpretation of intrusive thoughts and related beliefs should also bring about a more complete and thorough change, as well as being more likely to engage the patient in treatment with a consequent reduction in treatment refusal and dropout.

TREATMENT OF OBSESSIONS WITHOUT OVERT COMPULSIVE BEHAVIOR

Obsessions without overt compulsions can be considered a difficult category of OCD in which avoidance and compulsive activity are almost totally covert and are therefore especially difficult to gain access to and control. The term *obsessional ruminations* is confusing because it has been used indiscriminately to describe both obsessions and mental neutralizing (Salkovskis & Westbrook, 1989). For example, a patient reported that she had thoughts and images about her family dying; she would ruminate about these thoughts for periods of up to 3 hours at a time. Careful questioning elicited two functionally different types of thoughts: First she had intrusive thoughts such as, "My son is dead." If she had thoughts like this, she would neutralize it by making herself have the thought, "My son is not dead" and by forming a clear image of her son carrying out normal activities.

The psychological models of obsessions described here require only slight extension, acknowledging the role of mental neutralizing and avoidance behaviors that are difficult to detect and control. Both obsessions and neutralizing thoughts are mixed together in the cognitive domain, and discriminating between them is crucial to treatment. Obsessional thinking is defined as intrusive, involuntary cognitions (usually associated with discomfort) that are differentiated from neutralizing cognitions in that the patient deliberately initiates these latter thoughts by voluntary effort. They are also intended by the person to reduce the risk of being responsible for harm and, sometimes, discomfort. Covert avoidance behaviors, such as attempts not to think particular thoughts, have similar characteristics, but do not follow from the occurrence of intrusive cognitions. Avoidance is not defined in terms of how successful it is in preventing anxiety, but rather in terms of what the behavior is intended to do; that is, reducing perceived responsibility for harm. Covert avoidance and neutralizing are assessed by asking the patient about any mental efforts that are made because of the problem and by the intentions associated with these responses.

For example, a patient felt compelled to think every "bad" thought an even number of times. He spent much of his day trying not to have bad thoughts (avoidance); these efforts were frequently followed by thoughts such as, "I never liked my father" (obsession). If such a thought occurred, the patient was concerned that he had condemned himself to hell because he had failed to control his own thoughts. To wipe out this responsibility, he would then have to think, "I never liked my father" again when in a contrite frame of mind (neutralizing) and try to stop the recurrence of the intrusion (cognitive avoidance). This cycle was then repeated. In some instances, the patient may make himself think the obsessional thought before it has occurred spontaneously to be certain that the thought did not occur unnoticed.

TREATMENT PROCEDURES

A great deal of effort has recently been devoted to devising effective treatment procedures for obsessional ruminations (Freeston, 1994; Salkovskis, 1983; Salkovskis & Westbrook, 1989). In assessment, the therapist focuses on a description of a recent episode of rumination and identifying within that episode the specific sequence that occurred. Considerable emphasis is placed on identifying the significance the patient attaches to intrusive thoughts and the impact of such appraisals on subsequent efforts to neutralize, suppress, or otherwise control the intrusive thoughts. The impact of such control attempts on the occurrence of thoughts is also highlighted, often by demonstrating the counterproductive effects of such behavior. By the end of this phase, two targets should have been reached: A formulation or shared understanding of the problem should be agreed and the goals of therapy should be negotiated. This should include short-term, medium-term, and long-term goals. It is very important to emphasize with patients suffering from obsessional ruminations that the type of goal being considered would not include getting rid of the thoughts entirely; intrusive thoughts are a normal phenomenon that can and will continue to occur after the completion of treatment but without the previously associated distress and discomfort.

The therapist and patient thus reach a shared understanding or formulation intended to clarify the mechanisms by which the problem with intrusive thoughts is being maintained. The patient is helped to understand the significance of his or her intrusive thoughts. There are several ways of doing this including:

1. Discussing the fact that a range of intrusive cognitions occur in everyone and probably have important normal functions, such as helping problem solving, generating new ideas, and so on. This discussion can be used to highlight the fact that intrusions do not start as negative, positive, or neutral, but their significance is a product of appraisal and evaluation once they have occurred.

2. Discussing who would experience particular types of negative intrusive thoughts (e.g., Who is likely to experience upsetting blasphemous thought? What do the occurrence of these thoughts mean about that person?).

3. Discussion of "worries" as a type of intrusion. When someone worries, what do they worry about? Are worries focused on positive things, or on the person's worst fears?

4. Considering the possible usefulness of having negative intrusive thoughts in unusual situations (e.g., thoughts of doing something violent when one's family is being physically attacked) and the way in which never having such thoughts could be problematic.

5. Considering ways in which apparently positive intrusions could be evaluated negatively were they to occur in an inappropriate context can help the patient understand the importance of the way in which the intrusions are interpreted.

The importance of modifying any beliefs the patient has about the significance of his or her intrusive thoughts is clarified, and the role of audiotaped exposure in doing this is explained. At the same time, the importance of preventing any kind of neutralizing behavior is explained and discussed. A key intrusive thought is elicited and anxiety or discomfort rated. It is important that this intrusive thought elicit a considerable amount of discomfort. The intrusive thought is then recorded onto loop tape in the patient's own voice. The loop tape (or an ordinary tape recorded from a loop tape to simulate the same effect) is played back and any urges to neutralize are identified. Response prevention is initiated with a cognitive-behavioral rationale. In session, habituation is begun with recording of discomfort and any further difficulties in response prevention identified and dealt with. Homework is set up with charts and full instructions. Belief modification continues during this phase at every opportunity. The purpose of treatment remains to allow the patient to experience intrusive thoughts without attaching undue significance to them. The patient is asked what he or she makes of any changes that are occurring and how this fits with each of the two alternatives. Subsequent sessions involve different thoughts and moving the practice from regular sessions in the patient's own home at set times to using the tape in situ using a personal stereo.

The next stage is to have the patient use the natural occurrence of intrusive thoughts as a cue for triggering the use of the tape. The patient is asked to be aware of any occurrence of the intrusive thought (especially if it is associated with any urges to neutralize) and to then listen to the personal stereo at that time. The aim is to achieve exposure and reappraisal at times when the intrusive thought is relatively more salient, as indexed by the wish to neutralize. The patient is asked to use the tape for at least 5 minutes at this time, or until his or her discomfort has decreased to its original level, whichever is longer.

During the later stages of the tape's sequence, self-directed ERP for other thoughts is initiated and recorded. Possible future difficulties are identified and a setback pack is compiled by the patient. Throughout therapy the patient should record a "what I have learned during therapy" tape.

The formulation and the patient's beliefs about his or her thoughts are the key guide to the conduct of therapy as an exercise in belief change. Discussion and behavioral experiments should weave together the notion of the alternative explanation ("my problem is worry") and behavioral experiments designed to reinforce this idea. Examples would be imagery or thought restructuring, catastrophizing imagery or verbal exercises as a demonstration of ways in which these ideas worsen discomfort and distress; pie charts that tackle the idea of responsibility; thought experiments in which the person thinks up ways of bringing about the event he or she fears responsibility for; pros and cons of being obsessional and not being obsessional; and cumulative probability downward arrows.

The effectiveness of this type of treatment has recently been shown in a study by Freeston et al. (1997) in a comparison with a waiting-list control. Our own group is presently conducting a comparison of cognitive-behavioral treatment in ruminations compared with a waiting-list control and an equally credible alternative psychological treatment based on principles of stress management.

HYPOCHONDRIASIS

It has been suggested that there are a range of disorders directly related to OCD, the so-called OCD spectrum (Hollander & Wong, 1995). The notion of spectrum is based on the observation that the various disorders involved appear to share features and symptoms of the core disorder. On a more theoretical basis, it has also been suggested that systematic variations in neurotransmitter activity and relative levels of a particular neurotransmitter (particularly serotonin) account for the commonalities observed among disorders such as OCD, tic disorders, hypochondriasis, and others.

An alternative hypothesis has been proposed by Salkovskis (1996c), who suggested that many of the similarities noted are superficial rather than fundamental. In some instances, it can be argued that similarities between diagnoses are observed as a result of basic and normal psychological processes. For example, in many different disorders a degree of avoidance is prominent (e.g., agoraphobia and OCD). It has been suggested (Salkov-skis, 1988, 1991, 1996a) that this is best accounted for by the person actively attempting to avoid or escape a perceived threat (in the same way as the person who does not suffer from anxiety would seek to avoid a situation he or she perceives as threatening, such as a dangerous area). It is clear that there are marked similarities between OCD and hypochondriasis (see Salkovskis & Warwick, 1986). These may be accounted for by similarities in the type of threat perceived; unlike panic and social phobia, in which the threat is perceived as imminent, a much more prolonged or delayed time course is usually involved in both OCD and hypochondriasis (Salkovskis, 1996b). It seems likely that this difference in time course of the perceived threat accounts for common features of these disorders such as the repetitive seeking of reassurance and checking behaviors. There are also important common features in treatment, particularly the relative emphasis on helping sufferers to test the veracity of alternative explanations rather than trying to convince them of the inaccuracy of their previously held threat-based beliefs.

Hypochondriasis is a controversial disorder. Although not diagnostically part of the anxiety disorders group, there is evidence to suggest that the main problem is anxiety focused on health, based on misinterpretation of benign physical symptoms as indicating severe physical illness. It is clear that this definition is cognitive, with close similarities in the definition to the cognitive theory of panic (Clark, 1986; Salkovskis & Clark, 1991). Differences between panic and hypochondriasis are readily identifiable in terms of the speed with which the feared catastrophe is anticipated (immediately in panic, in the more distant future in hypochondriasis), in the symptoms that form the main focus of misinterpretation (panic involving symptoms that are more likely to be increased by anxiety itself), and in the behaviors the patient adopts to increase his or her safety (avoidance and escape in panic, checking and reassurance seeking in hypochondriasis; Salkovskis & Clark, 1993). Thus, the similarities between the phenomenology and symptoms of hypochondriasis and panic and OCD appear to arise because hypochondriasis shares the catastrophic misinterpretation of physical symptoms with panic disorder, whereas it shares the (usually) more prolonged time course of the feared catastrophe with OCD. The pattern of symptoms and comorbidity are certainly consistent with the notion of a panic–hypochondriasis–OCD continuum. This is not a spectrum, but an indication of shared features.

Conceptualizing hypochondriasis as an extreme instance of anxiety about health allows the extension of previous cognitive treatments of both panic and OCD to the previously untreatable problem of hypochondriasis. Since the 1970s, a number of case reports, single-case experiments, and case series have been reported, indicating that treatment can be effective in some instances. For example, Salkovskis and Warwick (1986) reported the treatment of two patients who erroneously believed themselves to be suffering from life-threatening illnesses; in both patients, a baseline was established, during which evidence for the anxiogenic effects of medical reassurance was gathered through diary recording. This information was presented to the patients as the outcome of a behavioral experiment indicating the possible role of reassurance seeking and associated checking behaviors. The patients showed substantial and sustained improvement once they engaged in treatment. In a larger case series including both illness phobics and patients with high levels of disease conviction, Warwick and Marks (1988) used a strategy based on ERP and belief change with good effects. More recently, a similar cognitive-behavioral treatment delivered in the context of group therapy was found to be effective in an uncontrolled study with general hospital patients (Stern & Fernandez, 1991).

Two controlled trials of cognitive-behavioral therapy have now been conducted. In the first, Warwick, Clark, Cobb, and Salkovskis (1996) compared 16 sessions of cognitive-behavioral treatment with a waiting-list control of comparable duration. On 23 of 24 measures, the treated group improved significantly more than the waiting-list group, with a mean assessor-rated improvement of 5% in the waiting list group as opposed to 76% in those treated with cognitive-behavioral therapy. Treatment gains were mostly maintained at 3-month follow-up. The second trial, also conducted in Oxford, indicates similar results, and also that cognitive therapy is superior to an equally credible alternative psychological treatment (behavioral stress management; Clark et al., 1998).

CONCLUSION

The cognitive–behavioral theory is based on the idea that the way a person appraises or interprets a situation is crucial. The specific beliefs someone holds about a situation therefore determine his or her reaction to that situation. There is a growing body of evidence supporting the notion that different types of psychological and psychiatric problems are characterized by different types of beliefs. Linking these beliefs with information-processing factors such as memory and attention is beginning to help make sense of clinical problems. Advances are likely to be made by the development of comprehensive integrative biopsychosocial models of problems such as OCD that do not rely solely on concepts of structural brain impairment or biochemical imbalances.

ACKNOWLEDGMENTS

Paul Salkovskis is Wellcome Trust Senior Research Fellow; Candida Richards and Elizabeth Forrester are also supported by the Wellcome Trust.

REFERENCES

Abel, J. L. (1993). Exposure with response prevention and serotonergic antidepressants in the treatment of obsessive compulsive disorder: A review and implications for interdisciplinary treatment. *Behaviour Research and Therapy, 31*, 463–478.

Abramowitz, J. S. (1996). Variants of exposure and response prevention in the treatment of obsessive-compulsive disorder: A meta-analysis. *Behavior Therapy, 27*(4), 583–600.

Brown, H. D., Kosslyn, S. M., Breiter, H. C., Baer, L., & Jenike, M. A. (1994). Can patients with obsessive-compulsive disorder discriminate between percepts and mental images? *Journal of Abnormal Psychology, 103*, 445–454.

Christensen, H., Hadzi-Pavlovic, D., Andrews, G., & Mattick, R. (1987). Behavior therapy and tricyclic medication in the treatment of obsessive-compulsive disorder: A quantitative review. *Journal of Consulting and Clinical Psychology, 55*, 701–711.

Clark, D. M. (1986). A cognitive approach to panic. *Behaviour Research and Therapy, 24*, 461–470.

Clark, D. M., Salkovskis, P. M., Mackmann, A., Wells, A., Fennell, M., Ludgate, J., Ahmad, S., Richards, H. C., & Gelder, M. (1998). Two psychological treatments for hypochondriasis: A randomised controlled trial. *British Journal of Psychiatry, 173*, 218–225.

Foa, E. B., & Goldstein, A. (1978). Continuous exposure and strict response prevention in the treatment of obsessive-compulsive neurosis. *Behavior Therapy, 9*, 821–829.

Freeston, M. (1994). *Characteristiques et traitement de l'obsession sans compulsion manifeste* [Characteristics & treatment of obsessions without overt compulsions]. Unpublished thesis, Universite Laval, Quebec City, Canada.

Freeston, M. H., Ladouceur, R., Gagnon, F., Thibodeau, N., Rheaume, J., Letarte, H., & Bujold, A. (1997). Cognitive-behavioral treatment of obsessive thoughts: A controlled study. *Journal of Consulting and Clinical Psychology, 65*(3), 405–413.

Freeston, M. H., Rheaume, J., & Ladouceur, R. (1996). Correcting faulty appraisals of obsessional thoughts. *Behaviour Research and Therapy, 34*, 433–446.

Hollander, E., & Wong, C. M. (1995). Obsessive-compulsive spectrum disorders. *Journal of Clinical Psychiatry, 56*(Suppl. 4), 3–6.

Kasvikis, Y., & Marks, I. M. (1988). Clomipramine, self-exposure, and therapist-accompanied exposure in obsessive-compulsive ritualizers: Two year follow-up. *Journal of Anxiety Disorders, 2*, 291–298.

McNally, R. J., & Kohlbeck, P. A. (1993). Reality monitoring in obsessive-compulsive disorder. *Behaviour Research and Therapy, 31*, 249–253.

Meyer, V. (1966). Modification of expectations in cases with obsessional rituals. *Behaviour Research and Therapy, 4*, 273–280.

Rachman, S. J. (1993). Obsessions, responsibility and guilt. *Behaviour Research and Therapy, 31*, 149–154.

Rachman, S. J., & de Silva, P. (1978). Abnormal and normal obsessions. *Behaviour Research and Therapy, 16*, 233–238.

Rachman, S. J., de Silva, P., & Roper, G. (1976). The spontaneous decay of compulsive urges. *Behaviour Research and Therapy, 14*, 445–453.

Rachman, S. J., & Hodgson, R. (1980). *Obsessions and compulsions*. Englewood Cliffs, NJ: Prentice-Hall.

Roper, G., & Rachman, S. J. (1975). Obsessional-compulsive checking: Replication and development. *Behaviour Research and Therapy, 13,* 25–32.

Roper, G., Rachman, S. J., & Hodgson, R. (1973). An experiment on obsessional checking. *Behaviour Research and Therapy, 11,* 271–277.

Salkovskis, P. M. (1983). Treatment of an obsessional patient using habituation to audiotaped ruminations. *British Journal of Clinical Psychology, 22,* 311–313.

Salkovskis, P. M. (1985). Obsessional-compulsive problems: A cognitive-behavioural analysis. *Behaviour Research and Therapy, 25,* 571–583.

Salkovskis, P. M. (1988). Phenomenology, assessment and the cognitive model of panic. In S. J. Rachman & J. Maser (Eds.), *Panic: Psychological perspectives* (pp. 111–136). Hillsdale, NJ: Lawrence Erlbaum Associates.

Salkovskis, P. M. (1989a). Cognitive-behavioural factors and the persistence of intrusive thoughts in obsessional problems. *Behaviour Research and Therapy, 27,* 677–682.

Salkovskis, P. M. (1989b). Obsessions and compulsions. In J. Scott, J. M. G. Williams, & A. T. Beck (Eds.), *Cognitive therapy: A clinical casebook* (pp. 50–77). London: Croom Helm.

Salkovskis, P. M. (1989c). Obsessions and intrusive thoughts: Clinical and non-clinical aspects. In P. Emmelkamp, W. Everaerd, F. Kraaymaat, & M. van Son (Eds.), *Anxiety disorders: Annual series of European research in behaviour therapy* (Vol. 4, pp. 197–212). Amsterdam: Swets.

Salkovskis, P. M. (1991). The importance of behaviour in the maintenance of anxiety and panic: A cognitive account. *Behavioural Psychotherapy, 19,* 6–19.

Salkovskis, P. M. (1996a). Avoidance behaviour is motivated by threat beliefs: A possible resolution of the cognition-behaviour debate. In P. M. Salkovskis (Ed.), *Trends in cognitive and behavioural therapy* (Vol. 1, pp. 27–41). Chichester, UK: Wiley.

Salkovskis, P. M. (1996b). The cognitive approach to anxiety: Threat beliefs, safety seeking behavior and the special case of health anxiety and obsessions. In P. M. Salkovskis (Ed.), *Frontiers of cognitive therapy: The state of the art and beyond* (pp. 48–74). New York: Guilford.

Salkovskis, P. M. (1996c). Cognitive-behavioral approaches to the understanding of obsessional problems. In R. Rapee (Ed.), *Current controversies in the anxiety disorders* (pp. 103–133). New York: Guilford.

Salkovskis, P. M. (1999). Understanding and treating obsessive compulsive disorder. *Behaviour Research and Therapy, 37,* 529–552.

Salkovskis, P. M., & Campbell, P. (1994). Thought suppression in naturally occurring negative intrusive thoughts. *Behaviour Research and Therapy, 32,* 1–8.

Salkovskis, P. M., & Clark, D. M. (1991). Cognitive therapy for panic attacks. *Journal of Cognitive Psychotherapy: An International Quarterly, 5,* 215–226.

Salkovskis, P. M., & Clark, D. M. (1993). Panic and hypochondriasis. *Advances in Behaviour Research and Therapy, 15,* 23–48.

Salkovskis, P. M., & Harrison, J. (1984). Abnormal and normal obsessions: A replication. *Behaviour Research and Therapy, 22,* 549–552.

Salkovskis, P. M., & Kirk, J. (1989). Obsessional disorders. In K. Hawton, P. M. Salkovskis, J. Kirk, & D. M. Clark (Eds.), *Cognitive-behavioural treatment for psychiatric disorders: A practical guide* (pp. 129–168). Oxford, UK: Oxford University Press.

Salkovskis, P. M., Rachman, S. J., Ladouceur, R., & Freeston, M., Taylor, S., Kyrios, M., & Sica, C. (1996). *Proceedings of the Smith College Women's Room: An addendum to Toronto Cafeteria*. Unpublished manuscript.

Salkovskis, P. M., Richards, H. C., & Forrester, E. (1995). The relationship between obsessional problems and intrusive thoughts. *Behavioural and Cognitive Psychotherapy, 23,* 281–299.

Salkovskis, P. M., & Warwick, H. M. C. (1985). Cognitive therapy of obsessive-compulsive disorder—Treating treatment failures. *Behavioural Psychotherapy, 13,* 243–255.

Salkovskis, P. M., Warwick, H. M. C. (1986). Morbid preoccupations, health anxiety and reassurance: A cognitive-behavioural approach to hypochondriasis. *Behaviour Research and Therapy, 24,* 597–602.

Salkovskis, P. M., & Warwick, H. M. C. (1988). Cognitive therapy of obsessive-compulsive disorder. In C. Perris, I. M. Blackburn, & H. Perris (Eds.), *The theory and practice of cognitive therapy.* Heidelberg, Germany: Springer.

Salkovskis, P. M., & Westbrook, D. (1989). Behaviour therapy and obsessional ruminations: Can failure be turned into success? *Behaviour Research and Therapy, 27,* 149–160.

Salkovskis, P. M., Westbrook, D., Davis, J., Jeavons, A., & Gledhill, A. (1997). Effects of neutralizing on intrusive thoughts: An experiment investigating the etiology of obsessive-compulsive disorder. *Behaviour Research and Therapy, 35,* 211–219.

Solomon, R. L., & Wynne, L. C. (1960). Traumatic avoidance learning: The principles of anxiety conservation and partial irreversibility. *Psychological Review, 61,* 353–385.

Stanley, M. A., & Turner, S. M. (1995). Current status of pharmacological and behavioral treatment of obsessive-compulsive disorder. *Behavior Therapy, 26,* 163–186.

Steketee, G., & Foa, E. B. (1985). In D. H. Barlow (Ed.), *Clinical handbook of psychological disorders: A step by step treatment manual* (pp. 173–204). New York: Guilford.

Stern, R., & Fernandez, M. (1991). Group cognitive and behavioural treatment for hypochondriasis. *British Medical Journal, 303,* 1229–1230.

Teasdale, J. D. (1983). Negative thinking in depression: Cause, effect or reciprocal relationship? *Advances in Behaviour Research and Therapy, 5,* 3–25.

Trinder, H., & Salkovskis, P. M. (1994). Personally relevant intrusions outside the laboratory: Long term suppression increases intrusion. *Behaviour Research and Therapy, 32,* 833–842.

van Oppen, P., de Haan, E., van Balkom, A. J., Spinhoven, P., Hoogduin, K., & van Dyck, R. (1995). Cognitive therapy and exposure in vivo in the treatment of obsessive-compulsive disorder. *Behaviour Research and Therapy, 33,* 379–390.

Warwick, H. M. C., Clark, D. M., Cobb, A., & Salkovskis, P. M. (1996). A controlled trial of cognitive-behavioural treatment of hypochondriasis. *British Journal of Psychiatry, 169,* 189–195.

Warwick, H. M., & Marks, I. M. (1988). Behavioural treatment of illness phobia and hypochondriasis: A pilot study of 17 cases. *British Journal of Psychiatry, 152,* 239–241.

Wegner, D. M. (1989). *White bears and other unwanted thoughts; Suppression, obsession and the psychology of mental control.* New York: Viking.

12

Inpatient Treatment of Refractory Obsessive-Compulsive Disorder

C. Alec Pollard
Saint Louis University School of Medicine
Saint Louis Behavioral Medicine Institute

With the availability of potent serotonin reuptake inhibitors (SRIs) and behavioral treatment featuring exposure and response prevention, the majority of individuals with obsessive-compulsive disorder (OCD) can be successfully treated on an outpatient basis (Dar & Greist, 1992; Jenike, 1992; Steketee & Foa, 1993; Sturgis & Meyer, 1980). However, a substantial minority of patients still refuse or withdraw prematurely from treatment, or complete treatment with little or no benefit. It has been suggested that some outpatients resist or fail to respond to therapy because their natural environment does not adequately facilitate recovery. In such cases, the limitations of outpatient care may be remediated by inpatient treatment.

The purpose of this chapter is to review the literature and discuss issues relevant to the inpatient treatment of refractory OCD. First, prior research examining the efficacy of inpatient treatment is reviewed. Clinical indications for inpatient care are then outlined and suggestions for future research are provided.

OUTCOME RESEARCH

There is little reason to doubt that OCD can be effectively treated with appropriate inpatient care. In fact, the first reports documenting the value of behavior therapy as a treatment for OCD involved studies conducted primarily on inpatient units (Catts & McConaghy, 1975; Marks, Hodgson,

223

& Rachman, 1975; Meyer, 1966; Meyer, Levy, & Schnurer, 1974). Subsequently, several additional authors have reported successful outcomes
with inpatient treatment. (Calvocoressi et al., 1993; Dahlgren, Pollard, &
Brown, 1994; Friedmann & Silvers, 1977; Jacob, Ford, & Turner, 1985;
Pollard, Merkel, & Obermeier, 1986; Scahill, Walker, Lechner, & Tynan,
1993; Thornicroft, Colson, & Marks, 1991; Van den Hout, Emmelkamp,
Kraaykamp, & Griez, 1988). It should be noted there is no evidence that
hospitalization by itself is helpful for OCD. Patients described in these
reports were all treated on units that provided specialized behavioral and,
in some cases, pharmacologic intervention for OCD. However, because
these same interventions have been successfully administered on an outpatient basis at considerably less expense (Van den Hout et al., 1988),
demonstrations of efficacy alone are insufficient to establish a role for
inpatient care in the treatment of OCD.

The cost of hospitalization might be justified if inpatient care was
proportionately more effective than outpatient care. Case studies suggest
continuous supervision by nursing staff can be helpful in the treatment
of some individuals receiving intensive behavior therapy (Mills, Agras,
Barlow, & Mills, 1973; Turner, Hersen, Bellack, & Wells, 1979). One sample
of inpatients, many of whom had OCD, rated individual sessions with
nurse behavior therapists as the most valuable component of care (Merkel
& Weiner, 1986). Nonetheless, few studies have directly compared inpatient and outpatient treatment. Investigators that have contrasted the two
levels of care found no differences. Foa, Steketee, Grayson, Turner, and
Latimer (1984) reported that equivalent percentages of 10 inpatients and
22 outpatients with OCD responded well to behavioral treatment. Another
study (Van den Hout et al., 1988) found no differences in treatment
response between 22 patients who received 5.4 months of inpatient behavior therapy and 43 patients who received 20 outpatient sessions of
behavior therapy. Although additional research with larger patient samples is needed, these two studies suggest that in many cases the expense
of inpatient treatment can be avoided without sacrificing efficacy.

Failure to demonstrate the general superiority of inpatient treatment
is not surprising. Even proponents suggest inpatient care should be reserved for only the most severe or complicated cases, patients who are
also among the most refractory to therapy (Calvocoressi et al., 1993; Frank,
1990; Hoffman & Neziroglu, 1993; Pollard, 1994). It is this refractory
subpopulation that particularly needs effective alternatives to standard
outpatient treatment. Before inpatient intervention can be established as
a preferred option, however, controlled outcome studies are needed in
which well-defined samples of patients with refractory OCD are randomly
assigned to inpatient and outpatient conditions. Thus far, no study of this
nature has been conducted. In the two studies involving outpatient com-

parison groups, the inpatient group was either more clinically severe (Van den Hout et al., 1988) or clinically equivalent but not necessarily refractory (Foa et al., 1984).

In the absence of definitive comparisons between inpatient and outpatient care, evaluation of the utility of inpatient approaches to refractory OCD should include consideration of studies that examine treatment outcome with outpatient nonresponders. Inpatients with OCD have typically had more chronic and clinically severe OCD than their outpatient counterparts (Marks, 1995; Van den Hout et al., 1988). In fact, patient samples described in reports of successful inpatient treatment consist largely of individuals who had already failed or were considered too severe for outpatient care (Calvocoressi et al., 1993; Dahlgren et al., 1994; Pollard et al., 1986; Thornicroft et al., 1991). The fact that clinical investigators report success with such a clinically challenging group of patients does suggest there is a role for inpatient care in the treatment of refractory OCD. Nonetheless, it is still possible these successfully treated inpatients would have fared as well with another trial of outpatient therapy. Further research is clearly needed.

CLINICAL INDICATIONS FOR INPATIENT TREATMENT

Given that hospitalization is not indicated for most cases of OCD, it would be useful for clinicians to know which patients are most likely to benefit from inpatient treatment. Currently, there are no widely accepted practice guidelines with hospital admission criteria for OCD, and research designed to determine factors that predict responsivity to inpatient care has yet to be conducted. In the absence of empirically based guidelines, the decision to hospitalize a patient with OCD must be based on clinical judgment. However, there are some guidelines in the clinical literature to assist practitioners. Several authors have discussed clinical indications for the inpatient treatment of OCD (Calvocoressi et al., 1993; Dahlgren et al., 1994; Foa, 1996; Frank, 1990; Hoffman & Neziroglu, 1993; Jacob et al., 1985; Megens & Vandereycken, 1988; Pollard, 1994; Van den Hout et al., 1988; Weir & Fasnacht, 1983). Their recommendations are summarized in this section of the chapter.

Reasons to consider admitting a patient with OCD to the hospital can be grouped into three categories. The first indication for inpatient treatment is when outpatient care is unsafe (Frank, 1990; Hoffman & Neziroglu, 1993; Pollard, 1994). The most obvious example is the suicidal patient. However, other dangers can be associated with OCD. Compulsions can be so pervasive and disruptive that an individual is unable to eat or engage in other necessary activities of daily living. Medication adjustments in patients with medical or psychiatric complications may occasionally be more safely performed on an inpatient unit. Similar precautions may be indicated for experimental or high-risk medication approaches such as intravenous or high-dose clomipramine. In other instances, a patient may be hospitalized to protect others. For example, a small minority of individuals with OCD become aggressive when confronted with obsessive stimuli or when interrupted during the performance of rituals and these individuals may pose a threat to family members, particularly during the early stages of exposure and response prevention.

A second indication for inpatient care is when outpatient treatment is impractical (Calvocoressi et al., 1993; Dahlgren et al., 1994; Foa, 1996; Frank, 1990; Hoffman & Neziroglu, 1993; Jacob et al., 1985; Megens & Vandereycken, 1988; Pollard, 1994; Van den Hout et al., 1988). For example, patients unable to conduct activities of daily living because of debilitating compulsions or obsessional slowness may need too much assistance to be successfully treated on an outpatient basis. In some cases, they are unable to get to the outpatient clinic because of the severity of their condition. Other patients cannot adequately participate in therapy because of obstacles in their natural environment. Patients living with a chaotic or highly stressful family situation may find it too difficult to adhere to an exposure and response prevention regimen. Inpatient treatment may also be indicated for some individuals with obsessions about harming others. When the severity of the fear is extremely high, some patients are willing to risk engaging in therapy only on an inpatient unit, where they feel hospital staff could prevent them from acting on their obsession.

The third indication for inpatient treatment is failure of outpatient therapy (Frank, 1990; Pollard, 1994; Van den Hout et al., 1988). A few caveats should be noted, however, when assessing the potential benefit of inpatient treatment for an outpatient nonresponder. Before determining that outpatient treatment has failed, it is important to ensure that the patient's treatment history includes adequate outpatient trials of both pharmacologic and behavioral intervention. For example, subtherapeutic doses of an SRI medication or administration of the drug for less than 8 to 12 weeks would not be considered an adequate drug trial (Jefferson & Greist, 1996; Rasmussen, Eisen, & Pato, 1993). Similarly, psychological intervention without properly administered exposure and response prevention is not an adequate trial of behavior therapy (Foa, 1996).

In some cases, the advantageous aspects of an inpatient environment also present a therapeutic challenge. Some patients respond differently in a hospital than they do at home. For example, a patient with washing compulsions may not be very concerned about contaminants while in the hospital or an individual with checking rituals may not worry about making mistakes when hospital staff are there to assume responsibility. Successful treatment requires creative interventions to address the differences between inpatient and home environments (e.g., making home visits, bringing contaminants from home to the hospital, creating situations at the hospital in which the patient feels responsible, going out on day passes to conduct exposure therapy, etc.).

Another caveat is that failure of outpatient treatment, by itself, does not automatically qualify a patient for hospitalization. All treatment failures are not due to factors associated with level of care (Foa, 1979; Foa, Steketee, Grayson, & Doppelt, 1983). Patients with overvalued ideation, for example, are not likely to surrender maladaptive beliefs simply because they are in the hospital. Before proceeding with inpatient care, there should be reason to believe that treatment failure was due to something lacking in outpatient care that can be provided more adequately on an inpatient basis. For example, inpatient treatment for OCD can provide patients with closer supervision, more social support and personal assistance, a more structured and facilitative environment, and more hours of behavior therapy per day than that typically available in outpatient settings. It is for access to these elements of inpatient care that outpatient nonresponders should be considered for hospitalization.

RECOMMENDATIONS FOR FURTHER RESEARCH

In light of the recent emphasis on health care cost containment, it is not surprising little research attention has been given to expensive forms of care like inpatient treatment. There has been a steady decline over the past 20 years in the number of patients hospitalized for OCD (Thomsen & Jensen, 1994). Nonetheless, the long-term personal and economic costs of refractory OCD are substantial (Hollander et al., 1996). Any therapeutic option with the potential to reduce these costs should be studied further.

The primary focus of future inpatient research should be on refractory conditions of OCD, in particular, patients who have failed to respond to adequate trials of established outpatient treatments. It is this subgroup of OCD sufferers for whom the relatively high initial cost of inpatient care may be justifiable. Although reports of successful inpatient treatment of outpatient nonresponders are promising, controlled studies are needed that adequately demonstrate the superiority of inpatient care with this group of patients. To improve on prior research, these studies will need to clearly specify criteria used to define refractory status, randomly assign participants to inpatient and outpatient groups, and measure outcome with well-studied instruments such as the Yale–Brown Obsessive Compulsive Scale (Goodman, Price, Rasmussen, Mazure, Delgado, et al., 1989; Goodman, Price, Rasmussen, Mazure, Fleischmann, et al., 1989).

If the value of inpatient treatment for refractory OCD is adequately demonstrated, it will then be useful to identify the critical components of hospital-based treatment. It has been proposed that critical components of inpatient care are those that directly facilitate exposure and response prevention, such as contingent reinforcement from nursing staff and a highly structured environment (Dahlgren et al., 1994). However, deciphering the contributions of each of these components is no simple task. Inpatient units usually offer a variety of adjunctive interventions including family therapy, activities therapy, group therapy, and community meetings. These ancillary program services may also contribute positively to outcome (Megens & Vandereycken, 1988). There are, in fact, numerous ways in which inpatient and outpatient care differ. Determining the essential ingredients of effective inpatient treatment will require systematic assessment of each component of care. Despite these challenges, component analysis research should be attempted. Identifying the critical components of care could improve the cost-effectiveness of inpatient programs by providing information necessary to allocate resources judiciously.

In addition to examining treatment components, it will also be useful to study other elements of successful inpatient care. Although some aspects of clinical philosophy (e.g., emphasis on reducing rituals and avoidance) are consistent across inpatient units that treat OCD, other aspects vary. For example, some authors believe high-quality exposure and response prevention is best administered on a specialized, behaviorally oriented unit (Pollard et al., 1986). Others have suggested behavioral treatment can be successfully conducted on a general psychiatric service (Calvocoressi et al., 1993). Programs also differ in the extent of therapist assistance provided. Some units provide a great deal of staff support and individual attention (e.g., Dahlgren et al., 1994), whereas other programs deemphasize therapist assistance as much as possible (e.g., Thornicroft et al., 1991). Differences between programs may be more a matter of emphasis than substance and the success of various programs suggests it is unlikely that any single approach will be found universally superior. Nonetheless, further research might indicate which approaches are most effective for which types of patients.

Achieving clinical improvement at discharge will be of limited importance if the benefits of treatment are not maintained once patients return to their natural environment. It will, therefore, be important to study the long-term outcome of inpatient treatment. Furthermore, research should attempt to discern what factors facilitate maintenance of initial treatment gains. Several questions will need to be addressed: What level and amount of outpatient follow-up care are necessary for maintenance of inpatient treatment gains? What strategies (e.g., family involvement, home visits) best facilitate the transition from inpatient to outpatient care? How soon can patients be phased into day treatment, intensive outpatient, or home-based care without sacrificing progress? Answers to these questions could help health care systems determine how to integrate inpatient services effectively into a comprehensive continuum of care for OCD sufferers.

CONCLUSIONS

Although inpatient care is not more effective than outpatient care for the general population of OCD sufferers, there is preliminary evidence that specialized inpatient treatment should be considered for refractory cases. Because of the lower cost and comparable efficacy of outpatient treatments with nonrefractory OCD, hospitalization should only be considered when outpatient care is unsafe, impractical, or ineffective. Further research is needed to elucidate the potential value of inpatient care and to decipher the active components of successful treatment.

REFERENCES

Calvocoressi, L., McDougle, C. I., Wasylink, S., Goodman, W. K., Trufan, S. J., & Price, L. H. (1993). Inpatient treatment of patients with severe obsessive-compulsive disorder. *Hospital and Community Psychiatry, 44,* 1150–1154.

Catts, S., & McConaghy, M. (1975). Ritual prevention in the treatment of obsessive-compulsive neurosis. *Australian and New Zealand Journal of Psychiatry, 9,* 37–41.

Dahlgren, L., Pollard, C. A., & Brown, S. (1994). The behavioral medicine unit at Saint Louis University Health Sciences Center. In P. W. Corrigan & R. P. Liberman (Eds.), *Behavior therapy in psychiatric hospitals* (pp. 129–148). New York: Springer.

Dar, R., & Greist, J. H. (1992). Behavior therapy for obsessive compulsive disorder. *The Psychiatric Clinics of North America, 15,* 885–894.

Foa, E. B. (1979). Failure in treating obsessive-compulsives. *Behaviour Research and Therapy, 17,* 169–176.

Foa, E. B. (1996). The efficacy of behavioral therapy with obsessive-compulsives. *The Clinical Psychologist, 49,* 19–22.

Foa, E. B., Steketee, G., Grayson, J. B., & Doppelt, A. G. (1983). Treatment of obsessive-compulsives: When do we fail? In E. B. Foa & P. M. G. Emmelkamp (Eds.), *Failures in behavior therapy* (pp. 10–34). New York: Wiley.

Foa, E. B., Steketee, G., Grayson, J. B., Turner, R., & Latimer, P. (1984). Deliberate exposure and blocking of obsessive-compulsive rituals: Immediate and long-term effects. *Behavior Therapy, 15,* 450–472.

Frank, M. (1990). Inpatient behavioral treatment. *OCD Newsletter, 4,* 1–2, 4–5.

Friedmann, C. T. H., & Silvers, F. M. (1977). A multi modal approach to inpatient treatment of obsessive-compulsive disorder. *American Journal of Psychotherapy, 31,* 456–465.

Goodman, W. K., Price, L. H., Rasmussen, S. A., Mazure, C., Delgado, P., Heninger, G. R., & Charney, D. S. (1989). The Yale–Brown Obsessive Compulsive Scale (Y–BOCS): II. Validity. *Archives of General Psychiatry, 46*, 1012–1016.

Goodman, W. K., Price, L. H., Rasmussen, S. A., Mazure, C., Fleischmann, R. L., Hill, C. L., Heninger, G. R., & Charney, D. S. (1989). The Yale–Brown Obsessive Compulsive Scale (Y–BOCS): I. Development, use, and reliability. *Archives of General Psychiatry, 46*, 1006–1011.

Hoffman, J., & Neziroglu, F. A. (1993). Inpatient treatment of OCD and related conditions. *OCD Newsletter, 7*, 9–10.

Hollander, E., Stein, D., Kwon, J., Broatch, J., Himelein, C., & Rowland, C. (1996). A pharmacoecomonic and quality-of-life study of OCD. *OCD Newsletter, 10*, 7.

Jacob, R. G., Ford, R. R., & Turner, S. M. (1985). Obsessive-compulsive disorder. In M. Hersen (Ed.), *Practice of inpatient behavior therapy: A clinical guide* (pp. 61–91). Philadelphia: Grune & Stratton.

Jefferson, J. W., & Greist, J. H. (1996). The pharmacotherapy of obsessive-compulsive disorder. *Psychiatric Annals, 26*, 207–209.

Jenike, M. A. (1992). Pharmacologic treatment of obsessive compulsive disorder. *The Psychiatric Clinics of North America, 15*, 895–920.

Marks, I. (1995). Rapid audit of clinical outcome and cost by computer. *Australian and New Zealand Journal of Psychiatry, 29*, 32–37.

Marks, I., Hodgson, R., & Rachman, S. (1975). Treatment of chronic obsessive-compulsive neurosis *in vivo* exposure, a 2 year follow-up and issues in treatment. *Bristish Journal of Psychiatry, 127*, 349–364.

Megens, J., & Vandereycken, W. (1988). Hospitalization of obsessive-compulsive patients: The "forgotten" factor in the behavior therapy literature. *Comprehensive Psychiatry, 30*, 161–169.

Merkel, W. T., & Weiner, R. L. (1986). Relationships between patients' perceived improvement and their evaluations of treatment components on a behaviorally oriented psychiatric unit. *Behavioral Residential Treatment, 1*, 255–263.

Meyer, V. (1966). Modifications of expectations in cases with obsessional rituals. *Behaviour and Research Therapy, 4*, 273–280.

Meyer, V., Levy, R., & Schnurer, A. (1974). The behavior treatment of obsessive-compulsive disorders. In H. R. Beech (Ed.), *Obsessional states* (pp. 233–258). London: Methuen.

Mills, H. L., Agras, W. S., Barlow, D. H., & Mills, J. R. (1973). Compulsive rituals treated by response prevention: An experimental analysis. *Archives of General Psychiatry, 28*, 534–529.

Pollard, C. A. (1994). When should inpatient treatment be considered for obsessive-compulsive disorder? *OCD Newsletter, 8*, 6.

Pollard, C. A., Merkel, W. T., & Obermeier, H. J. (1986). Inpatient behavior therapy: The Saint Louis University model. *Journal of Behavior Therapy and Experimental Psychiatry, 17*, 233–243.

Rasmussen, S. A., Eisen, J. L., & Pato, M. T. (1993). Current issues in the pharmacologic management of obsessive compulsive disorder. *Journal of Clinical Psychiatry, 54*, 4–9.

Scahill, L., Walker, R. D., Lechner, S. N., & Tynan, K. E. (1993). Inpatient treatment of obsessive-compulsive disorder in childhood: A case study. *Journal of Child and Adolescent Psychiatric and Mental Health Nursing, 6*, 5–14.

Steketee, G., & Foa, E. B. (1993). Obsessive-compulsive disorder. In D. H. Barlow (Ed.), *Clinical handbook of psychological disorders* (pp. 189–240). London: Guilford.

Sturgis, E. T., & Meyer, V. (1981). Obsessive-compulsive disorder. In S. M. Turner, K. S. Calhoun, & H. E. Adams (Eds.), *Handbook of clinical behavior therapy* (pp. 68–102). New York: Wiley.

Thomsen, P. H., & Jensen, J. (1994). Obsessive compulsive disorder: Admission patterns and diagnostic stability. A case-register study. *Acta Psychiatrica Scandinavica, 90,* 19–24.

Thornicroft, G., Colson, L., & Marks, I. (1991). An inpatient behavioral psychotherapy unit: Description and audit. *British Journal of Psychiatry, 158,* 362–367.

Turner, S. M., Herson, M., Bellack, A. S., & Wells, K. C. (1979). Behavioral treatment of obsessive compulsive neurosis. *Behaviour Research and Therapy, 17,* 95–106.

Van den Hout, M., Emmelkamp, P., Kraaykamp, H., & Griez, E. (1988). Behavioral treatment of obsessive compulsives: Inpatient vs outpatient. *Behaviour Research and Therapy, 26,* 331–332.

Weir, D. C., & Fasnacht, G. (1983). Obsessive-compulsive disorder. In L. I. Sederer (Ed.), *Inpatient psychiatry: diagnosis and treatment* (pp. 101–116). Baltimore: Williams & Wilkins.

13

Cognitive and Behavioral Treatment of Obsessive-Compulsive Spectrum Disorders

Fugen A. Neziroglu
Kevin P. Stevens
Brett Liquori
Jose A. Yaryura-Tobias
Institute for Bio-Behavioral Therapy and Research

A discussion of the cognitive and behavioral treatment of the obsessive-compulsive (OC) spectrum disorders necessitates a conceptual distinction between obsessive-compulsive disorder (OCD) spectrum disorders and those traditionally referred to as comorbid conditions. The OC spectrum, as presently conceived, is a series of major psychiatric disorders clinically related by significant obsessions or compulsions as core symptomatology. *Comorbidity* refers to the simultaneous coexistence of two or more psychiatric disorders that may or may not be related. Spectrum disorders may, therefore, be in addition considered comorbid when they coexist.

Currently, the following conditions are OCD-related disorders within the spectrum: eating disorders, body dysmorphic disorder (BDD), hypochondriasis, Tourette's syndrome, and some forms of trichotillomania (Yaryura-Tobias & Neziroglu, 1997b). Some researchers (e.g., Hollander & Benzequen, 1996) argue for an even broader conceptualization that would include depersonalization, pathological gambling, a range of sexual impulse control disorders, borderline personality, and other characterological disorders. Recent empirical and theoretical research has also highlighted schizophrenia and psychotic symptomatology as perhaps an aspect of the OCD spectrum (Eisen & Rasmussen, 1993; Huber & Gross, 1982; Hwang & Hollander, 1993; Insel & Akiskal, 1986; Jenike, Baer, Minichiello, Schwartz, & Carey, 1986; Yaryura-Tobias, Campisi, McKay, & Neziroglu, 1995; Yaryura-Tobias & Neziroglu, 1997b; Yaryura-Tobias, Stevens, Neziroglu, & Grunes, 1997).

OC symptoms cut across an array of defined nosological boundaries set forth by the *Diagnostic and Statistical Manual of Mental Disorders* (4th ed. [*DSM–IV*]; American Psychiatric Association, 1994). For example, obsessional states are common in somatoform disorders such as hypochondriasis, BDD, and the various eating disorders, whereas ritualized and complex motor compulsions are commonly seen in impulse control (e.g., trichotillomania) and tic disorders such as Tourette's syndrome. For researchers operating within the spectrum paradigm, the phenomenological experience of obsessional states and enactment of compulsive behaviors is the manifestation of a pathophysiological continuum underlying a number of psychopathological disturbances (Yaryura-Tobias & Neziroglu, 1983; Yaryura-Tobias, 1990; Yaryura-Tobias, Todaro, et al., 1997). Experientially, this continuum may embrace compulsive–impulsive, risk seeking–risk avoiding, and ego-dystonic–ego-syntonic dimensions. An in-depth and up-to-date review of spectrum disorders was provided by Yaryura-Tobias and Neziroglu (1997a, 1997b), who discussed the phenomenology as well as pharmacological and psychological treatment outcome studies. Various chapters in this volume also address the spectrum concept.

Additional support for the spectrum concept is further provided by empirical data suggesting that conditions falling within this cluster may respond similarly to specific pharmacological and behavioral treatments such as selective serotonin reuptake inhibitors and exposure and response prevention (ERP), respectively (Neziroglu & Yaryura-Tobias, 1995; Yaryura-Tobias & Neziroglu, 1997a, 1997b). Furthermore, epidemiological data indicate higher familial loadings for one or more spectrum disorders among those presently diagnosed, relative to controls.

A behavioral or functional description of the continuum conceptualizes both obsessional ideation and morbid images as aversive discriminative stimuli. Repetitive behaviors, rituals, and tics are all functionally analogous in their roles in reducing or removing these aversive antecedent stimuli. Therefore, compulsions are to varying degrees perpetuated through processes of negative reinforcement.

This chapter is devoted to an explication of the cognitive- and exposure-based behavioral treatment of several OC spectrum disorders. The discussion is confined to the following disorders, which have been the most represented within the behavioral literature: OCD, BDD, hypochondriasis, and trichotillomania. For each disorder, a description of phenomenology is given, followed by a brief review of current epidemiological estimates. Finally, a presentation of the cognitive and behavioral treatment indicated is provided, along with results of any relevant empirical outcome studies.

OCD PHENOMENOLOGY

The primary symptoms of OCD include obsessions, compulsions, and according to some investigators, doubting (Legrand du Saulle, 1875; Westphal, 1878; Yaryura-Tobias & Neziroglu, 1983). Obsessions are experienced as intrusive and ego-dystonic thoughts, images, sounds, or impulses that are difficult to dismiss or resist. Typically, the obsessions revolve around contamination, religion, sexual behavior, and morbid and aggressive themes (e.g., Barlow, 1988; Riggs & Foa, 1993). Morbid and aggressive themes encompass incestuous or bestial sexual obsessions and violent, homicidal thoughts, images, and impulses. Obsessions may also involve magical thinking, which is the belief that one's thoughts can create or undo events. The patient usually recognizes the obsessions as absurd, although this insight need not always be present.

Poor insight into the nature of obsessions has been referred to in the literature as overvalued ideas (OVIs; e.g., Riggs & Foa, 1993) and has been debated since the early 1900s (Wernicke, 1906). Obsessional ideas might be overvalued. OVIs are essentially affect-driven misperceptions guided by entrenched and distorted cognitions and may represent the pars intermedia between OCD and psychotic experiences (Yaryura-Tobias, 1995; Yaryura-Tobias, Campisi, et al., 1995; Yaryura-Tobias, Stevens, Neziroglu, & Grunes, 1997). They are rigid, stable, and affect-laden ideas that are highly resistant to modification (Wernicke, 1906). Few scales have been developed to assess the extent of OVIs, which have been reported to be a poor prognostic variable in the treatment of OCD (Foa, 1979; Foa & Kozak, 1986; Neziroglu, McKay, & Stevens, 1996; Neziroglu, McKay, Stevens, & Yaryura-Tobias, 1998; Neziroglu, Yaryura-Tobias, Stevens, & Anderson, 1997; Riggs & Foa, 1993). OVIs should be considered separately from other treatment variables such as severity of OCD (Neziroglu, McKay, & Stevens, 1996). A new scale assessing overvalued ideas is developed (Neziroglu, McKay, Yaryura-Tobias, Stevens, & Todaro, 1999).

Compulsions can be either mental or motoric in nature. Ideational or mental compulsions such as counting, arithomania, mentally checking or patterning objects, and ritualistic prayers are discreet compulsions that are difficult to treat. Not only may they occur automatically; response prevention may also be difficult to control in therapy (Neziroglu, 1994).

Motor compulsions can comprise verbally and physically aggressive urges, such as corprolalia and self-mutilating behaviors such as slashing, digging, biting, and hair pulling (Yaryura-Tobias & Neziroglu, 1978; Yaryura-Tobias, Neziroglu, & Kaplan, 1995). Compulsions may also be physiological in nature, such as the compulsive need to swallow, defecate, urinate, spit, or engage in continuous sexual activities. Bodily movement compulsions involve the urge to touch, tap, and rub objects in certain ways or at certain frequencies. Echokinetic and stereotyped movements may also fall in this category. Ceremonial compulsions relate to purification and decontamination rituals and include familiar acts such as washing, cleaning, and sterilizing. Other compulsions include ordering, arranging, hoarding, rereading, rewriting, and retracing one's steps. Compulsions, mental or motor, may be performed repetitively, according to superstitious rules, without purpose, or to undo some anticipated disastrous consequence. It is likely that compulsions in any form or purpose and in spite of their maladaptive consequences have cognitive or somatic anxiety-reducing properties.

As mentioned earlier, some researchers have purported that doubting is a very important symptom of OCD. Unfortunately, it has been largely overlooked. Although doubting may be masked by the presence of iterative questioning or checking, the experience of doubting revolves around the uncertainty of a belief or opinion and affects decision making and performance. As a result, the patient experiences a loss of evidence and meaning, along with control (Yaryura-Tobias & Neziroglu, 1997a, 1997b). LeGrand du Saulle (1875) went as far as calling OCD the disease of the doubt.

OCD carries with it many secondary symptoms such as sexual disturbances, anger, depression, perceptual disturbances, and phobias (Beech, 1971; Cammer, 1973; Kendall & DiScipio, 1970; Yaryura-Tobias, 1977; Yaryura-Tobias & Neziroglu, 1978, 1983; Yaryura-Tobias, Neziroglu, & Kaplan, 1995). In addition, patients with OCD often present with serious personality pathology (Jenike et al., 1986; McKay, Neziroglu, Todaro, & Yaryura-Tobias, 1996).

Epidemiology

OCD is a chronic and often debilitating disorder that occurs in approximately 2.5% of the population (Reiger et al., 1988). To date, there are no prevalence data on the spectrum disorders. OCD has been observed worldwide (Bertschy & Ahyi, 1991; Chen, Wong, & Lee, 1993; Haffner & Miller, 1990; Hayaschi, 1992; Horwath, Johnson, & Hornig, 1993; Karno, Golding, & Burnam, 1989; Ronchi, Abbruzzese, & Erzegovesi, 1992), leading researchers and clinicians alike to view OCD as a cross-cultural and cross-socioeconomic phenomenon (Kringlen, 1965; Neziroglu, Yaryura-Tobias, Lemli, & Yaryura, 1994). This seems to be true for the spectrum disorders as well.

OCD affects males and females equally (Kringlen, 1965; Muller, 1957; Neziroglu et al., 1994; Okasha, Kamel, & Hassan, 1968; Pacella, 1944; Pollitt, 1957; Pujol & Savy, 1968; Rosenberg, 1968; Rudin, 1953). Although the age of onset has been placed at between 10 and 30 years old (Chakraborty & Banerji, 1975; Ingram, 1961; Taschev, 1970), persons with OCD typically do not seek treatment for several years afterward (Pollitt, 1957; Pujol & Savy, 1968). The age of onset for BDD, by contrast, appears to be in early adolescence, at about age 15 (Neziroglu & Yaryura-Tobias, 1993b; Phillips, McElroy, Keck, Pope, & Hudson, 1993). Trichotillomania characteristically appears even earlier during the formative years of early childhood and adolescence (Greenberg & Sarner, 1965; Muller, 1957). Hypochondriasis, on the other hand, typically develops later in life, at about age 30 to 39 for men and 40 to 49 for women (Kenyon, 1964).

With respect to OCD, the first consultation is frequently sought only after the severity of the disorder has obviated adaptive social, occupational, and academic functioning (Neziroglu et al., 1994). Despite persons with OCD typically obtaining high Verbal IQ scores (Ballus, 1971; Ingram, 1961; Lo, 1967), up to 26% of those with OCD cannot function or work in an adaptive or viable manner (Neziroglu et al., 1994). Recent data collected by the authors of this chapter suggest that the IQ profiles of those with OCD form a bimodal distribution. Those with primary OCD typically show high verbal IQs and strengths in the areas of vocabulary, information, and comprehension. Those with other comorbid conditions and perhaps "organic" cases typically show only low average verbal IQs (Stevens, 1996). In addition, there is a high celibacy rate among those with OCD (Neziroglu et al., 1994; Rudin, 1953).

Both genetic and social-learning cognitive factors should be considered in the etiology, as well as the maintenance of the disorder (Woodruff & Pitts, 1964). High concordance rates for monozygotic twins have been found (Inouye, 1965); however, these rates do not completely explain the illness, indicating that learning factors play an important role in OCD.

Psychological Treatment

The psychological treatment of choice for OCD is behavior therapy. Specifically, ERP has been found to be effective (Boulougouris & Bassiakos, 1973; Catts & McConaghy, 1975; Emmelkamp & Kraanen, 1977; Foa & Goldstein, 1978; Marks, Hodgson, & Rachman, 1975; Meyer, Levy, & Schnurer, 1974; Rabavilas, Boulougouris, & Stefanis, 1976; Roper, Rachman, & Marks, 1975). ERP entails exposing patients to anxiety-provoking stimuli, such as dirt and germs, in an incremental and systematic fashion, preventing the compulsion from occurring. The patient learns that the anxiety evoked dissipates spontaneously and without the assumed necessary compulsion. Both exposure and response prevention are necessary to treat OCD. In addition, massed trials as opposed to spaced trials tend to produce better outcomes. Gains are generally maintained longer and generalize further when treatment is intensive (90-minute sessions, three to five times per week, for several weeks) and includes exposure in imagination as well as in vivo exposure.

ERP treatment success rates of 60% to 80% have been reported for motivated patients who engage in intensive therapy with compliance (Barlow, 1988; Foa & Steketee, 1979; Riggs & Foa, 1993; Yaryura-Tobias & Neziroglu, 1983). Unfortunately, the probability of at least moderate improvement decreases rapidly in noncompliant patients. In addition, refractory cases and patients presenting with comorbid conditions, personality pathology, and OVIs generally improve less and are more likely to relapse (Jenike et al., 1986; McKay, Neziroglu, et al., 1996; McKay, Todaro, Neziroglu, & Yaryura-Tobias, 1996; Neziroglu, Hoffman, Yaryura-Tobias, Veale, & Cottraux, 1996). For a review of how to conduct ERP see Steketee (1994), Neziroglu (1994), and Yaryura-Tobias and Neziroglu (1997a).

Cognitive therapy for the treatment of OCD has been researched, although less so than behavior therapy. Traditional forms of cognitive therapy, such as Rational Emotive Behavior Therapy (REBT; Ellis, 1962, 1994), may be too general in their attempt to challenge and replace core faulty or distorted cognitions, although the approach may be effective in modifying OCD beliefs and ideas such as demands for certainty and perfection (Emmelkamp, Visser, & Hoekstra, 1988; Ladoucer, Freeston, Gagnon, Thibodeau, & Dumont, 1995). Recent theoretical work in cognitive therapy for OCD has led to the development of a cognitive model by Salkovskis (1985). This model was later expanded on by van Oppen and Arntz (1994) and their treatment targets core beliefs typically held by persons with OCD (i.e., overestimation of responsibility and thought–action fusion). In a controlled study, they found cognitive therapy to be equally effective as ERP. Others also have emphasized the appraisal of the thought (obsession) and have postulated that it is the appraisal that maintains the disorder. Several researchers have found that modifying the appraisal of the thought in pure obsessional patients with no overt compulsions was effective in reducing obsessions and increasing functioning levels (Freeston et al., 1997; Neziroglu & Neuman, 1990).

An international cognitive beliefs work group identified the following beliefs to be specific to OCD: an overinflated sense of responsibility, the fusion of thoughts and actions, the overestimation of threat, the need to control thoughts, the overimportance of thoughts, and the intolerance of uncertainty (Obsessive Compulsive Cognitions Working Group, 1997). A meta-analysis comparing the efficacy of Salkovskis' cognitive model and ERP in the treatment of OCD suggests that cognitive therapy is at least equal to traditional ERP (van Oppen et al., 1995).

BDD PHENOMENOLOGY

BDD has undergone numerous conceptual revisions and nosological changes. The term *dysmorphia* means abnormal shape and literally refers to ugliness related to facial appearance (Philippopoulos, 1979). As early as 1891, the term *dysmorphophobia* was used to denote the subjective deformity despite a normal appearance (Morselli, 1891). The obsessive nature of the symptoms was apparent and noted by the early scholars. In addition to pathological doubt surrounding the perceived deformity, dysmorphophobia entails a rigidly fixed belief system, possibly bordering on delusional disorder (McKay, Neziroglu, & Yaryura-Tobias, 1997; Morselli, 1891; Neziroglu & Anderson, 1995; Neziroglu & Yaryura-Tobias, 1997).

Dysmorphophobia was replaced in the *Diagnostic and Statistical Manual of Mental Disorders* (3rd ed., rev. [*DSM–III–R*]; American Psychiatric Association, 1987) by BDD, which refers to an intense preoccupation, obsession, OVI, or delusion with regard to body shape. Our understanding of BDD, whether as a symptom, syndrome, or spectrum disorder, is still relatively poor (Birtchnell, 1988; deLeon, Bott, & Simpson, 1989; Neziroglu & Yaryura-Tobias, 1993a, 1993b; Phillips et al., 1993).

BDD involves a faulty or disturbed belief as well as body misperception. BDD patients tend to be shy and avoidant, and they attempt to camouflage their perceived ugliness by wearing hats or sunglasses, or by undergoing plastic surgery. It is common for such patients to remain homebound for years and to withdraw socially, leading to functional impairment in social and occupational arenas. The symptom cohort includes fixed ideas, reference ideas, schizoid traits, self-centered behavior, and severe distress (McKay, Todaro, et al., 1996; Neziroglu & Yaryura-Tobias, 1997). Hypochondriacal symptoms and tactile hallucinations may also be present (Andreasen & Barduch, 1977; McKay, Neziroglu, & Yaryura-Tobias, 1997; Phillips et al., 1993).

BDD typically involves the face, hair, skin, and eyes (Hollander & Phillips, 1993; Neziroglu & Yaryura-Tobias, 1993b; Phillips et al., 1993). Patients obsessed with facial deformities may resort to face picking and skin digging, which ironically, leave permanent scarring or tissue loss. In addition, patients with BDD may present with obsessionality unrelated to body image. Typically such obsessions wax and wane, whereas BDD-related obsessions tend to be durable, intense, and nearly impossible to resist (McKay, Stevens, Neziroglu, & Yaryura-Tobias, 1997). Magical thinking is also frequently observed in such individuals as they compulsively mirror check and simultaneously wish their ugliness to suddenly disappear.

BDD patients present well-described OC symptoms. Although the notion of delusional pathology is currently not favored, such persons are characterized by extreme OVIs to such a degree that it is difficult to modify their body image. Insight appears to be minimal, although judgment remains intact in other areas. Neurological and executive functions also appear to be normal.

Epidemiology

Epidemiological data on BDD are quite sparse. The few studies seem to place the age of onset in middle adolescence, between ages 14 and 16 (Neziroglu & Yaryura-Tobias, 1993b; Phillips et al., 1993). The ratio of males to females appears about equal, although the few studies conducted indicate slightly more males than females. Celibacy and unemployment rates are high in persons with BDD, similar to those with OCD. IQ data suggest that persons who present solely with BDD tend to exhibit greater Performance scores than Verbal scores (Neziroglu, personal communication, 1992); however, persons with comorbid OCD or other spectrum disorders tend to exhibit the typical Verbal greater than Performance profiles of general psychiatric patients (Neziroglu & Yaryura-Tobias, 1993a).

Psychological Treatment

The behavior therapy literature for BDD is still not very well developed and consists largely of case studies and single-participant designs. Munjack (1978) reported success using systematic desensitization. ERP for the treatment of BDD is functionally similar to the treatment for OCD. Therapy consists of exposing patients to increasingly intense anxiety-provoking stimuli, preventing the person from behaving in ways that artificially reduce the experienced anxiety or distress.

For example, a therapist who is treating a patient who perceives physical defects with his face may construct different hierarchies for each deformity (e.g., hairline, nose, complexion, etc.). Considering the obsession with the hairline, the therapist lists the various situations that would require progressively increased exposure to the deformed area. At first, this may entail imagining one's hair and hairline, familiar people seeing this, strangers seeing this, and other variations on this imaging. Actual in vivo exposure might involve the patient first removing hats, scarves, and other articles that cover the hair and hairline. After habituation has occurred, increased exposure to the actual hairline may take place. This could be done, for instance, by gradually pulling the hair back to expose more and more fully the actual hairline. Exposure should encompass all associated thoughts, feelings, and images to allow habituation to occur for the entire stimulus complex. Within each hierarchy, the exposure increases in intensity: The next item is exposed after habituation to the previous item has occurred.

The response prevention segment of treatment calls for the prevention of any activity or behavior that offers reassurance or somehow reduces anxiety. This might be attained by having patients refrain from mirror checking, camouflaging, consulting dermatologists and surgeons, or asking for reassurance from friends and family members.

Patients who willingly engage in the exposure sessions are encouraged to self-monitor the spontaneous dissipation of anxiety or distress. For example, patients may consent to having their picture taken and observe the reactions of others as these are publicly displayed. Additional between-session homework assignments may include patients agreeing to leave their home and engage the public arena without attempting to cover up their "deformed" faces. It is important to note that, unlike OCD patients, BDD patients tend to be less willing to engage in the exposure sessions. This might be due to a higher level of OVIs. In addition to tenuous compliance issues, persons with BDD may experience sudden and profound depression and distress, rather than fear or anxiety, when they are exposed. Therapists should treat persons with BDD at a slower and more cautious pace than they typically can do with OCD patients. Furthermore, our experience with BDD patients reveals that a majority eventually report or admit to histories of sexual and emotional abuse following the ERP phase. Although this needs to be empirically verified and referenced against other OCD spectrum disorders, therapists should consider applying certain cognitive techniques to address issues of abuse and depression during the intensive ERP segment of therapy.

Marks and Mishan (1988) treated five chronic BDD patients using ERP, but a question concerning whether these patients were, in fact, delusional somatic type has been raised. In addition, several of the patients were receiving medication, making it difficult to determine the effects of behavior therapy alone.

Neziroglu and Yaryura-Tobias (1993b) reported on the effects of ERP and cognitive therapy in BDD patients without simultaneous drug therapy. Three patients received intensive ERP (90-minute sessions, five times per week), and an additional two received the same treatment weekly. Overall, four of the five patients improved functionally. In addition, clinical decreases in scores on the Yale–Brown Obsessive Compulsive Scale and the overvalued ideas scale (OVIS), a measure of OVIs were obtained.

Braddock (1982) reported the successful treatment of an adolescent with BDD, whose chief complaint was a "funny and crinkly nose" and forehead. Braddock reported employing a behavioral approach in which all references to the deformed areas were avoided. In addition, the approach employed social skills and assertiveness training, although these skills were not formally taught. Avoiding references to deformed areas, including behaviors such as mirror checking, serves as a response prevention. Jerome (1987) observed the efficacy of avoidance as a method of response prevention in cases of BDD patients who sought cosmetic surgery and reported improvement despite the surgery offering no objective change. Because of the dressings applied after surgery, the patients were prevented from checking their deformities, thus allowing for the associated anxiety to spontaneously dissipate.

As stated earlier, BDD patients do not readily engage in ERP compared to OCD patients. In addition, it is our experience that ERP is effective in obtaining behavioral change (e.g., patients are more willing to expose their "defects"), but not necessarily perceptual or cognitive change. Patients continue to hold on to their beliefs. Cognitive therapy aimed at challenging specific BDD beliefs seems to be effective. Specific beliefs center around the need to be noticed, the need to be perfect, and the belief that attractiveness will lead to the attainment of all desired outcomes (Veale et al., 1996; Yaryura-Tobias & Neziroglu, 1997a, 1997b). The first controlled study for cognitive-behavior therapy for BDD found that participants' responses to treatment, consisting of psychoeducation, thought stopping, relaxation training, cognitive restructuring, and exposure exercises, was significantly better than no treatment on several measurements (Rosen, Reiter, & Orasan, 1995). However, because several modes of therapy were employed, the unique effect of each is impossible to discern. More studies are needed in this area.

HYPOCHONDRIASIS PHENOMENOLOGY

Hypochondriasis' core symptom is the perception of having a serious disease based on the misinterpretation of one or more bodily signs and symptoms (American Psychiatric Association, 1994). The term *hypochondriasis* was first used by Galen of Pergamon in the second century, and with minor modification, the original connotation remains. During the modern era, hypochondriasis became entrenched as the disease of the Western world's middle and upper classes (Idzorek, 1975).

Hypochondriasis seems to overlap numerous clinical entities that should be considered for the purpose of differential diagnosis. These include hysteria, conversion hysteria, prodromal schizophrenia, somatization disorder, major depression, generalized anxiety disorder, OCD, somatoform pain disorder, BDD, monosymptomatic delusion, and factitious disorder. Common to these conditions seems to be a faulty perception or an impaired cognition resting on dubious somatic complaints. At first glance, it appears that this is a group of disparate psychiatric disorders; however, on closer examination, most are similar in that they involve physical symptoms presumably caused by psychological distress (Cantor & Fallon, 1996; Turner, Jacob, & Morrison, 1984).

The intense preoccupation or worry about being ill and seeking continuous medical reassurance reminds us of OCD similitude. For hypochondriasis to be an OCD variant, other OC symptoms must be present (e.g., compulsions, doubting, etc.). Therefore, if patients obsess over being ill, compulsively check for physical evidence of disease, and need reassurance because of their doubting, then it is fair to raise the question of hypochondriasis being a spectrum disorder. It is common to see a combination of hypochondriasis and OCD symptoms (Cantor & Fallon, 1996).

Epidemiology

Although most patients present for treatment in general medical practices, epidemiological and prevalence data on hypochondriasis are contradictory. *DSM–IV* provides prevalence estimates that hover between 4% and 9%. Other estimates of up to 20% have been reported in the literature. Hypochondriasis seems to afflict females more so than males and reports of sex ratios indicate that between 60% and 75% of hypochondriacs are female (Barsky, Wyshak, & Klerman, 1986; Kellner, 1985). However, other studies have not revealed any sex ratio differences (Barsky & Wyshak, 1989). The most common comorbid conditions with hypochondriasis are major depression (54.6%), generalized anxiety disorder (33.6%), and specific phobias (31.1%; Brown, Golding, & Smith, 1990). Hypochondriacal complaints are rooted in verifiable physical illnesses, such as thyroid disease, organic brain syndrome, and systemic lupus erthematosis in about 15% of cases (Ladee, 1966). In another study, most complaints revolved around head and neck problems, the abdomen, and the chest (Yaryura-Tobias & Anderson, 1995).

Psychological Treatment

The treatment of hypochondriasis has varied. Traditionally, the intervention employed was supportive or reassurance based (Warwick & Salkovskis, 1990). This technique involved a physician or qualified medical professional reassuring the patient with extreme health anxiety that no etiology for the presenting problem was identified. Medical tests and specialized exams would be employed as a means of allaying the patient's fears. This type of intervention helped only temporarily, if at all, as the health concerns would inevitably return shortly thereafter, or would shift to another somatic concern. Research investigating the effects of reassurance on hypochondriasis sufferers indicates that reassurance will decrease anxiety for only a few hours (Salkovskis & Warwick, 1986). Over longer periods, however, reassurance serves the paradoxical function of increasing the severity of hypochondriasis symptomatology. Reassurance-seek-

ing behavior in those with hypochondriasis may be functionally analogous to a compulsion in OCD patients.

Cognitive and behavior therapy is indicated in the treatment for hypochondriasis (Marks, 1981; Salkovskis & Warwick, 1986; Warwick &
Salkovskis, 1985). In primary hypochondriasis, various behavioral therapies such as systematic desensitization, thought stopping, implosion, and
ERP have been used (Warwick & Marks, 1988). Cognitive therapy assumes
that persons with hypochondriasis misinterpret bodily signs and symptoms as dangerous and that particular illnesses are more probable than
they really are (e.g., Salkovskis & Warwick, 1986). Thus, we see the
overestimation of threat as well as the overimportance of thoughts, which
are two cognitive distortions typically seen in OCD. Salkovskis and Warwick (1986) proposed a cognitive model explaining the development of
hypochondriasis. Their model has six basic steps: previous experience,
formation of dysfunctional assumptions, a critical incident, activation of
assumptions, negative thoughts and imagery, and hypochondriasis. The
model assumes, consistent with our experience, that most hypochondriacs
report a critical physical ailment or complaint that triggered their obsessions and compulsive behaviors. In addition, it is important to note that
most hypochondriacs are more concerned with the ramifications and
meanings of their somatic symptoms, rather than their mere presence and
subsequent treatment needs. That is, the hypochondriac is more concerned
over the meaning of chronic headaches (e.g., is it a tumor?) than how to
go about treating them (Neziroglu, 1995; Neziroglu & Anderson, 1995).

ERP strategies are implemented in a similar manner to procedures
employed in the treatment for OCD (Neziroglu & Anderson, 1995). Prior
to the initiation of treatment, the patient is required to undergo a complete
physical examination to rule out organic etiologies or disease processes.
As in traditional approaches to ERP, the patient is gradually and progressively exposed to those stimuli that evoke fears and anxiety. For the
patient with hypochondriasis, these are often somatic pains and sensations
or other physical signs associated with ailment or disease.

Neziroglu and Anderson (1995) described the successful use of ERP with
a patient who interpreted any sensation felt in her head as an indication
that something was terribly wrong (e.g., aneurysms, tumors, embolisms,
etc.). The patient reportedly experienced near-constant anxiety in response
to these obsessive preoccupations, and engaged in a range of anxiety-reducing avoidance behaviors to prevent any catastrophic outcome from
occurring. Blood pressure and pulse were measured throughout the day,
and she refrained from all exercise as she believed that an accelerated heart
rate would cause the aneurysm in her brain to burst. Certain foods were
avoided because of the belief that they caused tumors. Shopping would
take hours as the patient felt compelled to read every ingredient for each

item purchased. Professional reassurance was continually sought, and despite the fact that the results of four MRIs and two positron emission tomography scans were negative, her fears remained unallayed. Instead, she believed that she had not been correctly diagnosed or treated. Her health concerns permeated all spheres of her life and greatly restricted her ability to function both socially and occupationally.

Behavioral treatment focused on exposing the patient to all internal and external stimuli associated with fear and anxiety. Interoceptive cue exposure involved deliberately increasing her heart rate through rigorous exercise. All attempts at reassurance seeking from family members and professionals were prevented. Imaginal flooding typically involved envisioning that her headaches were indeed an indication of a malignant tumor and that she was dying. As is typical of behavioral treatment, the patient's level of anxiety was initially intense but eventually plateaued and subsided as she internalized the belief that her fears were indeed irrational. Research has demonstrated ERP to be effective with other cases similar to this one (Neziroglu, 1995; Neziroglu & Anderson, 1995).

The cognitive approach for hypochondriasis appears to center around reviewing the patient's evidence for physical illness and then identifying testable alternative explanations for the symptoms that are experienced. This technique allows for the hypochondriacal assumptions to be most effectively challenged, which is then conducive to attempts at cognitive restructuring (Warwick & Salkovskis, 1990). As with most complex cases of OC spectrum disorders, cognitive therapy becomes an essential tool in producing the so-called cognitive shift. In the absence of a cognitive shift, patients are likely to relapse at some point in spite of the behavioral changes that are shaped in ERP sessions. Increasing evidence is emerging that each of the spectrum disorders evidence their own particular and highly specific cognitive distortions that must be targeted to maintain treatment gains.

TRICHOTILLOMANIA

Phenomenology

A diagnosis of trichotillomania, as currently defined within the *DSM–IV* (American Psychiatric Association, 1994), requires that the patient engages in the recurrent pulling of hair resulting in noticeable hair loss; experiences an increasing sense of tension immediately before pulling out the hair or when attempting to resist the behavior; and pleasure, gratification, or relief upon hair pulling. The patient's hair pulling may not be accounted for by another psychological disorder (e.g., in response to a delusion or hallucination) and is not due to a general medical condition. For many patients, this condition may be accompanied by inspection of the hair root, hair twirling, pulling the strand between the teeth, or trichophagia (the ingestion of hair).

Although trichotillomania is presently characterized as an impulse control disorder, the diagnostic criteria are consistent with an OC model. The patient typically experiences an increasing sense of tension immediately prior to, or when attempting to resist hair pulling. This is functionally analogous to the anxiety and ritualistic urges commonly associated with obsessional ideation, in that both affective states are discriminative stimuli for compulsive responding. Immediately after pulling, the patient experiences a positive change in affect. Those with OCD typically experience a reduction of unpleasant emotion after engaging in a compulsive ritual. Some researchers suggest it might be a form of OCD (Jenike, 1990; Philippopoulos, 1961; Primeau & Fontaine, 1987; Tynes, White, & Steketee, 1990), whereas others state that it is not an OCD variant (Christenson, Pyle, & Mitchell, 1991; Stanley et al., 1992; Winchel, Jones, & Stanley, 1992).

Stanley et al. (1992) suggested that the experience of pleasure reported by many patients during hair pulling differentiates this population from those with OCD, who typically experience no pleasure during ritual performance. This would suggest that hair pulling is shaped, strengthened, and maintained as a function of both negatively reinforcing consequences (i.e., reduction in unpleasant affect) and through positive reinforcement as well.

Other differentiating features reported by these researchers are the lower incidence of obsessions and compulsions and lower levels of anxiety and depression reported by patients with trichotillomania relative to those with OCD. Other researchers postulate it is a separate syndrome similar to other maladaptive habits such as thumb sucking, nail biting, and nose picking (Azrin, Nunn, & Frantz, 1980; Delgado & Mannino, 1969; Greenberg & Sarner, 1965).

Epidemiology

There have been no extensive epidemiological studies of trichotillomania. Data available are equivocal, as some researchers have reported an extremely low incidence (Anderson & Dean, 1956; Mannino & Delgado, 1969), whereas others have estimated a much higher rate of occurrence (Azrin & Nunn, 1980; Christenson et al., 1991; Greenberg & Sarner, 1965; Tynes & Winstead, 1992). In a study of freshman college students ($N = 2,534$), Christenson et al. (1991) reported a lifetime prevalence of 0.6%. This is significantly lower than the estimate provided by DSM–IV (American Psychiatric Association, 1994), which suggests that 1% to 2% of college students have a past or current history of trichotillomania.

Trichotillomania is noted predominantly in females and occurs more often in children than adults. Onset later in life is associated with more severe psychopathology. The age of onset is most frequently between early childhood and adolescence (Greenberg & Sarner, 1965; Muller, 1987). The scalp is the most frequently reported hair-pulling site, followed by the eyebrows, eyelashes, pubic region, face, trunk, and lower extremities (Yaryura-Tobias & Neziroglu, 1997b).

To explore a possible relation between trichotillomania and OCD, 65 of 69 first-degree relatives of 16 female probands with severe chronic trichotillomania were compared with OCD, control groups and trichotillomania patients (Lenane, Swedo, & Rapoport, 1992). Three of 16 trichotillomania probands had at least one first-degree relative with a lifetime OCD history and an age-correlated rate of 6.4% of first-degree relatives with OCD. No relatives in the normal control group met OCD criteria. The authors concluded the higher OCD rate in trichotillomania families suggests that trichotillomania is an OCD spectrum disorder along with other pathological grooming behaviors.

Psychological Treatment

The first reported behavioral intervention for trichotillomania described a program of self-monitoring with response chain interruption. This program entailed instruction in behavioral self-monitoring coupled with verbal instructions to patients' hands to "stop" (Taylor, 1963). Other interventions reported include counting and recording hair pulls (Saper, 1971) and contingent punishment. Researchers investigating the latter intervention strategy have utilized denial of privileges and the application of eye drops (Epstein & Peterson, 1973) and aversive self-stimulation with a rubber band. Although Saper (1971) reported some decline in OCD-like symptoms, patients from the other studies reported zero hair-pulling rates at the end of treatment.

Other behavior therapies reported to result in at least moderate improvement include such treatments as covert desensitization (Levine, 1976) and attention reflection and response prevention by cutting hair close to the scalp (Massong, Edwards, & Range-Sitton, 1980). In general, treatment packages that include self-monitoring and some form of response prevention appear to be common to all behavioral treatments.

The most successful behavioral treatment in the remediation of hair pulling is known as *habit reversal training*. This was first introduced by Azrin and Nunn (1980) as a self-management treatment for nervous habits like tics, thumb sucking, and stuttering. This protocol includes 13 components: (a) Competing response training focuses on teaching the patient a behavioral response that precludes the performance of the hair-pulling response.

A typical strategy requires the patient clench his or her fists together and keep his or her arms locked and firmly buttressed against the sides. (b) Habit awareness training teaches the patient to be aware of the specific bodily movements involved in the hair pulling, and (c) Self-monitoring techniques and daily records help to make the patient aware of rate, frequency, and intensity of the hair pulling; to assist in (d) Identifying response precursors such as face touching, hair straightening or twirling; and (e) Identifying habit-prone situations that may be sedentary activities such as watching TV, studying, or being home alone, as well as stress-inducing situations related to work, family, and social functioning. (f) Relaxation training is taught to assist in the management of urges and anxiety. (g) Response prevention involves practicing a competing response for 3 minutes when a response precursor or habit-prone situation has been identified. (h) Habit interruption involves engaging in the competing response to interrupt hair pulling and is designed to allow the patient's experience of urges and anxiety to dissipate in the absence of hair pulling, in a manner consistent with most ERP-based treatment approaches. Azrin and Nunn (1980) further recommended the use of (i) Positive attention and overcorrection (e.g., positive hair care), (j) Practicing competing responses in front of a mirror to ensure inconspicuousness of the response, and (k) Solicitation of social support, which involves praise from significant others for behavioral success. Finally, they recommended that treatment be concluded with (l) Habit inconvenience review, which is a discussion of the ways in which the patient's condition interferes with life functioning, and (m) Display of improvement. The latter component stresses deliberate and prolonged exposure to situations previously avoided.

Azrin et al. (1980) replicated their original work in a study comparing habit reversal training to negative practice in 34 hair pullers. Negative practice requires that the patient enact and exaggerate the hair-pulling response with great frequency, while refraining from actually pulling hair from the scalp. The theoretical rationale posits that continued responding in the absence of reinforcement will ultimately result in extinction. Results indicated that patients engaged in 90% less hair pulling with habit reversal, compared to 50% with negative practice.

CONCLUSION

OC symptoms appear to be related to, or associated with, several neuropsychiatric entities. This association cluster makes us believe OCD is a continuum segment, rather than one clinical entity. When several of these illnesses appear in the nosological panorama at the same time, it is referred to as *comorbidity* or *parallel emergents*.

We see many psychiatric OCD patients presenting with more than one major mental illness. This mosaic of symptoms validates the practice of viewing the brain as one indivisible system that, if lesioned or in a state of disequilibrium, affects many aspects of cerebral functioning.

Therefore, we define OCD as an open-ended mulitvariate phenomenon affecting the individual's biopsychosocial architecture. This framework organizes various nosological constructs under one consolidating pathophysiology. This energy flows in time and space, determining the duration and trajectory of the illness.

OCD is an entity of gradual onset and growth that, if untreated, becomes chronic. We think reversibility is a function of the OCD phenomenon, unless the condition remains unattended or is treated at a later evolutionary stage. The clinician must treat OCD and its spectrum. Generally, the prognosis seems to be guarded, and the pathology involved usually requires medication, behavior therapy, and cognitive therapy. The usage of a combination of these may alter the prognosis. Research supporting the efficacy of a behavioral component in case management continues to mount, although more outcome studies, especially with respect to the spectrum conditions, are warranted. Until we get answers, a multidisciplinary approach seems advisable and a biopsychosocial model concept should be applied.

REFERENCES

American Psychiatric Association. (1987). *Diagnostic and statistical manual of mental disorders* (3rd ed., rev.). Washington, DC: Author.

American Psychiatric Association. (1994). *Diagnostic and statistical manual of mental disorders* (4th ed.). Washington, DC: Author.

Anderson, F. W., & Dean, H. C. (1956). Some aspects of child guidance and clinical intake policy and practices: A study of 500 cases at the Los Angeles child guidance clinics. *CA Public Health Monograph, 42*, 1–14.

Andreason, R. A., & Barduch, J. (1977). Dysmorphophobia: Symptom or disease? *American Journal of Psychiatry, 134*, 673–675.

Azrin, N. H., & Nunn, R. G. (1980). Habit reversal: A method of eliminating nervous habits and tics. *Behavior Research and Therapy, 11*, 619–628.

Azrin, N. H., Nunn, R. G., & Frantz, S. E. (1980). Treatment of hair pulling (trichotillomania): A comparative study of habit reversal and negative practice training. *Journal of Behavior Therapy and Experimental Psychiatry, 11*, 13–20.

Ballus, C. (1971). Etiologia y patogenia [Etiology and pathology]. In S. Monserrat-Esteve, J. M. Costa-Molinari, & C. Ballus (Eds.), *Pathologia obsesiva* (pp. 81–114). Malaga, Spain: Graficase.

Barlow, D. H. (1988). *Anxiety and its disorders*. New York: Guilford.

Barsky, A. J., & Wyshak, F. (1989). Hypochondriasis and related health attitudes. *Psychosomatics, 30*, 412–420.

Barsky, A. J., Wyshak, F., & Klerman, L. L. (1986). Hypochondriasis: An evaluation of the DSM–III–R criteria for medical outpatients. *Archives of General Psychiatry, 43*, 493–500.

Beech, H. R. (1971). Ritualistic activity in patients. *Journal of Psychosomatic Research, 15,* 417–422.

Bertschy, G., & Ahyi, R. G. (1991). Obsessive compulsive disorder in Benin: Five case reports. *Psychopathology, 24,* 398–401.

Birtchnell, S. A. (1988). Dysmorphophobia—A centenary discussion. *British Journal of Psychiatry, 153,* 41–43.

Boulougouris, J. C., & Bassiakos, L. (1973). Prolonged flooding in cases with obsessive-compulsive neurosis. *Behavior Research and Therapy, 11,* 227–231.

Braddock, L. E. (1982). Dysmorphophobia in adolescence: A case report. *British Journal of Psychiatry, 140,* 199–201.

Brown, F. W., Golding, J. M., & Smith, G. R. (1990). Psychiatric comorbidity in primary care somatization disorder. *Psychosomatic Medicine, 52,* 445–451.

Cammer, L. (1973). Antidepressants as a prophylaxis against depression in the obsessive-compulsive person. *Psychosomatics, 14,* 201–206.

Cantor, C., & Fallon, B. A. (1996). *Phantom illness.* New York: Houghton-Mifflin.

Catts, S., & McConaghy, N. (1975). Ritual prevention in the treatment of obsessive-compulsive neurosis. *Australian and New Zealand Journal of Psychiatry, 9,* 37–41.

Chakraborty, A., & Banerji, G. (1975). Ritual, a culture specific neurosis, and obsessional states in Bengali culture. *Indian Journal of Psychiatry, 17*(4), 273–283.

Chen, C. N., Wong, J., & Lee, N. (1993). The Shatin community mental health survey in Hong Kong: Major findings. *Archives of General Psychiatry, 50,* 125–133.

Christenson, G. A., Pyle, R. L., & Mitchell, J. E. (1991). Estimated lifetime prevalence of trichotillomania in college students. *Journal of Clinical Psychiatry, 52,* 415–417.

deLeon, J., Bott, A., & Simpson, G. M. (1989). Dysmorphophobia: Body dysmorphic disorder or delusional disorder, somatic type? *Comprehensive Psychiatry, 30,* 457–472.

Delgado, R. A., & Mannino, F. V. (1969). Some observations on trichotillomania in children. *Journal of the American Academy of Child Psychiatry, 81,* 229–246.

Eisen, J. L., & Rasmussen, S. A. (1993). Obsessive compulsive disorder with psychotic features. *Journal of Clinical Psychiatry, 54,* 373–379.

Ellis, A. (1962). *Reason and emotion in psychotherapy.* New York: Lyle Stuart.

Ellis, A. (1994). Rational emotive behavioral therapy approaches to obsessive compulsive disorder. *Journal of Rational Emotive Cognitive Behavior Therapy, 12,* 121–141.

Emmelkamp, P. M. G., & Kraanen, J. (1977). Therapist controlled exposure in-vivi vs. self controlled exposure in-vivo: A comparison with obssesive-compulsive patients. *Behavior Research and Therapy, 21,* 341–346.

Emmelkamp, P. M. G., Visser, S., & Hoekstra, R. J. (1988). Cognitive therapy vs. exposure in vivo in the treatment of obsessive compulsive disorder. *Cognitive Therapy Research, 12,* 103–114.

Epstein, L. H., & Peterson, G. L. (1973). The control of undesired behavior by self imposed contingencies. *Behavior Therapy, 4,* 91–95.

Foa, E. B. (1979). Failure in treating obsessive compulsives. *Behavior, Research and Therapy, 9,* 821–829.

Foa, E. B., & Goldstein, A. (1978). Continuous exposure and complete response prevention in the treatment of obsessive-compulsive neurosis. *Behavior Research and Therapy, 9,* 821–829.

Foa, E. B., & Kozak, M. J. (1986). Emotional processing of fear: Exposure to corrective information. *Psychological Bulletin, 99,* 20–35.

Foa, E. B., & Steketee, G. S. (1979). Obsessive-compulsives: Conceptual issues and treatment interventions. *Progress in Behavior Modification, 8,* 1–15.

Freeston, M. H., Ladouceur, R., Gagnon, F., Thibodeau, N., Rheaume, J., Letarte, H., & Bujold, A. (1997). Cognitive-behavioral treatment of obsessive thoughts: A controlled study. *Journal of Consulting and Clinical Psychology, 65,* 405–413.

Greenberg, H. R., & Sarner, C. A. (1965). Trichotillomania: A review. *Comprehensive Psychiatry, 26*, 123–128.

Haffner, R. J., & Miller, R. J. (1990). Obsessive compulsive disorder: An exploration of some unresolved clinical issues. *Australian and New Zealand Journal of Psychiatry, 24*, 480–485.

Hayaschi, N. (1992). Neurotic symptoms of borderline patients: A case review study. *Sieshin Shinkeigaku Zasshi -Japanese Psychiatry and Neurology, 94*, 648–681.

Hollander, E. H., & Benzequen, S. (1996). Is there a distinct OCD spectrum? *CNS Spectrums, 1*, 17–26.

Hollander, E. H., & Phillips, K. A. (1993). Body image and experience disorders. In E. H. Hollander (Ed.), *Obsessive compulsive related disorders* (pp. 100–125). Washington, DC: American Psychiatric Association.

Horwath, E., Johnson, J., & Hornig, C. D. (1993). Epidemiology of panic disorder in African-Americans. *American Journal of Psychiatry, 150*, 465–469.

Huber, G., & Gross, G. (1982). Zwangssyndrome bbei Schizophrenie [Compulsive syndromes with schizophrenia]. *Schwerpunktmedizin, 2*, 12–19.

Hwang, M. H., & Hollander, E. H. (1993). Schizo-obsessive disorders. *Psychiatric Annals, 23*, 396–401.

Idzorek, S. (1975). A functional classification of hypochondriasis with specific recommendations for treatment. *South Medical Journal, 68*, 1326–1332.

Ingram, I. M. (1961). Obsessional illness in mental hospital patients. *Journal of Mental Sciences, 107*, 382–396.

Inouye, E. (1965). Similar and dissimilar manifestations of obsessive-compulsive neurosis in monozygotic twins. *American Journal of Psychiatry, 121*, 1171–1175.

Insel, T., & Akiskal, H. (1986). Obsessive compulsive disorder with psychotic features: A phenomenologic analysis. *American Journal of Psychiatry, 143*, 1527–1533.

Jenike, M. A. (1990). Psychotherapy of obsessive compulsive personality disorder. In M. A. Jenike & B. L. Miniciello (Eds.), *Obsessive compulsive disorders: Theory and management* (pp. 295–305). Chicago: Year Book Medical.

Jenike, M. A., Baer, L., Minichiello, W. E., Schwartz, C. E., & Carey, R. J. (1986). Concomitant obsessive compulsive disorder and schizotypal personality disorder. *American Journal of Psychiatry, 143*, 530–532.

Jerome, L. (1987). Anorexia nervosa or dysmorphophobia? *British Journal of Psychiatry, 150*, 560–561.

Karno, M., Golding, J. M., & Burnam, M. A. (1989). Anxiety disorder among Mexican Americans and non-Hispanic Whites in Los Angeles. *Journal of Nervous and Mental Disease, 177*, 202–209.

Kellner, R. (1985). Functional somatic symptoms and hypochondriasis. *Archives of General Psychiatry, 42*, 821–833.

Kendall, R. E., & DiScipio, W. J. (1970). Obsessional symptoms and obsessional personality traits in patients with depressive illness. *Psychological Medicine, 1*, 65–72.

Kenyon, F. E. (1964). Hypochondriasis: A clinical study. *British Journal of Psychiatry, 110*, 478–488.

Kringlen, E. (1965). Obsessional neurotics. *British Journal of Psychiatry, 111*, 709–772.

Ladee, G. A. (1966). *Hypochondriacal syndromes*. New York: Elsevier.

Ladoucer, R., Freeston, M. H., Gagnon, F., Thibodeau, N., & Dumont, J. (1995). Congitive behavioral treatment of obsessions. *Behavior Modification, 19*, 247–257.

Legrand du Saulle, H. (1875). *La folie du doute avec delire du toucher* [The disease of doubt with desire to touch]. Paris: Delahaye.

Lenane, M. C., Swedo, S. E., & Rapoport, J. L. (1992). Rates of obsessive compulsive disorder in first degree relatives of patients with trichotillomania: A research note. *Journal of Child Psychology and Psychiatry and Allied Disciplines, 33*, 925–933.

Levine, B. A. (1976). Treatment of trichotillomania by covert sensitization. *Journal of Behavior Therapy and Experimental Research, 7,* 75–76.

Lo, W. H. (1967). A follow-up study of obsessional neurotics in Hong Kong Chinese. *British Journal of Psychiatry, 113,* 823–832.

Mannino, F. V., & Delgado, R. A. (1969). Trichotillomania in children: A review. *American Journal of Psychiatry, 126,* 505–511.

Marks, I. M. (1981). *Cure and care of neuroses.* New York: Wiley.

Marks, I. M., Hodgson, R., & Rachman, S. (1975). Treatment of obsessive-compulsive neurosis by in-vivo exposure: A two yearfollow up and issues in treatment. *British Journal of Psychiatry, 127,* 674–678.

Marks, I., & Mishan, J. (1988). Dysmorphophobic avoidance with disturbed body perception: A pilot study of exposure therapy. *British Journal of Psychiatry, 152,* 674–678.

Massong, S. R., Edwards, R. P., & Range-Sitton, L. (1980). A case of trichotillomania in a three-year-old boy treated by response prevention. *Journal of Behavior Therapy and Experimental Psychiatry, 11,* 223–225.

McKay, D., Neziroglu, F. A., Todaro, J., & Yaryura-Tobias, J. A. (1996). Changs in personality disorders following behavior therapy for obsessive compulsive disorder. *Journal of Anxiety Disorders, 10,* 47–57.

McKay, D., Neziroglu, F. A., & Yaryura-Tobias, J. A. (1997). Comparison of clinical characteristics in obsessive compulsive disorder and body dysmorphic disorder. *Journal of Anxiety Disorders, 11,* 1–8.

McKay, D., Stevens, K. P., Neziroglu, F. A., & Yaryura-Tobias, J. A. (1997, November). *Cognitive functioning in obsessive compulsive disorder and body dysmorphhic disorder.* Paper presented at the annual meeting of the Association for the Advancement of Behavior Therapy, Miami, FL.

McKay, D., Todaro, J., Neziroglu, F. A., & Yaryura-Tobias, J. A. (1996). Evaluation of a naturalistic maintenance program in the treatment of obsessive compulsive disorder: A preliminary investigation. *Journal of Anxiety Disorders, 10,* 211–217.

Meyer, V., Levy, R., & Schnurer, A. (1974). The behavioral treatment of obsessive-compulsive disorder. In H. R. Beech (Ed.), *Obsessional states* (pp. 233–258). London: Methuen.

Morselli, E. (1891). Sulla dismorfofobia e sulla tafefobia [On dysmorphophobia and on the fear of being buried alive]. *Bolletino della Academia di Genova, 6,* 110–119.

Muller, S. A. (1957). Trichotillomania. *Clinical Dermatology, 5*(3), 595–601.

Munjack, D. J. (1978). The behavioral treatment of dysmorphophobia. *Journal of Behavior Therapy and Experimental Psychiatry, 9,* 53–56.

Neziroglu, F. A. (1994). Complexities and lesser known aspects of obsessive compulsive and related disorders. *Journal of Cognitive and Behavioral Practice, 1,* 133–157.

Neziroglu, F. A. (1995, November). *Hypochondriasis: Its diagnosis and treatment.* Paper presented at the 29th Annual Convention of the Association for the Advancement of Behavior Therapy, Washington, DC.

Neziroglu, F. A., & Anderson, M. C. (1995). *The effect of exposure based treatment of hypochondriasis.* Paper presented at the 29th annual convention of the Association for the Advancement of Behavior Therapy, Washington, DC.

Neziroglu, F. A., Hoffman, J., Yaryura-Tobias, J. A., Veale, D., & Cottraux, J. (1996). Current issues in behavior and cognitive therapy for obsessive compulsive disorder. *CNS Spectrums, 1,* 47–54.

Neziroglu, F. A., McKay, D., & Stevens, K. P. (1996, November). *Overvalued ideas in obsessive compulsive disorder.* Symposium conducted at the 30th annual meeting of the Association for the Advancement of Behavior Therapy, New York.

Neziroglu, F., McKay, D., Stevens, K. P., & Yaryura-Tobias, J. A. (1998, November). Effects of overvalued ideas on treatment outcome in patients diagnosed with body dysmorphic disorder. Paper presented at the 32nd annual meeting of the Association for the Advancement of Behavior Therapy, Miami, Florida.

Neziroglu, F. A., McKay, D., Yaryura-Tobias, J. A., Stevens, K. P., & Todaro, J. (in press). The overvalued ideas scale: Development, reliability, and validity in obsessive compulsive disorder. *Journal of Behavior Research and Therapy.*

Neziroglu, F. A., & Neuman, J. (1990). Three approaches to the treatment of obsessions. *International Journal of Cognitive Therapy, 4,* 377–392.

Neziroglu, F. A., & Yaryura-Tobias, J. A. (1993a). Body dysmorphic disorder: Phenomenology and case descriptions. *Behavioural Psychotherapy, 21,* 27–36.

Neziroglu, F. A., & Yaryura-Tobias, J. A. (1993b). Exposure, response prevention and cognitive therapy in the treatment of body dysmorphic disorder. *Journal of Behavior Therapy, 24,* 431–438.

Neziroglu, F. A., & Yaryura-Tobias, J. A. (1995). *Over and over again: Understanding obsessive compulsive disorder.* New York: The Free Press.

Neziroglu, F. A., & Yaryura-Tobias, J. A. (1997). A review of cognitive behavioral and pharmacological treatment of body dysmorphic disorder. *Behavior Modification, 21,* 324–340.

Neziroglu, F., Yaryura-Tobias, J. A., Lemli, J., & Yaryura, R. (1994). Estudio demografico del trastarno obseso-compulsivo [A large demographic study of obsessive-compulsive disorder]. *Acta Psquiatrica Latinoamericano, 40*(3), 217–223.

Neziroglu, F. A., Yaryura-Tobias, J. A., Stevens, K., & Anderson, M. (1997). Overvalued ideas and their impact on treatment outcome of obsessive compulsive disorder in patients. Symposium conducted at the 31st annual meeting of the Association for the Advancement of Behavior Therapy, Miami.

Obsessive Compulsive Cognitions Working Group. (1997). Cognitive assessment of obsessive compulsive disorder. *Behaviour Research and Therapy, 35,* 667–691.

Okasha, A., Kamel, M., & Hassan, A. H. (1968). Preliminary psychiatric observations in Egypt. *British Journal of Psychiatry, 114,* 949–955.

Pacella, B. (1944). Clinical and electroencephalographic studies of obsessive-compulsive states. *American Journal of Psychiatry, 100,* 830–838.

Philippopoulos, G. S. (1961). A case of trichotillomania (hair pulling). *Acta Psychiatrica et Psychosomatica, 9,* 304–312.

Philippopoulos, G. S. (1979). The analysis of a case of dysmorphophobia. *Canadian Journal of Psychiatry, 24,* 397–401.

Phillips, K. A., McElroy, S. L., Keck, P. E., Pope, H. G., & Hudson, J. (1993). Body dysmorphic disorder: 30 cases of imagined ugliness. *American Journal of Psychiatry, 150,* 302.

Pollitt, J. (1957). Natural history of obsessional states: A study of 150 cases. *British Medical Journal, 1,* 194–198.

Primeau, F., & Fontaine, R. (1987). Obsessive disorder with self mutilation: A subgroup responsive to pharmacotherapy. *Canadian Journal of Psychiatry, 32,* 699–701.

Pujol, R., & Savy, L. (1968). *Le devenir de l'obsede* [Becoming obsessional]. Paris, France: Masson et Cie.

Rabavilas, A. D., Boulougouris, J. C., & Stefanis, D. (1976). Duration of flooding sessions in the treatment of obsessive-compulsive patients. *Behavior Research and Therapy, 14,* 349–355.

Reiger, D. A., Boyd, H. H., Burke, J. D., Rae, D. S., Meyer, J. K., Kramer, M., Robins, L. N., George, L. K., Karno, M., & Locke, B. Z. (1988). One month prevalence of mental disorders in the United States. *Archives of General Psychiatry, 45,* 977–978.

Riggs, D. S., & Foa, E. B. (1993). Obsessive compulsive disorder. In D. H. Barlow (Ed.), *Clinical handbook of psychological disorders* (2nd ed., pp. 57–65). New York: Guilford.

Ronchi, P., Abbruzzese, M., & Erzegovesi, S. (1992). The epidemiology of obsessive compulsive disorder in an Italian population. *European Psychiatry, 7,* 53–59.

Roper, G., Rachman, S., & Marks, I. M. (1975). Passive and participant modelling in exposure treatment of obsessive-compulsive neurotics. *Behavior Research and Therapy, 13,* 271–279.

Rosen, J. C., Reiter, J., & Orasan, P. (1995). Cognitive-behavioral body image therapy for body dysmorphic disorder. *Journal of Consulting and Clinical Psychology, 63,* 263–269.

Rosenberg, C. M. (1968). Complications of obsessional neurosis. *British Journal of Psychiatry, 114,* 477.

Rudin, E. (1953). Ein Beitrag zur Frage der Zwang Krankheit insbesondere ihrer hereditaren bezielungen [A contribution to the question of obsessive-compulsive disorder, especially with regard to its genetic aspects]. *Archives of Psychiatric Illness, 191,* 14–54.

Salkovskis, P. M. (1985). Obsessional-compulsive problems: A cognitive-behavioural analysis. *Behaviour Research and Therapy, 23,* 571–583.

Salkovskis, P. M., & Warwick, H. M. C. (1986). Morbid preoccupations, health anxiety and reassurance: A cognitive behavioral approach to hypochondriasis. *Behaviour Research and Therapy, 24,* 597–602.

Saper, B. (1971). A report on behavior therapy with outpatient clinic patients. *Psychiatric Quarterly, 45,* 209–215.

Stanley, M. A., Swann, A. C., & Bowers, T. C. (1992). A comparison of clinical features in trichotillomania and obsessive compulsive disorder. *Behaviour Research and Therapy, 30,* 39–44.

Steketee, G. S. (1994). *Treatment of obsessive compulsive disorder.* New York: Guilford.

Stevens, K. P. (1996). *Verbal I.Q. profiles in OCD.* Unpublished manuscript and data.

Taschev, T. (1970). Zur Klinik der Zwangszustande [On compulsive episodes]. *Journal of Neurology and Psychiatry, 38,* 89–110.

Taylor, J. G. (1963). A behavioural interpretation of obsessive compulsive neurosis. *Behaviour Research and Therapy, 1,* 237–244.

Turner, S. M., Jacob, R. G., & Morrison, R. (1984). Somatoform and factitious disorders. In H. E. Adams & P. B. Sutker (Eds.), *Comprehensive handbook of psychopathology* (pp. 150–172). New York: Plenum.

Tynes, L. L., White, K., & Steketee, G. S. (1990). Toward a nosology of obsessive compulsive disorder. *Comprehensive Psychiatry, 31,* 465–480.

Tynes, L. L., & Winstead, D. K. (1992). Behavioral aspects of trichotillomania. *Journal of the Louisiana State Medical Society, 144,* 459–463.

van Oppen, P., & Arntz, A. (1994). Cognitive therapy for obsessive compulsive disorder. *Behaviour Research and Therapy, 32,* 79–87.

van Oppen, P., de Haan, E., van Balkom, A., Spinhoven, P., Hoogduin, K., & van Dijk, R. (1995). Cognitive therapy and exposure in vivo in the treatment of obsessive compulsive disorder. *Behavior, Research and Therapy, 33,* 379–390.

Veale, D., Gournay, K., Dryden, W., Boocock, A., Shah, F., Willson, R., & Walburn, J. (1996). Body dysmorphic disorder: A cognitive behavioural model and pilot randomised controlled study. *Behaviour Research and Therapy, 9,* 717–729.

Warwick, H. M. C., & Marks, I. M. (1988). Behavioral treatment of illness phobia. *British Journal of Psychiatry, 152,* 239–241.

Warwick, H. M. C., & Salkovskis, P. M. (1985). Reassurance. *British Medical Journal, 290,* 1028.

Warwick, H. M. C., & Salkovskis, P. M. (1990). Hypochondriasis. *Behaviour Research and Therapy, 28,* 105–117.

Wernicke, C. (1906). *Grundrisse der Psychiatrie* [Foundations of psychiatry]. Leipzig, Germany: Verlag.

Westphal, C. (1878). Uber Zwangsvorstellungen [About hallucinations]. *Archiven fur Psychiatrischen and Nervenkrankheiten* [*Archives of Psychiatric and Neurasthenic Disorders*], *8,* 734–750.

Winchel, R. M., Jones, J. S., & Stanley, B. (1992). Clinical characteristics of trichotillomania and its response to fluoxetine. *Journal of Clincial Psychiatry, 53,* 304–308.

Woodruff, R., & Pitts, F. N. (1964). Monozygotic twins with obsessional illness. *American Journal of Psychiatry, 120,* 1075–1080.

Yaryura-Tobias, J. A. (1977). Obsessive compulsive disorders: A serotonergic hypothesis. *Journal of Orthomolecular Psychiatry, 6,* 317–326.

Yaryura-Tobias, J. A. (1990). A unified theory of obsessive compulsive disorder. In C. N. Stefanis, A. D. Rabavilas, & C. R. Soldatos (Eds.), *Psychiatry, A world perspective* (pp. 568–571). Amsterdam: Elsevier Science.

Yaryura-Tobias, J. A. (1995). *Thinking in the obsessive compulsive disorder.* Paper presented at the 11th Argentine Congress of Psychiatry, Bariloche, Argentina.

Yaryura-Tobias, J. A., & Anderson, M. C. (1995, November). *Clinical features of hypochondriasis.* Paper presented at the 29th Annual Convention of the Association for the Advancement of Behavior Therapy, Washington, DC.

Yaryura-Tobias, J. A., Campisi, T. A., McKay, D., & Neziroglu, F. A. (1995). Schizophrenia and obsessive compulsive disorder: Shared aspects of pathology. *Neurology, Psychiatry and Brain Research, 3,* 143–148.

Yaryura-Tobias, J. A., & Neziroglu, F. A. (1978). Compulsions, aggression, and self mutilation: A hypothalamic disorder? *Journal of Orthomolecular Psychiatry, 7,* 114–117.

Yaryura-Tobias, J. A., & Neziroglu, F. A. (1983). *Obsessive compulsive disorders: Pathogenesis, diagnosis and treatment.* New York: Marcel Dekker.

Yaryura-Tobias, J. A., & Neziroglu, F. A. (1997a). *Bio-behavioral treatment and management of obsessive compulsive spectrum disorders.* Boston: Norton.

Yaryura-Tobias, J. A., & Neziroglu, F. A. (1997b). *The obsessive compulsive disorder spectrum.* Washington, DC: American Psychiatric Press.

Yaryura-Tobias, J. A., Neziroglu, F. A., & Kaplan, S. (1995). Self mutilation, anorexia, and dysmenorrhea in obsessive compulsive disorder. *International Journal of Eating Disorders, 17*(1), 33–38.

Yaryura-Tobias, J. A., Stevens, K. P., Neziroglu, F. A., & Grunes, M. (1997). Obsessive compulsive disorder and schizophrenia: A phenomenological perspective of shared pathology. *CNS Spectrums, 2,* 21–25.

Yaryura-Tobias, J. A., Todaro, J., Grunes, M., McKay, D., Neziroglu, F. A., & Stockman, R. (1997). *The sequential time of OCD spectrum disorders.* Manuscript submitted for publication.

14

Predicting Treatment Outcome for Obsessive-Compulsive Disorder: Effects of Comorbidity

Gail Steketee
Boston University

Nathan J. Henninger
C. Alec Pollard
Saint Louis University School of Medicine

This chapter summarizes findings regarding comorbidity and its relation to treatment outcome in patients with obsessive-compulsive disorder (OCD). OCD frequently co-occurs with other anxiety disorders, depression, and personality disorders and traits. Obsessive-compulsive (OC) symptomology has also been commonly reported in patients with eating disorders and Tourette's syndrome, but the prevalence of these conditions in patients with primary OCD has not been clearly established. Research on comorbidity and treatment outcome has had mixed and somewhat confusing results in relation to depressed and anxious mood and various personality traits, including schizotypal, borderline, dependent and passive-aggressive. Surprisingly, little of this research has focused on the effects of actual clinical comorbid diagnoses on outcome.

A recent study sponsored by the National Institute of Mental Health conducted by the first author examined comorbidity as a predictor of outcome for patients with OCD in a 16-week behavioral treatment program. Findings indicate that the concurrent presence of major depression predicted poor outcome for OCD symptoms at posttest, and that personality traits were also problematic for immediate but not longer term outcome. Generalized anxiety disorder (GAD) was related to more dropout and was also associated with poor outcome at follow-up. No other Axis I or II diagnoses or Axis II personality traits predicted outcome. Limitations of this research and future directions for study and intervention for comorbid OCD are suggested.

Behavioral treatments that include exposure and blocking of rituals have demonstrated considerable efficacy in ameliorating the symptoms of OCD, substantially reducing symptoms in approximately 75% of patients who elected it. However, it is apparent that not all patients benefit from this treatment approach. In fact, even for intensive programs that include 15 to 30 sessions, approximately one quarter to one third of patients have failed to benefit or to sustain their therapeutic gains (for review of these studies see Steketee & Lam, 1993). To develop more effective therapies, it is essential to examine carefully which patients benefit and which ones fail, with particular attention to factors likely to be amenable to additional or alternative treatments. Efforts to examine predictors associated with success and failure after treatment and at follow-up have burgeoned recently, probably precisely because of the availability of relatively effective treatments studied across multiple clinical settings. As previously pointed out (Steketee & Chambless, 1992), there are significant methodological problems with this literature, but it is nonetheless instructive.

Despite the substantial advances in exposure treatment efficacy and the availability of detailed manuals, clinicians complain that treatments do not address the complicated chronic and comorbid conditions that they often observe in their patients. Many variables have been studied in relation to behavioral treatment outcome, including demographics, symptom chronicity and severity, comorbidity, expectancy, motivation, insight, habituation, and family functioning, but relatively few of these have proven predictive. One exception, however, is comorbidity in its various forms, particularly affective and personality disorder comorbidity.

This chapter briefly summarizes the OCD comorbidity literature with particular emphasis on those Axis I and Axis II disorders that have been found to be commonly comorbid with OCD. Findings on the effects of these various disorders and related traits on the immediate and long-term outcome of behavioral treatments for OCD are then reviewed. We also present new findings regarding the effects of such comorbidity on a sample of OCD patients treated with a 16-week trial of exposure and response prevention and followed up 6 months later. In addition to the research findings, therapists' observations regarding characteristics of treatment failures are included to provide some clinical examples. We conclude with suggestions for further research needed to provide useful clinical directives.

COMORBIDITY OF OCD

Other Anxiety Disorders

OCD frequently co-occurs with other anxiety disorders. Epidemiologic data from North American samples suggest approximately half of those who suffer from OCD have had at least one additional anxiety disorder sometime during their lifetime (Weissman et al., 1994). Comorbidity rates in other parts of the world are more variable, ranging from 24.5% to 69.6% (Weissman et al., 1994). When specific anxiety disorders are examined separately, results vary, but are generally higher than would be expected. Percentages of OCD samples with another anxiety disorder have ranged from 19% to 46.5% for simple or specific phobia, 13.8% to 42% for social phobia, and 12% to 54% for panic disorder (Austin, Lydiard, Fossey, & Sealberg, 1990; Crino & Andrews, 1996; Karno, Golding, Sorenson, & Burnam, 1988; Rasmussen & Eisen, 1991).

Depression

Depression is another condition that frequently co-occurs with OCD. Comorbidity rates have varied considerably, depending on the nature of the sample and the criteria and methods used to measure depression. Nonetheless, lifetime prevalence of depression among OCD samples is comparatively high. Prevalence rates have ranged from 12% to 80%, but most studies suggest at least one third of individuals with OCD have a history of clinically significant depression (Crino & Andrews, 1996; Insel, 1982; Karno et al., 1988; Koloda, Bland, & Newman, 1994; Rasmussen & Eisen, 1991; Rasmussen & Tsuang, 1986; Weissman et al., 1994).

Personality Disorders

Most studies suggest that approximately half of individuals with OCD have at least one comorbid personality disorder, with reported percentages ranging from 33% to 91.7% (Baer & Jenike, 1992; Baer, Jenike, Ricciardi, & Holland, 1990; Black, Noyes, Pfohl, & Goldstein, 1993; Black, Yates, Noyes, & Pfohl, 1989; Cassano, del-Buono, & Catapano, 1993; Joffee, Swinson, & Regan, 1988; Maina, Bellino, Bogetto, & Ravizza, 1993; Mavissakalian, Hamann, & Jones, 1990a; McKay, Neziroglu, Todaro, & Yaryura-Tobias, 1996; Okasa, Saad, Khalil, Dawla, & Seif, 1994; Sciuto et al., 1991; Steketee, 1990; Thomsen & Mikkelsen, 1993). Findings regarding specific personality disorders are inconsistent, probably due in large part to the variety of measures used in different studies. It should also be noted that most of this research has involved rather modest sample sizes. Currently, the literature suggests a variety of personality disorders can co-occur with OCD, but consistently high comorbidity has yet to be found for any single disorder. Among Axis II disorders, dependent personality disorder has been most frequently reported across studies as highly comorbid with OCD.

Eating Disorders

There does appear to be some evidence of an association between OCD and eating disorders (Rubenstein, Altemus, & Pigott, 1995). OC symptomology is common in samples with eating disorders (Kaye, Weltzin, & Hsu, 1993). However, eating disorders may not be equally prevalent among OCD patients. The few existing studies suggest that between 8% and 11.4% of OCD patients also suffer from either anorexia or bulimia (Fahy, Osacar, & Marks, 1993; Rasmussen & Eisen, 1991).

Tourette's Syndrome

In clinical studies, OC symptoms have been reported in 30% to 90% of patients suffering from Tourette's syndrome (Frankel, 1986; Leckman, 1993; Steingard & Dillon-Stout, 1992). Considerably less evidence exists, however, regarding the incidence of tic disorders among OCD patients. In one study (Rasmussen & Eisen, 1992), only 6% to 7% of a clinical sample of OCD patients had a history of Tourette's syndrome.

Other Disorders

Epidemiologic research (e.g., Karno et al., 1988) suggests that other disorders may afflict a substantial portion of OCD sufferers in the general population. For example, alcohol abuse and schizophrenia were found in 24% and 12%, respectively, of the OCD sample. However, there are few comorbidity data available regarding these disorders in clinic patients. Similarly, little is known about the co-occurrence of OCD and what have been referred to as the OCD spectrum disorders, such as hypochondriasis, body dysmorphic disorder, and impulse control disorders (Hollander, 1992). Further research is needed regarding the prevalence of these disorders in OCD patients and the clinical implications of the various combinations of comorbidity.

RESEARCH ON COMORBIDITY AND TREATMENT OUTCOME

Depression

Among comorbid conditions, depressive diagnoses have not been studied as predictors for behavioral treatment. In the several medication trials that have used depression diagnoses as predictors, most outcomes have been unaffected (e.g., Goodman, Price, Rassmussen, & Delgado, 1989; Pigott, Pato, L'Heureux, & Hill, 1991), although Mavissakalian and Michelson (1983) found unexpected positive effects. Depressed mood has received considerable attention as a predictor for both exposure and drug trials. However, researchers have disagreed sharply over whether depression predicts outcome for OCD.

With respect to behavioral therapies, Rabavilas and Boulougouris (1979) examined the predictive capacity of patients' histories of mood fluctuations prior to treatment. Those with mood fluctuations responded well after behavior therapy, but relapsed more often than those without a history of such changes. It is not clear whether mood fluctuations in this study were connected with manic phases or might have been reactions to disturbing life events. Although the findings are intriguing, the absence of rigorous methodology reduces their utility for predicting patient outcomes. Fals-Stewart and Schafer (1993) observed that compliance with behavior therapy (defined somewhat narrowly by the number of sessions missed) was associated with higher depression scores on the Minnesota Multiphasic Personality Inventory, suggesting that the effect of some comorbidity might occur via negative effects on treatment compliance.

As shown in Table 14.1, several researchers have found that higher initial depressed mood assessed via various measures was related to less improvement after behavioral therapy (Cottraux, Messy, Marks, Mollard, & Bouvard, 1993; Emmelkamp, Hoekstra, & Visser, 1985; Foa, 1979; Foa et al., 1983; Keijsers, Hoogduin, & Schaap, 1994; Marks, Stern, Mawson, Cobb, & McDonald, 1980). This was also evident at follow-up according to one study (Foa et al., 1983). Among patients who received combined behavioral and pharmacological intervention, those who scored higher on depression took more medications at follow-up (Jenike, 1990; O'Sullivan, Noshirvani, Marks, Monteiro, & Lelliott, 1991). Further, worse outcome was also observed in unmedicated depressed OCD patients compared to those who received clomipramine (Marks et al., 1980).

In contrast to these findings, however, in several other studies of comparable quality, depression failed to predict outcome after behavior therapy (Basoglu, Lax, Kasvikis, & Marks, 1988; Castle et al., 1994; Hoogduin & Duivenvoorden, 1988; Riggs, Hiss, & Foa, 1992) or at follow-up (Emmelkamp et al., 1985; Orloff et al., 1994; O'Sullivan et al., 1991; Steketee, 1988). Studies of medication (mainly serotonergic) effects have also mainly showed no effect of depressed mood on outcome (e.g., Goodman et al., 1989; Pigott et al., 1991; Tollefson, Rampey, Potvin, & Jenike, 1994). One study by Ackerman, Greenland, Bystritsky, and Morgenstern (1994) indicated that the relation was nonlinear with moderate scores associated with worse outcome. However, too few participants scored in the clinically depressed range to confidently state that high scores were not predictive. Indeed, several medicated trials excluded individuals who were significantly depressed, making interpretation of nonsignificant findings questionable.

TABLE 14.1
Studies on Outcome of Treatment for OCD With Comorbid Depression

Study	N	Diagnostic Method	Treatment Groups	Posttest
Foa (1979)	10	Independent assessor	ERP	Negative
Marks et al. (1980)	40	WSADI, HAM-D	Clomipramine	Positive
			Relaxation	
			ERP	
Foa et al. (1983)	54	Independent assessor	ERP	Negative
Mavissakalian & Michelson (1983)	8	DSM-III, HAM-D	Imipramine	Positive
			Clomipramine	Positive
Emmelkamp et al. (1985)	42	ZSRDS	ERP	Negative
Foa et al. (1987)	37	DSM-III, BDI	Imipramine	No effect
Basoglu et al. (1988)	49	HAM-D, BDI	ERP	No effect
		(Dysphoria factor)	Clomipramine	
Hoogduin & Duivenvoorden (1988)	60	ZSRDS	ERP	No effect
Steketee (1988)	43	BDI	ERP	No effect
Goodman et al. (1989a)	42	DSM-III, HAM-D	Fluvoxamine	No effect
Fogelson & Bystritsky (1991)	19	DSM-III-R	Imipramine	Negative
O'Sullivan et al. (1991)	34	WSADI, HAM-D	ERP + Clomipramine	No effect
Pigott et al. (1991)	16	DSM-III-R, HAM-D	Clomipramine + an adjuvant	No effect

Study	N	Measure	Treatment	Effect
Foa et al. (1992)	38	BDI, *HAM-D*	ERP + Imipramine	No effect
Riggs et al. (1992)	54	BDI	ERP	No effect
Cottraux et al. (1993)	37	HAM-D	Fluvoxamine	No effect
			ERP	No effect
			Fluroxamine + ERP	Negative trend
Demal et al. (1993)	62	HAM-D, ZSRDS	Varied	Negative
Ackerman et al. (1994)	520	HAM-D	Clomipramine	Nonlinear, generally negative
Buchanan et al. (1996)	127	BDI	ERP	Negative
Castle et al. (1994)	178	FQ-D	ERP	No effect
Keijsers et al. (1994)	40	HAM-D	ERP	Negative
Orloff et al. (1994)	85	BDI	SRIs (+ ERP for 29%)	No effect
Tollefson et al. (1994)	281	HAM-D	Fluoxetine	No effect
Steketee et al. (1999)	106*	SCID	ERP	MDD had negative effect

Note. WSADI = Wakefield Self-Assessment Depression Inventory; HAM-D = Hamilton Rating Scale for Depression; DSM (III or III–R) = the Diagnostic and Statistical Manual criteria with nonstructured or semistructured clinician interview; ZSRDS = Zung Self-Rating Depression Scale; BDI = Beck Depression Inventory; FQ–D = Fear Questionnaire Depression; MDD = major depression disorder; SCID = Structured Clinical Interview for DSM–IV; ERP = exposure and response prevention; SRIs = serotonin reuptake inhibitors.

*n = 63 OCD and 43 agoraphobic patients. Regression analyses tested for diagnostic group (OCD/agoraphobia) effects.

Methodologies in these studies varied widely, but large samples and multivariate statistics were employed in research on both sides of the issue. Foa and her colleagues provided perhaps the most definitive study of the effects of depressed mood, and the only one with a prospective design (Foa, Kozak, Steketee, & McCarthy, 1992). Patients who scored high or low on depressed mood were given either antidepressant medication (imipramine) or placebo prior to an intensive behavioral treatment. Neither the level of depression nor the antidepressant effect of the medication influenced outcome at posttest or at follow-up.

Unfortunately, this body of research leaves clinicians in the dark about the effects of depression on treatment outcome for patients with OCD. Depressed mood is a common accompaniment to OCD, especially to severe OCD, as it is for other serious anxiety disorders such as agoraphobia and posttraumatic stress disorder. It may merely be a side effect of the debilitation and restrictions that typically accompany severe anxiety symptoms. If so, depressed mood would be likely to improve with effective treatment of obsessions and compulsions, without specific treatment for mood. Such outcomes have in fact been observed (e.g., Foa et al., 1983; Marks et al., 1980), and several researchers have found that reduction in OCD symptoms correlated significantly with reduction in depressed mood (Basoglu et al., 1988; Marks et al., 1988; Steketee, 1993). Interestingly, a high level of depression after exposure treatment was strongly related to relapse at follow-up (Steketee, 1993), but it was not clear whether this could be accounted for by persistent OCD symptoms.

The conflicting findings about depression as a predictor of outcome could be due to differences in measurement of depression and outcome or to procedural differences in treatment application. Alternatively, depression may only be predictive at high levels because it leads to over-reactivity and inadequate habituation of obsessive anxiety (Foa et al., 1983). One might predict, for example, that the concurrent presence of a major depressive disorder would interfere with outcome, especially for behavioral treatments, whereas dysthymia would not. Few studies have examined the effects of concurrent diagnoses of affective disorders on treatment outcome for OCD. One study found no prediction of follow-up evaluation, but most of the patients in the study had not received formal behavioral treatment (Orloff et al., 1994). A recent trial conducted by Steketee, Chambless, and Tran (1999) examined the effects of dysthymia and major depression on outcome for 63 OCD and 43 agoraphobic patients who received 22 sessions of behavioral treatment. Regression analyses included diagnosis to examine whether OCD or agoraphobic patients differed in the association of comorbid conditions to outcome. Potential confounding variables including sex, socioeconomic status, global functioning, initial severity, and duration of symptoms were examined in relation to outcome. Dysthymia showed no association with the immediate or 6-month effects of exposure treatment, but major depression (MDD) was a significant predictor of poor immediate and follow-up outcome, especially for target fears. When MDD was included with other Axis I and II comorbidity in combined regression analyses, it adversely influenced social functioning but not target fears at posttest and predicted poor outcome on both measures at follow-up. These findings suggest that the presence of major depression at intake may require special measures to ensure a good outcome for the patient.

Anxiety

Studies of anxiety as a predictor of outcome have confined attention to anxious mood rather than diagnoses of comorbid anxiety disorders. This literature contains both positive and negative findings. Most studies have observed no association of pretreatment anxious mood with behavioral outcome immediately after therapy (Boulougouris, 1977; Castle et al., 1994; Emmelkamp et al., 1985; Hoogduin & Duivenvoorden, 1988; Rabavilas & Boulougouris, 1979) or at follow-up (Emmelkamp et al., 1985; O'Sullivan et al., 1991; Steketee, 1988, 1993). However, a path analysis by Foa et al. (1983) indicated that pretreatment anxiety was related to immediate outcome, but was only indirectly related to long-term gains through its association with posttest outcome. Overall, then, general anxious mood does not appear to have a strong influence on immediate or follow-up outcome of exposure treatments. Likewise, pretreatment anxious mood appeared to exercise little influence on gains for medication treatment (e.g., Mavissakalian & Michelson, 1983), although very few studies have reported on this question. One could argue that, for individuals with anxiety disorders, measures of anxious mood merely reflect symptom severity. Indeed, an analysis of severity of symptoms as a predictor of outcome for OCD leads to virtually identical conclusions (Steketee & Shapiro, 1995).

Studies of the effect of comorbid anxiety disorders on outcome of medication trials are rare. Orloff et al. (1994) observed no effect of the presence of comorbid anxiety on outcome of serotonergic drugs. Fewer than half of their sample had received behavior therapy. Steketee et al. (1999) tested the effects of concurrent anxiety disorders, including social phobia and generalized anxiety disorder (GAD) on OCD and agoraphobic patients. Neither disorder influenced immediate outcome, but GAD predicted dropout and worse target symptoms at 6-month follow-up. Interestingly, both MDD and GAD contributed independently to the adverse outcome, indicating that OCD patients with GAD may also require additional intervention to ensure that they continue in treatment and maintain their gains.

Two studies have examined the effects of posttreatment anxious mood on follow-up outcome. Both Emmelkamp et al. (1985) and Steketee (1988) reported that patients with OCD whose anxiety remained elevated at the end of behavioral treatment tended to relapse over time. In the Emmelkamp et al. (1985) study, however, the measure of anxiety appeared to be identical to the measure of outcome and thus a strong association would be expected statistically. Even when measured differently, the concern about the overlap of anxious mood and severity of OCD symptoms remains, and thus the failure at follow-up of patients who do not succeed at posttest seems neither surprising nor particularly interesting. In the only study of the effects of comorbid anxiety disorder diagnoses on outcome, Orloff et al. (1994) found no prediction at follow-up evaluation at least 1 year later, but only 29% of their patients had received behavioral treatment.

Personality Disorders and Traits

In one early study of behavioral treatment effects, patients with premorbid obsessional personality traits (previously often mistaken for OCD) tended to respond more favorably immediately after exposure treatment compared to those without obsessional features (Rabavilas, Boulougouris, Perissaki, & Stefanis, 1979). Surprisingly, these investigators also found that dependent personality traits were associated with better immediate gains. Perhaps both personality traits had positive effects because of better compliance with the therapist's instructions during treatment, although this might not extend to better long-term outcome. In contrast, passive-aggressive traits (which might interfere with compliance) were associated with adverse behavior therapy outcomes (Steketee, 1990). Castle et al.'s (1994) analysis of a large sample of behaviorally treated patients indicated no influence of meticulous or anxious personality traits.

Findings from studies using standardized diagnostic assessment of personality disorder are depicted in Table 14.2. Although Steketee (1990) and Orloff et al. (1994) did not find that the presence of any personality disorder predicted outcome for exposure or serotonin reuptake inhibitor treatment, AuBuchon and Malatesta (1994) found the converse. They also observed that OCD patients with comorbid personality disorder more often dropped out and were more difficult to treat, implying that personality disorders introduced more complexity into the treatment process. Particular types of personality disorders, including avoidant, borderline, and paranoid (Cottraux et al., 1993; Jenike, 1990), have also predicted negative outcomes. Hermesh, Shahar, and Munitz (1987) observed that all eight of their patients with OCD and borderline personality disorder failed with behavioral treatment and with medications (clomipramine)

TABLE 14.2
Studies on Outcome of Treatment of
OCD With Comorbid Personality Disorder

Study	N	Diagnostic Method	Treatment Groups	Associated Outcome (Disorder/Variable)
Jenike et al. (1986)	43	DSM–III	ERP +/or Medication	Negative (Schizotypal)
Hermesh et al. (1987)	39	DSM–III	ERP +/or Clomipramine	Negative (Borderline)
Mavissakalian et al. (1990b)	27	DSM–III, PDQ	Clomipramine	No effect (All disorders)
Baer et al. (1992)	55	SIPD	Clomipramine	Negative (total number of disorders; Borderline; Schizotypal; Avoidant)
Orloff et al. (1994)	85	SCID	SRIs	No effect (all disorders)[a]
AuBuchon & Malatesta (1994)	31	DSM–III–R	ERP	Negative (one or more disorders)
Steketee et al. (1999)	106*	SCID	ERP	Negative at posttest (Anxious, dramatic) No effect at follow-up

Note. DSM (III or III–R) = the *Diagnostic and Statistical Manual* criteria with nonstructured or semistructured clinician interview; PDQ = Personality Diagnostic Questionnaire; SIDP = Structured Interview for *DSM–III* Personality Disorders; SCID = Structured Clinical Interview for *DSM*; ERP = exposure and response prevention; SRIs = serotonin reuptake inhibitors.
[a]One schizotypal patient worsened.
*n = 63 OCD and 43 agoraphobic patients. Regression analyses tested for diagnostic group (OCD/agoraphobia) effects.

because of poor compliance and possibly dropout. Rasmussen and Tsuang (1987) speculated that these patients, as well as those with histrionic personality, responded poorly to behavioral and drug treatment, but they provided no data supporting this statement. Because these personality traits are relatively rare among patients with OCD, their effects have been difficult to determine.

Jenike and colleagues have provided evidence linking schizotypal personality disorder to poor outcome for both behavioral and pharmacological treatment. Using retrospective chart reviews, they found that 90% of their nonschizotypal patients with OCD improved at least moderately, in contrast to only 7% of those with schizotypal personality (Jenike et al., 1986; Minichiello, Baer, & Jenike, 1987). The number of schizotypal traits was also correlated strongly with negative outcome ($r = -.74$). This research is flawed by retrospective diagnoses, but findings are nonetheless interesting. These investigators suggested that these traits interfered with compliance and probably signaled the presence of overvalued ideas about obsessive fears. These features in OCD patients who are male, have an onset age in their early teens, and show perceptual aberration, magical ideation, and social maladjustment argue for a connection to psychotic disorders, as several investigators have noted (Eisen & Rasmussen, 1993; Stanley, Turner, & Borden, 1990). The addition of support, limit setting, family therapy, structured living settings, cognitive therapy, and neuroleptics to behavioral treatment have been proposed (Jenike, 1990; Stanley & Turner, 1995).

In a study of personality criteria from the anxious, dramatic and odd clusters, Steketee et al. (1999) observed that OCD and agoraphobic patients with more anxious, dramatic and odd traits fared worse after behavioral treatment. However, when these criteria were combined with MDD in a single regression analysis, only anxious and dramatic clusters predicted worse immediate outcomes on social functioning. At 6-months follow-up, however, none of these Axis II predictors was significant alone or in combination with other comorbid conditions.

Comment

Findings from the previously described research on general comorbid anxiety and depressive mood state in OCD do not point to a need to intervene directly to reduce negative mood. This is particularly true for anxious mood, which may be confounded with obsessive anxiety itself. The picture for depressive symptoms is less clear, although the prospective study by Foa et al. (1983) argues against such a need. In this research there is little information about the predictive effect of comorbid diagnoses of depressive disorders (e.g., dysthymia, major depression, bipolar states) and anxiety disorders (e.g., social phobia, panic disorder, GAD), despite the frequent comorbidity of some of these disorders with OCD (see Karno et al., 1988; Rasmussen & Eisen, 1989). In one study of diagnostic comorbidity, Steketee et al.'s recent report does not point to a role of dysthymia in determining outcome, but major depression predicted gains at posttest. The hypothesis that only severe depression, evident in MDD, heralds fewer gains was supported, but the findings are not pronounced and join the ranks of those showing some adverse effects of depression. This is mixed news for patients whose OCD symptoms are accompanied by significant depression. Most patients, even those with major depression, benefitted from standard exposure treatment, but some modification to address serious depression may be in order. Note, however, that study findings do not shed light on the effect of bipolar disorders or of major depression that predates OCD onset. More information is needed on the predictive capacity of these conditions.

Among anxiety conditions, GAD was a consistent predictor, associated with more dropout and poor outcome at 6-month follow-up, especially on target ratings. Although some investigators have likened obsessions to the pervasive worries that mark GAD (e.g, Tallis & de Silva, 1992), these disorders differ significantly in the content and form of mental symptoms (Turner, Beidel, & Stanley, 1992), and do not commonly co-occur (Brown, Moras, Zinbarg, & Barlow, 1993). The number of OCD patients with GAD (n = 5) was quite small in the Steketee et al. (1999) study and findings should therefore be interpreted cautiously. If similar negative outcomes are found in other studies, it is of interest to determine the process by which this occurs. For example, such pervasive anxiety might reduce compliance with exposure instructions or homework assignments, interfering with willingness to tolerate anxiety-provoking treatments, capacity to habituate during these therapies, shifts in attitude toward danger, and ability to maintain gains once the therapist is no longer available. Information about such processes might assist in recommendations for alternative and adjunctive interventions. Obviously, more study of the effect of comorbid Axis I conditions is needed, particularly as clinicians clamor for information about how to treat the refractory, difficult patients who commonly present with multiple disorders.

The literature on personality features includes the study of the effects of both traits and disorders on behavioral treatment outcome. Given the difficulty of establishing personality diagnoses reliably, it is not clearly advantageous to study diagnoses over traits. Drawing conclusions from the available research on the effects of personality on outcome of OCD treatment is difficult. Many of the disorders and traits occur relatively infrequently in this heterogeneous population (e.g., schizotypal., borderline, histrionic, passive-aggressive), making study of individual Axis II disorders difficult without very large samples of OCD patients. It is somewhat surprising that the more common anxious cluster personality traits and disorders are not more studied in this regard.

Among personality features, anxious personality traits are most common across studies, present in a quarter or more of OCD patients. Although anxious personality traits did predict immediate outcome for patients in Steketee et al.'s (1999) trial, they did not do so at follow-up. Likewise, dramatic personality traits were associated with adverse outcomes at posttest but not at follow-up. Odd features had minimal or no effects. Thus, neither cluster nor overall personality traits were strongly associated with outcome across available studies. The personality disorders that have been found predictive in other studies, such as borderline personality disorder (Hermesh et al., 1987) and schizotypal (Minichiello et al., 1987) are often too rare in small sample studies to permit analysis. It seems evident that only with very large samples will we be able to detect the effects of particular personality disorders.

SUMMARY AND FUTURE DIRECTIONS

A number of Axis I and II disorders have been found to be comorbid with OCD. Anxiety and depressive disorders are particularly common among individuals with OCD. Personality disorders are also common, but the strength of the association between OCD and any specific Axis II disorder has varied substantially across studies. Further research is needed to clarify the association between OCD and several other disorders, including substance abuse, eating disorders, Tourette's syndrome, schizophrenia, and the OCD spectrum disorders. Despite evidence that OCD is often accompanied by additional psychopathology, surprisingly little is known about the implications of comorbidity on treatment.

Several variables that have predicted outcome for other disorders have not been adequately examined for OCD. Although Axis I and II comorbidity is common, its influence on outcome has rarely been studied. Some research has addressed anxious and depressed mood states, but little attention has been paid to commonly occurring depressive and anxiety disorders, or to less frequent but potentially problematic concurrent substance abuse and personality disorders. Such concurrent problems seem likely to at least complicate the treatment process, if not derail it, necessitating specialized concurrent or sequential interventions. However, the problematic influence of comorbidity has not yet been clearly demonstrated. More research on larger samples with adequate diagnostic procedures and outcome measures is needed. Almost none of the existing research, including our own, is prospective in nature, deliberately comparing samples selected for comorbidity or applying treatments to address comorbid conditions. This is likely to require greater flexibility in treatment delivery to include therapies that will yield maximum benefits.

For example, Jenike et al. (1986), among others, described the particular difficulties faced by socially inadequate single men with severe OCD, sometimes concurrent with OC or schizotypal personality disorder or features. Even if they respond to behavioral or pharmacological treatment, these men (often young) often do so only partially, and remain socially isolated with limited prospects for effective occupational, social, and home functioning. Indeed, social isolation was the only predictor of negative outcome in men in one study (Castle et al., 1994). Testing of specific treatments designed for this and other identified subgroups of OCD patients who do not respond adequately to existing treatments is clearly needed (e.g., see Walker, Freeman, & Christensen, 1994). Such research, however, is not likely to lend itself to group designs and multivariate analyses, but will instead require multiple single-subject designs or the participation of multiple sites. A coordinated research agenda from private and federal sources will be needed.

REFERENCES

Ackerman, D. L., Greenland, S., Bystritsky, A., & Morgenstern, H. (1994). Predictors of treatment response in obsessive-compulsive disorder: Multivariate analyses from a multicenter trial of clomipramine. *Journal of Clinical Psychopharmacology, 14,* 247–254.

AuBuchon, P. G., & Malatesta, V. J. (1994). Obsessive compulsive patients with comorbid personality disorder: Associated problems and response to a comprehensive behavior therapy. *Journal of Clinical Psychiatry, 55,* 448–453.

Austin, L. S., Lydiard, R. B., Fossey, M. D., & Sealberg, J. J. (1990). Panic and phobic disorders in patients with obsessive compulsive disorder. *Journal of Clinical Psychiatry, 51,* 456–458.

Baer, L., & Jenike, M. A. (1992). Personality disorders in obsessive compulsive disorder. *Psychiatric Clinics of North America, 15,* 803–812.

Baer, L., Jenike, M. A., Black, D. W., & Treece, C. (1992). Effects of Axis II diagnosis on treatment outcome with clomipromine in 55 patients with obsessive-compulsive disorder. *Archives of General Psychiatry, 49,* 862–866.

Baer, L., Jenike, M. A., Ricciardi, J. N., & Holland, A. D. (1990). Standardized assessment of personality disorders in obsessive-compulsive disorder. *Archives of General Psychiatry, 47,* 826–830.

Basoglu, M., Lax, T., Kasvikis, Y., & Marks, I. M. (1988). Predictors of improvement in obsessive-compulsive disorder. *Journal of Anxiety Disorders, 2,* 299–317.

Black, D. W., Noyes, R., Pfohl, B., & Goldstein, R. B. (1993). Personality disorder in obsessive-compulsive volunteers, well comparison subjects, and their first degree relatives. *American Journal of Psychiatry, 150,* 1226–1232.

Black, D. W., Yates, W. R., Noyes, R., & Pfohl, B. (1989). DSM–III personality disorder in obsessive-compulsive study volunteers: A controlled study. *Journal of Personality Disorders, 3,* 58–62.

Boulougouris, J. (1977). Variables affecting the behavior modification of obsessive-compulsive patients treated by flooding. In J. C. Boulougouris & A. D. Rabavilas (Eds.), *Phobia and obsessive compulsive disorders* (pp. 73–84). New York: Pergamon.

Brown, T. A., Moras, K., Zinbarg, R. E., & Barlow, D. H. (1993). Diagnostic and symptom distinguishability of generalized anxiety disorder and obsessive-compulsive disorder. *Behavior Therapy, 24,* 227–240.

Buchanan, A. W., Meng, K. S., & Marks, I. M. (1996). What predicts improvement and compliance during the behavioral treatment of obsessive compulsive disorder? *Anxiety, 2,* 22–27.

Cassano, D., del-Buono, G., & Catapano, F. (1993). The relationship between obsessive-compulsive personality and obsessive-compulsive disorder: Data obtained by the Personality Disorder Examination. *European Psychiatry, 8,* 219–221.

Castle, D. J., Deale, A., Marks, I. M., Cutts, F., Chadhoury, Y., & Stewart, A. (1994). Obsessive-compulsive disorder: Prediction of outcome from behavioural psychotherapy. *Acta Psychiatrica Scandanavica, 89,* 393–398.

Cottraux, J., Messy, P., Marks, I. M., Mollard, E., & Bouvard, M. (1993). Predictive factors in the treatment of obsessive-compulsive disorders with fluvoxamine and or behavior therapy. *Behavioral Psychology, 21,* 45–50.

Crino, R. D., & Andrews, G. (1996). Obsessive-compulsive disorder and Axis I comorbidity. *Journal of Anxiety Disorders, 10,* 37–46.

Demal, U., Lenz, G., Mayrhofer, A., & Zapotoczky, H. G. (1993). Obsessive-compulsive disorder and depression: A retrospective study on course and interaction. *Psychopathology, 26,* 145–150.

Eisen, J. L., & Rasmussen, S. A. (1993). Obsessive compulsive disorder with psychotic features. *Journal of Clinical Psychiatry, 54,* 373–379.

Emmelkamp, P. M. G., Hoekstra, R. J., & Visser, A. (1985). The behavioral treatment of obsessive-compulsive disorder: Prediction of outcome at 3.5 years follow-up. In P. Pichot, P. Berner, R. Wolf, & K. Thau (Eds.), *Psychiatry: The state of the art* (pp. 265–270). New York: Plenum.

Fahy, T. A., Osacar, A., & Marks, I. (1993). History of eating disorders in female patients with obsessive-compulsive disorder. *International Journal of Eating Disorders, 14,* 439–443.

Fals-Stewart, W., & Schafer, J. (1993). MMPI correlates of psychotherapy compliance among obsessive-compulsives. *Psychopathology, 26,* 1–5.

Foa, E. B. (1979). Failure in treating obsessive-compulsive disorder. *Behaviour Research and Therapy, 17,* 169–176.

Foa, E. B., Grayson, J. B., Steketee, G. S., Doppelt, H. G., Turner, R. M., & Latimer, P. R. (1983). Success and failure in the behavioral treatment of obsessive-compulsives. *Journal of Consulting and Clinical Psychology, 51,* 287–297.

Foa, E. B., Kozak, M. J., Steketee, G. S., & McCarthy, P. R. (1992). Treatment of depressive and obsessive-compulsive symptoms in OCD by imipramine and behaviour therapy. *British Journal of Clinical Psychology, 31,* 279–292.

Foa, E. B., Steketee, G., Kozak, M., & Dugger, D. (1987). Effects of imipramine on depression and obsessive-compulsive symptoms. *Psychiatry Research, 21,* 123–136.

Fogelson, D. L., & Bystritsky, A. (1991). Imipramine in the treatment of obsessive-compulsive disorder with and without major depression. *Annals of Clinical Psychiatry, 3,* 233–237.

Frankel, M. (1986). Obsessions and compulsions in Gilles de la Tourette's syndrome. *Neurology, 36,* 378–382.

Goodman, W. K., Price, L. H., Rassmussen, S. A., & Delgado, P. L. (1989). Efficacy of fluvoxamine in obsessive-compulsive disorder: A double-blind comparison with placebo. *Archives of General Psychiatry, 46,* 36–44.

Hermesh, H., Shahar, A., & Munitz, H. (1987). Obsessive-compulsive disorder and borderline personality disorder. *American Journal of Psychiatry, 144,* 120–121.

Hollander, E. (1992). *Obsessive-compulsive related disorders.* Washington, DC: American Psychiatric Press.

Hoogduin, C. A. L., & Duivenvoorden, H. J. (1988). A decision model in the treatment of obsessive-compulsive neurosis. *British Journal of Psychiatry, 152,* 516–521.

Insel, T. R. (1982). The dexamethasone suppresion test in patients with primary obsessive-compulsive disorder. *Psychiatry Research, 6,* 153–160.

Jenike, M. A. (1990). Predictors of treatment failure. In M. A. Jenike, L. Baer, & W. E. Minichiello (Eds.), *Obsessive-compulsive disorders: Theory and management* (pp. 306–311). Chicago: Year Book Medical.

Jenike, M. A., Baer, L., Minichiello, W. E., Schwartz, C. E., & Carey, R. J. (1986). Concomitant obsessive-compulsive disorder and schizotypal personality disorders. *American Journal of Psychiatry, 143,* 530–532.

Joffee, R. T., Swinson, R. P., & Regan, J. J. (1988). Personality features in obsessive-compulsive disorder. *American Journal of Psychiatry, 145,* 1127–1129.

Karno, M., Golding, J. M., Sorenson, S. B., & Burnam, A. (1988). The epidemiology of obsessive-compulsive disorder in five US communities. *Archives of General Psychiatry, 45,* 1094–1099.

Kaye, W. H., Weltzin, T. E., & Hsu, L. G. (1993). Relationship between anorexia nervosa and obsessive compulsive behaviors. *Psychiatric Annals, 23,* 365–373.

Keijsers, G. P. J., Hoogduin, C. A. L., & Schaap, C. P. (1994). Predictors of treatment outcome in the behavioral treatment of obsessive-compulsive disorder. *British Journal of Psychiatry, 165*(6), 781–786.

Koloda, J. L., Bland, R. C., & Newman, S. C. (1994). Obsessive-compulsive disorder. *Acta Psychiatrica Scandinavica, 89*(376, Suppl.), 24–35.

Leckman, J. F. (1993). Tourette's syndrome. In E. Hollander (Ed.), *Obsessive-compulsive related disorders* (pp. 113–138). Washington, DC: American Psychiatric Press.

Maina, G., Bellino, S., Bogetto, F., & Ravizza, L. (1993). Personality disorders in obsessive-compulsive patients. *European Journal of Psychiatry, 7,* 155–163.

Marks, I. M., Lelliott, P., Basoglu, M., Noshirvani, H., Monteiro, W., Cohen, D., & Kasvikis, Y. (1988). Clompiramine, self-exposure and therapist-aided exposure for obsessive-compulsive rituals. *British Journal of Psychiatry, 152,* 522–534.

Marks, I. M., Stern, R. S., Mawson, D., Cobb, J., & McDonald, R. (1980). Clomipramine and exposure for obsessive-compulsive rituals. *British Journal of Psychiatry, 136,* 1–25.

Mavissakalian, M., Hamann, M. S., & Jones, B. (1990a). A comparison of DSM–III personality disorders in panic, agoraphobia and obsessive-compulsive disorder. *Comprehensive Psychiatry, 31,* 238–244.

Mavissakalian, M., Hamann, M. S., & Jones, B. (1990b). DSM–III personality disorders in obsessive-compulsive disorder: Changes with treatment. *Comprehensive Psychiatry, 31*(5), 432–437.

Mavissakalian, M., & Michelson, L. (1983). Tricyclic antidepressants in obsessive-compulsive disorder: Antiobsessional or antidepressant agents? *Journal of Nervous and Mental Disease, 171,* 301–306.

McKay, J., Neziroglu, F., Todaro, J., & Yaryura-Tobias, J. A. (1996). Changes in personality disorders following behavioral therapy for obsessive-compulsive disorder. *Journal of Anxiety Disorders, 10,* 47–57.

Minichiello, W., Baer, L., & Jenike, M. A. (1987). Schizotypal personality disorder: A poor prognostic indicator for behavior therapy in the treatment of obsessive-compulsive disorder. *Journal of Anxiety Disorders, 1,* 273–276.

Okasha, A., Saad, A., Khalil, A. H., Dawla, A., & Seif, E. (1994). Phenomenology of obsessive-compulsive disorder: A transcultural study. *Comprehensive Psychiatry, 35,* 191–197.

Orloff, L. M., Battle, M. A., Baer, L., Ivanjack, L., Petit, A. R., Buttolph, L., & Jenike, M. A. (1994). Long-term follow-up of 85 patients with obsessive-compulsive disorder. *American Journal of Psychiatry, 151,* 441–442.

O'Sullivan, G., Noshirvani, H., Marks, I., Monteiro, W., & Lelliott, P. (1991). Six-year follow-up after exposure and clomipramine therapy for obsessive compulsive disorder. *Journal of Clincial Psychiatry, 52,* 150–155.

Pigott, T. A., Pato, M. T., L'Heureux, F., & Hill, J. L. (1991). A controlled comparison of adjuvant lithium carbonate or thyroid hormone in clomipramine-treated patients with obsessive-compulsive disorder. *Journal of Clinical Psychopharmacology, 11,* 242–248.

Rabavilas, A. D., & Boulougouris, J. C. (1979). Mood changes and flooding outcome in obsessive-compulsive patients: Report of a 2-year follow-up. *The Journal of Nervous and Mental Disease, 167,* 495–496.

Rabavilas, A. D., Boulougouris, J. C., Perissaki, C., & Stefanis, C. (1979). Pre-morbid personality traits and responsiveness to flooding in obsessive-compulsive patients. *Behaviour Research and Therapy, 17,* 575–580.

Rasmussen, S. A., & Eisen, J. L. (1989). Clinical features and phenomenology of obsessive compulsive disorder. *Psychiatric Annals, 19,* 67–73.

Rasmussen, S., & Eisen, J. L. (1991). Phenomenology of OCD: Clinical subtypes, heterogeneity, and coexistence. In J. Zohar, T. Insel, & S. Rasmussen (Eds.), *The psychobiology of obsessive-compulsive disorder.* New York: Springer.

Rasmussen, S. A., & Eisen, J. L. (1992). The epidemiology and clinical features of obsessive compulsive disorder. *Psychiatric Clinics of North America, 15,* 743–758.

Rasmussen, S., & Tsuang, M. T. (1986). Epidemiology and clinical features of obsessive compulsive disorder. In M. A. Jenike, L. Baer, & W. E. Minichiello (Eds.), *Obsessive-compulsive disorders: A theory of management* (pp. 13–42). Littleton, MA: PSG.

Rasmussen, S. A., & Tsuang, M. T. (1987). Obsessive-compulsive disorder and borderline personality disorder. *American Journal of Psychiatry, 144,* 121–122.

Riggs, D. S., Hiss, H., & Foa, E. B. (1992). Marital distress and the treatment of obsessive compulsive disorder. *Behavior Therapy, 23,* 585–597.

Rubenstein, C. S., Altemus, M., & Pigott, T. A. (1995). Symptom overlap between OCD and bulemia nervosa. *Journal of Anxiety Disorders, 9,* 1–9.

Sciuto, G., Diaferia, G., Battaglia, M., Perna, G., Gabriele, A., & Bellodi, L. (1991). DSM–III–R personality disorders in panic and obsessive-compulsive disorder: A comparison study. *Comprehensive Psychiatry, 32,* 450–457.

Stanley, M. A., & Turner, S. M. (1995). Current status of pharmacological and behavioral treatment of obsessive-compulsive disorder. *Behavior Therapy, 26,* 163–186.

Stanley, M. A., Turner S. M., & Borden, J. W. (1990). Schizotypal features in obsessive-compulsive disorder. *Comprehensive Psychiatry, 31,* 511–518.

Steingard, R., & Dillon-Stout, D. (1992). Tourette's syndrome and obsessive compulsive disorder: Clinical aspects. *Psychiatric Clinics of North America, 15,* 849–860.

Steketee, G. (1988). Intra- and interpersonal characteristics predictive of long-term outcome following behavioral treatment of obsessive compulsive disorder. In I. Hand & H.-U. Wittchen (Eds.), *Panic and phobias II* (pp. 221–232). New York: Springer-Verlag.

Steketee, G. (1990). Personality traits and disorders in obsessive-compulsives. *Journal of Anxiety Disorders, 4*(4), 351–364.

Steketee, G. (1993). Social support as a predictor of follow-up outcome following treatment for OCD. *Journal of Behavioural Psychotherapy, 21,* 81–95.

Steketee, G., & Chambless, D. L. (1992). Methodological issues in prediction of treatment outcome. *Clinical Psychology Review, 12,* 387–400.

Steketee, G., Chambless, D. L., & Tran, G. (1999). *The effects of Axis I and II comorbidity on behavior therapy outcome for OCD and agoraphobia.* Unpublished manuscript.

Steketee, G., & Lam, J. (1993). Obsessive compulsive disorder. In T. R. Giles (Ed.), *Handbook of effective psychotherapy: A comparative outcome approach* (pp. 253–278). New York: Plenum.

Steketee, G., & Shapiro, L. (1995). Predicting behavioral treatment outcome for agoraphobia and obsessive compulsive disorder. *Clinical Psychiatry Review, 15,* 317–346.

Tallis, F., & de Silva, P. (1992). Worry and obsessional symptoms: A correlational analysis. *Behaviour Research and Therapy, 30,* 103–105.

Thomsen, P. H., & Mikkelsen, H. U. (1993). Development of personality disorders in children and adolescents with obsessive-compulsive disorder: A 6 to 22 year follow-up study. *Acta Psychiatrica Scandinavica, 87,* 456–462.

Tollefson, G. D., Rampey, A. H., Potvin, J. H., & Jenike, M. A. (1994). A multicenter investigation of fixed-dose fluoxetine in the treatment of obsessive-compulsive disorder. *Archives of General Psychiatry, 51,* 559–567.

Turner, S. M., Beidel, D. C., & Stanley, M. A. (1992). Are obsessional thoughts and worry different cognitive phenomena? *Clinical Psychology Review, 12,* 257–270.

Walker, W. R., Freeman, R. F., & Christensen, D. K. (1994). Restricting environmental stimulation (REST) to enhance cognitive behavioral treatment for obsessive compulsive disorder with schizotypal personality disorder. *Behavior Therapy, 25,* 709–719.

Weissman, M. M., Bland, R. C., Canino, G. J., Greenwald, S., Hwu, H., Lee, C. K., Newman, S. C., Oakley-Brown, M. A., Rubio-Stipec, M., Wickramaratne, P. J., Wittchen, H., & Yeh, E. (1994). The cross national epidemiology of obsessive-compulsive disorder: The Cross National Collaborative Group. *Clinical Psychiatry, 55*(Suppl.), 5–10.

V

DRUG AND OTHER
SOMATIC TREATMENTS

15

Pharmacotherapy of Obsessive-Compulsive Disorder: Overview and Treatment-Refractory Strategies

Teresa A. Pigott
Sheila Seay
University of Texas Medical Branch

Obsessive-compulsive disorder (OCD) generally follows a chronic, fluctuating clinical course. Few ($\leq$ 10%) patients meeting full criterion for OCD will experience a symptom-free period of more than 1 month without symptomatology (Goodman, McDougle, & Price, 1992; Rasmussen & Eisen, 1992). As a result, OCD is often associated with considerable morbidity, psychosocial impairment, and occupational disability (Dupont, Rice, Shiraki, & Rowland, 1995). Fortunately first-line anti-OCD medication(s) are associated with symptom reduction in most patients with OCD (Goodman et al., 1992; Jenike & Rauch, 1994; Pigott & Seay, in press). In this chapter we provide a review of: (a) acute pharmacotherapy for OCD, (b) maintenance pharmacotherapy for OCD, and (c) pharmacotherapeutic strategies for treatment-refractory OCD.

THE ACUTE PHARMACOTHERAPY OF OCD

Measuring Efficacy in OCD

The most widely accepted instrument for assessing anti-OCD efficacy is the Yale–Brown Obsessive Compulsive Rating Scale (Y–BOCS). The Y–BOCS is a 10-item, observer-rated scale that was developed to assess change in obsessive thoughts and compulsive behaviors, respectively, in patients with OCD. The range of total scores on the Y–BOCS is between 0 (none) and 40 (most severe). A mean reduction greater than 25% to 35% from baseline as measured by the Y–BOCS is generally considered a "response" in patients with OCD (Goodman & Price, 1990; Goodman, Price, Rasmussen, Mazure, Delgado, et al., 1989; Goodman, Price, Rasmussen, Mazure, Fleischmann, et al., 1989).

First-Line Medications for OCD: Serotonin Reuptake Inhibitors

Relatively few medications are effective in the treatment of OCD. For example, controlled trials of tricyclic antidepressants (TCAs) such as imipramine (Volavka, Neziroglu, & Yaryura-Tobias, 1985), doxepin (Ananth, Solyom, & Solyom, 1975), amitriptyline (Ananth, Pecknold, van den Steen, & Engelsman, 1981), and desipramine (Goodman, Price, Rasmussen, Delgado, Heninger, & Charney, 1989; Insel et al., 1983; Leonard, Swedo, Rapoport, Coffey, & Cheslow, 1988; Zohar & Insel, 1987) failed to demonstrate significant anti-OCD effects. Most trials of monoamine oxidase inhibiting (MAOI) antidepressants have failed to demonstrate efficacy in most patients with OCD (Insel et al., 1983; Jain, Swinson, & Thomas, 1970). In fact, only the antidepressants clomipramine, fluoxetine, fluvoxamine, sertraline, and paroxetine, respectively, have demonstrated efficacy in placebo-controlled, multicenter trials conducted in patients with primary OCD (Clomipramine, 1991; Greist, 1992; Goodman, Kozak, Liebowitz, & White, 1996; Tollefson, Rampey, et al., 1994; Wheadon, Bushnell, & Steiner, 1993). Clomipramine is a TCA and the remaining four medications are classified as serotonin reuptake inhibitors (SRIs).

Most TCAs nonselectively block the neuronal reuptake of norepinephrine and serotonin. Clomipramine is distinguished from other TCAs by its ability to potently block serotonin reuptake (Benfield, Harris, & Luscombe, 1980; Stern, Marks, Wright, & Luscombe, 1980). Because both clomipramine and the SRIs possess selective or potent effects on serotonin reuptake, they have been labeled serotonin transport inhibitors by Greist (Greist, Jefferson, Kobak, Katzelnick, & Serlin, 1995). The SRIs remain the only medications that have consistently demonstrated efficacy in the treatment of OCD. The preferential efficacy of SRIs, in comparison to nonserotonin selective antidepressants, has implicated central serotonin (5-HT) pathways in the pathophysiology of OCD (Barr, Goodman, Price, McDougle, & Charney, 1992; Greist, Jefferson, Kobak, Katzelnick, & Serlin, 1995; Insel, Mueller, Alterman, Linnoila, & Murphy, 1985; Insel et al., 1983; Pigott, 1996; Zohar & Insel, 1987).

Fortunately, most patients with OCD will experience significant benefit from SRI therapy. As a result, SRIs are generally considered first-line pharmacotherapy for patients with OCD (Goodman et al., 1992; Jenike, 1992; Jenike & Rauch, 1994).

SRI Medications: Efficacy and Safety in OCD

Results of each of the placebo-controlled, multicenter trials that have been conducted in patients with primary OCD are briefly summarized in this section.

Clomipramine. Clomipramine was first reported as efficacious in the treatment of OCD in the early and mid-1980s (Ananth, 1986; Ananth et al., 1981; Asberg, Thoren, & Bertilsson, 1982; Insel et al., 1985; Montgomery, 1980; Stern et al., 1980; Thoren, Asberg, Crohnholm, Jornestedt, & Trachman, 1980; Volavka et al., 1985; Zohar & Insel, 1987). The most extensively studied anti-OCD medication worldwide, clomipramine has remained the gold standard by which any other medication is inevitably judged in the treatment of OCD. The pharmacologic effects of clomipramine are complex. For example, serotonin reuptake is potently blocked by the parent compound clomipramine, but its major metabolite, desmethyl-clomipramine, is an inhibitor of norepinephrine reuptake (Benfield et al., 1980). Clomipramine also has a relatively high affinity for adrenergic and histamine central receptors (Hall & Ogren, 1981). Both clomipramine and desmethyl-clomipramine also potently block acetylcholine receptors. Many of the adverse effects observed during clomipramine administration can be attributed to these multiple receptor effects (Nierenberg & Cole, 1992). Clomipramine's side effects such as sedation, orthostasis, dry mouth, delayed cardiac conduction, and weight gain can be particularly problematic, resulting in poor tolerance or medication discontinuation (Pato, Hill, & Murphy, 1990; Pigott et al., 1990).

Over 400 patients with OCD, based on criteria from the *Diagnostic and Statistical Manual of Mental Disorders* (3rd ed., rev. [*DSM–III–R*]; American Psychiatric Association, 1987), participated in the multicenter clomipramine versus placebo study (Clomipramine, 1991). As measured by the Y–BOCS, clomipramine was associated with a significantly greater reduction in OCD symptoms (37%) in comparison to placebo (8%) administration. There was no difference in response between the depressed versus nondepressed patients with OCD during the multicenter clomipramine study. Dry mouth, dizziness, tremor, fatigue, somnolence, constipation, and nausea were the most common side effects endorsed during the multicenter study. Clomipramine subsequently received Food and Drug Administration approval and became the first medication in the United States to have a specific indication for the treatment of OCD.

Most studies have suggested that 150 to 250 mg/day of clomipramine is a standard effective dose for patients with OCD (Clomipramine, 1991; Mavissakalian, Jones, Olsen, & Perel, 1990; Thoren, Asberg, Chronholm, et al., 1980). Doses of clomipramine over 250 mg/day are associated with a relatively high rate of seizures. Although plasma clomipramine concentration monitoring is commercially available, a specific concentration range that correlates with anti-OCD efficacy has not been determined. Instead, a significant relation between clomipramine plasma levels and anti-OCD response has been reported in some studies (Insel et al., 1985; Mavissakalian et al., 1990; Stern et al., 1980), but has been absent in others (Flament, Rapaport, Murphy, Lake, & Berg, 1987; Kasvikis & Marks, 1988; Thoren, Asberg, Bertelsson, et al., 1980). There is some evidence that response to clomipramine may be enhanced by an elevated plasma concentration of clomipramine versus desmethyl-clomipramine (Mavissakalian et al., 1990).

Fluoxetine. Fluoxetine is a bicyclic antidepressant that selectively blocks reuptake of 5-HT and has minimal affinity for histaminic, muscarinic, adrenergic, and serotonergic receptors (Wong, Bymaster, Reid, & Threlkeld, 1983). Fluoxetine has an active metabolite, norfluoxetine (DeVane, 1994).

A 13-week, fixed-dose, multicenter study of fluoxetine (Tollefson, Rampey, et al., 1994) compared 20, 40, and 60 mg daily doses of fluoxetine to placebo in 355 patients with OCD (*DSM–III–R* criteria). Each dose of fluoxetine was significantly more effective than placebo in reducing OCD symptoms. As measured by the Y–BOCS, there was a trend suggesting greater efficacy for fluoxetine at 60 mg/day (mean Y–BOCS reduction = 27%) versus 20 mg/day (mean Y–BOCS reduction = 20%) or 40 mg/day (mean Y–BOCS reduction = 22%). A second multicenter OCD study (Montgomery et al., 1993) was conducted outside of the United States ($N =$ 222). The same protocol design was used, except that the OCD patients received a shorter duration (8 instead of 13 weeks) of fluoxetine (20, 40, or 60 mg/day) or placebo administration. There was a significant decrease in Y–BOCS from baseline to endpoint in each treatment group. However, only the 60 mg fluoxetine was significantly more effective than the placebo. Side effects endorsed significantly more by the fluoxetine group, in comparison to the placebo group were nausea, dry mouth, or tremor. As noted during the clomipramine multicenter study, baseline levels of depressive symptoms did not correlate with subsequent changes in the Y–BOCS during the fluoxetine study (Tollefson, Rampey, et al., 1994).

The multicenter studies suggest that 20 to 60 mg/day of fluoxetine is effective in OCD, but that higher doses may be associated with greater symptom reduction. In fact, several studies have suggested that 80 mg/day of fluoxetine is effective and well tolerated in patients with OCD. Plasma fluoxetine concentration monitoring is commercially available, but is of limited value. Higher plasma concentrations of fluoxetine have been associated with a greater reduction in OCD symptoms. However, there was no significant difference in plasma concentrations of fluoxetine in responders versus nonresponders in the multicenter OCD study (Tollefson, Rampey, et al., 1994).

Sertraline. Sertraline is an SRI that is more potent and more selective for blockade of serotonin versus norepinephrine reuptake in comparison to fluoxetine (Koe, Weissman, Welch, & Browne, 1983). Sertraline has no demonstrable effects on norepinephrine or dopamine reuptake and also lacks direct adrenergic or cholinergic receptor effects. Sertraline's active metabolite, desmethyl-sertraline, has substantially less therapeutic activity than its parent compound (DeVane, 1994).

A 12-week, multicenter, fixed-dose study of sertraline hydrochloride (50, 100, or 200 mg/day) versus placebo was conducted in 324 patients with OCD (Greist, 1992). Sertraline at 50 mg/day and at 200 mg/day, but not at 100 mg/day, was significantly more effective than placebo administration. Reductions in OCD symptoms were greatest at doses of sertraline of 50 mg/day (24%) or at 200 mg/day (28%), whereas 100 mg/day of sertraline (19%) and placebo (15%) resulted in similar and nonsignificant changes in OCD symptoms. Although to some extent puzzling, this statistical anomaly may be somewhat attributed to the large placebo response rate. Side effects experienced at a significantly higher rate in the sertraline versus the placebo-treated group during the study were diarrhea, insomnia, decreased libido, nausea, anorexia, ejaculation failure, tremor, increased sweating, and increased weight gain.

Fluvoxamine. Fluvoxamine is a unicyclic SRI antidepressant that has minimal affinity for histaminic, muscarinic, adrenergic, and serotonergic receptors (Benfield & Ward, 1986). Fluvoxamine lacks active metabolites (DeVane, 1994).

Over 300 patients with OCD participated in a 10-week, multicenter, flexible-dose study of fluvoxamine maleate (mean dose = 249 mg/day) versus placebo (Goodman et al., 1996). Reductions in OCD symptoms during fluvoxamine treatment (20%) were significantly greater than during placebo (5%) administration as measured by the Y–BOCS. The most common side effects experienced at a significantly higher rate in the fluvoxamine group versus the placebo-treated group were insomnia, nausea, asthenia, somnolence, abnormal ejaculation, nervousness, and dry mouth.

Paroxetine. Paroxetine is a phenylpiperidine derivative that is structurally distinct from other SRIs. In comparative studies, paroxetine is a relatively more potent and selective SRI than fluoxetine, fluvoxamine, sertraline, zimelidine, or clomipramine (Crewe, Lennard, Tucker, Woods,

& Haddock, 1992). Paroxetine demonstrates little affinity for adrenergic, dopamine, or histamine receptors, it lacks active metabolites (DeVane, 1994), and it has significant muscarinic blocking effects.

A 12-week, fixed-dose, multicenter study (Wheadon et al., 1993) of 20 mg/day, 40 mg/day, and 60 mg/day versus placebo was conducted in 263 patients with OCD (*DSM–III–R* criteria). Paroxetine at 40 mg/day and 60 mg/day, but not at 20 mg/day, were significantly more effective than placebo administration. The greatest reduction in OCD symptoms occurred at 40 (mean Y–BOCS reduction = 25%) and at 60 mg/day (mean Y–BOCS reduction = 29%) As measured by the Y–BOCS, there was no significant difference in symptom reduction between 20 mg/day of paroxetine (17%) and placebo (13%) administration during the study. The most common side effects reported during paroxetine administration were nausea, somnolence, headache, constipation, fatigue, sweating, and dizziness.

These multicenter studies provide strong support for the efficacy of clomipramine and the SRIs in the treatment of patients with OCD. In addition, each of the SRIs was well tolerated and discontinuation rates were relatively low in the multicenter OCD studies (Greist et al., 1995). Because each of these studies was conducted separately, the comparative efficacy and safety of clomipramine versus the SRIs was not assessed. The next section reviews the available studies that have directly compared clomipramine to an SRI in the treatment of OCD.

Direct Comparisons of SRIs

Eleven OCD patients participated in a 26-week, randomized, double-blind, cross-over study of clomipramine and fluoxetine administration (Pigott et al., 1990). All of the patients received 2 weeks of placebo followed by 10 weeks of either clomipramine or fluoxetine administration, 4 weeks of placebo substitution, and then 10 weeks of the second medication. Similar and significant reductions from baseline in OCD symptoms were noted during clomipramine (mean dose = 210 mg/day) and fluoxetine (mean dose = 75 mg/day) administration. During the placebo-substitution phase between the active medication phases, substantial relapses in both OCD and depressive symptoms occurred. These relapses occurred despite the presence of substantial reductions in OCD symptoms during the initial medication treatment period and persisted until at least 6 weeks of treatment with the second medication. Individual responses to clomipramine versus fluoxetine were also assessed. Evidence of a preferential response (> 25% difference in OCD symptom reduction between clomipramine versus fluoxetine treatment) was demonstrated in 7 of 11 of the OCD patients: More improvement was noted during clomipramine in five patients and two patients had more improvement during fluoxetine treatment.

In the second part of the same study (Pigott et al., 1990), 21 OCD patients who had been receiving chronic clomipramine therapy (mean duration of clomipramine treatment = 14 months) were switched to fluoxetine in a double-blind fashion. Seventeen of the OCD patients (85%) achieved a similar level after 10 weeks of fluoxetine therapy as they had achieved during clomipramine treatment as measured by the Y–BOCS. More side effects were endorsed during clomipramine in comparison to fluoxetine administration in both studies.

Another study (Pigott, L'Heureux, & Murphy, 1993) retrospectively assessed response to clomipramine versus fluoxetine in 81 patients with OCD. Using a 25% or greater reduction from baseline on the Y–BOCS as criteria for "response": (a) more patients responded to clomipramine than fluoxetine treatment; (b) if a patient responded to clomipramine, there was a 65% chance that he or she would respond to subsequent trial of fluoxetine; (c) if a patient did not respond to clomipramine, there was only a 20% chance that he or she would respond to a subsequent trial of clomipramine; (d) if a patient responded to fluoxetine, there was an 80% chance that he or she would respond to a subsequent trial of clomipramine; and (e) 20% to 25% of the OCD patients failed to respond to either clomipramine or fluoxetine therapy (Table 15.1).

Jenike, Baer, and Greist (1990) reported a retrospective comparison of side effects during fluoxetine versus clomipramine treatment in a group of OCD patients. Fluoxetine, in comparison to clomipramine administration, was associated with a lower incidence of side effects. Moreover, 43% of the fluoxetine-treated patients denied side effects, whereas side effects were absent in only 3% of the clomipramine-treated patients.

Clomipramine has been compared to fluvoxamine in three separate controlled studies conducted in patients with OCD. In 10 patients with OCD, there were no significant differences between clomipramine and fluvoxamine treatment (Smeraldi, Erzegovesi, et al., 1992). Two subsequent multicenter, randomized, parallel-cell design studies compared

TABLE 15.1
OCD: Clomipramine vs. Fluoxetine (Pigott et al., 1993, n = 81)

If an OCD pt. responds to clomipramine, what are the chances that they will respond to fluoxetine? *65%*

If an OCD pt responds to fluoxetine, what are the chances that they will respond to clomipramine? *80%*

If an OCD pt *does not* respond to clomipramine, what are the chances that they will respond to fluoxetine? *20%*

---

clomipramine to fluvoxamine in patients with OCD (Freeman, Trimble, Deakin, Stokes, & Ashford, 1994; Koran et al., 1996). Clomipramine and fluvoxamine administration were associated with similar and significant reductions in OCD symptoms from baseline in both the first ($n = 79$) and second ($n = 66$) studies. There was no difference in the frequency of adverse events noted during clomipramine versus fluvoxamine treatment. Postural hypotension, dry mouth, dizziness, tremor, and anorgasmia were more common in the clomipramine-treated group and complaints of insomnia were more common in the fluvoxamine-treated group.

A double-blind, parallel design comparison of sertraline versus clomipramine in 86 patients with OCD was also recently reported (Flament & Bisserbe, 1997). Significant Y–BOCS reductions from baseline were noted after sertraline and clomipramine treatment. A statistically greater reduction in OCD symptoms was noted in the sertraline-treated patients versus the clomipramine-treated patients. There were more dropouts during clomipramine treatment (26%) than sertraline treatment (11%). However, it is important to note that the mean dose of clomipramine (90 mg/day) during the study was likely to have been inadequate and as such, may have significantly reduced clomipramine's effectiveness. The results from this study therefore require replication before any definitive conclusions are made concerning the comparative efficacy of sertraline and clomipramine.

Further direct comparisons of clomipramine versus the SRIs in the treatment of OCD have not yet been reported. However, the comparative efficacy of medications can also be examined by conducting a meta-analyses of pooled data from multiple studies. The next section reviews results from meta-analyses of studies conducted in patients with OCD.

Meta-Analyses of SRIs in the Treatment of OCD

Jenike and colleagues (Jenike et al., 1989) conducted a meta-analysis of data from separate placebo-controlled trials of clomipramine, fluoxetine, fluvoxamine, and sertraline conducted in OCD patients at the same site. According to this meta-analysis, the medication associated with the greatest reduction in OCD symptoms was clomipramine, followed by fluoxetine, fluvoxamine, and sertraline, respectively. A larger and more recent meta-analysis (Piccinelli, Pini, Bellantuono, & Wilkinson, 1995) of placebo-controlled OCD studies conducted with SRIs concluded that clomipramine was more effective than fluoxetine, fluvoxamine, or sertraline treatment; and there was no significant difference in efficacy between fluoxetine, fluvoxamine, or sertraline administration.

A meta-analysis of pooled data from the multicenter, placebo-controlled trials of clomipramine, fluoxetine, fluvoxamine, and sertraline, respec-

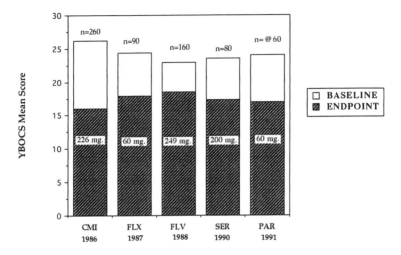

FIG. 15.1. SRIs in OCD: "Best" dose comparison. Adapted with permission from Greist et al. (1995) and Pigott (1996).

tively, in patients with OCD was also recently reported (Greist, Jefferson, Kobak, Katzelnick, & Serlin, 1995). Results suggested that: (a) the greatest improvement in OCD symptoms occurred during clomipramine admini- stration (39%) in comparison to fluoxetine (27%), sertraline (26%), or fluvoxamine (20%) administration, respectively; (b) a significantly greater percentage of patients treated with clomipramine were rated "much" or "very much" improved than were patients treated with fluoxetine, flu- voxamine, or sertraline; (c) the total dropout rate (side effects plus lack of efficacy and other causes) associated with clomipramine was signifi- cantly less than the dropout rates associated with the SRI antidepressants; and (d) similar dropout rates attributed solely to side effects were noted between the different anti-OCD agents (clomipramine, 8%; fluoxetine, 12%; fluvoxamine, 15%; and sertraline, 10%). Figure 15.1 illustrates the reduction in OCD symptoms associated with the "most effective dose" of clomipramine, fluoxetine, fluvoxamine, sertraline (based on the Greist meta-analyses), and paroxetine (adapted from Wheadon et al., 1993).

Although results from these meta-analyses suggest that clomipramine may be associated with a relatively greater reduction in OCD symptoms than the SRIs, several mitigating factors should be considered when interpreting these data. For example, SRIs were not available at the time that the clomipramine OCD study was conducted. In contrast, at least 20% of the OCD patients enrolled in the SRIs studies had failed to respond to or tolerate treatment with clomipramine or at least one SRI-antidepressant (Greist, 1992; Goodman et al., 1996). Therefore, the relatively smaller reductions in OCD symptoms associated with SRI therapy may in fact be secondary to the inclusion of more treatment-refractory patients in each successive trial that was conducted after the inaugural (clomipramine) trial.

First-Line Medication Guidelines
for the Acute Treatment of OCD

In the treatment of patients with OCD, controlled medication trials suggest that clomipramine, fluoxetine, sertraline, fluvoxamine, and paroxetine treatment are effective in reducing OCD symptomatology, although the response is generally partial (mean Y–BOCS reduction from baseline = 25–40%). An adequate trial of an anti-OCD agent consists of at least 10 to 12 weeks of treatment and relatively higher maintenance dosages (clomipramine, 150–250 mg/day; fluoxetine, 60–80 mg/day; fluvoxamine, 150–300 mg/day; sertraline, 150–200 mg/day; and paroxetine, 40–60 mg/day) may be required to attain efficacy in OCD. Clomipramine appears to be associated with more side effects than the SRIs.

Few controlled comparisons of clomipramine versus SRIs have been conducted in patients with OCD. Significant differences in anti-OCD efficacy have not been detected in the direct comparisons of clomipramine to fluoxetine or clomipramine versus fluvoxamine, respectively. Meta-analyses of placebo-controlled studies conducted in OCD patients have suggested that clomipramine may be associated with a relatively greater reduction in OCD symptoms in comparison to the SRIs and that no significant differences in anti-OCD efficacy exist between the individual SRI agents. However, there are a number of methodological issues that limit the interpretation of results from meta-analyses.

Although there have been few systematic investigations of cross-response between clomipramine and the SRIs, clinical experience suggests that nonresponse to one SRI does not preclude response to other SRIs in patients with OCD. Therefore, separate trials of clomipramine, fluoxetine, fluvoxamine, sertraline, and paroxetine are necessary to determine optimal anti-OCD efficacy in the individual OCD patient. Once the most effective medication for an individual with OCD is established, a treatment duration of at least 9 to 12 months is generally recommended (Table 15.2).

TABLE 15.2
Medication Response in OCD

Partial response = usual response
  40% mean reduction in OCD from baseline
Total remission is very rare (≤ 10%)
Relapse is common after medication is discontinued (≥ 80%)
20%–25% of patients do not respond* to SRIs

---

*0–25% reduction in OCD symptoms from baseline

MAINTENANCE PHARMACOTHERAPY FOR OCD

Because OCD is a chronic illness that can be associated with substantial anxiety and impairment, long-term medication treatment is often indicated and recommended. This section reviews the efficacy of maintenance pharmacotherapy for OCD and relapse rates after discontinuation of effective anti-OCD medication.

Long-Term Efficacy of SRI Treatment

There are comparatively few published data on the efficacy of SRIs or clomipramine for periods longer than 20 weeks in the treatment of OCD. Therefore, limited data are available concerning the long-term efficacy and tolerability of effective medications for the treatment of OCD.

Patients judged to be responders during the multicenter clomipramine study were eligible to participate in a double-blind extension study (De-Veaugh-Geiss, Landau, & Katz, 1989; Katz, DeVeaugh-Geiss, & Landau, 1990). The OCD patients treated with clomipramine maintained significant improvement as long as they remained on the medication. In addition, significantly more of the OCD patients receiving clomipramine (72%) were rated as "very much improved" or "much improved" in comparison to the patients receiving placebo (17%) during the 1-year extension phase. There is evidence that the daily dose of clomipramine may be decreased during chronic (> 1 year) administration of OCD without a substantial decrement in response (Ananth, 1986; Pato et al., 1990). Data from these studies suggest that the maintenance dose of clomipramine may be substantially less than dosages required for acute treatment of OCD symptoms.

There have been a few reports of chronic fluoxetine treatment in patients with OCD. Levine, Hoffman, Knepple, and Kenin (1989) treated 75 OCD patients with fluoxetine with good results including 15 patients who were administered fluoxetine for 5 months or longer. They concluded that incremental reductions in OCD symptoms occurred during treatment with fluoxetine and that the improvement persisted over the 5-month period of the study. Frenkel, Rosenthal, Nezu, and Winston (1990) reported a 32-week, open-label study of fluoxetine conducted in 10 patients with OCD. Significant reductions in OCD symptoms were noted during the study and the improvement remained stable as long as the medication was continued.

Patients ($n = 76$) who responded during the acute phase of the multicenter fluoxetine OCD study maintained their improvement during the 24-week continuation study (Tollefson, Birkett, Koran, & Genduso, 1994). Moreover, two thirds of the patients who did not respond during the core phase of the fluoxetine study ($n = 198$) achieved a clinical response when switched to open-label fluoxetine during the extension phase (Tollefson,

Birkett, et al., 1994). Maintenance dosages for fluoxetine in patients with OCD have not been systematically studied, but appear to be lower than dosages utilized in acute treatment (Dominguez, 1992).

Extension phases were also included in the multicenter OCD studies of sertraline, fluvoxamine, and paroxetine, respectively. Sertraline was safe and efficacious in the 1-year controlled extension trial in patients with OCD (Greist, Chouinard, et al., 1995). In addition, preliminary results of continuation phases conducted after the acute multicenter studies support the long-term efficacy of fluvoxamine and paroxetine in the treatment of OCD patients (Goodman et al., 1996; Steiner, Bushnell, Gergel, & Wheadon, 1995).

Relapse After Medication Discontinuation

Although most patients with OCD maintain improvement in their OCD symptoms with continued SRI treatment, there have been few studies that have addressed relapse rates after the discontinuation of effective pharmacotherapy. Two double-blind studies have specifically assessed the risk of relapse after clomipramine discontinuation (Leonard et al., 1991; Pato, Zohar-Kadouch, Zohar, & Murphy, 1988). Substantial recurrences of OCD symptoms occurred within 7 weeks of placebo substitution in 16 of 18 patients who had been chronically maintained on clomipramine treatment (Pato et al., 1988). Leonard et al. (1991) subsequently conducted a double-blind study of continued clomipramine versus substitution of desipramine in clomipramine-treated patients with OCD. When desipramine was substituted for clomipramine, 8 of 11 OCD patients relapsed within 8 weeks. In contrast, only 2 of 11 patients with OCD relapsed when clomipramine was continued over the same comparison period.

In an open study of 43 fluoxetine-treated (12–20 months) patients with OCD who discontinued their medication, only 8 (23%) were reported to have relapsed at the 1-year follow-up appointment (Fontaine & Chouinard, 1989). Although this report suggests that fluoxetine treatment may be associated with lower relapse rates than clomipramine, more recent studies have suggested that fluoxetine treatment in patients with OCD is also associated with substantial rates of relapse (Dominguez, 1992; Pigott et al., 1990). Double-blind discontinuation studies after long-term administration of sertraline and paroxetine are currently underway.

Summary: Long-Term Medication Treatment for OCD

Most patients require chronic, ongoing treatment with anti-OCD agents. Fortunately, patients with OCD appear to maintain improvement in their symptoms as long as they are continued on either clomipramine or SRI treatment. Available data suggests that most patients with OCD who are treated with anti-OCD medication will rapidly relapse after the medication is discontinued. Because of the swift return of OCD symptoms in most patients once they discontinue medication (regardless of the extent of anti-OCD response attained in patients with OCD), standard treatment of at least 12 months is preferred by clinicians.

PHARMACOTHERAPEUTIC STRATEGIES FOR TREATMENT-REFRACTORY OCD

Factors in Treatment Failure

Common factors associated with treatment failure in patients with OCD are reviewed in this section (Table 15.3). A number of disorders can masquerade as OCD (Table 15.4). Obsessive-compulsive personality disorder (OCPD) is characterized by some features such as perfectionism, rigidity, control, and preoccupation with details and rules that can resemble OCD symptoms (American Psychiatric Association, 1994). However, the prominent anxiety and distress that are readily endorsed in patients with OCD are generally absent in OCPD. Ruminations and ritualistic behaviors can occur in depression with psychotic features, but the mood disturbance should predate the onset of OCD symptoms and a history of premorbid OCD should be absent. OCD-like symptoms such as stereo-

TABLE 15.3
OCD: Treatment Resistant?

Accurate Diagnosis?
Comorbid Conditions?
Adequate Treatment Trials?
Integrated Treatment Regimen?
Treatment Compliance?
Unreasonable Expectations?

TABLE 15.4
OCD: Diagnosis Dilemmas

OCPD
Depression with psychotic features
Other anxiety disorders
Psychotic disorders
Stimulant abuse/intoxication
Neurological disorders/injury
Developmental D/O's with stereotypies

typic behaviors can also be secondary to stimulant abuse, neurological illness, brain trauma, or central nervous system neoplasm (Croisile, Tourniaire, Confavreux, Trillet, & Aimard, 1989; Hollander, Schiffman, et al., 1990; Kettle & Marks, 1986; Koizumi, 1985; Rosse et al., 1993). These disorders should be excluded by a careful and comprehensive history and appropriate diagnostic testing.

Comorbid diagnoses are common in patients with OCD and can contribute to treatment failure in patients with OCD. In fact, over 50% of patients with primary OCD will also meet criteria for a comorbid mood or additional anxiety disorder diagnoses (Austin et al., 1990; Foa & Kozak, 1995; Jenike, 1992; Jenike & Rauch, 1994; Karno, Golding, Sorenson, & Burnam, 1988; Pigott, L'Heureux, Dubbert, Bernstein, & Murphy, 1994; Rasmussen & Eisen, 1990, 1992). At the time of initial evaluation, 30% of OCD patients will also meet criteria for a major depressive episode. Lifetime prevalence rates are 60% to 80% for major depressive disorder and 13% for bipolar affective disorder in patients with primary OCD. Moreover an additional anxiety disorder diagnosis is present in 40% to 60% of patients with primary OCD. Elevated lifetime prevalence rates for eating disorders, somatoform disorders, and alcohol abuse have also been reported in OCD patients.

The presence of concurrent psychiatric disorders may impact treatment choice in patients with OCD. For example, combined treatment with an SRI and a mood stabilizer may be indicated for a patient with OCD and bipolar disorder. Augmenting agents such as lithium carbonate or nonselective antidepressants may also be specifically beneficial in patients with OCD and mood disorders who experience breakthrough depressive symptoms during SRI therapy (Hollander et al., 1991; Pigott et al., 1991). OCD patients with comorbid anxiety disorders may be particularly sensitive to the "activating" properties of SRI medications. Moreover there is some evidence that patients with OCD and social phobia may be less likely to respond to SRI therapy (Carrasco, Hollander, Schneier, & Liebowitz, 1992). As illustrated by these examples, concurrent psychiatric disorders can alter treatment choice and outcome, as well as contribute to nonresponse in patients with primary OCD.

Inadequate doses or duration of medication treatment can also contribute to treatment failure in patients with OCD. Considerable data suggests that a 10- to 12-week trial is required before lack of efficacy is established for an anti-OCD medication (Goodman et al., 1992; Jenike, 1992; Jenike & Rauch, 1994; Pigott et al., 1993). There is less consensus concerning an adequate dose for anti-OCD medications. Flexible dosing was used during the multicenter OCD trials of clomipramine (Clomipramine, 1991) and fluvoxamine (Goodman et al., 1996), so the lowest effective dose cannot be assessed from these studies. In contrast, a fixed-dose design can assist in the determination of the lowest effective dose for a particular medication. A fixed-dose design was used during the fluoxetine (Tollefson, Rampey, et al., 1994), sertraline (Greist, Jefferson, Kobak, Chouinard, et al., 1995), and paroxetine (Wheadon et al., 1993) multicenter OCD studies. Data obtained from these fixed-dose studies suggest that there is no statistical difference in anti-OCD efficacy between (a) 20, 40, and 60 mg/day of fluoxetine; (b) 40 and 60 mg/day of paroxetine; or (c) 50 and 100 mg/day of sertraline. These results suggest that a dose of fluoxetine at 20 mg/day, paroxetine at 40 mg/day, and sertraline at 50 mg/day constitutes the required dose to adequately assess efficacy in patients with OCD. However, this conclusion may be misleading. Further examination of the data from the multicenter OCD trials reveals a "trend" for the higher doses of each medication to be associated with the greatest symptom reduction. For example, the 60 mg/day groups, in comparison to the lower daily dose of medication groups had the greatest degree of OCD improvement during both the fluoxetine and paroxetine studies, respectively. Moreover, Greist, Jefferson, Kobak, Katzelnick, and Serlin's (1995) meta-analyses of "best dose" (i.e., the dose associated with the greatest improvement in OCD symptoms) for each of the SRIs designated relatively high optimal doses for clomipramine (226 mg/day), fluoxetine (60 mg/day), fluvoxamine (249 mg/day), sertraline (200 mg/day), and paroxetine (60 mg/day).

Preliminary studies and clinical experience suggest that an individual patient with OCD may have a differential response to clomipramine versus the various SRI antidepressants. In addition, some patients with OCD will respond to one SRI but not to another SRI (Greist, 1995; Greist et al., 1995; Jenike & Rauch, 1994; Pigott et al., 1993; Goodman et al., 1996). Unfortunately, factors that can reliably predict subsequent response to clomipramine or a specific SRI have not been identified (Baer, 1994; DeVeaugh-Geiss, Katz, Landau, Goodman, & Rasmussen, 1990; Goodman et al., 1992). These data suggest that a patient with OCD should not be considered treatment-resistant unless he or she has failed to respond to separate trials (≥ 10 weeks in duration and at the maximum tolerated dose) of clomipramine and at least three of the four SRIs (fluoxetine, fluvoxamine, sertraline, and paroxetine) (Table 15.5).

Treatment compliance and outcome expectations should always be considered in any patient who fails to respond to conventional treatment interventions. Appropriate explanation, easily understood instructions, availability of psychoeducational materials, and a sincere commitment to establishing a collaborative therapeutic relationship with patients can help to enhance compliance to recommended treatment regimens. Unreasonable expectations for treatment outcome can also contribute to poor results. Despite considerable progress in pharmacologic interventions for OCD, most patients will attain only partial symptom reduction. Some

TABLE 15.5
OCD: Adequate Treatment Trials?

Four separate medication trials:
Clomipramine + 3 SRIs
Duration of Trials: at least 10 wks.
Dosage: maximum tolerated
Clomipramine: $\leq$ 250 mg/day
Fluvoxamine: $\leq$ 300 mg/day
Paroxetine: $\leq$ 60 mg/day
Fluoxetine: $\leq$ 80 mg/day
Sertraline: $\leq$ 200 mg/day

patients designated as treatment failures are in fact treatment responders who do not know, or cannot accept, that partial symptom reduction is the usual response in OCD.

Augmentation Strategies

Because partial response is generally the rule in OCD pharmacotherapy, potential adjuvant or augmentation agents are commonly prescribed in OCD patients. Various medications have been reported to successfully augment clomipramine or the SRIs as potential adjuvant agents in the treatment of patients with OCD. However, few controlled trials of augmentation agents have been reported. This section reviews data from controlled trials, open studies, and case reports concerning the use of augmentation strategies in patients with OCD.

Controlled trials of adjuvant lithium carbonate, buspirone, neuroleptics, thyroid hormone, and clonazepam have been conducted in patients with OCD. Lithium augmentation has been reported to further reduce OCD symptoms in clomipramine-treated patients in several case reports (Feder, 1988; Golden, Morris, & Sack, 1988; Howland, 1991; Rasmussen, 1984). However, controlled studies have not supported the efficacy of lithium augmentation in patients with OCD (McDougle, Price, Goodman, Charney, & Heninger, 1991; Pigott et al., 1991). No further reduction in OCD symptoms was noted after lithium carbonate was added in a placebo-controlled, double-blind fashion to patients receiving ongoing clomipramine (Pigott et al., 1991) or fluvoxamine (McDougle et al., 1991) treatment. However, some of the clomipramine-treated OCD patients (6 of 16) did have further significant reductions in depressive symptoms after lithium carbonate was added. In the same report, double-blind addition of thyroid hormone to clomipramine-treated OCD patients was not associated with any further significant OCD or depressive symptom reduction (Pigott et al., 1991).

Further improvement in OCD symptoms was reported after the addition of buspirone to ongoing fluoxetine therapy in two open-label studies (Jenike, Baer, & Buttolph, 1991; Markovitz, Stagno, & Calabrese, 1990). However separate controlled trials conducted in patients receiving ongoing clomipramine (Pigott, L'Heureux, Hill, et al., 1992), fluoxetine (Grady et al., 1993), or fluvoxamine (McDougle et al., 1993) treatment failed to demonstrate evidence of further symptom reduction after the addition of buspirone. In fact, there was no difference between adjuvant buspirone and placebo administration in these studies.

No benefit was noted during a double-blind study of the addition of the 5-HT3 receptor antagonist ondansetron to fluvoxamine-treated patients with OCD (Smeraldi, Mundo, & Erzegovesi, 1992). Similarly, OCD patients receiving ongoing fluvoxamine treatment also did not benefit from the addition of the 5-HT2 antagonist ritanserin (Erzegovesi, Rhonchi, & Smeraldi, 1992).

A double-blind, crossover comparison of adjuvant clonazepam versus placebo administration did reveal some promising results in OCD patients receiving ongoing (> 20 weeks) clomipramine or fluoxetine treatment (Pigott, L'Heureux, Bernstein, Rubenstein, et al., 1992). Adjuvant clonazepam, but not placebo administration, resulted in further significant reductions in anxiety symptoms during the study. Moreover, significant reductions in OCD symptoms were noted on one of the three OCD rating scales during the study. Although promising, further studies are needed before clonazepam can be established as an effective augmentation strategy for patients with OCD.

The addition of a neuroleptic to ongoing SRI therapy in patients with OCD has yielded the most promising results concerning augmentation strategies for OCD. In a double-blind study, significant reductions in OCD symptoms were noted when adjuvant haloperidol was added to fluvoxamine in OCD patients with comorbid tics or Tourette's syndrome (McDougle, Goodman, et al., 1994). However, OCD patients without tics did not benefit from neuroleptic augmentation (McDougle et al., 1994).

A number of other augmentation strategies have been reported to be effective in OCD in open studies and case reports. Several medications with serotonergic effects such as fenfluramine (Hollander et al., 1990; Hollander & Liebowitz, 1988; Judd, Chua, Lynch, & Norman, 1991), trazodone (Hermesh, Alzenberg, & Munitz, 1990; Prasad, 1984), and tryptophan (Rasmussen, 1984; Yaryura-Tobias & Bhagavan, 1977) have been reported to be effective as augmentation agents in patients with OCD. Pretreatment with the anticonvulsant valproate (Deltito, 1994) has been reported to be effective in the treatment of patients with OCD who are refractory to conventional anti-OCD medications. There have also been reports that the atypical neuroleptic risperidone (Jacobsen, 1995; McDougle

TABLE 15.6
Augmentation Regimens*

OCD + tics: haloperidol beneficial
OCD + depression: lithium reduces depressive symptoms
OCD + anxiety: clonazepam reduces anxiety

*Adjuvant agent added to clomipramine or SRI in controlled trials with OCD patients

et al., 1994), the corticosteroid inhibitor aminoglutethimide (Chouinard, Belanger, Beauclair, Sultan, & Murphy, 1996), and the adrenergic blocker clonidine (Hollander, Fay, & Liebowitz, 1988; Lipsedge & Prothero, 1987), are effective augmentation strategies for treatment-refractory OCD patients stabilized on SRI therapy.

These results suggest that, with the exception of OCD patients with comorbid tics or Tourette's syndrome (McDougle et al., 1994), controlled trials have failed to support the routine use of augmentation agents in most OCD patients. Some augmenting agents such as clonazepam (Pigott, L'Heureux, Bernstein, Rubenstein, et al., 1992) have provided evidence of enhanced anxiolytic and possibly anti-OCD benefit when combined with ongoing SRI medication in patients with OCD. However, additional controlled studies are necessary before the specific indications for augmentation strategies can be determined (Table 15.6).

Alternative Primary Agents

A number of medications have been suggested as alternatives for patients with OCD who fail to respond to SRI medications. A double-blind, crossover comparison of buspirone versus clomipramine (Pato et al., 1991) was conducted in 20 patients with primary OCD (*DSM–III* criteria). Similar and significant reductions in OCD symptoms were associated with buspirone (mean dose = 58 mg/day) and clomipramine (mean dose = 225 mg/day) administration during the study. Although these results are surprising, several issues should be considered when interpreting the results of this study: the duration of medication treatment was only 6 weeks, and a significant order effect prevented analyses of the results from the second half of the study. In addition, an open trial failed to support the efficacy of buspirone in OCD (Jenike & Baer, 1988). These results suggest that a trial of buspirone may be reasonable in patients with OCD who fail to respond to conventional pharmacotherapy, but compelling evidence that buspirone is effective in most patients with OCD is currently absent.

MAOI antidepressants should be considered in OCD patients who fail to respond to standard pharmacotherapeutic interventions. Although trials of the MAOIs phenelzine (Jain et al., 1970) and clorgyline (Insel et al.,

1983) were ineffective in reducing OCD symptoms, a more recent study (Vallejo, Olivares, Marcos, Bulbena, & Menchon, 1992) reported beneficial results. Phenelzine (75 mg/day) and clomipramine (225 mg/day) were associated with significant and similar reductions in OCD symptoms in the double-blind, placebo-controlled study conducted in 30 patients with OCD (Vallejo et al., 1992). In addition, open studies have suggested that MAOIs may be particularly beneficial in patients with OCD who have primary somatic and bowel obsessions or concurrent social phobia, panic disorder, or somatic and bowel obsessions (Carrasco et al., 1992; Jenike, 1982; Jenike & Rauch, 1994; Jenike et al., 1983).

Several reports suggest that the benzodiazepine clonazepam may possess efficacy in OCD (Bacher, 1990; Bodkin & White, 1989; Hewlett, Vinogradov, & Agras, 1990, 1992; Pigott, L'Heureux, Bernstein, Rubenstein, et al., 1992). A controlled, crossover design study (Hewlett et al., 1992) compared clonazepam, diphenhydramine (Benadryl), clomipramine, and clonidine in patients with OCD. Clonazepam, diphenhydramine, and clomipramine, but not clonidine, were associated with significant reductions in OCD symptoms from baseline. These results are intriguing, but several methodological issues complicate the interpretation of these results: (a) the interval between the medication treatments was variable for each patient; and (b) the medication used as an active control (i.e., placebo), diphenhydramine, resulted in significant reductions in OCD symptoms. Nonetheless, these results coupled with evidence from case reports and the previously discussed augmentation study suggest that clonazepam represents a reasonable alternative for patients with OCD refractory to SRI treatment.

Although several reports have suggested that trazodone is beneficial in patients with OCD (Hermesh et al., 1990; Kim, 1987; Lydiard, 1986; Prasad, 1984, 1985), a controlled trial (Pigott, L'Heureux, Rubenstein, et al., 1992) found no difference between trazodone and placebo administration in 18 patients with OCD. Preliminary results from an open trial of another phenylpiperazine, nefazodone, were also discouraging. However, the 5-HT2 agonist, m-chlorophenylpiperazine, was associated with significant reductions in OCD symptoms from baseline in a controlled comparison with clomipramine (Pigott, L'Heureux, Bernstein, Grover, et al., 1992).

Combined Pharmacotherapy

Combined clomipramine–SRI or SRI–SRI regimens have been the focus of considerable interest recently. Despite apparent widespread clinical use, there have been few case reports of combined clomipramine and SRI treatment for OCD (Browne, Horn, & Jones, 1993; Simeon, Thatte, & Wiggins, 1990). This combined strategy may offer certain advantages such as: (a) enhanced tolerability (attenuation of SRI activation or insomnia with low-dose clomipramine or sedating SRI); (b) lower dose and reduced cost of medication (concomitant administration of SRI will raise plasma concentration of clomipramine); and (c) increased efficacy (synergistic effects?). Although promising, further studies are needed to address this potential new strategy.

Summary: Strategies for Treatment-Refractory OCD

A number of factors such as inaccurate diagnoses, presence of complicating, concurrent psychiatric disorders, and inadequate duration and dosage should be considered in any patient with OCD who appears resistant to standard pharmacotherapy. An OCD patient should not be considered resistant to first-line pharmacotherapy unless he or she has failed to respond to separate trials ($\geq$ 10 weeks in duration and at the maximum tolerated dose) of clomipramine and at least three of the four SRIs (fluoxetine, fluvoxamine, sertraline, and paroxetine). Unfortunately, a substantial portion (20% to 25%) of patients with OCD will fail to respond to standard first-line pharmacotherapy with SRI medications. Augmentation strategies and MAOI monotherapy should be considered in patients with OCD who fail to respond to SRI therapy. SRI augmentation with a neuroleptic appears to be particularly beneficial in OCD patients with comorbid tic disorders. However, controlled trials of other augmentation strategies suggest that further, significant reductions in OCD symptoms are rare in most patients with OCD. MAOI monotherapy may be particularly beneficial to OCD patients with concurrent anxiety disorders. Although preliminary, combined SRI treatment may also represent a promising alternative for patients with refractory OCD. Future research is needed to conduct controlled trials of promising treatment alternatives for OCD such as combined SRI regimens, identify new pharmacologic strategies for treatment-resistant patients, and identify predictors of treatment response.

REFERENCES

American Psychiatric Association. (1987). *Diagnostic and statistical manual of mental disorders* (3rd ed., rev.). Washington, DC: Author.

American Psychiatric Association. (1994). *Diagnostic and statistical manual of mental disorders* (4th ed.). Washington, DC: Author.

Ananth, J. (1986). Clomipramine: An antiobsessive drug. *Canadian Journal of Psychiatry, 31,* 253–258.

Ananth, J., Pecknold, J., van den Steen, N., & Engelsmann, F. (1981). Double-blind study of clomipramine and amitriptyline in obsessive neurosis. *Progress in Neuropsychopharmacology, 5,* 257–262.

Ananth, J., Solyom, L., & Solyom, C. (1975). Doxepin in the treatment of obsessive-compulsive disorder. *Psychosomatics, 16,* 185–187.

Asberg, M., Thoren, P., & Bertilsson, L. (1982). Clomipramine treatment of obsessive-compulsive disorder: Biochemical and clinical aspects. *Psychopharmacology Bulletin, 18*(3), 13–21.

Austin, L., Lydiard, R., Fossey, M., Zealberg, J., Laraia, M., & Ballenger, J. (1990). Panic and phobic disorders in patients with OCD. *Journal of Clinical Psychiatry, 51*(11), 456–458.

Bacher, N. (1990). Clonazepam treatment of OCD. *Journal of Clinical Psychiatry, 51,* 168–169.

Baer, L. (1994). Factor analysis of symptom subtypes of obsessive-compulsive disorder and their relation to personality and tic disorders. *Journal of Clinical Psychiatry, 55,* 18–23.

Barr, L., Goodman, W., Price, L., McDougle, C., & Charney, D. (1992). The serotonin hypothesis of obsessive-compulsive disorder: Implications of pharmacologic challenge studies. *Journal of Clinical Psychiatry, 53*(4), 17–28.

Benfield, D., Harris, C., & Luscombe, D. (1980). Some psychopharmacological aspects of desmethylclomipramine. *Postgraduate Medicine, 56*(1), 13–18.

Benfield, P., & Ward, A. (1986). Fluvoxamine: A review of its pharmacokinetic properties and therapeutic efficacy in depression. *Drugs, 32,* 313–334.

Bodkin, A., & White, K. (1989). Clonazepam in the treatment of OCD. *Journal of Clinical Psychiatry, 50,* 265–266.

Browne, M., Horn, E., & Jones, T. (1993). The benefits of clomipramine-fluoxetine combination in OCD. *Canadian Journal of Psychiatry, 38,* 242–243.

Carrasco, J., Hollander, E., Schneier, F., & Liebowitz, M. (1992). Treatment outcome of OCD with comorbid social phobia. *Journal of Clinical Psychiatry, 53,* 387–391.

Chouinard, G., Belanger, M., Beauclair, L., Sultan, S., & Murphy, B. (1996). Potentiation of fluoxetine by aminoglutethimide, an adrenal steroid suppressant in OCD resistant to SSRIs: A case report. *Progress in Neuropsychopharmacology and Biological Psychiatry, 20,* 1067–1079.

Clomipramine Collaborative Study Group (1991). Clomipramine in the treatment of patients with OCD. *Archives of General Psychiatry, 48,* 730–738.

Crewe, H., Lennard, M., Tucker, G., Woods, F., & Haddock, R. E. (1992). The effect of selective serotonin re-uptake inhibitors on cytochrome P4502D6 activity in human liver microsomes. *British Journal of Clinical Pharmacology, 34,* 262–265.

Croisile, B., Tourniaire, D., Confavreux, C., Trillet, M., & Aimard, G. (1989). Bilateral damage to the head of the caudate nuclei. *Annals of Neurology, 25,* 313–314.

Deltito, J. (1994). Valproate pretreatment for the difficult to treat patient with OCD. *Journal of Clinical Psychiatry, 55,* 500.

DeVane, C. (1994). Pharmacogenetics and drug metabolism of newer antidepressant agents. *Journal of Clinical Psychiatry, 55*(12), 38–45.

DeVeaugh-Geiss, J., Katz, R., Landau, P., Goodman, W., & Rasmussen, S. (1990). Clinical predictors of treatment response in OCD: Exploratory analyses from multi-center trials of clomipramine. *Psychopharmacology Bulletin, 26,* 54–59.

DeVeaugh-Geiss, J., Landau, P., & Katz, R. (1989). Preliminary results from a multi-center trial of clomipramine in OCD. *Psychopharmacology Bulletin, 25*(2), 36–40.

Dominguez, R. (1992). Serotonergic antidepressants and their efficacy in OCD. *Journal of Clinical Psychiatry, 53*(10), 56–59.

Dupont, R. L., Rice, D. P., Shiraki, S., & Rowland, C. R. (1995). Pharmacoeconomics: Economic costs of OCD. *Medical Interface, 4,* 102–109.

Erzegovesi, S., Rhonchi, P., & Smeraldi, E. (1992). 5-HT2 receptor and fluvoxamine effect in OCD. *Human Psychopharmacology, 7,* 287–289.

Feder, R. (1988). Lithium augmentation of clomipramine. *Journal of Clinical Psychiatry, 49,* 458.

Flament, M., & Bisserbe, J. C. (1997). Pharmacologic treatment of OCD: Comparative studies. *Journal of Clinical Psychiatry, 58*(12), 18–22.

Flament, M., Rapaport, J., Murphy, D., Lake, C., & Berg, C. (1987). Biochemical changes during clomipramine treatment of childhood obsessive-compulsive disorder. *Archives of General Psychiatry, 44,* 219–225.

Foa, E., & Kozak, M. (1995). DSM–IV field trial: Obsessive-compulsive disorder. *American Journal of Psychiatry, 152*(1), 90–96.

Fontaine, R., & Chouinard, G. (1989). Fluoxetine in the longterm maintenance treatment of OCD. *Psychiatric Annals, 19,* 88–91.

Freeman, C., Trimble, M., Deakin, J., Stokes, T., & Ashford, J. (1994). Fluvoxamine versus clomipramine in the treatment of OCD: A multi-center, randomized, double-blind, parallel group comparison. *Journal of Clinical Psychiatry, 55,* 301–305.

Frenkel, A., Rosenthal, J., Nezu, A., & Winston, A. (1990). Efficacy of long-term fluoxetine treatment of OCD. *Mt. Sinai Journal of Medicine, 57*(6), 348–352.

Golden, R., Morris, J., & Sack, D. (1988). Combined lithium-tricyclic treatment of OCD. *Biological Psychiatry, 23,* 181–185.

Goodman, W., Kozak, M., Liebowitz, M., & White, K. (1996). Treatment of OCD with fluvoxamine: A multicentre, double-blind, placebo-controlled trial. *International Journal of Clinical Psychopharmacology, 11,* 21–30.

Goodman, W., McDougle, C., & Price, L. (1992). Pharmacotherapy of obsessive-compulsive disorder. *Journal of Clinical Psychiatry, 53*(4), 29–37.

Goodman, W., & Price, L. (1990). Rating scales for OCD. In M. Jenike, L. Baer, & W. Minichiello (Eds.), *Obsessive-compulsive disorders: Theory and management* (pp. 154–166). St. Louis, MO: Mosby Year Book.

Goodman, W., Price, L., Rasmussen, S., Mazure, C., Delgado, P., Heninger, G. R., & Charney, D. S. (1989). The Yale–Brown Obsessive Compulsive Scale (Y–BOCS): II. Validity. *Archives of General Psychiatry, 46,* 1012–1016.

Goodman, W. K., Price, L. H., Rasmussen, S. A., Delgado, P. L., Heninger, G. R., & Charney, D. S. (1989). Efficacy of fluvoxamine in OCD: A double-blind comparison with placebo. *Archives of General Psychiatry, 46,* 36–42.

Goodman, W. K., Price, L. H., Rasmussen, S. A., Mazure, C., Fleischmann, R. L., Hill, C. L., Heninger, G. R., & Charney, D. S. (1989). The Yale–Brown Obsessive Compulsive Scale (Y–BOCS): I. Development, use, and reliability. *Archives of General Psychiatry, 46,* 1006–1011.

Grady, T. A., Pigott, T. A., L'Heureux, F., Hill, J. L., Bernstein, S. E., & Murphy, D. L. (1993). A double-blind study of adjuvant buspirone hydrochloride in fluoxetine-treated patients with OCD. *American Journal of Psychiatry, 150,* 819–821.

Greist, J., Chouinard, G., DuBoff, E., Halaris, A., Kim, S., Koran, L., Liebowitz, M., Lydiard, R., Rasmussen, S., & White, K. (1995). Double-blind parallel comparison of three dosages of sertraline and placebo in outpatients with OCD. *Archives of General Psychiatry, 52,* 289–295.

Greist, J., Jefferson, J., Kobak, K., Chouinard, G., DuBoff, E., Halaris, A., Kim, S., Koran, L., Liebowitz, M., & Lydiard, R. (1995). A 1-year double-blind placebo-controlled fixed dose study of sertraline in the treatment of OCD. *International Journal of Clinical Psychopharmacology, 10,* 57–65.

Greist, J., Jefferson, J., Kobak, K., Katzelnick, D., & Serlin, R. (1995). Efficacy and tolerability of serotonin transport inhibitors in obsessive-compulsive disorder: A meta-analysis. *Archives of General Psychiatry, 52,* 53–60.

Hall, H., & Ogren, S. (1981). Effects of antidepressant drugs on different receptors in the rat brain. *European Journal of Pharmacology, 70,* 393–407.

Hermesh, H., Aizenberg, D., & Munitz, H. (1990). Trazodone treatment in clomipramine-resistant OCD. *Clinical Neuropharmacology, 13,* 322–328.

Hewlett, W., Vinogradov, S., & Agras, W. (1990). Clonazepam treatment of obsessions and compulsions. *Journal of Clinical Psychiatry, 51*, 158–161.

Hewlett, W., Vinogradov, S., & Agras, W. (1992). Clomipramine, clonazepam, and clonidine treatment of OCD. *Journal of Clinical Psychopharmacology, 12*, 420–430.

Hollander, E., DeCaria, C., Schneider, F., Schneier, F., Schneier, H., Liebowitz, M., & Klein, D. (1990). Fenfluramine augmentation of serotonin reuptake blockade antiobsessional treatment. *Journal of Clinical Psychiatry, 51*, 119–123.

Hollander, E., Fay, M., & Liebowitz, M. (1988). Clonidine and clomipramine in OCD. *American Journal of Psychiatry, 145*, 388–389.

Hollander, E., & Liebowitz, M. (1988). Augmentation of antiobsessional treatment with fenfluramine. *American Journal of Psychiatry, 145*, 1314–1315.

Hollander, E., Mullen, L., DeCaria, C., Skodol, A., Schneier, F., Liebowitz, M., & Klein, D. (1991). OCD, depression, and fluoxetine. *Journal of Clinical Psychiatry, 52*, 418–422.

Hollander, E., Schiffman, E., Cohen, B., River Stein, A., Rosen, W., Gorman, J., Fyer, A., Papp, L., & Liebowitz, M. (1990). Signs of central nervous system dysfunction in obsessive-compulsive disorder. *Archives of General Psychiatry, 48*, 278–279.

Howland, R. (1991). Lithium augmentation of fluoxetine in the treatment of OCD and major depression: A case report. *Canadian Journal of Psychiatry, 36*, 154–155.

Insel, T., Mueller, E., Alterman, I., Linnoila, M., & Murphy, D. (1985). Obsessive-compulsive disorder and serotonin: Is there a connection? *Biological Psychiatry, 20*, 1174–1188.

Insel, T., Murphy, D., Cohen, R., Alterman, I., Kilts, C., & Linnoila, M. (1983). OCD: A double-blind trial of clomipramine and clorgyline. *Archives of General Psychiatry, 40*, 605–612.

Jacobsen, E. (1995). Risperidone for refractory OCD (case report). *Journal of Clinical Psychiatry, 56*, 423–429.

Jain, V., Swinson, R., & Thomas, J. (1970). Phenelzine in obsessional neurosis. *British Journal of Psychiatry, 117*, 237–238.

Jenike, M. (1982). Use of monoamine oxidase inhibitors in OCD. *British Journal of Psychiatry, 140*, 159.

Jenike, M. (1992). Pharmacologic treatment of obsessive-compulsive disorder. *Psychiatric Clinics of North America, 15*, 895–919.

Jenike, M., & Baer, L. (1988). Buspirone in OCD: An open trial. *American Journal of Psychiatry, 145*, 1285–1286.

Jenike, M., Baer, L., & Buttolph, L. (1991). Buspirone augmentation of fluoxetine in patients with OCD. *Journal of Clinical Psychiatry, 52*, 13–14.

Jenike, M. A., Baer, L., & Greist, J. H. (1990). Clomipramine versus fluoxetine in obsessive-compulsive disorder: A retrospective comparison of side effects and efficacy. *Journal of Clinical Psychopharmacology, 10*, 122–124.

Jenike, M., Hyman, S., Baer, L., Holland, A., Minichiello, W., Buttolph, L., Summergrad, P., Seymour, R., & Ricciardi, J. (1989). A controlled trial of fluvoxamine in OCD: Implications for a serotonergic theory. *American Journal of Psychiatry, 147*, 1209–1215.

Jenike, M., & Rauch, S. (1994). Managing the patient with treatment-resistant obsessive-compulsive disorder: Current strategies. *Journal of Clinical Psychiatry, 55*, 11–17.

Jenike, M., Surman, O., Cassem, N., Zusky, P., & Anderson, W. (1983). Monoamine oxidase inhibitors in OCD. *Journal of Clinical Psychiatry, 44*, 131–132.

Judd, F., Chua, P., Lynch, C., & Norman, T. (1991). Fenfluramine augmentation of clomipramine treatment of OCD. *Australian and New Zealand Journal of Psychiatry, 25*, 412–414.

Karno, M., Golding, J., Sorenson, S., & Burnam, M. (1988). The epidemiology of obsessive-compulsive disorder in five U.S. communities. *Archives of General Psychiatry, 45*, 1094–1099.

Kasvikis, Y., & Marks, I. (1988). Clomipramine in obsessive-compulsive ritualizers treated with exposure therapy: Relations between dose, plasma levels, outcome, and side effects. *Psychopharmacology, 95,* 113–118.

Katz, R., DeVeaugh-Geiss, J., & Landau, P. (1990). Clomipramine in OCD. *Biological Psychiatry, 28*(5), 401–414.

Kettle, P., & Marks, I. (1986). Neurological factors in obsessive-compulsive disorder: Two case reports and a review of the literature. *British Journal of Psychiatry, 149,* 315–319.

Kim, S. (1987). Trazodone in the treatment of OCD. *Journal of Clinical Psychopharmacology, 7,* 278–288.

Koe, B., Weissman, A., Welch, W., & Browne, R. G. (1983). Sertraline, a new uptake inhibitor with selectivity for serotonin. *Journal of Pharmacology and Experimental Therapeutics, 226,* 686–670.

Koizumi, H. (1985). Obsessive-compulsive symptoms following stimulants. *Biological Psychiatry, 20,* 1332–1333.

Koran, L., McElroy, S., Davidson, J., Rasmussen, S., Hollander, E., & Jenike, M. (1996). A double-blind, multicenter comparison of fluvoxamine and clomipramine in patients with OCD. *Journal of Clinical Psychopharmacology, 16,* 121–129.

Leonard, H., Swedo, S., Lenane, M., Rettew, D., Cheslow, D., Hamburger, S., & Rapaport, J. (1991). A double-blind desipramine substitution during long-term clomipramine treatment in children and adolescents with obsessive-compulsive disorder. *Archives of General Psychiatry, 48,* 922–927.

Leonard, H., Swedo, S., Rapoport, J., Coffey, M., & Cheslow, D. (1988). Treatment of childhood obsessive-compulsive disorder with clomipramine and desmethyl-imipramine: A double-blind crossover comparison. *Psychopharmacology Bulletin, 24,* 43–45.

Levine, R., Hoffman, J., Knepple, E., & Kenin, M. (1989). Long-term fluoxetine treatment of a large number of obsessive-compulsive disorder. *Journal of Clinical Psychopharmacology, 9,* 281–283.

Lipsedge, M., & Prothero, W. (1987). Clonidine and clomipramine in OCD. *American Journal of Psychiatry, 144,* 965–966.

Lydiard, R. (1986). OCD successfully treated with trazodone. *Psychsomatics, 27,* 858–859.

Markovitz, P., Stagno, S., & Calabrese, J. (1990). Buspirone treatment of fluoxetine in OCD. *American Journal of Psychiatry, 147,* 798–800.

Mavissakalian, M., Jones, B., Olson, S., & Perel, J. M. (1990). Clomipramine in obsessive-compulsive disorder: Clinical response and plasma level. *Journal of Clinical Psychopharmacology, 5,* 207–212.

McDougle, C., Fleischmann, R., Epperson, C., Wasylink, S., Leckman, J., & Price, L. (1995). Risperidone addition in fluvoxamine-refractory OCD: Three cases. *Journal of Clinical Psychiatry, 56,* 526–528.

McDougle, C., Goodman, W., Leckman, J., Holzer, J., Barr, L., McCance-Katz, E., Heninger, G., & Price, L. (1993). Limited therapeutic effect of the addition of buspirone in fluvoxamine-refractory OCD. *American Journal of Psychiatry, 150,* 647–649.

McDougle, C., Goodman, W., Leckman, J., Lee, N., Heninger, G., & Price, L. (1994). Haloperidol addition in fluvoxamine-refractory obsessive-compulsive disorder: A double-blind, placebo-controlled study in patients with and without tics. *Archives of General Psychiatry, 51,* 302–308.

McDougle, C., Price, L., Goodman, W., Charney, D., & Heninger, G. (1991). A controlled trial of lithium augmentation in fluvoxamine-refractory obsessive-compulsive disorder: Lack of efficacy. *Journal of Clinical Psychopharmacology, 11,* 175–184.

Montgomery, S. (1980). Clomipramine in obsessional neurosis. *Pharmacological Medicine, 1,* 189–192.

Montgomery, S., McIntyre, A., Osterheider, M., Sarteschi, P., Zitterl, W., Zohar, J., Birkett, M., & Wood, A. (1993). A double-blind, placebo-controlled study of fluoxetine in patients with DSM–III–R OCD. *European Neuropsychopharmacology, 3*(2), 143–152.

Nierenberg, A., & Cole, J. (1992). Antidepressant adverse drug reactions. *Journal of Clinical Psychiatry, 52*(6), 40–47.

Pato, M., Hill, J., & Murphy, D. (1990). A clomipramine dosage reduction study in the course of long-term treatment of OCD patients. *Psychopharmacology Bulletin, 26,* 211–214.

Pato, M. T., Pigott, T. A., Hill, J. L., Grover, G. N., Bernstein, S. E., & Murphy, D. L. (1991). Controlled comparison of buspirone and clomipramine in obsessive-compulsive disorder. *American Journal of Psychiatry, 148,* 127–129.

Pato, M., Zohar-Kadouch, R., Zohar, J., & Murphy, D. (1988). Return of symptoms after discontinuation of clomipramine in patients with obsessive-compulsive disorder. *American Journal of Psychiatry, 145,* 1521–1525.

Piccinelli, M., Pini, S., Bellantuono, C., & Wilkinson, G. (1995). Efficacy of drug treatment in OCD: A meta-analytic review. *British Journal of Psychiatry, 166,* 424–443.

Pigott, T. A. (1996). OCD: Where the serotonin selectivity story begins. *Journal of Clinical Psychiatry, 57,* 11–20.

Pigott, T. A., L'Heureux, F., Bernstein, S. E., Grover, G. N., Dubbert, B., Hill, J. L., & Murphy, D. L. (1992, May). *A controlled comparison of clomipramine and m-chlorophenylpiperazine in patients with OCD.* Paper presented at the NCDEU Annual Meeting, Key Biscayne, FL.

Pigott, T., L'Heureux, F., Bernstein, S., Rubenstein, C., Dubbert, B., & Murphy, D. (1992). A controlled trial of adjuvant clonazepam in clomipramine and fluoxetine treated patients with OCD. In *145th Annual American Psychiatric Association Meeting, NR 144* (p. 82). Washington, DC: American Psychiatric Press.

Pigott, T., L'Heureux, F., Dubbert, B., Bernstein, S., & Murphy, D. (1994). Obsessive-compulsive disorder: Comorbid conditions. *Journal of Clinical Psychiatry, 55*(10), 15–27.

Pigott, T. A., L'Heureux, F., Hill, J. L., Bihari, K., Bernstein, S. E., & Murphy, D. L. (1992). A double-blind study of adjuvant buspirone hydrochloride in clomipramine-treated OCD patients. *Journal of Clinical Psychopharmacology, 12,* 11–18.

Pigott, T., L'Heureux, F., & Murphy, D. (1993, March). Pharmacological approaches to treatment-resistant OCD patients. Paper presented at the *1st International OCD Conference Abstracts, Isle of Capri (Italy)* (pp. 123–125).

Pigott, T. A., L'Heureux, F., Rubenstein, C. S., Bernstein, S. E., Hill, J. L., & Murphy, D. L. (1992). A double-blind, placebo controlled study of trazodone in patients with obsessive-compulsive disorder. *Journal of Clinical Psychopharmacology, 12*(3), 156–162.

Pigott, T. A., Pato, M. T., Bernstein, S. E., Grover, G. N., Hill, J. L., Tolliver, T. J., & Murphy, D. L. (1990). Controlled comparisons of clomipramine and fluoxetine in the treatment of obsessive-compulsive disorder. *Archives of General Psychiatry, 47,* 1543–1550.

Pigott, T. A., Pato, M. T., L'Heureux, F., Hill, J. L., Grover, G. N., Bernstein, S. E., & Murphy, D. L. (1991). A controlled comparison of adjuvant lithium carbonate or thyroid hormone in clomipramine-treated OCD patients. *Journal of Clinical Psychopharmacology, 11*(4), 242–248.

Pigott, T., & Seay, S. (in press). Comparable efficacy of SSRIs in OCD. *Journal of Clinical Psychiatry.*

Prasad, A. (1984). OCD and trazodone. *American Journal of Psychiatry, 141,* 612–613.

Prasad, A. (1985). Efficacy of trazodone as an antiobsessional agent. *Pharmacology, Biochemistry, and Behavior, 22,* 347–348.

Rasmussen, S. (1984). Lithium and tryptophan augmentation in clomipramine-resistant OCD. *American Journal of Psychiatry, 141,* 1283–1285.

Rasmussen, S., & Eisen, J. (1990). Epidemiology and clinical features of OCD. In M. Jenike, L. Baer, & W. Minichiello (Eds.), *Obsessive-compulsive disorders: Theory and management* (pp. 10–27). St. Louis, MO: Mosby Year Book.

Rasmussen, S., & Eisen, J. (1992). The epidemiology and clinical features of obsessive-compulsive disorder. *Psychiatric Clinics of North America, 15*(4), 743–758.

Rosse, R., Fay-McCarthy, M., Collins, J., Risher-Flowers, D., Alim, T., & Deutsch, S. (1993). Transient compulsive foraging behavior associated with crack cocaine use. *American Journal of Psychiatry, 150*, 155–156.

Simeon, J., Thatte, S., & Wiggins, D. (1990). Treatment of adolescent OCD with a clomipramine-fluoxetine combination. *Psychopharmacology Bulletin, 26*, 285–290.

Smeraldi, E., Erzegovesi, S., Bianchi, I., Bellodi, L., Sciuto, G., & Diaferia, G. (1992). Fluvoxamine versus clomipramine treatment in OCD: A preliminary study. *New Trends in Experimental and Clinical Psychiatry, 8*, 63–65.

Smeraldi, E., Mundo, E., & Erzegovesi, S. (1992). 5-HT3 receptor and antiobsessional effect. *Human Psychopharmacology, 7*, 291–292.

Steiner, M., Bushnell, W., Gergel, I., & Wheadon, D. (1995, May). *Long-term treatment and prevention of relapse of OCD with paroxetine.* Paper presented at the annual meeting of the American Psychiatric Association, Miami, FL.

Stern, R., Marks, I., Wright, J., & Luscombe, D. (1980). Clomipramine: Plasma levels, side effects, and outcome in obsessive-compulsive neurosis. *Postgraduate Medical Journal, 56*(Suppl. 1), 134–139.

Thoren, P., Asberg, M., Bertilsson, L., Mellstrom, B., Sjoqvist, F., & Traskman, L. (1980). Clomipramine treatment of OCD: II. Biochemical aspects. *Archives of General Psychiatry, 37*, 1289–1294.

Thoren, P., Asberg, M., Crohnholm, B., Jornestedt, L., & Trachman, L. (1980). Clomipramine treatment of obsessive-compulsive disorder: I. A controlled clinical trial. *Archives of General Psychiatry, 37*, 1281–1285.

Tollefson, G., Birkett, M., Koran, L., & Genduso, L. (1994). Continuation treatment of OCD: Double-blind and open-label experience with fluoxetine. *Journal of Clinical Psychiatry, 55*, 69–78.

Tollefson, G., Rampey, A., Potvin, J., Jenike, M., Rush, A., Dominguez, R., Koran, L., Shear, M., Goodman, W., & Genduso, L. (1994). A multi-center investigation of fixed-dose fluoxetine in the treatment of obsessive-compulsive disorder. *Archives of General Psychiatry, 51*(7), 559–567.

Vallejo, J., Olivares, J., Marcos, T., Bulbena, A., & Menchon, J. (1992). Clomipramine versus phenelzine in obsessive-compulsive disorder: A controlled clinical trial. *British Journal of Psychiatry, 161*, 665–670.

Volavka, J., Neziroglu, F., & Yaryura-Tobias, J. (1985). Clomipramine and imipramine in obsessive-compulsive disorder. *Psychiatry Research, 14*, 85–93.

Wheadon, D., Bushnell, W., & Steiner, M. (1993, December). *A fixed-dose comparison of 20, 40, or 60 mg paroxetine to placebo in the treatment of obsessive-compulsive disorder.* Paper presented at the American College of Neuropsychopharmacology (ACNP) annual meeting, San Juan, PR.

Wong, D., Bymaster, F., Reid, L., & Threlkeld, P. (1983). Fluoxetine and two other serotonin uptake inhibitors without affinity for neuronal receptors. *Biochemistry and Pharmacology, 32*, 1287–1293.

Yaryura-Tobias, J., & Bhagavan, H. (1977). L-tryptophan in OCD. *American Journal of Psychiatry, 134*, 1298–1299.

Zohar, J., & Insel, T. (1987). Obsessive-compulsive disorder: Psychobiological approaches to diagnosis, treatment, and pathophysiology. *Biological Psychiatry, 22*, 667–687.

16

Preferential Efficacy of Serotonergic Medication in Obsessive-Compulsive Disorder: From Practice to Theory

Iulian Iancu
Pinhas N. Dannon
Michal Lustig
Yehuda Sasson
Joseph Zohar
Sheba Medical Center, Tel Hashomer Tel Aviv University

Until the early 1980s, obsessive-compulsive disorder (OCD) was considered a treatment-refractory, chronic condition of psychological origins. Treatment strategies included dynamic psychotherapy, which in general was of little benefit, and a variety of pharmacological treatments that had been tried without much success (Salzman & Thaler, 1981). The observation that clomipramine, a tricyclic antidepressant with a serotonergic profile, is effective in treating symptoms of OCD has resulted in intense interest in the relation between serotonin and this disorder (Fernandez-Cordoba & Lopez-Ibor, 1967; Renynghe de Voxrie, 1968; Yaryura-Tobias, Neziroglu, & Bergman, 1976).

Today, substantial evidence suggests that OCD is unique among psychiatric disorders as only serotonergic medications appear to be effective in treating this disorder (Dolberg, Iancu, Sasson, & Zohar, 1996). Nonserotonergic drugs, such as desipramine, a potent antidepressant and antipanic agent, are ineffective in treating OCD (Goodman et al., 1990; Leonard et al., 1991; Zohar & Insel, 1987). In this chapter, we present the clinical data supporting the unique response to selective serotonin reuptake inhibitors (SSRIs) and the implications of these well-established clinical findings to the development of the hypothesis that dysregulation of serotonergic neurons is the underlying etiology of OCD.

THE ROLE OF SEROTONIN IN DEPRESSION
AND ANXIETY DISORDERS

The major evidence for serotonin (5-HT) alterations in depression and anxiety derives from the symptomatic change following treatments that alter the serotonergic system. The utilization of SSRIs such as fluoxetine, fluvoxamine, paroxetine, sertraline, and citalopram, of 5-HT precursors such as L-tryptophan and 5-HT receptor agonists, such as buspirone, has provided some evidence that 5-HT function may be altered in depression and anxiety.

Certainly, many alterations in 5-HT function have been demonstrated in depression and anxiety (Heninger, 1995), but because of the complicated interdependency of the 5-HT system with other neurotransmitters and biochemical systems, these changes may easily be secondary to more primary abnormalities in other systems. In many instances, active treatments that alter 5-HT function are known to produce beneficial therapeutic effects even though abnormalities of the 5-HT system have not been clearly demonstrated for that clinical condition (e.g., treatment with serotonergic drugs for diabetic neuropathy; Heninger, 1995).

Serotonergic and noradrenergic drugs are equally effective in treating depressive symptoms (Anderson & Tomenson, 1994). Current evidence does not support the hypothesis that depression is associated with a primary disorder in only one neurotransmitter system (e.g., serotonin or norepinephrine). However, biological subtypes may exist and some patients may respond to a serotonergic drug, whereas others will respond only to a noradrenergic drug. Overall, the rate of response is equal for serotonergic and noradrenergic drugs.

For panic disorder, there is also evidence for efficacy of both serotonergic and noradrenergic drugs (Johnson, Lydiard, & Ballenger, 1995). However, serotonergic drugs have gained wider acceptance in the treatment of these patients and this is not only due to a reduction in their spectrum of side effects. Interestingly, the SSRI zimelidine was found to be superior to imipramine in treating panic disorder patients (Evans, Kenardy, Schneider, & Hoey, 1986). Similarly, the tricyclic clomipramine, which combines potent serotonin uptake inhibition with some noradrenergic uptake inhibition, has been shown not only to be an effective antipanic treatment (Johnston, Troyer, & Whitsett, 1988), but may also be more effective than imipramine (Modigh, Westberg, & Eriksson, 1992). This suggests that the efficacy of imipramine is probably related to its serotonin reuptake inhibition effect, rather than to its noradrenergic effect. This possibility is supported by the finding that the plasma level of imipramine, but not of desipramine, was correlated with clinical improvement in panic patients. That is, improvement correlated with the more serotonergic imipramine rather than with the predominantly noradrenergic agent desipramine (Mavissakalian, Perez, & Michelson, 1984).

OCD is the primary psychiatric disorder that displays a clearly specific response to serotonergic drugs rather than to noradrenergic drugs (Dolberg et al., 1996). This specificity has been found in other psychiatric illnesses, such as trichotillomania, onychophagia, and autism, in which clomipramine was reported to be more effective than desipramine (Swedo, Leonard, & Rapoport, 1989). The specific response to serotonergic drugs has paved the way to further research on the pathogenesis of OCD and OCD-related disorders, and needless to say, has improved the prognoses of these patients.

THE PHARMACOLOGICAL TREATMENT OF OCD

The outlook for the treatment of patients with OCD was not very promising in the early 1980s. However, since then, several potent serotonin reuptake inhibitors (SRIs) have been studied extensively in OCD. Aggregate statistics for all SRIs suggest that 70% of treatment-naive patients will improve at least moderately (Rasmussen & Pato, 1993).

Amongst the variety of medications used in the treatment of OCD patients, clomipramine was the first to be studied. Clomipramine was reported to be an effective medication for OCD in the late 1960s (Fernandez-Cordoba & Lopez-Ibor, 1967; Renynghe de Voxrie, 1968). Since then, numerous placebo-controlled studies have clearly shown the drug's effectiveness (Ananth, Pecknold, Van den Steen, & Engelsmann, 1981; Flament et al., 1985; Insel et al., 1983; Marks, Stern, Mawson, Cobb, & McDonald, 1980; Montgomery, 1980; Thoren, Asberg, Gronholm, Jornestedt, & Traskman, 1980; Volavka, Neziroglu, & Yaryura-Tobias, 1985; Zohar & Insel, 1987). This research direction culminated in the multicenter, controlled U.S. trial ($N = 520$) that conclusively confirmed clomipramine's effectiveness (Clomipramine Collaborative Study Group, 1991).

Besides clomipramine, other nontricyclic SRIs, such as fluoxetine (Montgomery et al., 1993; Tollefson et al., 1994), fluvoxamine (Greist, Jenike, Robinson, & Rasmussen, 1995; Mallya, White, Waternaux, & Quay, 1992), paroxetine (Wheadon, Bushnell, & Steiner, 1993; Zohar, Judge, and the OCD Paroxetine Study, 1996), and sertraline (Chouinard et al., 1990; Greist et al., 1993; Greist, Chouinard, et al., 1995) have gained acceptance as effective alternatives for the treatment of OCD.

FURTHER EVIDENCE FOR A SEROTONERGIC
MECHANISM OF ACTION

The effect of clomipramine on central monoaminergic neurons was investigated in vivo by Thoren, Asberg, Bertilsson, et al. (1980), who measured cerebrospinal fluid (CSF) concentrations of monoamine metabolites in patients with severe OCD before and after 3 weeks of treatment with clomipramine. They reported that patients who responded to clomipramine had higher pretreatment levels of 5-hydroxyindoleacetic acid (5-HIAA, a metabolite of 5-HT serving as an index of 5-HT turnover) than the nonresponders, and clinical improvement was positively correlated with the decrease in CSF concentration of 5-HIAA.

Further biochemical evidence for the role of the serotonergic system in OCD was given by Flament, Rapoport, Murphy, Berg, and Lake (1987). This group examined peripheral measures of serotonergic and noradrenergic function in adolescents with OCD participating in a double-blind, placebo-controlled study with clomipramine. Flament et al. reported that clinical improvement during drug therapy closely correlated with pretreatment platelet serotonin concentration and monoamine oxidase (MAO) activity, as well as with the decrease in both measures during clomipramine administration. These findings suggested that the effects of clomipramine on serotonin function are pertinent to the antiobsessional action observed.

Additional support for the importance of serotonin in the pathophysiology of OCD was given by Benkelfat et al. (1989). This group of investigators administered the serotonin receptor antagonist metergoline and placebo to 10 patients with OCD in a double-blind crossover study. Patients receiving clomipramine on a long-term basis responded with greater anxiety to a 4-day administration of metergoline when compared to the placebo phase. Obsessive-compulsive (OC) symptoms also peaked during the metergoline phase. Metergoline lowered plasma prolactin concentrations, providing further evidence of physiologically significant 5-HT antagonism.

EFFICACY OF SEROTONERGIC VERSUS
ADRENERGIC ANTIDEPRESSANTS

Anecdotal reports have suggested that clinical benefit can be obtained with a range of antidepressant medications, but consistent effectiveness has only been demonstrated for the SRIs. Although the superiority of clomipramine to placebo in the treatment of OCD is well documented, fewer studies have directly compared clomipramine to other drugs classified as antidepressants. Nonetheless, a consistent pattern emerges: Antidepressant drugs that are less potent SRIs than clomipramine are generally ineffective in treating OCD (Ananth et al., 1981; Insel et al., 1983; Leonard et al., 1989; Thoren, Asberg, Gronholm, et al., 1980; Zohar & Insel, 1987).

For example, in one double-blind study, clomipramine but not nortryptiline (a weak SRI) was significantly better than placebo in reducing the severity of OC symptoms (Thoren, Asberg, Gronholm, et al., 1980). Imipramine, for example, was reported to be of lesser efficacy compared to clomipramine (Volavka et al., 1985). In two additional double-blind crossover trials, clomipramine was found to be more effective than the relatively selective norepinephrine reuptake inhibitor desipramine (Leonard et al., 1991; Zohar & Insel, 1987).

Zohar and Insel (1987) assigned 10 patients to either clomipramine or desipramine for 6 weeks, followed by a 4-week placebo phase, leading to a switch of medications. Desipramine was found to be entirely ineffective as an antiobsessional agent, whereas clomipramine was significantly potent in reducing OC symptoms.

Goodman et al. (1990) treated 40 OCD adult patients with fluvoxamine ($n = 21$) or desipramine ($n = 19$) in a double-blind study. Goodman and associates (1990) found that fluvoxamine was more effective in reducing OC symptoms. Eleven of 21 patients were responders to fluvoxamine, compared with 2 of 19 who were responders to desipramine. The researchers concluded that their findings strengthen the hypothesis that inhibition of serotonin neural transport is relevant to antiobsessive efficacy.

Leonard et al. (1989) compared the efficacy of clomipramine and desipramine in a 10-week crossover, double-blind, controlled study in children and adolescents. Clomipramine was clearly superior to desipramine in the treatment of OCD symptoms. The patients had higher Hamilton Depression scores while taking desipramine and lower scores while on clomipramine, possibly due to superimposed depression on the OCD. In this study, 64% of patients receiving clomipramine as their first active treatment relapsed at least partially after being switched to desipramine. However, 38% of the sample had not responded to a previous trial of tricyclic antidepressant before entering the study, which may have negatively biased the group's response to desipramine.

Leonard and associates (1991) examined the effect of desipramine substitution during a long-term clomipramine treatment in 26 children and adolescents with OCD (mean treatment duration = 17 months). All had shown improvement in their symptoms with clomipramine, which had been continued for 4 to 32 months, at a dose of 50 to 250 mg, before entry into the study. Half of the patients were blindly assigned to 2 months of desipramine treatment, and then clomipramine was reintroduced. Almost

90% relapsed during the 2-month substitution period in comparison with only 18% of those kept on clomipramine. The study confirms that long-term clomipramine treatment is necessary in young patients with OCD. Altogether these results support the hypothesis that the serotonin reuptake properties of an antidepressant agent may be crucial to its efficacy as an anti-OCD agent.

OTHER PHARMACOLOGICAL APPROACHES

The treatment of resistant OCD patients has also contributed to the understanding that serotonergic tricyclics and SSRIs are important in the management of these patients. Providing further support for the importance of serotonin neurotransmission in the pathophysiology and treatment of OCD are early observations regarding the effectiveness of isocarboxazid, and more recently phenelzine, that are MAO inhibitors having prominent effects on serotonin metabolism. In an early study, Insel et al. (1983) compared the efficacy of clomipramine and clorgyline, a MAO-A inhibitor, in a controlled crossover study in OCD patients. Although clomipramine was effective, patients on clorgyline did not improve at all. Vallejo, Olivares, Marcos, Bulbena, and Menchon (1992) conducted a controlled clinical trial of the efficacy of clomipramine and phenelzine in 30 OCD patients. They reported improvement in both groups, but the lack of placebo controls and the small size of the study groups limit the applicability of these findings.

Clonazepam, a benzodiazepine with substantial serotonin effects, has shown some benefit in treating OCD, although the weight of evidence suggests that these effects are smaller than those found with long-term clomipramine treatment. Hewlett, Vinogradov, and Agras (1992) reported in a small ($N = 28$), double-blind, randomized, multiple crossover study, that clonazepam was as effective as clomipramine and superior to diphenhydramine (a control medication). The role of trazodone and buspirone has been studied in several open studies, as well as in a few controlled trials. Thus, Hermesh, Aizenberg, and Munitz (1990) reported improvement with trazodone in nine refractory OCD patients, whereas Pigott, L'Heureux, Rubenstein, et al. (1992) did not confirm trazodone's efficacy in a controlled study ($n = 21$). Buspirone's efficacy was reported in only one double-blind study comparing it with clomipramine (Pato et al., 1991). The small number of patients in this study limits the generalizability of its findings, and indeed this efficacy was not found in further open (Jenike, Baer, & Buttolph, 1991) and controlled studies (Grady et al., 1993; McDougle et al., 1993; Pigott, L'Heureux, Hill, & Murphy, 1992).

Fenfluramine, a serotonergic agent known to release serotonin into the synapse and also to block its reuptake, has been reported to alleviate OCD symptoms when used in combination with SSRI treatment (Hollander et al., 1990; Judd, Chua, Lynch, & Norman, 1991). However, controlled studies are needed to confirm fenfluramine's efficacy in this disorder. Lithium, which also has serotonergic activity, has shown efficacy in several case studies (Rasmussen, 1984) without confirmation in a double-blind study (McDougle, Price, Goodman, Charney, & Heninger, 1991). Due to the well-known limitations of open studies and the overrepresentation of positive reports in these studies, double-blind studies are crucial to conclusions on the efficacy of drugs in OCD.

SUMMARY

The treatment of OCD was characterized by pessimism until the mid-1980s, when effective treatments using behavior therapy and SRIs were developed. Although introduced for OCD in 1967, it was only in the 1980s that double-blind studies confirmed the efficacy of clomipramine, an SRI, for this disorder. This was followed by the further introduction of SSRIs, which also proved effective for OCD patients (Greist, Jefferson, Kobak, Katzelnick, & Serlin, 1995). The antiobsessive activity of these drugs was found to be independent from the drugs' antidepressant effect, as established by efficacy both in depressed and nondepressed patients. Overall, serotonergic therapies have enabled a better outlook for these patients and have increased our understanding of the pathophysiology of this disorder (Dolberg et al., 1996; Zohar & Insel, 1987).

Previously thought to be a rare and untreatable disorder, OCD is now recognized as common, and there is now good reason to expect that OCD patients will benefit substantially from behavior therapy and potent SRIs. Unfortunately, some OCD patients do not seek treatment and the disease tends to be chronic.

The efficacy of the SRIs together with the lack of efficacy on the part of adrenergic antidepressants as medications for OCD have suggested that serotonin is involved in the pathophysiology of OCD. This relation was validated only later by research on serotonergic markers in OCD and by the challenge paradigm (Dolberg et al., 1996).

Which type of serotonergic receptor is involved in the pathogenesis or the mechanism of action of antiobsessional drugs is yet unclear. The studies of Lesch et al. (1991) with ipsapirone, a 5-HT1A ligand, have shown that ipsapirone had no notable effect on behavioral measures, nor did it produce thermoregulatory and neuroendocrine responses that were significantly different from the placebo. Moreover, the lack of therapeutic effectiveness of the 5HT1A agent buspirone (Jenike et al., 1991) adds to the impression that this receptor is not involved in the pathophysiology and management of OCD.

However, it is important to stress that not all serotonergic drugs are effective in treating this disorder. Thus, the serotonin precursor tryptophan exhibited only mixed efficacy (Mattes, 1986; Rasmussen, 1984). Further studies of the serotonergic system involvement in OCD are crucial to elucidating the role of this neurotransmitter in the pathophysiology and management of OCD.

REFERENCES

Ananth, J., Pecknold, J. C., van den Steen, N., & Engelsmann, F. (1981). Double blind comparative study of clomipramine and amitriptyline in obsessive neurosis. *Progress in Neuropsychopharmacology and Biological Psychiatry, 5*, 257–262.

Anderson, I. M., & Tomenson, B. M. (1994). The efficacy of selective serotonin reuptake inhibitors in depression: A meta-analysis of studies against tricyclic antidepressants. *Journal of Psychopharmacology, 8*, 238–249.

Benkelfat, C., Murphy, D. L., Zohar, J., Hill, J. L., Grover, G., & Insel, T. R. (1989). Clomipramine in obsessive compulsive disorder: Further evidence for a serotonergic mechanism of action. *Archives of General Psychiatry, 46*, 23–28.

Chouinard, G., Goodman, W. K., Greist, J., Jenike, M., Rasmussen, S., White, K., Hackett, E., Gaffney, M., & Bick, P. A. (1990). Results of a double-blind placebo controlled trial of a new serotonin reuptake inhibitor, sertraline, in the treatment of obsessive compulsive disorder. *Psychopharmacology Bulletin, 26*, 279–284.

Clomipramine Collaborative Study Group. (1991). Clomipramine in the treatment of patients with obsessive compulsive disorder. *Archives of General Psychiatry, 48*, 730–738.

Dolberg, O. T., Iancu, I., Sasson, Y., & Zohar, J. (1996). The pathogenesis and treatment of obsessive compulsive disorder. *Clinical Neuropharmacology, 19*, 129–147.

Evans, L., Kenardy, J., Schneider, P., & Hoey, H. (1986). Effect of a selective serotonin uptake inhibitor in agoraphobia with panic attacks: A double-blind comparison of zimelidine, imipramine and placebo. *Acta Psychiatrica Scandinavica, 73*, 49–53.

Fernandez-Cordoba, E., & Lopez-Ibor, A. J. (1967). La monoclorimiprimina en enfermos psiquiatricos resistentes a otros tratamientos [Monochlorimipramine in the treatment of psychiatric patients resistant to other treatments]. *Actas Luso Espanolas Neurologia Psiquiatria y Ciencias Afinas, 26*, 119–147.

Flament, M. F., Rapoport, J. L., Berg, C. J., Sceery, W., Kilts, C., Mellstrom, B., & Linnoila, M. (1985). Clomipramine treatment of childhood obsessive compulsive disorder: A double-blind study. *Archives of General Psychiatry, 42*, 977–983.

Flament, M. F., Rapoport, J. L., Murphy, D. L., Berg, C. J., & Lake, C. R. (1987). Biochemical changes during clomipramine treatment of childhood obsessive compulsive disorder. *Archives of General Psychiatry, 44*, 219–225.

Goodman, W. K., Price, L. H., Delgado, P. L., Palumbo, J., Krystal, J. H., Nagy, L. N., Rasmussen, S. A., Heninger, G. R., & Charney, D. S. (1990). Specificity of serotonin reuptake inhibitors in the treatment of obsessive compulsive disorder: Comparison of fluvoxamine and desipramine. *Archives of General Psychiatry, 47*, 577–585.

Grady, T. A., Pigott, T. A., L'Heureux, F., Hill, J. L., Bernstein, S. E., & Murphy, D. L. (1993). Double-blind study of adjuvant buspirone for fluoxetine-treated patients with obsessive-compulsive disorder. *American Journal of Psychiatry, 150,* 819–821.

Greist, J. H., Chouinard, G., DuBoff, E., Halaris, A., Kim, S., Koran, L., Liebowitz, M., Lydiard, R., McElroy, S., Mendels, J., Rasmussen, S., & Flicker, C. (1993, June). *Long-term sertraline treatment of obsessive compulsive disorder.* Paper presented at the Ninth World Congress of Psychiatry, Rio de Janeiro, Brazil.

Greist, J., Chouinard, G., DuBoff, E., Halaris, A., Kim, S. W., Koran, L., Liebowitz, M., Lydiard, R. B., Rasmussen, S., White, K., & Sikes, C. (1995). Double blind parallel comparison of three doses of sertraline and placebo in outpatients with obsessive compulsive disorder. *Archives of General Psychiatry, 52,* 289–295.

Greist, J. H., Jefferson, J. W., Kobak, K. A., Katzelnick, D. J., & Serlin, R. C. (1995). Efficacy and tolerability of serotonin transport inhibitors in obsessive compulsive disorder: A meta-analysis. *Archives of General Psychiatry, 52,* 53–60.

Greist, J. H., Jenike, M. A., Robinson, D., & Rasmussen, S. A. (1995). Efficacy of fluvoxamine in obsessive-compulsive disorder: Results of a multicentre, double-blind placebo-controlled trial. *European Journal of Clinical Research, 7,* 195–204.

Heninger, G. R. (1995). The role of serotonin in clinical disorders. In F. E. Bloom & D. J. Kupfer (Eds.), *Psychopharmacology: The fourth generation of progress* (pp. 471–482). New York: Raven.

Hermesh, H., Aizenberg, D., & Munitz, H. (1990). Trazodone treatment of clomipramine resistant obsessive compulsive disorder. *Clinical Neuropharmacology, 13,* 322–328.

Hewlett, W. A., Vinogradov, S., & Agras, W. S. (1992). Clomipramine, clonazepam, and clonidine treatment of obsessive-compulsive disorder. *Journal of Clinical Psychopharmacology, 12,* 420–430.

Hollander, E., DeCaria, C. M., Schneier, F., Schneier, H., Liebowitz, M. R., & Klein, D. F. (1990). Fenfluramine augmentation of serotonin reuptake blockade antiobsessional treatment. *Journal of Clinical Psychiatry, 51,* 119–123.

Insel, T. R., Murphy, D. L., Cohen, R. M., Alterman, I., Kilts, C., & Linnoila, M. (1983). Obsessive-compulsive disorder: A double-blind trial of clomipramine and clorgyline. *Archives of General Psychiatry, 40,* 605–612.

Jenike, M. A., Baer, L., & Buttolph, L. (1991). Buspirone augmentation of fluoxetine in patients with obsessive compulsive disorder. *Journal of Clinical Psychiatry, 52,* 13–14.

Johnson, M. R., Lydiard, R. B., & Ballenger, J. C. (1995). Panic disorder: Pathophysiology and drug treatment. *Drugs, 49,* 328–344.

Johnston, D., Troyer, I., & Whitsett, S. (1988). Clomipramine treatment of agoraphobic women. *Archives of General Psychiatry, 45,* 453–459.

Judd, F. K., Chua, P., Lynch, C., & Norman, T. (1991). Fenfluramine augmentation of clomipramine treatment of obsessive compulsive disorder. *Australian and New Zealand Journal of Psychiatry, 25,* 412–414.

Leonard, H. L., Swedo, S. E., Lenane, M. C., Rettew, D. C., Cheslow, D. L., Hamburger, S. D., & Rapoport, J. L. (1991). A double-blind desipramine substitution during long-term clomipramine treatment in children and adolescents with obsessive compulsive disorder. *Archives of General Psychiatry, 48,* 922–927.

Leonard, H. L., Swedo, S. E., Rapoport, J. L., Koby, E., Lenane, M. C., Cheslow, D. L., & Hamburger, S. D. (1989). Treatment of obsessive compulsive disorder with clomipramine and desipramine in children and adolescents: A double-blind crossover comparison. *Archives of General Psychiatry, 46,* 1088–1092.

Lesch, K. P., Hoh, A., Disselkamp-Tietze, J., Wiesmann, M., Osterheider, M., & Schultz, H. M. (1991). 5-hydroxytryptamine 1A receptor responsivity in obsessive compulsive disorder: Comparison of patients and controls. *Archives of General Psychiatry, 48,* 540–547.

Mallya, G. K., White, K., Waternaux, C., & Quay, S. (1992). Short and long-term treatment of obsessive compulsive disorder with fluvoxamine. *Annals of Clinical Psychiatry, 4,* 77–80.

Marks, I. M., Stern, R. S., Mawson, D., Cobb, J., & McDonald, R. (1980). Clomipramine and exposure for obsessive compulsive rituals. *British Journal of Psychiatry, 136,* 1–25.

Mattes, J. A. (1986). A pilot study of combined trazodone and tryptophan in obsessive-compulsive disorder. *International Clinical Psychopharmacology, 1,* 170–173.

Mavissakalian, M., Perez, J., & Michelson, L. (1984). The relationship of plasma imipramine and N-desmethylimipramine to improvement in agoraphobia. *Journal of Clinical Psychopharmacology, 4,* 36–40.

McDougle, C. J., Goodman, W. A., Leckman, J. F., Holzer, J. C., Barr, L. C., McCance-Katz, E., Heninger, G. R., & Price, L. H. (1993). Limited therapeutic effect of addition of buspirone in fluvoxamine-refractory obsessive-compulsive disorder. *American Journal of Psychiatry, 150,* 647–649.

McDougle, C. J., Price, L. H., Goodman, W. K., Charney, D. S., & Heninger, G. R. (1991). A controlled trial of lithium augmentation in fluvoxamine-refractory obsessive-compulsive disorder: Lack of efficacy. *Journal of Clinical Psychopharmacology, 11,* 175–184.

Modigh, K., Westberg, P., & Eriksson, E. (1992). Superiority of clomipramine over imipramine in the treatment of panic disorder: A placebo-controlled trial. *Journal of Clinical Psychopharmacology, 12,* 251–261.

Montgomery, S. A. (1980). Clomipramine in obsessional neurosis: A placebo controlled trial. *Pharmaceutical Medicine, 1,* 189–192.

Montgomery, S. A., McIntyre, A., Osterheider, M., Sarteschi, P., Zitterl, W., Zohar, J., Birkett, M., Wood, A. J., & the Lilly European OCD Study Group. (1993). A double-blind, placebo-controlled study of fluoxetine in patients with DSM–III–R obsessive-compulsive disorder. *European Neuropsychopharmacology, 3,* 143–152.

Pato, M. T., Pigott, T. A., Hill, J. L., Grover, G. N., Bernstein, S., & Murphy, D. L. (1991). Controlled comparison of buspirone and clomipramine in obsessive-compulsive disorder. *American Journal of Psychiatry, 148,* 127–129.

Pigott, T. A., L'Heureux, F., Hill, J. L., & Murphy, D. L. (1992). A double-blind study of adjuvant buspirone hydrochloride in clomipramine-treated patients with obsessive-compulsive disorder. *Journal of Clinical Psychopharmacology, 12,* 11–18.

Pigott, T. A., L'Heureux, F., Rubenstein, C. S., Bernstein, S. E., Hill, J. L., & Murphy, D. L. (1992). A double-blind, placebo controlled study of trazodone in patients with obsessive compulsive disorder. *Journal of Clinical Psychopharmacology, 12,* 156–162.

Rasmussen, S. A. (1984). Lithium and tryptophan augmentation in clomipramine-resistant obsessive compulsive disorder. *American Journal of Psychiatry, 141,* 1283–1285.

Rasmussen, S. A., & Pato, M. T. (1993). Current issues in the pharmacologic management of obsessive compulsive disorder. *Journal of Clinical Psychiatry, 53,* 4–10.

Renynghe de Voxrie, G. V. (1968). Anafranil (G4586) in obsessive compulsive neurosis. *Archiva Neurologica Belgica, 68,* 787–792.

Salzman, L., & Thaler, F. H. (1981). Obsessive compulsive disorder: A review of the literature. *American Journal of Psychiatry, 138,* 286–296.

Swedo, S. E., Leonard, H. L., & Rapoport, J. L. (1989). A double-blind comparison of clomipramine and desipramine in the treatment of trichotillomania (hair pulling). *New England Journal of Medicine, 321,* 497–501.

Thoren, P., Asberg, M., Bertilsson, L., Mellstrom, B., Sjoqvist, F., & Traskman, L. (1980). Clomipramine treatment of obsessive compulsive disorder: Biochemical aspects. *Archives of General Psychiatry, 37,* 1289–1294.

Thoren, P., Asberg, M., Gronholm, B., Jornestedt, L., & Traskman, L. (1980). Clomipramine treatment of obsessive compulsive disorder: A controlled clinical trial. *Archives of General Psychiatry, 37,* 1281–1285.

Tollefson, G. D., Rampey, A. H., Potvin, J. H., Jenike, M. A., Rush, A. J., Dominguez, R. A., Koran, L. M., Shear, M. K., Goodman, W., & Genduso, L. A. (1994). A multicenter investigation of fixed-dose fluoxetine in the treatment of obsessive-compulsive disorder. *Archives of General Psychiatry, 51,* 559–567.

Vallejo, J., Olivares, J., Marcos, T., Bulbena, A., & Menchon, J. M. (1992). Clomipramine versus phenelzine in obsessive compulsive disorder. A controlled clinical trial. *British Journal of Psychiatry, 161,* 665–670.

Volavka, J., Neziroglu, F., & Yaryura-Tobias, J. A. (1985). Clomipramine and imipramine in obsessive compulsive disorder. *Psychiatry Research, 14,* 85–93.

Wheadon, D. E., Bushnell, W. D., & Steiner, M. (1993, December). *A fixed dose comparison of 20, 40, or 60mg paroxetine to placebo in the treatment of obsessive compulsive disorder.* Poster presented at the American College of Neuropharmacology Meeting, San Juan, PR.

Yaryura-Tobias, J. A., Neziroglu, F., & Bergman, L. (1976). Chlorimipramine for obsessive-compulsive neurosis: An organic approach. *Current Therapy Research, 20,* 541–548.

Zohar, J., & Insel, T. R. (1987). Obsessive compulsive disorder: Psychobiological approaches to diagnosis, treatment and pathophysiology. *Biological Psychiatry, 22,* 667–687.

Zohar, J., Judge, R., & the OCD Paroxetine Study. (1996). Paroxetine versus clomipramine in the treatment of obsessive compulsive disorder. *British Journal of Psychiatry, 172,* 468–475.

17

Clomipramine in the Treatment of Obsessive-Compulsive Disorder

Joseph DeVeaugh-Geiss
Glaxo Wellcome Inc.

Richard Katz
Novartis Pharmaceuticals Corporation

It has now been more than a decade since the initiation of the first industry-sponsored, multicenter, clinical investigations of a pharmacologic treatment for obsessive-compulsive disorder (OCD). This clinical development program was conceived in early 1986 and that summer the clinical trials were begun, under the sponsorship of CIBA-Geigy. At that time, because of very limited availability of effective treatments, it was difficult to successfully treat OCD. Behavioral therapy was an option for some patients, and a variety of pharmacologic approaches had been tried with varying degrees of success, but in the 1980s no medication had yet received U.S. Food and Drug Administration approval for treatment of OCD. Indeed, it is no exaggeration to say that OCD was mainly regarded at that time as a treatment-refractory disorder. It is, therefore, a privilege to be able to review here the development of the first drug approved in the United States for the treatment of OCD, and to know that the approval of clomipramine, and other drugs that followed, has contributed to a change in status for this disorder, from a mainly treatment-refractory to a mainly treatable condition.

HISTORY OF CLOMIPRAMINE

The development of clomipramine represents a combination of rational drug discovery at a preclinical level and clinical serendipity. At the time of the drug's development, CIBA had introduced the first tricyclic antidepressant, imipramine, and Geigy had introduced two structurally and therapeutically related drugs, opipramol and desipramine. Thus, antidepressant effects associated with the iminodibenzyl nucleus were clinically established, and the major remaining psychopharmacological goal for this structural series was therapeutic optimization. The specific approach employed in the case of clomipramine rested on structural analogy with the phenothiazine nucleus. The iminodibenzyl and phenothiazine ring structures are similar, and prior demonstration that addition of a three-position chlorine to the latter transformed a sedative antihistamine to a specific antipsychotic made the homologous substitution of particular interest. Structurally, clomipramine is to imipramine what chlorpromazine is to promazine.

Initial antidepressant findings for clomipramine were to a substantial degree predictable and, indeed, clinically confirmed. However, a broader and unanticipated spectrum of psychopharmacological activity was noted quite early in clinical trials. In particular, within the year following its first registration, anecdotal reports recognized significant antiphobic and antiobsessional effects for clomipramine (Fernandez-Cordoba & Lopez-Ibor Alino, 1967; Jimenez-Garcia, 1967; Lopez-Ibor Alino, 1969; Marshall, 1971). Among these early anecdotal reports, 36 to 61 patients were reported to have improved (Ananth, 1985). Although findings of improvement were generally consistent, some failures were noted (e.g., Laboucarie, Rascol, Jorda, Guraud, & Leinadier, 1967). In addition, even positive findings required substantial qualification. Findings generally represented clinical impressions only, in populations frequently admixed with other anxiety states or depression. For example, Escobar, Teeter, Tuason, and Schiele (1976), in a study of depressives, noted improvements on the OC item of an extended Hamilton Depression Rating Scale (HDRS). These early trials had a dual significance. They established a need to investigate the effects of clomipramine in a spectrum of phobic-anxiety states under better controlled conditions. Moreover, the issues identified in early investigations—therapeutic specificity, diagnostic overlap, and measurement of specific improvement—set the stage philosophically and methodologically for two decades of increasingly sophisticated clinical investigations.

CONTROLLED CLINICAL TRIALS PRIOR TO 1990

In 1980, five reports of controlled clinical trials with clomipramine appeared. Jaskari (1980) compared clomipramine ($n = 9$), mianserin ($n = 10$), and placebo ($n = 6$) in a double-blind, randomized, parallel-group study of

4 weeks' duration. Both clomipramine and mianserin were found to be superior to placebo. Marks, Stern, Mawson, Cobb, and McDonald (1980) compared clomipramine (n = 20) and placebo (n = 20) in a randomized, parallel-group design of 10 weeks' duration. Clomipramine was found to be superior to placebo. Montgomery (1980) compared clomipramine and placebo in a crossover design (n = 14) with 4 weeks of exposure to each treatment arm, finding clomipramine superior to placebo. Thoren, Asberg, Cronholm, Jornestedt, and Traskman (1980) compared clomipramine, nortriptyline, and placebo (n = 8 per group) in a randomized, parallel-group design of 5 weeks' duration. Both clomipramine and nortriptyline were superior to placebo. A preliminary report by Rapoport, Elkins, and Mikkelsen (1980) of a randomized, crossover study in children and adolescents found no significant differences between clomipramine and desmethylimipramine. Subsequent reports from this same group, however, demonstrated the effectiveness of clomipramine in the child and adolescent population in two 5-week, randomized, crossover design studies. The first (Flament et al., 1985), compared clomipramine and placebo (n = 19), and the second trial (Leonard et al., 1989) compared desmethylimipramine and clomipramine (n = 48). In these studies, clomipramine was found to be superior to placebo and desmethylimipramine.

Additional reports of clomipramine's effectiveness in controlled studies with adult patients appeared throughout the 1980s. Ananth, Pecknold, Van Den Steen, and Engelsmann (1981) compared clomipramine and amitriptyline in a 4-week, randomized, parallel-group study (n = 10 per group). Clomipramine (n = 12), clorgyline (n = 11), and placebo (n = 12) were compared in a 6-week, randomized, crossover study (Insel et al., 1983). Clomipramine (n = 7) and placebo (n = 5) were compared in a 12-week, randomized, parallel-group study (Mavissakalian, Turner, Michelson, & Jacob, 1985). Volavka, Neziroglu, and Yaryura-Tobias (1985) compared clomipramine and imipramine (n = 8 per group) in a 12-week, randomized, parallel-group study. Zohar and Insel (1987) used a randomized, crossover, six-week trial with 10 patients to compare clomipramine and desmethylimipramine. Finally, Marks et al. (1988) compared clomipramine (n = 37) and placebo (n = 12) in a 27-week randomized, parallel-group trial. In each of these trials, clomipramine-treated patients showed significant improvements compared to the control groups (placebo, amitriptyline, clorgyline, imipramine, and desmethylimipramine). Although it had been known that some OCD patients would respond to some of the antidepressant drugs, it was becoming clear during the early 1980s that the effectiveness of clomipramine in patients with OCD could be consistently and reliably demonstrated. Table 17.1 summarizes the published controlled clinical trials in OCD from 1980 to 1988.

TABLE 17.1
Controlled Trials of Clomipramine in OCD Prior to 1990

Reference	Treatments	n	Design	Outcome
Jaskari (1980)	CMI	9	Parallel	CMI > PBO
	Mianserin	10		Mianserin > PBO
	PBO	8		
Marks et al. (1980)	CMI	20	Parallel	CMI > PBO
	PBO	20		
Montgomery (1980)	CMI	14	Crossover	CMI > PBO
	PBO	14		
Rapoport et al. (1980)[a]	CMI	8	Crossover	No differences
	DMI	8		
	PBO	8		
Thoren et al. (1980)	CMI	8	Parallel	CMI > PBO
	Nortriptyline	8		Nortriptyline > PBO
	PBO	8		
Ananth et al. (1981)	CMI	10	Parallel	CMI > Amitriptyline
	Amitriptyline	10		
Insel et al. (1983)	CMI	12	Crossover	CMI > Clorgyline
	Clorgyline	11		CMI > PBO
	PBO	12		
Flament et al. (1985)[a]	CMI	19	Crossover	CMI > PBO
	PBO	19		
Mavissakalian et al. (1985)	CMI	7	Parallel	CMI > PBO
	PBO	5		
Volavka et al. (1985)	CMI	8	Parallel	CMI > Imipramine
	Imipramine	8		
Zohar & Insel (1987)	CMI	10	Crossover	CMI > DMI
	DMI	10		
Marks et al. (1988)	CMI	37	Parallel	CMI > PBO
	PBO	12		
Leonard et al. (1989)[a]	CMI	48	Crossover	CMI > DMI
	DMI	48		

Note. CMI = clomipramine; DMI = desmethylimipramine; PBO = placebo.
[a]Studies in children and adolescents; all others are adults.

CIBA-Geigy Pharmaceuticals, the inventor of clomipramine, recognized the importance of these findings from controlled clinical trials and convened a panel of OCD experts early in 1986 to discuss the methodological issues that would be confronted in initiating a drug development program in OCD. Although small-scale clinical trials were being reported in the literature, no large-scale drug development program in OCD had yet been undertaken. Furthermore, at that time OCD was still considered rare and the ability to enroll the large numbers of patients required for such a program was uncertain. The clinical trials program was initiated in the summer of 1986.

MULTICENTER, CONTROLLED CLINICAL TRIALS

Studies in Adults

Two studies in adults (Protocols 59 and 61) were sponsored by CIBA-Geigy in the United States. These were both multicenter, double-blind, randomized, parallel-group, placebo-controlled studies, designed to assess the efficacy and safety of clomipramine in the treatment of OCD. A total of 575 patients entered the two studies, 262 in Protocol 59, and 313 in Protocol 61. Patients were men and women with a diagnosis of OCD by *Diagnostic and Statistical Manual of Mental Disorders* (3rd ed., American Psychiatric Association, 1980) criteria. These studies were similar in design and included a 2-week single-blind placebo run-in, followed by randomization to either drug or placebo. Randomized treatment occurred over a period of 10 weeks, with dosing beginning at 25 mg daily and rising in 25 mg increments to 100 mg daily in the second week. Weekly increments of 50 mg were then permitted to a maximum of 250 mg daily. This maximum daily dose of 250 mg was established based on cumulative data from more than 4,000 patients treated with clomipramine in U.S. clinical studies in which a higher incidence of seizure was reported at dosages that exceeded 250 mg daily. For patients not responding to 250 mg daily, a total daily dose of 300 mg was allowed after consultation with the CIBA-Geigy clinical monitor. Approximately 30% of the clomipramine-treated patients received this higher dose.

The primary efficacy variable was the Yale–Brown Obsessive Compulsive Scale (Y–BOCS; Goodman et al., 1989a, 1989b), which was administered weekly during the study period. A number of secondary efficacy variables were also assessed. Additional details on the study design and methods have been published elsewhere (the Clomipramine Collaborative Study Group, 1991). Y–BOCS scores were compared, using analysis of covariance, for the clomipramine and placebo groups at each week of treatment.

The Y–BOCS score results from Protocols 59 and 61 are presented in Figs. 17.1 and 17.2, respectively. As the figures illustrate, there was a minimal placebo response. After 10 weeks of placebo treatment, the reductions in Y–BOCS scores from baseline were 3% and 5% in Protocols 59 and 61, respectively. The clomipramine-treated patients showed a clinically and statistically significant improvement, with statistically significant differences from placebo observed at all weeks of treatment in Protocol 59 and at Weeks 2 through 10 in Protocol 61. At Week 10 (the end of randomized treatment), the mean reductions from baseline in Y–BOCS scores for the clomipramine-treated patients were 38% in Pro-

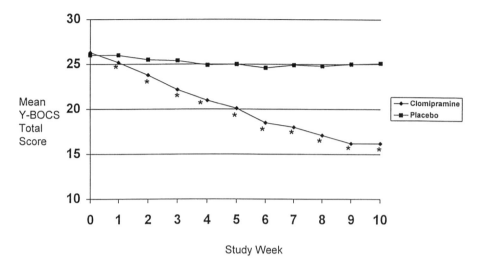

FIG. 17.1. Protocol 59—Adults (*p < .05 difference from placebo).

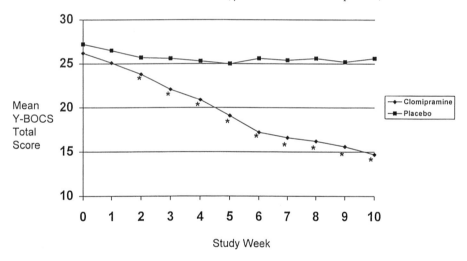

FIG. 17.2. Protocol 61—Adults (*p < .05 difference from placebo).

tocol 59 and 44% in Protocol 61. The secondary efficacy variables also showed similar improvements for clomipramine with minimal to no placebo effects (see Clomipramine Collaborative Study Group, 1991).

Adverse events were observed frequently in the clomipramine group. The most common adverse events were dry mouth, dizziness, tremor, fatigue, somnolence, and constipation. In addition, ejaculation failure was observed frequently in men treated with clomipramine. The most frequent adverse events are summarized in Table 17.2.

TABLE 17.2
Frequently Reported Medical Problems
(Percentage of Patients Reporting)[a]

	Adult Studies		Child and Adolescent Study	
Medical Problems	CMI	PBO	CMI	PBO
Dry mouth	80	17	63	16
Dizziness	53	11	41	14
Tremor	53	2	33	2
Fatigue	38	13	35	9
Somnolence	49	14	46	11
Constipation	44	9	22	2
Ejaculation failure[b]	41	4	5	0
Nausea	27	10	9	11
Increased sweating	24	2	9	0
Headache	24	16	28	34

Note. CMI = clomipramine; PBO = placebo.
[a]Includes adverse events and concomitant illnesses. [b]Male patients only.

Study in Children and Adolescents

Concurrent with Protocols 59 and 61 in adult patients, we conducted a multicenter, placebo-controlled trial (Protocol 64) of clomipramine versus placebo in a population of children and adolescents, aged 10 through 17. The study design was very similar to that of Protocols 59 and 61. Other than the difference in the age of the patients, the two important differences in this study were that the randomized treatment period was 8 weeks in duration (compared to 10 weeks in Protocols 59 and 61) and the maximum daily dose was set at 200 mg daily or 3 mg per kg, whichever was smaller. The same assessments, efficacy criteria, and statistical methods were used in Protocol 64 as described for Protocols 59 and 61, with the Y–BOCS modified for use with children and adolescents. Details of this study have been published elsewhere (DeVeaugh-Geiss et al., 1992). A total of 60 patients (31 clomipramine, and 29 placebo) were randomized to double-blind treatment and included in the efficacy analyses. The clomipramine group showed a statistically significantly greater improvement than the placebo group at Week 3 and Weeks 5 through 8. The mean reduction from baseline on the Y–BOCS score at Week 8 was 37% in the clomi-pramine group, compared with 8% reduction in the placebo group. Secondary efficacy variables showed improvements similar to those seen with the Y–BOCS and, in general, the outcome of this trial was similar to the results from the adult trials. Figure 17.3 illustrates the changes in Y–BOCS for Protocol 64. In general, the child and adolescent population

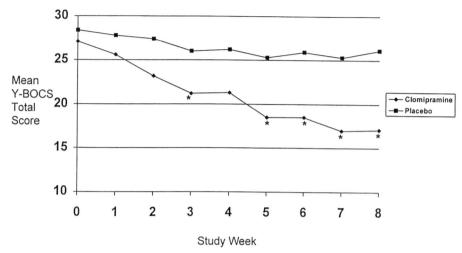

FIG. 17.3.   Protocol 64—Children and adolescents ($*p < .05$ difference from
placebo).

tolerated clomipramine as well or better than the adults. Again, the
frequently reported adverse events included dry mouth, somnolence,
dizziness, fatigue, and tremor. The percentages of patients experiencing
these adverse events were slightly lower than the percentages of the adult
patients experiencing these adverse events. Table 17.2 summarizes the
frequently reported adverse events for Protocols 59, 61, and 64.

Long-Term Efficacy

Protocols 59 and 61 were followed by a double-blind, continuation treatment phase that lasted 1 year and Protocol 64 was followed by a 1-year
open-label continuation phase. In general, during the double-blind continuation treatment in the adult protocols, there was a high rate of discontinuation in the placebo treatment groups, whereas the clomipramine
treatment groups did not experience as high a rate of discontinuation.
The disproportionate discontinuation rates precluded any statistical
analyses of these blinded continuations. Nevertheless, the continuation
phase of both adult studies demonstrated clearly that benefits observed
at the end of 10 weeks of treatment were maintained in the clomipramine
treatment groups during the 1-year period of continuation. Similarly, in
the open-label continuation of Protocol 64, the child and adolescent study,
benefits observed at Week 8 in the clomipramine-treated patients were
maintained for up to 1 year. It is not appropriate to draw any conclusions
from the continuation phases of these trials; however, benefit was maintained, as measured by Y–BOCS, and patients continued to tolerate clomipramine for the extended treatment, up to 1 year. Additionally, many

patients were allowed to participate in an open-label, humanitarian protocol and, subsequently, in a treatment Investigational New Drug (IND) protocol that permitted open-ended clomipramine treatment. Again, although it would not be appropriate to draw any conclusions, a large number of patients continued treatment for periods well beyond 1 year and continued to tolerate clomipramine well, with no apparent loss of therapeutic benefit.

SUMMARY OF CLOMIPRAMINE DEVELOPMENT PROGRAM

The clomipramine development program, initiated in 1986, was comprised of eight large clinical trials. Three of these were double-blind, placebo-controlled trials (two in adults and one in children and adolescents), three were extensions of these double-blind trials, and two offered open-label treatment (first a humanitarian protocol, then a treatment IND protocol) that enabled patients to receive clomipramine while it was still investigational. Table 17.3 summarizes these studies. The New Drug Application for clomipramine was submitted to the U.S. Food and Drug Administration in June 1989, and was approved in December 1989. Clomipramine was marketed in the United States as Anafranil® in early 1990.

COMPARISON TO OTHER SEROTONIN REUPTAKE INHIBITORS

Although direct, head-to-head comparisons of clomipramine and other treatments for OCD would give clinicians a reliable view on the relative efficacy and safety of these treatments, such studies would be large and expensive. Some small studies have attempted such comparisons, but have methodologic limitations such as not including a placebo arm. Although

TABLE 17.3
Clomipramine Phase 111 Development Program

Protocol	n	Population	Design
59	262	Adults	DB, placebo controlled, 10 weeks
59E	85	Adults	DB, extension of above, 52 weeks
61	313	Adults	DB, placebo controlled, 10 weeks
61E	127	Adults	DB, extension of above, 52 weeks
64	60	Children and adolescents	DB, placebo controlled, 8 weeks
64A	47	Children and adolescents	OL, extension of above, 52 weeks
62	498	Adults, adolescents, and children	OL, open-ended
67	>1,000	Adults, adolescents, and children	OL, open-ended, treatment IND

these types of studies are useful, they do not have the rigor of the multicenter, prospectively randomized, placebo-controlled, parallel-group design used in the assessment of these treatments for the purpose of regulatory approval. Fortunately, several serotonin reuptake inhibitors (SRIs) have been studied using the same design and methodology as the clomipramine multicenter trials. The similarity of the study designs facilitates comparison by meta-analysis, although it must be emphasized that the technique of meta-analysis is also limited and less reliable than a concurrent parallel-group comparison of two or more drugs and placebo. Greist, Jefferson, Kobak, Katzelnick, and Serlin (1995) relied on published and unpublished data from studies in OCD to compare clomipramine, fluvoxamine, fluoxetine, and sertraline. The methods and other details of this meta-analysis were described by Greist et al. (1995). They concluded that the treatment effect size for clomipramine is significantly greater than for the other SRIs. In addition, they found that there were fewer discontinuations with clomipramine. Independent analyses by Piccinelli, Pini, Bellantuono, and Wilkinson (1995) using a somewhat different database and different statistical methods appear quite similar to those of Greist et al. (1995). Because the clinical trials used in these analyses were conducted at different times, it is possible that the populations of patients recruited into these different clinical trials were not fully comparable. It is also possible that the availability of clomipramine as a treatment for OCD since 1990 could have influenced the conduct of clinical trials with other SRIs. However, most of these trials were conducted prior to the approval of clomipramine. It is also possible that the different pharmacological profile of clomipramine (i.e., not as highly selective as the other drugs for serotonin reuptake inhibition) could contribute to a different clinical profile for clomipramine. Although all of the SRIs appear to be effective in OCD, it is not certain whether some patients might respond better to one or another of these medications. Therefore, it is probably advisable that patients not responding to a selective SRI be given a trial of clomipramine before their condition is described as treatment-resistant or treatment-refractory. Additionally, because improvement continues over 8 to 10 weeks, a minimum trial of this length is required before determining that a medication is ineffective.

EFFICACY OF CLOMIPRAMINE IN OBSESSIVE-COMPULSIVE SPECTRUM DISORDERS

Hollander's identification of an obsessive-compulsive (OC) spectrum (Hollander, 1993; Hollander & Wong, 1995, chap. 1, this volume) provides a useful framework to examine additional OC-related clomipramine effects. OC spectrum disorders are a behaviorally heterogeneous group of

TABLE 17.4
Obsessive-Compulsive Spectrum Disorders

Risk spectrum
    Obsessive-compulsive disorder
    Trichotillomania/onychophagia
    Hypochondriasis (multi-/monosymptomatic)
    Body dysmorphic disorder
    Compulsive buying
    Compulsive gambling
    Sexual compulsions
Neurological spectrum
    Autism
    Huntington's disease
    Tourette's syndrome

Note. See Hollander and Wong (1995) for a full discussion of obsessive-compulsive spectrum disorders.

psychiatric conditions sharing certain clinical (e.g., recurrent thoughts and behavior) and treatment response characteristics with OCD. The OC spectrum includes a range of motive states, from risk-avoidant compulsivity (e.g., hypochondriasis) to risk-seeking impulsivity (e.g., compulsive gambling or sexual compulsions). Although individual conditions are rare, the OC spectrum is a broad one, and up to 10% of the U.S. population may be affected. Table 17.4 provides a list of relevant spectrum conditions. Of these, clomipramine has been reported to be of clinical benefit in hypochondriasis, dysmorphophobia, trichotillomania, onychophagia, pathological gambling and sexual exhibitionism, and autism. Additional benefits have been reported for two other extended-spectrum disorders: posttraumatic stress disorder (PTSD) and stuttering.

Effects on OC Spectrum Compulsive Behaviors (Risk-Averse Types)

There are no well-controlled studies of clomipramine in hypochondriasis. Three case reports suggest that the drug may be of benefit in multi- or monosymptomatic hypochondriasis. For example, a 31-year-old man suffered from debilitating chronic fears of fatal illness (heart attack, AIDS, brain tumor). His hypochondriasis resulted in frequent emergency room visits and severe restriction of his ability to work and travel (due to a need to be near medical facilities). Treatment with a variety of anxiolytics, antidepressants, lithium, and antipsychotics did not ameliorate his preoccupation. Fluoxetine 40 mg produced a limited response, whereas clomipramine 200 to 225 mg allowed a gradual reduction of worries and emergency room visits accompanied by employment seeking (Stone,

1993). Similar findings were noted for a 26-year-old man with monosymptomatic delusions of genital retraction ("koro") who did not respond to pimozide. After a suicide attempt, he received 200 mg of clomipramine daily and improved to an essentially symptom-free state (Fernando, 1988). Similarly, a 41-year-old woman with a monosymptomatic delusion of emitting a bad odor was treated first with pimozide and then with trazodone, with limited success in each trial. However, after a suicide attempt, 200 mg of clomipramine daily produced a resolution of depression and the odor obsession (Ross, Siddiqui, & Matas, 1987). These cases are anecdotal but consistent, and are characterized by a general failure of other classes of drugs, notably antipsychotics. In an open trial involving several SRIs, including clomipramine, Hollander, Liebowitz, Winchel, Klumker, and Klein (1989) also reported improvement in several cases of body dysmorphic disorder, which is also a somatoform disorder.

Effects on OC Spectrum Impulse Disorders
(Neuroethological and Risk Seeking Types)

Compulsive hair pulling and nail biting resemble OCD in sharing a core impulsivity with a repetitive and highly stereotyped behavioral focus. In a 10-week double-blind trial of clomipramine in comparison with desmethylimipramine in 13 women with trichotillomania, clomipramine was clinically and statistically superior to desmethylimipramine in improving hair pulling symptoms and severity, as well as associated anxiety and depression. In addition, nine patients received long-term clomipramine treatment. At 4 to 5 months, symptoms for these patients remained significantly reduced, with three patients essentially free of symptoms (Swedo et al., 1989). A subsequent report indicates some variability in degree of sustained improvement (Pollard et al., 1991).

Compulsive nail biting is a distinct but related spectrum disorder. In their report of clomipramine versus desmethylimipramine treatment for adolescent OCD, Leonard, Lenane, Swedo, Rettwe, and Rapoport (1991) noted a clomipramine-specific reduction in compulsive nail biting (onychophagia). As a consequence they conducted a double-blind, crossover trial of clomipramine with desmethylimipramine in a population of non-OC nail biters. This trial was characterized by a high proportion of discontinuations (14 completers out of 25 patients); however, for completers, clomipramine was more effective in reducing nail biting. The authors suggest that findings for hair pulling and nail biting are consistent with an ungoverned neuroethological mechanism for grooming. Indeed, this appears to be directly confirmed in a veterinary setting, at least for the case of canine acral lick dermatitis (Goldberger & Rapoport, 1991).

Effects of clomipramine on sexual impulse disorders have been investigated in a variety of settings. A double-blind crossover trial compared clomipramine with desmethylimipramine in a relatively small and heterogeneous group of paraphiliacs (Kruesi, Fine, Valladares, Phillips, & Rapoport, 1992). The trial was characterized by a substantial discontinuation rate (8 completers out of 15 patients randomized) and, in counterdistinction to OCD and other spectrum conditions, by nondifferential improvement across treatments. Absence of a differential response across conditions may, in part, reflect patient characteristics and exigencies of trial conduct; however, this also may indicate a possible difference in response pattern in comparison with other spectrum disorders.

Four other case reports suggest that clomipramine may be of benefit in sexual impulse disorders including exhibitionism, obsessive sexual preoccupations, and paraphilic conditions. For example, a man with a 10-year history of exhibitionism and multiple arrests was treated with 150 mg of clomipramine. The drive to expose himself diminished over 3 to 4 weeks, but returned on brief discontinuation (Wawrose & Sisto, 1992). Similar outcomes in a total of four patients, including one with sadomasochistic acting out, have been reported by two other groups (Casals-Ariet & Cullen, 1993; Rubey, Brady, & Norris, 1993). In addition, severe and compulsive sexual preoccupations in two patients remitted within 2 to 3 weeks following initiation of clomipramine treatment. Specifically for the treatment of sexual disorders, one factor that may affect both the onset of therapeutic effect and willingness to continue therapy is the presence of anorgasmia as a side effect. Several of the case reports noted this effect as potentially contributory. Finally, clomipramine has also been reported to improve symptoms of obsessional jealousy (Stein, Hollander, & Josephson, 1994) and possibly compulsive gambling (Hollander, Frenkel, DiCaria, Trungold, & Stein, 1992).

Clomipramine in OC Spectrum-Neurologic and Extended Spectrum Disorders

Autism and a variety of tic disorders (e.g., Tourette's syndrome) are included as neurologic disorders within an OC spectrum. Neither PTSD nor stuttering currently are formally included within an OC spectrum, although each of the latter shares certain key elements with spectrum diseases. PTSD entails a core pathological reexperiencing, including recurrent intrusive images and memories. Stuttering involves a disruption of fluency due to repeated stereotyped utterances. Clomipramine has been demonstrated to be of some benefit in each of these conditions.

Twelve autistic patients participated in a double-blind crossover trial of clomipramine versus desmethylimipramine and a second group of 12 patients was exposed to clomipramine versus a placebo (Gordon, Rapoport, Hamburger, State, & Mannheim, 1992; Gordon, State, Nelson, Hamburger, & Rapoport, 1993). Clomipramine was superior to both placebo and desmethylimipramine on symptom ratings (including stereotypes) and ritualized behaviors. Both drugs were equally superior to placebo in reducing hyperactivity. Two other preliminary reports are consistent with effects on autistic stereotypy (Brasic et al., 1994; McDougle et al., 1992).

Gordon et al. (1995) also compared clomipramine and desmethylimipramine in a randomized crossover trial in 17 psychiatrically normal stutterers. Clomipramine was superior on 5 of 10 self-report measures including severity and preoccupation. The intrusive reexperiencing of significant aspects of a traumatic event in the context of PTSD may qualitatively resemble intrusive images of OCD. In a brief trial, clomipramine reduced obsession and intrusion scores of six of seven war veterans with PTSD (Chen, 1991). Findings from these reports including well-controlled trials suggest that clomipramine may be effective in both OCD and a variety of OC spectrum disorders, and possibly within extensions of the OC spectrum.

ANCILLARY STUDIES AND PREDICTION OF THERAPEUTIC OUTCOME

At the time the CIBA-Geigy pivotal trials for clomipramine in OCD were initiated, both CIBA-Geigy and the clinical investigators recognized the unusual and potentially unique opportunities afforded in creating a large national data set of OCD patients. This recognition led to an early commitment to support a series of collaborative and individual efforts among investigators. Table 17.5 recognizes the breadth of these efforts. We focus here on possible modifiers of therapeutic responsiveness.

Initial examination of the CIBA-Geigy data set indicated a general absence of factors that might predict outcome. Age, sex, illness severity

TABLE 17.5
Ancillary Studies From the CIBA Pivotal Trials

Scale properties and validation
Family study-risks, heritability
Brain abnormalities-neuropsychological, soft signs
Physiological changes-psychophysiology, arousal
Personality and outcome
Baseline predictors of outcome, demographics, depression
Other predictors of outcome-adverse effects, plasma levels
Biological concomitants of OCD

or chronicity, and proportion of obsessions versus compulsions failed to predict a differential clomipramine response. A clinically significant correlation with initial severity of depression on the HDRS was noted (De-Veaugh-Geiss, Katz, Landau, Goodman, & Rasmussen, 1990). Subsequent logistic regression analyses by Ackerman and colleagues (Ackerman, Greenland, Bystritsky, & Katz, 1996; Ackerman, Greenland, Bystritsky, Morgenstern, & Katz, 1994) identified two predictors of response. Patients with later onset of illness tended to have better outcomes to treatment with clomipramine, and patients with relatively low or high HDRS scores fared better than patients with intermediate scores. In a separate study, Baer et al. (1992) noted an influence of initial degree of personality pathology and Cluster A pathology on poorer outcome. Although all findings are limited by the methodological constraints inherent in assembling a relatively homogeneous group of patients for study, they nonetheless suggest some possible basis for differential sensitivity to treatment.

CONCLUSIONS

The large multicenter trials of clomipramine in OCD suggest several paradoxes inherent in the drug development process. Examination of Table 17.1 suggests that 12 of 13 published trials antedating Protocols 59 and 61 had demonstrated clinical benefit for the drug. The pivotal trials were more than large-scale replicates, however. Beyond any immediate notions of proof of efficacy they established a technology of assessment that was subsequently applied to other compounds (e.g., fluvoxamine, fluoxetine, sertraline, etc.).

One unexpected finding was the continuing improvement over 10 weeks of treatment with clomipramine. This observation has had considerable impact on the design of subsequent clinical trials and the clinical management of OCD.

The trials additionally established a large representative database that allowed several outstanding unresolved issues to be revisited; for example, the role of depression in outcome and the influence of personality factors.

The trials also opened a door to consideration of psychiatrically related states and, to a degree, encouraged these states to be viewed as systemically related. Perhaps most significant to our minds, however, more than 10 years later, is the remarkable alliance of investigators, industry, regulators, and patients (including the OC Foundation) that served as the basis of success. Such collaboration, although not unique to the development of clomipramine (DeVeaugh-Geiss, 1991), is an uncommon but productive model for future endeavors.

REFERENCES

Ackerman, D. L., Greenland, S., Bystritsky, A., & Katz, R. J. (1996). Relationship between early side effects and therapeutic effects of clomipramine therapy in obsessive-compulsive disorder. *Journal of Clinical Psychopharmacology, 16,* 324–328.

Ackerman, D. L., Greenland, S., Bystritsky, A., Morgenstern, H., & Katz, R. J. (1994). Predictors of treatment response in obsessive-compulsive disorder: Mutivariate analyses from a multicenter trial of clomipramine. *Journal of Clinical Psychopharmacology, 14,* 247–254.

American Psychiatric Association. (1980). *Diagnostic and statistical manual of mental disorders* (3rd ed.). Washington, DC: Author.

Ananth, J. (1985). Pharmacotherapy of obsessive-compulsive disorder. In M. Mavissakalian, S. M. Turner, & L. Michelson (Eds.), *Obsessive-compulsive disorder psychological and pharmacological treatment* (pp. 167–211). New York: Plenum.

Ananth, J., Pecknold, J. C., van den Steen, N., & Engelsmann, F. (1981). Double-blind comparative study of clomipramine and amitriptyline in obsessive neurosis. *Progress in Neuropsychopharmacology and Biological Psychiatry, 5,* 257–262.

Baer, L., Jenike, M. A., Black, D. W., Treece, C., Rosenfeld, R., & Greist, J. (1992). Effect of Axis II diagnoses on treatment outcome with clomipramine in 55 patients with obsessive-compulsive disorder. *Archives of General Psychiatry, 49,* 862–866.

Brasic, J. R., Barnett, J. Y., Kaplan, D., Shierman, B. B., Aisemberg, B. P., Lafargue, R. T., Kowalik, S., Clark, A., Tsaltas, M. O., & Young, J. G. (1994). Clomipramine ameliorates adventitious movements and compulsions in prepubertal boys with autistic disorder and severe mental retardation. *Neurology, 44,* 1309–1312.

Casals-Ariet, C., & Cullen, K. (1993). Exhibitionism treated with clomipramine. *American Journal of Psychiatry, 150,* 1273–1274.

Chen, C. J. (1991). The obsessive quality and clomipramine treatment in PTSD. *American Journal of Psychiatry, 148,* 1087–1088.

Clomipramine Collaborative Study Group. (1991). Clomipramine in the treatment of patients with obsessive-compulsive disorder. *Archives of General Psychiatry, 48,* 730–738.

DeVeaugh-Geiss, J. (1991). Academic medical center/industry collaboration. *Archives of General Psychiatry, 48,* 754–756.

DeVeaugh-Geiss, J., Katz, R., Landau, P., Goodman, W., & Rasmussen, S. (1990). Clinical predictors of treatment response in obsessive-compulsive disorder: Exploratory analyses from multicenter trials of clomipramine. *Psychopharmacology Bulletin, 26,* 54–59.

DeVeaugh-Geiss, J., Moroz, G., Biederman, J., Cantwell, D., Fontaine, R., Greist, J., Reichler, R., Katz, R., & Landau, P. (1992). Clomipramine hydrochloride in child and adolescent obsessive-compulsive disorder—A multicenter trial. *Journal of the American Academy of Child and Adolescent Psychiatry, 31,* 45–49.

Escobar, J., Teeter, R. R., Tuason, V. B., & Schiele, B. C. (1976). Intravenous clomipramine and depressive subtypes. *Diseases of the Nervous System, 37,* 325–328.

Fernandez-Cordoba, E., & Lopez-Ibor Alino, J. (1967). La monoclorimipramina en enfermos psiquiatricos resistentes a otros tratamientos [Chlorimipramine in psychiatric patients resistant to other treatments]. *Actas Luso-Espanolas de Neurologia y Psychiatria, 26,* 119–147.

Fernando, N. (1988). Monosymptomatic hypochondriasis treated with a tricyclic antidepressant. *British Journal of Psychiatry, 152,* 851–852.

Flament, M. F., Rapoport, J. L., Berg, C. J., Sceery, W., Kilts, C., Mellstrom, B., & Linnoila, M. (1985). Clomipramine treatment of childhood obsessive-compulsive disorder: A double-blind controlled study. *Archives of General Psychiatry, 42,* 977–983.

Goldberger, E., & Rapoport, J. L. (1991). Canine acral lick dermatitis: Response to the antiobsessional drug clomipramine. *Journal of the American Animal Hospital Association, 27,* 179–182.

Goodman, W. K., Price, L. H., Rasmussen, S. A., Mazure, C., Fleishmann, C., Hill, C., Heninger, G., & Charney, D. (1989a). The Yale–Brown Obsessive Compulsive Scale (Y–BOCS): I. Development, use and reliability. *Archives of General Psychiatry, 46,* 1006–1011.

Goodman, W. K., Price, L. H., Rasmussen, S. A., Mazure, C., Fleishmann, C., Hill, C., Heninger, G., & Charney, D. (1989b). The Yale–Brown Obsessive Compulsive Scale (Y–BOCS): II. Validity. *Archives of General Psychiatry, 46,* 1012–1016.

Gordon, C. T., Cotelingham, G. M., Stager, S., Ludlow, C. L., Hamburger, S. D., & Rapoport, J. L. (1995). A double blind comparison of clomipramine and desipramine in the treatment of developmental stuttering. *Journal of Clinical Psychiatry, 56,* 238–242.

Gordon, C. T., Rapoport, J. L., Hamburger, S. D., State, R. C., & Mannheim, G. B. (1992). Differential response of seven subjects with autistic disorder to clomipramine and desipramine. *American Journal of Psychiatry, 149,* 363–366.

Gordon, C. T., State, R. C., Nelson, J. E., Hamburger, S. D., & Rapoport, J. L. (1993). A double-blind comparison of clomipramine, desipramine, and placebo in the treatment of autistic disorder. *Archives of General Psychiatry, 50,* 441–447.

Greist, J., Jefferson, J. W., Kobak, K., Katzelnick, D. J., & Serlin, R. C. (1995). Efficacy and tolerability of serotonin transport inhibitors in obsessive-compulsive disorder: A meta-analysis. *Archives of General Psychiatry, 52,* 53–60.

Hollander, E. (1993). *Obsessive-compulsive related disorders.* Washington, DC: American Psychiatric Press.

Hollander, E., Frenkel, M., DiCaria, C., Trungold, S., & Stein, D. J. (1992). Treatment of pathological gambling with clomipramine. *American Journal of Psychiatry, 149,* 710–711.

Hollander, E., Liebowitz, M. R., Winchel, R., Klumker, A., & Klein, D. (1989). Treatment of body-dysmorphic disorder with serotonin reuptake blockers. *American Journal of Psychiatry, 146,* 768–770.

Hollander, E., & Wong, C. M. (1995). Obsessive-compulsive spectrum disorders. *Journal of Clinical Psychiatry, 56*(Suppl. 4), 3–6.

Insel, T. R., Murphy, D. L., Cohen, R. M., Alterman, L., Kilts, C., & Linnoila, M. (1983). Obsessive-compulsive disorder: A double-blind trial of clomipramine and clorgyline. *Archives of General Psychiatry, 40,* 605–612.

Jaskari, M. O. (1980). Observations on mianserin in the treatment of obsessive neuroses. *Current Medical Research Opinion, 6,* 128–132.

Jimenez-Garcia, P. (1967). Experiencia clinica con clomipramina en enfermos psychiatricos [Clinical experience with clomipramine in psychiatric patients]. *Libro de Becas Cursos, 58,* 179–201.

Kruesi, M. J., Fine, S., Valladares, L., Phillips, R. A., Jr., & Rapoport, J. L. (1992). Paraphilias: A double-blind cross over trial of clomipramine vs desipramine. *Archives of Sexual Behavior, 21,* 587–593.

Laboucarie, J., Rascol, A., Jorda, P., Guraud, R., & Leinadier, H. (1967). New prospects in the treatment of melancholic states: Therapeutic study of a major antidepressant, chlorimipramine. *Revue Medicale de Toulouse, 3,* 863–872.

Leonard, H. L., Lenane, M. C., Swedo, S. E., Rettwe, D. C., & Rapoport, J. L. (1991). A double-blind comparison of clomipramine and desipramine treatment of severe onychophagia (nail biting). *Archives of General Psychiatry, 48,* 821–827.

Leonard, H., Swedo, S., Koby, E. V., Rapoport, J. L., Lenane, M. C., Cheslow, D. L., & Hamburger, S. D. (1989). Treatment of obsessive-compulsive disorder with clomipramine and desmethylimipramine in children and adolescents: A double-blind, crossover comparison. *Archives of General Psychiatry, 46,* 1088–1092.

Lopez-Ibor Alino, J. J. (1969). Intravenous perfusion of monochlorimipramine: Techniques and results. In *Proceedings of the International College of CINP Teragone April 1968* (International Congress Series 180, p. 519). Amsterdam: Excerpta Medica.

Marks, I. M., Lelliott, P., Basoglu, M., Noshirvani, H., Monteiro, W., Cohen, D., & Kasvikis, Y. (1988). Clomipramine, self-exposure and therapist-aided exposure for obsessive-compulsive rituals. *British Journal of Psychiatry, 152*, 522–534.

Marks, I. M., Stern, R. S., Mawson, D., Cobb, J., & McDonald, R. (1980). Clomipramine and exposure for obsessive-compulsive rituals. *British Journal of Psychiatry, 136*, 1–25.

Marshall, W. K. (1971). Treatment of obsessional illness and phobic anxiety state with clomipramine. *British Journal of Psychiatry, 119*, 467–468.

Mavissakalian, M., Turner, S. M., Michelson, L., & Jacob, R. (1985). Tricyclic antidepressants in obsessive-compulsive disorder: Antiobsessional or antidepressant agents? *American Journal of Psychiatry, 142*, 572–576.

McDougle, C. J., Price, L. H., Volkmar, F. R., Goodman, W. K., Ward-O'Brien, D., Nielsen, J., Bregman, J., & Cohen, D. J. (1992). Clomipramine in autism: Preliminary evidence of efficacy. *Journal of the American Academy of Child and Adolescent Psychiatry, 31*, 746–750.

Montgomery, S. A. (1980). Clomipramine in obsessional neurosis: A placebo-controlled trial. *Pharmaceutical Medicine, 1*, 189–192.

Piccinelli, M., Pini, S., Bellantuono, C., & Wilkinson, G. (1995). Efficacy of drug treatment in obsessive-compulsive disorder: A meta-analytic review. *British Journal of Psychiatry, 166*, 424–433.

Pollard, C. A., Ibe, I. O., Krojanker, D. N., Kitchen, A. D., Bronson, S. S., & Flynn, T. M. (1991). Clomipramine treatment of trichotillomania: A follow up report on four cases. *Journal of Clinical Psychiatry, 52*, 128–130.

Rapoport, J., Elkins, R., & Mikkelsen, E. (1980). Clinical controlled trial of chlorimipramine in adolescents with obsessive-compulsive disorder. *Psychopharmacology Bulletin, 16*, 61–65.

Ross, C. A., Siddiqui, A. R., & Matas, M. (1987). DSM–III: Problems in diagnosis of paranoia and obsessive compulsive disorder. *Canadian Journal of Psychiatry, 32*, 146–148.

Rubey, R., Brady, K. T., & Norris, G. T. (1993). Clomipramine treatment of sexual preoccupation. *Journal of Clinical Psychopharmacology, 13*, 158–159.

Stein, D. J., Hollander, E., & Josephson, S. C. (1994). Serotonin uptake blockers for the treatment of obsessional jealousy. *Journal of Clinical Psychiatry, 55*, 30–33.

Stone, A. B. (1993). Treatment of hypochondriasis with clomipramine. *Journal of Clinical Psychiatry, 54*, 200–201.

Swedo, S. E., Leonard, H. L., Rapoport, J. L., Lenane, M. C., Goldberger, E. L., & Cheslow, D. L. (1989). A double-blind comparison of clomipramine and desipramine in the treatment of trichotillomania (hair pulling). *New England Journal of Medicine, 321*, 497–501.

Thoren, P., Asberg, M., Cronholm, B., Jornestedt, L., & Traskman, L. (1980). Clomipramine treatment of obsessive-compulsive disorder: I. A controlled clinical trial. *Archives of General Psychiatry, 37*, 1281–1285.

Volavka, J., Neziroglu F., & Yaryura-Tobias, J. A. (1985). Clomipramine and imipramine in obsessive-compulsive disorder. *Psychiatry Research, 14*, 85–93.

Wawrose, F. E., & Sisto, T. M. (1992). Clomipramine and a case of exhibitionism. *American Journal of Psychiatry, 149*, 843.

Zohar, J., & Insel, T. (1987). Obsessive-compulsive disorder: Psychobiological approaches to diagnosis, treatment, and pathophysiology. *Biological Psychiatry, 22*, 667–687.

18

Biological Approaches to Treatment-Resistant Obsessive-Compulsive Disorder

Wayne K. Goodman
Herbert E. Ward
Anita S. Kablinger
Tanya K. Murphy
University of Florida College of Medicine

Obsessive-compulsive disorder (OCD) is usually chronic, often debilitating, and more common than previously believed. Not long ago, it was widely viewed as untreatable. The 1980s witnessed renewed optimism about the prognosis of OCD as new, more effective forms of pharmacotherapy (i.e., potent serotonin reuptake inhibitors [SRIs]) and behavior therapy (i.e., exposure and response prevention) were introduced and successfully tested. Despite these advances in treatment, a substantial number of patients with OCD remain symptomatic or show no improvement at all. The effectiveness of SRIs is well established in OCD, but between 40% and 60% of patients are nonresponders (Greist, Jefferson, Kobak, Katzelnick, & Serlin, 1995). Even among "responders" to SRIs, the magnitude of response is usually incomplete, with few patients becoming asymptomatic. In clinical trials, a 25% to 35% decrease in mean Yale–Brown Obsessive Compulsive Scale (Y–BOCS; Goodman, Price, Rasmussen, Mazure, Delgado, et al., 1989; Goodman, Price, Rasmussen, Mazure, Fleischmann, et al., 1989) scores from baseline is often used to define the threshold for a categorical response to treatment. Although this degree of change may represent a clinically meaningful reduction in symptom severity, there remains considerable room for further improvement.

This chapter focuses on biological approaches to the patient with OCD who is either a nonresponder or partial responder to treatment with SRIs. The current state of knowledge regarding the efficacy of these approaches is summarized and recommendations are proposed based on empirical evidence and our clinical experience. Although we refer to behavior therapy at various times throughout this chapter, a comprehensive discussion of the role of behavior therapy alone or in combination with SRIs is beyond the scope of this work.

DEFINITIONS OF TREATMENT RESISTANCE

Various terms have been used to refer to patients who have failed treatment, but there is no universal agreement on a recommended nomenclature. For the purposes of this review of biological therapies, the term *treatment-resistant* will generally be applied to those patients who have not shown a satisfactory response to adequate trials of at least two SRIs. The terms *treatment-refractory* and *intractable* connote greater degrees of treatment resistance as reflected in failure to respond to a variety of anti-obsessive-compulsive (OC) treatment strategies (including combinations of agents) and behavior therapy.

The classification of patients as treatment failures is critically dependent on the definition of response that is used. Most recent studies have used change scores on the 10-item Y–BOCS with a range from 0 (no symptoms) to 40 (extreme symptoms) as the primary outcome measure. The majority of large-scale drug trials have used a 25% or greater decrease from baseline in Y–BOCS score to define a responder. The clomipramine multicenter trials set a higher threshold of a 35% reduction in Y–BOCS scores to meet response criteria. Some studies have required responders to achieve a "much" or "very much improved" rating on the Clinical Global Impressions (CGI) scale in addition to meeting Y–BOCS criteria. Nevertheless, a problem with using change criteria alone is that a patient who is classified as a responder may still have clinically significant symptoms of OCD at the conclusion of the trial. For example, a patient who started out very severe (baseline Y–BOCS = 30) may be counted as a responder using a 35% reduction in Y–BOCS scores but still have moderate symptoms (Y–BOCS = 19.5). The latter example might be better categorized as a partial responder, reserving the term *responder* for those who achieve an endpoint below a preestablished severity level (e.g., Y–BOCS = 16).

REASONS FOR TREATMENT RESISTANCE

Different factors may account for the failure of a patient with OCD to respond to a potent SRI. First, the adequacy of the acute drug trial must be evaluated. Was the duration of the trial long enough or the dose sufficient? There is consensus among experts that the duration of an adequate medication trial must be between 10 and 12 weeks, but there is less uniformity of opinion with regard to what constitutes an adequate dose. Some (Wheadon, Bushnell, & Steiner, 1993), but not all (Greist, Chouinard, et al., 1995; Tollefson et al., 1994), fixed-dose trials of selective SRIs indicate that higher doses are significantly superior to lower doses in the treatment of OCD. In the case of paroxetine, 20 mg daily did not separate from placebo; the lowest effective dose was 40 mg daily. By and large, studies of fluoxetine suggest that 60 mg daily is more effective than 20 mg daily, but that 20 mg and 40 mg daily are still more effective than placebo. As the 60 mg daily dose of fluoxetine is associated with more side effects than lower doses, the preferred clinical practice is to leave patients on 40 mg for about 8 weeks before increasing the dose further. In the final analysis, the criteria for an adequate trial must be defined in terms of the medication(s) in question. Adequate trials of clomipramine, fluvoxamine, fluoxetine, sertraline, and paroxetine would be 10 to 12 weeks of treatment with a minimum mean daily dose of 150 mg, 150 mg, 40 mg, 150 mg, and 40 mg, respectively, for at least 8 weeks. Although a trial of fluoxetine with 40 mg daily for 8 to 12 weeks might be deemed adequate, a nonresponder to such a trial should probably not be labeled as fluoxetine-resistant until the dose is increased to 80 mg daily as tolerated.

Some estimate of compliance is helpful in determining whether the trial was adequate, as indicated by drug plasma levels or pill counts. To date, clinical trials have failed to demonstrate a direct relation between SRI plasma levels and response in OCD. However, as discussed later, it may be advisable to monitor clomipramine plasma levels when this drug is used in combination with fluvoxamine. Drug plasma levels may also be useful in identifying patients who are rapid metabolizers. Plasma concentrations should be measured when medications, such as, valproic acid or lithium, with established therapeutic and toxic ranges are prescribed.

Once the adequacy of a trial has been established, other explanations should be sought for cases of treatment resistance. Possible reasons for variability in drug response include effects of cormorbid conditions, differences in underlying biology, and psychosocial factors that can impact treatment. There is evidence that certain comorbid conditions are associated with a lower treatment response rate. OCD patients with schizotypal personality disorder appear to have a relatively worse outcome (Baer et al., 1992; Jenike, Baer, Minichiello, Schwartz, & Carey, 1986; Ravizza, Barzega, Bellino, Bogetto, & Maina, 1995). OCD patients with neurological soft signs may also do less well with SRIs (Hollander, Schiffman, et al., 1990). In contrast, most studies indicate that the response of OC symptoms to SRIs is generally independent of the presence or severity of coexisting depression (Katz & DeVeaugh-Geiss, 1990; Mavissakalian, Turner, Michelson, & Jacob, 1985).

Another study suggests that the response rate to SRI monotherapy is lower in OCD patients with a chronic tic disorder (McDougle, Goodman, Leckman, Barr, et al., 1993). Using a retrospective case-controlled design, treatment response to the SRI fluvoxamine was compared in patients with (n = 33) or without (n = 33) a comorbid chronic tic disorder. Although both groups of patients demonstrated statistically significant reductions in OC, depressive, and anxiety symptoms with fluvoxamine treatment, the frequency and magnitude of response of OC symptoms was significantly different between the two groups. A clinically meaningful improvement in OC symptoms occurred in only 21% of patients with comorbid chronic tics compared with a 52% response rate in patients without chronic tics. Those with a concurrent chronic tic disorder showed only a 17% reduction in Y–BOCS scores compared to a 32% decrease in severity of OC symptoms in those patients without chronic tics.

A careful differential diagnostic assessment should precede a drug trial. It is especially important to distinguish between OCD and the Axis II condition obsessive-compulsive personality disorder (OCPD), because there is little evidence that the latter responds to pharmacotherapy. In devising a treatment plan, one should make the distinction between OCD as a primary disturbance and OC-like symptoms as part of the clinical picture of another disorder, such as autism (McDougle et al., 1992), mental retardation (McNally & Calamari, 1989; Vitiello, Spreat, & Behar, 1989), or schizophrenia (Bark & Lindenmayer, 1992; Fenton & McGlashan, 1986). It is noteworthy that OC-like symptoms may indeed respond to SRIs in the presence of autism (Gordon, Rapoport, Hamburger, State, & Mannheim, 1992; McDougle, Price, & Goodman, 1990; McDougle et al., 1992), or mental retardation (Cook, Rowlett, Jaselskis, & Levanthal, 1992), or schizophrenia (see Byerly, Goodman, & Cuadros, chap. 4, this volume). Because it is presently unrealistic to expect all the primary and associated symptoms of the underlying disorder to respond equally well to SRI treatment, it is important to indicate which symptoms are being targeted for treatment.

Even apparently classic and uncomplicated cases of OCD demonstrate a variable response to SRI monotherapy. Variablility in drug response raises the possibility that OCD is heterogeneous with respect to pathogenesis. Accidents of nature furnish direct evidence for this premise. Numerous clinical reports document that injury to structures of the basal ganglia can be associated with the development of OC symptoms (Cummings & Cunningham, 1992; Goodman, McDougle, Price, et al., 1990; Jelliffe, 1932; Wise & Rapoport, 1989). However, one cannot rely on putative clinical subtypes of OCD to predict whether or not an individual patient will respond to SRI treatment.

The influence of an OCD patient's family environment on treatment outcome or long-term course has only recently become the subject of formal study. A family member's reaction can range from complete compliance with the patient's rituals to total opposition to the symptomatic behaviors (Livingston-Van Noppen, Rasmussen, & Eisen, 1990). Clinicians have reported that either extreme response may contribute to exacerbation of OC symptoms, posing a formidable countervailing force to otherwise effective treatment. In most instances, family members are advised to encourage the patient to resist his or her OC symptoms, but they are discouraged from extreme reactions to the patient's behaviors (i.e., either hostile opposition or performing compulsions on his or her behalf). The possible contribution of family factors to treatment resistance was explored in studies led by Calvocoressi et al. (1995).

In a study by Mawson, Marks, and Ramm (1982), the anti-OC effects of clomipramine were partially neutralized by instructing patients not to expose themselves to situations that would elicit OC symptoms. These antiexposure instructions contrast with the usual practice of advising patients to confront feared situations without performing compulsions. The impact of antiexposure instructions on outcome is more a theoretical than a clinical issue, because most patients conduct self-exposure despite instructions to the contrary (Cottraux et al., 1990).

DOSAGE ESCALATION AND SWITCHING ANTIDEPRESSANTS

If a patient has had a limited response but few side effects with an SRI, the next logical step is to increase to the highest recommended dose. Fortunately, selective serotonin reuptake inhibitors (SSRIs), such as fluvoxamine, fluoxetine, paroxetine, and sertraline, are generally safe even at high doses. In contrast, clomipramine should not be administered in doses greater than 250 mg daily without careful medical monitoring (e.g., serial electrocardiograms) and unless clinically indicated (see later discussion about combination treatments). The risk of seizures associated with clomipramine increases significantly with doses greater than 250 mg daily. As with all tricyclic antidepressants, the metabolism of clomipramine can vary tremendously from patient to patient. At least one steady state blood level is necessary to ensure that a particular dose is therapeutic for a given patient and to avoid toxicity in patients who are slow metabolizers. The anti-OC efficacy of supramaximal (higher than recommended) doses of SSRIs has not been formally studied, although case reports have shown beneficial results using this approach (Byerly, Goodman, & Christensen, 1996).

Although there is debate in the literature regarding the value of prescribing a different potent SRI after an OCD patient has not responded to clomipramine (Mattes, 1994; Pigott & Murphy, 1991; Tamimi & Mavissakalian, 1991), there are numerous anecdotal examples of therapeutic success with one SRI following failure with a different SRI, including clomipramine. Several different authors of literature reviews on the pharmacotherapy of OCD have advocated changing to a different SRI if there has been no improvement at all following an adequate trial with one SRI; if there have been partial gains, a combination treatment approach is generally recommended instead. However, we are unaware of any controlled data substantiating this intuitively appealing approach: Whether partial responders do better than nonresponders to SRIs during a subsequent combination treatment trial has yet to be formally examined. Considerations of power are likely to necessitate a multicenter collaborative study to investigate this question. Naturally, if the patient does not tolerate one SRI it is advisable to try a different one, selected on the basis of expected side effect profile.

Based on some intriguing case reports (Jenike, Surman, Cassem, Zusky, & Anderson, 1983), a trial with a monoamine oxidase inhibitor (MAOI) showed promise in OCD patients with comorbid panic disorder. In a 12-week double-blind trial, both phenelzine and clomipramine were found to be effective in reducing symptoms as reflected on two of four OC measures (Vallejo, Olivares, Marcos, Bulbena, & Menchon, 1992). None of the patients in this study had panic disorder. This study suggested that MAOIs may be helpful in some patients with OCD even in the absence of panic disorder. More recently, Jenike tested the hypothesis that comorbid anxiety may predict response to an MAOI in a 10-week double-blind, placebo-controlled trial of phenelzine (60 mg daily) versus fluoxetine (80 mg daily; Jenike, Baer, Minichiello, Rauch, & Buttolph, 1997). Fluoxetine was significantly superior to both placebo and phenelzine in this trial. Phenelzine was no more effective than placebo even when the subset of patients with prominent anxiety symptoms was included. In an early comparison trial, clomipramine, but not the MAOI clorgyline, resulted in significant OC symptom reduction (Insel, Murphy, et al., 1983). Together, these reports suggest some patients with OCD may show improvement on phenelzine, but it is difficult to predict who will respond based on baseline clinical characteristics. It is the opinion of the senior author of this chapter that MAOIs should be reserved as a distant second-line approach in treatment-refractory OCD.

Recently, several novel medications have been introduced for the treatment of depression, but their value in the treatment of OCD has not yet been established. Venlafaxine inhibits the reuptake of both serotonin (5-hydroxytryptamine; 5-HT) and norepinephrine without significant affinity for muscarinic, histaminergic, or noradrenergic receptors (Nierenberg, Feighner, Rudolph, Cole, & Sullivan, 1994). A case of comorbid depression and OCD showed improvement in both domains during treatment with venlafaxine (Zajecka, Fawcett, & Guy, 1990). Grossman and Hollander (1996) reported successful venlafaxine treatment in a patient with OCD who was unable to tolerate clomipramine or paroxetine. Ananth, Burgoyne, Smith, and Swartz (1995) also reported two OCD cases that responded to venlafaxine after either intolerance or poor response to SRIs. Likewise, Rauch and colleagues reported that 12 weeks of open treatment with venlafaxine in 10 OCD patients produced significant improvement ($\geq$ 35% reduction in Y–BOCS and 1 or 2 on the CGI scale) in 30% (three of nine completers) of patients (Rauch, O'Sullivan, & Jenike, 1996). In contrast, venlafaxine was not significantly better than placebo in a double-blind trial in 30 patients with OCD (Yaryura-Tobias & Neziroglu, 1996). The relatively short 8-week duration of treatment is a limitation of this study. Together, these published reports seem to warrant additional testing of venlafaxine in OCD under double-blind conditions for 10 to 12 weeks of treatment.

Nefazodone is structurally related to trazodone, but has a somewhat different pharmacologic profile and less propensity for inducing sedation (Fontaine et al., 1994). Early pilot studies of nefazodone in OCD were suspended, apparently because of lack of efficacy (Pigott, Goodman, & Rasmussen, personal communication, 1991). Nefazodone was implicated in the emergence of OC symptoms in a patient being treated for depression (Sofuoglu & Debattista, 1996).

COMBINATION STRATEGIES: ADDING ANOTHER TREATMENT TO THE SRI

The patient who has had a partial response to SRI monotherapy or failed to show any improvement following two consecutive trials with different SRIs is a candidate for combination treatment.

SRI Plus Behavior Therapy

It is believed that a combination of an SRI and exposure and response prevention is the most broadly effective treatment for OCD (Goodman, Rasmussen, Foa, & Price, 1994), but support from double-blind, placebo-controlled studies is still sparse (for recent meta-analyses review, see Cox, Swinson, Morrison, & Lee, 1993; Stanley & Turner, 1995; van Balkom et al., 1994). In fact, few studies have adequately addressed the question of whether a potent SRI plus behavior therapy is superior to either treatment alone. The studies that have examined this question either suffer from methodological shortcomings that hamper data interpretation or they do not show clear advantages of combined SRI and behavior therapy over SRI therapy alone. For example, Marks, Stern, Mawson, Cobb, and McDonald (1980) studied the combination of clomipramine and behavior therapy in 40 patients with OCD who received 4 weeks of drug or placebo, followed by 3 weeks of behavior therapy for all patients while clomipramine or placebo was continued. The authors found a large behavior therapy effect and a small additive effect of drug and behavior therapy. The brief drug-only period (4 weeks) may have resulted in an underestimation of the efficacy of drug therapy alone. Moreover, drug and behavior therapy were compared after 7 weeks of treatment, when the maximum effect of medication may still not yet have occurred. A study by Cottraux et al. (1990) found only a minimal anti-OC advantage of combined fluvoxamine and behavior therapy over fluvoxamine alone.

It is anticipated that the findings from a study sponsored by the National Institute of Mental Health being conducted by Foa and Liebowitz will shed light on the comparative efficacy of clomipramine plus behavior therapy, clomipramine alone, and behavior therapy alone. Apart from considerations of acute treatment efficacy, there may be other advantages to the combination of an SRI and behavior therapy. For example, clinical experience suggests that concomitant behavior therapy may decrease the likelihood of relapse in OCD patients after drug discontinuation. Although the emphasis of this chapter is on biological approaches to OCD, behavioral therapy should be integrated into the overall treatment plan. (For additional discussion of combined drug and behavioral therapy, see Kozak, Liebowitz, & Foa, chap. 25, this volume.)

SRI Plus Agents That May Affect Serotonin Function

To date, the rationale for the majority of drug combination strategies has been to add agents to ongoing SRI therapy that may modify serotonergic function, such as tryptophan, fenfluramine, lithium, or buspirone. The addition of clonazepam, pindolol, or another SRI is also discussed in this section.

Adding Tryptophan. Addition of tryptophan, the amino acid precursor of 5-HT, has been reported helpful in an OCD patient on clomipramine (Rasmussen, 1984), but ineffective in OCD patients on trazodone (Mattes, 1986). Trazodone is a selective, but weak, inhibitor of 5-HT reuptake (Marek, McDougle, Price, & Seiden, 1992). Adverse neurological reactions resembling the 5-HT syndrome seen in laboratory animals have been reported when tryptophan is used in combination with fluoxetine (Steiner & Fontaine, 1986). At present, oral tryptophan supplements are not readily available in the United States because of evidence linking some of these preparations to the eosinophilia myalgia syndrome, a serious and potentially fatal hematologic and connective tissue illness (Hertzman et al., 1990). In Canada, where tryptophan is widely available, Blier and Bergeron (1996) described the benefits of adding tryptophan to a subgroup of patients with OCD taking a combination of an SRI and pindolol (discussed later).

Adding Fenfluramine. In an open-label study, Hollander, DeCaria, et al. (1990) reported that addition of the 5-HT releaser and reuptake blocker d,l-fenfluramine (Pondimen) to ongoing treatment with various SRIs led to improvement in OCD symptoms in six of seven patients. Subsequently, Judd, Chua, Lynch, and Norman (1991) reported that two clomipramine-treated patients improved after addition of dexfenfluramine (Redux). D-fenfluramine is thought to have more specific effects on 5-HT transport and release than the racemic mixture. Both d,l-fenfluramine and dexfenfluramine have been associated with primary pulmonary hypertension (Abenhaim et al., 1996) and, accordingly, there have been strict guidelines for use of dexfenfluramine in obesity. Clinicians should also be aware that administration of d-fenfluramine is neurotoxic to 5-HT neurons in some studies of laboratory animals, including nonhuman primates (Kleven & Seiden, 1989; McCann, Seiden, Rubin, & Ricaurte, 1997; Scheffel et al., 1992). The absence of evidence that fenfluramine is neurotoxic in humans may reflect the difficulty in assessing subtle neurological changes in the living human. In animal studies, preadministration of an SRI appears to prevent fenfluramine-induced neurotoxicity by blocking entry of fenfluramine into 5-HT nerve terminals (Clineschmidt et al., 1978). This finding suggests that SRI–fenfluramine cotherapy may be safer than fenfluramine monotherapy with respect to 5-HT neuronal damage. On the other hand, the package insert for dexfluramine warns against its concomitant use with SRIs, purportedly out of concern for development of 5-HT syndrome. Given the aforementioned safety concerns (i.e., primary pulmonary hypertension, possible neurotoxicity, and 5-HT syndrome) we are reluctant to recommend the routine use of the SRI–fenfluramine combination until its anti-OC efficacy is confirmed in controlled trials. For the time being, this combination should be reserved for seriously ill OCD patients with well-documented treatment resistance. The patient should be advised about potential risks of fenfluramine before it is prescribed. (In September 1997, the manufacturer [Wyeth-Ayerst] of Pondimen and Redux voluntarily removed these products from the market after reports of cardiac complications [carcinoid-like valvular changes; Connolly et al., 1997].)

Adding Lithium. Coadministration of lithium is a proven method for enhancing the thymoleptic action of antidepressants in patients with depression (Heninger, Charney, & Sternberg, 1983). Lithium has been hypothesized to potentiate antidepressant-induced increases in 5-HT neu-rotransmission by enhancing presynaptic 5-HT release in some brain regions (Blier & de Montigny, 1992). The success of lithium augmentation in depression and the hypothesized role of 5-HT in OCD has prompted studies of the anti-OC efficacy of this approach.

Lithium has been reported in individual cases to augment the anti-OC effect of chronic treatment with imipramine (Stern & Jenike, 1983), clomi-pramine (Feder, 1988; Golden, Morris, & Sack, 1988; Rasmussen, 1984), desipramine (Eisenberg & Asnis, 1985), and doxepin (Golden et al., 1988). In a small open case series, the addition of lithium to ongoing fluoxetine treatment reportedly led to an improvement in OC symptoms in three of four patients with OCD (Ruegg, Evans, & Comer, 1990). In contrast, no significant improvement in OC symptoms was observed by Pigott et al. (1991) following 4 weeks of double-blind addition of lithium to ongoing clomipramine treatment in 16 patients who had demonstrated a partial response to clomipramine. Using stringent treatment response criteria, McDougle, Price, Goodman, Charney, and Heninger (1991) found that only 2 of 11 (18%) fluvoxamine-refractory patients responded to a 2-week double-blind, placebo-controlled trial of lithium addition to ongoing flu-voxamine treatment. There were significant, but small, decreases in OC symptom severity as measured on the Y–BOCS in the lithium group compared to the placebo group (McDougle et al., 1991). In a companion study, McDougle et al. (1991) tried to extend their findings by examining the effects of a 4-week fluvoxamine–lithium combination treatment in 10 patients refractory to fluvoxamine alone. In the latter study, lithium was no better than placebo. Thus, on the basis of controlled trials, the efficacy of lithium addition in patients with OCD does not appear to approach the rate or quality of response that is typically observed when this strategy is employed in patients with treatment-resistant depression (Price, Charney, & Heninger, 1986). Although the overall yield is low in OCD, individual patients, particularly those with marked depressive symptoms, may benefit from lithium augmentation. In both the Pigott et al. (1991) and McDougle et al. (1991) studies there was some improvement in depression ratings with addition of lithium. That lithium augmentation seems useful in depression, but not in OCD, may reflect regional brain differences in lithium's effects on 5-HT neurotransmission (Blier & de Montigny, 1992).

Adding Buspirone.   In two open-label studies (Jenike, Baer, & Buttolph, 1991; Markovitz, Stagno, & Calabrese, 1990), addition of the 5-HT type 1A agonist buspirone to ongoing fluoxetine treatment in patients with OCD led to greater improvement in OC symptoms than did continued treatment with fluoxetine alone. These initially encouraging findings have not been corroborated by three subsequent double-blind trials. Pigott, L'Heureux, Hill, et al. (1992) studied 14 patients who had experienced partial symptom relief after at least 3 months of clomipramine mono-therapy. Ten weeks of adjuvant buspirone treatment (up to 60 mg daily) did not produce significant improvement in OC ratings compared to base-line (i.e., before the start of a 2-week placebo run-in period). Using a parallel-group design, McDougle, Goodman, Leckman, Holzer, et al. (1993) reported that buspirone added to the treatment of 33 patients who were refractory to fluvoxamine was no better than placebo in reducing OC, depressive, or anxiety symptoms. In the latter study, either buspirone (up to a maximal daily dose of 60 mg) or placebo was combined with fluvoxamine for 6 weeks in patients already on fluvoxamine for 8 weeks. Grady et al. (1993) randomized 13 fluoxetine-treated patients to adjuvant buspirone or placebo for 4 weeks. There were no differences between the two treatment groups with respect to OC, depressive, or anxiety symptoms. Together, these controlled studies suggest that addition of buspirone to SRI therapy is not an effective treatment strategy for most OCD patients. It should also be noted that addition of buspirone to fluoxetine produced a paradoxical worsening of OC symptoms in one case report (Tanquary & Masand, 1990). Although the SRI–buspirone combination is generally well tolerated, there is a case report of a patient with OCD who experienced a seizure when buspirone was added to fluoxetine (Grady, Pigott, L'Heureux, & Murphy, 1992).

Despite these rather discouraging efficacy data, it appears that a minority of patients do experience some improvement in OC symptoms with combined SRI–buspirone treatment. In the study of Pigott, L'Heureux, Hill, et al. (1992), 29% of the 14 patients reported at least a 25% reduction in Y–BOCS scores after addition of buspirone. Buspirone addition may thus occasionally be helpful in reducing OC symptoms in OCD patients with comorbid generalized anxiety disorder. Controlled studies with sufficient numbers of OCD patients with comorbid general-ized anxiety disorder would be required to test the validity of these observations.

Adding Clonazepam.   The benzodiazepine clonazepam is not generally considered a serotonergic agent. However, there is evidence from studies in both animals and humans that clonazepam may possess serotonergic properties not shared by other benzodiazepines (Wagner, Reches, Yablon-skaya, & Fahn, 1986). For example, unlike diazepam, clonazepam will induce certain animal behaviors that are blocked by serotonergic agents but not by benzodiazepine antagonists (Pranzatelli, 1989). In humans, the antimyoclonic effects of clonazepam are blocked by 5-HT antagonists (Hwang & Van Woert, 1979).

A number of clinicians maintain that addition of clonazepam to ongoing SRI therapy is helpful in reducing symptoms of OCD, but substantiation by published reports is scarce. The Harvard group (Jenike, 1990) found that only one of seven (14%) patients with OCD improved more than 20% on the Y–BOCS when clonazepam (1–1.5 mg daily) was added to ongoing fluoxetine. In a double-blind, placebo-controlled crossover trial, Pigott, L'Heureux, Rubenstein, et al. (personal communication) studied the anti-OC effects of adding 4 weeks of clonazepam (3–4 mg daily) to either fluoxetine or clomipramine in 18 patients with OCD. They found significant improvement on one of three measures of OCD in the clonazepam group. No significant improvement was shown on the Y–BOCS. The clonazepam group showed significant improvement in anxiety. In a single case of an adolescent with refractory OCD, a combination of fluoxetine and clonazepam produced a marked improvement (Leonard et al., 1994). Although existing literature furnishes limited support for the anti-OC efficacy of adjuvant clonazepam, it seems worthwhile to conduct additional studies with longer durations of combined treatment.

A controlled trial by Hewlett, Vinogradov, and Agras (1992), in which clonazepam alone was as effective as clomipramine alone, gives further impetus to investigating the role of clonazepam in OCD. However, apart from this study, most other evidence for the anti-OC efficacy of benzodiazepine monotherapy is limited to case reports (Bacher, 1990; Bodkin & White, 1989; Hewlett, Vinogradov, & Agras, 1990). Furthermore, the Hewlett et al. (1992) study is subject to several design limitations. Treatment duration was brief (6 weeks) and high doses of clonazepam ($M = 6.85$ mg daily) were used. The efficacy of clomipramine may have been underestimated as a result of the trial's relatively short duration. The marked side effects on clonazepam (which seemed to resemble intoxication) may have produced only an apparent improvement in OCD. Until further studies of clonazepam alone or as an adjunct in OCD are conducted, the physician should use benzodiazepines sparingly in this condition. In our clinical experience, benzodiazepines may help secondary anxiety, but are rarely useful for the core symptoms of OCD; when they do seem to work, the anti-OC benefit is rarely sustained. Furthermore, a theoretical, albeit unproven, disadvantage of benzodiazepines is that they may impede the therapeutic effects of behavior therapy (Jensen, Hutchings, & Poulsen, 1989). (Hewlett provides a comprehensive review of benzodiazepines in the treatment of OCD elsewhere in chap. 21, this volume.)

Adding Trazodone. In addition to weakly inhibiting 5-HT reuptake, the antidepressant trazodone and its major metabolite m-chlorophenylpiperazine are active at a number of different neuroreceptors, including several 5-HT receptor subtypes and alpha adrenergic receptors

(Marek et al., 1992). Several open-label reports suggested that trazodone may reduce symptoms of OCD when used either alone (Baxter et al., 1987; Haresh, Aizenberg, & Munitz, 1990; Kim, 1987; Lydiard, 1986) or in combination (Swerdlow & Andia, 1989) with an SRI. However, a placebo-controlled, double-blind trial failed to confirm the efficacy of trazodone monotherapy (Pigott, L'Heureux, Rubenstein, et al., 1992). In clinical practice, low-dose trazodone is often used as a sedative-hypnotic in conjunction with activating SRIs such as fluoxetine (Nierenberg, Adler, Peselow, Zornberg, & Rosenthal, 1994). Whether this combination confers any direct anti-OC benefit remains to be established in controlled studies.

Adding Pindolol. Studies in laboratory animals suggest that antidepressant-induced enhancement of 5-HT neurotransmission does not occur immediately because of 5-HT autoreceptor-mediated inhibition of firing rate and release. As these autoreceptors desensitize during chronic antidepressant administration, both firing rate and release recover, leading to a net increase in 5-HT neurotransmission. Artigas, Perez, and Alvarez (1994) hypothesized that addition of an agent that blocks somatodendritic 5-HT$_{1A}$ autoreceptors might accelerate or augment the action of antidepressants in humans. Pindolol is a nonselective β-adrenergic antagonist that binds with high affinity to the 5-HT$_{1A}$ receptor (Hoyer, 1988) and antagonizes the presynaptic actions of 5-HT$_{1A}$ agonists (Anderson & Cowen, 1992; Coccaro, Gabriel, & Siever, 1990; Tricklebank, Forler, & Fozard, 1984). These authors conducted an open-label study on the effects of pindolol augmentation of SRIs or MAOIs in patients with major depression (Artigas et al., 1994). The results were encouraging in both newly treated and treatment-resistant depressed patients. Further evidence that pindolol addition accelerates the antidepressant effect of SSRIs is furnished by an open-label trial from Blier and Bergeron (1995) and a double-blind, placebo-controlled trial from Artigas, Romero, de Montigny, and Blier (1996). On the other hand, the Yale group of Berman, Darnell, Miller, Anand, and Charney (1997) failed to replicate these findings in their double-blind, placebo-controlled trial. Adding pindolol (for 6 weeks) to fluoxetine did not hasten antidepressant response in 43 patients with major depression (Berman et al., 1997).

An open-label study by Koran, Mueller, and Maloney (1996) combined pindolol with an SRI in eight OCD patients who did not show a satisfactory response to the SRI alone; only one of the eight responded. The one who responded had a 20-year history of moderately severe OC symptoms that improved rapidly and dramatically (with a corresponding drop in Y–BOCS score to 0) after addition of pindolol 2.5 mg three times per day (TID). In another open-label trial, Blier and Bergeron (1996) added pindolol (2.5 mg TID) to ongoing SRI treatment of 13 patients who had not improved on SRIs alone. Four weeks of combined pindolol–SRI treatment had an antidepressant effect in patients with depressive symptomatology, but did not reduce severity of OC symptoms as reflected in mean scores on the Y–BOCS. Examination of individual Y–BOCS score data did reveal clinical improvement of OC symptoms in 4 of 13 patients, but overall there was no significant group effect of pindolol addition. Addition of tryptophan to the SRI–pindolol combination was associated with significant improvement in OC symptoms after 4 weeks of treatment (Blier & Bergeron, 1996). These encouraging results with triple therapy (SRI–pindolol–tryptophan) need to be verified in double-blind, placebo-controlled trials. (For a more comprehensive discussion of this and related topics, see Blier et al., chap. 27, this volume.)

Combining SRIs

In clinical practice, a number of SRI-resistant OCD patients receive simultaneous treatment with two selective SRIs. However, there is scant empirical or theoretical support for this strategy. There is one report in abstract form of four cases of treatment-refractory OCD in which combined fluoxetine–fluvoxamine seemed effective and well-tolerated (Palova, 1996). The advantage of dual SSRI therapy over a higher dose of a single agent is hard to explain based on our current understanding of their pharmacodynamic properties (i.e., common mode of action via inhibition of 5-HT transport). Suitable empirical studies would require a high-dose SSRI monotherapy control group and double-blind conditions.

A more interesting strategy is the combination of an SSRI and clomipramine. There have been encouraging case reports of coadministering fluoxetine and clomipramine in adolescents (Simeon, Thatte, & Wiggins, 1990) and adults (Browne, Horn, & Jones, 1993) with OCD. Based on a randomized but open-label trial in 33 patients with OCD, addition of sertraline 50 mg/day to clomipramine 150 mg/day was reported better tolerated and more effective than increasing the clomipramine dose from 150 to 250 mg/day (Ravizza, Barzega, Bellino, Bogetto, & Maina, 1996). Another group (Szegedi, Wetzel, Leal, Hartter, & Hiemke, 1996) examined the safety and tolerability of combining fluvoxamine and clomipramine in 22 adults with major depression or OCD who had been nonresponders to 4 weeks of monotherapy. Fluvoxamine, a potent inhibitor of cytochrome P4501A2, inhibits the N-demethylation of clomipramine to desmethylclomipramine and thereby reverses the ratio of desmethylclomipramine to clomipramine such that the concentration of the parent exceeds that of its metabolite (Brosen, Skjelbo, Rasmussen, Paulsen, & Loft, 1993). Serum clomipramine levels reached 500 to 1,200 ng/ml in half of the patients. Two patients developed myoclonic jerks. Four patients had alterations in intracardiac conduction, but without clinical cardiac symptoms. The authors concluded that in this sample of 22 patients, this combination was generally well tolerated. However, in light of marked elevations in clomipramine (the parent compound) they recommended careful monitoring of the tricyclic antidepressant serum levels, electroencephalogram, and electrocardiogram. With combined treatment, 17 patients (not all OCD) scored "much improved" or "very much improved" on the CGI by unblinded raters. The possible enhanced therapeutic effects of combining fluvoxamine and clomipramine may rest in the selective elevation of the more serotonergic parent compound. In comparison to clomipramine, desmethylclomipramine has greater potency for blocking norepinephrine uptake.

At this point, there seems to be little rationale for the combination of two SSRIs for treating OCD refractory to monotherapy. However, further study of the combination of fluvoxamine and clomipramine using double-blind, placebo-controlled methods seems justified. Safety remains a major concern with this combination and will have to be addressed in parallel with future efficacy studies.

Adding Desipramine

The scientific literature indicates little or no therapeutic benefit of noradrenergic medications in OCD. The only exception is the tricyclic/SRI clomipramine, the major metabolite of which blocks norepinephrine reuptake as well as 5-HT. Meta-analytic studies (Greist, Jefferson, et al., 1995; Jenike et al., 1990) have suggested clomipramine may be more effective in reducing OC symptoms as compared to agents that more selectively inhibit 5-HT reuptake. (For discussion of comparative efficacy of SRIs in OCD see Pigott & Seay, chap. 15, this volume.) This observation led to the proposal that the anti-OC efficacy of clomipramine may be attributed to its dual actions on 5-HT and norepinephrine transport. If true, then one might predict that a combination of SSRI and a selective norepinephrine reuptake inhibitor would mimic the effects of clomipramine. Barr, Goodman, Anand, McDougle, and Price (1997) investigated the addition of desipramine or placebo in a double-blind fashion to 23 fluvoxamine-, fluoxetine-, or sertraline-treated OCD patients who failed to respond to 10 weeks of monotherapy with the SSRI. The antidepressant desipramine was selected because of its relatively specific inhibition of norepinephrine reuptake and its lack of efficacy in reducing OC symptoms when administered as a single agent (Goodman, Price, et al., 1990). The mean final desipramine dose was 150.9 mg/day ($SD = 69.7$) with a mean final plasma desipramine level of 148.3 ng/ml ($SD = 82.0$). No significant overall differences were found between the two treatment groups in either

OC or depressive symptoms (Barr et al., 1997). These data suggest that the norepinephrine reuptake blocking properties of clomipramine do not contribute to its anti-OC efficacy.

SRI–Antipsychotic Combinations

Conventional Neuroleptics. These agents alone do not appear effective in OCD (Goodman, McDougle, et al., 1990), but there is emerging evidence that conjoint SRI–neuroleptic treatment may be beneficial in a subset of patients with OCD (McDougle et al., 1994). To date, the putative subgroup that has received the most attention has been OCD with a comorbid chronic tic disorder. This research has been based on the phenomenologic, family-genetic, neurochemical, and neuroanatomic data between OCD and Tourette's syndrome (TS), and the extensive preclinical literature documenting anatomic and functional interactions between the 5-HT and dopamine (DA) systems in the brain (Goodman, McDougle, et al., 1990; Leckman, Pauls, & Cohen, 1995; Pauls, Towbin, Leckman, Zahner, & Cohen, 1986). TS is a chronic neuropsychiatric disorder of childhood onset that is characterized by multiple motor and phonic tics that wax and wane in severity, and by an array of behavioral problems, including symptoms of attention deficit hyperactivity disorder and OCD. Conventional neuroleptics (dopamine-2 [D2] antagonists) such as haloperidol and pimozide have been the mainstay of treatment for TS (Shapiro et al., 1989).

Riddle, Leckman, Hardin, Anderson, and Cohen (1988) reported on the anti-OC benefits of adding an SRI to a neuroleptic in two cases of concomitant TS and OCD. Subsequently, Delgado, Goodman, Price, Heninger, and Charney (1990) reported on a young man with coexisting TS and OCD who showed marked improvement in his OC symptoms as well as tics when pimozide was added to fluvoxamine. Of interest, OC symptoms returned and tics remained suppressed when fluvoxamine was discontinued and the patient was left on pimozide alone. This suggested that adequate control of his OC symptoms required coadministration of an SRI and a DA antagonist, whereas tics could be managed with a DA antagonist alone. This case was followed up with an open case series in which low-dose neuroleptic (haloperidol or pimozide) was added to ongoing treatment in 17 nonpsychotic OCD patients unresponsive to fluvoxamine (McDougle, Goodman, et al., 1990). Nine of 17 (53%) patients were judged responders after combined SRI–DA antagonist treatment; responders experienced a 62% decrease in Y–BOCS scores. Seven of eight (88%) patients with comorbid tic spectrum disorders or schizotypal personality disorder were responders, whereas only two of nine (22%) patients without these comorbid diagnoses were responders.

Results from a double-blind, placebo-controlled study of haloperidol addition to fluvoxamine-refractory patients lend further support to the efficacy of this combination treatment strategy (McDougle et al., 1994). Sixty-two patients received single-blind placebo treatment for 1 week, followed by 8 weeks of single-blind treatment with fluvoxamine. Thirty-four of these had an unsatisfactory response to 8 weeks of fluvoxamine monotherapy and were then randomized (double-blind) to either 4 weeks of haloperidol ($n = 17$) or placebo ($n = 17$) in addition to a fixed daily dosage of fluvoxamine. A comorbid diagnosis of chronic tics or TS was present in eight patients in the haloperidol group and seven patients in the placebo group. Mean daily dose of haloperidol at the end of the 4-week trial was 6.2 mg ($SD = 3.0$). Benztropine 0.5 mg twice a day (BID) was administered prophylactically to both the haloperidol and placebo groups. For the purpose of the ratings, tics were distinguished from tic-like compulsions (e.g., compulsive touching or blinking) based on whether the patient attached a purpose or meaning to the behavior. For example, if a patient felt an urge to repeatedly touch an object this would be rated as a compulsion only if it was preceded by a need to neutralize an obsessive thought or image; otherwise it would be labeled a complex motor tic.

The fluvoxamine–haloperidol combination was significantly superior to the fluvoxamine–placebo combination on the basis of both stringent categorical response criteria and mean change in weekly Y–BOCS scores. Eleven of 17 (65%) of the patients who received haloperidol were responders, whereas none of the placebo-treated group showed a response. In responders to addition of haloperidol, Y–BOCS scores decreased significantly from a mean of 25.1 ($SD = 6.0$) to 15.5 ($SD = 9.1$), or 39%. As predicted, most of the benefit of haloperidol addition to fluvoxamine occurred in the OCD patients with a chronic tic disorder. In those patients with a comorbid chronic tic disorder, Y–BOCS scores decreased from a mean of 25.5 ($SD = 4.7$) to 13.6 ($SD = 8.0$), or 47% following haloperidol addition. Eight of eight (100%) patients with a current comorbid tic disorder were responders to haloperidol addition, whereas three out of nine (33%) patients without a tic disorder were responders. There were no significant differences in plasma fluvoxamine levels between the fluvoxamine–haloperidol and fluvoxamine–placebo groups at the end of the 4-week trial. Thus, it is seems unlikely that the therapeutic action of haloperidol addition was mediated through pharmacokinetic effects.

The aforementioned double-blind trial (McDougle et al., 1994) had insufficient power to determine whether SRI-resistant OCD patients with comorbid schizotypal personality show a significant improvement after addition of neuroleptic. Despite the widespread clinical impression that neuroleptics are useful in treating OCD with psychotic symptoms, there are no controlled trials in this population.

Newer Neuroleptics. Because of the limited effectiveness and safety of conventional neuroleptics in TS, clinicians have turned to a new generation of neuroleptics that have been introduced for the treatment of schizophrenia. Risperidone, a member of a class of antipsychotics that blocks both DA and 5-HT receptors, has been established as superior to placebo and equal, or superior, to haloperidol in the treatment of schizophrenia (Chouinard et al., 1993; Marder & Meibach, 1994). Risperidone has a more favorable side effect profile than conventional neuroleptics and may have less potential for producing tardive dyskinesia. Compared to haloperidol, fewer extrapyramidal side effects are observed with risperidone in doses of 6 mg daily or less. Risperidone is currently being widely used by clinicians to treat tic disorders as encouraging reports appear in the literature (Bruun & Budman, 1996; Lombroso et al., 1995; Stammenkovic, Aschauer, & Kasper, 1994; Van der Linden, Bruggeman, & Van Woerkom, 1994).

Might risperidone earn a place in the treatment of OCD, particularly TS-related OCD? A number of preliminary reports suggest that risperidone might alleviate OC symptoms when added to ongoing SRI therapy. In one study, one of three children with TS and comorbid OCD showed substantial improvement in OC symptoms when risperidone was added to paroxetine (Lombroso et al., 1995). McDougle, Fleischmann, et al. (1995) reported that three of three patients with primary OCD who were unresponsive to fluvoxamine alone showed marked improvement after risperidone was added to fluvoxamine. None of the patients had a history of tics, although one had a son with a chronic motor tic disorder. In a separate report of five cases with SRI-refractory OCD, addition of risperidone was associated with a 44% decrease in mean Y–BOCS scores (Jacobsen, 1995). In another case series, risperidone was added to 14 OCD patients who were refractory to clomipramine 250 mg/day ($n = 7$) or sertraline 50 mg/day and clomipramine 150 mg/day ($n = 7$; Ravizza et al., 1996). Seven (50%) of these patients "showed good clinical improvement and good tolerability" after risperidone was added (Ravizza et al., 1996). Saxena, Wang, Bystritsky, and Baxter (1996) combined risperidone with ongoing SRI treatment in 21 SRI-refractory OCD patients and found that 14 of 16 completers had "substantial" reductions in OC symptoms. Patients with horrific mental imagery had the best response, whereas patients with comorbid tic disorders had the poorest rate of response (only one of five improved) and the highest rate of akathisia (Saxena et al., 1996). In a separate case report, a combination of risperidone and fluoxetine was reported highly effective in a patient with comordid OCD and TS who had failed to respond to a number of other agents (Giakas, 1995). Taken together, the literature suggests that risperidone addition to an SRI may be effective in treating SRI-refractory OCD patients. Specific clinical features predictive of response to a risperidone–SRI combination remain to be established.

With few exceptions, it appears that risperidone alone is not beneficial in OCD. A group from the Netherlands reported that three of five TS patients experienced improvement in their OC behavior during risperidone treatment (Van der Linden et al., 1994). Two shortcomings of this report, however, are a very small sample size and the absence of OC-specific rating scales. Another study found that risperidone monotherapy was of no benefit in several adolescents with OCD (Simeon, Carrey, Wiggins, Milin, & Hosenbocus, 1995). As has been reported for clozapine (discussed later), there are an increasing number of reports that risperidone can either exacerbate existing (Dryden-Edwards & Reiss, 1996; Kopala & Honer, 1994; Remington & Adams, 1994) or induce new (Alzaid & Jones, 1997; Ames et al., 1996) OC symptoms when given for the treatment of psychotic symptoms. The mechanism by which this may occur or what subpopulation may be more at risk for the development of OC symptoms with risperidone is not yet known.

The prototypic "atypical" neuroleptic clozapine appears ineffective in both TS (Caine & Polinsky, 1979) and OCD (McDougle, Barr, et al., 1995). There are two positive case reports involving treatment-resistant adults (Steinert, Schmidt-Michel, & Kaschka, 1996; Young, Bostic, & McDonald, 1994), but negative findings in an open-label study of 12 treatment-resistant patients (McDougle, Barr, et al., 1995). In the open-label study, none of the 10 completers was a responder. The open-label study did not address whether conjoint SRI–clozapine treatment might be effective in some cases of OCD. Clozapine, like risperidone, antagonizes both DA and 5-HT receptors (Breier, 1995), but it has a much lower affinity for D2 receptors, a property that may be critical to tic suppression, and perhaps, alleviation of OC symptoms in some cases of OCD as well. It is noteworthy that clozapine (and risperidone) has been associated with exacerbation or induction of OCD in patients with schizophrenia. At present, more than a dozen cases from six independent centers have been reported in which OC symptoms emerged during the course of clozapine treatment of patients with schizophrenia (Allen & Tejera, 1994; Baker et al., 1992; Cassady & Taker, 1992; Eales & Layeni, 1994; Patel & Tandon, 1993; Patil, 1992). Emergence of OCD in clozapine-treated schizophrenics may be related to withdrawal from chronic D2 blockade (Baker et al., 1992). Indirect evidence suggests that increased D2 activity may produce OC-like behavior in animals or humans (for review, see Goodman, McDougle, et al., 1990). Alternatively, it has been suggested that blockade of 5-HT$_2$ receptors may be involved (Dursun & Reveley, 1994). It is of interest that coadministration of an SRI has been shown to reverse OC symptoms in cases of clozapine- (Allen & Tejera, 1994; Cassady & Taker, 1992; Kopala & Honer,

1994; Patel & Tandon, 1993) or risperidone-induced (Kopala & Honer, 1994) OC symptoms—although some authors have had more variable success (Steingard, Chengappa, Baker, & Schooler, 1993).

Novel and Experimental Drug Treatments

A variety of alternative drug treatments have been used in OCD. Of those considered here, intravenous clomipramine is the only treatment supported by a reasonable degree of empirical evidence. Several open-label trials suggest that intravenous administration of clomipramine may be helpful in OCD patients refractory to oral clomipramine (Fallon et al., 1992; Thakur, Remillard, Meldrum, & Gorecki, 1991; Warneke, 1989). To date, two double-blind trials of intravenous clomipramine have been published, and one of these (Fallon, Campeas, Schneier, Davies, & Liebowitz, 1994; Fallon, Liebowitz, Campeas, Schneier, & Davies, 1993) has appeared as an interim report only. In these double-blind studies, 38 treatment-refractory patients were randomly assigned to 14 consecutive weekday infusions of either clomipramine or placebo (saline). At 1 week postintravenous treatment, 35.7% of the clomipramine group were responders whereas no one in the placebo group was a responder. In another double-blind study, Koran, Sallee, and Pallanti (1997) compared pulse-loaded intravenous or oral clomipramine in OCD patients who had been ill at least 1 year. At 4.5 days after the second pulse-loaded dose, six of seven patients given intravenous clomipramine and only one of eight receiving oral clomipramine showed a response. Four of six responders to intravenous pulse loading of clomipramine maintained their response after 8 weeks of oral clomipramine. As many of the responders had failed previous trials with orally administered SRIs, intravenous pulse loading of clomipramine may be useful in treating refractory patients. A disadvantage of this experimental technique is its limited availability. (For a detailed discussion of intravenous clomipramine, see Fallon & Liebowitz, chap. 20, this volume.)

The alpha-2 adrenergic agonist clonidine has been found effective in suppressing motor tics (Leckman et al., 1991) and an early report suggested it was helpful for treating obsessions in some patients with TS (Cohen, Detlor, Young, & Shaywitz, 1980). Except for a few case reports of successful treatment with oral clonidine alone (Knesevich, 1982) or in combination with clomipramine (Lipsedge & Prothero, 1987), most published evidence points to the ineffectiveness of clonidine for OCD when used alone (Hewlett et al., 1992; Hollander, Fay, & Liebowitz, 1988) or in combination with other medications (Jenike, 1990). One investigative group reported that a single dose of intravenous clonidine reduced symptoms, but cautioned that the apparent anti-OC effect might have been due to clonidine-induced sedation (Hollander, Fay, Cohen, et al., 1988).

Moreover, clonidine seems to be poorly tolerated, with sedation prompting discontinuation in many patients (Jenike, 1990).

There is scant support for the efficacy of anticonvulsant agents in the treatment of OCD (Jenike, 1990; Joffe & Swinson, 1987). If there is a role for carbamazepine in OCD, it may be in patients with electroencephalogram or clinical evidence of a seizure disorder (Jenike & Brotman, 1984; Khanna, 1988). The anti-OC efficacy of combined SRI–carbamazepine treatment has not been adequately studied. Sodium valproate was found ineffective in two cases of OCD (McElroy, Keck, & Pope, 1987; McElroy & Pope, 1988). However, one author has suggested that divalproex may be a useful pretreatment for OCD patients who might otherwise tolerate SRIs poorly (Deltito, 1994). The anticonvulsant clonazepam was discussed earlier in this chapter.

There is a paucity of empirical data on psychostimulants as a possible treatment for OCD. What does exist consists mostly of pharmacological challenge findings or anecdotal reports. There is an early report that single doses of d-amphetamine induced transient improvement in obsessional symptoms in a group of 12 patients (Insel, Hamilton, Guttmacher, & Murphy, 1983). Another group, also using a challenge paradigm, confirmed that single doses of oral d-amphetamine reduced OC symptoms (Joffe, Swinson, & Levitt, 1991), but found that oral methylphenidate had no overall effect (Joffe et al., 1991; Swinson & Joffe, 1988). Another group of investigators found that intravenous administration of methylphenidate produced a worsening of symptoms in three of five patients with OCD (Lemus, Robinson, Kronig, et al., 1991). In a study of hyperactive boys, a trial with dextroamphetamine was associated with production of compulsive behaviors (Borcherding, Keysor, Rapoport, Elia, & Amass, 1990). In addition, numerous anecdotal reports suggest that recreational use of stimulants can exacerbate OC symptoms (Goodman, McDougle, et al., 1990; Koizumi, 1985), in some cases persistently (Frye & Arnold, 1981). Discrepancies in the literature regarding the effects of psychostimulants on OC symptoms may be related to differences in dosing, route of administration, or clinical characteristics of the individuals. To our knowledge, the effects of chronic administration of psychostimulants on OC symptoms have not been evaluated in a controlled trial.

An open-label case series described a significant reduction in OC and depressive symptoms during chronic treatment with the DA receptor agonist bromocriptine (12.5–30 mg/day) in three of four adults with OCD and comorbid depression (Ceccherini-Nelli & Guazzelli, 1994). Controlled studies of bromocriptine in OCD are needed to verify the efficacy of this approach.

The possible role of hormones and neuropeptides in the treatment of OCD has begun to be explored, but preliminary findings are not encouraging. Four weeks of adjuvant triiodothyronine treatment was ineffective in 16 patients who had had a partial response to clomipramine (Pigott et al., 1991). Preclinical studies suggest that the neuropeptide oxytocin mediates a number of behavioral effects that may be related to OC behavior in humans (Leckman et al., 1994), including inhibiting the acquisition of aversive conditioning (Insel, 1992). Ansseau et al. (1987) reported a case in which 4 weeks of intranasal administration of oxytocin led to improvement in OC symptoms, but the side effects were profound, including memory disturbances, psychosis, and osmotic abnormalities. In a more recent publication, oxytocin was ineffective in reducing symptoms (Den Boer & Westenberg, 1992). In a small study of women, the antiandrogen cyproterone acetate seemed to exert an anti-OC effect, but it was not sustained (Casas et al., 1986). An attempt by another group to replicate this finding in a woman with severe OCD was unsuccessful (Feldman, Noshirvani, & Chu, 1988).

Recent studies on the therapeutic use of the second messenger precursor inositol have been extended to OCD. The design was based on the successful inositol treatment of depression (Levine et al., 1995) and panic disorder (Benjamin et al., 1995) under double-blind, placebo-controlled conditions. Fux, Levine, Aviv, and Belmaker (1996) entered 15 patients (who had failed previous treatment with clomipramine or SSRIs) into a double-blind, controlled crossover trial of 18 g/day of inositol or placebo for 6 weeks each. There were no reported side effects and 13 patients completed the protocol. Y–BOCS scores were significantly lower when participants were taking inositol compared to when they were on placebo. The mechanism of action of inositol is unclear but warrants continued interest and replication.

Addition of the steroid suppressant aminoglutethimide to fluoxetine led to significant improvement in a case of treatment-refractory OCD (Chouinard, Belanger, Beauclair, Sultan, & Murphy, 1996). The rationale for this approach was based on evidence that steroids contribute to the maintainance of the depressed mood state and that steroid suppressant agents may be useful in cases of treatment-resistant depression.

It has been proposed that some cases of childhood-onset OCD may be related to an infection-triggered autoimmune process similar to that of Sydenham's chorea, a late manifestation of rheumatic fever (Swedo, Leonard, & Kiessling, 1994). More than 70% of cases of Sydenham's chorea have OC symptoms (Swedo et al., 1989). The etiology of Sydenham's chorea is thought to involve the development of antibodies to group A β-hemolytic strepococcal (GABHS) infection that cross-react with basal ganglia and other brain areas (Murphy et al., 1997). Swedo coined the acronym PANDAS (Pediatric Autoimmune Neuropsychiatric Disorders Associated with Strep) to describe cases of childhood-onset OCD that resemble Sydenham's chorea with respect to acute onset following a GABHS infection, accompanying neurological signs, and an episodic course (Swedo et al., 1994). Various trials with immunomodulatory treatments (e.g., prednisone, plasmapheresis, iv immunoglobins) or antimicrobial prophylaxis (e.g., penicillin) are underway at the National Institute of Mental Health and elsewhere for putative PANDAS cases. This exciting new avenue of research will undoubtedly be the subject of intense investigation over the next few years.

NONPHARMACOLOGIC BIOLOGICAL APPROACHES

Nonpharmacological biological treatments of OCD have included electroconvulsive therapy (ECT), neurosurgery, sleep deprivation, phototherapy, and repetitive transcranial magnetic stimulation (rTMS). ECT, regarded as the gold standard for treating depression, is generally viewed as having limited benefit in OCD (Jenike & Rauch, 1995) despite sporadic reports of its success in treatment-resistant cases (Casey & Davis, 1994; Husain, Lewis, & Thornton, 1993; Khanna, Gangadhar, & Sinha, 1988; Mellman & Gorman, 1984). In some instances the favorable response to ECT was short-lived (Casey & Davis, 1994; Khanna et al., 1988). Khanna et al. (1988) described nine treatment-refractory OCD patients (without depression) who underwent ECT, resulting in a decline in global OCD ratings exceeding 20%. However, all had returned to their baseline illness by 4 months. In a retrospective review, Maletzky, McFarland, and Burt (1994) examined the response to ECT in 32 patients with treatment-refractory OCD. Comparison of pre- and post-ECT measures of symptom severity (as measured by the Maudsley Obsessional-Compulsive Inventory) revealed a significant improvement. As noted by the authors, limitations of this report include its retrospective design, the shortcomings of the outcome measures, and the application of "unevenly applied and diverse behavioral, cognitive, and chemotherapies" (Maletzky et al., 1994, p. 40) during the post-ECT evaluation period. ECT should certainly be considered in the treatment of depressive symptoms in the treatment-refractory OCD patient at risk of suicide. A sham-controlled trial of ECT in OCD (with and without depression) seems long overdue, although fraught with ethical and practical difficulties. Additionally, randomization of OCD patients to ECT or serotonergic medications with repeated, blind evaluations could prove valuable. (See Rudorfer, chap. 22, this volume, for a comprehensive review of ECT in OCD.)

To many, the mere mention of neurosurgical treatment of psychiatric illness (sometimes euphemistically called psychosurgery) evokes troubling thoughts about a notorious period in the history of mental health care when frontal lobotomies were performed indiscriminantly on patients with all forms of pathology, leaving them with profound and permanent alterations in personality and intellect (Stagno, Smith, & Hassenbusch, 1994). However, modern stereotactic surgical procedures should not be equated with the relatively crude neurosurgical approaches of the past. As a professional faced with a patient suffering from malignant and intractable OCD, we may be asked to consider all available treatment options dispassionately and objectively, including neurosurgery. Recent evidence suggests that stereotactic lesions of the cingulum bundle (cingulotomy; Jenike, Baer, Ballantine, et al., 1991) or anterior limb of the internal capsule (capsulotomy; Mindus, Rasmussen, & Lindquist, 1994) may produce substantial clinical benefit in some patients without causing appreciable morbidity. In a retrospective follow-up study of 33 patients who underwent cingulotomy, Jenike, Baer, Ballentine, et al. (1991) found that 25% to 30% of the patients experienced substantial benefit according to conservative criteria. In a more recent prospective study, Baer et al. (1995) evaluated 18 patients before and 6 months after bilateral cingulotomy. Five patients (28%) met conservative criteria for treatment response. A number of unanswered questions about neurosurgical treatment of OCD remain:

1. What is the true (placebo-corrected) efficacy of surgery?
2. Which procedure (i.e., cingulotomy, capsulotomy, limbic leucotomy) is best?
3. What is the optimal placement of lesions?
4. Can we predict who are the best candidates for surgery?

Some of these questions could be addressed using a research protocol developed jointly by investigators at Harvard and Brown Universities. In this study, carefully screened treatment-refractory cases of severe OCD are randomized in a blinded fashion to anterior capsulotomy using a "gamma-knife" (radiosurgery) or to a sham procedure in which no gamma radiation is emitted. At present, stereotactic psychosurgery should be viewed as the option of last resort in the gravely ill patient with OCD who has not responded to well-documented adequate trials over a 5-year period with several SRIs (including clomipramine), exposure and response prevention, at least two combination strategies (including combined SRI and behavior therapy), an MAOI trial, a trial with a novel antidepressant (e.g., venlafaxine), and ECT (if depression is present). (For further discussion of the neurosurgical treatment of OCD, see Jenike, chap. 23, this volume.)

Sleep deprivation had no overall beneficial effect on OC symptoms or mood in 16 patients with OCD (Joffe & Swinson, 1988). Likewise, bright light therapy was ineffective in reducing severity of symptoms in a small group of patients with OCD (Yoney, Pigott, L'Heureux, & Rosenthal, 1991).

rTMS provides a relatively noninvasive probe of cortical function. In rTMS, a pulsatile high-intensity electromagnetic field emitted from a coil placed against the scalp induces focal electrical currents in the underlying cerebral cortex. Cortical activity can be stimulated or disrupted by rTMS. Its primary application to date has been investigations of the relation between regional cortical activity and function in health and disease, but some early studies suggest rTMS may have therapeutic value in depression (George et al., 1995) and perhaps OCD (Greenberg et al., 1997). In a preliminary controlled study, Greenberg et al. (1997) reported that a single session of rTMS applied to the right prefrontal cortex produced a transient reduction in compulsive urges. It is possible that the anti-OC effect of rTMS stemmed from its interference with ongoing neuronal activity mediating the compulsive urges. rTMS is not without risk, as seizures have been reported in at least six (of more than 250) patients undergoing the procedure (Wasserman, 1997). Local discomfort from activation of scalp musculature and nerves also occurs (Wasserman, 1997). Further evaluation of rTMS as an investigative and therapeutic tool seems justified.

SUMMARY

In summary, despite advances in the pharmacotherapy and behavior therapy of OCD, a number of patients experience minimal or no clinical gains. The first step in approaching the treatment-resistant case of OCD is to determine whether an adequate SRI trial has actually taken place and to evaluate what factors may have contributed to treatment resistance. Options in dealing with the SRI-resistant OCD patient include switching to a different SRI, combining another medication (or behavior therapy) with the SRI, considering novel or experimental drug treatments, or employing nonpharmacological biological approaches. A complete discussion of behavior therapy is beyond the scope of this chapter, but there is reason to believe that, in many cases, combined SRI and behavior therapy may be the most broadly effective treatment for OCD. How much more effective the combination is than SRI therapy alone or behavior alone remains an active area of study and the subject of considerable debate.

Unfortunately, none of the SRI–drug combination approaches to treatment-resistant OCD can be viewed as firmly established. In the case of SRI plus lithium or SRI plus buspirone, encouraging open-label reports have been followed up by mostly negative controlled trials. The lack of a mean between-group difference should not completely overshadow the observation that some individual patients do seem to benefit from lithium or buspirone addition. Potential clinical indicators for adding lithium or buspirone to an SRI are, respectively, prominent depressive symptoms or generalized anxiety disorder. The proposed predictor for buspirone needs to be evaluated prospectively in a controlled trial. The combination of fluvoxamine and clomipramine to capitalize on a drug–drug interaction (i.e., elevating plasma concentrations of clomipramine) deserves further research. Both an open-label and a double-blind trial have shown that a combination of fluvoxamine and a neuroleptic is effective in reducing OC symptoms in fluvoxamine-refractory OCD patients with comorbid tic disorders. The addition of neuroleptic to an SRI should also be considered if delusional ideation or schizotypal traits are present. Addition of fenfluramine should be avoided because of insufficient empirical support and safety concerns. Addition of clonazepam to SRI therapy may be worthy of consideration, but cannot be enthusiastically endorsed until more controlled trials appear. Several reports over a number of years suggest that intravenously administered clomipramine may have a place in the management of treatment-resistant OCD. ECT may have a role in the severely depressed patient with OCD who has been refractory to pharmacological and behavioral approaches. The physician should be cognizant of current evidence regarding the possible role of stereotactic neurosurgery in severe refractory OCD.

Identification of meaningful subtypes of OCD, and clinical or biological markers of those subtypes, presents an important challenge for the future. Subtype markers may serve as predictors of treatment response and help in the selection of appropriate treatment. At present, years can be lost before the best fit is found between the patient and the treatment. Future research is needed to develop new and better approaches for the treatment-refractory patient with OCD.

ACKNOWLEDGMENTS

This work was supported, in part, by National Institute of Mental Health Grants MH-45803, MH-56597 and by the State of Florida. We thank Donna Epting and Candy L. Hill for their expert assistance.

REFERENCES

Abenhaim, L., Moride, Y., Brenot, F., Rich, S., Benichou, J., Kurz, X., Higenbottam, T., Oakley, C., Wouters, E., Aubier, M., Simonneau, G., & Begaud, B. (1996). Appetite-suppressant drugs and the risk of primary pulmonary hypertension: International Primary Pulmonary Hypertension Study Group. *New England Journal of Medicine, 335*(9), 609–616.

Allen, L., & Tejera, C. (1994). Treatment of clozapine-induced obsessive-compulsive symptoms with sertraline [Letter]. *American Journal of Psychiatry, 151*(7), 1096–1097.

Alzaid, K., & Jones, B. D. (1997). A case report of risperidone-induced obsessive-compulsive symptoms. *Journal of Clinical Psychopharmacology, 17,* 58–59.

Ames, D., Wirshing, W. C., Marder, S. R., Hwang, S. S., German, C. A., Mintz, J., & Goldstein, D. (1996). Risperidone vs. haloperidole: Relative liabilities for OCD and depression. *Schizophrenia Research* [Abstract V.B.2], *18*(2–3), 129.

Ananth, J., Burgoyne, K., Smith, M., & Swartz, R. (1995). Venlafaxine for treatment of obsessive-compulsive disorder. *American Journal of Psychiatry, 152,* 1832–1833.

Anderson, I. M., & Cowen, P. J. (1992). Effect of pindolol on endocrine and temperature responses to buspirone in healthy volunteers. *Psychopharmacology, 106,* 428–432.

Ansseau, M., Legros, J. J., Mormont, C., Cerfontaine, J. L., Papart, P., Geenen, V., Adam, F., & Francek, G. (1987). Intranasal oxytocin in obsessive-compulsive disorder. *Psychoneuroendocrinology, 12,* 231–236.

Artigas, F., Perez, V., & Alvarez, E. (1994). Pindolol induces a rapid improvement of depressed patients treated with serotonin reuptake inhibitors. *Archives of General Psychiatry, 51,* 248–251.

Artigas, F., Romero, L., de Montigny, C., & Blier, P. (1996). Acceleration of the effect of selected antidepressant drugs in major depression by $5\text{-}HT_{1A}$ antagonists. *Trends in Neuroscience, 19*(9), 378–383.

Bacher, N. (1990). Clonazepam treatment of obsessive compulsive disorder [Letter to the editor]. *Journal of Clinical Psychiatry, 51,* 168–169.

Baer, L., Jenike, M. A., Black, D. W., Treece, C., Rosenfeld, R., & Greist, J. (1992). Effect of Axis II diagnoses on treatment outcome with clomipramine in 55 patients with obsessive compulsive disorder. *Archives of General Psychiatry, 49,* 862–866.

Baer, L., Rauch, S. L., Ballantine, T., Martuza, R., Cosgrove, R., Cassem, E., Giriunas, I., Manzo, P., Dimino, C., & Jenike, M. A. (1995). Cingulotomy for intractable obsessive-compulsive disorder. *Archives of General Psychiatry, 52,* 384–392.

Baker, R. W., Chengappa, K. N. R., Baird, J. W., Steingard, S., Christ, M. A. G., & Schooler, N. R. (1992). Emergence of obsessive compulsive symptoms during treatment with clozapine. *Journal of Clinical Psychiatry, 53,* 439–442.

Bark, N., & Lindenmayer, J. P. (1992). Ineffectiveness of clomipramine for obsessive-compulsive symptoms in a patient with schizophrenia [Letter to the editor]. *American Journal of Psychiatry, 149,* 136–137.

Barr, L. C., Goodman, W. K., Anand, A., McDougle, C. J., & Price, L. H. (1997). Addition of desipramine to serotonin reruptake inhibitors in treatment-resistant obsessive compulsive disorder. *American Journal of Psychiatry, 154*(9), 1293–1295.

Baxter, L. R., Jr., Thompson, J. M., Schwartz, J. M., Guze, B. H., Phelps, M. E., Mazziotta, J. C., Selin, C. E., & Moss, L. (1987). Trazodone treatment response in obsessive-compulsive disorder—Correlated with shifts in glucose metabolism in the caudate nuclei. *Psychopathology, 20*(1, Suppl.), 114–122.

Benjamin, J., Levine, J., Fux, M., Aviv, A., Levy, D., & Belmaker, R. H. (1995). Double-blind, placebo-controlled, crossover trial of inositol treatment for panic disorder. *American Journal of Psychiatry, 152,* 1084–1086.

Berman, R. M., Darnell, A. M., Miller, H. L., Anand, A., & Charney, D. S. (1997). Effect of pindolol in hastening response to fluoxetine in the treatment of major depression: A double-blind, placebo-controlled trial. *American Journal of Psychiatry, 154,* 37–43.

Blier, P., & Bergeron, R. (1995). Effectiveness of pindolol with selected antidepressant drugs in the treatment of major depression. *Journal of Clinical Psychopharmacology, 15,* 217–222.

Blier, P., & Bergeron, R. (1996). Sequential administration of augmentation strategies in treatment-resistant obsessive-compulsive disorder: Preliminary findings. *International Journal of Clinical Psychopharmacology, 11,* 37–44.

Blier, P., & de Montigny, C. (1992). Lack of efficacy of lithium augmentation in obsessive-compulsive disorder: The perspective of different regional effects of lithium on serotonin release in the central nervous system. *Journal of Clinical Psychopharmacology, 12*(1), 65–66.

Bodkin, J. A., & White, K. (1989). Clonazepam in the treatment of obsessive compulsive disorder associated with panic disorder in one patient. *Journal of Clinical Psychiatry, 50,* 265–266.

Borcherding, B. G., Keysor, C. S., Rapoport, J. L., Elia, J., & Amass, J. (1990). Motor/vocal tics and compulsive behaviors on stimulant drugs: Is there a common vulnerability? *Psychiatry Research, 33*(1), 83–94.

Breier, A. (1995). Serotonin, schizophrenia and antipsychotic drug action. *Schizophrenia Research, 14,* 187–202.

Brosen, K., Skjelbo, E., Rasmussen, B. B., Poulsen, H. E., & Loft, S. (1993). Fluvoxamine is a potent inhibitor of cytochrome P4501A2. *Biochemical Pharmacology, 45,* 1211–1214.

Browne, M., Horn, E., & Jones, T. T. (1993). The benefits of clomipramine-fluoxetine combination in obsessive compulsive disorder. *Canadian Journal of Psychiatry, 38*(4), 242–243.

Bruun, R. D., & Budman, C. L. (1996). Risperidone as a treatment for Tourette's syndrome. *Journal of Clinical Psychiatry, 57,* 29–31.

Byerly, M. J., Goodman, W. K., & Christensen, R. (1996). High doses of sertraline for treatment-resistant obsessive-compulsive disorder [Letter to the editor]. *American Journal of Psychiatry, 153*(9), 1232–1233.

Caine, E. D., & Polinsky, R. J. (1979). Haloperidol induced dysphoria in patients with Tourette syndrome. *American Journal of Psychiatry, 236,* 1216–1217.

Calvocoressi, L., Lewis, B., Harris, M., Trufan, S. J., Goodman, W. K., McDougle, C. J., & Price, L. H. (1995). Family accommodation in obsessive compulsive disorder. *American Journal of Psychiatry, 152*(3), 441–443.

Casas, M., Alvarez, E., Duro, P., Garcia-Ribera, C., Udina, C., Velat, A., Abella, D., Rodriguez-Espinosa, J., Salva, P., & Jané, P. (1986). Antiandrogenic treatment of obsessive-compulsive neurosis. *Acta Psychiatria Scandinavia, 73,* 221–222.

Casey, D. A., & Davis, M. H. (1994). Obsessive-compulsive disorder responsive to electroconvulsive therapy in an elderly woman. *Southern Medical Journal, 87,* 862–864.

Cassady, S. L., & Taker, G. K. (1992). Addition of fluoxetine to clozapine [Letter to the editor]. *American Journal of Psychiatry, 149*(9), 1274.

Ceccherini-Nelli, A., & Guazzelli, M. (1994). Treatment of refractory OCD with the dopamine agonist bromocriptine. *Journal of Clinical Psychiatry, 55*(9), 415–416.

Chouinard, G., Belanger, M.-C., Beauclair, L., Sultan, S., & Murphy, B. E. (1996). Potentiation of fluoxetine by aminoglutethimide, an adrenal steroid suppressant, in obsessive compulsive disorder resistant to SSRIs: A case report. *Progress in Neuro-Psychopharmacology and Biological Psychiatry, 20,* 1067–1079.

Chouinard, G., Jones, B., Remington, G., Bloom, D., Addington, D., MacEwan, G. W., LaBelle, A., Beauclair, L., & Arnott, W. (1993). A Canadian multicenter placebo-controlled study of fixed doses of risperidone and haloperidol in the treatment of chronic schizophrenic patients. *Journal of Clinical Psychopharmacology, 13*(1), 25–40.

Clineschmidt, B. V., Zacchei, A. G., Totaro, J. A., Pflueger, A. B., McGuffin, J. C., & Wishousky, T. I. (1978). Fenfluramine and brain serotonin. *Annals of the New York Acadademy of Science, 305,* 222–241.

Coccaro, E., Gabriel, S., & Siever, L. (1990). Buspirone challenge: Preliminary evidence for a role for central $5\text{-}HT_{1A}$ receptor function in impulsive aggressive behavior in humans. *Psychopharmacology Bulletin, 26,* 393–405.

Cohen, D. J., Detlor, J., Young, J. G., & Shaywitz, B. A. (1980). Clonidine ameliorates Gilles de la Tourette syndrome. *Archives of General Psychiatry, 37,* 1350–1357.

Connolly, H. M., Crary, J. L., McGoon, M. D., Hensrud, D. D., Brooks, B. S., Edwards, W. D., & Schaff, H. V. (1997). Valvular heart disease associated with fenfluramine-phentermine. *New England Journal of Medicine, 337*, 581–588.

Cook, E. H., Jr., Rowlett, R., Jaselskis, C., & Levanthal, B. L. (1992). Fluoxetine treatment of children and adults with autistic disorder and mental retardation. *Journal of the American Academy of Child & Adolescent Psychiatry, 31*(4), 739–745.

Cottraux, J., Mollard, E., Bouvard, M., Marks, I., Sluys, M., Nury, A. M., Douge, R., & Cialdella, P. (1990). A controlled study of fluvoxamine and exposure in obsessive-compulsive disorder. *International Journal of Clinical Psychopharmacology, 5*(1), 17–30.

Cox, B. J., Swinson, R. P., Morrison, B., & Lee, P. S. (1993). Clomipramine, fluoxetine and behavior therapy in the treatment of obsessive-compulsive disorder: A meta-analysis. *Journal of Behavioral Therapy and Experimental Psychiatry, 24*(2), 149–153.

Cummings, J. L., & Cunningham, K. (1992). Obsessive-compulsive disorder in Huntington's disease. *Biological Psychiatry, 31*, 263–270.

Delgado, P. L., Goodman, W. K., Price, L. H., Heninger, G. R., & Charney, D. S. (1990). Fluvoxamine/pimozide treatment of concurrent Tourette's and obsessive-compulsive disorder. *British Journal of Psychiatry, 157*, 762–765.

Deltito, J. A. (1994). Valproate pretreatment for difficult-to-treat patients with OCD. *Journal of Clinical Psychiatry, 55*(11), 500.

Den Boer, J. A., & Westenberg, G. M. (1992). Oxytocin in obsessive compulsive disorder. *Peptides, 13*(6), 1083–1085.

Dryden-Edwards, R. C., & Reiss, A. L. (1996). Differential response of psychotic and obsessive symptoms to risperidone in an adolescent. *Journal of Child & Adolescent Psychopharmacology, 6*, 139–145.

Dursun, S. M., & Reveley, M. A. (1994). Obsessive-compulsive symptoms and clozapine [Letter to the editor]. *British Journal of Psychiatry, 165*, 267–268.

Eales, M. G., & Layeni, A. O. (1994). Exacerbation of obsessive-compulsive symptoms associated with clozapine. *British Journal of Psychiatry, 164*, 687–688.

Eisenberg, J., & Asnis, G. (1985). Lithium as an adjunct treatment in obsessive-compulsive disorder. *American Journal of Psychiatry, 142*, 663.

Fallon, B. A., Campeas, R., Schneier, F., Davies, S., & Liebowitz, M. R. (1994). *IV clomipramine for refractory OCD: A controlled study. New Research 448.* Washington, DC: American Psychiatric Association.

Fallon, B. A., Campeas, R., Schneier, F. R., Hollander, E., Feerick, J., Hatterer, J., Goetz, D., Davies, S., & Liebowitz, M. R. (1992). Open trial of intravenous clomipramine in five treatment-refractory patients with obsessive-compulsive disorder. *Journal of Neuropsychiatry & Clinical Neuroscience, 4*, 70–75.

Fallon, B. A., Liebowitz, M. R., Campeas, R., Schneier, F., & Davies, S. (1993). *Treatment of refractory OCD with intravenous clomipramine.* Albany: New York State Office of Mental Health Research Conference.

Feder, R. (1988). Lithium augmentation of clomipramine. *Journal of Clinical Psychiatry, 49*, 458.

Feldman, J. D., Noshirvani, H., & Chu, C. (1988). Letter to the editor. *Acta Psychiatria Scandinavia, 78*(2), 254.

Fenton, W. S., & McGlashan, T. H. (1986). The prognostic significance of obsessive-compulsive symptoms in schizophrenia. *American Journal of Psychiatry, 143*(4), 437–441.

Fontaine, R., Ontiveros, A., Elie, R., Kensler, T. T., Roberts, D. L., Kaplita, S., Ecker, J. A., & Faludi, G. (1994). A double-blind comparison of nefazodone, imipramine, and placebo in major depression. *Journal of Clinical Psychiatry, 55*, 234–241.

Frye, P. E., & Arnold, L. E. (1981). Persistent amphetamine-induced compulsive rituals: Response to pyridoxine (B6). *Biological Psychiatry, 16*(6), 583–587.

Fux, M., Levine, J., Aviv, A., & Belmaker, R. H. (1996). Inositol treatment of obsessive-compulsive disorder. *American Journal of Psychiatry, 153,* 1219–1221.

George, M. S., Wasserman, E. M., Williams, W. A., Callahan, A., Ketter, T. A., Basser, P., Hallett, M., & Post, R. M. (1995). Daily repetitive transcranial magnetic stimulation (rTMS) improves mood in depression. *NeuroReport, 6,* 1853–1856.

Giakas, W. J. (1995). Risperidone treatment for a Tourette's disorder patient with comorbid obsessive-compulsive disorder. *American Journal of Psychiatry, 152,* 1097–1098.

Golden, R. N., Morris, J. E., & Sack, D. A. (1988). Combined lithium-tricyclic treatment of obsessive-compulsive disorder. *Biological Psychiatry, 23,* 181–185.

Goodman, W. K., McDougle, C. J., Price, L. H., Riddle, M. A., Pauls, D. L., & Leckman, J. F. (1990). Beyond the serotonin hypothesis: A role for dopamine in some forms of obsessive compulsive disorder? *Journal of Clinical Psychiatry, 51*(8, Suppl.), 36–43.

Goodman, W. K., Price, L. H., Delgado, P. L., Palumbo, J., Krystal, J. H., Nagy, L. M., Rasmussen, S. A., Heninger, G. R., & Charney, D. S. (1990). Specificity of serotonin reuptake inhibitors in the treatment of obsessive compulsive disorder: Comparison of fluvoxamine and desipramine. *Archives of General Psychiatry, 47,* 577–585.

Goodman, W. K., Price, L. H., Rasmussen, S. A., Mazure, C., Delgado, P., Heninger, G. R., & Charney, D. S. (1989). The Yale–Brown Obsessive Compulsive Scale (Y–BOCS): Part II. Validity. *Archives of General Psychiatry, 46,* 1012–1016.

Goodman, W. K., Price, L. H., Rasmussen, S. A., Mazure, C., Fleischmann, R. L., Hill, C. L., Heninger, G. R., & Charney, D. S. (1989). The Yale–Brown Obsessive Compulsive Scale (Y–BOCS): Part I. Development, use, and reliability. *Archives of General Psychiatry, 46,* 1006–1011.

Goodman, W. K., Rasmussen, S. A., Foa, E. B., & Price, L. H. (1994). Obsessive compulsive disorder. In R. F. Prien & D. S. Robinson (Eds.), *Clinical evaluation of psychotropic drugs: Principles and guidance* (pp. 431–466). New York: Raven.

Gordon, C. T., Rapoport, J. L., Hamburger, S. D., State, R. C., & Mannheim, G. B. (1992). Differential response of seven subjects with autistic disorder to clomipramine and desipramine. *American Journal of Psychiatry, 149,* 363–366.

Grady, T. A., Pigott, T. A., L'Heureux, F. L., Hill, J. L., Bernstein, S. E., & Murphy, D. L. (1993). Double-blind study of adjuvant buspirone for fluoxetine-treated patients with obsessive-compulsive disorder. *American Journal of Psychiatry, 150*(5), 819–821.

Grady, T. A., Pigott, T. A., L'Heureux, F., & Murphy, D. L. (1992). Seizure associated with fluoxetine and adjuvant buspirone therapy [Letter to the editor]. *Journal of Clinical Psychopharmacology, 12,* 70–71.

Greenberg, B. D., George, M. S., Martin, J. D., Benjamin, J., Schlaepfer, T. E., Altemus, M., Wassermann, E. M., Post, R. M., & Murphy, D. L. (1997). Effect of prefrontal repetitive transcranial magnetic stimulation in obsessive-compulsive disorder: A preliminary study. *American Journal of Psychiatry, 154*(6), 867–869.

Greist, J., Chouinard, G., DuBoff, E., Halaris, A., Kim, S. W., Koran, L., Liebowitz, M., Lydiard, R. B., Rasmussen, S., White, K., & Sikes, C. (1995). Double-blind parallel comparison of three dosages of sertraline and placebo in outpatients with obsessive-compulsive disorder. *Archives of General Psychiatry, 52,* 289–295.

Greist, J. H., Jefferson, J. W., Kobak, K. A., Katzelnick, D. J., & Serlin, R. C. (1995). Efficacy and tolerability of serotonin transport inhibitors in obsessive compulsive disorder: A meta-analysis. *Archives of General Psychiatry, 52,* 53–60.

Grossman, R., & Hollander, E. (1996). Treatment of obsessive-compulsive disorder with venlafaxine [Letter to the editor]. *American Journal of Psychiatry, 153,* 576–577.

Haresh, H., Aizenberg, D., & Munitz, H. (1990). Trazodone in clomipramine-resistant obsessive-compulsive disorder. *Clinical Neuropharmacology, 13,* 322–328.

Heninger, G. R., Charney, D. S., & Sternberg, D. E. (1983). Lithium carbonate augmentation of antidepressant treatment: An effective prescription for treatment-refractory depression. *Archives of General Psychiatry, 40,* 1335–1342.

Hertzman, P. A., Blevins, W. L., Mayer, J., Greenfield, B., Ting, M., & Gleich, G. J. (1990). Association of the Eosinophilia-Myalgia syndrome with the ingestion of tryptophan. *New England Journal of Medicine, 322,* 869–873.

Hewlett, W. A., Vinogradov, S., & Agras, W. S. (1990). Clonazepam treatment of obsessions and compulsions. *Journal of Clinical Psychiatry, 51,* 158–161.

Hewlett, W. A., Vinogradov, S., & Agras, W. S. (1992). Clomipramine, clonazepam, and clonidine treatment of obsessive-compulsive disorder. *Journal of Clinical Psychopharmacology, 12,* 420–430.

Hollander, E., DeCaria, C. M., Schneier, F. R., Schneier, H. A., Liebowitz, M. R., & Klein, D. F. (1990). Fenfluramine augmentation of serotonin reuptake blockade antiobsessional treatment. *Journal of Clinical Psychiatry, 51,* 119–123.

Hollander, E., Fay, M., Cohen, B., Campeas, R., Gorman, J. M., & Liebowitz, M. R. (1988). Serotonergic and noradrenergic sensitivity in obsessive-compulsive disorder: Behavioral findings. *American Journal of Psychiatry, 145,* 1015–1017.

Hollander, E., Fay, M., & Liebowitz, M. R. (1988). Clonidine and clomipramine in obsessive-compulsive disorder. *American Journal of Psychiatry, 145,* 388–389.

Hollander, E., Schiffman, E., Cohen, B., Rivera-Stein, M. A., Rosen, W., Gorman, J. M., Fyer, A. J., Papp, L., & Liebowitz, M. R. (1990). Signs of central nervous system dysfunction in obsessive-compulsive disorder. *Archives of General Psychiatry, 47,* 27–32.

Hoyer, D. (1988). Functional correlates of serotonin 5-HT1 recognition sites. *Journal of Recept Research, 8,* 59–81.

Husain, M. M., Lewis, S. F., & Thornton, W. L. (1993). Maintenance ECT for refractory obsessive-compulsive disorder [Letter to the editor]. *American Journal of Psychiatry, 150,* 1899–1900.

Hwang, E. C., & Van Woert, M. H. (1979). Antimyoclonic action of clonazepam: The role of serotonin. *European Journal of Pharmacology, 60,* 31–40.

Insel, T. R. (1992). Oxytocin—A neuropeptide for affiliation: Evidence from behavioral, receptor autoradiographic, and comparative studies. *Psychoneuroendocrinology, 17,* 3–35.

Insel, T. R., Hamilton, J. A., Guttmacher, L. B., & Murphy, D. L. (1983). D-amphetamine in obsessive-compulsive disorder. *Psychopharmacology, 80,* 231–235.

Insel, T. R., Murphy, D. L., Cohen, R. M., Alterman, I., Kilts, C., & Linnoila, M. (1983). Obsessive-compulsive disorder: A double-blind trial of clomipramine and clorgyline. *Archives of General Psychiatry, 40,* 605–612.

Jacobsen, F. M. (1995). Risperidone in the treatment of severe affective illness and refractory OCD. *Journal of Clinical Psychiatry, 56,* 423–429.

Jelliffe, S. E. (1932). Psychopathology of forced movements in oculogyric crises. *Journal of Nervous and Mental Disease, 76*(6), 631–633.

Jenike, M. A. (1990). Drug treatment of obsessive-compulsive disorder. In M. A. Jenike, L. Baer, & W. E. Minichiello (Eds.), *Obsessive compulsive disorders: Theory and management* (2nd ed., pp. 249–282). Chicago: Year Book Medical.

Jenike, M. A., Baer, L., Ballantine, H. T., Martuza, R. L., Tynes, S., Giriunas, L., Buttolph, M. L., & Cassem, N. H. (1991). Cingulotomy for refractory obsessive-compulsive disorder: A long-term follow-up of 33 patients. *Archives of General Psychiatry, 48,* 548–555.

Jenike, M. A., Baer, L., & Buttolph, L. (1991). Buspirone augmentation of fluoxetine in patients with obsessive compulsive disorder. *Journal of Clinical Psychiatry, 52,* 13–14.

Jenike, M. A., Baer, L., Minichiello, W. E., Rauch, S. L., & Buttolph, M. L. (1997). Placebo-controlled trial of fluoxetine and phenelzine for obsessive-compulsive disorder. *American Journal of Psychiatry, 154*(9), 1261–1264.

Jenike, M. A., Baer, L., Minichiello, W. E., Schwartz, C. E., & Carey, R. J., Jr. (1986). Concomitant obsessive-compulsive disorder and schizotypal personality disorder. *American Journal of Psychiatry, 143,* 530–533.

Jenike, M. A., & Brotman, A. W. (1984). The EEG in obsessive compulsive disorder. *Journal of Clinical Psychiatry, 45*, 122–124.

Jenike, M. A., Hyman, S., Baer, L., Holland, A., Minichiello, W. E., Buttolph, L., Summergrad, P., Seymour, R., & Ricciardi, J. (1990). A controlled trial of fluvoxamine in obsessive-compulsive disorder: Implications for a serotonergic theory. *American Journal of Psychiatry, 147*, 1209–1215.

Jenike, M. A., & Rauch, S. L. (1995). Managing the patient with treatment-resistant obsessive compulsive disorder: Current strategies. *Journal of Clinical Psychiatry, 56*(2), 81–82.

Jenike, M. A., Surman, O. S., Cassem, N. H., Zusky, P., & Anderson, W. H. (1983). Monoamine oxidase inhibitors in obsessive-compulsive disorder. *Journal of Clinical Psychiatry, 144*, 131–132.

Jensen, H. H., Hutchings, B., & Poulsen, J. C. (1989). Conditioned emotional responding under diazepam: A psychophysiological study of state-dependent learning. *Psychopharmacology, 98*, 392–397.

Joffe, R. T., & Swinson, R. P. (1987). Carbamazepine in obsessive-compulsive disorder. *Biological Psychiatry, 22*, 1169–1171.

Joffe, R. T., & Swinson, R. P. (1988). Total sleep deprivation in patients with obsessive-compulsive disorder. *Acta Psychiatria Scandinavia, 77*, 483–487.

Joffe, R. T., Swinson, R. P., & Levitt, A. J. (1991). Acute psychostimulant challenge in primary obsessive-compulsive disorder. *Journal of Clinical Psychopharmacology, 11*(4), 237–241.

Judd, F. K., Chua, P., Lynch, C., & Norman, T. (1991). Fenfluramine augmentation of clomipramine treatment of obsessive compulsive disorder. *Australian and New Zealand Journal of Psychiatry, 25*, 412–414.

Katz, R. J., & DeVeaugh-Geiss, J. (1990). The antiobsessional effects of clomipramine do not require concomitant affective disorder. *Psychiatry Research, 31*, 121–129.

Khanna, S. (1988). Carbamazepine in obsessive-compulsive disorder. *Clinical Neuropharmacology, 11*, 478–481.

Khanna, S., Gangadhar, B. N., & Sinha, V. (1988). Electroconvulsive therapy in obsessive-compulsive disorder. *Convulsive Therapy, 4*, 314–320.

Kim, S. W. (1987). Trazodone in the treatment of obsessive-compulsive disorder: A case report. *Journal of Clinical Psychopharmacology, 7*(4), 278–279.

Kleven, M. S., & Seiden, L. S. (1989). D-, L- and DL-fenfluramine cause long-lasting depletions of serotonin in rat brain. *Brain Research, 505*, 351–353.

Knesevich, J. W. (1982). Successful treatment of obsessive-compulsive disorder with clonidine hydrochloride. *American Journal of Psychiatry, 139*, 364–365.

Koizumi, H. M. (1985). Obsessive-compulsive symptoms following stimulants. *Biological Psychiatry, 20*(12), 1332–1333.

Kopala, L., & Honer, W. G. (1994). Risperidone, serotonergic mechanisms, and obsessive-compulsive symptoms in schizophrenia [Letter to the editor]. *American Journal of Psychiatry, 151*(1), 1714–1715.

Koran, L. M., Mueller, K., & Maloney, A. (1996). Will pindolol augment the response to a serotonin reuptake inhibitor in obsessive-compulsive disorder? [Letter to the editor]. *Journal of Clinical Psychopharmacology, 16*, 253–254.

Koran, L. M., Sallee, F. R., & Pallanti, S. (1997). Rapid benefit of intravenous pulse loading of clomipramine in obsessive-compulsive disorder. *American Journal of Psychiatry, 154*, 396–401.

Leckman, J. F., Goodman, W. K., North, W. G., Chappell, P. B., Price, L. H., Pauls, D. L., Anderson, G. M., Riddle, M. A., McDougle, C. J., Barr, L. C., & Cohen, D. J. (1994). The role of central oxytocin in obsessive compulsive disorder and related normal behavior. *Psychoneuroendocrinology, 19*(8), 723–749.

Leckman, J. F., Hardin, M. T., Riddle, M. A., Stevenson, J., Ort, S. I., & Cohen, D. J. (1991). Clonidine treatment of Gilles de la Tourette syndrome. *Archives of General Psychiatry, 48*, 324–328.

Leckman, J. F., Pauls, D. L., & Cohen, D. J. (1995). Tic disorders. In F. E. Bloom & D. J. Kupfer (Eds.), *Psychopharmacology: The fourth generation of progress* (pp. 1665–1674). New York: Raven.

Lemus, C. Z., Robinson, D. G., Kronig, M., et al. (1991). Behavioral responses to a dopaminergic challenge in obsessive-compulsive disorder. *Journal of Anxiety Disorders, 5*, 369–373.

Leonard, H. L., Topol, D., Bukstein, O., Hindmarsh, D., Allen, A. J., & Swedo, S. E. (1994). Clonazepam as an augmenting agent in the treatment of childhood-onset obsessive-compulsive disorder. *Journal of the American Academy of Child & Adolescent Psychiatry, 33*(6), 792–794.

Levine, J., Barak, Y., Gonzalves, M., Szor, H., Elizur, A., Kofman, O., & Belmaker, R. H. (1995). Double-blind controlled trial of inositol treatment of depression. *American Journal of Psychiatry, 152*, 792–794.

Lipsedge, M. S., & Prothero, W. (1987). Clonidine and clomipramine in obsessive-compulsive disorder. *American Journal of Psychiatry, 144*, 965–966.

Livingston-Van Noppen, B., Rasmussen, S. A., & Eisen, J. (1990). Family function and treatment of obsessive-compulsive disorder. In M. A. Jenike, L. Baer, & W. E. Minichiello (Eds.), *Obsessive-compulsive disorders: Theory and management* (2nd ed., pp. 325–340). Chicago: Year Book Medical.

Lombroso, P. J., Scahill, L., King, R. A., Lynch, K. A., Chappell, P. B., Peterson, B. S., McDougle, C. J., & Leckman, J. F. (1995). Risperidone treatment of children and adolescents with chronic tic disorders: A preliminary report. *Journal of the American Academy of Child & Adolescent Psychiatry, 34*, 1147–1152.

Lydiard, R. B. (1986). Obsessive-compulsive disorder successfully treated with trazodone. *Psychosomatics, 27*(12), 858–859.

Maletzky, B., McFarland, B., & Burt, A. (1994). Refractory obsessive-compulsive disorder and ECT. *Convulsive Therapy, 10*(1), 34–42.

Marder, S. R., & Meibach, R. C. (1994). Risperidone in the treatment of schizophrenia. *American Journal of Psychiatry, 151*(6), 825–835.

Marek, G. J., McDougle, C. J., Price, L. H., & Seiden, L. S. (1992). A comparison of trazodone and fluoxetine: Implications for a serotonergic mechanism of antidepressant action. *Psychopharmacology, 109*, 2–11.

Markovitz, P. J., Stagno, S. J., & Calabrese, J. R. (1990). Buspirone augmentation of fluoxetine in obsessive-compulsive disorder. *American Journal of Psychiatry, 147*, 798–800.

Marks, I. M., Stern, R. S., Mawson, D., Cobb, J., & McDonald, R. (1980). Clomipramine and exposure for obsessive compulsive rituals: I. *British Journal of Psychiatry, 136*, 1–25.

Mattes, J. A. (1986). A pilot study of combined trazodone and tryptophan in obsessive-compulsive disorder. *International Journal of Clinical Psychopharmacology, 1*, 170–173.

Mattes, J. A. (1994). Fluvoxamine in obsessive-compulsive nonresponders to clomipramine or fluoxetine [Letter to the editor]. *American Journal of Psychiatry, 151*(10), 1524.

Mavissakalian, M., Turner, S. M., Michelson, L., & Jacob, R. (1985). Tricyclic antidepressants in obsessive-compulsive disorder: Antiobsessional or antidepressant agents? II. *American Journal of Psychiatry, 142*, 572–576.

Mawson, D., Marks, I. M., & Ramm, L. (1982). Clomipramine for chronic obsessive compulsive rituals: Two year follow-up and further findings. *British Journal of Psychiatry, 140*, 11–18.

McCann, U., Seiden, L. E., Rubin, L. J., & Ricaurte, G. A. (1997). Brain serotonin neurotoxicity and primary pulmonary hypertension from fenfluramine and dexfenfluramine: A systematic review of the evidence. *Journal of the American Medical Association, 278*(8), 666–672.

McDougle, C. J., Barr, L. C., Goodman, W. K., Pelton, G. H., Aronson, S. C., Anand, A., & Price, L. H. (1995). Limited efficacy of clozapine monotherapy in refractory obsessive compulsive disorder. *American Journal of Psychiatry, 152*, 1812–1814.

McDougle, C. J., Fleischmann, R. L., Epperson, C. N., Wasylink, S., Leckman, J. F., & Price, L. H. (1995). Risperidone addition in fluvoxamine-refractory obsessive-compulsive disorder: Three cases. *Journal of Clinical Psychiatry, 56*, 526–528.

McDougle, C. J., Goodman, W. K., Leckman, J. F., Barr, L. C., Heninger, G. R., & Price, L. H. (1993). The efficacy of fluvoxamine in obsessive compulsive disorder: Effects of comorbid chronic tic disorder. *Journal of Clinical Psychopharmacology, 13*(5), 354–358.

McDougle, C. J., Goodman, W. K., Leckman, J. F., Holzer, J. C., Barr, L. C., McCance-Katz, E., Heninger, G. R., & Price, L. H. (1993). Limited therapeutic effect of addition of buspirone in fluvoxamine-refractory obsessive-compulsive disorder. *American Journal of Psychiatry, 150*, 647–649.

McDougle, C. J., Goodman, W. K., Leckman, J. F., Lee, N. C., Heninger, G. R., & Price, L. H. (1994). Haloperidol addition in fluvoxamine-refractory obsessive-compulsive disorder: A double-blind, placebo-controlled study in patients with and without tics. *Archives of General Psychiatry, 51*, 302–308.

McDougle, C. J., Goodman, W. K., Price, L. H., Delgado, P. L., Krystal, J. H., Charney, D. S., & Heninger, G. R. (1990). Neuroleptic addition in fluvoxamine-refractory obsessive compulsive disorder: An open case series. *American Journal of Psychiatry, 147*, 652–654.

McDougle, C. J., Price, L. H., & Goodman, W. K. (1990). Fluvoxamine treatment of coincident autistic disorder and obsessive compulsive disorder: A case report. *Journal of Autism & Developmental Disorders, 20*, 537–543.

McDougle, C. J., Price, L. H., Goodman, W. K., Charney, D. S., & Heninger, G. R. (1991). A controlled trial of lithium augmentation in fluvoxamine-refractory obsessive-compulsive disorder: Lack of efficacy. *Journal of Clinical Psychopharmacology, 11*, 175–184.

McDougle, C. J., Price, L. H., Volkmar, F. R., Goodman, W. K., Ward-O'Brien, D., Nielsen, J., Bergman, J., & Cohen, D. J. (1992). Clomipramine in autism: Preliminary evidence of efficacy. *Journal of the American Academy of Child & Adolescent Psychiatry, 31*(4), 746–750.

McElroy, S. L., Keck, P. E., & Pope, H. G. (1987). Sodium valproate: Its use in primary psychiatric disorders. *Journal of Clinical Psychopharmacology, 7*, 16–24.

McElroy, S. L., & Pope, H. G. (1988). *Use of anticonvulsants in psychiatry: Recent advances.* Clifton, NJ: Oxford Health Care.

McNally, R. J., & Calamari, J. E. (1989). Obsessive-compulsive disorder in a mentally retarded woman. *British Journal of Psychiatry, 155*, 116–117.

Mellman, L. A., & Gorman, J. M. (1984). Successful treatment of obsessive-compulsive disorder with ECT. *American Journal of Psychiatry, 141*, 596–597.

Mindus, P., Rasmussen, S. A., & Lindquist, C. (1994). Neurosurgical treatment for refractory obsessive-compulsive disorder: Implications for understanding frontal lobe function. *Journal of Neuropsychiatry, 6*, 467–477.

Murphy, T. K., Goodman, W. K., Fudge, M. W., Williams, R. C., Ayoub, E. M., Dalal, M., Lewis, M. H., & Zabriskie, J. B. (1997). B lymphocyte antigen D8/17: A peripheral marker for Tourette's syndrome and childhood-onset obsessive compulsive disorder? *American Journal of Psychiatry, 154*, 402–407.

Nierenberg, A. A., Adler, L. A., Peselow, E., Zornberg, G., & Rosenthal, M. (1994). Trazodone for antidepressant-associated insomnia. *American Journal of Psychiatry, 151*, 1069–1072.

Nierenberg, A. A., Feighner, J. P., Rudolph, R., Cole, J. O., & Sullivan, J. (1994). Venlafaxine for treatment-resistant unipolar depression. *Journal of Clinical Psychopharmacology, 14*(6), 419–423.

Palova, E. (1996). Combination of two SSRIs in long-term treatment of patients with OCD: Four case reports. *European Neuropsychopharmacology, 6*(Suppl. 4), 148.

Patel, B., & Tandon, R. (1993). Development of obsessive-compulsive symptoms during clozapine treatment. *American Journal of Psychiatry, 150*(5), 836.

Patil, V. J. (1992). Development of transient obsessive-compulsive symptoms during treatment with clozapine. *American Journal of Psychiatry, 149*(2), 272.

Pauls, D. L., Towbin, K. E., Leckman, J. F., Zahner, G. E. P., & Cohen, D. J. (1986). Gilles de la Tourette's syndrome and obsessive-compulsive disorder: Evidence supporting a genetic relationship. *Archives of General Psychiatry, 43*, 1180–1182.

Pigott, T. A., L'Heureux, F., Hill, J. L., Bihari, K., Bernstein, S. E., & Murphy, D. L. (1992). A double-blind study of adjuvant buspirone hydrochloride in clomipramine-treated patients with obsessive-compulsive disorder. *Journal of Clinical Psychopharmacology, 12*, 11–18.

Pigott, T. A., L'Heureux, F., Rubenstein, C. S., Bernstein, S. E., Hill, J. L., & Murphy, D. L. (1992). A double-blind, placebo-controlled study of trazodone in patients with obsessive-compulsive disorder. *Journal of Clinical Psychopharmacology, 12*(3), 156–162.

Pigott, T. A., & Murphy, D. L. (1991). In reply to "Are effective antiobsessional drugs interchangeable?" [Letter to the editor]. *Archives of General Psychiatry, 48*, 858–859.

Pigott, T. A., Pato, M. T., L'Heureux, F., Hill, J. L., Grover, G. N., Bernstein, S. E., & Murphy, D. (1991). A controlled comparison of adjuvant lithium carbonate or thyroid hormone in clomipramine-treated patients with obsessive-compulsive disorder. *Journal of Clinical Psychopharmacology, 11*, 242–248.

Pranzatelli, M. R. (1989). Benzodiazepine-induced shaking behavior in the rat: Structure-activity and relation to serotonin and benzodiazepine receptors. *Experimental Neurology, 104*, 241–250.

Price, L. H., Charney, D. S., & Heninger, G. R. (1986). Variability of response to lithium augmentation in refractory depression. *American Journal of Psychiatry, 143*, 1387–1392.

Rasmussen, S. A. (1984). Lithium and tryptophan augmentation in clomipramine resistant obsessive-compulsive disorder. *American Journal of Psychiatry, 141*, 1283–1285.

Rauch, S. L., O'Sullivan, R. L., & Jenike, M. A. (1996). Open treatment of obsessive-compulsive disorder with venlafaxie: A series of ten cases. *Journal of Clinical Psychopharmacology, 16*, 81–84.

Ravizza, L., Barzega, G., Bellino, S., Bogetto, F., & Maina, G. (1995). Predictors of drug treatment response in obsessive compulsive disorder. *Journal of Clinical Psychiatry, 56*, 368–373.

Ravizza, L., Barzega, G., Bellino, S., Bogetto, F., & Maina, G. (1996). Therapeutic effect and safety of adjunctive risperidone in refractory obsessive-compulsive disorder (OCD). *Psychopharmacology Bulletin, 32*(43), 677–682.

Remington, G., & Adams, M. (1994). Risperidone and obsessive-compulsive symptoms [Letter to the editor]. *Journal of Clinical Psychopharmacology, 14*(5), 358–359.

Riddle, M. A., Leckman, J. F., Hardin, M. T., Anderson, G. M., & Cohen, D. J. (1988). Fluoxetine treatment of obsessions and compulsions in patients with Tourette's syndrome. *American Journal of Psychiatry, 145*, 1173–1174.

Ruegg, R. G., Evans, D. L., & Comer, W. S. (1990). Lithium plus fluoxetine treatment of obsessive compulsive disorder [Abstract NR 92, 81]. *New Research Program and Abstracts of the 143rd Annual Meeting of the American Psychiatric Association*. Washington, DC: American Psychiatric Association.

Saxena, S., Wang, D., Bystritsky, A., & Baxter, L. R. (1996). Risperidone augmentation of SRI treatment for refractory obsessive-compulsive disorder. *Journal of Clinical Psychiatry, 57*, 303–306.

Scheffel, U., Dannals, R. F., Cline, E. J., Ricaurte, G. A., Carroll, F. I., Abraham, P., Lewin, A. H., & Kuhar, M. J. (1992). [123/125I]RTI-55, an in vivo label for the serotonin transporter. *Synapse, 11*(2), 134–139.

Shapiro, E., Shapiro, A. K., Fulop, G. K., Hubbard, M., Mandeli, J., Nordlie, J., & Phillips, R. A. (1989). Controlled study of haloperidol, pimozide and placebo for the treatment of Gilles de la Tourette's syndrome. *Archives of General Psychiatry, 46*, 722–730.

Simeon, J. G., Carrey, N. J., Wiggins, D. M., Milin, R. P., & Hosenbocus, S. N. (1995). Risperidone effects in treatment-resistant adolescents: Preliminary case reports. *Journal of Child & Adolescent Psychopharmacology, 5*, 69–79.

Simeon, J. G., Thatte, S., & Wiggins, D. (1990). Treatment of adolescent obsessive-compulsive disorder with a clomipramine-fluoxetine combination. *Psychopharmacology Bulletin, 26,* 285–290.

Sofuoglu, M., & Debattista, C. (1996). Development of obsessive symptoms during nefazodone treatment [Letter to the editor]. *American Journal of Psychiatry, 153,* 577–578.

Stagno, S. J., Smith, M. L., & Hassenbusch, S. J. (1994). Reconsidering "psychosurgery": Issues of informed consent and physician responsibility. *Journal of Clinical Ethics, 5,* 217–223.

Stammenkovic, M., Aschauer, H., & Kasper, S. (1994). Risperidone for Tourette's syndrome. *Lancet, 344,* 1577–1578.

Stanley, M. A., & Turner, S. M. (1995). Current status of pharmacological and behavioral treatment of obsessive-compulsive disorder. *Behavioral Therapy, 26,* 162–186.

Steiner, W., & Fontaine, R. (1986). Toxic reaction following the combined administration of fluoxetine and L-tryptophan: Five case reports. *Biological Psychiatry, 21,* 1067–1071.

Steinert, T., Schmidt-Michel, P. O., & Kaschka, W. P. (1996). Considerable improvement in a case of obsessive-compulsive disorder in an emotionally unstable personality disorder, borderline type under treatment with clozapine. *Pharmacopsychiatry, 29*(3), 111–114.

Steingard, S., Chengappa, K. N. R., Baker, R. W., & Schooler, N. R. (1993). Clozapine, obsessive symptoms, and serotonergic mechanisms [Letter to the editor]. *American Journal of Psychiatry, 150*(9), 1435.

Stern, T. A., & Jenike, M. A. (1983). Treatment of obsessive-compulsive disorder with lithium carbonate. *Psychosomatics, 24,* 671–673.

Swedo, S. E., Leonard, H. L., & Kiessling, L. S. (1994). Speculations on antineuronal antibody-mediated neuropsychiatric disorders of childhood. *Pediatrics, 93*(2), 323–326.

Swedo, S. E., Rapoport, J. L., Cheslow, D. L., Leonard, H. L., Ayoub, E. M., Hosier, D. M., & Wald, E. R. (1989). High prevalence of obsessive-compulsive symptoms in patients with Sydenham's chorea. *American Journal of Psychiatry, 146*(2), 246–249.

Swerdlow, N. R., & Andia, A. M. (1989). Trazodone-fluoxetine combination for treatment of obsessive-compulsive disorder. *American Journal of Psychiatry, 146,* 1637.

Swinson, R. P., & Joffe, R. T. (1988). Biological challenges in obsessive compulsive disorder. *Progress in Neuro-Psychopharmacology & Biological Psychiatry, 12*(2–3), 369–375.

Szegedi, A., Wetzel, H., Leal, M., Hartter, S., & Hiemke, C. (1996). Combination treatment with clomipramine and fluvoxamine: Drug monitoring, safety, and tolerability data. *Journal of Clinical Psychiatry, 57,* 257–264.

Tamimi, R. R., & Mavissakalian, M. R. (1991). Are effective antiobsessional drugs interchangeable? [Letter to the editor]. *Archives of General Psychiatry, 48,* 857–858.

Tanquary, J., & Masand, P. (1990). Paradoxical reaction to buspirone augmentation of fluoxetine [Letter to the editor]. *Journal of Clinical Psychopharmacology, 10,* 377.

Thakur, A. K., Remillard, A. J., Meldrum, L. H., & Gorecki, D. K. (1991). Intravenous clomipramine and obsessive-compulsive disorder. *Canadian Journal of Psychiatry, 36,* 521–524.

Tollefson, G. D., Rampey, A. H., Jr., Potvin, J. H., Jenike, M. A., Rush, A. J., Dominguez, R. A., Koran, L. M., Shear, M. K., Goodman, W. K., & Genduso, L. A. (1994). A multicenter investigation of fixed-dose fluoxetine in the treatment of obsessive-compulsive disorder. *Archives of General Psychiatry, 51,* 559–567.

Tricklebank, M., Forler, C., & Fozard, J. (1984). The involvement of subtypes of the 5-HT1 receptor and of catecholaminergic systems in the behavioral response to 8-hydroxy-2-(di-n-propylamino) tetralin in the rat. *European Journal of Pharmacology, 106,* 271–282.

Vallejo, J., Olivares, J., Marcos, T., Bulbena, A., & Menchon, J. M. (1992). Clomipramine versus phenelzine in obsessive-compulsive disorder. A controlled clinical trial. *British Journal of Psychiatry, 161,* 665–670.

van Balkom, A. J. L. M., van Oppen, P., Vermeulen, A. W. A., van Dyck, R., Nauta, M. C. E., & Vorst, H. C. M. (1994). A meta-analysis on the treatment of obsessive-compulsive disorder: A comparison of antidepressants, behavior, and cognitive therapy. *Clinical Psychology Review, 14*(5), 359–381.

Van der Linden, C., Bruggeman, R., & Van Woerkom, T. (1994). Serotonin-dopamine antagonist and Gilles de La Tourette's syndrome: An open pilot dose-titration study with risperidone. *Movement Disorders, 9*(6), 687–688.

Vitiello, B., Spreat, S., & Behar, D. (1989). Obsessive-compulsive disorder in mentally retarded patients. *Journal of Nervous & Mental Disease, 177*, 232–236.

Wagner, H. R., Reches, A., Yablonskaya, E., & Fahn, S. (1986). Clonazepam-induced up-regulation of serotonin-1 and serotonin-2 binding sites in rat frontal cortex. *Advances in Neurology, 43*, 645–651.

Warneke, L. B. (1989). Intravenous chlorimipramine therapy in obsessive-compulsive disorder. *Canadian Journal of Psychiatry, 34*, 853–859.

Wasserman, E. M. (1997). Repetitive transcranial magnetic stimulation: An introduction and overview. *CNS Spectrums, 2*, 21–25.

Wheadon, D. E., Bushnell, W. D., & Steiner, M. (1993, December). *A fixed dose comparison of 20, 40, or 60 mg paroxetine to placebo in the treatment of obsessive-compulsive disorder.* Paper presented at the 32nd annual meeting of the American College of Neurophsychophar-macology, Honolulu, HI.

Wise, S. P., & Rapoport, J. L. (1989). Obsessive compulsive disorder: Is it basal ganglia dysfunction? In J. L. Rapoport (Ed.), *Obsessive-compulsive disorder in children and adolescents* (pp. 327–344). Washington, DC: American Psychiatric Press.

Yaryura-Tobias, J. A., & Neziroglu, F. A. (1996). Venlafaxine in obsessive-compulsive disorder [Letter to the editor]. *Archives of General Psychiatry, 53*(7), 653–654.

Yoney, T. H., Pigott, T. A., L'Heureux, F., & Rosenthal, N. E. (1991). Seasonal variation in obsessive-compulsive disorder: Preliminary experience with light treatment. *American Journal of Psychiatry, 148*, 1727–1729.

Young, C. R., Bostic, J. Q., & McDonald, C. L. (1994). Clozapine and refractory obsessive-compulsive disorder: A case report. *Journal of Clinical Psychopharmacology, 14*(3), 209–210.

Zajecka, J. M., Fawcett, J., & Guy, C. (1990). Coexisting major depression and obsessive-compulsive disorder treated with venlafaxine [Letter to the editor]. *Journal of Clinical Psychopharmacology, 10*, 152–153.

19

The Role of Neuroleptics in Treatment-Refractory Obsessive-Compulsive Disorder

Christopher J. McDougle
Indiana University School of Medicine

C. Neill Epperson
Yale University School of Medicine

Lawrence H. Price
Brown University School of Medicine

Although serotonin reuptake inhibitors (SRIs) have clearly been established as the first-line pharmacotherapy for obsessive-compulsive disorder (OCD), between 40% and 60% of patients remain unimproved after an adequate trial with these drugs. Adding agents that enhance serotonin (5-HT) neurotransmission to ongoing treatment in SRI-refractory patients has not yielded impressive results. The addition of neuroleptic medication to the regimens of treatment-refractory patients appears to be a potentially useful strategy for the specific subgroup of OCD patients with a comorbid chronic tic disorder (e.g., Tourette's syndrome). Controlled investigations of neuroleptic addition to ongoing SRI therapy are needed in OCD patients with concomitant symptoms of psychosis or schizotypal personality disorder (SPD) as well as in SRI-refractory trichotillomania and body dysmorphic disorder (BDD). Preliminary results from studies of the atypical neuroleptic risperidone indicate that it may be effective in subgroups of SRI-refractory OCD patients, and perhaps better tolerated than typical neuroleptics. One interpretation of emerging drug treatment response data is that both the 5-HT and dopamine (DA) systems may be critical to the treatment, and possibly the pathophysiology, of some forms of OCD.

Although OCD has traditionally been viewed as resistant to a variety of therapeutic interventions, significant advances have been made in the psychopharmacology of this disabling condition. The clear efficacy of SRIs, such as clomipramine (DeVeaugh-Geiss et al., 1991), fluvoxamine (Goodman, Price, Rasmussen, Delgado, et al., 1989), fluoxetine (Tollefson et al., 1994), and sertraline (Greist et al., 1995), has now been established in double-blind, placebo-controlled studies. Consistent with these drug response data are the hypotheses that changes in 5-HT function are critical to the treatment of OCD and perhaps involved in the pathophysiology of at least some patients with the disorder (Insel, Mueller, Alterman, Linnoila, & Murphy, 1985).

Despite success with potent SRIs, as many as 40% to 60% of OCD patients are clinically unchanged after an adequate trial with these agents (McDougle, Goodman, Leckman, & Price, 1993). The lack of improvement in obsessive-compulsive (OC) symptoms in this large group of OCD patients suggests that OCD may be a neurobiologically heterogeneous disorder and that many patients require treatment strategies other than SRI monotherapy for symptom control.

One approach to this SRI-refractory group has been to add agents such as tryptophan (Rasmussen, 1984), fenfluramine (Hollander et al., 1990), lithium (McDougle, Price, Goodman, Charney, & Heninger, 1991; Pigott et al., 1991), and buspirone (Grady et al., 1993; McDougle, Goodman, Leckman, Holzer, et al., 1993; Pigott et al., 1992), which may act by enhancing 5-HT function, to ongoing treatment with SRIs. Controlled studies of adding lithium (McDougle et al., 1991; Pigott et al., 1991) or buspirone (Grady et al., 1993; McDougle, Goodman, Leckman, Holzer, et al., 1993; Pigott et al., 1992), however, have demonstrated that this is not usually an effective approach and this has suggested that pharmacotherapy targeted at other or multiple neurochemical systems may be necessary in subgroups of patients with OCD.

THE ROLE OF DOPAMINE IN SOME FORMS OF OCD

Although the role of 5-HT in the treatment of OCD has been established, several lines of evidence from preclinical and clinical investigations implicate DA in the mediation of some forms of OC phenomena. In particular, the occurrence of OC symptoms in stimulant abusers, patients with comorbid chronic tic disorders, and some patients with psychotic spectrum disorders provides indirect evidence for the role of DA in some forms of OCD.

The Relation Between OC Phenomena and Stimulant Abuse

A proposed animal model for compulsive behavior involves pharmacologic provocation with direct- or indirect-acting DA receptor agonists that facilitate DA transmission and produce repetitive behavior in animals. Ellinwood and Escalante (1970) observed compulsive behavior, usually consisting of repetitive sniffing in the same area continuously for 3 to 4 hours, after amphetamine injection in cats. The relevance of these preclinical data to humans is supported by the observation that seemingly purposeful and complex repetitive behaviors may emerge, and at times persist, with stimulant abuse. Ellinwood (1967) described patients who assembled and disassembled objects repeatedly in a ritualized manner subsequent to the abuse of high-dose amphetamine. Schiorring (1975) described repetitive cleaning, washing, grooming, and hoarding behaviors, which he termed *punding*, in a sample of stimulant abusers. Cocaine, which potentiates the effects of DA by blocking presynaptic reuptake (Gawin & Ellinwood, 1988), has been reported to exacerbate OC symptoms in patients with OCD (McDougle, Goodman, Delgado, & Price, 1989) and to induce such behaviors in individuals with a family history, but no personal history, of OCD (Satel & McDougle, 1991). In addition, Rosse et al. (1993) described cocaine-induced compulsive foraging behavior in 33 out of 41 crack cocaine addicts who were interviewed. These individuals would compulsively search for pieces of crack cocaine that they believed they may have dropped or misplaced. The behavior would typically begin after the individual had exhausted his supply of crack cocaine and would last for approximately 90 minutes. Although stimulants have potent effects on neurotransmitter systems other than DA, these indirect data suggest that increased DA tone may contribute to some types of OC symptoms.

The Relation Between OCD and Tourette's Syndrome

Tourette's syndrome (TS) is a chronic neuropsychiatric disorder of childhood onset that is characterized by multiple motor and one or more phonic tics that wax and wane in severity (American Psychiatric Association, 1994). In addition to tics, many patients with TS have interfering OC symptoms. Although the tics of TS are often suppressed with neuroleptics (D_2 DA receptor antagonists) such as haloperidol and pimozide (Shapiro et al., 1989), comorbid OC symptoms are typically resistant to treatment with neuroleptic alone. Similarly, the frequency and intensity of OC symptoms in patients with a principal diagnosis of OCD are rarely decreased with neuroleptic monotherapy (see later discussion).

That OCD and TS are related conditions is not a new observation. Pitman, Green, Jenike, and Mesulam (1987) reported that 38% of OCD patients studied met criteria for some type of tic disorder. Frankel et al. (1986) reported OC symptoms in 52%, Pitman et al. (1987) in 63%, Nee, Caine, Polinsky, Eldridge, and Ebert (1980) in 68%, and Stefl (1984) in 74% of TS patients studied. Family-genetic studies provide evidence that

TS and some forms of OCD are etiologically related (Pauls, Alsobrook, Goodman, Rasmussen, & Leckman, 1995; Pauls & Leckman, 1986).

Although the etiology of TS remains unknown, neurobiological (Cohen, Shaywitz, Caparulo, Young, & Bowers, 1978) and pharmacologic (Shapiro et al., 1989) data implicate the DA system in the neurochemical dysfunction, and the basal ganglia and related structures in the neuropathology (Singer, Hahn, & Moran, 1991) of the disorder. As noted earlier, the DA receptor antagonists haloperidol and pimozide partially reduce the tics of TS (Shapiro et al., 1989), whereas stimulants can acutely exacerbate such symptoms in some patients with TS (Mesulam, 1986). DA uptake carrier sites were significantly increased in number compared to normal controls in postmortem striatum from three adults with TS (Singer et al., 1991). Furthermore, DA uptake sites were determined to be significantly elevated in adults with TS compared with matched healthy adults in a recent single photon emission computed tomography neuroimaging study (Malison et al., 1995). Abnormalities in basal ganglia and related brain regions have also been implicated in the pathophysiology of some forms of OCD (Goodman et al., 1990).

The Relation Between OCD and Psychosis

For years, clinicians have noted a relation between OC phenomena and psychotic spectrum disorders. The subgroup of patients with primary OCD with associated psychotic symptoms has been given diagnoses such as obsessive psychosis (Solyom, DiNicola, Phil, Sookman, & Luchins, 1985) and OCD with psychotic features (Insel & Akiskal, 1986). Those patients with primary OCD and comorbid SPD have been referred to as schizo-obsessive (Jenike, Baer, Minichiello, Schwartz, & Carey, 1986). In general, this group of patients has been described as having severe, debilitating OC symptoms that may approach delusional proportions.

In a review of the relation between OCD and symptoms of psychosis, Insel and Akiskal (1986) found that delusions emerging during the course of OCD do not usually signify a schizophrenic process, but rather represent a reactive affective or paranoid psychosis that is typically transient in nature. The shift from an obsession to a delusion occurs when resistance (the internal struggle against an obsessional urge or idea) is abandoned and insight is lost. They further posited that OCD represents a psychopathological spectrum varying along a continuum of insight, with patients at the severe end of the spectrum best described as having an OC psychosis. With the relaxation of *Diagnostic and Statistical Manual of Mental Disorders* (4th ed. [*DSM–IV*]; American Psychiatric Association, 1994) diagnostic criteria for OCD around the issue of insight, these patients may now qualify for a formal diagnosis of OCD as long as they exhibit good insight at some point during the illness.

Fenton and McGlashan (1990) described the long-term outcome of seven patients with primary OCD who had comorbid psychotic symptoms, which they labeled *OCD psychosis*. Based on a global functioning scale that rated a patient's success in reentering "the usual concourse of living" (p. 760) over a 15-year follow-up period, only 29% of OCD psychosis patients compared to 46% and 69% of schizophrenic patients and affective disorder patients, respectively, were rated as achieving a score of moderate or better on this scale.

Other investigators have completed preliminary systematic clinical assessments of patients with OCD and comorbid SPD. Stanley, Turner, and Borden (1990), for example, found that 8% of a sample of adults with primary OCD met *Diagnostic and Statistical Manual of Mental Disorders* (3rd ed., rev. [*DSM–III–R*]; American Psychiatric Association, 1987) criteria for a comorbid diagnosis of SPD, and that an additional 20% of the sample had notable schizotypal features. Using *Diagnostic and Statistical Manual of Mental Disorders* (3rd ed. [*DSM–III*]; American Psychiatric Association, 1980) criteria, Baer et al. (1990) found that 5% of 96 adults with OCD met criteria for a comorbid diagnosis of SPD. Preliminary findings suggest that OCD patients with comorbid SPD may be particularly refractory to standard pharmacotherapy and behavior therapy (Jenike et al., 1986).

NEUROLEPTIC MONOTHERAPY IN OCD

To our knowledge, there have been no published controlled trials of neuroleptics alone in the treatment of OCD as it is currently defined in *DSM–IV*. Most experienced clinicians agree that, in general, neuroleptics alone are not effective in the treatment of the core symptoms of OCD (Goodman et al., 1990). In fact, it is not uncommon for patients to present to our clinics who have been misdiagnosed as having schizophrenia and whose OC symptoms have not improved with neuroleptic treatment alone. There have, however, been some open-label reports describing the effectiveness of monotherapy with neuroleptic medication in some patients with OCD (Altschuler, 1962; Dally, 1967; Lopez-Ibor & Lopez-Ibor, 1973; McDougle, Southwick, & Rohrbaugh, 1990; O'Regan, 1970a, 1970b; Rivers-Bulkeley & Hollender, 1982). A 21-year-old man with intense OC symptoms, for example, responded rapidly to loxapine 100 mg/day, although the authors acknowledged that his schizophrenic features might have been partly, or even substantially, responsible for his favorable response (Rivers-Bulkeley & Hollender, 1982). Hussain and Ahad (1970), however, reported the lack of efficacy of haloperidol and triperidol in three patients with severe chronic OC neurosis.

Controlled studies of neuroleptic alone and neuroleptic in combination with clomipramine have been reported, although the diagnoses of patients studied do not appear to be consistent with OCD as it is currently defined in *DSM–IV*. Trethowan and Scott (1955) described results from a study in which 59 out of 70 outpatients suffering from neurotic disorders with obsessive-compulsive features completed a double-blind, placebo-controlled trial of chlorpromazine 150 to 200 mg/day for varying durations of time. A significant global response to chlorpromazine was observed in 46% of patients compared to placebo. No improvement in compulsive rituals was observed, although aggressive urges toward self or others and obsessive-hypochondriacal ideas improved significantly.

A 60-day multicenter controlled trial of clomipramine 125 mg/day, alone and in combination with haloperidol 5 mg/day or diazepam 20 mg/day, was conducted in 54 adults with phobic-obsessive psychoneurosis (Cassano et al., 1981). For the 40 patients who completed the study, OC symptomatology responded best to clomipramine alone, whereas phobic symptoms were most successfully treated with the clomipramine–haloperidol combination. The authors concluded that clomipramine in combination with haloperidol or diazepam was no better than clomipramine alone in the treatment of phobic-obsessive psychoneurosis. The diagnostic criteria employed, the lack of outcome measures specific for measuring change in OC symptoms, the dosage of clomipramine administered, the duration of treatment, and the limited statistical power, however, make this investigation difficult to interpret with respect to more current pharmacologic trials in patients with OCD.

COMBINED SRI–NEUROLEPTIC TREATMENT IN OCD

There is emerging evidence that the combination of an SRI and a neuroleptic may benefit some patients with OCD. To date, the group that has received the most attention with regard to this combination treatment strategy has been OCD patients with a comorbid chronic tic disorder. This research has been based on the phenomenologic, genetic, neurochemical, and neuroanatomic overlap between OCD and TS, and the extensive preclinical literature documenting functionally coupled interactions between the 5-HT and DA systems in the brain (Korsgaard, Gerlach, & Christensson, 1985). Riddle, Leckman, Hardin, Anderson, and Cohen (1988) reported on the anti-OC benefits of adding the SRI fluoxetine to neuroleptic in two cases of concomitant TS and OCD. Subsequently, the case of a 25-year-old man with comorbid TS who presented for treatment of OCD at the Yale OCD Clinic was described (Delgado, Goodman, Price,

Heninger, & Charney, 1990). The SRI fluvoxamine worsened tics and did not help the OC symptoms. The addition of the DA receptor antagonist pimozide, however, dramatically reduced both OC and tic symptoms. Double-blind sequential discontinuation and placebo substitution of fluvoxamine and pimozide confirmed that pimozide alone reduced only tics and the combination of fluvoxamine and pimozide was required for the improvement in OCD.

In an open case series by the group at Yale (McDougle, Goodman, et al., 1990), neuroleptic (6.5 mg/day, pimozide equivalents) was added to ongoing treatment in 17 OCD patients unresponsive to fluvoxamine with or without lithium. These cases were reviewed by a rater blind to treatment outcome to determine whether comorbid tic spectrum disorders or SPD were associated with a positive response to neuroleptic addition. According to conservative criteria, 9 of 17 (53%) patients were judged responders to this combination treatment strategy. A concurrent diagnosis of chronic tics or SPD was associated with a positive response to addition of neuroleptic. Seven of eight (88%) patients with these comorbid diagnoses were responders, whereas only two of nine (22%) patients without these comorbid diagnoses were responders.

In a double-blind, placebo-controlled study in OCD patients with and without comorbid chronic tics, haloperidol (6.2 ± 3.0 mg/day) was significantly more effective than placebo when added to ongoing fluvoxamine treatment in OCD patients unresponsive to fluvoxamine alone (McDougle et al., 1994). In those patients with chronic tics (motor or phonic), OC symptoms, rather than tics, were the predominant presenting complaint. Tics were distinguished from tic-like compulsions (such as compulsive touching or blinking) based on whether the patient attached a meaning or purpose to the behavior. This definition allowed raters to distinguish true tics from tic-like compulsions so that Yale–Brown Obsessive Compulsive Scale (Y–BOCS; Goodman, Price, Rasmussen, Mazure, Delgado, et al., 1989; Goodman, Price, Rasmussen, Mazure, Fleischmann, et al., 1989) scores reflected changes in severity of obsessions and compulsions rather than tics. Sixty-two patients received placebo for 1 week, followed by 8 weeks of fluvoxamine in identical-appearing capsules. Thirty-four of these patients were refractory to fluvoxamine monotherapy and were entered into a 4-week, double-blind, placebo-controlled haloperidol addition phase (Fig. 19.1). The patients continued on the same dose of fluvoxamine during haloperidol addition. Assignment to haloperidol or placebo was random, with patients, treating staff (including prescribing physicians), and raters blind to assignment. Patients were given benztropine 0.5 mg BID (twice daily) as prophylaxis against extrapyramidal symptoms and in an attempt to preserve blind treatment conditions. Blood samples were collected before and after the 4-week, double-blind

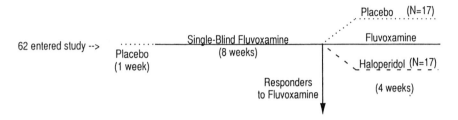

FIG. 19.1. Study design for double-blind, placebo-controlled investigation
of haloperidol addition in fluvoxamine-refractory OCD. (From *Archives of
General Psychiatry*, 51, 302–308, 1994).

trial to determine if coadministration of haloperidol increased fluvoxamine blood levels, and to determine if treatment response was related
to a pharmacokinetic effect.

The superiority of fluvoxamine–haloperidol over fluvoxamine–placebo
in reducing the severity of OC symptoms was shown with the Y–BOCS.
Fluvoxamine–haloperidol was significantly better than fluvoxamine–placebo beginning at Week 4 of treatment (Fig. 19.2). In the fluvoxamine–
haloperidol group, the reduction in total Y–BOCS ratings was highly
significant by Week 3, and by Week 4, the decrease was even greater,
representing a 26% reduction from baseline. In contrast, there were no
significant changes in Y–BOCS scores for any week following baseline in
the fluvoxamine–placebo group. Based on stringent treatment response
criteria, 11 of 17 (65%) patients randomly assigned to receive fluvoxamine–
haloperidol were rated as responders after 4 weeks of treatment, compared with none of 17 patients who received fluvoxamine–placebo. In
responders, Y–BOCS scores decreased by 39%, from a baseline of 25.3
(*SD* = 6.0) to a final score of 15.5 (*SD* = 9.1) following 4 weeks of haloperidol. Those OCD patients with a concurrent chronic tic disorder, such
as TS, demonstrated a preferential response to the fluvoxamine–haloperidol combination treatment strategy (Fig. 19.3). In fact, eight out of eight
patients with comorbid chronic tic disorders (TS *n* = 4, chronic motor tic
disorder *n* = 4) responded to double-blind haloperidol addition to ongoing
fluvoxamine treatment. In contrast, combined fluvoxamine–haloperidol
treatment was of benefit in significantly fewer OCD patients without
comorbid tics (33%), usually effecting only partial improvement when
any response occurred. In comparing the effects of fluvoxamine–haloperidol on OC symptoms between patients with and without tics, fluvoxamine–haloperidol proved significantly better in patients with tics beginning at Week 2 of treatment (Fig. 19.4). This effect was even more
pronounced after Weeks 3 and 4 of fluvoxamine–haloperidol. In the group
of patients with tics, Y–BOCS scores decreased by 47%, from 25.5 (*SD* =
4.7) to 13.6 (*SD* = 8.0) following 4 weeks of haloperidol addition to

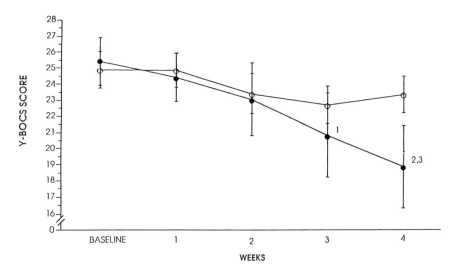

FIG. 19.2. Change in severity of OC symptoms in patients given haloperidol (closed circles) or placebo (open circles) for 4 weeks; measured on the Yale–Brown Obsessive Compulsive Scale (range: 0 = no symptoms, 40 = most severe).
[1]$p < .006$, change from baseline (haloperidol), paired t test. [2]$p < .001$, change from baseline (haloperidol), paired t test. [3]$p < .008$, change from baseline, haloperidol vs. placebo, Student's t test. All tests are two-tailed. (From *Archives of General Psychiatry, 51*, 302–308, 1994).

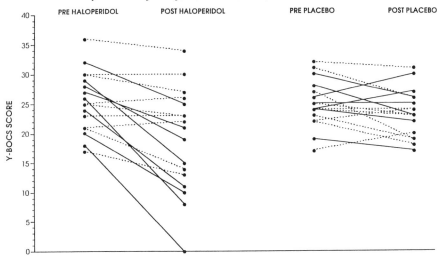

FIG. 19.3. Change in Y–BOCS scores for OCD patients with (solid lines) and without (dotted lines) comorbid chronic tic disorder given haloperidol or placebo for 4 weeks in addition to ongoing fluvoxamine treatment. (From *Archives of General Psychiatry, 51*, 302–308, 1994).

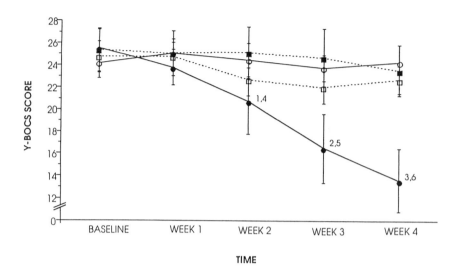

FIG. 19.4. Change in severity of OC symptoms on the Y–BOCS in patients with tics given haloperidol (—●—) or placebo (—○—) and in patients without tics given haloperidol (--■--) or placebo (--□--) for 4 weeks. [1]$p < .05$, change from baseline in patients with tics (haloperidol), paired t test. [2]$p < .003$, change from baseline in patients with tics (haloperidol), paired t test. [3]$p < .0002$, change from baseline in patients with tics (haloperidol), paired t test. [4]$p < .04$, change from baseline, patients with vs. without tics (haloperidol), Student's t test. [5]$p < .001$, change from baseline, patients with vs. without tics (haloperidol), Student's t test. [6]$p < .0001$, change from baseline, patients with vs. without tics (haloperidol), Student's t test. All tests are two-tailed. (From *Archives of General Psychiatry, 51*, 302–308, 1994).

TABLE 19.1
Potential for Use of SRI–Neuroleptic Combination Treatment in OCD

Diagnosis	Evidence for Efficacy
OCD with comorbid chronic tic disorder	McDougle et al. (1994) + + +
OCD with comorbid schizotypal personality disorder	McDougle, Goodman, et al. (1990) + +
OCD with psychotic features	+
SRI-refractory trichotillomania	Stein & Hollander (1992) + +
SRI-refractory body dysmorphic disorder	+

Note. OCD = obsessive-compulsive disorder; SRI = serotonin reuptake inhibitor. Rating of evidence for efficacy reflects a composite score based on consideration of the following factors: (a) weight of published evidence in favor of efficacy, (b) degree of methodologic rigor (controlled vs. open-label study design), and (c) our consensual clinical impression, where + + + = multiple reports of efficacy including one controlled trial, + + = promising preliminary evidence, and + = rationale is clear but evidence is lacking.

fluvoxamine. Although fluvoxamine blood levels increased after 4 weeks of haloperidol and placebo, these increases were not statistically significant, nor did changes in levels between the two groups differ. Furthermore, fluvoxamine blood levels did not correlate with treatment response. These results suggest that OCD patients with a comorbid chronic tic disorder may represent a clinically meaningful subtype of OCD that requires conjoint SRI–neuroleptic therapy for effective symptom reduction. Moreover, these drug response data indicate that both the brain 5-HT and DA systems may contribute to the treatment response and, perhaps, the pathophysiology of this tic-related subtype of OCD.

OTHER POSSIBLE INDICATIONS
FOR NEUROLEPTICS IN OCD

In addition to the demonstrated efficacy of combined fluvoxamine–haloperidol treatment in OCD patients with comorbid chronic tic disorders (McDougle et al., 1994), it is possible that other forms of OCD may benefit from neuroleptic addition (Table 19.1). One group of patients in whom neuroleptic addition may prove useful is OCD patients with comorbid SPD. These patients are often resistant to standard pharmacological and behavioral treatment approaches. For example, in a retrospective analysis of 43 treatment-resistant patients in their OCD clinic, Jenike et al. (1986) found that 33% had SPD, and only one of these patients showed an improvement in symptoms following short-term medication and behavior therapy. Based on data suggesting that low-dose neuroleptics may be useful in some patients with SPD (Hymowitz, Frances, Jacobsberg, Sickles, & Hoyt, 1986) and the generally poor outcome of OCD patients with comorbid SPD (Jenike et al., 1986), studies of neuroleptic addition to ongoing SRI therapy in OCD patients with comorbid SPD are needed. As mentioned earlier, we showed in an open-label study that the addition of pimozide to ongoing fluvoxamine treatment led to a significant improvement in OCD patients with comorbid SPD. In our controlled study of haloperidol addition in fluvoxamine-refractory OCD (McDougle et al., 1994), however, it was not possible to make definitive conclusions about the usefulness of this treatment strategy in this population because our sample included only two such patients. Systematic studies of neuroleptic addition in SRI-refractory OCD patients whose obsessions have reached delusional proportions are also needed.

Trichotillomania, currently classified as an impulse control disorder in *DSM–IV* (American Psychiatric Association, 1994), is characterized by chronic hair pulling. Because the hair pulling is often a repetitive, purposeful, but stereotyped behavior that is experienced as both anxiety relieving and excessive, some consider the disorder to fall on a spectrum

of OC-related disorders. In a double-blind crossover study, Swedo et al.
(1989) found the SRI clomipramine significantly better than the relatively
selective norepinephrine reuptake inhibitor desipramine in reducing hair
pulling in adult women with trichotillomania. More recently, Stein and
Hollander (1992) reported that the addition of the DA receptor antagonist
pimozide (1–3 mg/day) to treatment of patients with incomplete responses to SRI monotherapy led to an improvement in hair pulling in six
out of seven adults with trichotillomania. Thus, SRI-refractory trichotillomania appears to be another condition for which systematic investigation of neuroleptic addition to ongoing SRI therapy may prove useful.

BDD, the preoccupation with some imagined defect in appearance in
a normal-appearing person, is classified as a somatoform disorder in
DSM–IV (American Psychiatric Association, 1994). Open-label reports
have suggested that SRIs such as clomipramine and fluoxetine may be
an effective treatment for this disorder (Hollander, Liebowitz, Winchel,
Klumker, & Klein, 1989). Some authors have stated that BDD and monosymptomatic hypochondriacal psychosis, a disorder in which thoughts of
a defect in appearance reach delusional intensity, may be two variants of
the same disorder (Brotman & Jenike, 1985). Interestingly, there are numerous open-label reports describing the efficacy of pimozide in the treatment of monosymptomatic hypochondriacal psychosis (Munro &
Chmara, 1982). Controlled studies of low-dose neuroleptic addition in
SRI-refractory patients with BDD whose bodily preoccupations have
shifted to delusional intensity appear warranted.

Although neuroleptic addition has been found effective in reducing
OC symptoms in some patients with OCD, it should not be used indiscriminately, as these patients often require prolonged pharmacotherapy
for continued symptom reduction. Because of the risks of tardive dyskinesia, adequate trials of two or more SRIs (including clomipramine)
should be completed before neuroleptic addition is considered. Furthermore, a time-limited trial of neuroleptic addition should be attempted,
with reassessment of the risk–benefit ratio of ongoing neuroleptic treatment at regular intervals. The recent development of alternative drug
treatments that modulate DA transmission without the risks of toxic extrapyramidal side effects (e.g., clozapine, risperidone, olanzapine, and
quetiapine) may prove useful in some patients with OCD.

ATYPICAL NEUROLEPTICS IN OCD

Clozapine

Clozapine is an atypical neuroleptic that is effective for treatment-resistant
schizophrenia (Kane, Honigfeld, Singer, Meltzer, & the Clozaril Collaborative Study Group, 1988). The drug's ability to block $5\text{-}HT_2A$, $5\text{-}HT_2C$,

5-HT$_3$ and DA D$_1$-D$_4$ receptors has been proposed as its mechanism of action. Based on the efficacy of combined SRI/DA D$_2$ receptor antagonist treatment in refractory OCD (McDougle et al., 1994) and clozapine's neurochemical profile, we conducted a 10-week systematic investigation of clozapine monotherapy in treatment-refractory adults with OCD (McDougle, Barr, et al., 1995).

All patients were free of psychotropic medications for at least 3 weeks before starting the study and met the following criteria for refractoriness: (a) a minimum dose of clomipramine 200 mg/day for at least 8 weeks; (b) a minimum dose of fluoxetine 60 mg/day or fluvoxamine 200 mg/day for at least 8 weeks; (c) the combination of clomipramine, fluoxetine, or fluvoxamine with a typical neuroleptic, such as haloperidol, for a minimum of 4 weeks; and (d) a trial of behavior therapy while on medication, with less than 35% improvement on the Y–BOCS or a Y–BOCS score of 16 or greater, no better than minimal improvement on the global improvement item of the Clinical Global Impression scale (CGI), and consensus of the primary investigators that the patient was unimproved.

Six women and six men, of whom nine were inpatients and three outpatients 19 to 56 years old ($M = 34.8$, $SD = 2.2$) were entered into the study. Ten of the 12 patients completed the 10-week trial of clozapine. Two patients discontinued the trial prematurely due to sedation (100 mg/day for 3 weeks) and hypotension (125 mg/day for 2 weeks), respectively. The mean dose of clozapine in the 10 completers was 462.5 mg/day ($SD = 93.7$). Two of the patients had comorbid *DSM–III–R* diagnoses of major depression; two chronic motor tic disorder with mixed and borderline personality disorder, respectively; one dysthymia; one a past history of alcohol dependence; and one SPD with a history of anorexia nervosa.

Clozapine was not associated with statistically significant improvement on the Y–BOCS total score ($M = 29.2$, $SD = 6.7$ to $M = 26.3$, $SD = 6.9$), the Y–BOCS Obsession subscale score ($M = 14.6$, $SD = 3.4$ to $M = 14.1$, $SD = 2.8$), the Y–BOCS Compulsion subscale score ($M = 14.6$, $SD = 3.7$ to $M = 12.2$, $SD = 5.0$), the Hamilton Depression Rating Scale ($M = 27.0$, $SD = 12.9$ to $M = 20.0$, $SD = 9.7$), or the CGI ($M = 4.0$, $SD = 0.0$ to $M = 3.8$, $SD = 0.4$). The two patients with chronic motor tic disorder showed no significant reduction in Yale Global Tic Severity Scale scores. None of the patients were classified as treatment responders and none of the patients had an exacerbation of OC symptoms with clozapine. Side effects included sedation ($n = 6$), hypotension ($n = 2$), nocturnal enuresis ($n = 2$), dizziness ($n = 1$), constipation ($n = 1$), nausea ($n = 1$), and weight gain ($n = 1$). No significant decreases in white blood cell count were obtained.

The results of this systematic investigation suggest that clozapine monotherapy is not an effective intervention for most adult patients with treatment-refractory OCD. Neither the group as a whole, the two patients with comorbid chronic tics, nor the one with SPD showed any significant change in OC symptoms.

To our knowledge, there has been only one previous report of clozapine treatment in primary OCD (Young, Bostic, & McDonald, 1994). The patient was a 21-year-old man who had received treatment with multiple drugs, behavior therapy, electroconvulsive therapy (ECT), and psychosurgery (capsulotomy) without improvement. Following 4 months of clozapine 600 mg/day, the patient's Y–BOCS score decreased from 36 to 19, meeting criteria for a partial response. LaPorta (1994) described a 38-year-old man with chronic schizophrenia and moderate mental retardation, previously unresponsive to high doses of typical neuroleptics, who demonstrated a marked reduction in interfering repetitive grooming habits on clozapine 300 mg/day.

Baker et al. (1992) and others (B. Patil & Tandon, 1993; V. J. Patil, 1992) have found that up to 10% of schizophrenic patients develop obsessions and/or compulsions during clozapine treatment. Buckley, Sajatovic, and Meltzer (1994) reported a similar phenomenon in a patient with delusional disorder treated with clozapine. More recently, in a retrospective chart review of 142 clozapine-treated inpatients with a broad range of psychiatric disorders, Ghaemi, Zarate, Popli, Pillay, and Cole (1995) identified no definitive cases of the induction or exacerbation of OC symptoms.

Clozapine's ability to reduce psychosis yet induce or exacerbate OC symptoms in some schizophrenics, although showing limited efficacy in primary OCD, parallels differences in results from our pharmacological challenge studies between these diagnostic groups. Our data indicate that m-chlorophenylpiperazine (mCPP), a $5\text{-HT}_2\text{C}$ receptor agonist/5-HT_3 receptor antagonist, exacerbates psychosis in schizophrenics (Krystal et al., 1993) with no consistent effect on obsessions and compulsions in OCD patients (Goodman et al., 1995). Although the mechanisms of action of clozapine and mCPP are complex and not fully understood, the differential treatment and behavioral response to clozapine and mCPP, respectively, between patients with schizophrenia and OCD provide indirect evidence that 5-HT_2 receptor function may be different in these disorders.

The results of this preliminary study are limited by the relatively small sample size and the open-label design. Nevertheless, they suggest that clozapine monotherapy is not effective in adults with treatment-refractory OCD. The role of clozapine addition in the treatment of SRI-refractory OCD remains undetermined.

Risperidone

Risperidone is a highly potent and selective 5-HT_2 receptor antagonist that also acts as an antagonist at the alpha-$_1$, histamine-$_1$, DA D$_2$, and alpha-$_2$ receptor sites (Leysen et al., 1988). It has no peripheral or central anticholinergic activity, nor does it have significant interactions with opioid, benzodiazepine, substance P, or neurotensin receptors (Moller, Pelzer, Kissling, Riehl, & Wernicke, 1991). Thus, its side effect profile appears to be much more tolerable and safer than that of DA D_2 receptor antagonists currently used to treat SRI-refractory OCD, such as haloperidol and pimozide. Importantly, only a limited number of cases of tardive dyskinesia have been reported with risperidone administration to date. We recently reported three cases of fluvoxamine-refractory OCD responsive to the addition of risperidone to ongoing fluvoxamine treatment (McDougle, Fleischmann, et al., 1995).

The first patient was a 52-year-old married woman who first developed OC symptoms at age 20. Her primary symptoms consisted of contamination and sexual obsessions and repeating and washing compulsions. Despite numerous medication trials and ECT, her OC symptoms persisted without significant improvement for 32 years. She had no personal lifetime history of tics, although her son had chronic motor tic disorder and OCD.

Risperidone 1 mg/day was added to fluvoxamine 250 mg/day and within 2 weeks, the patient reported a marked reduction in her level of anxiety, improved mood, and increased ability to resist performing compulsions. She showered unassisted for the first time in 3 years, ate dinner with her husband in a restaurant for the first time in 8 years, had sex with her husband for the first time in 6 years, began assisting her housekeeper in cleaning her home, and began to look for volunteer work. Four weeks following risperidone addition, she had a reduction in her Y–BOCS score from 31 to 11. Mild sedation was the only side effect.

The second patient, a 34-year-old single man, developed OC symptoms consisting of sexual and contamination obsessions and washing, counting, checking, and arranging compulsions at age 13. He had no personal or family history of chronic tics. Prior to presenting to our clinic for treatment, he had received a 4-month trial of fluoxetine 80 mg/day with no effect. At the time of admission, he had a Y–BOCS score of 32 and met criteria for SPD and secondary major depression. The patient's symptoms were so interfering that he was fired from his job as a television cameraman. He was treated with a 12-week course of fluvoxamine 300 mg/day with no change in his OC symptoms. He then received an additional 10-week course of fluvoxamine plus desipramine 150 mg/day with no improvement. Subsequently, the patient was treated with fluvoxamine plus haloperidol up to 4 mg/day, again with no reduction in OC symptoms.

The patient was next treated with fluvoxamine 300 mg/day plus risperidone 1 mg/day. One week later, he reported that his obsessions were gone, that his compulsions were markedly reduced, and that he no longer felt depressed. His Y–BOCS score decreased from 32 to 14. Although the patient appeared less cognitively disorganized, he continued to demonstrate eccentric behavior and digressive speech. No significant side effects occurred.

The third patient, a 28-year-old single woman, developed OC symptoms at age 19. Her symptoms were characterized by a morbid preoccupation with her facial complexion, repeated checking of her appearance in the mirror, repetitive picking at facial blemishes, and various rituals that she performed hoping that her complexion would improve. She had no personal or family history of chronic tics.

Prior to presenting to our clinic, the patient had received unsuccessful 8- to 12-week trials of fluoxetine 80 mg/day, fluoxetine plus lithium 1,200 mg/day, various tricyclics (including nortriptyline, desipramine, doxepin, and clomipramine, all with adequate blood levels), and buspirone 30 mg/day. She was hospitalized on our unit where she received a 12-week trial of fluvoxamine 300 mg/day without effect. Risperidone 1 mg/day was added to the fluvoxamine and within 1 week, the patient reported that "she could care less" about her appearance and that her mood was "much improved." Although she continued to check herself in the mirror on occasion, she described the anxiety and distress associated with the OC symptoms as markedly reduced. Within 4 weeks of risperidone addition, the patient's Y–BOCS score decreased from 30 to 17. The risperidone was reduced to 0.5 mg/day due to moderate sedation and the response was maintained.

In reviewing these three cases, it is interesting that Case 1 had a family history of chronic tics, Case 2 had a personal history of SPD, and Case 3 had comorbid BDD, a syndrome that can reach delusional proportions. Based on our preliminary experience with risperidone addition, we have initiated a double-blind, placebo-controlled investigation of risperidone addition in SRI-refractory OCD. This study is designed to determine whether risperidone addition is a truly effective treatment for refractory OCD, and if particular subtypes of OCD show a preferential response to this combination treatment strategy.

SUMMARY

Additional research is necessary to further investigate the role of typical and atypical neuroleptics in the treatment of OCD and the interactions between DA and 5-HT systems in the pathophysiology of the disorder. The development of pharmacologic challenge probes of DA function and DA transporter and neuroreceptor radioligands with high affinity and specificity for use in brain imaging studies (Malison et al., 1995) will be critical in further defining these relations. Such research will be instrumental in the identification of homogenous clinical and biological subgroups of patients with OCD, paving the way for more specifically targeted pharmacotherapies.

ACKNOWLEDGMENTS

This work was supported in part by Grants MH30929, MH25642, T32 MH18268, and MH49351 from the National Institute of Mental Health, the State of Connecticut Department of Mental Health and Addiction Services, National Alliance for Research on Schizophrenia and Depression Young Investigator Awards to Christopher J. McDougle (Seaver Investigator) and C. Neill Epperson, and the Stanley Foundation Research Awards Program to Lawrence H. Price and Christopher J. McDougle. The authors wish to thank Betsy Kyle for her assistance in the preparation of the chapter.

REFERENCES

Altschuler, M. (1962, October). Massive doses of trifluoperazine in the treatment of compulsive rituals. *Clinical Notes*, October, 367–368.

American Psychiatric Association. (1980). *Diagnostic and statistical manual of mental disorders* (3rd ed.). Washington, DC: Author.

American Psychiatric Association. (1987). *Diagnostic and statistical manual of mental disorders* (3rd ed., rev.). Washington, DC: Author.

American Psychiatric Association. (1994). *Diagnostic and statistical manual of mental disorders* (4th ed.). Washington, DC: Author.

Baer, L., Jenike, M. A., Ricciardi, J. N., II, Holland, A. D., Seymour, R. J., Minichiello, W. E., & Buttolph, M. L. (1990). Standardized assessment of personality disorders in obsessive-compulsive disorder. *Archives of General Psychiatry, 47*, 826–830.

Baker, R. W., Chengappa, K. N. R., Baird, J. W., Steingard, S., Christ, M. A. G., & Schooler, N. R. (1992). Emergence of obsessive compulsive symptoms during treatment with clozapine. *Journal of Clinical Psychiatry, 53*(12), 439–442.

Brotman, A. W., & Jenike, M. A. (1985). Reply to CA Thomas: Dysmorphophobia and monosymptomatic hypochondriasis [Letter]. *American Journal of Psychiatry, 142*, 1121.

Buckley, P. F., Sajatovic, M., & Meltzer, H. Y. (1994). Treatment of delusional disorders with clozapine [Letter]. *American Journal of Psychiatry, 151*(9), 1394–1395.

Cassano, G. B., Castrogiovanni, P., Mauri, M., Rutigliano, G., Pirro, R., Cerone, G., Nielsen, N. P., Reitano, S., Guidotti, N., Bedarida, D., Marchetti, F. P., Catalano, A., Benecchi, M. V., Amabile, G., Zanasi, M., Pugliese, L., Rocco, M. L., Balestrieri, A., Tansella, M., Burti, L., & Pariante, F. (1981). A multicenter controlled trial in phobic-obsessive psychoneurosis: The effect of clomipramine and of its combinations with haloperidol and diazepam. *Progress in Neuro-Psychopharmacology & Biological Psychiatry, 5*, 129–138.

Cohen, D. J., Shaywitz, B. A., Caparulo, B., Young, J. G., & Bowers, M. B., Jr. (1978). Chronic, multiple tics of Gilles de la Tourette's disease: CSF acid monoamine metabolites after probenecid administration. *Archives of General Psychiatry, 35*, 245–250.

Dally, P. (1967). *Chemistry of psychiatric disorders*. London: Logos Press.

Delgado, P. L., Goodman, W. K., Price, L. H., Heninger, G. R., & Charney, D. S. (1990). Fluvoxamine/pimozide treatment of concurrent Tourette's and obsessive compulsive disorder. *British Journal of Psychiatry, 157*, 762–765.

DeVeaugh-Geiss, J., Katz, R., Landau, P., Akiskal, H., Ananth, J., Ballenger, J., Betts, W. C., Diamond, B., Feiger, A., Foa, E., Fogelson, D., Goodman, W., Greist, J., Himmelhoch, J., Hoehn-Saric, R., Jenike, M., Kim, S. W., Liebowitz, M., Mavissakalian, M., Noyes, R., Ramussen, S., Ringold, A., & Shear, K. (1991). Clomipramine in the treatment of patients with obsessive-compulsive disorder. *Archives of General Psychiatry, 48*, 730–738.

Ellinwood, E. H., Jr. (1967). Amphetamine psychosis: I. Description of the individuals and process. *Journal of Nervous and Mental Disease, 144*, 273–283.

Ellinwood, E. H., Jr., & Escalante, O. (1970). Chronic amphetamine effect on the olfactory forebrain. *Biological Psychiatry, 2*, 189–203.

Fenton, W. S., & McGlashan, T. H. (1990). Long-term outcome of obsessive-compulsive disorder with psychotic features. *Journal of Nervous and Mental Disease, 189*, 760–761.

Frankel, M., Cummings, J. L., Robertson, M. M., Trimble, M. R., Hill, M. A., & Benson, D. F. (1986). Obsessions and compulsions in Gilles de la Tourette's syndrome. *Neurology, 36*, 378–382.

Gawin, F., & Ellinwood, E. H., Jr. (1988). Cocaine and other stimulants: Actions, abuse, and treatment. *New England Journal of Medicine, 318*(18), 1173–1182.

Ghaemi, S. N., Zarate, C. A., Jr., Popli, A. P., Pillay, S. S., & Cole, J. O. (1995). Is there a relationship between clozapine and obsessive-compulsive disorder? A retrospective chart review. *Comprehensive Psychiatry, 36*(4), 267–270.

Goodman, W. K., McDougle, C. J., Price, L. H., Barr, L. C., Hills, O. F., Caplik, J. F., Charney, D. S., & Heninger, G. R. (1995). M-chlorophenylpiperazine in patients with obsessive compulsive disorder: Absence of symptom exacerbation. *Biological Psychiatry, 38*, 138–149.

Goodman, W. K., McDougle, C. J., Price, L. H., Riddle, M. A., Pauls, D. L., & Leckman, J. F. (1990). Beyond the serotonin hypothesis: A role for dopamine in some forms of obsessive compulsive disorder? *Journal of Clinical Psychiatry, 51*, 36–43.

Goodman, W. K., Price, L. H., Rasmussen, S. A., Delgado, P. L., Heninger, G. R., & Charney, D. S. (1989). Efficacy of fluvoxamine in obsessive-compulsive disorder: A double-blind comparison with placebo. *Archives of General Psychiatry, 46*, 36–43.

Goodman, W. K., Price, L. H., Rasmussen, S. A., Mazure, C., Delgado, P., Heninger, G. R., & Charney, D. S. (1989). The Yale–Brown Obsessive Compulsive Scale (Y–BOCS): Part II. Validity. *Archives of General Psychiatry, 46*, 1012–1016.

Goodman, W. K., Price, L. H., Rasmussen, S. A., Mazure, C., Fleischmann, R., Hill, C., Heninger, G. R., & Charney, D. S. (1989). The Yale–Brown Obsessive Compulsive Scale (Y–BOCS): Part 1. Development, use, and reliability. *Archives of General Psychiatry, 46*, 1006–1011.

Grady, T. A., Pigott, T. A., L'Heureux, F., Hill, J. L., Bernstein, S. E., & Murphy, D. L. (1993). Double-blind study of adjuvant buspirone for fluoxetine-treated patients with obsessive-compulsive disorder. *American Journal of Psychiatry, 150*, 819–821.

Greist, J., Chouinard, G., DuBoff, E., Halaris, A., Kim, S. W., Koran, L., Liebowitz, M., Lydiard, R. B., Rasmussen, S., White, K., & Sikes, C. (1995). Double-blind parallel comparison of three dosages of sertraline and placebo in outpatients with obsessive-compulsive disorder. *Archives of General Psychiatry, 52*, 289–295.

Hollander, E., DeCaria, C. M., Schneier, F. R., Schneier, H. A., Liebowitz, M. R., & Klein, D. F. (1990). Fenfluramine augmentation of serotonin reuptake blockade antiobsessional treatment. *Journal of Clinical Psychiatry, 51*, 119–123.

Hollander, E., Liebowitz, M. R., Winchel, R., Klumker, A., & Klein, D. F. (1989). Treatment of body-dysmorphic disorder with serotonin reuptake blockers. *American Journal of Psychiatry, 146*, 768–770.

Hussain, M. Z., & Ahad, A. (1970). Treatment of obsessive-compulsive neurosis [Letter]. *Canadian Medical Association Journal, 103,* 649–650.

Hymowitz, P., Frances, A., Jacobsberg, L. B., Sickles, M., & Hoyt, R. (1986). Neuroleptic treatment of schizotypal personality disorders. *Comprehensive Psychiatry, 27,* 267–271.

Insel, T. R., & Akiskal, H. S. (1986). Obsessive-compulsive disorder with psychotic features: A phenomenologic analysis. *American Journal of Psychiatry, 143,* 1527–1533.

Insel, T. R., Mueller, E. A., Alterman, A., Linnoila, M., & Murphy, D. L. (1985). Obsessive-compulsive disorder and serotonin: Is there a connection? *Biological Psychiatry, 20,* 1174–1188.

Jenike, M. A., Baer, L., Minichiello, W. E., Schwartz, C. E., & Carey, R. J. (1986). Concomitant obsessive-compulsive disorder and schizotypal personality disorder. *American Journal of Psychiatry, 143,* 530–532.

Kane, J., Honigfeld, G., Singer, J., Meltzer, H., & and the Clozaril Collaborative Study Group. (1988). Clozapine for the treatment-resistant schizophrenic. *Archives of General Psychiatry, 45,* 789–796.

Korsgaard, S., Gerlach, J., & Christensson, E. (1985). Behavioral aspects of serotonin-dopamine interaction in the monkey. *European Journal of Pharmacology, 118,* 245–252.

Krystal, J. H., Seibyl, J. P., Price, L. H., Woods, S. W., Heninger, G. R., Aghajanian, G. K., & Charney, D. S. (1993). m-Chlorophenylpiperazine effects in neuroleptic-free schizophrenic patients: Evidence implicating serotonergic systems in the positive symptoms of schizophrenia. *Archives of General Psychiatry, 50,* 624–635.

LaPorta, L. D. (1994). More on obsessive-compulsive symptoms and clozapine. *Journal of Clinical Psychiatry, 55*(7), 312.

Leysen, J. E., Gommeren, W., Eens, A., De Chaffoy, De Courcelles, D., Stoof, J. C., & Janssen, P. A. J. (1988). Biochemical profile of risperidone, a new antipsychotic. *Journal of Pharmacology and Experimental Therapeutics, 247,* 661–670.

Lopez-lbor, J. J., & Lopez-lbor, J. M. (1973). Tratamiento psicofarmacologico de las neurosis obsessivas. *Actas Luso Esp Neurol Psiquiatria, 1*(6), 767.

Malison, R. T., McDougle, C. J., van Dyck, C. H., Scahill, L., Baldwin, R. M., Seibyl, J. P., Price, L. H., Leckman, J. F., & Innis, R. B. (1995). [123I]B-CIT SPECT imaging demonstrates increased striatal dopamine transporter binding in Tourette's syndrome. *American Journal of Psychiatry, 152,* 1359–1361.

McDougle, C. J., Barr, L. C., Goodman, W. K., Pelton, G. H., Aronson, S. C., Anand, A., & Price, L. H. (1995). Lack of efficacy of clozapine monotherapy in refractory obsessive compulsive disorder. *American Journal of Psychiatry, 152,* 1812–1814.

McDougle, C. J., Fleischmann, R. L., Epperson, C. N., Wasylink, S., Leckman, J. F., & Price, L. H. (1995). Risperidone addition in fluvoxamine-refractory obsessive compulsive disorder: Three cases. *Journal of Clinical Psychiatry, 56,* 526–528.

McDougle, C. J., Goodman, W. K., Delgado, P. L., & Price, L. H. (1989). Pathophysiology of obsessive-compulsive disorder [Letter to the editor]. *American Journal of Psychiatry, 146,* 1350–1351.

McDougle, C. J., Goodman, W. K., Leckman, J. F., Holzer, J. C., Barr, L. C., McCance-Katz, E. F., Heninger, G. R., & Price, L. H. (1993). Limited therapeutic effect of addition of buspirone in fluvoxamine-refractory obsessive compulsive disorder. *American Journal of Psychiatry, 150,* 647–649.

McDougle, C. J., Goodman, W. K., Leckman, J. F., Lee, N. C., Heninger, G. R., & Price, L. H. (1994). Haloperidol addition in fluvoxamine-refractory obsessive compulsive disorder: A double-blind, placebo-controlled study in patients with and without tics. *Archives of General Psychiatry, 51,* 302–308.

McDougle, C. J., Goodman, W. K., Leckman, J. F., & Price, L. H. (1993). The psychopharmacology of obsessive compulsive disorder: Implications for treatment and pathogenesis. *Psychiatric Clinics of North America, 16*(4), 749–766.

McDougle, C. J., Goodman, W. K., Price, L. H., Delgado, P. L., Krystal, J. H., Charney, D. S., & Heninger, G. R. (1990). Neuroleptic addition in fluvoxamine-refractory obsessive-compulsive disorder. *American Journal of Psychiatry, 147,* 652–654.

McDougle, C. J., Price, L. H., Goodman, W. K., Charney, D. S., & Heninger, G. R. (1991). A controlled trial of lithium augmentation in fluvoxamine-refractory obsessive compulsive disorder: Lack of efficacy. *Journal of Clinical Psychopharmacology, 11,* 175–184.

McDougle, C. J., Southwick, S. M., & Rohrbaugh, R. M. (1990). Tourette's disorder and associated complex behaviors: A case report. *Yale Journal of Biology and Medicine, 63,* 209–214.

Mesulam, M. M. (1986). Cocaine and Tourette's syndrome. *New England Journal of Medicine, 315,* 398.

Moller, H. J., Pelzer, E., Kissling, W., Riehl, T., & Wernicke, T. (1991). Efficacy and tolerability of a new antipsychotic compound (risperidone): Results of a pilot study. *Pharmacopsychiatry, 24,* 185–189.

Munro, A., & Chmara, J. (1982). Monosymptomatic hypochondriacal psychosis: A diagnostic checklist based on 50 cases of the disorder. *Canadian Journal of Psychiatry, 27,* 374–376.

Nee, L. E., Caine, E. D., Polinsky, R. J., Eldridge, R., & Ebert, M. H. (1980). Gilles de la Tourette syndrome: Clinical and family study of 50 cases. *Annals of Neurology, 7,* 41–49.

O'Regan, J. B. (1970a). Treatment of obsessive compulsive neurosis [Letter]. *Canadian Medical Association Journal, 103,* 650–651.

O'Regan, J. B. (1970b). Treatment of obsessive-compulsive neurosis with haloperidol. *Canadian Medical Association Journal, 103,* 167–168.

Patil, B., & Tandon, R. (1993). Development of obsessive-compulsive symptoms during clozapine treatment. *American Journal of Psychiatry, 150*(5), 836.

Patil, V. J. (1992). Development of transient obsessive-compulsive symptoms during treatment with clozapine [Letter]. *American Journal of Psychiatry, 149,* 272.

Pauls, D. L., Alsobrook, J. P., Goodman, W., Rasmussen, S., & Leckman, J. F. (1995). A family study of obsessive-compulsive disorder. *American Journal of Psychiatry, 152,* 76–84.

Pauls, D. L., & Leckman, J. F. (1986). The inheritance of Gilles de la Tourette's syndrome and associated behaviors: Evidence for autosomal dominant transmission. *New England Journal of Medicine, 315,* 993–997.

Pigott, T. A., L'Heureux, F., Hill, J. L., Bihari, K., Bernstein, S. E., & Murphy, D. L. (1992). A double-blind study of adjuvant buspirone hydrochloride in clomipramine-treated patients with obsessive-compulsive disorder. *Journal of Clinical Psychopharmacology, 12,* 11–18.

Pigott, T. A., Pato, M. T., L'Heureux, F., Hill, J. L., Grover, G. N., Bernstein, S. E., & Murphy, D. L. (1991). A controlled comparison of adjuvant lithium carbonate or thyroid hormone in clomipramine-treated patients with obsessive-compulsive disorder. *Journal of Clinical Psychopharmacology, 11,* 242–248.

Pitman, R. K., Green, R. C., Jenike, M. A., & Mesulam, M. M. (1987). Clinical comparison of Tourette's disorder and obsessive-compulsive disorder. *American Journal of Psychiatry, 144,* 1166–1171.

Rasmussen, S. A. (1984). Lithium and tryptophan augmentation in clomipramine-resistant obsessive-compulsive disorder. *American Journal of Psychiatry, 141,* 1283–1285.

Riddle, M. A., Leckman, J. F., Hardin, M. T., Anderson, G. M., & Cohen, D. J. (1988). Fluoxetine treatment of obsessions and compulsions in patients with Tourette's syndrome [Letter to the editor]. *American Journal of Psychiatry, 145,* 1173–1174.

Rivers-Bulkeley, N., & Hollender, M. H. (1982). Successful treatment of obsessive-compulsive disorder with loxapine. *American Journal of Psychiatry, 139,* 1345–1346.

Rosse, R. B., Fay-McCarthy, M., Collins, J. P., Jr., Risher-Flowers, D., Alim, T. N., & Deutsch, S. I. (1993). Transient compulsive foraging behavior associated with crack cocaine use. *American Journal of Psychiatry, 150,* 155–156.

Satel, S. L., & McDougle, C. J. (1991). Obsessions and compulsions associated with cocaine abuse [Letter to the editor]. *American Journal of Psychiatry, 148,* 947.

Schiorring, E. (1975). Changes in individual and social behavior induced by amphetamine and related compounds in monkeys and man. *Behaviour, 43,* 481–521.

Shapiro, E., Shapiro, A. K., Fulop, G., Hubbard, M., Mandell, J., Nordlie, J., & Phillips, R. A. (1989). Controlled study of haloperidol, pimozide, and placebo for the treatment of Gilles de la Tourette's syndrome. *Archives of General Psychiatry, 46,* 722–730.

Singer, H. S., Hahn, I.-H., & Moran, T. H. (1991). Abnormal dopamine uptake sites in post-mortem striatum from patients with Tourette's syndrome. *Annals of Neurology, 30,* 558–562.

Solyom, L., DiNicola, V. F., Phil, M., Sookman, D., & Luchins, D. (1985). Is there an obsessive psychosis? Aetiological and prognostic factors of an atypical form of obsessive compulsive neurosis. *Canadian Journal of Psychiatry, 30,* 372–379.

Stanley, M. A., Turner, S. M., & Borden, J. W. (1990). Schizotypal features in obsessive-compulsive disorder. *Comprehensive Psychiatry, 31,* 511–518.

Stefl, M. E. (1984). Mental health needs associated with Tourette syndrome. *American Journal of Public Health, 74,* 1310–1313.

Stein, D. J., & Hollander, E. (1992). Low-dose pimozide augmentation of serotonin reuptake blockers in the treatment of trichotillomania. *Journal of Clinical Psychiatry, 53,* 123–126.

Swedo, S. E., Leonard, H. L., Rapoport, J. L., Lenane, M. C., Goldberger, E. L., & Cheslow, D. L. (1989). A double-blind comparison of clomipramine and desipramine in the treatment of trichotillomania (hair pulling). *New England Journal of Medicine, 321,* 497–501.

Tollefson, G. D., Rampey, A. H., Jr., Potvin, J. H., Jenike, M. A., Rush, A. J., Dominguez, R. A., Koran, L. M., Shear, M. K., Goodman, W., & Genduso, L. A. (1994). A multicenter investigation of fixed-dose fluoxetine in the treatment of obsessive-compulsive disorder. *Archives of General Psychiatry, 51,* 559–567.

Trethowan, W. H., & Scott, P. A. L. (1955). Chlorpromazine in obsessive-compulsive and allied disorders. *The Lancet,* April 16, 781–785.

Young, C. R., Bostic, J. Q., & McDonald, C. L. (1994). Clozapine and refractory obsessive-compulsive disorder: A case report. *Journal of Clinical Psychopharmacology, 14,* 209–210.

Intravenous Clomipramine for Obsessive-Compulsive Disorder

Brian A. Fallon
Michael R. Liebowitz
The New York State Psychiatric Institute
Columbia University

Recent studies have enhanced our knowledge of the treatment and pathophysiology of obsessive compulsive-disorder (OCD; Greist, Jefferson, Koback, Katzelnick, & Serlin, 1995; Leonard, 1997; Liebowitz & Hollander, 1991). With pharmacological agents such as clomipramine, fluoxetine, sertraline, paroxetine, citalopram, and fluvoxamine, pharmacological augmenting strategies, such as dopamine antagonists for patients with concurrent tic disorders or schizotypal features, and nonpharmacological techniques, such as behavioral therapy, approximately 60% to 70% of patients significantly improve. Given recent indications of prevalence (Karno, Sorensen, & Burnam, 1988; Weissman et al., 1994), however, this still leaves hundreds of thousands of patients failing to show any benefit from treatment. In addition, even among the patients who improve, treatment response may be meaningful but limited, such that the patient is still left with marked or severe OCD. The overly optimistic view of outcome in OCD of the recent past has been replaced by a sobering awareness that a significant number of OCD patients either do not benefit at all from current therapies or achieve only a limited improvement in morbidity. In the United States, these treatment-refractory patients have only one other treatment option: neurosurgery. Although neurosurgery for OCD is a potentially valuable treatment option, it is not widely available, has not yet been tested in a well-controlled design, and may lead to secondary frontal lobe dysfunction (Mindus, Rasmussen, & Lindquist, 1994). Expanding the options for these treatment-refractory patients is critical.

The intravenous (IV) administration of clomipramine might represent a major alternative treatment for patients with refractory OCD. The potential benefit of IV clomipramine for treatment-refractory patients has been suggested by: (a) clinical reports from Canada (Thakur, Remillard, Meldrum, & Gorecki, 1991; Warneke, 1984, 1985, 1989), where it is being studied in open trials; (b) reports from Europe (Capstick, 1971; Koran, Faravelli, & Pallanti, 1994; Rack, 1973, 1977; Walter, 1973), where it is extensively used; and (c) open and controlled clinical trials (Fallon et al., 1992, 1998; Koran, Sallee, & Pallanti, 1997). These reports suggest that IV clomipramine may be an effective treatment for oral clomipramine-refractory patients. In addition, clomipramine administered intravenously may result in a more rapid improvement in OCD than when given orally (Fallon et al., 1992; Fallon et al., 1998; Koran et al., 1994, 1997; Warneke, 1984).

Pulse dosing of IV clomipramine has been studied in the United States for the treatment of major depression (Pollock, Perel, Nathan, & Kupfer, 1989) and has recently been tested in a controlled comparison of oral versus IV clomipramine to "jump start" the oral treatment of OCD (Koran et al., 1997). This work suggests that pulse dosing of IV clomipramine may result in a significantly faster reduction in OCD symptoms than occurs with pulse oral clomipramine, occurring within days rather than weeks.

The hypothesized mechanism for the preferential efficacy of IV over oral clomipramine rests on the assumption that because IV clomipramine avoids the first-pass hepato-enteric metabolism, the bioavailability of the serotonergic parent compound (nondesmethylated clomipramine) over its more noradrenergic metabolite (desmethylclomipramine) is greater to the central nervous system by the IV route than orally. Prior reports have confirmed that when clomipramine is given intravenously rather than orally, significantly higher plasma ratios of clomipramine to desmethylclomipramine are attained (Thakur et al., 1991). The gradual administration of IV clomipramine starting at a low dose of 25 mg and increasing over 14 infusions to 250 mg/day results in the predominance of clomipramine over desmethylclomipramine for the first 9 to 10 days with a transition to increasing concentrations of desmethylclomipramine during the last 5 days (Fallon, Liebowitz, Campeas, Schneier, & Davies, 1993). Hypotheses have been made to account for the more rapid clinical response that has been suggested by the IV pulse-dosing studies. First, as was suggested by Pollock et al. (1989), the high-dose pulse strategy might allow for more rapid down-regulation of postsynaptic receptors because of the more rapid delivery of the higher dosages of medication that are normally needed for a therapeutic response. Additionally, Koran et al. (1997) speculated that IV pulse loading may initiate changes in postsynaptic neurons (G-protein signal transduction, cyclase and phosphatidyl-inositol second messenger activity, or gene expression) that may then be maintained by oral clomipramine. Pulse dosing in which treatment consists of 2 high-dose infusions (75–150 mg for the first infusion and 200 mg for the second infusion) results in a rapid, high-dosage delivery of the more serotonergic nondesmethylated clomipramine compound. Gradual and pulse dosing IV clomipramine strategies may exert different biological and clinical effects.

This chapter reviews the literature on the use of IV clomipramine for OCD, making use of published articles and abstracts presented at scientific conferences.

IV CLOMIPRAMINE

Many of the reports on the use of IV clomipramine for OCD suffer severe limitations, such as the lack of operationalized diagnostic criteria, the use of clinical impression rather than reliable rating instruments to assess treatment progress and outcome, the lack of placebo controls, and sample sizes that are small and heterogeneous with regard to concomitant depressive and anxiety states.

Clinical Reports and Uncontrolled Series

Capstick (1971) treated 16 obsessional patients with IV clomipramine up to 150 mg/day with an average of 12 infusions; nine patients (56%) made moderate to marked improvement, one of whom had previously failed to respond to an oral trial of clomipramine 225 mg/day. Walter (1973) treated five obsessional patients with IV clomipramine up to 250 mg/day with 12 to 14 infusions; two of five patients were judged to be much improved to symptom free and three of five minimally to definitely improved. Rack (1973) gave IV clomipramine up to 200 mg/day to 21 oral clomipramine-refractory patients, 16 of whom had OCD; 12 (57%) had good to excellent outcomes, one after failing to benefit from placebo infusions. In a later series, Rack (1977) treated 11 OCD patients with IV infusions up to 200 mg/day, all of whom had either no response or only a partial response to oral clomipramine 150 mg/day; five patients (45%) had good to excellent outcomes. However, Rack did not specify the length of his prior oral clomipramine trials, and 150 mg/day is a low maximum oral dose by current standards.

In three separate reports that detail the treatment of a total of nine oral clomipramine-unresponsive OCD patients, Warneke (1984, 1985, 1989) reported that all responded well to 14 IV clomipramine infusions up to 350 mg/day. These patients all had unsuccessful trials of oral clomipramine previously—two at 250 to 350 mg/day for several weeks, one at 150 mg/day for an unspecified period, two at 200 mg/day for several months, one adolescent at 200 mg/day for a few weeks, one at an unspecified dose responded but relapsed on the same dose, and two could not tolerate more than 100 mg/day. Again, it should be noted that only two of these participants may have been truly refractory patients, in that only two of the nine patients were treated with at least 200 mg/day for more than 8 weeks. Even these patients may have responded to higher doses of oral clomipramine. Thakur et al. (1991) used the same treatment protocol as Warneke to treat a 62-year-old woman with refractory OCD who had failed to respond to 175 mg of clomipramine given for an unspecified duration. This patient did extremely well and maintained her improvement at 3-year follow-up. The dosage and duration criticisms, however, apply to that report as well.

In reviewing the treatment of more than 60 OCD patients with IV clomipramine, Warneke (1989, 1992) emphasized the following points. The treatment did not produce any serious adverse reactions. The usual course of therapy consisted of up to 14 daily infusions (given every weekday) beginning with 25 mg and building up to 350 mg per infusion—a dose greater than the 250 mg/day maximum approved in the United States for oral dosing. Side effects consisted of drowsiness during the infusion, myoclonic jerks treated with nightly sedatives, and mild superficial phlebitis at infusion sites corrected by increasing the dilution of the infusions, and, where necessary, using indwelling heparinized catheters or anti-inflammatory drugs. Only two patients had side effects that required premature termination of the course of IV treatment; these side effects consisted of induration and inflammation at the infusion site. Several patients unable to take more than 100 mg/day of oral clomipramine because of postural hypotension, drowsiness, and dry mouth tolerated much higher IV doses and could subsequently tolerate maintenance oral clomipramine up to 350 mg/day without side effects. Maintenance oral clomipramine was routinely given following response to IV clomipramine to prevent relapse. Although some patients showed improvement in OCD during the 14 days of IV infusion treatment, most patients had a delayed response occurring a few weeks later. The exact time course for response among the delayed responders in Warneke's studies was not clear. If the response occurred within 1 or 2 weeks after the infusion, then one would more likely attribute the improvement to the effect of the IV clomipramine. If, on the other hand, the improvement occurred 4 weeks or more after the infusion ended, one would be left wondering whether the improvement was more likely due to the oral clomipramine administered after the infusion rather than to the IV clomipramine. Warneke's articles suggest that the former more rapid time course was the case among his patients. This uncontrolled open treatment data pointed to the necessity for placebo-controlled trials of IV clomipramine as the data suggested that IV clomipramine was safe, well-tolerated, and effective among some oral clomipramine-refractory or oral clomipramine-intolerant patients. In addition, IV clomipramine treatment may enable a patient to tolerate higher doses of oral clomipramine than previously possible.

There have been six published reports on the use of IV clomipramine for OCD that have used *Diagnostic and Statistical Manual of Mental Disorders* (3rd ed., rev. [*DSM–III–R*]; American Psychiatric Association, 1987) diagnoses and standardized rating instruments to assess treatment response (Fallon et al., 1992, 1998; Koran et al., 1994; Koran, Pallanti, Paiva, & Quercioli, 1996; Koran et al., 1997; Sallee, Pollock, Perel, Ryan, & Stiller, 1989). Although each of these reports represents an improvement over prior work in that standardized rating scales were used to assess change, only one was a double-blind placebo-controlled study (Fallon et al., 1998). Each of the reports are summarized here, as the results are promising and support the need for additional controlled studies.

Sallee et al. (1989) conducted an open trial of IV pulse loading of clomipramine among five adolescents with depression. In this sample, three adolescents also had comorbid OCD, two of whom had failed to respond to previous treatment with tricyclic antidepressants. A pulse-loading strategy was used in an attempt to shorten the length of time required to reach a therapeutic plasma concentration. The treatment consisted of two consecutive nightly infusions of clomipramine (75 mg and 200 mg, respectively) administered over 90 minutes. The 75-mg infusion was administered in 250 cc of 0.9% saline and the 200-mg dose was given in 500 cc of 0.9% saline. The patients were then free from medication for 7 days before beginning maintenance oral pharmacotherapy. One of the non-OCD depressed patients could not tolerate the second infusion because of pronounced nausea and vomiting. There were no significant electrocardiogram changes during or immediately after the IV infusions. Among the three depressed adolescents with concurrent OCD, clinically significant improvement in obsessive-compulsive and depressive symptoms was seen at the 36-hour postinfusion rating, as measured by the self-report Leyton Obsessional Inventory and the clinician-administered Hamilton Depression Scale (Hamilton, 1960) and National Institute of Mental Health (NIMH) Obsessive Compulsive Rating Scale with the improvement in the former two scales reaching statistical significance. The improvement was sustained at 6-month follow-up on 350 mg/day of oral clomipramine. It should be noted that the adolescents entered into this trial had not had prior treatment with either oral clomipramine or any of the selective serotonin reuptake inhibitors (SRIs).

Fallon et al. (1992) reported on the open treatment of five patients with *DSM–III–R* OCD using gradual IV clomipramine infusions in which doses started at 25 mg/day and increased by 25 mg at each infusion up to a maximum dose of 250 mg/day by the 10th infusion. Treatment was given for 14 consecutive weekdays. Clomipramine was administered in 500 cc of 0.9% saline, infused over 1 hour. Patients were observed by a physician with a continuous cardiac monitor. Ratings consisted of the Yale–Brown Obsessive Compulsive Scale (Goodman et al., 1989), the NIMH Obsessive Compulsive Scale, the Physician's Clinical Global Impression Scale (Guy, 1976), and the Hamilton Depression Scale. Three of the five patients were rated as much improved after the 14 infusions, experiencing a mean improvement of 39% on the Y–BOCS. Of the responders, one patient had reported absolutely no response to a prior adequate trial of oral clomipramine. Another patient who reported a partial response to oral clomipramine in the past reported 50% more improvement with the IV form. The third responder also had shown a partial response to oral clomipramine in the past, but discontinued it due to a 50-lb. weight gain. All of the patients tolerated the IV form well, experienced no significant electrocardiogram changes, and reported fewer side effects than recalled from their experience with oral clomipramine. At 6-month follow-up on oral clomipramine, two of the responders had relapsed during the interim. One responder and one minimal responder had made further gains and were rated as much improved at the 6-month evaluation. Noteworthy is that the two patients who relapsed had been started on oral clomipramine at 25 mg after the infusions and increased to 250 mg over several weeks, whereas the two patients who made further progress after the infusions had been brought to a dose of 250 mg of oral clomipramine by Day 5 post-IV infusion.

Koran et al. (1994) reported on the use of 6 to 7 weeks of daily IV clomipramine in five OCD patients with concomitant major depression treated in a private outpatient practice in Italy. None of these patients had adequate prior pharmacologic treatment for OCD. One of the five had been unable to tolerate an oral clomipramine dose of greater than 50 mg. Patients received IV clomipramine mixed in 500 cc of 0.9% saline infusions over 3 hours, 6 days per week. Patients were treated initially with 25 mg of clomipramine in 250 ml of normal saline and increased every 2 to 3 days by 25 to 50 mg up to a maximum dose of 200 mg at Week 5. The mean percentage improvement on the Y–BOCS increased with time from 33% after 3 weeks, to 40% after 4 weeks and 71% after 6 to 7 weeks. As noted previously by Warneke (1992) and Fallon et al. (1992), improvement accrued over time. This degree of improvement is greater and faster than that reported in studies of oral clomipramine (DeVeaugh-Geiss, Landau, & Katz, 1989). Side effects consisted of mild to moderate dry mouth, fatigue, drowsiness, nausea, sweating, and sexual dysfunction. No patient needed to discontinue IV treatment due to side effects. At 6- to 12-month follow-up, all patients maintained at least their maximum IV clomipramine response.

Koran et al. (1996) reported a nonrandomized, open treatment comparison of pulse IV clomipramine versus gradual IV clomipramine among OCD patients who would not be considered treatment refractory. Seven treatment-naive OCD patients were treated with pulse-loaded IV clomipramine and 20 similar OCD outpatients were treated with gradually increased IV doses. The pulse-loaded patients received 150 mg of IV clomipramine on Day 1 and 200 mg of clomipramine on Day 2. The gradually treated IV patients received 25 mg/day increasing to 200 mg/day over 2 weeks and continued IV treatment at maximum tolerated dose for a mean of 43 days. After the IV infusions, both groups received oral clomipramine for 6 months. Using nonblind ratings, the pulse-loaded IV group had a mean Y–BOCS drop of 32% from the baseline score 5 days postinfusion, whereas the gradual IV group had no improvement at that point (Day 7 of gradual treatment). Over the 6-month period, the pulse-loaded group had statistically significantly greater improvement than the gradually treated group.

Controlled Trials of IV Clomipramine

Fallon and colleagues (1998) reported on a double-blind placebo-controlled study of IV clomipramine for patients who were refractory to oral clomipramine, where refractory was defined as a partial or complete nonresponse to an 8-week trial of clomipramine with at least 2 weeks at a dose of 200 mg/day. Of the 54 patients, 5 patients had been unable to tolerate an adequate oral clomipramine trial due to side effects. All but 1 of the 54 patients had also failed to respond to at least one selective SRI and more than half had not responded to a trial of behavior therapy. Patients received 14 consecutive weekday infusions of either placebo or clomipramine in 500 cc of 0.9% saline. Ratings were conducted by a blind evaluator at baseline, the seventh infusion, and the 14th infusion. There were no responders in either group at the seventh infusion. After the 14th infusion, 21% of the patients randomized to clomipramine were responders, whereas none of the patients assigned to placebo showed even minimal improvement ($p < .02$). One week post-IV, 43% of the IV clomipramine patients were responders with no IV placebo patients responding ($p = .002$). These placebo-controlled results obtained under double-blind conditions at Infusion 14 and single-blind conditions 1-week postinfusion suggest that IV clomipramine may be an important option for patients with OCD who are not responding to currently available treatments. Among those patients re-evaluated one month post-infusion, 55% were responders. Patients who recalled never having had even a partial response to oral clomipramine were just as likely to respond to IV clomi-pramine treatment as patients who previously had had a partial oral clomipramine response.

Koran et al. (1997) conducted a double-blind trial of pulse IV versus pulse oral clomipramine for 15 patients with OCD. Pharmacologic non-response was not an entry criteria for the study, but 8 of the 15 patients had a history of poor response to a trial of oral clomipramine of 200 mg or more for at least 8 weeks and 10 of the 15 had failed to respond to adequate trials of at least two other SRIs. All 15 patients received 150 mg of clomipramine on Day 1 and 200 mg on Day 2, seven IV and eight oral. Of the 15 patients in the study, four of the prior oral clomipramine nonresponders were randomized to pulse IV therapy and four were randomized to pulse oral therapy. Patients were subsequently treated with oral clomipramine for 8 weeks, starting at 150 mg/day and increasing over 16 days to 250 mg. The results showed that 4.5 days after the second pulse dose of treatment, six of seven pulse IV patients versus one of eight pulse oral clomipramine patients were responders (Y–BOCS improvement of at least 25%) at Day 7 ($p = .009$, two-tailed Fisher's Exact Test). Among the patients randomized to pulse IV clomipramine, two of the four oral clomipramine-refractory patients were IV responders. One IV patient had a panic attack and one an episode of hypotension and bradycardia. During the 8 weeks of subsequent oral clomipramine treatment for all patients, four of the six IV responders maintained or improved their response but two relapsed. Four of the eight pulse oral clomipramine patients were responders by the end of Week 8; one of these four oral clomipramine responders had previously been unresponsive to oral clomipramine. These results indicate that pulse IV clomipramine may work faster than pulse oral clomipramine, that marked improvement can be seen within 1 week after only two pulse infusions, and that some patients with a history of poor response to oral clomipramine may benefit from pulse IV treatment. However, this study did not demonstrate any response differ-ence at the 8-week end-of-treatment point between patients who had been given pulse IV or pulse oral therapy.

CONCLUSIONS

Placebo-controlled data now indicate that IV clomipramine is more effec-tive than IV placebo among OCD patients with a history of poor response to oral clomipramine. The Fallon et al. (1998) study, however, did not extend double-blind ratings beyond the last infusion, thus leaving unan-swered questions about the actual number of patients capable of benefit-ing from IV clomipramine treatment. In the single-blind 1-week post-IV ratings, the number of patients responding increased with time after the last infusion. This finding is comparable to the reports of Warneke (1992) and Koran et al. (1994). Both controlled studies relied on the patients' recollections of their nonresponse to oral clomipramine, leaving open the question about the potentially confounding negative effect of a historical recall bias among patients who are still sick (Fallon et al., 1998; Koran et al., 1997). Additional double-blind research is needed to address both the degree of improvement over time and the actual superiority of IV clomipramine over oral clomipramine among patients refractory to oral clomipramine by history.

The double-blind trial by Koran et al. (1997) among patients with general OCD (i.e., not restricted to treatment-refractory patients) suggested that two infusions of IV clomipramine can lead to a more rapid improvement in OCD than possible with pulse oral dosing. Two of the four historically oral clomipramine-refractory patients responded to the pulse IV clomipramine infusions. These promising findings need to be examined with a larger sample size under well-controlled conditions to assess speed of response and degree and durability of improvement. Because one of the pulse IV clomipramine patients had an episode of bradycardia and hypotension within 10 minutes of the second double-blind infusion, questions remain about the safety of high-dose pulse infusions. If these findings among OCD patients in general can be confirmed and extended in controlled trials to oral pharmacotherapy-refractory patients in particular, clinical and economic considerations would suggest that pulse IV clomipramine may be the treatment of choice.

At present, the aqueous form of clomipramine mixed in the IV saline infusions is not approved by the Food and Drug Administration (FDA) for use in the United States. However, IV clomipramine is being used by psychiatrists in Europe, Canada, and Asia. Should additional controlled trials support the results suggested by the studies reported here, then the combined efforts of OCD advocacy groups and private enterprise should make it possible for IV clomipramine to win FDA approval for use in the United States.

A review of these studies on IV clomipramine for treatment-refractory OCD patients revealed that the results section in each paper did not provide a detailed description of the patients who had failed to respond to IV clomipramine. These patients, having failed oral SRIs and IV clomipramine, would be considered truly pharmacologically refractory. Had these patients ever received an adequate trial of behavior therapy? Also not known is whether these pharmacologically refractory patients were more likely to have a personality disorder, other Axis I comorbidity, a longer course of illness, an enmeshed family system that strengthened the OCD behaviors, neurological soft signs, neurophysiological or neuroimaging abnormalities, lower peak or trough levels of clomipramine, or a type of OCD more characterized by the "just right" dimension (touching, ordering, symmetry) than by the harm-avoidance dimension (washing, checking). Future research should examine these issues, as a better understanding of factors that affect outcome may lead to the development of more effective treatment strategies.

In summary, clomipramine administered intravenously is a valuable, alternative treatment that appears to act rapidly and is effective among some patients with OCD who have had a history of poor response to oral clomipramine.

REFERENCES

American Psychiatric Association. (1987). *Diagnostic and statistical manual of mental disorders* (3rd ed., rev.). Washington, DC: Author.

Capstick, N. (1971). Chlorimipramine in obsessional states (A pilot study). *Psychosomatics, 12*, 332–335.

DeVeaugh-Geiss, J., Landau, P., & Katz, R. (1989). Preliminary results from a multicenter trial of clomipramine in obsessive-compulsive disorder. *Psychopharmacology Bulletin, 25*, 36–40.

Fallon, B. A., Liebowitz, M. R., Campeas, R., Schneier, F. R., Marshall, R., Davies, S., Goetz, D., & Klein, D. F. (1998). IV clomipramine for obsessive-compulsive disorder refractory to oral clomipramine: A placebo-controlled study. *Archives of General Psychiatry, 55*, 918–924.

Fallon, B. A., Campeas, R., Schneier, F. R., Hollander, E., Feerick, J., Hatterer, J., Goetz, D., Davies, S., & Liebowitz, M. R. (1992). An open trial of IV clomipramine in 5 treatment refractory patients with OCD. *Journal of Neuropsychiatry and Clinical Neurosciences, 4*, 70–75.

Fallon, B. A., Liebowitz, M. R., Campeas, R., Schneier, F., & Davies, S. (1993, December). *Treatment of refractory OCD with intravenous clomipramine.* Paper presented at the New York State Office of Mental Health Research Conference, Albany, NY.

Goodman, W. K., Price, L. H., Rasmussen, S. A., Mazure, C., Fleischmann, R., Hill, C., Henninger, G. R., & Charney, D. S. (1989). The Yale–Brown Obsessive Compulsive Scale (Y–BOCS), Part I: Development, use, and reliability. *Archives of General Psychiatry, 46*, 1006–1011.

Greist, J. H., Jefferson, J. W., Kobak, K. A., Katzelnick, D. J., & Serlin, R. C. (1992). Efficacy and tolerability of serotonin transport inhibitors in obsessive-compulsive disorder. *Archives of General Psychiatry, 52*, 53–60.

Guy, W. (1976). *ECDEU assessment manual for psychopharmacology* (DHHS Pub. No. 76-338). Washington, DC: U.S. Government Printing Office.

Hamilton, M. (1960). A rating scale for depression. *Journal of Neurology, Neurosurgery, and Psychiatry, 23*, 56–62.

Karno, M. G., Sorenson, S. B., & Burnam, A. (1988). The epidemiology of OCD in five U.S. communities. *Archives of General Psychiatry, 45*, 1094–1099.

Koran, L. K., Faravelli, C., & Pallanti, S. (1994). Intravenous clomipramine for OCD [Letter to editor]. *Journal of Clinical Psychopharmacology, 14*, 216–218.

Koran, L. K., Pallanti, S., Paiva, R., & Quercioli, L. (1996). Pulse loading vs gradual dosing of intravenous clomipramine in obsessive-compulsive disorder. *European Neuropsychopharmacology, 96,* 121–126.

Koran, L. K., Sallee, F. R., & Pallanti, S. (1997). Rapid benefit of intravenous pulse loading of clomipramine in obsessive-compulsive disorder. *American Journal of Psychiatry, 154,* 396–401.

Leonard, H. L. (1997). New developments in the treatment of obsessive-compulsive disorder. *Journal of Clinical Psychiatry, 58*(S14), 39–45.

Liebowitz, M. R., & Hollander, E. (1991). Obsessive-compulsive disorder: Psychobiological integration. In J. Zohar, T. Insel, & S. Rasmussen (Eds.), *The psychobiology of OCD* (pp. 227–255). New York: Springer.

Mindus, P., Rasmussen, S. A., & Lindquist, C. (1994). Neurosurgical treatment for refractory obsessive-compulsive disorder: Implications for understanding frontal lobe function. *Journal of Neuropsychiatry and Clinical Neurosciences, 6,* 467–477.

Pollock, B. G., Perel, J. M., Nathan, R. S., & Kupfer, D. J. (1989). Acute antidepressant effect following pulse loading with intravenous and oral clomipramine. *Archives of General Psychiatry, 46,* 29–35.

Rack, P. H. (1973). Clomipramine (Anafranil) in the treatment of obsessional states with special reference to the Leyton Obsessional Inventory. *Journal of International Medical Research, 1,* 397–402.

Rack, P. H. (1977). Clinical experience in the treatment of obsessional states (2). *Journal of International Medical Research, 5,* 81–90.

Sallee, F. R., Pollock, B. G., Perel, J. M., Ryan, N. D., & Stiller, R. L. (1989). Intravenous pulse loading of clomipramine in adolescents with depression. *Psychopharmacology Bulletin, 25,* 114–118.

Thakur, A. K., Remillard, A. J., Meldrum, L. H., & Gorecki, D. K. (1991). Intravenous clomipramine and OCD. *Canadian Journal of Psychiatry, 36,* 521–523.

Walter, C. S. (1973). Clinical impressions on treatment of obsessional states with intravenous clomipramine (Anafranil). *Journal of International Medical Research, 1,* 413–416.

Warneke, L. B. (1984). The use of intravenous chlorimipramine in the treatment of obsessive compulsive disorder. *Canadian Journal of Psychiatry, 29,* 135–141.

Warneke, L. B. (1985). Intravenous chlorimipramine in the treatment of obsessional disorder in adolescence: Case report. *Journal of Clinical Psychiatry, 46,* 100–103.

Warneke, L. B. (1989). Intravenous chlorimipramine therapy in obsessive-compulsive disorder. *Canadian Journal of Psychiatry, 34,* 853–859.

Warneke, L. B. (1992). Intravenous clomipramine for OCD [Letter]. *Canadian Journal of Psychiatry, 53,* 522–523.

Weissman, M. M., Bland, R. C., Canino, G. J., Greenwald, S., Hwu, H., Lee, C. K., Newman, S. C., Oakley-Browne, M. A., Rubio-Stipec, M., Wickramaratne, P. R., Wittchen, H. U., & Yeh, E. K. (1994). The cross national epidemiology of OCD. *Journal of Clinical Psychiatry, 55,* 5–10.

21

Benzodiazepines in the Treatment of Obsessive-Compulsive Disorder

William A. Hewlett
Vanderbilt University School of Medicine

ANXIETY, OBSESSIVE-COMPULSIVE DISORDER, AND THE BENZODIAZEPINES

The *Diagnostic and Statistical Manual of Mental Disorders* (4th ed. [*DSM–IV*]; American Psychiatric Association, 1994) defines *anxiety* as the "apprehensive anticipation of future danger or misfortune accompanied by a feeling of dysphoria or somatic symptoms of tension" (p. 764). Unfortunately, this definition encompasses multiple experiential and biological states ranging from nonspecific agitative states to panic. The most common usage of the term refers to preparative or anticipatory anxiety characterized by worries and dysphoric autonomic arousal.

Benzodiazepines have been employed for decades to treat excessive anticipatory anxiety (Bethume, 1964; Tobin, Bird, & Boyle, 1960). Benzodiazepines are known to act in the central nervous system (CNS) at γ-aminobuteric acid $(GABA)_A$ receptors to facilitate GABAergic neurotransmission (see Costa, Corda, Epstein, Forchetti, & Guidotti, 1983). Benzodiazepine treatment affects numerous neurotransmitter systems, including GABA, norepinephrine, corticotrophin releasing factor (CRF), cholecystokinin (CCK), and serotonin receptive neurons that are thought to mediate symptoms of anxiety (see Nutt, 1991). Treatment with benzodiazepines is efficacious in reducing the worries and dysphoric emotional and autonomic components of anticipatory anxiety. These effects are immediate, and can nearly eliminate symptoms of anxiety associated with generalized anxiety disorder (GAD) with acute treatment. Benzodiazepines are also used as first- or second-line agents for every other anxiety disorder (see Kaplan & Sadock, 1990; Rosenbaum & Gelenberg, 1991), except one—obsessive-compulsive disorder (OCD).

OCD is classified as an anxiety disorder by the *DSM–IV*; however, it has its own separate diagnostic category in the International Classification of Diseases and Related Health Problems (10th rev. [ICD–10]; Janca et al., 1996; World Health Organization, 1993). The cognitive and emotional experiences of OCD are qualitatively different from the anxiety encountered in GAD. Worries almost always have a realistic component and are usually related to events in the future. They tend to be ruminative, drawn out in time as the mind reviews adverse scenarios that might occur. Worries are normally not associated with rituals. One may engage in preparatory behavior for future events as a result of worries, but the experience lacks the dreadful urgency and immediacy that characterizes obsessive-compulsive (OC) symptoms.

Obsessions are intrusive aversive experiences of dread, uncertainty, or a distressing sense that something is "not right" or is incomplete. Obsessions differ from worries in that the individual usually recognizes that these perceptions are out of proportion to real circumstances; however, the experiences are so aversive that the individual feels compelled to act on them to reduce their intensity. In contrast to worries, in which various scenarios are played out in time as cognitive preparation, obsessive mental images are often brief, intrusive, horrific experiences that the individual tries to avoid.

Unlike the other anxiety disorders, the most efficacious agents for the treatment of OCD are potent preferential serotonin reuptake inhibitors (PSRIs).[1] These medications may only reduce the symptoms of OCD by 30% to 70%, and unlike benzodiazepines, require 6 to 12 weeks of treatment to exert their therapeutic benefits. Treatment of OCD with benzodiazepines in general has had marginal success; however, a clear understanding of the efficacy of benzodiazepines in OCD requires a critical review of the literature, and careful consideration of the methodologies used for treatment and evaluation.

EARLY BENZODIAZEPINE STUDIES

Case reports describing the utility of high-dose benzodiazepines for obsessive neurosis first appeared in early 1960s. Breitner (1960) treated a group of patients with chlordiazepoxide (25–75 mg),[2] four of whom ex-

---

[1]PSRIs include the selective serotonin reuptake inhibitors (SSRIs) and clomipramine.
[2]All medication doses are given as daily totals.

perienced symptoms consistent with a diagnosis of OCD. All four achieved significant improvement on the medication. Bethume (1964) reported a patient having an "obsessive compulsive state" who "feared the weather," and as a result, "her life was devoted to studying in detail the weather patterns and its vicissitudes" (p. 154). Treatment with diazepam (15 mg) "completely cleared her symptoms." Rao (1964) studied eight participants, who by his description, appeared to have OCD. Six of these responded to treatment with diazepam. Criteria for improvement were based on clinical judgment, but appeared to be at least as stringent as those used today. Hussain and Ahad (1970) described the treatment of 11 patients with chronic obsessive-compulsive neurosis of such severity that the patients were referred for psychosurgery. Two of these patients reportedly improved on high-dose chlordiazepoxide (100 mg) and one with high-dose diazepoxide. No measure of improvement was given. It was noted that one patient remitted without medication.

Case reports in this era are complicated by a lack of standard measurement for improvement. One report (Denham, 1963), typical of the problems in the early literature, described the use of psychotherapy assisted by chlordiazepoxide (30–60 mg) in 18 "severe obsessional" patients and another 15 with both "phobic and obsessional" symptoms. He reported good results in 60% of all cases within 6 months. The remainder showed marked improvement. The paper provided a description of two of these cases that would suggest that any improvement was open to interpretation. One patient was troubled by compulsive checking that was felt to be related to "hostility against his employer" and "resentment against his frigid wife." Within 1 month this patient had "adjusted to his work conditions" and "was ready to solve his marital conflict" (pp. 195–197). No mention was made of whether the checking behaviors were at all changed. A second case involved a man troubled by "compulsive swearing in the presence of women" and "aggression of a homicidal tendency." Even though he began each session complaining of continued symptoms, his therapy was described as successful because he would finish the session citing "incidences confirming improvement." Although the author claimed good results or marked improvement in these cases, it is unclear that either case experienced a true reduction in core OCD symptoms. The second case also illustrates the diagnostic confusion of the time, because it is unclear that this individual would qualify for a diagnosis of OCD using modern criteria.

Early therapeutic trials of benzodiazepines included multiple diagnostic categories under a general heading of psychoneurosis, and although they included individuals with obsessional and compulsive neuroses, the results for these subgroups were not separately specified (Bethume, 1964; Gilbert, 1965; Laffranchini, 1975; Sonne & Holm, 1975). There was a tendency to rate obsessive symptoms across diagnostic categories, rather than focus on the disorder itself.

Haward (1979) examined the effects of lorazepam (2–15 mg) on symptom clusters in 69 outpatients. He found a poor association of improvement with obsessionality and high association with phobic symptoms. Ananth and Van den Steen (1983) compared intramuscular lorazepam (.05 mg/kg), diazepam (.14 mg/kg), and placebo in 24 patients with neurotic anxiety. Patients were not broken down by psychiatric diagnosis. Lorazepam was superior to diazepam and placebo in the Obsessive Compulsive Phobic Cluster of the Wittenborn Psychiatric Rating Scale (Wittenborn, 1974) during the first 12 hours after injection. The only obsessive neurotic patient in the study improved with lorazepam treatment. No specific measure of improvement was cited.

Orvin (1967) conducted a complex crossover placebo-controlled study with oxazepam (30–120 mg), chlordiazepoxide (30–90 mg), and placebo in 25 patients with OC and phobic reactions. Two patients had schizophrenia with OC features. The author concluded that oxazepam was significantly more effective than chlordiazepoxide. Aside from the diagnostic uncertainties of the study, analysis was complicated because only 12 of the patients crossed over to any other condition, only seven patients received both benzodiazepines, and three patients repeated trials of the same medication. It was not possible to determine actual response frequencies from the reported data; however, 7 of 19 oxazepam trials resulted in a 70% or greater reduction in symptoms. An additional six oxazepam trials and two diazepam trials had a reduction in symptoms of greater than 50%. No placebo trial had a satisfactory response. Responses were measured on a scale containing mostly non-OCD-related symptoms, raising the question of whether there was any actual improvement in core symptoms.

In the early 1970s, enthusiasm surrounded a new benzodiazepine, bromazepam (Ro 5-3350, Lexotan™, Lexotanil™, Medazepam™), a medication with purported efficacy in OC neurosis. In open trials, Okuma, Nakao, Ogura, Kishimoto, and Majima (1971) found that 9 of 18 patients with OC neurosis achieved "effective" or "markedly effective" improvement on bromazepam. Burrell, Culpan, Newton, Ogg, and Short (1974) treated 220 patients with bromazepam (3–36 mg). Forty-four of 63 patients (70%) with severe obsessive ruminations and 23 of 32 patients (72%) with compulsive rituals showed marked or moderate improvement. Salmoni, Amati, Giambelluca, and Vacca (1973) described the use of bromazepam (12–96 mg) in 15 patients having obsessions with or without phobias. Three achieved complete remission of symptoms and an additional three achieved partial remission. De Giacomo and Pierri (1974) described the treatment of 20 patients with bromazepam (5–72 mg). Thirteen of these were described as obsessive or phobic-obsessive. For the entire group, there was a 38% improvement in obsessive ideation and a 40% improvement in obsessive behavior; however, only four of the patients with obsessional features had a good response to treatment. Interestingly, one of the patients with a positive response had previously failed a trial of clomipramine.

Lin and Chen (1979) conducted a placebo-controlled trial of bromazepam (36 mg) in 35 patients with OC neurosis in a complicated double- and single-blind protocol. Patients either received medication or placebo for 2 weeks, then received bromazepam for 6 weeks, followed by bromazepam or placebo for 2 weeks, and then 2 weeks of placebo. Ratings were obtained using the 5-item Obsessive-Compulsive subscale of the Symptom Checklist–90 (SCL–90; Derogatis, Lipman, & Covi, 1973; Kim, Dysken, & Kuskowski, 1992), as well as global improvement in obsessive symptoms. Both bromazepam and placebo produced a statistically significant decrement in symptoms; however, bromazepam was significantly more effective than placebo. Eight dropouts were not included in the analysis. Higher doses appeared to have significantly more benefit; however, no attempt was made to control for time on medication. Sixteen patients (59% of trial completers) were deemed to be improved, with eight rated as markedly improved (66–100% decrease in overall symptoms) and eight rated as moderately improved (33–66% decrease in symptoms.) In contrast to these overall ratings, there was only a 14% drop in the mean symptom score for obsessions for trial completers over the course of treatment, suggesting again that most of the rated symptoms were not related to OCD.

A number of investigators compared bromazepam to other benzodiazepines in an attempt to demonstrate a selective antiobsessive effect of the newer medication. Grattarola and Morgando (1973) reported a double-blind comparison of diazepam and bromazepam treatment in phobic-obsessive psychoneurotics. Four of nine patients showed good improvement in obsessive behavior and ideas on bromazepam (5 mg), whereas only 1 of 11 patients showed such improvement on diazepam (5 mg). A second open-label trial of bromazepam (5–15 mg) at a higher dose found 10 of 19 patients experienced a good response for both obsessional ideas and behavior. Two of these patients experienced an "optimal" response in obsessions, and one an optimal response in obsessional behavior. Lens (1974) compared bromazepam and diazepam in 49 psychoneurotic patients at doses ranging from 7.5 to 40 mg. Of four patients with obsessional neurosis, two experienced excellent and good responses on bromazepam, whereas only one experienced an excellent response on diazepam. Draper (1975) reported an open trial of bromazepam in 15 patients, 6 of whom had a diagnosis that included obsessional neurosis. Four of these showed a distinct response and a fifth showed some improvement. A small but complex double-blind A-B-A crossover trial comparing chlordiazepoxide (30 mg) and bromazepam (30 mg) in 10 patients was also reported in the same publication. Only four of these patients were categorized as obsessional. There was a definite improvement in two of the four obsessionals on bromazepam, but no patient showed such improvement on chlordiazepoxide. On the average, obsessionals were slightly better on bromazepam, and unchanged on chlordiazepoxide. Sonne and Holm (1975) cited an unpublished study by Deberdt (1974) comparing bromazepam (15 mg) and diazepam (15 mg) in 19 patients with obsessive and phobic anxiety symptoms. No differences were found between treatment groups. In an unspecified crossover analysis, however, results for bromazepam were interpreted as significantly better than those for diazepam.

Cassano, Carrara, and Castrogiovanni (1975) conducted a 3-week comparison of bromazepam (20–25 mg) and diazepam (20–25 mg) in 58 psychoneurotic patients, 20 of whom were classified as obsessives. Four of 10 obsessives taking bromazepam achieved marked or moderate improvement by clinical assessment, with five patients dropping out of the trial. Seven of 10 patients taking diazepam achieved such a response, with one dropping out. Overall, the diazepam group showed significant improvement for the obsessions item on the Wittenborn Psychiatric Rating Scale (Wittenborn, 1974), and there was a marked change in obsessive ideas and a significant change in the obsessive symptoms complex subscale for the obsessive group. No significant results were reported for bromazepam treatment. No other significant changes in symptoms possibly related to OCD were reported for either medication in three other psychiatric rating scales. The study did report that obsessives responded less to benzodiazepine treatment than did neurotics, and no difference in drug efficacy was found for the two treatments.

Only one early study compared the efficacy of the serotonergic reuptake inhibitor clomipramine with a benzodiazepine (diazepam; Waxman, 1977). Clomipramine was significantly more effective than diazepam in treating ruminations (83% vs. 47% reduction) and rituals (38% vs. 7% reduction). The only early study of benzodiazepine augmentation of clomipramine treatment found that 6-week clomipramine monotherapy was more effective in reducing obsessive symptoms and rituals than diazepam-augmented therapy in 54 patients (Cassano et al., 1981). In fact, the combination of diazepam and clomipramine treatment eliminated the statistical improvement in ritual reduction seen with clomipramine monotherapy.

Summary of Early Trials

There is considerable difficulty in assessing the validity of the early literature on benzodiazepines in OCD. The most significant concern involves the refinement in our definition of OCD over the years. The early studies included patients having ruminations, phobias, panic, and fantasies, as well as behaviors that we now associate with OC personality disorder and impulse control disorders. A second problem is that early studies lacked adequate means for quantifying the severity of OCD symptoms. Improvement was often measured by general clinical judgment. Patients having secondary or multiple psychiatric symptoms were rated as improved, without any recorded evidence of changes in core OCD symptoms. Additionally, improvement was often measured by the number rather than the severity of OCD symptoms. Improvement in misclassified symptoms, such as ruminations, was analyzed as improvement in the overall OCD condition. Finally, there has been a change in the definition of successful treatment. In early studies, small reductions in obsessions accompanied by significant decreases in anxiety would be seen as significant improvement, as there was little else at that time that had any effect on the condition. With the advent of more effective treatments, the PSRIs, a new standard for efficacy developed that was far more stringent. It is unclear that all patients rated as improved in the earlier studies would meet these more stringent criteria. Largely because of these methodological difficulties, the earlier studies are of more historical than practical interest.

MODERN TRIALS

Modern trials have focused on two novel benzodiazepines, alprazolam and clonazepam. Tesar and Jenike (1984) described alprazolam treatment (12 mg) for a panic attack in a patient having almost constant OCD symptoms. This patient experienced only occasional obsessions at 2-month follow-up. Tollefson (1985) treated four patients with alprazolam at doses ranging from 1.25 to 6 mg daily. Only one of these four patients appears to have had classic OCD symptoms. Descriptions of symptomatology suggest that the other three patients suffered from an OC personality disorder, from panic associated with claustrophobic imagery, and from a mixture of paranoid and obsessive ideation. Ketter, Chun, and Lu (1986) described an unusual 56-year-old insulin-dependent diabetic with fecal and urinary incontinence having obsessions and compulsions involving contamination. The patient experienced anxiety and depression described as secondary to his OCD. No history of panic symptoms was described. Alprazolam (3 mg) reportedly alleviated his OCD symptoms. Although it was not stated explicitly, this patient also appeared to have a dementing illness, as he was subsequently discharged to a skilled nursing facility where he required treatment with intermittent haloperidol for agitation. Hardy (1986) described a 57-year-old patient with a 25-year history of OCD by *DSM–III* criteria who suffered from ruminations and verification compulsions. This patient had previously been treated with clomipramine with unknown benefit, but stopped due to weight gain. After 10 days of treatment with alprazolam at 0.75 mg per day, this patient was described as having symptoms sufficiently diminished to begin normal activities that had been precluded by his symptoms.

Stein, Hollander, Mullen, DeCaria, and Liebowitz (1992) conducted the only reported clinical trial of alprazolam (3–10 mg) in OCD in an open-label 12-week study involving 14 patients. Only two of these patients responded to treatment, suggesting that this medication may have only limited usefulness in OCD. It was not reported whether any of these participants were refractory to SSRI treatment, thus it is not known whether the two individuals that did respond were uniquely responsive to benzodiazepines.

The other benzodiazepine that has attracted significant modern-day attention in the treatment of OCD is clonazepam. Such attention is due in part to the unique serotonergic effects of clonazepam, first appreciated in animal models (Hwang & Van Woert, 1979; Jenner, Chadwick, Reynolds, & Marsden, 1975; Pranzatelli, Dailey, Levy, & Dollison, 1991; Pratt, Jenner, Reynolds, & Marsden, 1979; Wagner, Reches, Yablonskaya, & Fahn, 1986). Unlike classical benzodiazepines such as diazepam, clonazepam will induce a serotonergic behavioral syndrome in animals, indistinguishable from that induced by serotonergic agonists. Behaviors induced by clonazepam are blocked by serotonergic agents, but not by benzodiazepine receptor antagonists (Nakamura & Carney, 1983; Nakamura & Fukushima, 1976; Pranzatelli, 1989; Pranzatelli et al., 1991). In humans, chronic treatment with diazepam has an inhibitory effect, if any, on the serotonergic stimulation of prolactin (Nutt & Cowen, 1987). Chronic treatment of OCD patients with clonazepam, however, significantly augments serotonergic prolactin responses induced by fenfluramine (Hewlett, Berman, & Martin, 1991). Clonazepam, but not diazepam, will transiently reduce myoclonic symptoms in the subset of patients whose symptoms are alleviated by the serotonin (5-HT) precursor, 5-hydroxytryptophan (Chadwick et al., 1977; Chadwick, Jenner, Harris, Reynolds, & Marsden, 1975; Jenner et al., 1975). In animal models, such antimyoclonic effects of clonazepam are potentiated by serotonergic reuptake inhibitors, and blocked by serotonergic antagonists (Hwang & Van Woert, 1979). Although benzodiazepines exert their action through enhancing GABAergic neurotransmission, GABAergic antagonists are ineffective in blocking the action of clonazepam in these serotonergic models (Hwang & Van Woert, 1979; Pranzatelli, 1989).

Clinically, there are four case studies describing the efficacy of clonazepam as a monotherapy in OCD. Five of six patients described in these reports failed trials of other benzodiazepines. Bodkin and White (1989) described the treatment of a patient having both OCD and panic attacks. Two weeks of treatment with clonazepam (3 mg) completely eliminated the compulsions in this patient, and significantly reduced his obsessions. Improvement was maintained over a period of 6 months. The improvement was not simply a benzodiazepine effect, because lorazepam (3 mg) produced no benefit for his OCD symptoms, although it effectively treated his panic symptoms. Likewise, diazepam and chlordiazepoxide had no effect on the OCD symptoms in this patient.

A second case study (Hewlett, Vinogradov, & Agras, 1990) described the efficacy of clonazepam (4–5 mg) in three patients having OCD and depressive symptoms. One patient who had failed numerous trials of psychotropics, including tranylcypromine and alprazolam, had a significant response in her OCD symptoms within 2 weeks of initiating clonazepam treatment. The reduction of symptoms at 4 weeks in this patient (5 mg) exceeded that achieved in a previous 8-week trial of clomipramine. This trial was terminated prior to completion due to significant problems with disinhibition. A second patient in this series suffered from food contamination fears so severe that she would induce vomiting when contaminated. This patient also had failed multiple trials of psychotropics including phenelzine and diazepam, but achieved a gradual, significant reduction of OCD symptoms on clonazepam over a period of 1 month. Her improvement was maintained for over a year, at which time she was lost to follow-up. The third patient, having OCD with aggressive obsessions, suffered from intermittent exacerbations of her symptoms in which she became psychotically paranoid. Tricyclic and neuroleptic treatment produced resolutions in her depressive and psychotic symptoms, but did not affect her obsessions or compulsions. Alprazolam treatment likewise had no effect on her OCD symptoms. Clonazepam treatment (3–5 mg), however, reduced her obsessions significantly within 1 week. Continued suppression of OCD symptoms was maintained over a 9-month follow-up period.

Bacher (1990) described efficacious treatment of a 60-year-old compulsive man with recurrent obsessional thinking using clonazepam at 1.5 mg daily. This individual had not responded to various other benzodiazepines. The diagnosis of OCD cannot be confirmed for this patient because symptomatic details were not provided. Finally, Ross and Pigott (1993) described the effective use of clonazepam (2 mg) in a 14-year-old boy with clear-cut obsessive fears. This latter report is notable in that the patient had failed previous trials of both fluoxetine and clomipramine, suggesting that a patient refractory to PSRI treatment could be treated effectively with clonazepam.

There is only one published controlled trial of clonazepam in OCD (Hewlett, Vinogradov, & Agras, 1992). This study compared the efficacy of clonazepam (4–10 mg), clomipramine (100–250 mg), and clonidine (0.4–1.0 mg), to that of an active placebo, diphenhydramine. The study had an unusual crossover design in which each participant attempted 6-week trials of all four medications in randomized order. After each trial, patients remained off medications until symptoms returned to prestudy levels to eliminate crossover effects. All participants were diagnosed by structured interview, meeting *DSM–III–R* criteria for OCD. Doses of clonazepam after 4 weeks of treatment averaged 6.9 mg daily. Clonazepam trials were initiated in 25 individuals. Twenty patients completed these trials. Clonazepam OCD scores at 5 and 6 weeks of treatment were significantly lower than those of either diphenhydramine or clonidine, and not statistically different from those of clomipramine. Average improvement over attempted clonazepam trials was 19%. Average improvement over completed clonazepam trials was 24%. In comparison, clomipramine improvement over completed trials averaged 28%.

The time course of improvement for clonazepam and clomipramine is contrasted with that of clonidine in Fig. 21.1. Statistically significant improvement with clonazepam occurred within 2 weeks and improvement on clonazepam appeared to level out after 3 weeks. Approximately half (48%) of the patients attempting clonazepam trials and 60% of those completing clonazepam trials achieved a clinically significant response, defined as a 25% reduction in symptoms on the Yale–Brown Obsessive Compulsive Scale (Y–BOCS; Goodman et al., 1989). In comparison, 54% of patients attempting clomipramine trials achieved a clinically significant response. Interestingly, there was a significant cross-response between clonazepam and clomipramine among patients who completed trials of both medications. Individuals who responded to one of these medications tended to respond to the other, whereas those that did not respond to one were less likely to respond to the other. It is also significant that 40% of clomipramine nonresponders had a significant response to clonazepam, averaging a 35% reduction in symptoms. Anxiety ratings on clonazepam at 6 weeks were slightly elevated from baseline, and uncorrelated with treatment outcome when controlled for level of depression, suggesting that a reduction in anxiety could not account for the decrease in OCD symptoms.

The Hewlett et al. (1992) study was limited in that medication trials only lasted 6 weeks. Ratings in patients treated with clomipramine and other PSRIs continue to improve for up to 12 weeks or longer (Goodman,

OCD IMPROVEMENT
(Y-BOCS RATING)

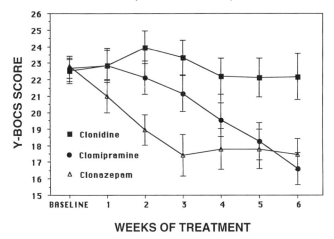

WEEKS OF TREATMENT

FIG. 21.1.   Average Y–BOCS scores ± *SEM* for baseline and weekly ratings for 6-week trials of clonazepam, clomipramine, and clonidine from double-blind crossover treatment study (from "Clomipramine, Clonazepam and Clonidine Treatment of Obsessive Compulsive Disorder," by W. Hewlett, S. Vinograd, and W. Agras, 1992, *Journal of Clinical Psychiatry*, *12*(6), 420–430. Reprinted by permission of Lippincott Williams & Wilkins).

McDougle, & Price, 1992). It is not known whether aggregate improvement on clonazepam would continue or diminish over that period. A second problem with the study was that there was no true placebo trial. Patients taking the active placebo, diphenhydramine, showed a statistical, but not clinically significant, response to this medication. In spite of its flaws, the study does suggest that high doses of clonazepam may result in significant relief for a subset of OCD patients. It would also suggest that a trial of clonazepam may be warranted in PSRI nonresponders. It should be noted that high-dose clonazepam produced significant side effects, including ataxia, disinhibition, and depression. No individual who experienced an exacerbation of depression achieved any benefit from clonazepam treatment. In fact, the patients who achieved the best responses on clonazepam in this study experienced a paradoxical activation on this medication.

The mechanism by which clonazepam might produce serotonin-mimetic effects that might be beneficial in OCD is not clear. Clonazepam does not appear to act through 5-HT$_1$ or 5-HT$_2$ receptors (Hwang & Van Woert, 1979; Pranzatelli, 1989; Wagner et al., 1986), nor via the 5-HT$_3$ receptor (Hewlett et al., 1998); nor does it act via inhibition of 5-HT reuptake (Hwang & Van

Woert, 1979; Pratt et al., 1979). Chronic clonazepam administration is associated with a decrease in 5-HT utilization (Pratt et al., 1979; Wagner et al., 1986), and an up-regulation of 5-HT_1 and 5-HT_2 receptors in frontal cortex (Pranzatelli et al., 1991; Wagner et al., 1986). One explanation for these findings would be that clonazepam may act as a serotonin-mimetic agent at 5-HT receptive neurons that mediate certain serotonergic actions, but that indirectly reduce 5-HT neuronal activity through negative feedback inhibition. Clonazepam could conceivably act through 5-HT_{4-7} receptors, or through a receptor for another neurotransmitter. Such interactions have not been explored. Clonazepam does not exert its unique serotonergic effects through central benzodiazepine sites, however (Hwang & Van Woert, 1979; Pranzatelli, 1989).

Enthusiasm for clonazepam as a monotherapy for OCD should be tempered by negative impressions of clonazepam efficacy that have been reported in clinical practice. Goodman, McDougle, Barr, Aronson, and Price (1993), reporting their experience with clonazepam, suggested that its beneficial effects were limited to anti-anxiety effects, and it was rarely effective for the core symptoms of OCD. In their experience, when anti-obsessive effects did occur, they were rarely sustained. They also pointed out an important potential drawback of benzodiazepines in OCD: In theory, they may disrupt processes necessary for effective behavioral treatment of OCD, specifically the therapeutic effects of exposure and response prevention (Goodman et al., 1993).

More recently, a double-blind placebo-controlled study found no benefit for clonazepam (3–6 mg) as a monotherapy (S. Stahl, personal communication, 1995). Only 1 of 15 patients experienced a significant improvement on this medication, whereas two patients improved on placebo. The average clonazepam dose in this study was significantly lower than in the previous study; thus higher doses of clonazepam may be required for therapeutic benefit. If this is true, it would further limit the usefulness of clonazepam as a monotherapy, because many patients cannot, or will not, tolerate the side effects of clonazepam at the higher doses. It should be noted that information regarding previous PSRI responses in these patients was not available, so it is not known if low-dose clonazepam lacked efficacy in a population that was treatment-refractory, or whether the study population consisted prominently of PSRI responders and partial responders. Such information is critical in determining the role of novel treatments for selected populations of OCD patients.

Treatment Efficacy in Individual Case Trials

In an effort to enumerate cases of benzodiazepine efficacy as a monotherapy in OCD, papers describing treatment of OC symptoms with benzodiazepines were searched for cases in which treatment outcome was specified. Care was taken to eliminate cases that clearly were not OCD by today's standards (e.g., cases of OC personality, depressive ruminations, etc.). In some cases, more than one benzodiazepine trial was described for a given patient. A total of 443 case trials of benzodiazepine treatment were found in 44 references describing treatment outcome for individual patients. Of these, 166 cases (38%) were judged to have a successful outcome (significant reduction in OCD symptoms; much improved, very much improved). The majority of treatment successes were cases described in papers written prior to the widespread use of PSRIs. Table 21.1 details successes and failures of benzodiazepine case trials before and after 1980. The success rate in case reports prior to 1980 was 53%. Since 1980 the success rate for benzodiazepine treatment of OCD in case reports has been substantially lower (16%), probably reflecting the more stringent standards of efficacy. It should also be noted that case reports by nature select for successful outcomes. As such, these data may reflect a higher success rate than that found in clinical practice.

To evaluate the use of benzodiazepines as monotherapies in current clinical practice, a retrospective poll of 12 OCD centers was recently conducted (Hewlett, 1997). Five centers reported using alprazolam as a monotherapy, but only 7 of 85 patients (8%) achieved a clinically significant response. Ten centers reported the use of clonazepam as a monotherapy for OCD; 37 of 123 patients (30%) achieved a clinically significant response. One center in the survey had a significantly higher response rate for clonazepam than the other centers. Without this center, 22 of 95 patients (23%) achieved a clinically significant response. Only one center reported the use of other benzodiazepines in 10 patients. None of these patients experienced significant improvement. Thus, modern clinical experience confirms that alprazolam is of little value in the treatment of OCD, but supports the suggestion that clonazepam could be useful as an alternative treatment for PSRI-refractory patients. Interpretive caution is advised, however, as this survey represents uncontrolled retrospective reports of treatment, without knowledge of doses, duration of treatment, or patient comorbid diagnoses. At this time there is only one limited, 6-week, controlled trial suggesting efficacy for clonazepam in OCD, and this trial only provides data regarding high-dose treatment.

ADJUNCTIVE TREATMENT

Benzodiazepine augmentation of antidepressant treatment for OCD has been recommended since the late 1960s (Dally, 1967). More recently, benzodiazepines have been used as adjuncts to PSRI treatment to treat symptoms of anxiety, panic, or drug-induced restlessness (Jenike, 1990).

TABLE 21.1
Benzodiazepine Case Trials, Published Outcomes in OCD

	Successes			Failures		
Benzodiazepines	Pre-1980	Post-1980	Total	Pre-1980	Post-1980	Total
Alprazolam	0	9[a]	9	0	15[b]	15
Bromazepam	80[c]	0	80	76[d]	1[e]	77
Chlordiazepoxide	30[f]	0	30	26[g]	6[h]	32
Clonazepam	0	18[i]	18	0	13[j]	13
Clorazepate	0	0	0	0	2[k]	2
Diazepam	14[l]	0	14	17[m]	13[n]	30
Diazepoxide	1[o]	0	1	0	0	0
Lorazepam	0	1[p]	1	0	3[q]	3
Oxazepam	14[r]	0	14	5[s]	1[t]	6
Unnamed benzo- diazepines	0	0	0	0	98[u]	98
Total	139	28	167	124	152	276

Note. Success and failure of benzodiazepine case trials tallied from 44 references providing medication trial outcome prior to or after 1980. Successful trials were defined as greater than 25% to 30% improvement in symptoms or better than moderate improvement when descriptors were used. Some cases had multiple trials of benzodiazepines.
[a]Hardy (1986); Ketter et al. (1986); Stein et al. (1992); Tesar & Jenike (1984); Tollefson (1985). [b]Flament et al. (1985); Hewlett et al. (1990); Stein et al. (1992). [c]Burrell et al. (1974); Cassano et al. (1975); De Giacomo & Pierri (1974); Draper (1975); Grattarola & Morgando (1973); Lens (1974); Lin & Chen (1979); Okuma et al. (1971); Salmoni et al. (1973). [d]Burrell et al. (1974); Cassano et al. (1975); De Giacomo & Pierri (1974); Draper (1975); Grattarola & Morgando (1973); Lin & Chen (1979); Okuma et al. (1971); Salmoni et al. (1973). [e]Ansseau et al. (1987). [f]Breitner (1960); Denham (1963); Hussain & Ahad (1970); Orvin (1967). [g]Bodkin & White (1989); Denham (1963); Draper (1975); Orvin (1967). [h]Bodkin & White (1989); Flament et al. (1985); Jenike, Surman, Cassem, Zusky, & Anderson (1983); Knesevich (1982); Snyder (1980); Tollefson (1985). [i]Bacher (1990); Bodkin & White (1989); Hewlett et al. (1990); Hewlett et al. (1992); Ross & Pigott (1993). [j]Hewlett et al. (1992). [k]Jenike & Brotman (1984); Jenike et al. (1983). [l]Bethume (1964); Cassano et al. (1975); Grattarola & Morgando (1973); Lens (1974); Rao (1964). [m]Cassano et al. (1975); Grattarola & Morgando (1973); Lens (1974); Rao (1964). [n]Bodkin & White (1989); Flament et al. (1985); Hewlett et al. (1990); Jenike (1981); Jenike et al. (1983); Knesevich (1982); Ross & Pigott (1993); Snyder (1980). [o]Hussain & Ahad (1970). [p]Ananth & Van den Steen (1983). [q]Ansseau et al. (1987); Bodkin & White (1989); Lydiard (1986). [r]Orvin (1967). [s]O'Regan (1970); Orvin (1967). [t]Flament et al. (1985). [u]Bacher (1990); Baxter (1985); Casas et al. (1986); Fallon et al. (1992); Farid & Bulto (1994); Jaskari (1980); Jenike & Baer (1988); Jenike et al. (1990); Koran, Faravelli, & Pallanti (1994); Lelliott & Monteiro (1986).

Indeed, this may be the most common usage of benzodiazepines in this disorder. Jenike (1990) described the use of alprazolam (0.5–2 mg) as an augmentation strategy in his review of treatment-refractory OCD; however, it was his impression that this strategy was only useful for enhancing a patient's tolerance of anxiety, particularly in the setting of behavior therapy. Jenike and Rauch (1994) recommended the use of clonazepam in patients who were agitated or had comorbid bipolar illness or insomnia. They also recommended the early use of clonazepam in doses up to 5 mg daily as an augmentation strategy in patients for whom anxiety was a prominent feature (Rauch & Jenike, 1994). In addition, they proposed clonazepam treatment for patients with comorbid tics or Tourette's syndrome, because of the reported benefits in these conditions (see Hewlett, 1993; Troung, 1988). It is unclear whether these recommendations were based on clinical experience or their literature review.

There are few case reports describing the use of benzodiazepines as adjuncts for the primary treatment of OCD symptoms. Fontaine and Chouinard (1985) described treatment of a single fluoxetine-refractory patient with clonazepam at an unreported dose. OC symptoms were remarkably improved, as rated by the SCL–90 and the OC scale for anxiety (Thoren, Asberg, Cronholm, Jornestedt, & Traskman, 1980), a subscale of the Comprehensive Psychopathological Rating Scale (Asberg & Schalling, 1979). Unfortunately, these scales include items that are no longer thought to be specific for OCD. Cohen and Rosenbaum (1987) described a case of an individual with intrusive thoughts without rituals, compulsions, or other anxiety or affective symptoms. This individual would ruminate about whether he was capable of committing violent acts, and dwell on horrific experiences of other individuals, imagining himself in their place. He "was unable to clear the thoughts from his mind" (p. 52). Treatment with imipramine (300 mg) produced partial improvement, but he was still troubled by intrusive thoughts. The addition of clonazepam (2 mg) eliminated these ruminations. Discontinuation of clonazepam led to a recurrence of ruminations that resolved with reinstitution of treatment. It is not clear from the case description, however, whether these intrusive thoughts were true obsessions or intrusive imaginal ruminations.

Leonard et al. (1994) described a third case of clonazepam augmentation in a 20-year-old man whose symptoms began in childhood with a compulsive tic-like vocalization. He subsequently developed "just right" compulsions, mental coprolalia, and urges to deface objects to which he succumbed "because he had to do it" (p. 793). Seven years after onset of his symptoms he developed contamination obsessions with hand washing and showering rituals, as well as obsessive ideas of reference. He was treated with separate 12-week trials of clomipramine (250 mg), fluoxetine (80 mg), and fluvoxamine (250 mg), which were without benefit, except for a 1-month symptom-free period following consumption of 1 gram of fluoxetine in a suicide attempt. A 10-month trial of buspirone augmentation (40 mg) of fluoxetine (60 mg) also failed. Augmentation with clonazepam, however at a dose of 6 mg/day produced a dramatic (75%) reduction of symptoms. A decrease in dose to 3 mg/day after 3 months resulted in an increase in symptoms that resolved when the dose was increased to 4 mg/day. The patient was described as having maintained an excellent clinical response on the combination of fluoxetine (60 mg) and clonazepam (4 mg) for 1 year. This case is notable in that the patient's symptom history began with vocalizations and maladaptive urges similar to those seen in Tourette's syndrome, for which clonazepam has been effectively used in treatment. It is also notable for the high doses of clonazepam that were required to effect and maintain a reduction in PSRI-refractory symptoms. It is not clear from the description whether fluoxetine cotreatment with clonazepam produced any benefit beyond what would have been achieved using high-dose clonazepam alone in this patient, pointing out one of the difficulties in determining therapeutic mechanisms in single augmentation trials.

Controlled studies of augmenting agents are even more difficult to conduct, because factors such as the degree of previous PSRI response and possible subpopulation mixes are confounding factors in the analysis. Jenike (1990) reported that seven of nine patients (78%) treated simultaneously with fluoxetine and clonazepam (1–3 mg) experienced a significant (20%) improvement in a 10-week open trial. Only one of seven patients, however, achieved improvement in a 4-week trial of clonazepam augmentation (1–3 mg) initiated after 10 weeks of fluoxetine treatment. It was not reported whether improvement was measured from the pre- or postfluoxetine reference point. He also reported that two patients failed a 4-week alprazolam augmentation trial (0.5 mg and 2.0 mg) after 10 weeks of fluoxetine treatment.

Pigott, L'Heureux, and Rubenstein (1992) conducted a double-blind, placebo-controlled crossover study involving 4-week clonazepam augmentation of chronic (20-week) clomipramine (dose $M = 191$ mg) and fluoxetine (dose $M = 80$ mg) treatment. Although there was no improvement on the Y–BOCS or the National Institute of Mental Health Obsessive-Compulsive rating scales (NIMH OC; Benkelfat et al., 1989), there was a significant reduction in NIMH Global Obsessive-Compulsive Scale (NIMH GOCS) ratings (Insel et al., 1983; Murphy, Pickar, & Alterman, 1982). The former scales rate separate severity measures of obsessions and compulsions, whereas the latter rates the clinician's overall assessment of OCD improvement. There was also significant improvement in the NIMH Global Anxiety ratings (Murphy et al., 1982); however, there was no correlation between the GOCS ratings and the Global Anxiety ratings, suggesting that OCD improvement was independent of changes in anxiety.

It is unclear why improvement was not uniformly consistent across OCD measurements in this study. There might have been elements of OCD that were not picked up well by the symptomatic measures, or alternatively, the Global ratings might have been contaminated by improvement not specifically related to OCD symptoms. It is also possible that the Global ratings were more susceptible to investigator bias, as doses of clonazepam used would have produced noticeable side effects that would affect the blind. Indeed, half of the patients in this study could not tolerate the maximum dose of clonazepam. This study also demonstrates the problems associated with augmentation protocols. The group of patients studied had already achieved a 35% reduction of symptoms on PSRIs prior to the augmentation trial, indicating that they were, on the average, PSRI responders. It is clear that serotonergic facilitation produces, at best, a partial reduction in OCD symptoms. It is possible that these patients could have achieved maximal serotonergic therapeutic benefit on the PSRI. If this were the case, any serotonergic augmentation by clonazepam would have no further benefit for these patients. Conversely, the lack of clonazepam response on the symptomatic measures could have resulted because PSRI nonresponders were underrepresented in the study. Such problems point out the importance of including previous PSRI response as a factor in the analysis of therapeutic trials of novel and adjunctive agents.

The report does suggest that clonazepam augmentation may have primary global benefits in OCD, independent of its anxiolytic action. It is not known, of course, whether an alternative benzodiazepine adjunct such as alprazolam might have produced similar benefits. The effective use of benzodiazepines as adjuncts in OCD will require more study to address such questions. At this point, however, there is little evidence that generic benzodiazepine augmentation has any benefit in the treatment of core symptoms of OCD. It should be noted that benzodiazepines can be helpful as adjunctive treatment in managing insomnia and agitation in the setting of OCD, particularly when such states occur as a consequence of SSRI treatment. Additionally, clonazepam can be used as prophylactic anticonvulsant treatment for patients requiring high doses of clomipramine, which have been associated with an increased risk of seizure, or when using clomipramine with medications that are known to increase clomipramine blood levels (e.g., fluvoxamine). Although these treatments may not affect the core symptoms of OCD, they represent important therapeutic uses of benzodiazepines in the setting of OCD.

OCD TREATMENT RESISTANCE AND BENZODIAZEPINE TREATMENT

PSRIs are the clear treatment of choice for OCD. To be considered treatment-refractory, OCD must, by definition, have failed adequate doses and durations of these agents. The question of benzodiazepine efficacy in treatment-refractory OCD is tied to factors that influence efficacy, and the

TABLE 21.2
Factors Affecting OCD Treatment Efficacy

Factors influencing perception of outcome
  Misdiagnosis
  Loose definition of efficacy
  Noncompliance
  Inadequate dose or duration of treatment
  Waxing and waning course of OCD
  Inappropriate expectations
  Positive or negative physician or patient medication bias
Secondary factors affecting outcome
  Stress
  Patient hypersensitivity to medication side effects
  Secondary gain
  Disruptive nature of change for individual or social system
Factors relating to biology of OCD
  Insufficient augmentation of serotonin neurotransmission
  Requirement for additional nonserotonergic treatment
  Serotonin-insensitive OCD

perception of efficacy, in treatment trials. Table 21.2 summarizes these factors.

Treatment efficacy is perceived in the context of expectations. One of the common problems occurring in the early literature, as well in clinical psychiatry outside specialized OCD treatment centers, is that treatment outcomes are mistakenly labeled effective or ineffective based on factors independent of OCD improvement. The most frequent reason for this is misdiagnosis. The early literature is replete with examples of phobic behaviors, impulse control disorders, excessive fantasizing, paranoid ideation, and even complex tics that have been mislabeled as OCD. Even today, physicians may misdiagnose features of the OC personality as OCD. Symptoms such as worries, ruminations, meticulous behavioral patterns, excessive persistence, and inflexibility may not show significant responses to PSRIs, leading to the perception of treatment failure. Benzodiazepines can reduce many of these symptoms and lead to an inappropriate perception of effectiveness. Outcomes in the early studies were also affected by inadequate definitions of efficacy. Treatments that produced minimal reductions in OCD symptoms were considered significant improvements in the context of what was available, leading to attributions of efficacy that are not valid by today's standards.

Physician and patient biases may also affect the perception of efficacy of both PSRI and benzodiazepine trials. Both disbelief and exaggerated expectations may have deleterious effects on the perceived efficacy of PSRI trials. Conversely, biases may adversely affect the perception of efficacy and the willingness to tolerate benzodiazepine trials. In one study (Hewlett et al., 1992), patients whose response to clonazepam exceeded their response to clomipramine declined chronic treatment with the benzodiazepine because of adverse associations. Patients perceived benzodiazepines as medications for individuals who were just too anxious, and viewed clonazepam treatment in that light. Similarly, physicians may avoid the use of benzodiazepines because of their addiction and abuse liability, or because of a bias in attributing true anti-obsessive effects to the anxiolytic or sedative actions of this benzodiazepine.

Treatment resistance may also be related to secondary factors unrelated to the inherent biology of OCD. Factors such as external stressors, side effects induced by PSRI treatment, and anxious concerns about lifestyle changes resulting from treatment may secondarily affect the outcome of PSRI trials. Each of these factors may be alleviated to some degree by the addition of benzodiazepines, resulting in a greater likelihood of trial efficacy without primary effects on the core symptoms themselves.

There are also biological factors that may influence treatment resistance, relating to the serotonergic responsivity of OCD symptoms. In this regard, one should consider three possible biologic variants. First, patients may not respond to PSRIs because of factors that limit the medication's ability to enhance serotonergic neurotransmission sufficiently. In such cases, treatments that further enhance serotonergic output may be necessary to improve treatment outcome. The ability of clonazepam to augment serotonergic effects could play a limited role in reducing symptoms in this subset of OCD patients.

In a second biologic variant, alterations in serotonergic tone may be necessary, but not sufficient, to effect changes in symptoms. It may be necessary to alter the output of an independent neuronal population in the manner of neuroleptic addition for OCD patients with comorbid tics (McDougle et al., 1994). Although clonazepam augmentation has not been specifically studied in this population, Rauch and Jenike (1994) suggested that clonazepam augmentation may also have unique benefits for this subgroup. The efficacy of clonazepam in PSRI-resistant OCD (Hewlett et al., 1992; Leonard et al., 1994) would indicate that a subset of PSRI-resistant patients may require a medication having an action beyond simple serotonergic enhancement.

Third, there might be a population for whom OCD symptoms are completely independent of serotonergic tone. Khanna (1988) and Joffe and Swinson (1987) reported patients resistant to either clomipramine or behavior therapy that responded to carbamazepine. For a small minority of OCD patients, it is conceivable that silent epileptic foci in brain regions affecting OC symptomatology might be unresponsive to PSRIs, but might respond to an anti-epileptic medication such as carbamazepine or clonazepam. In fact, the only approved indication for clonazepam is for the treatment of absence seizures, and clonazepam has been used effectively to treat patients with coexisting seizure disorders and OCD (Hewlett et al., 1990). To study treatment resistance with clonazepam or any other medication, it will be important to utilize the degree of previous PSRI response as a factor in the analyses so that biological populations that may require that medication for effective treatment can be better identified.

SUMMARY

Anxiety disorders, as defined by the *DSM–IV*, are a heterogeneous group of disorders, most of which may be effectively treated, at least in part, with benzodiazepines. In contrast, there is no benzodiazepine that should be considered a first-line medication in the treatment of OCD, and there is no indication that CNS benzodiazepine receptors, per se, have any role in the treatment of core OCD symptoms. PSRIs are clearly the treatment of choice for OCD. Any other pharmacologic treatment should be considered only in the context of PSRI-resistant treatment.

Clonazepam is the only medication belonging to the class of benzodiazepines that has shown limited promise in the treatment of this disorder. With the possible exception of its anti-epileptic effects, there is no indication that its purported anti-obsessive effects are related to an interaction at the $GABA_A$-benzodiazepine receptor complex. The anti-obsessive effects of clonazepam do not appear to be related to anxiety state. Although clonazepam may enhance serotonergic neurotransmission via a benzodiazepine-independent action, the mechanisms by which clonazepam might effect any anti-obsessive changes is not known.

Low-dose clonazepam monotherapy appears to have limited benefit in the primary treatment of OCD symptoms, and may interfere with the therapeutic value of behavioral treatments. There is some indication that global improvement can occur when clonazepam is used as an adjunct to PSRI treatment. Although high-dose clonazepam therapy may have substantial adverse effects, if tolerated, such treatment may reduce OCD symptoms in a subset of PSRI-refractory patients, and should be considered as a possible therapeutic course when other strategies have failed. Clearly, a trial of high-dose clonazepam should be considered before a patient is subjected to neurosurgical interventions, because the success or failure of such a trial can be appreciated in less than 4 weeks. Although evidence for efficacy is limited for this population, the possibility of therapeutic benefit becomes important when faced with a surgical alternative with potentially irreversible consequences. More extensive clinical experience in patients with documented PSRI treatment responses will be necessary to determine the long-term utility of this unique benzodiazepine in the treatment-refractory OCD population.

REFERENCES

American Psychiatric Association. (1994). *Diagnostic and statistical manual of mental disorders* (4th ed.). Washington, DC: Author.

Ananth, J., & van den Steen, N. (1983). Intramuscular lorazepam: A double-blind comparison with diazepam and placebo. *Neuropsychobiology, 9*(2–3), 139–141.

Ansseau, M., Legros, J. J., Mormont, C., Cerfontaine, J. L., Papart, P., Geenen, V., Adam, F., & Franck, G. (1987). Intranasal oxytocin in obsessive-compulsive disorder. *Psychoneuroendocrinology, 12*(3), 231–236.

Asberg, M., & Schalling, D. (1979). Construction of a new psychiatric rating instrument, the Comprehensive Psychopathological Rating Scale (CPRS). *Progress in Neuropsychopharmacology, 3*(4), 405–412.

Bacher, N. M. (1990). Clonazepam treatment of obsessive compulsive disorder. *Journal of Clinical Psychiatry, 51*(4), 168–169.

Baxter, L. (1985). Two cases of obsessive-compulsive disorder with depression responsive to trazodone. *Journal of Nervous & Mental Disorders, 173*(7), 432–433.

Benkelfat, C., Murphy, D. L., Zohar, J., Hill, J. L., Grover, G., & Insel, T. R. (1989). Clomipramine in obsessive-compulsive disorder: Further evidence for a serotonergic mechanism of action. *Archives of General Psychiatry, 46*(1), 23–28.

Bethume, H. (1964). A new compound in the treatment of severe anxiety states: Report on the use of diazepam. *New England Journal of Medicine, 63*, 153–156.

Bodkin, J. A., & White, K. (1989). Clonazepam in the treatment of obsessive compulsive disorder associated with panic disorder in one patient. *Journal of Clinical Psychiatry, 50*(7), 265–266.

Breitner, C. (1960). Drug therapy in obsessional states and other psychiatric problems. *Diseases of the Nervous System, 21*(Suppl.), 31–35.

Burrell, R. H., Culpan, R. H., Newton, K. J., Ogg, G. J., & Short, J. H. (1974). Use of bromazepam in obsessional, phobic and related states. *Current Medical Research Opinion, 2*(7), 430–436.

Casas, M., Alvarez, E., Duro, P., Garcia-Ribera, C., Udina, C., Velat, A., Abella, D., Rodriguez-Espinosa, J., Salva, P., & Jane, P. (1986). Antiandrogenic treatment of obsessive-compulsive neurosis. *Acta Psychiatria Scandinavia, 73*(2), 221–222.

Cassano, G. B., Carrara, S., & Castrogiovanni, P. (1975). Bromazepam versus diazepam in psychoneurotic inpatients. *Pharmakopsychiatrie and Neuropsychopharmakologie, 8*(1), 1–7.

Cassano, G. B., Castrogiovanni, P., Mauri, M., Rutigliano, G., Pirro, R., Cerone, G., Nielsen, N. P., Reitano, S., Guidotti, N., Bedarida, D., Marchetti, F. P., Catalano, A., Benecchi, M. V., Amabile, G., Zanasi, M., Pugliese, L., Rocco, M. L., Balestrieri, A., Tansella, M., Burti, L., & Pariante, F. (1981). A multicenter controlled trial in phobic-obsessive psychoneurosis: The effect of clomipramine and of its combinations with haloperidol and diazepam. *Progress in Neuropsychopharmacology, 5*(2), 129–138.

Chadwick, D., Hallett, M., Harris, R., Jenner, P., Reynolds, E. H., & Marsden, C. D. (1977). Clinical, biochemical, and physiological features distinguishing myoclonus responsive to 5-hydroxytryptophan, tryptophan with a monoamine oxidase inhibitor, and clonazepam. *Brain, 100*(3), 455–487.

Chadwick, D., Jenner, P., Harris, R., Reynolds, E. H., & Marsden, C. D. (1975). Manipulation of brain serotonin in the treatment of myoclonus. *Lancet, 2*(7932), 434–435.

Cohen, L., & Rosenbaum, J. (1987). Clonazepam: New uses and potential problems. *Journal of Clinical Psychiatry, 48*(10, Suppl.), 50–55.

Costa, E., Corda, M. G., Epstein, B., Forchetti, C., & Guidotti, A. (1983). GAGA-benzodiazepine interactions. In E. Costa (Ed.), *The benzodiazepines: From molecular biology to clinical practice* (pp. 117–136). New York: Raven.

Dally, P. (1967). *Chemotherapy of psychiatric disorders.* London: Logos.

Deberdt, R. (1974). *Le traitement des nevroses obsessionnelles et phobiques par le Ro 5-3350* [Treatment of obsessional and phobic neuroses with Ro 5-3350]. Unpublished manuscript.

De Giacomo, P., & Pierri, G. (1974). Clinical evaluation of bromazepam with special reference to obsessive syndromes and phobias. *Acta Neurologica (Napoli), 29*(3), 307–313.

Denham, J. (1963). Psychotherapy of obsessional neurosis assisted by lithium. *Topical Problems of Psychotherapy, 4,* 195–198.

Derogatis, L., Lipman, R., & Covi, L. (1973). SCL–90: An outpatient psychiatric rating scale—Preliminary report. *Psychopharmacology Bulletin, 9*(1), 13–28.

Draper, R. (1975). Clinical experience with Ro 5-3350 (bromazepam). *Journal of Internal Medicine Research, 3*(3), 214–222.

Fallon, B., Campeas, R., Schneier, F., Hollander, E., Feerick, J., Hatterer, J., Goetz, D., Davies, S., & Liebowitz, M. (1992). Open trial of intravenous clomipramine in five treatment-refractory patients with obsessive-compulsive disorder. *Journal of Neuropsychiatry, 4*(1), 70–75.

Farid, B., & Bulto, M. (1994). Buspirone in obsessional compulsive disorder: A prospective case study. *Pharmacopsychiatry, 27,* 207–209.

Flament, M. F., Rapoport, J. L., Berg, C. J., Sceery, W., Kilts, C., Mellstrom, B., & Linnoila, M. (1985). Clomipramine treatment of childhood obsessive-compulsive disorder: A double-blind controlled study. *Archives of General Psychiatry, 42*(10), 977–983.

Fontaine, R., & Chouinard, G. (1985). Antiobsessive effect of fluoxetine. *Psychiatry, 142*(8), 989.

Gilbert, M. M. (1965). Clinical trial of a new drug, analog of chlordiazepoxide, for treatment of anxiety and tension. *International Journal of Neuropsychiatry, 6,* 556–558.

Goodman, W. K., McDougle, C. J., Barr, L. C., Aronson, S. C., & Price, L. H. (1993). Biological approaches to treatment-resistant obsessive compulsive disorder. *Journal of Clinical Psychiatry, 54*(6, Suppl.), 16–26.

Goodman, W. K., McDougle, C. J., & Price, L. H. (1992). Pharmacotherapy of obsessive compulsive disorder. *Journal of Clinical Psychiatry, 53*(4, Suppl.), 29–37.

Goodman, W. K., Price, L. H., Rasmussen, S. A., Mazure, C., Fleischmann, R. L., Hill, C. L., Heninger, G. R., & Charney, D. S. (1989). The Yale–Brown Obsessive Compulsive Scale: I. Development, use, and reliability. *Archives of General Psychiatry, 46*(11), 1006–1011.

Grattarola, F. R., & Morgando, E. (1973). Clinical trial of a new derivative of the series of benzodiazepines: Bromazepam (Ro 5-3350) in the treatment of phobic obsessive symptoms. *Minerva Medica, 64*(40), 2107–2111.

Hardy, J. L. (1986). Obsessive compulsive disorder. *Canadian Journal of Psychiatry, 31*(3), 290.

Haward, L. R. C. (1979). Multivariate symptom analysis related to response to lorazepam treatment. *Current Medical Research Opinion, 6*(1), 20–23.

Hewlett, W. (1993). Use of benzodiazepines in obsessive compulsive disorder and Tourette's syndrome. *Psychiatric Annals, 23*(6), 309–316.

Hewlett, W. A. (1997). Novel pharmacologic treatments of obsessive compulsive disorder. In E. H. Hollander & D. Stein (Eds.), *Obsessive compulsive disorders* (pp. 161–201). New York: Marcel Dekker.

Hewlett, W. A., Berman, S., & Martin, K. (1991). Fenfluramine-stimulated prolactin release during serotonergic and non-serotonergic treatment of obsessive-compulsive disorder [Abstract]. *Biological Psychiatry, 29,* 73A.

Hewlett, W., Fridman, S., Trividi, B., Schmidt, D., de Paulis, T., & Ebert, M. (1998). Characterization of Desamino-5-[125I]Iodo-3-Methoxyzacopride ([125I]MIZAC) binding to 5-HT$_3$ receptors in the rat brain. *Progressive Neuro-Psychopharmacology and Biological Psychiatry, 22,* 397–410.

Hewlett, W. A., Vinogradov, S., & Agras, W. S. (1990). Clonazepam treatment of obsessions and compulsions. *Journal of Clinical Psychiatry, 51*(4), 158–161.

Hewlett, W., Vinogradov, S., & Agras, W. (1992). Clomipramine, clonazepam and clonidine treatment of obsessive compulsive disorder. *Journal of Clinical Psychiatry, 12*(6), 420–430.

Hussain, M., & Ahad, A. (1970). Treatment of obsessive-compulsive neurosis. *CMA Journal, 103,* 648–650.

Hwang, E. C., & Van Woert, M. H. (1979). Antimyoclonic action of clonazepam: The role of serotonin. *European Journal of Pharmacology, 60,* 31–40.

Insel, T. R., Murphy, D. L., Cohen, R. M., Alterman, I., Kilts, C., & Linnoila, M. (1983). Obsessive-compulsive disorder: A double-blind trial of clomipramine and clorgyline. *Archives of General Psychiatry, 40*(6), 605–612.

Janca, A., Kastrup, M., Katschnig, H., Lopez-Ibor, J., Mezzich, J., & Sartorius, N. (1996). The ICD–10 multiaxial system for use in adult psychiatry: Structure and applications. *Journal of Nervous & Mental Diseases, 184*(3), 191–192.

Jaskari, M. O. (1980). Observations on mianserin in the treatment of obsessive neuroses. *Current Medical Research Opinions, 6*(7, Suppl.), 128–131.

Jenike, M. A. (1981). Rapid response of severe obsessive-compulsive disorder to tranyl-cypromine. *American Journal of Psychiatry, 138*(9), 1249–1250.

Jenike, M. A. (1990). Drug treatment of obsessive-compulsive disorder. In M. A. Jenike, L. Baer, & W. E. Minichiello (Eds.), *Obsessive-compulsive disorders: Theory and management* (pp. 249–282). Littleton, MA: Year Book Medical.

Jenike, M. A., & Baer, L. (1988). An open trial of buspirone in obsessive-compulsive disorder. *American Journal of Psychiatry, 145*(10), 1285–1286.

Jenike, M. A., Baer, L., Summergrad, P., Minichiello, W. E., Holland, A., & Seymour, R. (1990). Sertraline in obsessive-compulsive disorder: A double-blind comparison with placebo. *American Journal of Psychiatry, 147*(7), 923–928.

Jenike, M. A., & Brotman, A. W. (1984). The EEG in obsessive-compulsive disorder. *Journal of Clinical Psychiatry, 41*(3), 122–124.

Jenike, M. A., & Rauch, S. L. (1994). Managing the patient with treatment-resistant obsessive compulsive disorder: Current strategies. *Journal of Clinical Psychiatry, 55*(3, Suppl.), 11–17.

Jenike, M. A., Surman, O. S., Cassem, N. H., Zusky, P., & Anderson, W. H. (1983). Monoamine oxidase inhibitors in obsessive-compulsive disorder. *Journal of Clinical Psychiatry, 44*(4), 131–132.

Jenner, P., Chadwick, D., Reynolds, E. H., & Marsden, C. D. (1975). Altered 5-HT metabolism with clonazepam, diazepam and diphenylhydantoin. *Journal of Pharmacy & Pharmacology, 27*(9), 707–710.

Joffe, R. T., & Swinson, R. P. (1987). Carbamazepine in obsessive-compulsive disorder. *Biological Psychiatry, 22*(9), 1169–1171.

Kaplan, H. I., & Sadock, B. I. (1990). *Pocket handbook of clinical psychiatry.* Baltimore: Williams & Wilkins.

Ketter, T., Chun, D., & Lu, F. (1986). Alprazolam in the treatment of compulsive symptoms. *Journal of Clinical Psychopharmacology, 6*(1), 59–60.

Khanna, S. (1988). Carbamazepine in obsessive-compulsive disorder. *Neuropharmacology, 11*(5), 478–481.

Kim, S., Dysken, M., & Kuskowski, M. (1992). The Symptom Checklist–90 Obsessive-compulsive subscale: A reliability and validity study. *Psychiatry Research, 41*(1), 37–44.

Knesevich, J. W. (1982). Successful treatment of obsessive-compulsive disorder with clonidine hydrochloride. *American Journal of Psychiatry, 139*(3), 364–365.

Koran, L. M., Faravelli, C., & Pallanti, S. (1994). Intravenous clomipramine for obsessive-compulsive disorder. *Journal of Clinical Psychopharmacology, 14*(3), 216–218.

Laffranchini, S. (1975). Experience de cinq annees en pratique psychiatrique ambulatoire avec un tranquillisant nouveau, le Lexotanil (Ro 5-3350) [Five years' experience with a new tranquilizer Lexotanil (Ro 5-3350) in ambulatory patients in a psychiatric practice]. *Therapeutische Umshau/Revue Therapeutique, 32*(11), 741–744.

Lelliott, P. T., & Monteiro, W. O. (1986). Drug treatment of obsessive-compulsive disorder. *Drugs, 31*(1), 75–80.

Lens, F. (1974). A new benzodiazepine screened in a parallel double-blind test. *Acta Psychiatria Belgica, 74*(3), 327–337.

Leonard, H. L., Topol, D., Bukstein, O., Hindmarsh, D., Allen, A. J., & Swedo, S. E. (1994). Clonazepam as an augmenting agent in the treatment of childhood-onset obsessive-compulsive disorder. *Journal of American Academy of Child & Adolescent Psychiatry, 33*(6), 792–794.

Lin, H. N., & Chen, C. C. (1979). A double-blind test on the effect of bromazepam in obsessive-compulsive neurosis. *Taiwan I Hsueh Hui Tsa Chih, 78*(3), 267–275.

Lydiard, R. B. (1986). Obsessive-compulsive disorder successfully treated with trazodone. *Psychosomatics, 27*(12), 858–859.

McDougle, C. J., Goodman, W. K., Leckman, J. F., Lee, N. C., Heninger, G. R., & Price, L. H. (1994). Haloperidol addition in fluvoxamine-refractory obsessive-compulsive disorder: A double-blind, placebo-controlled study in patients with and without tics. *Archives of General Psychiatry, 51*(4), 302–308.

Murphy, D., Pickar, D., & Alterman, I. (1982). Methods for the quantitative assessment of depressive and manic behavior. In E. Burdock, A. Sudilovsky, & S. Gershon (Eds.), *Quantitative techniques for the evaluation of the behavior of psychiatric patients* (pp. 355–392). New York: Marcel Dekker.

Nakamura, M., & Carney, J. M. (1983). Separation of clonazepam-induced head twitches and muscle relaxation in mice. *Pharmacology, Biochemistry, and Behavior, 19*(3), 549–552.

Nakamura, M., & Fukushima, H. (1976). Head twitches induced by benzodiazepines and the role of biogenic amines. *Psychopharmacology, 49,* 259–261.

Nutt, D. J. (1991). Anxiety and its therapy: Today and tomorrow. In M. Briley & S. E. File (Eds.), *New concepts in anxiety* (pp. 1–12). Boca Raton, FL: CRC.

Nutt, D. J., & Cowen, P. J. (1987). Diazepam alters brain 5-HT function in man: Implications for the acute and chronic effects of benzodiazepines. *Psychological Medicine, 17*(3), 601–607.

Okuma, T., Nakao, T., Ogura, C., Kishimoto, A., & Majima, K. (1971). Effect of 7-Bromo-5-(2-pyridyl)-3H-1, 4-benzodiazepine-2(1H)-one, Bromazepam (Ro 5-3350), a new minor tranquilizer, on psychoneurosis with special reference to the obsessive-compulsive symptoms. *Folia Psychiatrica et Neurologica, 25*(3), 181–193.

O'Regan, J. B. (1970). Treatment of obsessive-compulsive neurosis with haloperidol. *CMA Journal, 103,* 167–168.

Orvin, G. H. (1967). Treatment of the phobic obsessive-compulsive patient with oxazepam, an improved benzodiazepine compound. *Psychosomatics, 8,* 278–280.

Pigott, T. A., L'Heureux, F., & Rubenstein, C. S. (1992). A controlled trial of clonazepam augmentation in OCD patients treated with clomipramine or fluoxetine. In *New Research Program and Abstracts of the 145th Annual Meeting of the American Psychiatric Association* (Abstract NR #144, p. 82). Washington, DC: American Psychiatric Press.

Pranzatelli, M. R. (1989). Benzodiazepine-induced shaking behavior in the rat: Structure-activity and relation to serotonin and benzodiazepine receptors. *Experimental Neurology, 104*(3), 241–250.

Pranzatelli, M. R., Dailey, A., Levy, M., & Dollison, A. (1991). Absence of tolerance to the excitatory effects of benzodiazepines: Clonazepam-evoked shaking behavior in the rat. *Pharmacology, Biochemistry, and Behavior, 39*(4), 1021–1024.

Pratt, J., Jenner, P., Reynolds, E. H., & Marsden, C. D. (1979). Clonazepam induces decreased serotoninergic activity in the mouse brain. *Neuropharmacology, 18,* 791–799.

Rao, A. (1964). A controlled trial with "valium" in obsessive-compulsive state. *Journal of the Indian Medical Association, 42,* 564–567.

Rauch, S. L., & Jenike, M. A. (1994). Management of treatment-resistant obsessive compulsive disorder: Concepts and strategies. In E. Hollander, J. Zohar, D. Marazziti, & B. Olivier (Eds.), *Current insights in obsessive compulsive disorder* (pp. 227–244). New York: Wiley.

Rosenbaum, J. F., & Gelenberg, A. J. (1991). Anxiety disorders. In A. J. Gelenberg, E. L. Bassuk, & S. C. Schoonover (Eds.), *The practitioner's guide to psychoactive drugs* (pp. 190–204). New York: Plenum.

Ross, D., & Pigott, L. (1993). Clonazepam for OCD. *Journal of American Academy of Child & Adolescent Psychiatry, 32*(2), 470–471.

Salmoni, G., Amati, A., Giambelluca, A., & Vacca, L. (1973). Clinical and therapeutic considerations on the use of a benzodiazepine derivative, bromazepam (Ro 5-3350) in the treatment of obsessive-phobic disorders. *Acta Neurologica (Napoli), 28*(5), 588–609.

Snyder, S. (1980). Amitriptyline therapy of obsessive-compulsive neurosis. *Journal of Clinical Psychiatry, 41*(8), 286–289.

Sonne, L. M., & Holm, P. (1975). A comparison between bromazepam (Ro 5-3350, Lexotan) and diazepam (Valium) in anxiety neurosis: A controlled, double-blind clinical trial. *International Pharmacopsychiatry, 10*(2), 125–128.

Stein, D. J., Hollander, E., Mullen, L. S., DeCaria, C. M., & Liebowitz, M. R. (1992). Comparison of clomipramine, alprazolam and placebo in the treatment of obsessive-compulsive disorder. *Human Psychopharmacology, 7,* 389–395.

Tesar, G. E., & Jenike, M. A. (1984). Alprazolam as treatment for a case of obsessive-compulsive disorder. *American Journal of Psychiatry, 141*(5), 689–690.

Thoren, P., Asberg, M., Cronholm, B., Jornestedt, L., & Traskman, L. (1980). Clomipramine treatment of obsessive compulsive disorder: A controlled clinical trial. *Archives of General Psychiatry, 37,* 1281–1285.

Tobin, J. M., Bird, I. F., & Boyle, D. E. (1960). Preliminary evaluation of librium (Ro 5-0690) in the treatment of anxiety reactions. *Diseases of Nervous Systems, 21*(Suppl.), 11.

Tollefson, G. (1985). Alprazolam in the treatment of obsessive symptoms. *Journal of Clinical Psychopharmacology, 5*(1), 39–42.

Troung, D. D. (1988). Clonazepam, haloperidol, and clonidine in tic disorders. *Southern Medical Journal, 81,* 1103–1105.

Wagner, H. R., Reches, A., Yablonskaya, E., & Fahn, S. (1986). Clonazepam-induced up-regulation of serotonin1 and serotonin2 binding sites in rat frontal cortex. *Advanced Neurology, 43*(645), 645–651.

Waxman, D. (1977). A clinical trial of clomipramine and diazepam in the treatment of phobic and obsessional illness. *Journal of Internal Medicine Research, 5,* 99–110.

World Health Organization. (1993). *Manual of the international statistical classification of diseases, injuries, and causes of death.* Geneva: Author.

Wittenborn, J. (1974). The WPRS: A quantification of observable psychopathology. *Modern Problems of Pharmacopsychiatry, 7,* 33–49.

22

Electroconvulsive Therapy in Treatment-Refractory Obsessive-Compulsive Disorder

Matthew V. Rudorfer
National Institute of Mental Health

Despite the considerable advances in pharmacological and behavioral treatments over the past two decades, a significant minority of patients with obsessive-compulsive disorder (OCD) continue to respond minimally at best to currently available interventions (Goodman, McDougle, Barr, Aronson, & Price, 1993; Jenike, 1993). As documented throughout this volume, much current research is devoted to the study of new treatments or treatment combinations to help those suffering from refractory OCD. At the same time, questions have been raised about the potential utility of older treatments, most notably electroconvulsive therapy (ECT), in the modern therapeutic regimen for OCD (Maletzky, McFarland, & Burt, 1994).

Most contemporary treatment algorithms for OCD dismiss or ignore any role for ECT (American Psychiatric Association, 1990; Jefferson et al., 1995; Jenike, Baer, & Minichiello, 1987; Small, 1985). However, the persistence over several decades of occasional favorable reports in the literature (Maletzky et al., 1994; Martin, 1996) compels a reexamination of the evidence for any true anti-OCD efficacy of this venerable treatment modality.

EARLY CLINICAL EXPERIENCE

In contrast to the serendipity that has marked the discovery of most somatic treatments in psychiatry (Rudorfer, Linnoila, & Potter, 1987), the

431

introduction of convulsive therapy in the 1930s was predicated on the hypothesis, later disproved, of a biological antagonism between epilepsy and schizophrenia (Rudorfer, Henry, & Sackeim, 1997). Within several years, the unpredictable pharmacological initiation of seizures had evolved into a more titratable and controlled electrical induction of therapeutic convulsions (Rudorfer et al., 1997). The successful 1938 introduction of ECT in Rome demonstrated a key principle of the treatment: The therapeutic action results from the convulsive activity in the brain (or the resulting effects or adaptations), independent of the nature of the initiating stimulus or the resulting peripheral grand mal motor seizure activity (Fink, 1979; Rudorfer et al., 1997). Indeed, half a century later the serendipitous clinical improvement demonstrated by a patient with OCD who experienced a seizure associated with drug withdrawal led to a notable example of OCD treatment with ECT, as discussed later (Mellman & Gorman, 1984). By the early 1940s the new ECT had spread far beyond its origins in central Europe. With widespread clinical experience, the original indication of schizophrenia was modified with the observation that ECT was particularly effective for the treatment of severe mood disorders (American Psychiatric Association, 1990; Rudorfer et al., 1997).

Nonetheless, prior to and even following the psychopharmacological revolution of the 1950s, ECT continued to be used for the treatment of a number of disorders, including OCD, that were not responsive to the newly developed antipsychotic and antidepressive medications. The literature from that earlier era of clinical investigation is flawed by methodological limitations that include lack of diagnostic specificity, nonrandom assignment of treatment, nonblind raters, and absence of uniform treatment techniques. However, the careful clinical observations of the time remain informative.

It must be borne in mind that the concept of treatment resistance or refractoriness was very different from the modern-day concept as used throughout this volume. Until the first clinical trials of clomipramine (i.e., throughout the time of maximal use of ECT), no patients with OCD could have met today's criteria for treatment refractoriness due to the lack of availability of the late century's armamentarium of serotonergic medications. Thus, from one point of view, until recent years all OCD patients referred for ECT were potential responders; a countervailing force was the widespread belief of the time that OCD was a psychologically based disorder and thus preferentially treated with psychotherapy rather than somatic treatment (Korson, 1949).

Also related to the dominance of psychoanalytic theory at the time, many reports of the 1940s and 1950s attended more to psychological and personality constructs than to symptoms or the modern equivalent of diagnostic criteria. Thus, large, systematically conducted surveys of patients who had undergone ECT in both Britain (Hobson, 1953) and the United States (Kahn & Fink, 1959) identified premorbid obsessional personality traits as predictive of a positive clinical response to ECT, which may have been administered for any number of indications. The Maudsley Hospital study (Hobson, 1953), but not the Hillside Hospital survey (Kahn & Fink, 1959), also rated 150 ECT-treated inpatients for obsessive-compulsive (OC) symptoms, which were found not to correlate with outcome after convulsive therapy. However, patients in both of these studies were predominantly depressed, presumably with few suffering from primary OCD.

A more targeted approach was taken by the British investigator Grimshaw (1965), who reviewed the records of 100 patients with OCD and treated in the premodern psychopharmacology era between 1945 and 1959. Most patients were subsequently reinterviewed, with a mean follow-up period of 5 years. No effective anti-OCD medications were used; a minority of patients were treated symptomatically with chlorpromazine or a barbiturate, the latter sometimes combined with an amphetamine. Of the 31 patients who had been treated with ECT, results at follow-up were mixed: 16 were improved (including 9 judged much improved or recovered) and 15 were unchanged or worse. Interestingly, most of the improved patients reported that ECT had not been responsible for their clinical response, leading the author to conclude that ECT had little place in the treatment of primary OCD (Grimshaw, 1965). The favorable response to ECT of a few OCD patients in that series and in the occasional positive case report of the psychoanalytic era (Korson, 1949) remained unexplained.

The last-named report (Korson, 1949) is particularly interesting on several levels (Table 22.1). Although most of the paper is devoted to a psychoanalytic explanation of the patient and his symptoms, which are ascribed primarily to sexual conflict, a series of three somatic interventions are of note.

Pharmacoconvulsive therapy, consisting of six biweekly intravenous metrozal injections, produced the desired grand mal seizures, but with no effect on the core obsessions and compulsions. Throughout the sixth hospital year, the patient underwent weekly "narcosynthesis treatments" with intravenous sodium amytal. This was associated with a reduction in obsessions about harming people and an estimated 75% decline in compulsive hand washing.

At that point, daily ECT was instituted for 13 sessions. On the day of the final ECT session, the patient became acutely agitated, disoriented, and psychotic, with auditory and visual hallucinations. This delirious state cleared after 5 days, and 2 weeks after the final ECT, evidencing clear memory and orientation, the patient pronounced himself "cured." Korson (1949) ascribed the patient's complete (and apparently permanent) recovery to his achieving insight into the putative psychological origin of his OCD symptoms as well as the experience of "just punishment" in the form of ECT.

Although today this psychodynamic explanation of therapeutic response might be questioned, it is hard to read in this case any specific benefit of convulsive therapy. Indeed, the "clean" pharmacoconvulsive therapy trial was utterly ineffective, although six biweekly sessions would be unlikely to constitute adequate treatment. On the other hand, the 13 daily ECT sessions that concluded this man's treatment apparently were excessive, leading to neurotoxicity. Thus, despite all the time and effort that attended this patient's treatment, it would appear that he did not experience what by today's standards would be considered an adequate and appropriate ECT trial.

A cogent summary of the expert opinion of the efficacy of ECT in the treatment of OCD in the premedication era—a mixed, mostly negative verdict—was offered by Kalinowsky and Hoch (1952) in the revision of their classic textbook of somatic treatments in psychiatry:

> In obsessive-compulsive neurotics, results are uncertain. Most patients fail to show lasting improvement, but they do manifest some benefit temporarily. Even when compulsions and obsessions persist after the treatment, the emotional tension accompanying them is often lessened for a while and the patient is better able to adjust to his symptoms. Some patients become more accessible to psychotherapy at this stage. However, it is our experience that even though the symptoms may be obliterated . . . the symptoms in most cases return sooner or later with the same intensity. (p. 196)

Writing a decade later in London, Grimshaw (1965) agreed with this generally negative assessment. And with the passage of another 10 years, during which conventional treatment of OCD made great strides, Pollitt (1975) continued to observe that in true OCD, ECT, "while occasionally associated with temporary improvement, does not influence the natural history of the illness and often worsens the symptoms" (p. 139). The availability of effective pharmacotherapies for OCD did, however, change the treatment landscape with respect to ECT, both in shifting the latter down the treatment hierarchy such that candidates for ECT increasingly were medication-refractory, and in offering the possibility of combination treatments. The influence of these phenomena on the assessment of ECT in the treatment of OCD is considered next.

CLINICAL EXPERIENCE
IN THE PHARMACOTHERAPY ERA

In an unusual but important report, British investigators Walter, Mitchell-Heggs, and Sargant (1972) described their experience in treating hundreds of treatment-resistant patients during the 1960s with modified narcosis, often combined with additional medications and ECT. Their typical regimen consisted of chlorpromazine plus a sedative and an antidepressant, preferably a monoamine oxidase inhibitor (MAOI). Eighty patients with treatment-resistant OCD (more than half of whom had been referred to the authors for psychosurgery) were treated in this manner, with an average treatment course of 5½ weeks. Acute outcome ratings of recovery or much improvement were rendered for 40% of the obsessional neurosis group, with the best results seen in patients younger than age 45 and those with anxiety related to their rituals.

Consistent with the less enthusiastic investigators of earlier years (Grimshaw, 1965; Kalinowsky & Hoch, 1952), however, Walter et al. (1972) also noted that despite their encouraging short-term results for combined ECT and pharmacotherapy in refractory OCD, relapses were common. Ironically, relapses were felt to coincide with the clearing of ECT-associated memory loss (Walter et al., 1972); the hypothesized role of amnesia in the therapeutic mechanism of anti-OCD action, common in the older literature (Kalinowsky & Hoch, 1952), is considered further later.

Case Reports

Several caveats attend consideration of the case report literature describing the use of ECT in the treatment of OCD. As with any treatment, favorable outcomes are more likely to be submitted for publication. Inclusion and exclusion criteria are not uniform, and commonly are poorly defined in case material. Moreover, in the case of ECT, once antidepressant pharmacotherapy was developed, the common use of concomitant medication during a trial of ECT introduced an important new, typically uncontrolled confounding variable complicating evaluation of the efficacy of ECT itself (Kellner, Nixon, & Bernstein, 1991).

A further irony of the modern period of effective anti-OCD pharmacotherapy and behavior therapy is the continued existence of substantial amounts of treatment refractoriness that has encouraged clinicians to consider all available options for some patients, including ECT, in spite of the generally negative reports of the pre-selective serotonin reuptake inhibitor literature. This is exemplified in case reports by Mellman and

TABLE 22.1
ECT in OCD: Case Reports

| | | Patient Information | | | | | |
| | Sex | Age (yr) | OCD Duration (yr) | Comorbid Depression | Concurrent Meds | Number and Type of ECTs | Response | Comment |
Reference								
Korson (1949)	M	33	15	No	None	13 (daily)	Delirium, followed by complete recovery	ECT given after 6 years of hospitalization, including a year of weekly sodium amytal infusions, which had yielded clinical improvement
Mellman & Gorman (1984)	M	60	3	No	None	10 (bilateral, brief pulse)	Complete remission	Atypical features included late age of onset during period of grief; no compulsions
Soyka et al. (1991)	M	24	7	Yes	None	10 (6 uni-lateral, then switched to bi-lateral)	Complete remission	German-language report

Study	Sex	Age	Onset				Outcome	Comments
Sichel et al. (1993)	F	23	0 (2 weeks)	Yes	None	(Details not provided)	Antidepressant response, with continued obsessions	One of a series of 15 women with new-onset postpartum OCD, only this patient received ECT for severe secondary depression; mood improved post-ECT, leaving persistent obsessional thoughts (without compulsions), which required clomipramine
Husain et al. (1993)	F	65	13	Yes	Not specified	9, bilateral	Complete remission	Relatively advanced age of onset; no compulsions; return of obsessions 3 months post-ECT required second (successful) course of 9 bilateral ECTs
Casey & Davis (1994)	F	84	75	Yes	None	6, bilateral, brief pulse	Complete remission	Return of OCD symptoms without depression twice within 7 months after initial ECT required two additional courses of 4 and 6 bilateral brief pulse ECT treatments, again leading to complete, but transient, remissions

Gorman (1984) and others, documenting clear-cut responses to ECT in patients whose OCD had proven refractory to an adequate course of clomipramine (Table 22.1).

A striking aspect of that case was the absence of depression, which today is the cardinal indication for ECT (American Psychiatric Association, 1990; Fink, 1979; Rudorfer et al., 1997). Rather, the authors were prompted to consider ECT based on the fortuitous clinical improvement noted following an alprazolam withdrawal seizure experienced by the patient during medication discontinuation (Mellman & Gorman, 1984). Ten bilateral ECT sessions were associated with total resolution of obsessions, with response sustained over a 10-month follow-up period on maintenance nortriptyline and lithium. An older age of onset of OCD and its origin during a period of grief and a history of remission during haloperidol treatment were atypical aspects of the case (Jenike et al., 1987; Mellman & Gorman, 1984).

A subsequent German-language report (Soyka, Niederecker, & Meyendorf, 1991) described a 24-year-old man whose OCD, which had proven refractory to conventional treatments over a 3-year period, responded to six unilateral and four bilateral ECT treatments (Table 22.1). Following ECT, maintenance clomipramine was able to sustain remission during 18 months of follow-up (Soyka et al., 1991).

Again, a key limitation in interpreting such case reports is the unknown dimension of the denominator representing all OCD cases treated with ECT, with either a positive or a negative outcome. For example, when British clinicians Farid and Bulto (1994) described their successful use of the serotonergic anxiolytic, buspirone, in a man with OCD, ECT was listed as just one of a number of previously ineffective treatments. Although no details of the earlier ECT trial were presented, preventing any conclusions to be drawn about the appropriateness or adequacy of the convulsive therapy, it is fair to say that these authors, and an unknown number of others, saw no need to publish the failure of ECT to adequately treat their patients' OCD.

Systematic Series

Although still limited by small numbers of patients and open-label designs, two systematically collected case series over the past decade go well beyond single case reports in identifying the potential efficacy of ECT in uncomplicated treatment-refractory OCD (Table 22.2).

Khanna Gangadhar, Sinha, Rajendra, and Channabasavanna (1988) in India reported favorable short-term results with ECT in nine OCD patients who had failed to respond to antidepressant medication or behavior therapy. A strength of the design was the requirement that any associated

TABLE 22.2
ECT in OCD: Case Series

| | | Patient Information | | | | | | OCD Ratings | |
| | | | | | | | | | |
Reference	N	Sex	Age ($\overline{X}$, yr)	OCD Duration ($\overline{X}$, yr)	Comorbid Depression	Concurrent Meds	Number and Type of ECTs	Pre-ECT	Post-ECT
Khanna et al. (1988)	9	9 M 0 F	30	4.3	None	None routinely	Bilateral (most) or unilateral, brief pulse	42 (LOI)	33 (LOI)
Maletzky et al. (1994)	32	13 M 19 F	45.5	27.3	13/32	None routinely	Bilateral, multiple, brief pulse	21.7 (MOCI)	12.5 (MOCI)

Note. LOI = Leyton's Obsessional Inventory (Cooper, 1970); MOCI = Maudsley Obsessive Compulsive Inventory (Hodgson & Rachman, 1972).

439

depression, an important confounding variable in OCD treatment studies (discussed later) be nonmelancholic in severity and clearly temporally secondary to the OCD. However, the definition of treatment resistance was less strict than was implied; all patients had experienced an unsuccessful trial of a tertiary amine tricyclic antidepressant (Potter, Manji, & Rudorfer, 1998; Potter, Rudorfer, & Manji, 1991), but in only six patients did that include clomipramine. Similarly, the requisite trial of failed behavior therapy was not specified.

Following a course of 10 ECT sessions, all patients showed subjective improvement in ratings of both obsessions and compulsions, although two patients with less than average benefit reported no subjective positive changes (Khanna et al., 1988). The four patients who were treated with unilateral nondominant electrode placement (American Psychiatric Association, 1990; Fink, 1979; Rudorfer et al., 1997) showed clinical responses equivalent to the remaining participants treated with bilateral ECT, presumably arguing against the amnesia theory of ECT action in OCD (discussed later). Although some correlation was noted between reduction in depression and drop in interference ratings during the course of ECT, depression was not unusually prominent in these patients, with a mean Hamilton Depression Rating score hovering around 10 during the study.

In contrast to the older reports on depressed patients cited earlier, OCD patients with considerable OC personality traits tended to fare less well with ECT; agitation predicted positive treatment outcome (Khanna et al., 1988). Improvement was maximal at the conclusion of the ECT trial, with an average decline in global OCD ratings exceeding 20% (Table 22.2). Clinical response remained steady for an additional 1 to 4 months, by which time all patients had returned to their baseline level of illness. Three patients received maintenance amitriptyline following convulsive therapy, but all nine failed to sustain their improvement, returning to their pre-ECT condition by 6 months after treatment (Khanna et al., 1988; Table 22.3).

Similarly, five of seven OCD patients (out of 11 treated) who improved with multiple monitored ECT relapsed within 6 months (Maletzky, 1981); several responded again to retreatment. A larger series of 32 refractory OCD patients treated with multiple (three to five treatments per session) ECT over a 12-year period was later reported (Maletzky et al., 1994; Table 22.2). Although the severity and intransigence of these patients' disorders were well-established, only half had received clomipramine, which had not been routinely available in the United States during much of the study period. An average of 11 seizures, induced with bilateral electrode placement during a mean of 3.5 sessions, was associated with significant improvement in ratings of obsessions and compulsions within 5 days of

TABLE 22.3
Continuation Treatment After ECT in OCD

Reference	Patient Information			Continuation Meds	Continuation ECT	Duration of Continuation Tx	Response	Comment
	N	Sex	Age (yr)					
Korson (1949)	1	M	33	None	None	10-month follow-up	Continued remission	
Mellman & Gorman (1984)	1	M	60	Nortriptyline 100 mg/day, lithium 1,200 mg/day (blood level 0.8 mEq/L)	None	10 months	Continued remission	
Khanna et al. (1988)	3 of 9	M	Part of sample with average age of 30	Amitriptyline, mean dose 100 mg/day	None	6 months	Relapse in all	The 6 patients in sample who did not take medication after ECT also relapsed
Soyka et al. (1991)	1	M	24	Clomipramine	None	18 months	Continued remission	
Sichel et al. (1993)	1	F	23	Clomipramine 250 mg/day	None	<12 months	Further reduction in obsessions	At 1-year follow-up, patient had only residual obsessional symptoms, no longer on medication

(Continued)

TABLE 22.3
(Continued)

| Reference | Patient Information | | | Continuation Meds | Continuation ECT | Duration of Continuation Tx | Response | Comment |
	N	Sex	Age (yr)					
Husain et al. (1993)	1	F	65	None	Monthly bilateral treatment following almost 3 months of weekly to biweekly ECT	15 months	Continued remission	Maintenance ECT was instituted after second acute course of ECT (each consisting of 9 bilateral treatments); previously, continuation pharmacotherapy (phenelzine and lorazepam) after first course of ECT had failed to prevent relapse of OCD symptoms within 3 months post-ECT
Casey & Davis (1994)	1	F	84	Fluoxetine 40–60 mg/day	Repeat course of 4 sessions of bilateral brief pulse ECTs given after OCD relapse on maintenance pharmacotherapy	5 months	Complete remission for 2–3 months after first course of ECT, followed by gradual return of OCD but not depressive	The second course of acute ECT, given after failure of fluoxetine maintenance, led to 2-month remission, then relapse; a successful third

442

Study	n	Sex	Age	Treatment	Schedule	Duration	Outcome	Comments
							symptoms over next 2 months despite increased fluoxetine dosage to 60 mg/day	ECT course (6 bilateral brief pulse treatments) was followed by maintenance ECT (see next entry)
Casey & Davis (1994)	1	F	84	Clomipramine (dose not specified) replaced maintenance ECT after 1 year	2–3 bilateral brief pulse ECTs every 1–2 months	1 year, after which maintenance ECT was replaced with clomipramine	Trend toward briefer remissions during the year of maintenance ECT	With the availability of clomipramine for maintenance treatment, ECT was successfully discontinued
Maletzky et al. (1994)	32 of 32	13M 19F	45.5 ($\bar{X}$)	Clomipramine ($n = 23$), fluoxetine ($n = 9$) plus behavior therapy ($n = 32$)	Monthly multiple ECT (4 seizures) session, bilateral, brief pulse ($n = 5$, all also taking maintenance medication)	12 months	4 of 13 depressed and 4 of 19 nondepressed patients had remission at 3–4 months, then slow decline; 8 depressed and 10 nondepressed patients, including all 5 remitted patients on maintenance ECT, remained significantly improved at 12 months	

the last treatment in both depressed (whose mood improved as well) and nondepressed patients. Acutely, ECT was associated with a greater than 40% drop in OCD ratings, with little difference in depressed versus nondepressed patients. Although a slow erosion in clinical state was seen in some measures over a 1-year follow-up, even at that time point both depressed and nondepressed OCD participants retained significant changes from baseline on the Maudsley Obsessive Compulsive Inventory (MOCI) scores, and 8 (of 13) depressed and 10 (of 19) nondepressed patients were felt to maintain their "striking gains." The wide disparities in patient demographics, differences in treatment methodologies, and the use of nonblinded raters evaluating two popular, but distinct, British rating scales of OCD symptoms preclude meaningful comparison of the outcomes of what at present remain the two largest contemporary case series of ECT use in OCD (Table 22.2).

THE ROLE OF COMORBID DEPRESSION

Perhaps related to its generally early age of onset and its chronicity and associated disability, many people with OCD suffer from other concurrent mental disorders. Some investigators actively attempt to neutralize this potential confounding variable, such as the efforts of Khanna et al. (1988) to screen out OCD patients suffering from primary depression. More common is the example of Maletzky et al. (1994), who dealt with comorbid depression only in the course of data analysis by creating a separate cohort of patients with both OCD and depression to compare with the OCD-only group. Either approach is preferable to ignoring the potential presence of comorbid conditions, a danger in any anecdotal account of clinical practice.

Factoring out the role of depression, the most common comorbid condition associated with OCD, has proven challenging in clinical trials. It has now been established that the anti-obsessional action of serotonergic pharmacotherapy, such as clomipramine, is independent of the antidepressant effect of these compounds (Jenike, 1993; Mavissakalian, Turner, Michelson, & Jacob, 1985). In terms of ECT, the previously noted illustrations of the Khanna et al. (1988) and Maletzky et al. (1994) case series were able to demonstrate an anti-OCD effect of convulsive therapy independent of its antidepressant action. Much of the literature, however, is less clear.

Although Mellman and Gorman (1984) carefully documented the lack of overt depression in their patient, going so far as to interview family members, it remains notable that the onset of OCD in the man under study began relatively late in life in the context of acute grief. Although

some biological parameters—notably sleep and neuroendocrine dysregulation (Insel, 1984)—are shared by both OCD and depression, most investigators today do not regard the two disorders as pathophysiologically
related, treating the usual comorbidity of depression as secondary to the
OCD (Casey & Davis, 1994; Husain, Lewis, & Thornton, 1993; Maletzky
et al., 1994).

Concurrent depression at the time of ECT treatment of OCD complicates the interpretation of clinical response. This is illustrated in two
relatively recent cases of elderly women with comorbid OCD and depression (Casey & Davis, 1994; Husain et al., 1993; see Table 22.1). In both
instances, OCD was felt to be the primary disorder and, indeed, one
84-year-old patient had suffered from OCD since childhood (Casey &
Davis, 1994). The atypical onset of OCD in midlife in the other patient
(Husain et al., 1993), who received ECT at age 65 while suicidally depressed, raises more questions about whether the ECT, which was extremely effective in both cases, is acting as a specifically anti-obsessional
agent or via its more common antidepressant action (Fink, 1979; Rudorfer
et al., 1997). Earlier clinical data (Folstein, Folstein, & McHugh, 1973)
demonstrated an association between poor response to ECT and the
absence of certain depressive signs and symptoms, particularly in non-
mood disorders; however, it is not specified whether frank OCD was
present in any of the surveyed "neurotic" patients.

Husain et al. (1993) noted that earlier antidepressant treatments had
in fact improved their patient's mood without affecting her OCD symptoms, as was also true of two postpartum women with OCD who were
initially treated with the noradrenergic tricyclic antidepressant desipramine (Sichel, Cohen, Dimmock, & Rosenbaum, 1993). An unexplained
difference in these case reports is the positive response of Husain et al.'s
patient to ECT, suggesting that, in fact, ECT had exerted an anti-OCD
action beyond relief of associated dysphoria.

In contrast stands the one patient among a series of 15 women whose
OCD developed during the postpartum period (Sichel et al., 1993) who
received ECT. That patient, with no previous psychiatric history, developed a severe secondary depression and underwent a course of ECT with
some improvement, although residual symptoms remained (Table 22.1).
In this instance, ECT acted as did desipramine in the postpartum series,
improving mood symptoms but not core OCD pathology, which cleared
only with subsequent clomipramine treatment (Tables 22.1 and 22.3). The
other 14 postpartum OCD patients, most of whom also developed secondary depression, responded or remitted with serotonergic antidepressant medications without ECT (Sichel et al., 1993).

Consistent with most of the previous literature, both Husain et al.'s
(1993) and Casey and Davis' (1994) older patients relapsed within several

months following ECT despite continuation pharmacotherapy, in both cases responding again to reinitiation of convulsive therapy followed by successful maintenance ECT (Table 22.3). Casey and Davis (1994) noted that at the time of their elderly patient's second course of ECT, nearly complete remission from OCD symptoms was achieved, even though, in contrast to the time ECT was first used, she was no longer depressed.

Less typical presentations of concomitant OCD and depression have also been treated with ECT. For example, encephalitis lethargica, presenting with a characteristic triad of catatonic, obsessional, and depressive symptoms, was somewhat responsive to ECT (Johnson & Lucey, 1987).

POST-ECT CONTINUATION
AND MAINTENANCE TREATMENT

Relapse after a period of remission lasting no more than several months after completion of a course of ECT is no less a problem in OCD than in the more typical use of ECT in depression (Prudic et al., 1996; Rudorfer et al., 1997). Consequently, a number of treatment approaches have been utilized in an effort to maintain improvement in patients whose OCD symptoms have responded to an acute course of ECT. The results of these efforts have been divided, however (Table 22.3), and no clear consensus on the optimal protocol has emerged. Moreover, the naturalistic nature of the reported cases has prevented control of many potentially confounding variables.

For example, all 32 of Maletzky et al.'s (1994) OCD patients received pharmacotherapy after completion of ECT (Table 22.3). The best results were seen with clomipramine, fluoxetine, or MAOIs, even in cases in which these medications had failed prior to ECT (Maletzky et al., 1994); this outcome is contrary to a growing experience with pharmacotherapy for relapse prevention of depression after ECT (Prudic et al., 1996). Interpretation of these findings is complicated by the fact that all patients also received behavior therapy during the follow-up period. Moreover, five patients who, as in Khanna et al.'s (1988) series, suffered a rapid relapse within 1 to 3 months, remitted throughout the follow-up period with institution of maintenance ECT.

Published data on the major modes of continuation treatment after ECT (i.e., pharmacotherapy and maintenance ECT), as well as no active treatment, are presented in Table 22.3, which reveals their inconsistency. Thus, lack of continuation treatment after successful ECT in OCD did not undermine the clinical response of the young man reported by Korson (1949) but was associated with early relapse in two thirds of the more recent cases in the Khanna et al. (1988) series. However, pharmacotherapy after ECT did not prevent relapse in the other third of patients in the latter report (Khanna et al., 1988), nor in the elderly women described by Husain et al. (1993) and Casey and Davis (1994). In these last two cases, additional courses of ECT were necessary after failure of continuation pharmacotherapy, an approach that does not always work for OCD patients (M. Fink, personal communication, June 15, 1996). Only after a year of maintenance ECT—effective, but with progressively shortening periods of remission—was medication able to be successfully substituted in Casey and Davis' (1994) patient.

In contrast, at least three cases of clinical response of OCD to ECT being sustained by follow-up pharmacotherapy have been published (Mellman & Gorman, 1984; Sichel et al., 1993; Soyka et al., 1991; Table 22.3). As noted, Maletzky et al. (1994) achieved considerable success in maintaining improvement in OCD symptoms reached with multiple ECT sessions with the use of combined treatments, including behavior therapy, in all patients throughout the follow-up period. Although the impressive maintenance of clinical response in that relatively large patient series commands the attention of clinicians, the use of two or three concurrent active treatments in the unstructured clinical design that encompasses much of the literature on ECT in treatment-refractory OCD poses a common methodological problem in determining the actual agent(s) of therapeutic action.

PUTATIVE MECHANISMS OF ACTION

Without a definitive clinical trial demonstrating the efficacy of ECT in OCD, all theories regarding possible mechanisms of action of this treatment for this indication remain speculative. Indeed, although there is now case material suggesting an anti-obsessional therapeutic action of ECT in some nondepressed OCD patients (Casey & Davis, 1994; Khanna et al., 1988; Maletzky et al., 1994; Mellman & Gorman, 1984), much clinical opinion continues to call for reserving ECT treatment for individuals with severe (generally suicidal) secondary depression, suggesting that the mechanism of action is the usual antidepressant one, only indirectly benefiting the core OCD symptoms (Goodman et al., 1993; Jenike et al., 1987; Sichel et al., 1993). As posited by Pollitt (1975), "ECT given alone is likely to help only those whose obsessions are secondary to, or part of, a depressive illness demonstrable clinically" (p. 139).

A more extreme position was taken by Ottosson (1985), who opined that when ECT "is occasionally found to be effective" in the treatment of OCD, "the mechanism of action is probably suggestion" (p. 935). This reminds the field that absent a controlled study, a placebo effect, although historically extremely low in true OCD, cannot be ruled out completely for any treatment modality.

Theories related to an anti-OCD action of ECT have paralleled those put forth for the classical antidepressant efficacy of convulsive therapy (Rudorfer et al., 1997), ranging from the psychological to the biological. Early views conceptualizing convulsive therapy as painful and assaultive and emphasizing the resulting confusion and memory deficits, reflected unfortunate midcentury clinical realities that antedate modern ECT (Fink, 1979; Rudorfer & Goodwin, 1993; Rudorfer et al., 1997). An illustration of the psychoanalytic view of ECT interpreted by the patient as punishment was provided by Korson (1949):

> It was felt that the treatment situation was a repetition of an ancient interpersonal situation—the individual delivers himself into the hands of a strict but in the end forgiving parent figure, who will mete out punishment justly and thus allow atonement and delivery from all evil. The acceptance of punishment allows the patient to assuage his conscience, fear and anxiety becoming unnecessary when retribution has taken place. (p. 41)

More than anything, the advances in ECT methodology over the past generation have served to undermine these psychoanalytic concepts. The modern application of premedication with general anesthetics and muscle relaxants, along with the introduction of true informed consent, have eliminated most of the reality-based fear and sense of violation that were common a half-century ago (Consensus Conference, National Institutes of Health, 1985; Fink, 1979; Martin, 1996; Rudorfer & Goodwin, 1993; Rudorfer et al., 1997). Still, it has been argued that many patients continue to experience fear in anticipation of ECT and its unpleasant aftereffects, thereby making the ECT session into a type of aversive therapy (Gruber, 1971); this author went so far as to suggest that even the anesthetized, unconscious patient might experience as an unconditioned stimulus the unpleasant effects of succinylcholine or of the ECT itself, possibly even unconsciously feeling pain from the seizure during treatment.

Interestingly enough, Korson's (1949) patient did not experience the then-common amnesia after ECT (felt by some to be a therapeutic forgetting of the OC state). Instead, this young man was able to verbalize a psychodynamic understanding of his obsessions and compulsions as related to psychological conflicts about sexual feelings, consistent with the author's conclusion that psychoanalysis (not the ECT) was the treatment of choice for OCD (Korson, 1949).

Until relatively recent times, the application of the electrical stimulus in convulsive therapy entailed the use of high doses of a sine wave charge administered via bilaterally placed electrodes, resulting in considerable acute confusion and retrograde and anterograde memory disturbances (Consensus Conference, National Institutes of Health, 1985; Fink, 1979; Rudorfer et al., 1997). Although most commonly associated with the unwanted toxicities of ECT, at one time this generally unwanted state was felt to be potentially therapeutic in OCD. Korson (1949), for example, expressed the "hope that the repeated amnesias caused by the current would tend to converge and constitute a powerful aid in the removal of the conflictual material" (p. 41).

Thus, the clinical impression that confusion and memory loss were integral elements of a therapeutic anti-obsessional action of ECT at times led clinicians to deliberately induce what are today considered adverse effects of convulsive therapy (Walter et al., 1972). Kalinowsky and Hoch (1952) wrote of their experience with OC symptoms being "obliterated by the amnesia developing during a long course of closely spaced treatment" (p. 196), although they warned of the transient nature of such a response, with symptoms eventually returning at their original intensity. They also described the widespread use in the early days of ECT of an extreme form of the multiple ECT—intentionally causing regression to the point of delirium and incontinence—that would later be touted in modified form by Maletzky (1981). Results with such intense treatment were "disappointing, with the exception of a few obsessionals" (Kalinowsky & Hoch, 1952, p. 198).

A key argument against amnesia as the mechanism of action of ECT in OCD, as in depression, has been the successful development of ECT employing unilateral electrode placement (American Psychiatric Association, 1990; Consensus Conference, National Institutes of Health, 1985; Fink, 1979; Martin, 1996; Sackeim et al., 1993). With an adequate electrical stimulus initially applied over the nondominant cerebral hemisphere, unilateral ECT can result in generalized convulsions that for many, if not all, patients are therapeutic without appreciable confusion or memory loss (American Psychiatric Association, 1990; Consensus Conference, National Institutes of Health, 1985; Rudorfer et al., 1997; Sackeim et al., 1993). Recognizing this threat to the retrograde amnesia theory of ECT efficacy in OCD, Gruber (1971) wondered whether even in unilateral ECT amnesia might occur secondary to the barbiturate anesthesia that is an integral part of modern convulsive therapy. However, this does not appear to be the case (Rudorfer et al., 1997; Sackeim et al., 1993).

With better understanding of brain function and the neurobiology of OCD, more sophisticated hypotheses of the mechanisms of action of ECT have emerged in recent years. Khanna (1988) reviewed the preclinical and clinical evidence supporting a role of frontal lobe dysfunction in OCD, implying, although not directly demonstrating, that this neural substrate was related to his group's success in demonstrating short-term anti-obsessional activity of ECT (Khanna et al., 1988). Moreover, the serotonin hypothesis of OCD, extensively described throughout this volume, is consistent with a therapeutic role of ECT in this disorder. As reviewed in detail elsewhere (Fochtmann, 1994; Mann & Kapur, 1994; Rudorfer et al., 1997), in animal models electroconvulsive shock is associated with increased numbers of serotonin receptors and enhanced responsivity of serotonin-mediated behaviors; patients undergoing ECT show increased cerebrospinal fluid (CSF) concentrations of 5-hydroxy-indoleacetic acid (5-HIAA), the major metabolite of serotonin (Rudorfer et al., 1997). Casey and Davis (1994) hypothesized that "the overall increase in serotonergic function may be the common thread in the response of OCD to ECT and other somatic therapies" (p. 863).

A related area under intensive study is the putative role of dopamine, a catecholamine neurotransmitter, in the pathophysiology and treatment of OCD and other major mental disorders. Evidence from preclinical and clinical reports, the latter primarily including worsening of OC symptoms with chronic administration of dopaminergic agonists, has implicated this transmitter in mediating the symptomatology of OCD (Goodman et al., 1990). This connection is strengthened by the clinical utility of antipsychotic compounds in some subtypes of OCD, such as that associated with tic disorders (Goodman et al., 1993; Goodman et al., 1990; Jenike, 1993). Dopamine has also received attention in studies of the mechanisms of action of ECT. However, data showing enhanced dopaminergic-mediated behaviors in preclinical models of electroconvulsive shock (Fink, 1979; Fochtmann, 1994) and increased CSF concentrations of the major dopamine metabolite, homovanillic acid, in depressed patients treated with ECT (Mann & Kapur, 1994; Rudorfer et al., 1997) may not be consistent with a hyperdopaminergic model of illness. The challenges of studying the dopamine system in vivo (Goodman et al., 1990; Rudorfer et al., 1997) must be overcome to permit more definitive conclusions regarding the role of this transmitter in the pathophysiology of OCD and its response to treatment with ECT or pharmacotherapy (Goodman et al., 1993; Goodman et al., 1990; Jenike, 1993).

CONCLUSIONS

Even after 60 years of using ECT in clinical practice, little can be said with certainty regarding its value in the treatment of OCD. For the average patient with OCD, modern treatment entails administration of serotonergic pharmacotherapy, behavior treatment, or a combination of both, with no consideration of ECT. In the presence of concomitant severe depression or failure to respond to multiple conventional treatment trials, the situation is less clear. Under those more challenging circumstances, ECT may prove helpful. In some cases it appears that ECT is acting through its expected antidepressant mechanism, but some nondepressed OCD patients have reportedly been helped by ECT as well.

However, it must be recognized that an equally uncontrolled but sizable clinical database suggests that ECT is not—or is only transiently—useful in the treatment of the nondepressed OCD patient. The much-discussed obsessional man whose treatment with ECT by Mellman and Gorman (1984) was successful despite the apparent absence of depression highlights both the promise and the difficulty of translating the anecdotal literature into clinical practice. The possible interpretations of this case, ranging from ECT as a useful treatment for OCD to ECT as a useful treatment for the depression that may emanate from grief and present as pure obsessions (Jenike et al., 1987) each requires definitive study before being accepted and incorporated into treatment guidelines.

The chief obstacle to interpretation of the data gathered over the past several decades is the uncontrolled nature of the published reports, without any confirmatory controlled trials. The limitations of the anecdotal case reports and naturalistic patient series are legion, ranging from reporting bias and nonblinded raters to varying control over such confounding variables as comorbid conditions and medications.

In the absence of solid controlled data, clinical experience assumes special weight. In that light, the recent observations of M. Fink (personal communication, June 15, 1996) are of particular value in determining the effectiveness of ECT in the treatment of OCD in the clinical setting:

We treat 1–2 patients with OCD each year [with ECT]. In each instance, there is a dramatic response of OCD by the 6–8th treatment. We are often gratified by the response, the patient is enabled to make home visits, and self-congratulatory remarks surround the patient. Discharge planning begins and then all collapses. We have tried continuation ECT only to have OCD recur, occasionally with a vengeance, despite weekly ECT. In one instance, we repeated a course, only to fail to get relief. I can recall no case where an improvement persisted. In at least two recent instances, the family was willing to have us repeat the course of ECT, admitting the effects were transient, but arguing that the relief was helpful nevertheless. . . . Clinicians seem to have a favorite experience that ECT was helpful in severe OCD. But each clinician who has such a story, also states that he is reluctant to take on another case.

On balance, the present state of knowledge suggests that ECT has no role in the routine treatment of OCD. It may be helpful in the presence of significant secondary depression. For treatment-refractory OCD, clinical experience indicates that only a minority of patients are likely to respond. Defining and characterizing that subset of potential ECT responders should be subject to definitive controlled study.

Placebo-controlled trials with ECT, entailing so-called sham treatments with administration of premedications but no electrical stimulation (Rudorfer et al., 1997), are fraught with ethical and practical difficulties. However, particularly in view of the low placebo response rate of OCD, a straightforward clinical trial entailing randomization to ECT or to a serotonergic antidepressant, with repeated evaluation by raters blinded to treatment condition, would prove valuable. As a first step, the study of patients without a history of treatment refractoriness, but stratified for the presence of secondary depression could help establish a baseline of the true efficacy of ECT in OCD. Further comparisons of ECT with the various strategies outlined in this volume for treatment-refractory OCD could then address the issues of whether, when, and where to incorporate ECT into a treatment algorithm for refractory OCD.

As somatic treatments for mood and anxiety disorders evolve, their effects on OCD should be evaluated. For instance, early data have suggested a transient reduction in compulsive urges in patients with OCD undergoing repetitive transcranial magnetic stimulation (rTMS) (Greenberg et al., 1997), a novel subconvulsive intervention undergoing study primarily for antidepressant efficacy.

As with the more conventional use of ECT for depression (Rudorfer et al., 1997), continuation and maintenance treatment following any successful acute courses of ECT in OCD are important issues also requiring systematic study. Only with such scientifically sound data in hand can mental health professionals make optimal recommendations to their patients with OCD, and can individuals suffering from this disorder make truly informed decisions regarding their treatment.

REFERENCES

American Psychiatric Association. (1990). *The practice of electroconvulsive therapy: Recommendations for treatment, training, and privileging—A task force report.* Washington, DC: American Psychiatric Press.

Casey, D. A., & Davis, M. H. (1994). Obsessive-compulsive disorder responsive to electroconvulsive therapy in an elderly woman. *Southern Medical Journal, 87,* 862–864.

Consensus Conference, National Institutes of Health. (1985). Electroconvulsive therapy. *Journal of the American Medical Association, 254,* 2103–2108.

Cooper, J. E. (1970). Leyton's Obsessional Inventory. *Psychological Medicine, 1,* 47–64.

Farid, B. T., & Bulto, M. (1994). Buspirone in obsessional compulsive disorder: A prospective case study. *Pharmacopsychiatry, 27,* 207–209.

Fink, M. (1979). *Convulsive therapy: Theory and practice.* New York: Raven.

Fochtmann, L. J. (1994). Animal studies of electroconvulsive therapy: Foundations for future research. *Psychopharmacology Bulletin, 30,* 321–444.

Folstein, M., Folstein, S., McHugh, P. R. (1973). Clinical predictors of improvement after electroconvulsive therapy of patients with schizophrenia, neurotic reactions, and affective disorders. *Biological Psychiatry, 7,* 147–152.

Goodman, W. K., McDougle, C. J., Barr, L. C., Aronson, S. C., & Price, L. H. (1993). Biological approaches to treatment-resistant obsessive compulsive disorder. *Journal of Clinical Psychiatry, 54*(6, Suppl.), 16–26.

Goodman, W. K., McDougle, C. J., Price, L. H., Riddle, M. A., Pauls, D. L., & Leckman, J. F. (1990). Beyond the serotonin hypothesis: A role for dopamine in some forms of obsessive compulsive disorder? *Journal of Clinical Psychiatry, 51*(8, Suppl.), 36–43.

Greenberg, B. D., George, M. S., Martin, J. D., Benjamin, J., Schlaepfer, T. E., Altemus, M., Wassermann, E. M., Post, R. M., & Murphy, D. L. (1997). Effect of prefrontal repetitive transcranial magnetic stimulation in obsessive-compulsive disorder: A preliminary study. *American Journal of Psychiatry, 154,* 867–869.

Grimshaw, L. (1965). The outcome of obsessional disorder: A follow-up study of 100 cases. *British Journal of Psychiatry, 111,* 1051–1056.

Gruber, R. P. (1971). ECT for obsessive-compulsive symptoms (Possible mechanisms of action). *Diseases of the Nervous System, 32,* 180–182.

Hobson, R. F. (1953). Prognostic factors in electric convulsive therapy. *Journal of Neurology, Neurosurgery, and Psychiatry, 16,* 275–281.

Hodgson, R. J. & Rachman, S. (1972). Obsessional-compulsive complaints. *Behaviour Research and Therapy, 15,* 389–395.

Husain, M. M., Lewis, S. F., & Thornton, W. L. (1993). Maintenance ECT for refractory obsessive-compulsive disorder. *American Journal of Psychiatry, 150,* 1899–1900.

Insel, T. R., (Ed.) (1984). *Obsessive-compulsive disorder.* Washington, DC: American Psychiatric Press.

Jefferson, J. W., Altemus, M., Jenike, M. A., Pigott, T. A., Stein, D. J., & Greist, J. H. (1995). International psychopharmacology algorithm project report: E. Algorithm for the treatment of obsessive-compulsive disorder (OCD). *Psychopharmacology Bulletin, 31,* 487–500.

Jenike, M. A. (1993). Obsessive-compulsive disorder: Efficacy of specific treatments as assessed by controlled trials. *Psychopharmacology Bulletin, 29,* 487–499.

Jenike, M. A., Baer, L., & Minichiello, W. E. (1987). Somatic treatments for obsessive-compulsive disorders. *Comprehensive Psychiatry, 28,* 250–263.

Johnson, J., & Lucey, P. A. (1987). Encephalitis lethargica, a contemporary cause of catatonic stupor: A report of two cases. *British Journal of Psychiatry, 151,* 550–552.

Kahn, R. L., & Fink, M. (1959). Personality factors in behavioral response to electroshock therapy. *Journal of Neuropsychiatry, 1,* 45–49.

Kalinowsky, L. B., & Hoch, P. H. (1952). *Shock treatments, psychosurgery and other somatic treatments in psychiatry* (2nd ed.). New York: Grune & Stratton.

Kellner, C. H., Nixon, D. W., & Bernstein, H. J. (1991). ECT—Drug interactions: A review. *Psychopharmacology Bulletin, 27,* 595–609.

Khanna, S. (1988). Obsessive-compulsive disorder: Is there a frontal lobe dysfunction? *Biological Psychiatry, 24,* 602–613.

Khanna, S., Gangadhar, B. N., Sinha, V., Rajendra, P. N., & Channabasavanna, S. M. (1988). Electroconvulsive therapy in obsessive-compulsive disorder. *Convulsive Therapy, 4,* 314–320.

Korson, S. M. (1949). The successful treatment of an obsessive compulsive neurosis with narcosynthesis followed by daily electro-shocks. *Journal of Nervous and Mental Disease, 109,* 37–41.

Maletzky, B. M. (1981). *Multiple-monitored electroconvulsive therapy.* Boca Raton, FL: CRC.

Maletzky, B., McFarland, B., & Burt, A. (1994). Refractory obsessive compulsive disorder and ECT. *Convulsive Therapy, 10,* 34–42.

Mann, J. J., & Kapur, S. (1994). Elucidation of biochemical basis of the antidepressant action of electroconvulsive therapy by human studies. *Psychopharmacology Bulletin, 30,* 445–453.

Martin, B. A. (1996). Electroconvulsive therapy (ECT). In K. Z. Bezchlibnyk-Butler & J. J. Jeffries (Eds.), *Clinical handbook of psychotropic drugs* (6th ed., pp. 39–42). Seattle, WA: Hogrefe & Huber.

Mavissakalian, M., Turner, S. M., Michelson, L., & Jacob, R. (1985). Tricyclic antidepressants in obsessive-compulsive disorder: Antiobsessional or antidepressant agents? II. *American Journal of Psychiatry, 142,* 572–576.

Mellman, L. A., & Gorman, J. M. (1984). Successful treatment of obsessive-compulsive disorder with ECT. *American Journal of Psychiatry, 141,* 596–597.

Ottosson, J.-O. (1985). Use and misuse of electroconvulsive treatment. *Biological Psychiatry, 20,* 933–946.

Pollitt, J. (1975). Obsessional states. *British Journal of Psychiatry, 9,* 133–140.

Potter, W. Z., Manji, H. K., & Rudorfer, M. V. (1998). Tricyclics and tetracyclics. In A. F. Schatzberg & C. B. Nemeroff (Eds.), *The American Psychiatric Press textbook of psychopharmacology* (2nd ed., pp. 199–218). Washington, DC: American Psychiatric Press.

Potter, W. Z., Rudorfer, M. V., & Manji, H. K. (1991). The pharmacologic treatment of depression. *New England Journal of Medicine, 325,* 633–642.

Prudic, J., Haskett, R. F., Mulsant, B., Malone, K. M., Pettinati, H. M., Stephens, S., Greenberg, R., Rifas, S. L., & Sackeim, H. A. (1996). Resistance to antidepressant medications and short-term clinical response to ECT. *American Journal of Psychiatry, 153,* 985–992.

Rudorfer M. V., & Goodwin, F. K. (1993). Introduction. In C. E. Coffey (Ed.), *The clinical science of electroconvulsive therapy* (pp. xvii–xxi). Coffey CE, ed. Washington, DC: American Psychiatric Press.

Rudorfer, M. V., Henry, M. E., & Sackeim, H. A. (1997). Electroconvulsive therapy. In A. Tasman, J. Kay, & J. A. Lieberman (Eds.), *Psychiatry* (pp. 1535–1556). Philadelphia: Saunders.

Rudorfer, M. V., Linnoila, M., & Potter, W. Z. (1987). Accidental antidepressants: Search for specific action. In S. G. Dahl, L. F. Gram, S. M. Paul, & W. Z. Potter (Eds.), *Clinical pharmacology in psychiatry: IV. Selectivity in psychotropic drug action—Promises or problems?* (pp. 157–166). Heidelberg, Germany: Springer-Verlag.

Sackeim, H. A., Prudic, J., Devanand, D. P., Kiersky, J. E., Fitzsimons, L., Moody, B. J., McElhiney, M. C., Coleman, E. A., & Settembrino, J. M. (1993). Effects of stimulus intensity and electrode placement on the efficacy and cognitive effects of electroconvulsive therapy. *New England Journal of Medicine, 328,* 839–846.

Sichel, D. A., Cohen, L. S., Dimmock, J. A., & Rosenbaum, J. F. (1993). Postpartum obsessive compulsive disorder: A case series. *Journal of Clinical Psychiatry, 54,* 156–159.

Small, J. G. (1985). Efficacy of electroconvulsive therapy in schizophrenia, mania, and other disorders: II. Mania and other disorders. *Convulsive Therapy, 1,* 271–276.

Soyka, M., Niederecker, M., & Meyendorf, R. (1991). Erfolgreiche behandlung eines therapieresistenten zwangssyndroms durch elektrokrampftherapie [Successful treatment of a therapy-refractory compulsive syndrome by electroconvulsive therapy]. *Nervenarzt*, *62*, 448–450.

Walter, C. J. S., Mitchell-Heggs, N., & Sargant, W. (1972). Modified narcosis, ECT and antidepressant drugs: A review of technique and immediate outcome. *British Journal of Psychiatry, 120*, 651–662.

23

Neurosurgical Treatment of Obsessive-Compulsive Disorder

Michael A. Jenike
Harvard Medical School and Massachusetts General Hospital

With the use of appropriate medication and behavioral therapies to treat patients with obsessive-compulsive disorder (OCD), the outlook for the majority of patients is quite good. There are, however, a very small number of patients who not only remain refractory to all conventional treatments, but also are extremely ill and essentially nonfunctional. For such treatment-refractory and severely ill OCD patients, clinicians are obligated to consider any treatments, even neurosurgical options, that could possibly provide relief.

For over a decade I had not referred any OCD patients for neurosurgical intervention despite having one of the main centers performing these procedures in the same hospital. Conceptually, it did not seem logical that removing a small piece of brain tissue could improve the lives of such severely ill patients. In addition, we were aware of the controversial nature of these procedures and did not wish to get involved in such controversy unless there were likely to be tangible rewards for our patients. However, as our clinic followed an increasing number of patients, the population of refractory patients grew, and we eventually felt obliged to more fully investigate potential benefits of these operations. Our general principle has been this: Would I refer one of my close family members for such an operation or would I undergo it myself? If, after careful consideration of the available data, we could not answer in the affirmative, we would not recommend this option to our patients. Our retrospective (Jenike et al., 1991) and prospective (Baer et al., 1995) reviews of the outcomes and complications of one of these operations (cingulotomy) gave us reason for optimism (Jenike, Baer, & Minichiello, 1990).

OCD is one of the most commonly reported psychiatric disorders in the medical literature with regard to neurosurgical procedures (Mindus & Jenike, 1992). Modern stereotactic surgical interventions produce lesions only millimeters wide, which are placed with great precision in brain structures that appear to be important for symptom production. The clinician contemplating neurosurgical intervention for his or her otherwise intractable OCD patient will need to know general selection guidelines, indications and contraindications, the procedures available, their probable outcome, the hazards involved, what preoperative work-up is needed, and the rationale behind neurosurgery for OCD. It is also important to remember that the data are far from conclusive, that there remains much controversy, that all the published reports do not seem credible, and that there have been no controlled trials for these operations that likely have a significant placebo effect.

Several methodological issues must be borne in mind when interpreting studies from this field. Many earlier reports are problematic in that they are retrospective, diagnostic criteria have changed in the many years during which the studies were carried out, and outcome assessment instruments with documented validity and reliability were often not available at the time of the studies. Because the interventions are performed at only a few centers, very few physicians are experienced in the field. Accordingly, it is common that the same clinician responsible for the selection and the treatment of the patients also performed the determination of clinical outcome, sometimes after only a short period of observation.

Neurosurgical procedures are now routinely performed for intractable pain, Parkinson's disease, or uncontrollable epileptic seizures. However, only a few centers in the world have kept surgery as a therapeutic option for intractable mental illness (Snaith, 1987). Each center tends to favor one particular type of intervention, the choice of which most often seems determined by local tradition, rather than by comparison of the relative merits of different methods. Neurosurgical intervention for mental illness is prohibited in some countries, and citizens of these countries must go abroad for treatment. The operations most often reported in the treatment of refractory OCD are subcaudate tractotomy, limbic leucotomy, cingulotomy, and capsulotomy.

PATIENT SELECTION

It must be well documented that the illness is causing considerable suffering and the patient's psychosocial functioning is significantly reduced. Some of the severely ill candidates for such operations may suffer from a malignant form of OCD referred to by various terms such as *obsessional psychosis* (Insel & Akiskal, 1986; Robinson, Winnik, & Weiss, 1976; Solyom, DiNicola, Phil, Sookman, & Luchins, 1985) or a schizo-obsessive state (Jenike, Baer, Minichiello, Schwartz, & Carey, 1986), and the majority have comorbid conditions such as severe depression, body dysmorphic disorder, panic disorder, or personality disorders.

Patients must have failed all available and appropriate psychotropic medication trials as well as behavioral treatments. Each patient should have had adequate trials (at least 10 weeks at maximally tolerated dose) of clomipramine, fluoxetine, fluvoxamine, sertraline, paroxetine, and a monoamine oxidase inhibitor as well as augmentation of at least one of these drugs for 1 month with at least two of the following: lithium, clonazepam, and buspirone. If a patient has tics, a trial of augmentation with low-dose neuroleptic should be performed (McDougle et al., 1990). With recent preliminary data suggesting that venlafaxine may be helpful for OCD (Rauch, O'Sullivan, & Jenike, 1996), this should perhaps be added to the list of required medication trials. All patients must also have had an extended trial of behavior therapy consisting of exposure and response prevention. The illness must have been subject to intensive psychiatric treatment for such a lengthy period that it is, indeed, clearly refractory to standard treatment. In practice, most centers define this as a minimum of 5 years. Patients that meet these criteria may be candidates for neurosurgical intervention (see Table 23.1).

Contraindications (see Table 23.2) must be taken into consideration. Generally, these are not absolute contraindications and considerable clinical judgment and experience must be brought to bear on each case to determine who is and who is not a reasonable candidate. The use of multidisciplinary committees to evaluate these complicated patients is

TABLE 23.1
Indications for Neurosurgical Intervention

1. The patient fulfills the diagnostic criteria for OCD.
2. The duration of illness exceeds 5 years.
3. The disorder is causing substantial suffering.
4. The disorder is causing substantial reduction in the patient's psychosocial functioning.
5. Current treatment options tried systematically for at least 5 years have either been without appreciable effect on the symptoms, or must be discontinued due to intolerable side effects.
6. The prognosis, without neurosurgical intervention, is considered poor.
7. The patient gives informed consent.
8. The patient accepts participation in the preoperative evaluation program.
9. The patient accepts participation in the postoperative rehabilitation program.
10. There is a referring physician in the patient's local area willing to acknowledge responsibility for the postoperative long-term management of the patient.

TABLE 23.2
Contraindications for Neurosurgical Intervention

1. Age below 18 or over 65 years
2. The patient has another (current or lifetime) Axis I diagnosis (e.g., organic brain syndrome, delusional disorder, or current or recent alcohol or drug abuse) that substantially complicates function, treatment, or the patient's ability to comply with treatment, or leads to serious adverse events such as overdosage, suicide attempts, and so on. Some centers include somatoform disorders as a contraindication.
3. A complicating current Axis II diagnosis from Cluster A (e.g., paranoid personality disorder) or B (e.g., borderline, antisocial, or histrionic personality disorder) may constitute a relative contraindication. A current Cluster C personality disorder (e.g., avoidant or OC personality disorder) is generally not a contraindication because it may, in fact, disappear with successful treatment of the coexistent OCD.
4. The patient has a current Axis III diagnosis with brain pathology, such as moderate or marked cerebral atrophy, stroke, or tumor, or has undergone previous neurosurgical procedures that might produce complications.

crucial to ensure that patients meet inclusion and exclusion criteria, to eliminate all potential bias on the part of the treating clinicians, and to make certain that patients fully comprehend potential risks and benefits. The committee reviews each applicant's past psychiatric history including previous treatment in detail. They ensure that all inclusion and exclusion criteria are satisfied and adjudicate all cases in which questions arise; for example, whether or not a patient who has been through all the medication trials but, because of the illness, is unable to comply with reasonable trials of behavior therapy, should be allowed to undergo the operation. If deemed necessary, the committee meets with the patient and family.

AVAILABLE PROCEDURES

As noted, there are four procedures that are commonly used to treat severely ill OCD patients, including subcaudate tractotomy, limbic leucotomy, cingulotomy, and capsulotomy. The majority of these procedures are stereotactic interventions in which a device called a stereotactic frame is employed, permitting high accuracy (±1 mm in three dimensions) in placing bilateral lesions in intended targets, as determined with neuroradiological imaging. The operation may be performed under local anesthesia with light sedation, and while the targets are being lesioned, patients do not report subjective sensations. Neurosurgeons prefer to err on the conservative side by creating initial lesions that are quite small and performing a second intervention if warranted clinically.

Subcaudate Tractotomy

Subcaudate tractotomy was developed and is used in London. Unlike the majority of the other operations in which heated electrodes are used to make the lesions, in this procedure lesions are created by means of beta radioactive 90-Yttrium rods, 1 mm wide and 7 mm long, which are inserted stereotactically into the target area (Bartlett & Bridges, 1977; Göktepe, Young, & Bridges, 1975; Knight, 1972). Under general anesthesia bilateral burr holes 16 mm in diameter are made just above the frontal sinuses 15 mm from the midline. The targets, visualized by means of a ventriculogram, are located beneath the head of the caudate nucleus, in a brain region called the substantia innominata. The half-life of the beta emitter is approximately 60 hours, after which time the rods become ineffective. They are arranged as an array in two or three rows covering a volume approximately 20 mm wide, 18 mm long, and 5 mm thick. In the first few postoperative weeks the patient may suffer from episodes of confusion. The main indication for subcaudate tractotomy is not OCD, however, but unresponsive affective disorder (Göktepe et al., 1975; Lovett & Shaw, 1987). As of 1991, 1,200 psychiatric patients were reported to have undergone this procedure (Malizia, 1991).

There are only a couple of reports on the efficacy of this procedure in OCD patients. Strom-Olsen and Carlisle (1971) published results of 20 OCD patients who were operated on in the 1960s. Ten of these patients were reported to have either completely recovered or to have only slight residual symptoms without need for further treatment postoperatively (Chiocca & Martuza, 1990). However, the authors noted that four of these patients later relapsed. Göktepe et al. (1975) later reported on 18 OCD patients, 50% of whom reported total recovery or minimal symptoms. In these reports there were low rates of postoperative epilepsy and of adverse personality traits such as overeating, volubility, and extravagance.

In summary, clinical improvement was reported in 50% of 28 OCD patients who underwent this operation. The minimum period of follow-up was 1 year. There was no discussion in the reports about possible long-term effects from the radioactivity caused by the implanted yttrium seeds (Chiocca & Martuza, 1990).

Cingulotomy

Cingulotomy is, together with capsulotomy, the most commonly reported surgical procedure for the most severe anxiety disorders (Ballantine, Levy, Dagi, & Giriunas, 1977; Waziri, 1990) and has been the neurosurgical approach of choice since the 1970s in the United States and Canada not only for intractable pain and major depression (Ballantine, Bouckoms,

Thomas, & Giriunas, 1987; Bouckoms, 1991), but also for OCD (for a review, see Chiocca & Martuza, 1990; Mindus & Jenike, 1992). Cingulotomy is relatively benign, having a very low incidence of complications and transient or late side effects. It is not unusual, however, for a second operation (in which the lesion is extended) to be necessary. This is usually done 6 months to 1 year after the initial procedure when it is clear that no more benefit may be expected. The operation is performed under general anesthesia and involves only minimal hair shaving just behind the anterior hairline, usually causing no significant postoperative cosmetic problem. Bilateral burr holes approximately 12 mm in diameter are made and, with modern techniques, a magnetic resonance image is obtained to help visualize the targets. Electrodes are introduced stereotactically into two adjacent targets in the cingulate bundle on each side (see Fig. 23.1). Lesions are then created by the radio-frequency-induced heating of the tip of the electrodes to 80°C to 85°C for 100 seconds (Ballantine, 1985; Ballantine et al., 1987; Martuza, Chiocca, Jenike, Giriunas, & Ballantine, 1990).

One of the earliest reports of this operation was by Whitty, Duffield, and Tow (1952), who indicated that five OCD patients underwent open cingulotomy and four reportedly improved. The pronounced side effects on personality and behavior common with frontal lobotomy were not present with cingulotomy. Kullberg (1977) reported that 4 of 13 patients improved after cingulotomy. Foltz and White (1962) modified the operation by using the stereotactic method that was used by Ballantine et al. (1987) who reported that of 32 OCD patients, 25% were found to be functionally well and another 31% were markedly improved at follow-up.

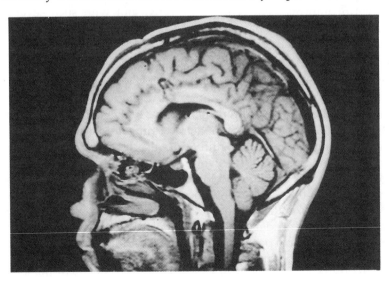

FIG. 23.1. Cingulotomy.

Side effects of this procedure include a 1% incidence of epilepsy that is controllable with anticonvulsant medication. There was no evidence of behavioral, emotional, or intellectual side effects.

Jenike and co-workers (1991) retrospectively evaluated 33 OCD patients who had undergone cingulotomy over a 25-year period. Using the Yale–Brown Obsessive Compulsive scale (Y–BOCS; Goodman, Price, Rasmussen, Mazure, Delgado, et al., 1989; Goodman, Price, Rasmussen, Mazure, Fleischmann, et al., 1989) as the dependent measure and very conservative criteria, the authors estimated that at least 25% to 30% of the patients benefited substantially from the intervention. Several patients attributed improvement primarily to postsurgery treatments. Excluding those participants, as many as 30% to 40% of these severely disabled patients believed they benefited substantially from the cingulotomy alone, and another 10% maintained that the surgery had augmented subsequent treatments. These operations were often done before the common usage of serotonin reuptake inhibitors, however; and with improved efficacy of nonsurgical treatment for OCD, future patients will likely be an even more refractory population than in previous studies.

In a recent prospective study (Baer et al., 1995), 18 severely ill OCD patients who underwent bilateral anterior cingulotomy were assessed by the same raters before surgery and 6 months later (using the Y–BOCS). Five patients (28%) met conservative criteria for treatment response, and three others (16%) were possible responders. The group improved significantly in mean functional status and no serious adverse events were found. In a disorder that characteristically waxes and wanes, fluctuation in level of improvement is to be expected, but with such severely ill patients, it is unlikely that they would improve significantly unless the intervention was helpful.

Limbic Leucotomy

In this multitarget procedure developed by Kelly (1972) and co-workers in the United Kingdom, subcaudate tractotomy lesions are produced, but in addition targets in the cingulum are also lesioned; this operation is basically a combination of the two previously described procedures. The proponents of this operation feel that lesions in both sites produce better results in OCD than lesions in either area alone (Mitchell-Heggs, Kelly, & Richardson, 1976; Richardson, 1973; for a review, see Kelly, 1980). After hair shaving, and under local or generalized anesthesia, bilateral burr holes are made 9.5 cm posterior to the nasion and 15 mm from the midline. Again, a ventriculogram is used to visualize the targets. Intraoperative stimulation of autonomic responses may be used to verify the accuracy of target placement, at least in the substantia innominata site (Kelly, 1972;

Mitchell-Heggs et al., 1976), although its usefulness has been questioned (Poynton, Bridges, & Bartlett, 1988). The cingulotomy lesions are produced by means of radio-frequency heated electrodes. Side effects include transient postoperative confusion and headache.

Mitchell-Heggs et al. (1976) reported 27 OCD patients, 89% of whom were improved 1 year postoperatively. This figure was disputed by Bartlett and Bridges (1977), who noted that the 89% improvement rate included patients who still had significant residual symptoms (Chiocca & Martuza, 1990). Transient side effects included headache, confusion, and perseverative behaviors, and there were no long-term personality changes or episodes of epilepsy. Including these patients, Kelly (1980) later provided an additional review of patients treated by limbic leucotomy and reported that 84% of 49 patients were improved at a mean of 20 months postoperatively.

Capsulotomy

Developed in Sweden, capsulotomy has been in use for more than three decades for the treatment of refractory anxiety OCD and has recently also been performed by neurosurgeons in the United States. Two surgical techniques for capsulotomy have been described, the radio frequency (RF) thermolesion, and the radiosurgical, or gamma capsulotomy.

Unfortunately, despite claims to the contrary, the Swedish group still does not know precisely where in the internal capsule the lesions should be made for optimal results and an open trial is now underway with the gamma knife in an effort to determine this (Rasmussen & Jenike, unpublished data).

In the RF thermolesion procedure, developed by the Swedish neurosurgeon Lars Leksell (Bingley, Leskell, Meyerson, & Rylander, 1977; Burzaco, 1981; for reviews, see Meyerson & Mindus, 1988; Mindus, 1991), the operation is performed under local anesthesia and light sedation. The coordinates of the target in the anterior limb of the internal capsule are determined with magnetic resonance imaging (MRI). Small bilateral burr holes are made just behind the coronary suture and monopolar electrodes with a diameter of 1.5 mm are inserted into the target area (see Fig. 23.2). Thermolesions are then produced by heating the uninsulated tip of the electrode for 75 seconds to approximately 75°C, creating a lesion approximately 4 mm wide and 15 to 18 mm long. While the lesions are being induced the patients do not report any subjective sensations. Postoperative headache is uncommon. As with other procedures in current use (with the possible exception of cingulotomy), a mild decrease in initiative and mental drive may be noted after RF capsulotomy during the first 2 to 3 postoperative months. This appears to correlate with circumlesional

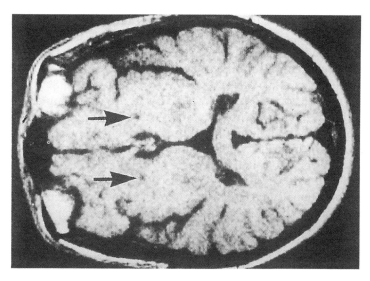

FIG. 23.2. Anterior capsulotomy.

edema, as determined with MRI, and disappears with resolution of edema (Mindus, unpublished results). After 3 months, initiative and mental drive have usually returned to preoperative levels.

The first report of the efficacy of this procedure was by Herner (1961), who found either good or fair results in 78% of 18 patients. A long-term follow-up by Bingley et al. (1977) reported that at a mean follow-up of 35 months, 71% of 35 patients were either free of symptoms or much improved. Of 24 patients who were unable to work preoperatively, 20 could resume work postoperatively. Kullberg (1977) reported that 10 of 13 patients improved with capsulotomy compared to only 4 of 13 cingulotomy patients. There was one serious side effect of capsulotomy, as one patient reportedly lost impulse control and became aggressive. In addition, several patients treated with capsulotomy demonstrated personality changes consisting of emotional shallowness, loss of initiative, diminution of inhibition, and mood elevation (Chiocca & Martuza, 1990). Fodstad, Strandman, Karlsson, and West (1982) reported two other patients who improved after capsulotomy.

The radiosurgical, or gamma capsulotomy technique, also developed by Leksell and co-workers (Leksell & Backlund, 1979; Mindus et al., 1987; Rylander, 1979), differs in that lesions are produced by cross-firing of approximately 200 narrow beams of 60-Cobalt gamma irradiation from a stereotactic gamma unit. Craniotomy and shaving are unnecessary. The biological effect of each individual gamma beam is negligible. At their point of focus, however, effects are combined to produce a radiosurgical lesion. The method has been successfully used now for more than 20 years in the treatment of acoustic neuromas, arteriovenous malformations, cancer pain, craniopharyngeomas, pituitary adenomas, and other deep-seated pathological processes. Gamma capsulotomy patients do not need to be hospitalized for postoperative care. As yet, the experience with gamma capsulotomy is considerably less extensive than that with the RF technique (Meyerson & Mindus, 1988; Mindus et al., 1987). The risk for radiation-induced malignancy is not elevated following this form of irradiation; no such case has been observed in the two decades during which the procedure has been in use.

In an ongoing investigation of gamma capsulotomy with a small number of patients, it appears that there is progressive improvement in OCD symptoms over 18 months at follow-up with a mean decrement in Y–BOCS scores of about 33% and similar improvement in depression and anxiety scores (Rasmussen & Jenike, unpublished data). It is important to keep in mind, however, that other postoperative treatments were not controlled and some of the patients had very intensive behavior therapy after the operation. For example, two of the patients with the best response actually lived with an experienced behavior therapist, who is involved in the study, for months after the operation.

With the advent of new technology, it is now clinically and ethically feasible to perform a sham operation as a control. With the gamma knife we are able to overcome ethical concerns that had prevented a controlled trial until now. With this technique, a small lesion can be precisely localized in a specific region of the brain without opening the cranium. Our group has proposed a study of 48 patients who are to be randomly assigned to receive either anterior capsulotomy ($n = 24$) or a sham procedure ($n = 24$). During the randomly assigned sham condition, each of the radiation ports is blocked with lead inserts by a research technician and even the surgeon is unaware if the ports are open or closed when he performs the operation. Patients and investigators performing examinations will remain blind to surgical condition, and clinical questionnaires, structured interviews, neuropsychological testing, and neuroimaging techniques (i.e., morphometric MRI) will be used to evaluate patients prior to the operation and again 6 months later to follow treatment response, adverse effects, and structural changes that may correlate with postoperative clinical improvement. At the 6-month point, the code (i.e., capsulotomy or sham procedure) is broken and the patient is then offered the capsulotomy operation if he or she received the sham procedure initially. This study has been approved by three Institutional Review Boards (Massachusetts General Hospital, Brown University, and Rhode Island Hospital) and will likely begin when the optimal lesion site in the anterior capsule has been determined by a currently ongoing dose finding trial (Rasmussen & Jenike, unpublished data).

WHICH IS THE BEST OPERATION?

Unfortunately, there have been few comparison studies of the operations already described. In addition, diagnostic criteria for OCD were not consistent across the studies, outcome standards varied among research groups, and complications were not always reported. Strikingly, there are essentially no negative reports of neurosurgical procedures reported in the medical literature, suggesting that only favorable or partly positive reports have been published. Keeping these variables and uncertainties in mind, it appears that limbic leucotomy was more effective than the other procedures, but there is considerable evidence from the literature that the group reporting these data was more liberal about their definitions of improvement than the other researchers. Certainly, no definitive conclusions about which procedure is best can be drawn without further research.

For reasons discussed later, most studies have not had control groups. Many investigators have instead compiled data from different reports, an approach marred by the obvious shortcoming that the procedures, including assessments of outcome and observation time, all vary considerably among studies. Moreover, outcome cannot be independently ascertained from some reports because the results are not given in sufficient detail. This makes direct comparison across studies difficult to interpret, but the method can provide an approximation of the outcome after various surgical interventions.

Some patients with only limited response to surgery report that treatment modalities that were ineffective before surgery seemed to give them at least some symptom relief postoperatively (Jenike et al., 1991; Mindus, 1991). This important information requires further study but offers some hope to the patient who has had a poor response to surgery alone.

SURGICAL RISKS

Neurosurgical complications include infection, hemorrhage, epileptic seizure, and weight gain. Despite occasional complications, Ballantine et al. (1987) reported no deaths in their series of 696 cingulotomies performed over a 25-year period in patients with various psychiatric disorders. Although infection and intracerebral hemorrhage cannot always be avoided, their sequelae can, provided that treatment is immediately instituted. The incidence of hemiplegia has been estimated at 0.03% following cingulotomy (Ballantine et al., 1987). No case of hemiplegia has been reported in relation to subcaudate tractotomy, limbic leucotomy, or capsulotomy. The risk of postoperative epilepsy following these interventions has been estimated to be less than 1% (Ballantine, 1985; Ballantine et al., 1987; Bingley & Person, 1978; Jenike et al., 1991), and these cases were usually easily controlled with antiseizure medications. Several authors have reported weight gain in capsulotomized patients (Bingley et al., 1977; Mindus, 1991), but it is unknown whether this phenomenon is specific for capsulotomy or occurs after other procedures as well.

The risk of neurosurgery for severe OCD compares favorably with that of stereotactic operations for nonpsychiatric illnesses; in one study on 243 consecutive stereotactic interventions for various neurological illnesses, 15 complications were noted including one death (Blaauw & Braakman, 1988).

Cognitive Alterations

The risk of negative effects on cognitive functioning following modern procedures have been carefully investigated by several independent researchers following cingulotomy (Ballantine, 1985; Corkin, 1980; Corkin & Hebben, 1981; Corkin, Twitchell, & Sullivan, 1979), subcaudate tractotomy (Bartlett & Bridges, 1977; Göktepe et al., 1975), limbic leucotomy (Mitchell-Heggs et al., 1976; for a review, see Kelly, 1980), and capsulotomy (Bingley et al., 1977; Burzaco, 1981; Vasko & Kullberg, 1979; for reviews, see Mindus, 1991; Sweet & Meyerson, 1990). Using identical or different psychometric tests pre- and postoperatively the authors found no evidence of reduced intellectual function related to surgery. On the contrary, patients tended to achieve better tests results after the operation, a finding for which several explanations have been advanced, including improved concentration ability, freedom from drugs, and practice effects of taking the tests a second time.

Specifically studying patients who had undergone cingulotomy, one group (Ballantine et al., 1987) noted that an independent study of a cohort of their patients was performed for the U.S. government by the Department of Psychology at the Massachusetts Institute of Technology, with reports indicating no evidence of lasting neurological, intellectual, personality, or behavioral deficits after cingulotomy (Corkin, 1980; Corkin et al., 1979). In fact, a comparison of preoperative and postoperative scores revealed modest gains in Wechsler IQ ratings (Lezak, 1995). The only apparent irreversible decrement identified by these investigators was a decrease in performance on the Taylor Complex Figure Test in patients over the age of 40 (Lezak, 1995).

Although not demonstrable with conventional tests, neurosurgical intervention may give rise to frontal lobe dysfunction. Therefore, it is important to evaluate the surgical candidate's cognitive functions, as a patient with preoperative abnormal or borderline test scores may run an elevated risk for postoperative changes.

Personality Alteration

It is of interest that postoperative side effects may, in fact, occur also in patients who do not undergo surgery. In their prospective, controlled study comparing the efficacy of intensive nonsurgical treatment with that of modified bimedial leucotomy in OCD, Tan, Marks, and Marset (1971) noted brusqueness and irritability (6 patients), apathy, laziness, and general blunting (two patients) among the 13 controls. In other words, symptoms and signs often regarded as postoperative side effects also appeared in the nonsurgery group.

According to anecdotal evidence, negative personality changes following current surgical procedures are rare. Because the interventions may be expected to influence, directly or indirectly, frontal lobe function and, hence, personality, more research is needed in this area. With regard to subcaudate tractotomy, tests were administered only at follow-up (Göktepe et al., 1975). Kelly (1980) gave the Leyton Obsessional Inventory (LOI; Cooper, 1970) to 26 OCD patients before and at 20 months after limbic leucotomy and found significant changes in obsessive features in the direction of normality. Unfortunately, the validity of the LOI is not well established.

A widely used personality instrument, the Eysenck Personality Inventory (Eysenck, 1965), was administered prospectively to 15 patients undergoing capsulotomy (Bingley et al., 1977; Rylander, 1979), and in no case were negative personality changes observed after capsulotomy.

It is well known that impulsiveness is one of the most conspicuous symptoms of frontal lobe dysfunction (for a review, see Stuss & Benson, 1986). For this reason, a method likely to detect negative personality changes following surgery must cover impulsiveness and related features such as psychopathy, hostility, and aggressiveness. One such instrument is the Karolinska Scales of Personality (KSP), developed by Schalling, Åsberg, Edman, and Oreland (1987). It contains scales measuring traits related to frontal lobe function and scales reflecting different dimensions of anxiety proneness. A large number of studies have been performed by independent investigators who have shown the KSP to differentiate between diagnostic subgroups and to correlate significantly with biological markers for vulnerability to certain psychopathological conditions. Mindus and Nyman (1991) gave the KSP to 24 consecutive patients before and at 1 year after RF capsulotomy. Before surgery, deviant scores were obtained on 5 of the 15 KSP scales, 4 of which are scales related to anxiety proneness. At 1 year after capsulotomy, statistically significant decreases were noted on eight of the scales with normal scores on all but two scales (which remained borderline). In particular, the scores on scales related to impulsiveness, psychopathy, hostility, and aggressiveness were within the normal range. Negative personality changes are not likely to occur after modern surgical procedures involving areas thought to be involved in OCD (Mindus, Nyman, Rosenquist, Rydin, & Meyerson, 1988).

It must be remembered, however, that these conclusions are based on observations made on groups of participants and do not preclude that negative changes could occur in individual patients.

Suicide

In the review by Waziri (1990) only 3% of the patients were reported to be worse or dead at follow-up. Among the dead was one suicide. It is important, however, to keep in mind that suicide may well be a complication of surgical procedures, at least in very depressed OCD patients, as Jenike et al. (1991) found that 4 of 33 patients who had undergone cingulotomy for OCD had died by suicide at follow-up averaging 13 years. Looking back over these patients' records, each patient that had committed suicide had been noted to suffer from severe depression with prominent suicidal ruminations when they were first evaluated for cingulotomy. Even though they all met criteria for OCD, they had extensive comorbid disease. None of the OCD patients who were not noted to be suicidal at baseline assessment became suicidal after the operation. It remains possible that disappointment secondary to failure of this last-resort treatment could have contributed to suicide in these predisposed patients. Ballantine et al. (1987) discussed in more detail the issue of suicide in psychiatric patients who have undergone cingulotomy.

Patients with a poor response to surgery may be at increased risk for suicide (Jenike et al., 1991). Therefore, these individuals should be informed of two things: First, treatments that were ineffective before surgery might be helpful postoperatively. Second, neurosurgeons prefer to err on the conservative side, creating only small initial lesions, permitting a second intervention if warranted clinically.

RISK OF NONINTERVENTION

In most surgery studies, patients have a duration of illness that averages more than 15 years. This tells something of the prognosis. The risk for social, somatic, and mental complication (including suicide) in this group of patients cannot be overrated. A small number of patients have been described, who were eligible for intervention but never operated on for different reasons (Ballantine et al., 1987; Mindus, 1991). Their conditions remained the same, and some of them eventually committed suicide. The physician with a patient with malignant OCD, for whom all therapeutic options have been exhausted, has the delicate task of weighing the risk of intervention against the risk of nonintervention. Deferring the decision to operate on a given patient may not spare him or her complications.

POSTOPERATIVE CARE

Neurosurgical intervention should be regarded as an adjunct to rehabilitation made possible through symptomatic modification. Therefore, the postoperative treatment program should be instituted early, preferably under the guidance of someone (e.g., the referring physician) who knows the patient well. Behavior treatment with exposure and response prevention should be reinstituted shortly after the operation.

NEUROBIOLOGIC RATIONALE FOR OPERATIONS

Although there are a number of hypotheses, it remains unknown why these procedures might improve symptoms in some patients and not in others. No clear predictors of which OCD patients might improve overall or if a specific operation may help one type of patient have been identified. It appears that different surgical approaches all have the common objective of severing interconnections between dorsolateral and the orbitomedial areas of the frontal lobes and limbic and thalamic structures. In man, it has been shown that lesions in the substantia innominata following subcaudate tractotomy cause extensive degeneration in the ventral portion of the internal capsule (Corsellis & Jack, 1973). The fiber tract degeneration can be traced back to the dorsomedial nucleus of the thalamus, which has extensive interconnections with various parts of the limbic system (Modell, Mountz, Curtis, & Greden, 1989). These observations indicate that lesions in one region may affect the function of other brain regions. Conversely, there is evidence to show that different approaches may affect similar clinical conditions. For example, lesions in the orbitofrontal area as in subcaudate tractotomy, or in the orbitofrontal-thalamic tract as in capsulotomy, or in the midline thalamic nuclei as in certain forms of thalamotomy (Hassler & Dieckman, 1973) all have been associated with improvement in OCD. In other words, although different surgical interventions have different stereotactic targets, they might affect, directly or indirectly, the same brain system(s).

Despite the lack of a specific identified brain abnormality in OCD, there is growing evidence that the syndrome has a biologic causation (see Rauch & Jenike, 1993, for review). Only recently have morphometric MRI analyses revealed that OCD patients (only studied in females thus far) have diminished white matter when their brains have been compared to carefully matched control individuals (Breiter et al., 1994; Jenike et al., 1996). It remains intuitively appealing to search for underlying localized brain pathology; however, current thinking has shifted away from ascribing complex tasks like speech or associative memory to particular areas of the brain. Instead, circuits in many different areas of the brain are called on to interact simultaneously using parallel distributed processing. This shift in thinking has been bolstered by neuroanatomical techniques that have demonstrated an ever increasing complexity of interconnectivity between any two areas of the brain. Abnormalities in frontal lobe and basal ganglia function (Jenike et al., 1990; Modell et al., 1989; Rauch & Jenike, 1993) in patients with OCD have led to hypotheses about the disorder's pathogenesis that emphasize possible aberrations in the neural circuits that connect these two regions.

Initially, interest in the neurologic basis of OCD focused on the basal ganglia. Several neurologic syndromes known to affect the basal ganglia have been associated with obsessive and compulsive symptoms (Cummings & Frankel, 1985; LaPlane et al., 1989; Weilburg et al., 1989; Williams, Owen, & Heath, 1988). Obsessions, compulsions, and tics were frequently found in patients who suffered from von Economos encephalitis. These patients often had neuropathologic lesions in the basal ganglia post mortem (Schilder, 1938). Osler noted obsessive-compulsive (OC) symptoms in patients with Sydenham's chorea, another illness that was subsequently found to involve basal ganglia pathology fever (Swedo, Rapoport, et al., 1989). Tourette's syndrome is another disease that probably involves the basal ganglia and is associated with a higher than expected frequency of OCD (Pitman, Green, Jenike, & Mesulam, 1987). Although clinical evidence is for the most part anecdotal, it supports the hypothesis that OCD involves abnormalities of the basal ganglia (Cummings & Frankel, 1985; Kellner et al., 1991; Luxenberg et al., 1988). The ego dystonic nature of obsessions and the resistance toward the compulsions exhibited by most patients fit well with this hypothesis because the basal ganglia are thought to be the site for automatic motor planning and fixed action patterns. Rapoport and colleagues proposed a neuroethologic model of OCD based on abnormalities in fixed action patterns in the basal ganglia. As Osler may have predicted, careful studies of Sydenham's chorea patients (where antibasal ganglia antibodies have been found) confirmed a higher than expected frequency of OCD in patients who developed this complication of rheumatic fever (Swedo, Rapoport, et al., 1989). Taken together, these data are suggestive of striatal abnormality in at least some patients with OCD. They do not, however, address whether the abnormal findings are reflective of primary pathology versus some compensatory or secondary process.

At the same time, evidence is accumulating that there are also abnormalities in frontal lobe function in OCD. The frontal lobes are associated with neuropsychological functions of programming, regulating, anticipating, controlling, and verifying behaviors. Frontal lobe pathology is correlated with inflexibility, decreased response inhibition, perseveration, and stereotypy—characteristics reminiscent of OCD symptomatology (Otto, 1990). Some neuropsychological investigations of OCD patients have implicated frontal lobe dysfunction (Behar et al., 1984; Flor-Henry, 1983; Flor-Henry, Yeudall, Koles, & Howarth, 1975), and others failed to demonstrate frontal findings but did find memory deficits (Otto, 1990; Zielinski, Taylor, & Juzwin, 1991). A controlled electrophysiological study of OCD patients demonstrated frontal cortical abnormalities in evoked potentials (Savage et al., 1994), and case reports have noted electroencephalogram abnormalities consistent with frontal epileptic foci (Ward, 1988). On the other hand, radiological studies have not revealed gross structural pathology in the frontal lobes of OCD patients (Behar et al., 1984; Garber, Ananth, Chiu, Griswold, & Oldendorf, 1989; Insel, 1992; Insel, Donnelly, Lalakea, Alterman, & Murphy, 1983; Jenike et al., 1996). There is, however, evidence suggesting subtle frontal metabolic or compositional abnormalities. Garber et al. (1989), comparing nuclear magnetic resonance brain images of 32 OCD patients and 14 normal controls, found that OCD patients had prolonged T1 relaxation time in right frontal white matter and increased right minus left frontal differences in white matter T1. Furthermore, right minus left T1 differences for orbitofrontal cortex correlated with OCD symptom severity in the subset of patients who were untreated or who had positive family histories of OCD. The underlying pathophysiological significance of these frontal findings is unknown. Nonetheless, the finding of a localized abnormality that correlates with symptom severity strongly suggests frontal involvement.

Perhaps the most compelling clinical evidence for implicating these neuroanatomically defined regions in the pathogenesis of OCD comes from positron emission tomography (PET) studies. Three groups have now found abnormalities in regional metabolic rates in the orbitomedial frontal and caudate nuclei of OCD patients versus controls. Baxter and colleagues (Baxter et al., 1987; Baxter et al., 1988) compared 14 OCD patients with equal numbers of normal controls and patients with unipolar major depression. In OCD patients, compared to the other two groups, 18-FDG PET revealed significantly elevated absolute glucose metabolic rates for the whole cerebral hemispheres, caudate nuclei, and orbital gyri. Furthermore, metabolic rates in the left orbital gyrus, divided by those of the ipsilateral hemisphere ("normalized" metabolic rates) were significantly higher than those found in normal controls. Nordahl et al. (1989) studied eight OCD patients and compared them with 30 normal volunteers. Again 18-FDG PET found normalized regional brain metabolic rates high in OCD patients compared with the controls in both orbital gyri, but normalized OCD caudate rates similar to those in normal controls. Swedo, Shapiro, et al. (1989) studied 18 childhood-onset OCD patients with 18-FDG and reported increased absolute glucose metabolism in left orbital and right sensorimotor regions and bilaterally in the anterior cingulate gyri (the site of cingulotomy lesioning) and lateral prefrontal areas. Normalized values were significantly increased in right lateral prefrontal and left anterior cingulate regions only. In addition there was a significant correlation between absolute and normalized right orbital glucose metabolic activity and severity of OCD symptoms. In addition, six patients, who failed to respond to a subsequent trial of clomipramine, had significantly higher right anterior cingulate and right orbital metabolism than 11 drug-responsive patients.

Rauch et al. (1994) found that when OCD patients are stimulated to have obsessional symptoms while in the PET scanner, there is significant activation compared to baseline in the orbital frontal regions, thalamus, and cingulate gyri, suggesting that there may be a circuit which influences OCD symptoms. This circuit may be interfered with by any of the neurosurgical procedures that are performed for refractory OCD. Whether changes in this circuit's activity occur postoperatively has not as yet been determined.

Two recent reports have found that there are regional decreases in metabolic activity that correlate with the decrease in severity of OC symptoms as measured by the Y–BOCS following successful pharmacologic or behavioral treatment (Baxter et al., 1992; Swedo et al., 1992). One reported decreases in caudate activity and the other decreases in right orbitofrontal metabolism. Furthermore, Baxter et al. (1992) found that in untreated patients with OCD, abnormal metabolic activity is significantly correlated across the ipsilateral orbitofrontal and caudate regions.

Neuroanatomic evidence that pointed to the existence of functional circuits that link cortical, striatal, and thalamic nuclei in a series of topographically defined feed-forward loops was pointed out by Alexander (1986). He described the basal ganglia as a funnel through which information between thalamus and cortex must pass. In this context, the basal ganglia separately influence at least five different pathways, each via a corresponding basal ganglia-thalamocortical circuit (motor, oculomotor, dorsolateral prefrontal, orbitofrontal, and anterior cingulate). In recent hypotheses for the pathoanatomical basis (or bases) of OCD, these loops between the basal ganglia, limbic system, and frontal lobes are ascribed important pathogenetic functions. These brain regions contain the targets of current neurosurgical intervention in OCD. For example, the limbs of one of these proposed loops, the frontal-striatal-pallidal-thalamic-frontal loop (Modell et al., 1989), are believed to pass through the anterior limb of the internal capsule, the target of capsulotomy. It has been suggested (Kelly, 1980; Martuza et al., 1990) that there may be two important components of the neuroanatomy of OCD: the OC component and an anxiety component mediated through the Papez circuit, which includes the cingulum bundle, the target of cingulotomy.

These findings prompted several authors to propose a neuroanatomic model of dysfunction in OCD that was based on the existence of abnormal activity in fronto-striatal-pallido-thalamic-frontal loops in the brain (Baxter, Schwartz, Guze, Bergman, & Szuba, 1990; Insel, 1992; Modell et al., 1989; Rapoport et al., 1981). The loop of primary interest to those interested in psychiatric symptoms has two components: an orbitofrontal-thalamic interconnection mediated by the excitatory neurotransmitter glutamic acid and an orbitofrontal-striatal-thalamic interconnection mediated by various neurotransmitters such as glutamate, dopamine, gamma-aminobutyric acid, and serotonin. Modell et al. (1989) hypothesized that the latter interconnection modulates the neuronal activity of the former. According to this model, overactivity in the orbitofrontal-thalamic interconnection would give rise to obsessive thoughts and compulsive rituals. In the normal state, the orbitofrontal area would at the same time stimulate the caudate, which in turn would stimulate the pallidum, which would in turn inhibit activity of the medial thalamic nuclei. This would modulate and correct the overactivity of the orbitofrontal-thalamic interconnection. In patients with OCD, dysfunctions arise in either the modulatory activity of the fronto-caudate-pallido-thalamic interconnection or in the primary activity of the orbitofrontal-thalamic interconnection. In theory, lesions in these circuits might serve to compensate for dysfunction associated with the clinical state of OCD.

As already noted, the surgical literature provides considerable anecdotal evidence for lessening of OCD symptoms in some patients following cingulotomy, limbic leucotomy, subcaudate tractotomy, and anterior capsulotomy. All of these procedures interrupt connections between the frontal lobes and thalamic nuclei with significant limbic input (dorsomedial and anterior thalamic nuclei). The percentage of neurons that participate in the previously mentioned circuits versus the percentage that project directly to the frontal lobe is presently unknown. As noted, the precise effect of neurosurgical intervention in OCD is also unknown. Anterior capsulotomy has the distinct advantage of being the most neuroanatomically discrete of the surgical procedures used to date. However, in spite of the technical precision of the procedure, the lesion placement and size has yet to be determined precisely. To date, size and placement of the lesion has not been guided by any empirical evidence from animal studies; and such studies are not likely to be helpful because these regions differ quite remarkably between nonhuman primates and humans.

Preliminary evidence suggests that OCD patients do not improve immediately after surgery, but that several weeks or months are required for positive clinical effects to be fully manifested. Thus, it is likely that secondary nerve degeneration or metabolic alterations in brain areas other than in the region that is actually lesioned are involved in the therapeutic effect. New methods utilizing magnetic resonance (MR) spectroscopy of N-acetyl-aspartate, a putative measure of neuron integrity, may allow for serial assessment of downstream effects of surgical lesions. The proposed pathogenetic imbalance of the functions of these brain regions appears to be somehow counteracted by neurosurgical intervention, the net effect being experienced by some patients as symptom relief.

CONCLUSIONS

As noted earlier, it is important to keep in mind that the data on neurosurgery for intractable and malignant OCD are far from conclusive, that there remains much controversy, that all the published reports do not seem credible, and that there have been no controlled trials for these operations that likely have a significant placebo effect. It is important to convey this uncertainty to patients so that they have an accurate perspective. When these operations have been oversold, some patients will not do the considerable work needed to get better with behavior therapy because they feel there is an easier way to improve.

We cannot be sure that rater bias was eliminated in any of the studies that have been reviewed or that the nonrandom treatment of patients with surgical procedures might not have affected the postoperative assessment to some degree. The theoretical ideal of a randomized double-blind trial would be required to solve these problems; however, the feasibility and ethics of such a study have been discussed. The gamma knife will eventually allow a controlled trial to be undertaken. Until now we had to rely on a more traditional method of evaluation by objectively reviewing the responses of patients who had already received these treatments.

Progressive improvement over time has been reported after some of these surgical procedures, and there is some evidence that other treatments, including pharmacotherapy and behavior therapy, are more likely to be successful after the operation than before. Because the vast majority of patients who have undergone surgery were severely and chronically disabled, it is possible that these procedures assisted in alleviating some of their symptoms, and the results of the cumulative studies strongly support the need for continued research in this area. It is currently impossible to determine which surgical procedure is best for a particular patient. Head-to-head comparison studies are not yet underway, and it may be years before we have comparative data. Until such data are available, clinicians should probably work with the surgical team closest to them.

When nonsurgical treatments have failed, there is evidence that at least partial relief can be obtained in some OCD patients by surgery. In the future, it will be important to maximize our understanding of these procedures. When the technology is available, prospective patients should be studied before and after surgery with single photon emission computed tomography or PET scans and with MRI. As already noted, usually patients do not benefit immediately; a few weeks or months are required for optimal improvement. Sequential scans might allow researchers to follow the course of metabolic and structural lesions in an effort to understand what parts of the brain are affected in patients who respond and also in those who are not helped. With modern technology it is possible to correlate lesion site and size with clinical outcome. The identification of clinical subgroups of patients with a particularly high likelihood of improvement after a neurosurgical procedure also merits further study.

REFERENCES

Alexander, G. E. (1986). Parallel organization of functionally segregated circuits linking basal ganglia and cortex. *Annual Review of Neuroscience, 9*, 357–381.

Baer, L., Rauch, S. L., Ballantine, H. T., Martuza, R., Cosgrove, R., Cassem, E., Giriunas, I., Manzo, P., Dimino, C., & Jenike, M. A. (1995). Cingulotomy for intractable obsessive-compulsive disorder: Prospective long-term follow-up of 18 patients. *Archives of General Psychiatry, 52*, 384–392.

Ballantine, H. T., Jr. (1985). Neurosurgery for behavioral disorders. In R. H. Wilkins & S. S. Rengachary (Eds.), *Neurosurgery* (p. 2527). New York: Elsevier/North-Holland Biomedical.

Ballantine, H. T., Jr., Bouckoms, A. J., Thomas, E. K., & Giriunas, I. E. (1987). Treatment of psychiatric illness by stereotactic cingulotomy. *Biological Psychiatry, 22*, 807–819.

Ballantine, H. T., Jr., Levy, B. S., Dagi, T. F., & Giriunas, I. B. (1977). Cingulotomy for psychiatric illness: Report of 13 years' experience. In W. Sweet, S. Obrador, & J. G. Martin-Rodriguez (Eds.), *Neurosurgical treatment in psychiatry, pain and epilepsy* (p. 333). Baltimore: University Park Press.

Bartlett, J. R., & Bridges, P. K. (1977). The extended subcaudate tractotomy lesion. In W. H. Sweet, S. Obrador, & J. G. Martin-Rodriguez (Eds.), *Neurosurgical treatment in psychiatry, pain, and epilepsy* (p. 387). Baltimore: University Park Press.

Baxter, L. R., Schwartz, J. M., Guze, B. H., Bergman, K., & Szuba, M. P. (1990). Neuroimaging in obsessive-compulsive disorder. In M. A. Jenike, L. Baer, & W. E. Minichiello (Eds.), *Obsessive compulsive disorders: Theory and management* (2nd ed., pp. 167–188). Chicago: Yearbook Medical.

Baxter, L. R., Phelps, M. E., Mazziotta, J. C., Guze, B. H., Schwartz, J. M., & Selin, C. E. (1987). Local cerebral glucose metabolic rates in obsessive-compulsive disorder. *Archives of General Psychiatry, 44*, 211–218.

Baxter, L. R., Schwartz, J. M., Bergman, K. S., Szuba, M. P., Guze, B. H., Mazziotta, J. C., Alazraki, A., Selin, C. E., Ferng, H. K., & Munford, P. (1992). Caudate glucose metabolic rate changes with both drug and behavior therapy for OCD. *Archives of General Psychiatry, 49*, 681–689.

Baxter, L. R., Schwartz, J. M., Mazziotta, J. C., Phelps, M. E., Pahl, J. J., Guze, B. H., & Fairbanks, L. (1988). Cerebral glucose metabolic rates in nondepressed patients with obsessive-compulsive disorder. *American Journal of Psychiatry, 145*, 1560–1563.

Behar, K., Rapoport, J. L., Berg, C. J., Denckla, M. B., Mann, L., Cox, C., Fedio, P., Zahn, T., & Wolfman, M. G. (1984). Computerized tomography and neuropsychological test measures in adolescents with obsessive-compulsive disorder. *American Journal of Psychiatry, 141*, 363–368.

Bingley, T., Leksell, L., Meyerson, B. A., & Rylander, G. (1977). Long term results of stereotactic capsulotomy in chronic obsessive-compulsive neurosis. In W. H. Sweet, S. Obrador, & J. G. Martin-Rodriguez (Eds.), *Neurosurgical treatment in psychiatry* (pp. 287–299). Baltimore: University Park Press.

Bingley, T., & Person, A. (1978). EEG studies on patients with chronic obsessive-compulsive neurosis before and after psychosurgery. *Electronenc Clin Neurophys, 44*, 691.

Blaauw, G., & Braakman, R. (1988). Pitfalls in diagnostic stereotactic brain surgery. *Acta Neurosurgery, 42*(Suppl.), 161.

Bouckoms, A. J. (1988). Ethics of psychosurgery. *Acta Neuroschirurgica, 44*(Suppl.), 173.

Bouckoms, A. J. (1991). The role of stereotactic cingulotomy in the treatment of intractable depression. In J. A. Amsterdam (Ed.), *Advances in neuropsychiatry and psychopharmacology 2: Refractory depression* (p. 2). New York: Raven Press.

Breiter, H. C. R., Filipek, P. A., Kennedy, K. N., Baer, L., Pitcher, D. A., Olivares, M. J., Renshaw, P. F., Caviness, V. S., Jr., & Jenike, M. A. (1994). Retrocallosal white matter abnormalities in patients with obsessive-compulsive disorder. *Archives of General Psychiatry, 51*, 663–664.

Burzaco, J. (1981). Stereotactic surgery in the treatment of obsessive-compulsive neurosis. In C. Perris, G. Struwe, & B. Jansson (Eds.), *Biological psychiatry* (p. 1103). Amsterdam: Elsevier/North-Holland Biomedical.

Chiocca, E. A., & Martuza, R. L. (1990). Neurosurgical therapy of obsessive-compulsive disorder. In M. A. Jenike, L. Baer, & W. E. Minichiello (Eds.), *Obsessive-compulsive disorders: Theory and management* (pp. 283–294). Chicago: Year Book Medical.

Cooper, J. (1970). The Leyton Obsessional Inventory. *Psychological Medicine, 1*, 48–64.

Corkin, S. (1980). A prospective study of cingulotomy. In E. S. Valenstein (Ed.), *The psychosurgery debate* (p. 264). San Francisco: Freeman.

Corkin, S., & Hebben, N. (1991). *Subjective estimates of chronic pain before and after psychosurgery or treatment in a pain unit.* Paper presented at the Third World Congress on Pain of the International Association for the Study of Pain, Edinburgh, Scotland.

Corkin, S., Twitchell, T. E., & Sullivan, E. V. (1979). Safety and efficacy of cingulotomy for pain and psychiatric disorder. In E. R. Hitchcock, H. T. Ballantine, & B. A. Myerson (Eds.), *Modern concepts in psychiatric surgery* (pp. 253–272). New York: Elsevier/North-Holland.

Corsellis, J., & Jack, A. B. (1973). Neuropathological observations on yttrium implants and on undercutting in the orbito-frontal areas of the brain. In L. V. Laitinen & K. E. Livingston (Eds.), *Surgical approaches in psychiatry* (p. 90). Baltimore: University Park Press.

Cummings, J. L., & Frankel, M. (1985). Gilles de la Tourette syndrome and the neurological basis of obsessions and compulsions. *Biological Psychiatry, 20*, 1117–1126.

Eysenck, S. B. (1965). A new scale for personality measurements in children. *British Journal of Educational Psychiatry, 35*, 362–367.

Flor-Henry, P. (1983). *Cerebral basis of psychopathology.* Boston: John Wright.

Flor-Henry, P., Yeudall, L. T., Koles, Z. J., & Howarth, B. G. (1975). Neuopsychological and power spectral EEG investigations of the obsessive compulsive syndrome. *Biological Psychiatry, 14,* 119–130.

Fodstad, H., Strandman, E., Karlsson, B., & West, K. A. (1982). Treatment of chronic obsessive-compulsive states with stereotactic anterior capsulotomy or cingulotomy. *Acta Neuroschirurgica, 62,* 1–23.

Foltz, E. L., & White, L. E. (1962). Pain relief by frontal cingulotomy. *Journal of Neurosurgery, 19,* 89.

Garber, H. J., Ananth, J. V., Chiu, L. C., Griswold, V. J., & Oldendorf, W. H. (1989). Nuclear magnetic resonance study of obsessive-compulsive disorder. *American Journal of Psychiatry, 146,* 1001–1005.

Göktepe, E. O., Young, L. B., & Bridges, P. K. (1975). A further review of the results of stereotactic subcaudate tractotomy. *British Journal of Psychiatry, 126,* 270.

Goodman, W. K., Price, L. H., Rasmussen, S. A., Mazure, C., Delgado, P., Heninger, G. R., & Charney, D. S. (1989). The Yale–Brown Obsessive Compulsive Scale (Y–BOCS): Part II. Validity. *Archives of General Psychiatry, 46,* 1012–1018.

Goodman, W. K., Price, L. H., Rasmussen, S. A., Mazure, C., Fleischmann, R., Hill, C. L., Heninger, G. R., & Charney, D. S. (1989). The Yale–Brown Obsessive Compulsive Scale (Y–BOCS): Part I. Development, use, and reliability. *Archives of General Psychiatry, 46,* 1006–1011.

Hassler, R., & Dieckman, G. (1973). Relief of obsessive-compulsive disorders, phobias and tics by stereotactic coagulation of the rostral intralaminar and medial-thalamic nuclei. In L. V. Laitinen & K. E. Livingston (Eds.), *Surgical approaches in psychiatry* (p. 206). Baltimore: University Park Press.

Insel, T. R. (1992). Toward a neuroanatomy of OCD. *Archives of General Psychiatry, 49,* 739–744.

Insel, T. R., & Akiskal, H. S. (1986). Obsessive-compulsive disorder with psychotic features: A phenomenologic analysis. *American Journal of Psychiatry, 143,* 1527.

Insel, T. R., Donnelly, E. F., Lalakea, M. L., Alterman, I. S., & Murphy, D. L. (1983). Neurological and neuropsychological studies of patients with obsessive-compulsive disorder. *Biological Psychiatry, 18,* 741–751.

Jenike, M. A., Baer, L., Ballantine, H. T., Martuza, R. L., Tynes, S., Giriunas, I., Buttolph, L., & Cassem, N. (1991). Cingulotomy for refractory obsessive-compulsive disorder: A long term follow-up of 33 patients. *Archives of General Psychiatry, 48,* 548.

Jenike, M. A., Baer, L., & Minichiello, W. E. (Eds.). (1998). *Obsessive-compulsive disorders: Practical management* (3rd ed.). Chicago: Mosby.

Jenike, M. A., Baer, L., Minichiello, W. E., Schwartz, C. E., & Carey, R. J. (1986). Coexistent obsessive-compulsive disorder and schizotypal personality disorder: A poor prognostic indicator. *Archives of General Psychiatry, 43,* 296.

Jenike, M. A., Breiter, H. C. R., Baer, L., Kennedy, K. N., Savage, C. R., Olivares, M. J., O'Sullivan, R. L., Shera, D. M., Rauch, S. L., Keuthen, N., Rosen, B. R., Caviness, V. S., & Filipek, P. A. (1996). Cerebral structural abnormalities in patients with obsessive-compulsive disorder: A quantitative morphometric magnetic resonance imaging study. *Archives of General Psychiatry, 53,* 625–632.

Kellner, C. H., Jolley, R. R., Holgate, R. C., Austin, L., Lydiard, R. B., Laraia, M., & Ballenger, J. C. (1991). Brain MRI in obsessive-compulsive disorder. *Psychiatry Research, 36,* 45–49.

Kelly, D. (1972). Physiological changes during operations on the limbic system in man. *Conditioned Reflex, 7,* 127.

Kelly, D. (1980). *Anxiety and emotions: Physiological basis and treatment.* Springfield, IL: Thomas.

Knight, G. C. (1972). Bifrontal stereotaxic tractotomy in the substantia innominata: An experience of 450 cases. In E. Hitchcock, L. Laitinen, & K. Vaernet (Eds.), *Psychosurgery* (p. 269). Springfield, IL: Thomas.

Kullberg, G. (1977). Differences in effects of capsulotomy and cingulotomy. In W. H. Sweet, W. S. Obrador, & J. G. Martin-Rodrigues (Eds.), *Neurosurgical treatment in psychiatry, pain, and epilepsy* (pp. 301–308). Baltimore: University Park Press.

LaPlane, E., Levasseur, M., Pillon, B., Dubois, B., Baulac, M., Mazoyer, B., Tran Dinh, S., Sette, G., Danze, F., & Baron, J. C. (1989). Obsessions-compulsions and behavioural changes with bilateral basal ganglia lesions: A neuropsychological, magnetic resonance imaging and positron tomography study. *Brain, 112*, 699–725.

Leksell, L., & Backlund, E. O. (1979). Stereotactic gamma capsulotomy. In E. R. Hitchcock, H. T. Ballantine, Jr., & B. A. Meyerson (Eds.), *Modern concepts in psychiatric surgery* (p. 213). Amsterdam: Elsevier/North-Holland Biomedical.

Lezak, M. D. (1995). *Neuropsychological assessment* (3rd ed.). Oxford: Oxford University Press.

Lovett, L. M., & Shaw, D. M. (1987). Outcome in bipolar affective disorder after stereotactic tractotomy. *British Journal of Psychiatry, 151*, 113.

Luxenberg, J. S., Swedo, S. E., Flament, M. F., Friedland, R. P., Rapoport, J., & Rapoport, S. I. (1988). Neuroanatomical abnormalities in obsessive-compulsive disorder detected with quantitative X-ray computed tomography. *American Journal of Psychiatry, 145*, 1089–1093.

Malizia, A. (1991). Indications for psychosurgery [Abstract S-13-12-02] *Biological Psychiatry*, (Suppl.), 11S.

Martuza, R. L., Chiocca, E. A., Jenike, M. A., Giriunas, I. E., & Ballantine, H. T. (1990). Stereotactic radiofrequency thermal cingulotomy for obsessive compulsive disorder. *Journal of Neuropsychiatry and Clinical Neurosciences, 2*, 331–336.

McDougle, C. J., Goodman, W. K., Price, L. H., Delgado, P. L., Krystal, J. H., Charney, D. S., & Heninger, G. R. (1990). Neuroleptic addition in fluvoxamine-refractory obsessive compulsive disorder: An open case series. *American Journal of Psychiatry, 147*, 552–554.

Meyerson, B. A., & Mindus, P. (1988). Capsulotomy as treatment of anxiety disorders. In L. D. Lunsford (Ed.), *Modern stereotactic neurosurgery* (p. 353). Boston: Martinus Nijhoff.

Mindus, P. (1991). *Capsulotomy in anxiety disorders: A multidisciplinary study*. Unpublished thesis, Karolinska Institute, Stockholm, Sweden.

Mindus, P., Bergström, K., Levander, S. E., Noren, G., Hindmarsh, T., & Thuomas, K. A. (1987). Magnetic resonance images related to clinical outcome after psychosurgical intervention in severe anxiety disorder. *Journal of Neurology, Neurosurgery, and Psychiatry, 50*, 1288.

Mindus, P., & Jenike, M. A. (1992). Neurosurgical treatment of malignant obsessive-compulsive disorder. *Psychiatric Clinics of North America, 15*(4), 921–938.

Mindus, P., & Nyman, H. (1991). Normalization of personality characteristics in patients with incapacitating anxiety disorders after capsulotomy. *Acta Psychiatr Scand, 83*, 283–291.

Mindus, P., Nyman, H., Rosenquist, A., Rydin, E., & Meyerson, B. A. (1988). Aspects of personality in patients with anxiety disorders undergoing capsulotomy. *Acta Neurochirurgica, 44*(Suppl.), 138.

Mitchell-Heggs, N., Kelly, D., & Richardson, A. (1976). Stereotactic limbic leucotomy—A follow-up at 16 months. *British Journal of Psychiatry, 128*, 226–240.

Modell, J. G., Mountz, J. M., Curtis, G. C., & Greden, J. F. (1989). Neurophysiologic dysfunction in basal ganglia/limbic striatal and thalamocortical circuits as a pathogenetic mechanism of obsessive-compulsive disorder. *Journal of Neuropsychiatry, 1*, 27–36.

Nordahl, T. E., Benkelfat, C., Semple, W. E., Gross, M., King, A. C., & Cohen, R. M. (1989). Cerebral glucose metabolic rates in obsessive-compulsive disorder. *Neuropsychopharmacology, 2*, 23–28.

Otto, M. (1990). Neuropsychology of obsessive-compulsive disorder. In M. A. Jenike, L. Baer, & W. E. Minichiello (Eds.), *Obsessive-compulsive disorders: Theory and management* (2nd ed., pp. 132–148). Chicago: Year Book Medical.

Pitman, R. K., Green, R. C., Jenike, M. A., & Mesulam, N. M. (1987). Clinical comparison of Tourette syndrome and obsessive-compulsive disorder. *American Journal of Psychiatry, 144*, 1166–1171.

Poynton, A., Bridges, P. K., & Bartlett, J. R. (1988). Psychosurgery in Britain now. *British Journal of Neurosurgery, 2,* 297.

Rapoport, J., Elkins, R., Langer, D. H., Sceery, W., Buchsbaum, M. S., Gillin, J. C., Murphy, D. L., Zahn, T. P., Lake, R., Ludlow, C., & Mendelson, W. (1981). Childhood obsessive-compulsive disorder. *American Journal of Psychiatry, 138,* 12.

Rauch, S. L., & Jenike, M. A. (1993). Neurobiological models of obsessive compulsive disorder. *Psychosomatics, 34,* 20–32.

Rauch, S. L., Jenike, M. A., Alpert, N. M., Baer, L., Breiter, H. C. R., & Fischman, A. J. (1994). Regional cerebral blood flow measured during symptom provocation in obsessive-compulsive disorder using 15-O labeled CO2 and positron emission tomography. *Archives of General Psychiatry, 1,* 62–70.

Rauch, S. L., O'Sullivan, R. L., & Jenike, M. A. (1996). Open treatment of obsessive-compulsive disorder with venlafaxine: A series of ten cases. *Journal of Clinical Psychopharmacology, 16,* 81–84.

Richardson, A. (1973). Stereotactic limbic leucotomy: Surgical technique. *Postgraduate Medical Journal, 49,* 860.

Robinson, S., Winnik, H. Z., & Weiss, A. A. (1976). Obsessive psychosis: justification for a separate clinical entity. *Israeli Annual of Psychiatry, 30,* 372.

Rylander, G. (1979). Stereotactic radiosurgery in anxiety and obsessive-compulsive states: Psychiatric aspects. In E. R. Hitchcock, H. T. Ballantine, Jr., & B. A. Meyerson (Eds.), *Modern concepts in psychiatric surgery* (p. 235). Amsterdam: Elsevier/North-Holland Biomedical.

Savage, C. R., Weilburg, J. B., Duffy, F. H., Baer, L., Shera, D., & Jenike, M. A. (1994). Low level sensory processing in obsessive-compulsive disorder: An evoked potential study. *Biological Psychiatry, 35,* 247–252.

Schalling, D., Åsberg, M., Edman, G., & Oreland, L. (1987). Markers of vulnerability to psychopathy: Temperament traits associated with platelet MAO activity. *Acta Psychiatr Scand, 16,* 172.

Schilder, P. (1938). The organic background of obsessions and compulsions. *American Journal of Psychiatry, 94,* 1397–1414.

Snaith, P. (1987). The case for psychosurgery [Letter]. *British Journal of Hospital Med, 8,* 147.

Solyom, L., DiNicola, V. F., Phil, M., Sookman, D., & Luchins, D. (1985). Is there an obsessive psychosis? Aetiological and prognostic factors of an atypical form of obsessive-compulsive neurosis. *Canadian Journal of Psychiatry, 30,* 372.

Strom-Olsen, R., & Carlisle, S. (1971). Bi-frontal stereotactic tractotomy: A follow-up study of its effects on 210 patients. *British Journal of Psychiatry, 118,* 141–154.

Stuss, D. T., & Benson, D. F. (1986). Personality and emotion. In D. T. Stuss & D. F. Benson (Eds.), *The frontal lobes* (p. 21). New York: Raven.

Swedo, S. E., Pietrini, P., Leonard, H. L., Schapiro, M. B., Rettew, D. C., Goldberger, E. L., Rapoport, S. I., Rapoport, J. L., & Grady, C. L. (1992). Cerebral glucose metabolism in childhood-onset OCD. *Archives of General Psychiatry, 49,* 690–694.

Swedo, S. E., Rapoport, J. L., Cheslow, D. L., Leonard, H. L., Ayoub, E. M., Hosier, D. M., & Wald, E. R. (1989). High prevalence of obsessive-compulsive symptoms in patients with Sydenham's chorea. *American Journal of Psychiatry, 146,* 246–249.

Swedo, S. E., Shapiro, M. B., Grady, C. L., Cheslow, D. L., Leonard, H. L., Kumar, A., Friedland, R., Rapoport, S. I., & Rapoport, J. L. (1989). Cerebral glucose metabolism in childhood-onset obsessive-compulsive disorder. *Archives of General Psychiatry, 46,* 518–523.

Sweet, W. H., & Meyerson, B. A. (1990). Neurosurgical aspects of primary affective disorders. In J. R. Youmans (Ed.), *Neurological surgery.* Philadelphia: Saunders.

Tan, E., Marks, I. M., & Marset, P. (1971). Bi-medial leucotomy in obsessive-compulsive neurosis: A controlled serial inquiry. *British Journal of Psychiatry, 118,* 155.

Vasko, T., & Kullberg, G. (1979). Results of psychological testing of cognitive functions in patients undergoing stereotactic psychiatric surgery. In E. R. Hitchcock, H. T. Ballantine, Jr., & B. A. Meyerson (Eds.), *Modern concepts in psychiatric surgery* (p. 303). Amsterdam: Elsevier/North-Holland Biomedical.

Ward, C. D. (1988). Transient feelings of compulsion caused by hemispheric lesions: Three cases. *Journal of Neurology, Neurosurgery, and Psychiatry, 51*, 266–268.

Waziri, R. (1990). Psychosurgery for anxiety and obsessive-compulsive disorders. In R. Noyes, Jr., M. Roth, & G. D. Burrows (Eds.), *Handbook of anxiety: Treatment of anxiety.* Amsterdam: Elsevier Science.

Weilburg, J. B., Mesulam, M. M., Weintraub, S., Buonnano, F., Jenike, M. A., & Stakes, J. W. (1989). Focal striatal abnormalities in a patient with obsessive-compulsive disorder. *Archives of Neurology, 46*, 233–235.

Whitty, C. W. M., Duffield, J. E., & Tow, P. M. (1952). Anterior cingulectomy in the treatment of mental disease. *Lancet, 1*, 475–481.

Williams, A. C., Owen, C., & Heath, D. A. (1988). A compulsive movement disorder with cavitation of caudate nucleus. *Journal of Neurology, Neurosurgery, and Psychiatry, 51*, 447–448.

Zielinski, C. M., Taylor, M. A., & Juzwin, K. R. (1991). Neuropsychological deficits in obsessive-compulsive disorder. *Neuropsychiatry, Neuropsychology, and Behavioral Neurology, 4*, 110–126.

VI

COMBINED TREATMENT

Combined Drug and Behavioral Treatments for Obsessive-Compulsive Disorder: Early Findings

David A. Spiegel
Center for Anxiety and Related Disorders, Boston University

Once considered to be a treatment-refractory condition, obsessive-compulsive disorder (OCD) has begun to yield to the application of new and improved treatments. As discussed in preceding chapters, treatments have evolved along two relatively independent lines. The first is the pharmacological, through the synthesis of serotonin reuptake inhibitors (SRIs) that possess anti-obsessional and anticompulsive properties, including clomipramine (Clomipramine Collaborative Study Group, 1991; Leonard et al., 1991; Leonard et al., 1989; Pigott et al., 1990), fluvoxamine (Freeman, Trimble, Deakin, Stokes, & Ashford, 1994; Goodman, Price, Rasmussen, Delgado, et al., 1989; Rasmussen et al., in press), and fluoxetine (Levine, Hoffman, Knepple, & Kenin, 1989; Pigott et al., 1990; Tollefson et al., 1994). The second is the psychosocial, primarily through the perfection of therapies that incorporate the procedures of in vivo exposure and response prevention (ERP) either as the principal therapeutic intervention (Baer & Minichiello, 1990; Foa, Steketee, & Ozarow, 1985; O'Sullivan & Marks, 1991; Steketee, 1993) or in conjunction with cognitive restructuring (Emmelkamp & Beens, 1991; van Oppen et al., 1995). Both approaches have enjoyed a substantial degree of success, so that most patients who engage in therapy now can expect to experience clinically significant improvement. Unfortunately, improvement generally is modest, and there exists a sizable minority of patients who either cannot tolerate a given treatment or fail to respond to it. Possibly because of the limitations of each individual treatment, the belief has grown among clinicians that a combination of drug and psychosocial therapies is the best treatment for OCD (Greist, Jefferson, Kobak, Katzelnick, & Serlin, 1995).

This chapter reviews the empirical evidence for that belief as of this writing, with the recognition that existing data are few and the conclusions therefore tentative. Studies are underway currently that will provide needed additional information. To provide points of reference for the discussion of combined treatments, the chapter begins with a brief comparative summary of the efficacy of pharmacological and psychosocial therapies, specifically behavior therapy, when they are given individually.

EFFICACY OF DRUG OR BEHAVIORAL TREATMENT

Experience from drug trials suggests that 10% to 25% of patients who accept treatment with serotonergic anti-obsessional drugs will drop out due to side effects or medical adverse events (Clomipramine Collaborative Study Group, 1991; Fontaine & Chouinard, 1989; Greist et al., 1995; Kasvikis & Marks, 1988a; Levine et al., 1989; Rasmussen et al., in press; Tollefson et al., 1994). Among those who complete treatment, the mean reduction in scores on the Yale–Brown Obsessive Compulsive Scale (Y–BOCS; Goodman, Price, Rasmussen, Mazure, Delgado, et al., 1989; Goodman, Price, Rasmussen, Mazure, Fleischmann, et al., 1989) is in the range of 20% to 40% (Clomipramine Collaborative Study Group, 1991; Greist et al., 1995; Leonard et al., 1991; Levine et al., 1989; Rasmussen et al., in press; Tollefson et al., 1994). Roughly half of pharmacologically treated patients do not improve sufficiently to be classified as treatment responders (Clomipramine Collaborative Study Group, 1991; Goodman, Price, Rasmussen, Delgado, et al., 1989; Greist et al., 1995; Pigott et al., 1990; Rasmussen et al., in press), generally defined as a 25% to 30% reduction in symptom severity or a rating of "much improved" or "very much improved" on the Clinical Global Impression of Improvement (CGI; Guy, 1976). For example, in the large multicenter drug trials, 60% of participants treated with clomipramine and 38% to 43% of those treated with fluoxetine, fluvoxamine, or sertraline were classified as responders at posttreatment based on the CGI improvement criterion (Greist et al., 1995).

Although responders tend to maintain their gains as long as medication is continued, most studies show a high percentage of patients relapsing within a few months after drugs are withdrawn. Reported relapse rates vary considerably (Asberg, Thoren, & Bertilsson, 1982; Fontaine & Chouinard, 1989; Insel et al., 1983; Leonard et al., 1991; Leonard et al., 1989; Pato, Zohar-Kadouch, Zohar, & Murphy, 1988; Thoren, Asberg, Cronholm, Jornestedt, & Traskman, 1980) but average about 80%.

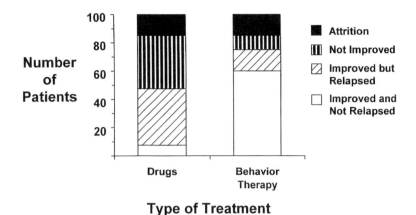

FIG. 24.1. Projected treatment outcomes for a hypothetical cohort of 100 OC ritualizers embarking on a course of pharmacotherapy or behavior therapy.

Figure 24.1 depicts how these percentages translate into numbers for a hypothetical cohort of 100 OCD patients who embark on a course of pharmacotherapy. In round numbers, approximately 15 patients will find the drug intolerable and will discontinue treatment. Of the remaining 85, at least 40 will fail to improve to a clinically significant degree. Of the 45 or so patients who do improve significantly, 35 to 40 will relapse if the drug is withdrawn, leaving only 5 to 10 of the original 100 improved after termination of treatment.

The outcome would be better, although still far from ideal, if these same 100 patients had been treated with behavior therapy. As with drug treatment, approximately 15% of treatment starters will drop out either in fact, or in effect, by refusing to comply with treatment instructions (Foa, Kozak, Steketee, & McCarthy, 1992; Greist, 1990; McDonald, Marks, & Blizzard, 1988). Among those who complete treatment, the mean reduction in symptom severity, typically assessed as the amount of time spent in individually identified target rituals, is approximately 60% (O'Sullivan & Marks, 1991). Only about 1 in 10 treatment completers fails to achieve at least a 30% reduction on this measure (Foa et al., 1985).

Patients who respond tend to maintain their gains during follow-up periods ranging up to 9 years, with relapse rates averaging about 20% (Foa et al., 1992; Foa et al., 1985; O'Sullivan & Marks, 1991). For example, O'Sullivan and Marks (1991) reviewed nine studies in which a total of 195 patients (87% of treatment completers) were reassessed an average of 3 years after treatment. Overall, 79% were rated as much improved or very much improved at follow-up.

Thus, with behavior therapy, among a hypothetical cohort of 100 obsessive-compulsive (OC) ritualizers who enter treatment, approximately 15 will drop out or be noncompliant and 10 will fail to improve to a clinically significant degree. Of the 75 or so who do improve, roughly 60 will maintain their improvements posttreatment.

It is difficult to compare the efficacies of drug and behavioral treatments beyond gross response estimates because of differences in the way improvement has been assessed in published trials. For example, as noted, most of the large drug trials have used the Y–BOCS to assess symptom severity. Although the Y–BOCS has been shown to be sensitive to symptom changes (Goodman, Price, Rasmussen, Mazure, Delgado, et al., 1989; Nakagawa, Marks, Takei, de Araujo, & Ito, 1996), it is a nonlinear measure combining ratings of the time occupied by symptoms, the degree to which symptoms interfere with normal functioning and cause distress, the extent to which the patient resists symptoms, and the degree of control the patient has over symptoms. A 20% to 40% reduction in Y–BOCS score does not necessarily correspond to a 20% to 40% reduction in time spent in obsessions or compulsions. In addition, cited improvement rates with behavior therapy often pertain to treatment completers, whereas those from drug trials are based more commonly on intention-to-treat analyses. Further, the control groups in drug and behavior therapy studies usually differ (e.g., a pill placebo in drug studies vs. relaxation therapy in behavioral treatment studies), confounding comparison of improvement rates that are calculated relative to the control treatment. Finally, participants in behavior therapy studies often have been permitted limited use of psychotropic medications, the effect of which typically has not been examined.

The preceding estimates of the efficacy of behavioral treatment assume that patients receive an adequate dose of therapy, which typically consists of 15 to 30 hours of therapist-supervised in vivo ERP. With such treatment, pre–post treatment effect sizes for OC symptoms, calculated as the posttreatment mean score minus the pretreatment mean score divided by the pretreatment standard deviation, generally fall in the range of 1.5 to 2.5 (Christensen, Hadzi-Pavlovic, Andrews, & Mattick, 1987; Cottraux et al., 1990; Foa et al., 1992; Rachman et al., 1979). Efficacy varies depending on the kind and amount of exposure. In one study (Rachman et al., 1979), the average effect size for six measures of OC symptoms was 1.9 after 11 hours of therapist-assisted exposure and 2.7 after 22 hours of the same treatment. The latter figure is similar to that found in a more recent trial in which participants received 30 hours of supervised exposure and may approach the upper limit for this form of treatment (Foa et al., 1992). By comparison, calculated effect sizes in pharmacotherapy trials are in the range of 0.8 to 2.3 (Cottraux et al., 1990; Jenike, Baer, & Greist, 1990;

Rasmussen et al., in press; Tollefson et al., 1994). Effect size drops to 0.4 to 1.5 when placebo responses are subtracted (Greist et al., 1995). These figures are somewhat smaller than for behavior therapy, but still quite respectable.

Abramowitz (1997) suggested that pre–post effect sizes may overestimate true treatment effects. He argued that because patients are more likely to seek treatment when their symptoms are more severe, natural fluctuations in symptom severity would tend to be in the direction of improvement. To avoid that confound, he analyzed only studies in which participants were randomly assigned to parallel treatment and control groups and calculated effect size as the difference between the two groups' mean posttreatment scores divided by the pooled standard deviation. Computed that way, the average effect size (across two studies) of exposure and response prevention versus a relaxation control treatment, based on clinician-rated outcome measures, was 1.18 (Abramowitz, 1997). Across eight trials involving psychological treatments, improvement was positively correlated ($r = .87$, $p = .005$) with the amount of time spent in therapist-guided exposure. The average effect size (across five studies) of SRIs versus a pill placebo was 1.09.

As encouraging as those data are, it is nonetheless the case that due to dropouts, noncompliance, and poor response, as many as one half of all patients who begin pharmacotherapy and one quarter of those who embark on a course of behavior therapy will fail to achieve a 25% to 35% reduction on measures of of OC symptoms. Those patients represent a considerable challenge for the clinician, who is often at a loss for how to proceed after the standard first-line treatments have been exhausted.

One approach for patients being treated pharmacologically is to try augmenting a partially effective serotonergic agent with another drug in the hope of boosting response. Although studies involving groups of OCD patients generally find little benefit from drug augmentation, it may be helpful in some patients. For patients being treated behaviorally, increasing the intensity of treatment may break an impasse (Beidel, 1991). However when both modalities are available, clinicians are increasingly turning to a combination of pharmacologic and behavioral treatments either as the treatment of first choice or when one or the other single therapy fails.

Given the independent efficacies of drug and behavior therapies for OCD and the likelihood that they produce their effects through different mechanisms of action, it seems reasonable to hope that those effects might be at least partially additive. If so, the combination of treatments should be superior to either one alone. As noted earlier, this supposition is widely presumed to be the case, although there are very few published trials that specifically address that question. Those studies are reviewed next.

CONTROLLED TRIALS OF SEROTONERGIC DRUGS
AND BEHAVIOR THERAPY

To date, there have been only three published controlled studies comparing a combination of effective drug and behavioral treatments to either component alone. In all three, behavioral treatment consisted of therapist-assisted, in vivo ERP and exposure homework. The drugs were either clomipramine or fluvoxamine at doses in the usual therapeutic range (up to 200 mg/day clomipramine and 300 mg/day fluvoxamine). The findings of those studies are discussed first for acute treatment and then for follow-up.

Acute Treatment Response

In the first trial (Marks, Stern, Mawson, Cobb, & McDonald, 1980; Mawson, Marks, & Ramm, 1982; O'Sullivan, Noshirvani, Marks, Monteiro, & Lelliott, 1991; Rachman et al., 1979; Stern, Marks, Mawson, & Luscombe, 1980), Marks and colleagues compared clomipramine plus daily exposure therapy to a drug placebo plus exposure, to clomipramine plus daily relaxation therapy (relaxation was selected as a psychological placebo treatment), and to a drug placebo plus relaxation (a double placebo control group). Clomipramine (dose $M = 164$ mg/day) or placebo was administered alone for 4 weeks before psychological treatment was added. For ethical reasons, patients assigned to the relaxation therapy cells were crossed over to receive exposure therapy after 3 weeks of relaxation therapy. The study design was therefore a 2 (clomipramine vs. pill placebo) × 2 (exposure therapy vs. relaxation) design for the first 7 weeks and a 2-group (clomipramine plus exposure vs. pill placebo plus exposure) design from Week 10 onward. Participants were 40 moderately depressed (mean score of 17 on the Hamilton Depression Rating Scale [HDRS]; Hamilton, 1960) OCD patients. Pharmacotherapy was given for 36 weeks, and follow-up assessments were conducted 1, 2, and 6 years posttreatment.

At the end of Week 7, improvement in OC symptoms was greatest among participants who received both clomipramine and exposure and least among those in the double placebo group. Clomipramine appeared to facilitate response to exposure therapy during Weeks 5 through 7. From Weeks 7 through 18, the combined treatment was superior to exposure plus pill placebo on measures of rituals (Fig. 24.2), depression, and social adjustment. The differences declined by Week 36, the point at which treatment was discontinued.

A few years later, Marks et al. conducted a second trial (Kasvikis & Marks, 1988a, 1988b; Marks et al., 1988) that differed from the earlier one

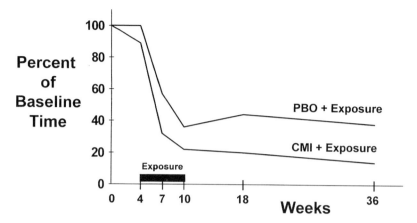

FIG. 24.2. Percentage of baseline time spent in four target rituals by patients treated with clomipramine (CMI) plus exposure or drug placebo (PBO) plus exposure: Average of self and assessor ratings (data from Marks et al., 1980).

in several respects: (a) it included a drug plus antiexposure cell in which participants were instructed to continue to engage in compulsive rituals while the drug had a chance to work; (b) the sample was not depressed (mean score of 10 on the HDRS); and (c) exposure therapy was delivered in a less intensive form (exposure homework plus up to 15 weekly, rather than daily, sessions with the therapist). The study was designed to compare the effects of exposure homework versus antiexposure instructions among participants receiving clomipramine and the effects of clomipramine versus placebo among participants receiving exposure therapy. Forty-nine individuals were enrolled. Treatment was administered for 27 weeks, with follow-up assessments 1 and 2 years posttreatment.

In the first comparison, participants receiving clomipramine plus exposure homework did markedly better than those receiving clomipramine plus antiexposure instructions. In the second comparison, at Week 8, clomipramine (dose $M = 157$ mg/day) plus exposure was better than pill placebo plus exposure on five measures of rituals, two measures of depression, and a measure of social leisure. However, the between-group differences were smaller than in the previous Marks et al. study and waned earlier. They had disappeared by Week 17.

Most recently, Cottraux and colleagues (Cottraux, Mollard, Bouvard, & Marks, 1991; Cottraux et al., 1990) reported a study comparing fluvoxamine plus weekly exposure with a drug placebo plus weekly exposure and with fluvoxamine plus antiexposure instructions. Participants were 60 moderately depressed (mean HDRS score of 19) patients, of whom 44 completed treatment. Treatment was administered for 24 weeks, with follow-up assessments 6 and 12 months posttreatment. Unlike the patients in the second Marks study (Marks et al., 1988), participants in this trial complied poorly with antiexposure instructions. Thus, of the three combined-treatment trials, the Cottraux et al. study comes closest to including a drug comparison group that was neutral with regard to exposure.

Patients who received fluvoxamine plus exposure showed a greater reduction in rituals at Week 8 (Fig. 24.3) and a greater reduction in depression at Week 24 than those who received placebo plus exposure. They also showed broader improvement overall than participants in either of the other two groups, achieving significant changes in all 13 measures of rituals and depression by treatment end, compared with 9 and 10 measures in the other two groups. Sixty-nine percent of participants in the combined treatment group were classified as successes at posttreatment, compared with 54% and 40%, respectively, in the drug-only and exposure-only groups.

Taken together, these three studies suggest that the therapeutic effects of serotonergic drugs and exposure therapy may be modestly additive during the early weeks or months of treatment, at least among initially depressed patients. A measure of treatment additivity is the effect size for the combined versus single treatment, calculated as the mean improvement from baseline to the point of interest in the combined treatment group minus the mean improvement in the single treatment group divided by the pretreatment standard deviation pooled across both groups.

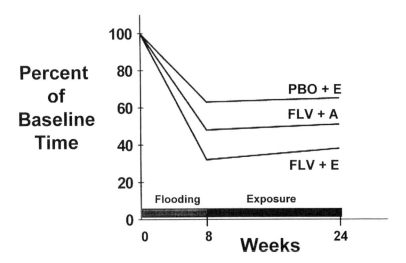

FIG. 24.3. Percentage of baseline time spent in four target rituals by patients treated with fluvoxamine plus exposure (FLV + E), drug placebo plus exposure (PBO + E), or fluvoxamine plus antiexposure instructions (FLV + A): Patient self-ratings (data from Cottraux et al., 1990).

Data reported for the first Marks et al. study and the Cottraux et al. study, both of which involved moderately depressed OCD patients, enabled calculation of mid- and posttreatment effect sizes for combined therapy versus exposure plus pill placebo for three patient-rated variables: depression and the time and discomfort associated with four main target rituals. The average midtreatment effect sizes, calculated at Week 7 in the Marks et al. study and Week 8 in the Cottraux et al. study, were 0.55, 0.75, and 0.95, respectively, for the ratings of depression and of the time and discomfort associated with rituals. All values favored the combined treatment over exposure plus pill placebo. At posttreatment (Week 36 in the Marks et al. study and Week 24 in the Cottraux et al. study), the corresponding values were 0.76, 0.82, and 0.78.

Long-Term Follow-Up

Although the advantage of combined therapies was apparent primarily during the initial phase of treatment, there is some very tentative evidence to suggest that patients who receive combined treatments may do slightly better in the long term than those who receive single treatments. In the first Marks et al. study, there was still a trend for the combined treatment to maintain its superiority over exposure alone at 1-year follow-up, although the differences were no longer significant (Marks et al., 1980). At 2-year follow-up, patients in the combined treatment group were rated as having significantly better leisure and social adjustment than those in the exposure plus pill placebo group (Mawson et al., 1982), and at 6-year follow-up they performed better on a behavioral avoidance test (O'Sullivan et al., 1991). As might be expected, a majority (70%) of these chronic patients had received some kind of psychotropic medication during the intervening years, many for relapses of depression, but drug use did not differ significantly between the two groups.

In the Cottraux et al. study, 82% of patients in the fluvoxamine plus exposure group were rated as improved at 1-year follow-up, compared with 72% in the exposure-only group, a nonsignificant trend in favor of combined treatment. Again, medication use in the two groups did not differ significantly during the follow-up period.

As noted earlier, relapse rates in pharmacotherapy trials tend to be high following drug discontinuation, suggesting that patients may need to be on drugs for extended periods if treatment gains are to be maintained. In contrast, relapse rates following behavior therapy are lower. What happens when the two treatments are combined?

The Cottraux et al. study allows the best comparison of relapse following combined versus single treatments. In that study, relapse was reported in two ways: as the percentage of participants who required

further treatment of any kind during the first 6 months of follow-up, and
as the percentage taking anti-obsessional drugs by 12-month follow-up.
As shown in Fig. 24.4, no participants in the combined treatment group
required further treatment of any kind by 6 months, compared with 56%
and 40%, respectively, in the fluvoxamine-only and exposure-only groups.
By 1 year, 60% of patients in the fluvoxamine-only group were back on
medication, compared with 17% and 18% on drugs in the combined
treatment and exposure-only groups. Thus, relapse following discontinuation of medication in the combined treatment group was no greater than
that following behavior therapy alone.

Further indication that combined treatment may confer more lasting
advantages than single treatments comes from a recent analysis by Hembree, Cohen, Riggs, Kozak, and Foa (1991), reporting naturalistic follow-
up data for 62 OC patients treated with pharmacotherapy (clomipramine
or fluvoxamine, $n = 24$), exposure therapy ($n = 23$), or a combination of
the two (n = 15). When assessed an average of 17 months posttreatment,
93% of the patients in the combined treatment group were rated as
improved with respect to rituals (defined as a 30% or greater reduction
from baseline), compared to 67% in the exposure-only group and 50% in
the drug-only group. However, 25 patients were taking psychotropic
drugs at the time of assessment. Considering only the patients who were
not taking drugs at follow-up, the percentages were 100%, 68%, and 22%,
respectively for combined treatment, exposure alone, and drug alone.
Thus, whether or not they were taking medication, the percentage of
patients who were improved at follow-up was greatest among those who
initially had received combined treatment.

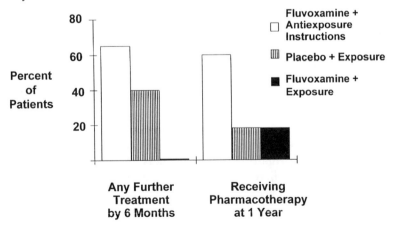

FIG. 24.4. Percentage of treatment completers who received additional
treatment for OCD during the first 6 months after the study and the
percentage taking drugs for OCD at 12-month follow-up (data from
Cottraux et al., 1991).

One of the difficulties in interpreting follow-up data from pharmacotherapy trials is that the drugs are typically withdrawn fairly rapidly according to a predetermined schedule. That procedure differs from the usual clinical practice, where extended drug maintenance periods are common and discontinuation, when attempted, is done more flexibly. The patients assessed in the Hembree et al. (1991) study were not taken off drugs as part of the study protocols, although 38% of those who received drugs during the active treatment phase were no longer taking them at follow-up. Thus, the outcome reported in that study (i.e., 93% of participants improved at follow-up) may be more representative of the outcome when a combined treatment approach is used that allows flexible medication management.

CONCLUSIONS

Although the outlook is better now than ever before for patients with OCD, still about one fourth of those who attempt behavior therapy and half who start a course of pharmacotherapy fail to achieve a one third reduction in symptoms. In many of those cases, failure is due to premature withdrawal from or noncompliance with treatment. Among treatment completers, improvement averages about 60% with behavior therapy and 30% with a single course of pharmacotherapy. Because patients often respond better to one serotonergic drug than another, the average improvement with pharmacotherapy probably is higher than 30% if multiple drug trials are given. Most patients who respond to medication when it is given alone lose their gains when it is discontinued.

To date, there have been few studies of concurrent drug and behavioral therapies, but the existing data suggest that combined approaches may offer some modest advantages over single treatments. Among initially depressed patients, the addition of a serotonergic antidepressant to exposure therapy may facilitate compliance with behavioral instructions (Marks et al., 1980) and promote earlier improvement of OC symptoms and mood than exposure alone. There is also some indication that combined treatments may yield a somewhat broader spectrum of improvement and a slightly higher proportion of responders than single treatments. In addition, responders may maintain their gains better posttreatment.

By far, the most robust finding from combined treatment trials is that the addition of behavior therapy to pharmacotherapy appears to reduce the likelihood of relapse when drugs are discontinued. Relapse rates following combined treatment appear to be comparable to those after behavior therapy alone and are substantially lower than those following pharmacotherapy alone.

Given the limited data available, these conclusions must be considered tentative until further studies are done. Currently, a collaborative study is underway at the Medical College of Pennsylvania and Columbia University comparing the combination of clomipramine and behavior therapy to each component alone and to a drug placebo control. In that study, behavior therapy is administered intensively, with most sessions occurring during the first month. Drug and behavior therapy begin together for patients in the combined treatment group. Preliminary results from that study have been less favorable to combined treatment than the trials reviewed here, although the effect of behavior therapy in reducing relapse following drug discontinuation is apparently being replicated.

If the collaborative study should fail to demonstrate other benefits for combined therapy, that would not necessarily mean there are none, although that is certainly a possibility. Other factors, including patient, treatment, and assessment variables could result in the failure of a study to show differences that are observed in clinical practice. It is possible, for example, that combined treatment might be more advantageous than behavior therapy alone for certain subtypes of OCD, or for patients with marked anxiety or depression, or for those who are reluctant to engage in exposure therapy. Given the length of time required for a therapeutic response to pharmacotherapy, combined treatment might be better than behavior therapy alone when the latter is done gradually over an extended period of time (e.g., weekly or less frequent treatment sessions) or if the drug is started before behavior therapy is begun. Combined therapy may also be advantageous in ways that are not measured by the usual efficacy variables. For example, it may lower the drug dose or number of exposure sessions needed for a given degree of improvement or lessen the patient's discomfort during exposure. Until more data are available, it is not clear for which patients, if any, combined therapy is best, how it is optimally administered, and what benefits it may offer. At present, its use seems most indicated for OCD patients with moderate to severe depression and patients who have improved with pharmacotherapy but wish to discontinue medication. Whether it may also be beneficial for patients with purported poor prognosis features such as overvalued ideation, severe anxiety, comorbid Axis I disorders, or prominent personality disorders has yet to be explored.

REFERENCES

Abramowitz, J. S. (1997). Effectiveness of psychological and pharmacological treatments for obsessive-compulsive disorder: A quantitative review. *Journal of Consulting and Clinical Psychology, 65,* 44–52.

Asberg, M., Thoren, P., & Bertilsson, L. (1982). Clomipramine treatment of obsessive-compulsive disorder: Biochemical and clinical aspects. *Psychopharmacology Bulletin, 18*, 13–21.

Baer, L., & Minichiello, W. E. (1990). Behavior therapy for obsessive-compulsive disorder. In M. A. Jenike, L. Baer, & W. E. Minichiello (Eds.), *Obsessive-compulsive disorders: Theory and management* (2nd ed., pp. 202–232). Chicago: Year Book Medical.

Beidel, D. C. (1991, April). *Identification of treatment refractory patients and maintenance of treatment gains: New directions for behavior therapy!* Paper presented at the 11th National Conference on Anxiety Disorders, Chicago.

Christensen, H., Hadzi-Pavlovic, D., Andrews, G., & Mattick, R. (1987). Behavior therapy and tricyclic medication in the treatment of obsessive-compulsive disorder: A quantitative review. *Journal of Consulting and Clinical Psychology, 55*, 701–711.

Clomipramine Collaborative Study Group. (1991). Clomipramine in the treatment of patients with obsessive-compulsive disorder. *Archives of General Psychiatry, 48*, 730–738.

Cottraux, J., Mollard, E., Bouvard, M., & Marks, I. M. (1991, November). *One year followup after exposure and/or fluvoxamine in depressed obsessive-compulsive disorder.* Paper presented at the 25th Annual Convention of the Association for Advancement of Behavior Therapy, New York.

Cottraux, J., Mollard, E., Bouvard, M., Marks, I., Sluys, M., Nury, A. M., Douge, R., & Cialdella, P. (1990). A controlled study of fluvoxamine and exposure in obsessive-compulsive disorder. *International Clinical Psychopharmacology, 5*, 17–30.

Emmelkamp, P. M. G., & Beens, H. (1991). Cognitive therapy with obsessive-compulsive patients: A comparative evaluation. *Behaviour Research and Therapy, 29*, 293–300.

Foa, E. B., Kozak, M. J., Steketee, G. S., & McCarthy, P. R. (1992). Treatment of depressive and obsessive-compulsive symptoms in OCD by imipramine and behavior therapy. *British Journal of Clinical Psychology, 31*, 279–292.

Foa, E. B., Steketee, G. S., & Ozarow, B. (1985). Behavior therapy with obsessive compulsives: From theory to treatment. In M. Mavissakalian, S. M. Turner, & L. Michelson (Eds.), *Obsessive-compulsive disorder: Psychological and pharmacological treatment* (pp. 49–129). New York: Plenum.

Fontaine, R., & Chouinard, G. (1989). Fluoxetine in the long-term maintenance treatment of obsessive compulsive disorder. *Psychiatric Annals, 9*, 88–91.

Freeman, C. P. L., Trimble, M. R., Deakin, J. F. W., Stokes, T. M., & Ashford, J. J. (1994). Fluvoxamine versus clomipramine in the treatment of obsessive-compulsive disorder: A multicenter, randomized, double-blind, parallel group comparison. *Journal of Clinical Psychiatry, 55*, 301–305.

Goodman, W. K., Price, L. H., Rasmussen, S. A., Delgado, P. L., Heninger, G. R., & Charney, D. S. (1989). Efficacy of fluvoxamine in obsessive-compulsive disorder: A double-blind comparison with placebo. *Archives of General Psychiatry, 46*, 36–44.

Goodman, W. K., Price, L. H., Rasmussen, S. A., Mazure, C., Delgado, P., Heninger, G. R., & Charney, D. S. (1989). The Yale–Brown Obsessive Compulsive Scale: II. Validity. *Archives of General Psychiatry, 46*, 1012–1016.

Goodman, W. K., Price, L. H., Rasmussen, S. A., Mazure, C., Fleischmann, C., Hill, C. L., Heninger, G. R., & Charney, D. S. (1989). The Yale–Brown Obsessive Compulsive Scale: I. Development, use, and reliability. *Archives of General Psychiatry, 46*, 1006–1011.

Greist, J. H. (1990). Treatment of obsessive compulsive disorder: Psychotherapies, drugs, and other somatic treatment. *Journal of Clinical Psychiatry, 51*(8, Suppl.), 44–50.

Greist, J. H., Jefferson, J. W., Kobak, K. A., Katzelnick, D. J., & Serlin, R. C. (1995). Efficacy and tolerability of serotonin transport inhibitors in obsessive-compulsive disorder: A meta-analysis. *Archives of General Psychiatry, 52*, 53–60.

Guy, W. (1976). *ECDEU assessment manual for psychopharmacology, revised* (DHEW Publication No. ADM 76-338). Washington, DC: U.S. Government Printing Office.

Hamilton, M. (1960). A rating scale for depression. *Journal of Neurology, Neurosurgery, and Psychiatry, 23,* 56–62.

Hembree, E. A., Cohen, A. C., Riggs, D. S., Kozak, M. J., & Foa, E. B. (1991). *The long-term efficacy of behavior therapy and serotonergic medications in the treatment of obsessive-compulsive ritualizers.* Unpublished manuscript.

Insel, T. R., Murphy, D. L., Cohen, R. M., Alterman, I., Kilts, C., & Linnoila, M. (1983). Obsessive-compulsive disorder: A double-blind trial of clomipramine and corgyline. *Archives of General Psychiatry, 40,* 605–612.

Jenike, M. A., Baer, L., & Greist, J. H. (1990). Clomipramine vs. fluvoxamine in obsessive-compulsive disorder: A retrospective comparison of side effects and efficacy. *Journal of Clinical Psychopharmacology, 10,* 122–124.

Kasvikis, Y., & Marks, I. M. (1988a). Clomipramine in obsessive-compulsive ritualizers treated with exposure therapy: Relations between dose, plasma levels, outcome and side effects. *Psychopharmacology, 95,* 113–118.

Kasvikis, Y., & Marks, I. (1988b). Clomipramine, self-exposure, and therapist-accompanied exposure in obsessive-compulsive ritualizers: Two-year follow-up. *Journal of Anxiety Disorders, 2,* 291–298.

Leonard, H. L., Swedo, S. E., Lenane, M. C., Rettew, D. C., Cheslow, D. L., Hamburger, S. D., & Rapoport, J. L. (1991). A double-blind desipramine substitution during long-term clomipramine treatment in children and adolescents with obsessive-compulsive disorder. *Archives of General Psychiatry, 48,* 922–927.

Leonard, H. L., Swedo, S. E., Rapoport, J. L., Koby, E. V., Lenane, M. C., Cheslow, D. L., & Hamburger, S. D. (1989). Treatment of obsessive-compulsive disorder with clomipramine and desipramine in children and adolescents. *Archives of General Psychiatry, 46,* 1088–1092.

Levine, R., Hoffman, J. S., Knepple, E. D., & Kenin, M. (1989). Long-term fluoxetine treatment of a large number of obsessive-compulsive patients. *Journal of Clinical Psychopharmacology, 9,* 281–283.

Marks, I. M., Lelliott, P., Basoglu, M., Noshirvani, H., Monteiro, W., Cohen, D., & Kasvikis, Y. (1988). Clomipramine, self-exposure and therapist-aided exposure for obsessive-compulsive rituals. *British Journal of Psychiatry, 152,* 522–534.

Marks, I. M., Stern, R. S., Mawson, D., Cobb, J., & McDonald, R. (1980). Clomipramine and exposure for obsessive-compulsive rituals: I. *British Journal of Psychiatry, 136,* 1–25.

Mawson, D., Marks, I. M., & Ramm, L. (1982). Clomipramine and exposure for chronic obsessive compulsive rituals: III. Two year follow- up and further findings. *British Journal of Psychiatry, 140,* 11–18.

McDonald, R., Marks, I. M., & Blizzard, R. (1988). Quality assurance of outcome in mental health care: A model for routine use in clinical settings. *Health Trends, 20,* 111–114.

Nakagawa, A., Marks, I. M., Takei, N., de Araujo, L. A., & Ito, L. M. (1996). Comparisons among the Yale–Brown Obsessive-Compulsive Scale, Compulsion Checklist, and other measures of obsessive-compulsive disorder. *British Journal of Psychiatry, 169,* 108–112.

O'Sullivan, G., & Marks, I. (1991). Follow-up studies of behavioral treatment of phobic and obsessive compulsive neuroses. *Psychiatric Annals, 2,* 386–373.

O'Sullivan, G., Noshirvani, H., Marks, I., Monteiro, W., & Lelliott, P. (1991). Six-year follow-up after exposure and clomipramine therapy for obsessive compulsive disorder. *Journal of Clinical Psychiatry, 52,* 150–155.

Pato, M. T., Zohar-Kadouch, R., Zohar, J., & Murphy, D. L. (1988). Return of symptoms after discontinuation of clomipramine in patients with obsessive-compulsive disorder. *American Journal of Psychiatry, 145,* 1521–1525.

Pigott, T. A., Pato, M. T., Bernstein, S. E., Grover, G. N., Hill, J. L., Tolliver, T. J., & Murphy, D. L. (1990). Controlled comparisons of clomipramine and fluoxetine in the treatment of obsessive-compulsive disorder: Behavioral and biological results. *Archives of General Psychiatry, 47,* 926–932.

Rachman, S., Cobb, J., Grey, B., McDonald, D., Mawson, D., Sartory, G., & Stern, R. S. (1979). The behavioral treatment of obsessional-compulsive disorders, with and without clomipramine. *Behaviour Research and Therapy, 17*, 467–478.

Rasmussen, S., Goodman, W. K., Greist, J. H., Jenike, M. A., Kozak, M. J., Liebowitz, M., Robinson, D. G., & White, K. L. (in press). Fluvoxamine in the treatment of obsessive-compulsive disorder: A multi-center double-blind placebo-controlled study in outpatients. *Journal of Clinical Psychopharmacology.*

Steketee, G. S. (1993). *Treatment of obsessive-compulsive disorder.* New York: Guilford.

Stern, R. S., Marks, I. M., Mawson, D., & Luscombe, D. K. (1980). Clomipramine and exposure for compulsive rituals: II. Plasma levels, side effects and outcome. *British Journal of Psychiatry, 136*, 161–166.

Thoren, P., Asberg, M., Cronholm, B., Jornestedt, L., & Traskman, L. (1980). Clomipramine treatment of obsessive compulsive disorder: I. A controlled clinical trial. *Archives of General Psychiatry, 37*, 1281–1285.

Tollefson, G. D., Rampey, A. H., Potvin, J. H., Jenike, M. A., Rush, A. J., Dominguez, R. A., Koran, L. M., Shear, M. K., Goodman, W., & Genduso, L. A. (1994). A multicenter investigation of fixed-dose fluoxetine in the treatment of obsessive-compulsive disorder. *Archives of General Psychiatry, 51*, 559–567.

van Oppen, P., de Haan, E., van Balkom, A. J. L. M., Spinhoven, P., Hoogduin, K., & van Dyck, R. (1995). Cognitive therapy and exposure *in vivo* in the treatment of obsessive compulsive disorder. *Behaviour Research and Therapy, 33*, 379–390.

Cognitive Behavior Therapy and Pharmacotherapy for Obsessive-Compulsive Disorder: The NIMH-Sponsored Collaborative Study

Michael J. Kozak
MCP and Hahnemann University

Michael R. Liebowitz
New York State Psychiatric Institute

Edna B. Foa
MCP and Hahnemann University

PREVALENCE AND COURSE OF OBSESSIVE-COMPULSIVE DISORDER

Formerly thought to be a rare disorder, obsessive-compulsive disorder (OCD) is now considered to afflict more than 500,000 individuals in the United States. Epidemiological data suggest a 6-month prevalence of 1% to 2% (Myers et al., 1984) and a lifetime prevalence of 2% to 3% (Karno, Golding, Sorenson & Burnam, 1988; Robins, Helzer, Weissman, & Orvaschel, 1984). Just more than half of those with OCD are female (Rasmussen & Tsuang, 1986). Age of onset of the disorder ranges from early adolescence to young adulthood, with somewhat earlier onset in males (modal onset 13–15 years old) than in females (modal onset 20–24 years old; Rasmussen & Eisen, 1990). Development of the disorder is usually gradual, but acute onset has been reported. Chronic waxing and waning of symptoms is typical; however, episodic and deteriorating courses have been observed in about 10% of patients (Rasmussen & Eisen, 1989).

Many individuals with OCD suffer for years before seeking treatment. Rasmussen and Tsuang (1986) found that on the average, individuals first presented themselves for psychiatric treatment more than 7 years after the onset of significant symptoms. The disorder is frequently associated with impairments in general functioning such as disruption of gainful employment and marital and other interpersonal relationships (Emmelkamp, de Haan, & Hoogduin, 1990; Riggs, Hiss, & Foa, 1992).

TREATMENT OF OCD

OCD was for some time considered intractable: Neither psychodynamic psychotherapy nor a wide variety of pharmacotherapies had been successful in treating it (Black, 1974). Now, however, there are two treatments of established efficacy: cognitive behavior therapy by prolonged exposure and pharmacotherapy with serotonin reuptake inhibitors (SRIs).

Cognitive-Behavior Therapy: Exposure and Ritual Prevention

Early behavioral intervention such as systematic desensitization had limited success (Beech & Vaughn, 1978; Cooper, Gelder, & Marks, 1965) as did other behavioral procedures such as aversion relief, imaginal flooding, paradoxical intention, satiation, and aversion procedures (for a review see Foa, Steketee, & Ozarow, 1985).

The prognosis has improved dramatically with the introduction of a treatment program called exposure and response prevention (ERP; Meyer, 1966). Excellent results were obtained first in two cases of OCD with prolonged exposure to obsessional cues and prevention of rituals (response prevention) and later in 10 of 15 cases. The treatment was somewhat effective in the other five cases. Durability of improvement was excellent: Only two patients relapsed after 5 to 6 years (Meyer & Levy, 1973; Meyer, Levy, & Schnurer, 1974). Uncontrolled and controlled studies of ERP reveal a consistent picture: A preponderance of cognitive behavior therapy completers are responders at posttreatment and follow-up (Foa & Kozak, 1996).

Cognitive-behavior therapy for OCD involves repeated and prolonged (up to 2 hours) confrontation with situations that provoke discomfort and prohibition of rituals, despite urges to ritualize. Exposure is gradual, with situations provoking moderate distress confronted before more difficult ones. Treatment may include both imaginal and actual (in vivo) exposure. Additional exposure practice between treatment sessions is also prescribed. Several manuals that detail the procedures of exposure treatment are available (Baer & Minichiello, 1990; Foa & Wilson, 1991; Kozak & Foa, 1996; Steketee, 1994).

Mechanism of Change During Exposure Therapy. Foa and Kozak (1985) hypothesized that the exposure modifies several types of fear structures in OCD patients as it targeted changes in unrealistic association between feared stimuli (e.g., toilet seats) and threat meaning (e.g., venereal disease). For other OCD patients, certain harmless stimuli are strongly associated with general distress without regard to harm, and it is hypothesized that these associations can also be modified via exposure. In other words, through ERP, patients with OCD learn to evaluate more realistically the threat they associated with situations or objects that evoke obsessional distress. They learn to adjust their subjective probability estimates of harm and they learn that anxiety does not stay forever even if they do not avoid, escape, or ritualize; rather it gradually decreases. Through imaginal exposure they learn to distinguish between thinking about threat and actually being exposed to danger.

The Efficacy of ERP Programs. Cognitive-behavior therapy by ERP, in which patients refrain from compulsive rituals, revolutionized the psychosocial treatment of OCD. Many studies report both significant and lasting improvement in obsessive thoughts and compulsive rituals after behavior therapy. The 12 outcome studies ($N = 330$) that reported number of treatment responders revealed that among treatment completers, an average of 83% were responders immediately after treatment. In 16 studies reporting long-term outcome ($N = 376$; mean follow-up interval of 29 months), 76% were responders (Foa & Kozak, 1996). In sum, ERP has been found to yield high responder rates, high degrees of improvement in responders, few adverse effects, and great durability of improvement following treatment discontinuation.

Limitations of Cognitive-Behavior Therapy. Although cognitive behavior therapy for OCD is a potent treatment, it does have notable limitations. Perhaps most important is a substantial treatment-refusal rate (e.g., about 30% at the MCP clinic over the last 10 years). In addition, not all patients who enter treatment complete it. For example, in our ongoing comparative study of treatment with behavior therapy and clomipramine, 22% of patients who were randomized to behavior therapy declined to begin exposure and 28% who began to receive cognitive behavior therapy dropped out before completing it. Studies of the efficacy of exposure-based therapy for OCD rarely document treatment refuser rates, or include treatment refusers in treatment efficacy samples. Thus, efficacy findings reported for behavior therapy with treatment completers underestimate its efficacy with the larger population.

Another significant issue is the limited availability of accomplished practitioners of exposure treatment for OCD. Evidence to date for the efficacy of cognitive-behavior therapy with OCD has come from centers specializing in this treatment, and there are only a handful in the United States. The specialty centers may be unusual not only in expertise, but also in the kinds of patients they attract. This would limit the generalizability of existing findings. Whether centers not specialized in cognitive-behavior therapy can obtain similar success with ERP awaits demonstration.

Clomipramine

Clomipramine still appears to be the most effective medication available for the treatment of OCD. Of 22 controlled trials for OCD in adults, clomipramine was found more effective than placebo or an active comparator in 17, and equally effective in 5 (Greist, Jefferson, Kobak, Katzelnick, & Serlin, 1995). In the most extensive study, a multicenter trial at 16 sites, clomipramine had a 61% response rate and 42% mean symptom reduction, compared with placebo, which had a 6% response rate and 5% mean symptom reduction (DeVeaugh-Geiss, Landau, & Katz, 1989; Clomipramine Study Group, 1991).

OCD patients are prone to relapse when clomipramine is discontinued (Thoren, Asberg, Chronholm, Jornestedt, & Traskman, 1980). In the only reported placebo substitution trial, 16 of 18 (89%) OCD patients relapsed within 7 weeks of clomipramine discontinuation (Pato, Zohar-Kadouch, Zohar, & Murphy, 1988). Length of treatment (5–27 months) was not related to relapse rate. The rapid 1-week clomipramine taper, however, might have exacerbated relapse. Although available estimates of relapse are restricted by limited sample size, they suggest that relapse is substantial upon drug withdrawal after acute response to clomipramine.

Selective Serotonin Reuptake Inhibitors

Several selective serotonin reuptake inhibitors (SSRIs) are of demonstrated efficacy for OCD. These drugs are more serotonergically selective than clomipramine, the principal metabolite of which (desmethylclomipramine) is a noradrenergic reuptake inhibitor. The SSRIs also generally exhibit more favorable side effect profiles than clomipramine. However, as discussed later, they may not be as effective as clomipramine for OCD.

The SSRI fluvoxamine has been approved by the U.S. Food and Drug Administration (FDA) for treatment of OCD after demonstrating superiority to placebo in three small controlled studies (Goodman, Price, Rasmussen, Delgado, et al., 1989; Perse, Greist, Jefferson, Rosenfeld & Dar, 1987; Price, Goodman, Charney, Rasmussen, & Heninger, 1987), and several larger trials (Greist, 1992; Goodman, Kozak, Liebowitz, & White, 1996). Recent controlled comparisons of fluvoxamine and clomipramine in OCD suggested similar efficacy and tolerability (Freeman, Trimble, Deakin, Stokes, & Ashford, 1994; Smeraldi et al., 1992; Tamimi, Mavissakalian, Jones, & Olson, 1991). However, these studies lack a placebo control group and are thereby vulnerable to potential positive response bias. An open trial assessing the efficacy of fluvoxamine in clomipramine nonresponders suggests slightly greater efficacy for clomipramine but slightly greater tolerability for fluvoxamine (Mattes, 1994). Meta-analytic comparisons of placebo-controlled trials (Greist, Jefferson, Kobak, Katzelnick, & Serlin, 1995) suggest greater efficacy for clomipramine than fluvoxamine, with no difference in tolerability.

Fluoxetine, another SSRI marketed as an antidepressant, is also FDA-approved for OCD. It was found useful in many open clinical trials (Fontaine & Chouinard, 1986, 1989; Jenike, Buttolph, Baer, Ricciardi, & Holland, 1989; Liebowitz et al., 1989; Turner, Jacob, Beidel, & Himmelhoch, 1985), as well as in two multicenter placebo-controlled studies (Montgomery et al., 1993; Tollefson et al., 1994). Two small direct comparisons of clomipramine and fluoxetine, without placebo-control conditions, found trends for clomipramine to have the greater efficacy (Pigott et al., 1990, cited by Greist et al., 1995). Meta-analytic studies of individual drugs (Greist et al., 1995; Jenike, Baer, & Greist, 1990) also suggest that clomipramine is more effective than fluoxetine for OCD; fluoxetine is often used first, however, because of its more favorable side effect profile.

Paroxetine is another SSRI that is approved for treating OCD. In a SmithKline Beecham-sponsored multicenter trial with 348 patients, 40 mg and 60 mg doses of paroxetine were found superior to placebo after 12 weeks, with 45% of the 60-mg group showing at least 25% reduction in OCD symptoms at endpoint (Paroxetine Study Group, 1996). A double-blind discontinuation study of a subset of the same patients in the multicenter trial found that 59% relapsed within 6 months after substitution of placebo for paroxetine. This relapse rate is lower than the almost universal relapse found after clomipramine withdrawal by Pato et al. (1988), but similar to the relapse rate found after fluoxetine withdrawal by Fontaine and Chouinard (1989).

Sertraline is the most recently FDA-approved SSRI for OCD. In a multicenter trial involving 324 patients, several dose levels of sertraline were superior to placebo (Greist, Chouinard, et al., 1995). Sertraline was found comparable to clomipramine in a comparative trial with no placebo control group, and in which responses to both drugs seemed high (Bisserbe, Wiseman, Flament, Goldberg, & Lane, 1995). However, sertraline appears less effective than clomipramine in meta-analytic comparisons (Greist, Jefferson, Kobak, Katzelnick, & Serlin, 1995).

Comparisons Among Medications. The available results on the comparability of clomipramine and the SSRIs are admittedly limited, in that there are few direct comparisons in which patients are randomly assigned to each treatment. Small double-blind trials have failed to demonstrate differences between the efficacy of clomipramine and fluoxetine (Pigott et al., 1990), and between clomipramine and fluvoxamine (Freeman et al., 1994). A large multicenter, double-blind comparison of paroxetine, clomipramine, and placebo found that paroxetine and clomipramine were superior to placebo, but did not differ from one another (Zohar, Judge, & the OCD Paroxetine Study Investigators, 1996).

A meta-analysis of the major multicenter trials of several of the individual drugs versus placebo, all of which used similar inclusion–exclusion criteria and outcome measures, found that the SSRIs fluvoxamine, fluoxetine, and sertraline were less effective than clomipramine for OCD (Greist, Jefferson, Kobak, Katzelnick, et al., 1995). Greist et al. (1995) found that clomipramine treatment resulted in both larger decrements in Yale–Brown Obsessive Compulsive Scale (Y–BOCS; Goodman, Price, Rasmussen, Mazure, et al., 1989) scores and larger percentages of responders than did the SSRIs. Effect size for clomipramine was 1.48, compared to 0.69 for fluoxetine, 0.50 for fluvoxamine, and 0.35 for sertraline. It is unclear why clomipramine emerged as superior in the meta analysis, but not in the available direct comparisons. Perhaps the samples for the SSRIs were somewhat different than that for the earlier clomipramine study, such that the later samples had more medication nonresponders who had unsuccessfully tried clomipramine and then tried subsequently available medications. However, if this were the case, one might expect that each subsequently available medication would yield a smaller effect size, but this does not seem to occur. Despite clomipramine's more troublesome side effects, dropout from side effects in the clomipramine multicenter trial was similar to that for the SSRIs, and overall dropout rate in the clomipramine multicenter trial was less than that of the SSRI trials.

The preceding conclusions were drawn from analyses of data collected for a number of different studies, conducted sometimes years apart and at different sites, and not from direct experimental comparisons of the various drugs. Therefore, a number of factors might account for Greist, Jefferson, Kobak, Katzelnick, et al.'s (1995) finding that clomipramine appears superior: (a) greater difficulty blinding evaluators to clomipramine than to the SSRIs because of the obvious side effects compared to inactive placebo, (b) greater baseline severity in the clomipramine study, and (c) a higher proportion of patients in the clomipramine study who had no previous treatment. Notably, statistical control for a number of these factors did not change the overall findings (Greist, Jefferson, Kobak, Katzelnick, et al., 1995). Moreover, as mentioned earlier, several small studies directly comparing clomipramine with other SSRIs also suggested the superiority of clomipramine without differences in tolerability or, alternatively, found no differences between clomipramine and the active comparator. Overall, our tentative conclusion about the currently available results is that clomipramine may have greater efficacy for OCD than the SSRIs.

Limitations of Medication Therapy. Despite the demonstrated efficacy of pharmacotherapy for OCD, the medications have several limitations. First, their acute efficacy is limited, as measured by both proportion of responders and degree of improvement: Estimates for clomipramine, arguably the most potent available compound, are about 50% responders and about 40% reduction in OCD symptom severity. Second, all the medications that have been found helpful with OCD can cause troubling side effects. Third, relapse is high when pharmacotherapy is discontinued, and many patients eventually stop taking their medication for a variety of reasons, such as prohibitive cumulative cost or pregnancy. Finally, just as with exposure therapy, many individuals who might profit from pharmacotherapy decline to accept and complete it. For example, in our ongoing comparative study of clomipramine and cognitive behavior therapy, 15% of those randomized to clomipramine declined to receive this treatment, and 22% of those who did begin it discontinued it prematurely.

Medication and Cognitive-Behavior Therapy

Perhaps because neither ERP nor serotonergic drugs alone have been found effective for all patients with OCD, their *combination* is increasingly recommended as a first-choice treatment. The availability of two treatments that are partially effective individually has spawned a handful of investigations of their combined efficacy. However, the evidence for the general superiority of such combined treatment is at best weak.

There are six published reports of studies that combined antidepressants with behavior therapy (Amin, Ban, Pecknold, & Klingner, 1977; Cottraux et al., 1990; Foa & Rowan, 1990; Marks et al., 1988; Marks, Stern, Mawson, Cobb, & McDonald, 1980; Neziroglu, 1979), but none of them allows strong conclusions about: the relative efficacy of serotonergic medication and behavior therapy, their combined acute efficacy versus the two monotherapies, or whether the addition of behavior therapy to pharmacotherapy reduces the problem of relapse after drug discontinuation.

Combined Behavioral and Pharmacotherapies

A number of studies have combined antidepressants and behavior therapy, but none allows a conclusive comparison of anti-obsessive medication plus behavior therapy, adequately examines their additive and interactive effects on obsessive-compulsive (OC) symptoms, or examines the additive and interactive effects of the two therapies on relapse with treatment continuation.

Amin et al.'s (1977) study of clomipramine and behavior therapy had only two and three individuals per group. Neziroglu's (1979) findings of additive effects of clomipramine and behavior therapy were based on an uncontrolled study of 10 patients, and the effect of drug discontinuation was not studied.

Behavior therapy was found by Marks et al. (1980) to be acutely superior to clomipramine, which had a small additive effect. However, the medication-only period was only 4 weeks, which is too short for optimal assessment of the efficacy of clomipramine alone. Notably, in the CIBA-Geigy multicenter trial of clomipramine, continued improvement on clomipramine was observed through 10 weeks (DeVeaugh-Geiss et al., 1989). In a subsequent comparison of clomipramine and exposure, Marks et al. (1988) found that adjunctive medication had a small transitory (8-week) additive effect, and again that exposure was more potent than clomipramine. Although the design of the study did not allow evaluation of the long-term effects of behavior therapy, a 6-year follow-up included in the study revealed no persistent drug effect, and long-term improvement was associated with good compliance during exposure treatment (O'Sullivan, Noshirvani, Marks, Monteiro, & Lelliott, 1991).

A study by Foa, Kozak, Steketee, and McCarthy (1992) explored the hypothesis that reducing comorbid depression via imipramine would enhance the efficacy of subsequent behavior therapy, because depression was suspected to inhibit habituation, a hypothesized mechanism of action of exposure-based behavior therapy. In this study, imipramine or placebo were combined with behavior therapy. Although the imipramine did reduce depression, it did not reduce OC symptoms or enhance the effect of behavior therapy. Of course this medication and behavior therapy comparison does not inform us about the anti-obsessive effects of serotonergic medication combined with behavior therapy.

Fluvoxamine and behavior therapy have been found to produce similar acute and 6-month reductions in OCD symptoms, and behavior therapy plus fluvoxamine led to slightly greater improvement in depression than did behavior therapy alone (Cottraux et al., 1990). This superiority of the combined treatment for depression, however, was not evident at follow-up.

At Allegheny University (formerly Medical College of Pennsylvania), an uncontrolled study examined the long-term effects ($M = 1.5$ years post-treatment) of intensive cognitive behavior therapy and fluvoxamine or clomipramine (Hembree, Cohen, Riggs, Kozak, & Foa, 1992). Patients had been treated with serotonergic drugs, intensive behavior therapy, or behavior therapy plus one of the two medications. Patients who were on medications at follow-up did equally well regardless of whether they had received cognitive behavior therapy in addition to medication or medication alone. However, patients who were free from medication at follow-up showed a different pattern: Those who had received cognitive behavior therapy alone or behavior therapy plus medication were less symptomatic than those who had only received medication. Thus, patients treated with cognitive behavior therapy maintained their gains more than patients treated with serotonergic medication that was subsequently withdrawn.

Several investigators have used meta-analyses to compare the efficacy of serotonergic medications with cognitive behavior therapy and found rough equivalence (Cox, Swinson, Morrison, & Lee, 1993; van Balkom et al., 1994), but any such conclusion is questionable because of nonoverlapping symptom severity measures. The nonequivalence of measures limits the strength of any conclusions about pretreatment severity and improvement.

The results of the studies described do suggest that cognitive-behavior therapy might indeed turn out to be the first-choice treatment for OCD, but only hint at the superiority of combined treatment. Cognitive-behavior therapy appears to produce larger acute improvement than medication, its efficacy is more lasting, and it has no continuing side effects. However, any conclusion of the outright superiority of cognitive-behavior therapy is mitigated by the reluctance of many patients to cooperate with exposure treatment because of their OCD-related fears. The extent to which differing rates of treatment refusal for cognitive-behavior therapy and pharmacotherapy biased the outcomes in these reviewed studies is unclear.

PREDICTORS OF TREATMENT OUTCOME

As already noted, although the majority of patients respond well to the available treatments, a substantial minority do not. What factors predict outcome?

Personality Disorders

Comorbid personality disorder was found to predict poor outcome of behavior therapy in two studies (AuBuchon & Malatesta, 1994; Fals-Stewart & Lucente, 1993). Schizotypal personality predicted poor outcome with serotonergic medication in several studies (Baer & Jenike, 1992; Baer et al., 1992; Jenike, Baer, & Carey, 1986; Minichiello, Baer, & Jenike, 1987; Ravizza, Barzega, Bellino, Bogetto, & Maina, 1995). Borderline and avoidant personalities, as well as total number of personality disorders, were found related to nonresponsiveness to clomipramine (Baer et al.,

1992). Only one study failed to find that personality disorder predicted poor response to clomipramine (Mavissakalian, Jones, Olson, & Perel, 1990). Thus, it appears that comorbid personality disorder, especially schizotypal and borderline personality, predicts poor outcome for both behavior therapy and pharmacotherapy.

Pretreatment OCD Severity

Several studies failed to find that overall pretreatment OCD severity predicted response to behavior therapy (Foa et al., 1983; Hoogduin & Duivenvoorden, 1988; Marks et al., 1980; O'Sullivan et al., 1991; Steketee, 1993). However, severity of specific OCD symptoms, such as behavioral avoidance, rituals, and obsessions, predicted poor outcome of treatment by clomipramine plus behavior therapy (Basoglu, Lax, Kasvikis, & Marks, 1988) and fluvoxamine plus behavior therapy (Cottraux, Mollard, Bouvard, & Marks, 1993). Severity of compulsions predicted poor outcome of treatment by clomipramine in one sample of 49 patients (Lax, Basoglu, & Marks, 1992). However, no relation was found between overall OCD severity and clomipramine outcome in the multicenter CIBA-Geigy study that included 519 patients (Ackerman, Greenland, Bystritsky, Morgenstern, & Katz, 1994). Only one study ($N = 45$) (Alarcon, Libb, & Spitler, 1993) found that higher overall pretreatment Y–BOCS scores predicted poor outcome of treatment with clomipramine.

Inconsistent findings were reported with respect to the predictive power of the type of ritual (washing versus checking). Some studies found no relation for outcome of behavior therapy (Foa & Chambless, 1978; Foa et al., 1983; Rachman, Marks, & Hodgson, 1973), one study found checking predicted good outcome (Drummond, 1993), three studies found washing predicted good outcome of behavior therapy (Basoglu et al., 1988; Boulougouris, 1977; Buchanan, Meng, & Marks, 1996), and one study found cleaning, but not hand washing, predicted poor outcome with clomipramine (Alarcon et al., 1993). In summary, it appears that overall OCD severity may not predict behavior therapy or clomipramine outcome, but certain specific OCD symptoms may be predictive.

Pretreatment Depression

Interest in depression and outcome of behavior therapy came from early observations that patients with severe depression responded poorly to behavior therapy (e.g., Marks, 1973). Interest in depression and outcome of pharmacotherapy stems in part from the claim that the reduction of OCD symptoms by antidepressant medication is mediated by the reduction in depression (Marks et al., 1980). A controlled prospective study investigating this hypothesis revealed that both depressed and nondepressed patients fared equally well with behavior therapy and that the reduction of depression by imipramine prior to behavior therapy did not enhance behavior therapy outcome for OCD (Foa et al., 1992). The literature is inconclusive about whether pretreatment depression predicts outcome of either behavior therapy or medication. In 6 of 10 available studies, depression was not predictive of behavior therapy outcome; in the other studies it predicted poor outcome (Buchanan et al., 1996; for review, see Steketee & Shapiro, 1995). Several studies examined the effects of pretreatment depression on outcome with SRIs and none found depression to influence outcome (e.g., Ravizza et al., 1995).

Because of the notion that depression influences outcome of medication treatment for OCD, CIBA-Geigy conducted two multicenter studies with clomipramine: One excluded patients with high depression and the other included them. Conflicting results emerged from two separate analyses of data from these studies. Combining the data from both studies, Deveaugh-Geiss et al. (1990) failed to find a relation of depression to outcome. However, in the study that included depressed patients, Ackerman et al. (1994) found that pretreatment depression predicted response to clomipramine, but in a nonlinear, u-shaped fashion: Patients with low and high scores on the Hamilton Depression Rating Scale (HDRS; Hamilton, 1960) did better than those in the middle range. Notably, the highest HDRS score in this sample was 21 (moderate depression).

In summary, the majority of findings reveal no relation between pretreatment depression and outcome of clomipramine or behavior therapy. However, some studies did find that depression forbode poorer outcome with behavior therapy.

Expectancy of Outcome

Patients' expectations of the benefit they would derive from treatment were found to predict outcome of behavior therapy in one study (Cottraux et al., 1993) but not in another (Lax et al., 1992). Studying treatment with clomipramine, Lax et al. (1992) found that patients with more severe symptoms had higher expectation but improved less than those with less severe symptoms and lower expectations. The pure effects of expectation on outcome of clomipramine were not ascertained from this study because symptom severity and expectation were correlated.

Motivation and Compliance With Behavior Therapy

Several studies investigated the influence of motivation (and compliance) on BT outcome (Hoogduin & Duivenvoorden, 1988; Keijsers, Hoogduin, & Schaap, 1994; Lax et al., 1992; O'Sullivan et al., 1991). All but Lax et al. (1992) found compliance or motivation to predict good outcome.

Evocation of Fear and its Decrease Within and Between Exposures

Foa and Kozak (1986) identified three indicators of emotional processing associated with successful outcome of exposure treatment for anxiety. First, patients who improve show physiological responding and fear ratings during exposure that evidence activation of anxiety. Second, their anxiety decreases gradually during confrontation with feared objects or situations. Third, intensity of the initial distress reaction at each exposure session decreases across sessions. Support for the validity of these predictors of successful outcome with exposure therapy can be found in treatment outcome studies with a number of anxiety disorders, and from laboratory experiments (see Foa & Kozak, 1986, for review).

Studying OCD specifically, Kozak, Foa, and Steketee (1988) explored the relation between the three indicators and therapy outcome with ERP. The first indicator, activation of anxiety, was evident in both self-report and physiological measures during exposure sessions, and predicted post-treatment improvement. Treatment was generally successful, and the second indicator, habituation within sessions, was also evident in both self-report and physiology for the group as a whole. This indicator did not, however, predict individual differences in outcome, perhaps because most patients habituated within sessions. Individual differences in the third indicator, habituation of anxiety across sessions, also predicted improvement.

THE NATIONAL INSTITUTE OF MENTAL HEALTH (NIMH) SPONSORED COLLABORATIVE COMPARISON OF CLOMIPRAMINE AND BEHAVIOR THERAPY FOR OCD

Aims and Design

This study is designed to compare the efficacy and durability of the two most established treatments for OCD, clomipramine and cognitive behavior therapy, to one another, to their combination, and to pill placebo. As noted in the preceding review, clomipramine and other medications for OCD have moderate efficacy, prominent side effects, and lack of durability after discontinuation. Studies of cognitive-behavior therapy indicate marked efficacy and durability. However, cognitive-behavior therapy is refused by a substantial number of patients. The available efficacy studies were conducted by cognitive-behavior therapy experts in specialty clinics, thus raising questions of its generalizability, and its relative efficacy compared to clomipramine has not been studied in a well-controlled design. Treatment that combines clomipramine and cognitive behavior therapy is widely believed to be superior to either treatment alone in efficacy and tolerability, although it has received little systematic investigation.

A study was begun in 1990 to compare all four treatments at a cognitive-behavior therapy-oriented site (Eastern Pennsylvania Psychiatric Institute at MCP and Hahnemann University; EPPI) and a pharmacologically oriented site (New York State Psychiatric Institute at Columbia University; NYSPI), providing treatment with both clomipramine and cognitive behavior therapy and methodologically rigorous assessments. The collaboration of pharmacotherapists and cognitive behavior therapists was intended to strengthen not only the scientific rigor of the study, but also its credibility among practioners of both types of treatment.

The primary goals of this project have been:

1. To compare the efficacy for OCD of treatment with clomipramine, exposure and ritual prevention, their combination, and pill placebo.
2. To compare the relapse rates after discontinuation of the treatments, and in particular, to examine whether ERP inhibits relapse after discontinuation of clomipramine.
3. To compare the efficacy of pharmacotherapy and psychosocial treatment for OCD at centers, each of which is known for expertise in one class of treatment: psychopharmacological treatment at NYSPI and cognitive-behavior therapy at EPPI.

Subsidiary goals have been to examine the relative effects of clomipramine, behavior therapy, and combined treatment on specific aspects of OCD such as obsessions, rituals, anxiety, and level of depression, and to explore predictors of response to treatment.

We believe that this study constitutes a model paradigm for pharmacotherapy–psychotherapy comparisons because experts in each modality deliver both treatment modalities, thus guarding against expert bias for either treatment. It is designed to yield definitive conclusions about the relative efficacy of ERP and clomipramine, the two treatments that have been considered the therapies of choice for OCD for the last decade. We hope that the results of this study will be informative about the generalizability of both treatments and influence clinical practice widely.

EXPERIMENTAL DESIGN

One hundred sixty-eight participants with OCD, half at each site (NYSPI and EPPI), meeting *Diagnostic and Statistical Manual of Mental Disorders* (4th ed. [*DSM–IV*]; American Psychiatric Association, 1994) criteria will participate in the study, approximately 120 of whom are expected to complete the treatment phase. A satellite site developed in Winnipeg (Murray Stein, MD and Vivienne Rowan, PhD) accrued a small number of patients that are subsumed in the NYSPI data. Other satellite sites are being considered to enhance the rate of patient accrual. Participants are randomly assigned to the following four groups: clomipramine (CMI), pill placebo (PBO), cognitive-behavior therapy (CBT), and clomipramine plus behavior therapy (CMI + CBT).

To date, a total of 549 individuals have been screened for the study. Of these, 99 were randomized into study conditions. Of the remainder, 247 did not meet study criteria: 68 did not have OCD or had subclinical OCD, 92 had already received adequate trials of behavior therapy or clomipramine, 17 were excluded for medical reasons, and 70 were excluded for comorbid diagnoses such as major depression. Another 203 individuals who otherwise met study eligibility criteria declined to participate: 36 were unwilling to participate in research, 39 refused to receive clomipramine, 29 refused to receive behavior therapy, 46 declined for other specified reasons, and 53 declined for unspecified reasons.

Preliminary analyses have been performed on data from the first 97 of the 99 randomized patients, and some of the results are summarized here. Of the 97 randomized, 14 withdrew at randomization, after they had learned their treatment condition, and before receiving any treatment: four from CMI, four from PBO, five from CBT, and one from CMI + CBT. There is no difference in refusal by treatment. It appears that these 14 postrandomization treatment refusers were covertly committed to a particular therapy, and despite their prior consent to accept random assignment, withdrew when they were assigned to an unwanted treatment. These 14 treatment refusers are not included in our preliminary results because they essentially declined to enter the study. Thus, 83 patients constitute the available intent-to-treat sample that actually began treatment. Twenty-two patients (27%) dropped out during treatment (five from CMI, four from PBO, five from CBT, and eight from CMI + CBT), yielding a completer sample of 61 patients.

The study is ongoing and we plan to enter additional patients as follows: 23 into CMI, 28 into CBT, 24 into CMI + CBT, and 9 into PBO. When combined with the previously accrued sample, these new entrants will sum to 46 per active treatment group and 29 in the placebo group. Fewer patients are needed in the placebo cell than in the active treatment cells because of the substantial differences expected between all active treatments and placebo. Assuming 28% dropout, we expect that this will yield approximately 31 completers per active treatment group and 22 completers in the placebo group.

Treatment and Assessment Schedule

Patients were randomized to one of four treatment conditions: CBT, CMI, CBT + CMI, and PBO. Active treatment lasted 3 months, followed by a 3-month no-treatment follow-up period.

Patients were evaluated at four major assessment points: pretreatment, 1 month (after intensive behavior therapy), 3 months (after clomipramine and behavior therapy), and 6 months (after 3 months of no treatment). The primary outcome measure of OCD was the severity score on the Y–BOCS. Various additional interview and questionnaire measures of anxiety, depression, and general functioning were also administered, but except for a Clinical Global Impressions rating (CGI) did not constitute primary outcome variables. Non-responders at 3 months were withdrawn from the trial and offered alternative treatment. Responders were defined as having a CGI rating of "much improved" or "very much improved." The much improved rating was defined as corresponding to at least 50% reduction in overall time spent on obsessions or compulsions, and very much improved meant near disappearance of these symptoms.

PROCEDURES

Screening

Patients deemed eligible following preliminary screening received a full explanation of study procedures and consent to participate was obtained. Participants were evaluated by a psychiatrist or psychologist via a structured diagnostic interview. Those meeting *DSM–IV* criteria for OCD were accepted into the study provided that the following inclusion and exclusion criteria were met:

- OCD was severe enough to rate 7 or higher on the NIMH global OCD scale and score 18 or higher on Items 1–10 of the Y–BOCS.
- Patients must not have both major depression and a HDRS score of more than 18.
- Eligible patients then underwent medical evaluation, after which medication-free patients were randomized. Otherwise eligible patients who were taking psychoactive medication underwent a 2-week drug-free period prior to the pretreatment assessment. Anti-OCD drugs such as SSRIs were discontinued 4 weeks prior to study randomization, except for fluoxetine, which was stopped for 6 weeks.

Pretreatment Assessment

After screening, patients received a pretreatment assessment by an independent evaluator, who also assessed the patient throughout the study, and who had no other contact with that patient.

Treatment

After their pretreatment assessment, patients began 12 weeks of treatment. Treatment procedures for each of the four conditions are summarized briefly here.

Clomipramine or Pill Placebo. Patients were seen weekly for 30 minutes by their research psychiatrist during this 12-week phase for medication adjustment, based on a standard dosage schedule. Treatment procedures are formalized in a manual. Patients were told by their psychiatrist that they had to expose themselves to phobic situations without ritualizing to overcome fear, and that the role of clomipramine is to make this easier. However, no systematic exposure instructions, nor any insight-oriented therapy was permitted. Dosage schedule was fixed for the first 5 weeks and flexible thereafter. The target dose was 250 mg/day; 12 weeks of treatment and at least 150 mg per day for 4 consecutive weeks was required for inclusion as a completer. At 12 weeks, all patients were withdrawn from their pills within 3 weeks (50 mg reduction every fifth day).

Cognitive-Behavior Therapy. The 3-month active treatment period included 4 phases: treatment planning, 3 weeks of intensive, 5-days-per-week imaginal and in vivo exposure of gradually increasing difficulty, a home visit, and eight weekly maintenance visits. Following two orientation and information-gathering sessions, exposure sessions were conducted daily for 2 hours on all weekdays for 15 sessions, and daily homework was assigned. Ritualizing was proscribed from the outset of the exposure sessions. During the fourth week, the therapist visited the patient's home for 2 hours on 2 consecutive days.

Clomipramine Plus Cognitive-Behavior Therapy. Patients in this group began both treatments in the same week, and continued to receive both contemporaneously, according to the procedures already described for CBT and clomipramine alone.

No-Treatment Follow-Up Period

Patients judged to be responders after Week 12 entered the 3-month treatment-free follow-up that began with a 3-week medication taper period for participants in both active and inactive pills conditions. Responders were defined as patients rated "much improved" or "very much improved" on the CGI scale by the independent evaluator. At 1-month intervals during the follow-up period, continuing patients were assessed. Criteria for relapse were that the patient returned to Week 0 CGI severity status or worse for 1 week; manifested a clinical state that made further study participation inadvisable, as judged by the independent evaluator; or receives psychotherapy or psychotropic medication for OCD from outside sources.

QUALITY CONTROL

The first 6 months of the project were devoted to instituting the study procedures. This included training cognitive-behavior therapists, pharmacotherapists, and independent evaluators. Cognitive behavior therapists from both sites received instruction at EPPI in the treatment protocol, observed experts conducting treatment, and performed a supervised intensive cognitive behavior therapy with at least one patient before beginning the protocol. Pharmacotherapists received instruction at NYSPI in medication management according to the study protocol. Independent evaluators received group training in the assessment instruments and performed practice ratings of taped interviews. Ratings of the evaluators were compared to one another in the group setting, discrepancies were discussed, and rules for rating were further explicated as needed to assure interrater agreement.

Pharmacotherapists at both sites audiotaped sessions and submitted them to NYSPI for weekly supervision by Dr. Campeas (via telephone for EPPI). Pharmacotherapists from both sites met periodically for supervised review of procedures. Medication dose levels were systematically recorded and medication blood levels were assessed at fixed time points to monitor compliance with medication.

Continuing supervision was arranged for cognitive behavior therapists and independent evaluators with Dr. Kozak at EPPI. Cognitive behavior therapists videotaped sessions and submitted tapes immediately to EPPI. NYSPI used overnight mail to submit tapes. At EPPI, tapes were viewed and sessions discussed with therapists several times per week (via telephone for NYSPI). Cognitive-behavior therapists from both sites met

together periodically for supervised review of tapes and therapy procedures.

Independent evaluators audiotaped their evaluation sessions and
evaluators from both sites met quarterly for review of procedures and
comparative rerating of randomly selected taped evaluations from both
sites. Discrepant ratings were discussed and rating rules explicated to
promote convergence. The rerating data are available for estimates of
interrater reliability.

PRELIMINARY RESULTS

Demographics

Our preliminary findings are based on 97 randomized patients. The average
age of the entrants was 34.8 years (range = 18 to 71); 52 were men and 45
were women. Seventy-five were White, three were African American, four
were Hispanic, two were Asian, four were Native-American, and ethnicity
was unavailable for nine participants. Fifty-one were single, 31 were
married, 6 were divorced, 1 was widowed, and marital status was unavailable for 8 participants. Education level was as follows: some high school, 2;
high school graduate, 17; some college, 30; undergraduate degree, 17; some
postgraduate school, 8; graduate degree, 12; and unknown, 11.

As noted earlier 97 patients were randomized. Of these, 14 refused to
start treatment, 22 others dropped out during treatment, and 61 completed
3 months of treatment. Of the 61 completers, 31 were categorized as
responders, and thus eligible to enter follow-up. Of these, 30 entered
follow-up: 8 from CMI, 1 from PBO, 11 from CBT, and 10 from CMI + CBT.
Twenty-four patients completed the follow-up phase: all of the CBT responders (11/11) and all but two (Week 20 dropouts) of the CMI + CBT
responders (8/10) completed the follow-up phase; five of eight CMI
responders also completed the follow-up phase and three dropped out at
Week 16; the one PBO responder dropped out of follow-up at Week 20.

OUTCOME

The intent-to-treat sample consists of the 83 participants who actually
began treatment in study protocols. The last available assessment (up to
3 months) was used. Pretreatment group differences appeared to be
minimal for the Y–BOCS, HDRS, CGI-Severity, and NIMH GOCS measures. Pre- and posttreatment scores for the Y–BOCS, the primary measure
of OCD symptoms, are summarized in Table 25.1.

TABLE 25.1
Treatment Outcome: Intent-to-Treat Sample

	PBO[a]	CMI[b]	CBT[c]	CMI + CBT[d]
Pretreatment	24.5 (3.9)	26.5 (4.0)	23.9 (5.2)	25.2 (4.8)
Posttreatment	23.2 (5.9)	19.1 (7.4)	15.3 (8.6)	13.3 (10.4)

[a]n = 20. [b]n = 23. [c]n = 18. [d]n = 22.

Participants were categorized as responders or nonresponders on the CGI improvement scale as described earlier. It appeared that treatment type affected responding. Responder rates (3 months) were: PBO (n = 20), 5.0%; CMI (n = 23), 39.1%; CBT (n = 18), 61.1%; CMI + CBT (n = 22), 45.5%.

Twenty-two patients (27%) dropped out during the 12 weeks after beginning treatment. These patients did not differ in initial severity from the 61 who completed treatment. There was no differential attrition by treatment group. Dropouts did not differ in initial severity from completers for any treatment condition.

There were five dropouts from CMI, four during the first week of treatment and one during Week 4. Reasons included side effects in four cases and "personal" reasons in one. Two of four PBO dropouts occurred during the first week, and the other two during Week 8. Reasons were lack of efficacy in two cases, "personal" in one case, and unknown in the last. Four of five CBT dropouts occurred during the first week, and the fifth during Week 4. Reasons were inability to comply in three cases, refusal to continue in a fourth case, and missing too many sessions in the fifth case. Four CMI + CBT dropouts occurred during the first week, two others during Week 4, and the last two during Week 8. Reasons were inability to comply with behavior therapy in one case, noncompliance in a second, side effects in three others, and unknown in the remaining three.

The completer sample consists of the 61 participants that completed the 3-month active treatment period. Pretreatment group differences appeared to be minimal for the Y–BOCS, HDRS, CGI Severity, and NIMH GOCS. At 1 month and 3 months, the groups appeared to differ on the Y–BOCS, CGI Severity, and NIMH GOCS. At 1 month, OCD symptom severity as measured by the Y–BOCS was lower for the CBT and CMI + CBT groups than for the CMI group, which was lower than for the PBO group. At 1 month on the CGI, CBT and CMI + CBT groups were superior to the CMI and PBO groups. At 1 month on the NIMH GOCS, the CBT and CMI + CBT groups were superior to the PBO group and the CMI and PBO groups did not differ. At 3 months, on the Y–BOCS, CGI, and NIMH GOCS, the CBT and CMI + CBT groups were superior to the CMI group, which itself was superior to the PBO group.

Patients were categorized as responders or nonresponders on the CGI improvement scale as previously described. All three active treatments were superior to placebo at 1 and 3 months. Behavior therapy was superior to clomipramine at 1 and 3 months, where clomipramine and behavior therapy were superior to clomipramine only at 1 month. Responder rates at 3 months were PBO (1/16), 6.3%; CMI (9/18), 50.0%; CBT (11/13), 84.6%; and CMI + CBT (10/14), 71.4%.

A patient was considered a relapser if he or she returned to Week 0 CGI severity status or worse for 1 week; manifested a clinical state that made further study participation inadvisable, as judged by the independent evaluator; or received psychotherapy or psychotropic medication for OCD from outside sources. Our impression from the 30 patients who entered the follow-up phase of the study is of substantial relapse among patients in the CMI group, compared to those in the CBT group alone or in the CMI + CBT group. Relapse rates were CMI (7/8), 87.5%; CBT, (0/11); and CMI + CBT (1/10), 10.0%. The small sample in each follow-up group however, yields such wide confidence intervals for estimating percentage relapse that conclusions about long-term outcome would be premature.

CLOMIPRAMINE DOSAGE AND BLOOD LEVELS

For patients in active medication conditions (CMI and CMI + CBT), the relation between clomipramine dosage and blood metabolites was examined. Due to differences in the way individuals metabolize clomipramine, two composite indicators were calculated. The first indicator was calculated by adding clomipramine and desmethylclomipramine blood levels at each time point (Weeks 4, 5, 12). This indicator correlated .50 (ns) with drug dosage at 4 weeks, .38 (ns) at 5 weeks, and .20 (ns) at 12 weeks. The second indicator, the ratio of clomipramine to desmethylclomipramine at each time point (Weeks 4, 5, 12), correlated $-.35$ (ns) with drug dosage at 4 weeks, $-.61$ ($p < .01$) at 5 weeks and $-.54$ (ns) at 12 weeks.

For the CMI and CMI + CBT groups individually, there were no differences between responders and nonresponders for blood levels or drug dosages. When the two groups were combined, there were no differences in blood levels or drug dosages between responders and nonresponders at Weeks 4 or 5. However, at 12 weeks there was a trend for the nonresponders to have a higher dosage (239 mg/day) than responders (214 mg/day). These results indicate that the lack of response was not due to lower dosage or blood levels in the nonresponders. The tendency for nonresponders to have higher dosages and higher blood levels suggests that psychiatrists were aware of their poor response and accordingly increased their medication. There was no difference between dosages administered to the CMI and CMI + CBT groups at Weeks 4 or 5. At Week 12, however, the CMI group (244 mg/day) had a higher dosage level then the CMI + CBT group (196 mg/day), suggesting that concomitant behavior therepy lowers the required clomipramine dosage.

INTERSITE COMPARISONS

Overall Sample

EPPI screened 362 patients and NYSPI screened 185. Of the 362 screened at EPPI, 134 (37%) were study eligible, versus 120 of the 185 (65%) at NYSPI. These proportions differed significantly. At EPPI, 46 of the 134 (34%) eligible patients were randomized into the study, compared to 51 of 120 (43%) at NYSPI, which did not differ significantly. At EPPI, 9 of 46 (20%) refused to accept the treatment to which they were randomized, compared to 5 of 51 (10%) at NYSPI. These proportions did not differ significantly. At EPPI, 37 of 134 (28%) eligible patients were randomized and actually began treatment, compared to 46 of 120 (38%) at NYSPI. These proportions also did not differ significantly. EPPI had 3 dropouts among its 37 entrants (8%) versus 19 dropouts from 46 entrants (41%) at NYSPI. These proportions differed significantly.

These data can be summarized as follows: EPPI screened a larger pool of potential patients; samples of study-eligible patients were similar in size at both sites; NYSPI and EPPI did not differ in proportions of eligible patients who entered the study or actually began treatment; and NYSPI had a higher dropout rate than did EPPI and this was not limited to any particular treatment. However, the relatively small sample accrued to date does not permit firm conclusions about site differences in drop-out rate.

Fidelity to Treatment

For the CMI group, there appeared to be no site differences in Week 12 doses or blood levels of clomipramine, desmethylclomipramine or the two combined. For the CMI + CBT, there were no significant differences between sites in blood levels, but NYSPI exceeded EPPI in dose. For the CMI group, NYSPI Week 12 doses averaged 245 mg/day ($SD = 16$), whereas EPPI averaged 244 mg/day ($SD = 18$). For the CMI + CBT group, NYSPI Week 12 doses averaged 230 mg/day ($SD = 45$) versus 175 mg/day ($SD = 38$) at EPPI.

Formal assessment of behavior therapy protocol adherence has been conducted on a sample of 16 cases from EPPI and 10 from NYSPI, including at least one case from each of the three behavior therapists involved at each site to date. Two raters who were not otherwise involved in the study viewed videotapes and inspected therapist charts to ascertain protocol adherence in 13 criteria areas and assigned a rating of 0 or 1 to each area depending on whether there was documentation of procedural compliance by the therapist. Thus, each case can be characterized by overall percentage of adherence to the 13 criteria areas. Inspection of the data suggests no site differences in treatment adherence. Proportion adherence was 91.6% for the NYSPI sample and 87.2% for the EPPI sample. Because of both the similar adherence ratings and similar behavior therapy outcome results at the two sites, it appears likely that intersite standardization of behavior therapy procedures has been achieved.

SUMMARY AND DISCUSSION
OF PRELIMINARY FINDINGS

The data and data analyses presented here cannot be considered definitive. Because of limited sample size many comparisons have limited power and some estimates have very wide confidence intervals. Thus, our preliminary results should be interpreted with caution.

The two most established treatments for OCD, behavior therapy and clomipramine, were again demonstrated to be effective. At the end of 1 month of treatment, both monotherapies and their combination were superior to placebo on various OCD measures.

The present direct comparison of clomipramine and ERP suggests that immediately following treatment, ERP appeared superior to clomipramine alone for OCD symptoms, as evidenced by significant differences on several analyses of both the intent-to-treat and completer samples.

As expected, clomipramine, ERP, and their combination were superior to placebo on OCD measures immediately after treatment for both the intent-to-treat and completer samples. However, in contrast to our expectations, evidence for the superiority of the combination treatment to the monotherapies was quite weak. ERP alone seemed just as successful as the combination treatment. The combination treatment did appear superior to clomipramine alone, as reflected in significant differences on dimensional measures of OCD symptoms and marginally significant trends on some of the categorical measures. Thus, it seems that adding clomipramine to ERP does little to enhance outcome, but adding ERP to clomipramine does more. The impression that the ERP contributes disproportionately more than clomipramine to the combination treatment is buttressed by the finding of a faster onset of action for both ERP alone and ERP plus clomipramine than for clomipramine alone.

Durability of improvement is better for ERP alone and ERP plus clomipramine than it is for clomipramine alone, as reflected in significant group differences in OCD symptoms 3 months after treatment discontinuation.

Our preliminary findings for clomipramine alone are similar to those of the large CIBA-Geigy multicenter trial that demonstrated that clomipramine is an effective treatment for OCD. We obtained a 50% responder rate to clomipramine versus a 6% responder rate to placebo (CGI ratings) in our completer sample, but somewhat less (39% vs. 5%) in the whole sample that received treatment. However, limitations in both proportions of patients responding and degree of improvement obtained, even in completer samples, highlight the need for more effective treatment regimens for OCD. For example, the mean total Y–BOCS score for the clomipramine completer group at the end of 12 weeks of treatment, although approximately 33% reduced from baseline, is still over 18, and thus in the range of clinical severity. As discussed later, behavior therapy and clomipramine with behavior therapy may represent two more effective regimens for OCD. Also, our preliminary findings for behavior therapy alone parallel those of previous studies of its efficacy. In the completer sample, we found an 85% responder rate to behavior therapy versus 6% for placebo, and in the intent-to-treat sample, a 61% responder rate versus 5% for placebo. Thus, the preliminary findings of this multisite double-blind comparison add further support to the impression from the literature that exposure-based therapy is a generally more potent treatment for OCD than are the available medications.

The present data do not suggest that the combination of intensive exposure therapy and clomipramine, applied simultaneously, afford an advantage over intensive exposure alone. Thus, the common claim that the most potent treatment for OCD is a combination of SRIs and behavior therapy seems premature. On the other hand, these data do not offer general support for the opposite conclusion that combination treatment affords no advantage either.

In addition to the modest sample size in this study, several considerations mitigate against an inference that combination therapy might not be superior for certain individuals. This study is probably not ideally designed to detect combination treatment effects because 3-month pharmacotherapy and the 1-month intensive exposure are begun simultaneously. However, sequential design where behavior therapy is added to clomipramine or placebo also would have complicated evaluation of the combination treatment because of expected differences in drop-out rate or severity between medication and placebo groups. The emergence of such differences at the end of the first treatment in the sequence would confound results of the second stage of treatment.

Our current design does test the efficacy of a form of combined treatment that many believe to be the optimal treatment for OCD (Abel, 1993) despite the paucity of supporting data. Notably, clomipramine does not show much effect until 6 to 10 weeks, at which point intensive behavior therapy is already completed. It is plausible that a combination therapy would be superior especially for individuals who were too fearful to begin exposure, providing that the SRI were administered 8 to 10 weeks prior to exposure onset. Also, because patients had to agree to accept randomization before entering the study, self-selection may have restricted the sample of refusers of behavior therapy alone, who could conceivably have gained most from a combination treatment.

Despite the apparent superiority of exposure treatment for OCD, several difficulties limit its utility. Although various estimates of its underuse vary in their details, there is general agreement that relatively few patients with OCD actually receive exposure treatment. One frequently cited clinical observation is that 30% of patients with OCD refuse to enter behavior therapy (Emmelkamp & Foa, 1983). Our preliminary findings also indicate the underuse of behavior therapy: Of approximately 450 treatment seekers with OCD screened over 4 years, only about 35% received behavior therapy either openly or in a controlled trial. Another problem that compromises the utility of behavior therapy is dropout. In our ongoing NIMH-sponsored controlled trial, 40% of those who began behavior therapy did not complete it.

The apparent underuse of cognitive-behavior therapy is at once puzzling and disturbing. One survey noted that the administration of cognitive-behavior therapy ranked 43rd in importance out of 50 professional content areas for psychiatrists (Langsley & Yager, 1988). According to the 1988–1989 American Psychiatrist Activities Survey, the vast majority of psychiatrists (90%) do not use behavior therapy (APA, 1989). Given its demonstrated efficacy with OCD, it is unfortunate that so few mental health service providers receive training in ERP procedures for OCD, and thus so rarely offer this successful treatment. The professional identity of many biologically oriented psychiatrists could in part account for their inattention to behavior therapy, but it does not explain the scarcity of psychologists and social workers with expertise in behavior therapy for OCD.

Besides the widespread unavailability of skilled providers, another factor that may mitigate the utility of cognitive-behavior therapy is patients' refusal to enter treatment because of obsessive fear of the exposure tasks. Many patients say that exposure is threatening, and a substantial minority refuse to enter treatment because of anticipatory anxiety. Others begin treatment but drop out because they cannot tolerate the anxiety evoked by confronting feared situations. A second barrier is the time and energy required for a month-long intensive behavior therapy program. Our successful intensive program requires daily 2-hour sessions, 5 days per week, plus daily homework practice, and travel to and from therapy. This requirement of 25 or more hours per week is often incompatible with employment or household obligations. The dose-response function for exposure with OCD has not been ascertained, and we do not know how much attenuation of the intensive treatment regimen studied here can be tolerated without important deterioration of efficacy. Perhaps only those individuals with mild OCD can achieve satisfactory improvement with truncated versions of the highly successful intensive exposure program.

Treatment refusal and dropout not only compromise treatment utility but also distort the samples in treatment outcome studies, limiting the generalizability of efficacy findings. Restrictive inclusion criteria also contribute to this problem. Such restrictive sampling is not peculiar to this NIMH study. OCD sufferers with comorbid mental disorders such as depression, tics, schizotypy, and borderline personality are typically excluded from large pharmaceutical-company-sponsored trials of medications, as well as from NIMH-sponsored treatment efficacy research. Thus, there is little information on how well the efficacy findings from this and other available controlled studies apply to "complicated" cases of OCD. Furthermore, as noted earlier, the Epidemiological Catchment Area (ECA) study has revealed its frequent comorbidity with other disorders. Notably, the estimated 80% efficacy for behavior therapy in these preliminary findings is based on 4% of the screened patients who met study entry criteria, accepted behavior therapy, and completed it.

Its limitations notwithstanding, the NIMH-sponsored behavior therapy–clomipramine comparison is a unique and pivotal study that constitutes a model for pharmacotherapy–psychotherapy comparisons, in that experts in each treatment deliver that treatment, thus guarding against expert bias toward a particular treatment. Data from the fully accrued sample should allow definitive conclusions about the relative efficacy of cognitive-behavior therapy and clomipramine, the two treatments that have been considered the therapies of choice for OCD for the last decade, and shed new light on the promise of combination treatment. We anticipate that because of the study's methodological appeal, these findings will have widespread credibility and will influence clinical practice broadly. NIMH support of such complex projects is invaluable: The knowledge to be derived from them is very much in the public interest, and because their expense is unlikely to be recouped in profits to some corporate underwriter, public sponsorship is essential.

REFERENCES

Abel, J. L. (1993). Exposure with response prevention and serotonergic antidepressants in the treatment of obsessive compulsive disorder: A review and implications for interdisciplinary treatment. *Behaviour Research and Therapy, 5,* 463–478.

Ackerman, D. L., Greenland, S., Bystritsky, A., Morgenstern, H., & Katz, R. J. (1994). Predictors of treatment response in obsessive-compulsive disorder: Multivariate analyses from a multicenter trial of clomipramine. *Journal of Clinical Psychopharmacology, 14,* 247–254.

Alarcon, R. D., Libb, J. W., & Spitler, D. (1993). A predictive study of obsessive-compulsive disorder response to clomipramine. *Journal of Clinical Psychopharmacology, 13,* 210–213.

American Psychiatric Association. (1989). *Psychiatrist Activity Survey (1988–1989).* Unpublished data.

American Psychiatric Association. (1994). *Diagnostic and statistical manual of mental disorders* (4th ed.). Washington, DC: Author.

Amin, M. D., Ban, T. A., Pecknold, J. C., & Klingner, A. (1977). Clomipramine (anafranil) and behavior therapy in obsessive-compulsive and phobic disorders. *Journal of International Medical Research, 5,* 33–37.

AuBuchon, P. G., & Malatesta, V. J. (1994). Obsessive compulsive patients with comorbid personality disorder: Associated problems and response to a comprehensive behavior therapy. *Journal of Clinical Psychiatry, 55,* 448–453.

Baer, L., & Jenike, M. A. (1992). Personality disorders in obsessive compulsive disorder. *Psychiatric Clinics of North America, 55,* 803–812.

Baer, L., Jenike, M. A., Black, D. W., Treece, C., Rosenfeld, R., & Greist, J. (1992). Effect of Axis II diagnoses on treatment outcome with clomipramine in 55 patients with obsessive-compulsive disorder. *Archives of General Psychiatry, 49,* 862–866.

Baer, L., & Minichiello, W. E. (1990). Behavior therapy for obsessive-compulsive disorder. In M. A. Jenike, L. Baer, & W. E. Minichiello (Eds.), *Obsessive compulsive disorders: Theory and management.* Chicago: Year Book Medical.

Basoglu, M., Lax, T., Kasvikis, Y., & Marks, I. M. (1988). Predictors of improvement in obsessive-compulsive disorder. *Journal of Anxiety Disorders, 2,* 299–317.

Beech, H. R., & Vaughn, M. (1978). *Behavioral treatment of obsessional states.* New York: Wiley.

Bisserbe, J. C., Wiseman, R., Flament, M., Goldberg, M., & Lane, R. (1995, May). *A double-blind comparison of sertraline and clomipramine in outpatients with obsessive-compulsive disorder.* Poster presented at the 148th Annual Meeting of the American Psychiatric Association, Miami, FL.

Black, A. (1974). The natural history of obsessional neurosis. In H. R. Beech (Ed.), *Obsessional states* (pp. 19–54). London: Methuen.

Boulougouris, J. (1977). Variables affecting the behaviour modification of obsessive-compulsive patients treated by flooding. In J. C. Boulougouris & A. D. Rabavilas (Eds.), *The treatment of phobic and obsessive-compulsive disorders* (pp. 73–84). Oxford, UK: Pergamon.

Buchanan, A. W., Meng, K. S., & Marks, I. M. (1996). What predicts improvement and compliance during the behavioral treatment of obsessive compulsive disorder? *Anxiety, 2,* 22–27.

Clomipramine Study Group. (1991). Clomipramine in the treatment of patients with obsessive-compulsive disorder. *Archives of General Psychiatry, 48,* 730–738.

Cooper, J. E., Gelder, M. G., & Marks, I. M. (1965). Results of behaviour therapy in 77 psychiatric patients. *British Medical Journal, 1,* 1222–1225.

Cottraux, J., Mollard, E., Bouvard, M., & Marks, I. (1993). Exposure therapy, fluvoxamine, or combination treatment in obsessive-compulsive disorder: One-year follow-up. *Psychiatry Research, 49,* 63–75.

Cottraux, J., Mollard, E., Bouvard, M., Marks, I., Sluys, M., Nury, A. M., Douge, R., & Ciadella, P. (1990). A controlled study of fluvoxamine and exposure in obsessive-compulsive disorder. *International Clinical Psychopharmacology, 5,* 17–30.

Cox, B. J., Swinson, R. P., Morrison, B., & Lee, P. S. (1993). Clomipramine, fluoxetine, and behavior therapy in the treatment of obsessive-compulsive disorder: A meta-analysis. *Journal of Behavior Therapy and Experimental Psychiatry, 24,* 149–153.

DeVeaugh-Geiss, J., Landau, P., & Katz, R. (1989). Treatment of OCD with clomipramine. *Psychiatric Annals, 19,* 97–101.

Drummond, L. M. (1993). The treatment of severe, chronic, resistant obsessive compulsive disorder: An evaluation of an in-patient program using behavioral psychotherapy in combination with other treatments. *British Journal of Psychiatry, 163,* 223–229.

Emmelkamp, P. M. G., de Haan, E., & Hoogduin, C. A. L. (1990). Marital adjustment and obsessive-compulsive disorder. *British Journal of Psychiatry, 156,* 55–60.

Emmelkamp, P. M. G., & Foa, E. B. (1983). Failures are a challenge. In E. B. Foa & P. M. G. Emmelkamp (Eds.), *Failures in behavior therapy* (pp. 1–9). New York: Wiley.

Fals-Stewart, W., & Lucente, S. (1993). An MCMI cluster typology of obsessive-compulsives: A measure of personality characteristics and its relationship to treatment participation, compliance and outcome in behavior therapy. *Journal of Psychiatric Research, 27*(2), 139–154.

Foa, E. B., & Chambless, D. L. (1978). Habituation of subjective anxiety during flooding in imagery. *Behavior Research and Therapy, 16,* 391–399.

Foa, E. B., Grayson, J. B., Steketee, G. S., Doppelt, H. G., Turner, R. M., & Latimer, P. R. (1983). Success and failure in the behavioral treatment of obsessive-compulsives. *Journal of Consulting and Clinical Psychology, 51,* 287–297.

Foa, E. B., & Kozak, M. J. (1985). Treatment of anxiety disorders: Implications for psychopathology. In A. H. Tuma & J. D. Maser (Eds.), *Anxiety and the anxiety disorders* (pp. 421–452). Hillsdale, NJ: Lawrence Erlbaum Associates.

Foa, E. B., & Kozak, M. J. (1986). Emotional processing of fear: Exposure to corrective information. *Psychological Bulletin, 99,* 20–35.

Foa, E. B., & Kozak, M. J. (1996). Psychological treatment for obsessive-compulsive disorder. In M. R. Mavissakalian & R. F. Prien (Eds.), *Long-term treatments of anxiety disorders* (pp. 285–309). Washington, DC: American Psychiatric Press.

Foa, E. B., Kozak, M. J., Steketee, G., & McCarthy, P. R. (1992). Treatment of depressive and obsessive-compulsive symptoms in OCD by imipramine and behavior therapy. *British Journal of Clinical Psychology, 31,* 279–292.

Foa, E. B., & Rowan, Y. (1990). Behavior therapy. In A. S. Belleck & M. Hersen (Eds.), *Handbook of comparative treatments for adult disorders* (pp. 256–265). New York: Wiley.

Foa, E. B., Steketee, G. S., & Ozarow, B. J. (1985). Behavior therapy with obsessive-compulsives: From theory to treatment. In M. Mavissakalian (Ed.), *Obsessive-compulsive disorders: Psychological and pharmacological treatments* (pp. 49–129). New York: Plenum.

Foa, E. B., & Wilson, R. (1991). *Stop obsessing! How to overcome your obsessions and compulsions.* New York: Bantam Doubleday Dell.

Fontaine, R., & Chouinard, G. (1986). An open clinical trial of fluoxetine in the treatment of obsessive-compulsive disorder. *Journal of Clinical Psychopharmacology, 6,* 98–101.

Fontaine, R., & Chouinard, G. (1989). Fluoxetine in the long-term maintenance treatment of obsessive compulsive disorder. *Psychiatric Annals, 19*(2), 88–91.

Freeman, C. P. L., Trimble, M. R., Deakin, J. F. W., Stokes, T. M., & Ashford, J. J. (1994). Fluvoxamine versus clomipramine in the treatment of obsessive compulsive disorder: A multicenter, randomized, double-blind, parallel group comparison. *Journal of Clinical Psychiatry, 55*(7), 301–305.

Goodman, W., Kozak, M. J., Liebowitz, M. R., & White, K. (1996). Treatment of obsessive compulsive disorder with fluvoxamine: A multicenter double blind, placebo controlled trial. *International Clinical Psychopharmacology, 11,* 21–29.

Goodman, W. K., Price, L. H., Rasmussen, S. A., Delgado, P. L., Heninger, G. R., & Charney, D. S. (1989). Efficacy of fluvoxamine in obsessive compulsive disorder: A double blind comparison with placebo. *Archives of General Psychiatry, 46,* 36–44.

Goodman, W. K., Price, L. H., Rasmussen, S. A., Mazure, C., Delgado, P., Heninger, G. R., & Charney, D. S. (1989). The Yale–Brown Obsessive Compulsive Scale: II. Validity. *Archives of General Psychiatry, 46*(11), 1012–1016.

Goodman, W. K., Price, L. H., Rasmussen, S. A., Mazure, C., Fleischmann, R. L., Hill, C. L., Heninger, G. R., & Charney, D. S. (1989). The Yale–Brown Obsessive Compulsive Scale: I. Development, use, and reliability. *Archives of General Psychiatry, 46*(11), 1006–1011.

Greist, J. H. (1992, June). *Fluvoxamine in OCD: A multicentre parallel design double-blind placebo-controlled trial.* Paper presented at the XVIIIth Collegium Internationale Neuro-Psychopharmacologicum Congress, Nice, France.

Greist, J., Chouinard, G., DuBoff, E., Halaris, A., Kim, S. W., Koran, L., Liebowitz, M., Lydiard, R. B., Rasmussen, S., White, K., & Sikes, C. (1995). Double-blind parallel comparison of three dosages of sertraline and placebo in outpatients with obsessive-compulsive disorder. *Archives of General Psychiatry, 52,* 289–295.

Greist, J. H., Jefferson, J. W., Kobak, K. A., Chouninard, G., DuBoff, E., Halaris, A., Kim, S. A., Koran, L., Liebowitz, M. R., Lydiard, R. B., Mendels, J., Rasmussen, S., White, K., & Flicker, C. (1995). A 1 year double-blind placebo-controlled fixed dose study of sertraline in the treament of obsessive-compulsive disorder. *International Clinical Psychopharmacology, 10*(2), 57–65.

Greist, J. H., Jefferson, J. W., Kobak, K. A., Katzelnick, D. J., & Serlin, R. C. (1995). Efficacy and tolerability of serotonin transport inhibitors in obsessive-compulsive disorder: A meta-analysis. *Archives of General Psychiatry, 52*(1), 53–60.

Hamilton, M. (1960). A rating scale for depression. *Journal of Neurological and Neurosurgical Psychiatry, 23,* 56–62.

Hembree, E. A., Cohen, A., Riggs, D., Kozak, M. J., & Foa, E. B. (1992). *The long-term efficacy of behavior therapy and serotonergic medications in the treatment of obsessive-compulsive ritualizers.* Unpublished manuscript.

Hoogduin, C. A., & Duivenvoorden, H. J. (1988). A decision model in the treatment of obsessive-compulsive neuroses. *British Journal of Psychiatry, 152,* 516–521.

Jenike, M. A., Baer, L., & Carey, R. J. (1986). Coexistent obsessive-compulsive disorder and schizotypal personality disorder: A poor prognostic indicator. *Archives of General Psychiatry, 43*(3), 296.

Jenike, M. A., Baer, L., & Greist, J. H. (1990). Clomipramine versus fluoxetine in obsessive-compulsive disorder: A retrospective comparison of side effects and efficacy. *Journal of Clinical Psychopharmacology, 10*(2), 122–124.

Jenike, M. A., Buttolph, L., Baer, L., Ricciardi, J., & Holland, A. (1989). Open trial of fluoxetine in obsessive-compulsive disorder. *American Journal of Psychiatry, 146*(7), 909–911.

Karno, M., Golding, J. M., Sorenson, S. B., & Burnam, M. A. (1988). The epidemiology of obsessive-compulsive disorder in five US communities. *Archives of General Psychiatry, 45*(12), 1094–1099.

Keijsers, G. P. J., Hoogduin, C. A. L., & Schaap, C. P. D. R. (1994). Predictors of treatment outcome in the behavioural treatment of obsessive-compulsive disorder. *British Journal of Psychiatry, 165*(6), 781–786.

Kozak, M. J., & Foa, E. B. (1996). Obsessive compulsive disorder. In V. B. V. Hasselt & M. Hersen (Eds.), *Sourcebook of psychological treatment manuals for adult disorders* (pp. 65–122). New York: Plenum.

Kozak, M. J., Foa, E. B., & Steketee, G. (1988). Process and outcome of exposure treatment with obsessive-compulsives: Psychophysiological indicators of emotional processing. *Behavior Therapy, 19,* 157–169.

Langsley, D. G., & Yager, J. (1988). The definition of a psychiatrist: Eight years later. *American Journal of Psychiatry, 4,* 469–475.

Lax, T., Basoglu, M., & Marks, I. M. (1992). Expectancy and compliance as predictors of outcome in obsessive-compulsive disorder. *Behavioural Psychotherapy, 20,* 257–266.

Liebowitz, M. R., Hollander, E., Schneier, F., Campeas, R., Hatterer, J., Papp, L., Fairbanks, J., Sandberg, D., Davies, S., & Stein, M. (1989). Fluoxetine treatment of obsessive-compulsive disorder: An open clinical trial. *Journal of Clinical Psychopharmacology, 9*(6), 423–427.

Marks, I. M. (1973). New approaches to the treatment of obsessive-compulsive disorder. *The Journal of Nervous and Mental Disease, 156,* 420–426.

Marks, I. M., Lelliott, P. T., Basoglu, M., Noshirvani, H., Monteiro, W., Cohen, D., & Kasvikis, Y. (1988). Clomipramine, self-exposure and therapist-aided exposure for obsessive-compulsive rituals. *British Journal of Psychiatry, 152,* 522–534.

Marks, I. M., Stern, R. S., Mawson, D., Cobb, J., & McDonald, R. (1980). Clomipramine and exposure for obsessive-compulsive rituals—I. *British Journal of Psychiatry, 136,* 1–25.

Mattes, J. A. (1994). Fluvoxamine in obsessive-compulsive non-responders to clomipramine or fluoxetine [Letter]. *Americal Journal of Psychiatry, 151*(10), 1524.

Mavissakalian, M., Jones, B., Olson, S. C., & Perel, J. M. (1990). The relationship of plasma clomipramine and N-desmethylclomipramine to response in obsessive-compulsive disorder. *Psychopharmacology Bulletin, 26*(1), 119–122.

Meyer, V. (1966). Modification of expectations in cases with obsessional rituals. *Behaviour Research and Therapy, 4,* 273–280.

Meyer, V., & Levy, R. (1973). Modification of behavior in obsessive-compulsive disorders. In H. E. Adams & P. Unikel (Eds.), *Issues and trends in behavior therapy* (pp. 77–136). Springfield, IL: Thomas.

Meyer, V., Levy, R., & Schnurer, A. (1974). The behavioural treatment of obsessive-compulsive disorders. In H. R. Beech (Ed.), *Obsessional states* (pp. 233–258). London: Methuen.

Minichiello, W. E., Baer, L., & Jenike, M. A. (1987). Schizotypal personality disorder: A poor prognostic indicator for behavior therapy in the treatment of obsessive-compulsive disorder. *Journal of Anxiety Disorders, 1*(3), 273–276.

Montgomery, S. A., McIntyre, A., Osterheider, M., Sarteschi, P., Zitterl, W., Zohar, J., Birkett, M., Wood, A. J., & Group, T. L. E. O. S. (1993). A double-blind, placebo-controlled study of fluoxetine in patients with DSM–III–R obsessive-compulsive disorder. *European Neuropsychopharmacology, 3*(2), 143–152.

Myers, J., Weissman, M., Tischler, G., Holzer, C., Leaf, P., Orvaschel, H., Anthony, J., Boyd, J., Burke, J., Kramer, M., & Stoltzman, R. (1984). Six-month prevalence of psychiatric disorders in three communities: 1980–1982. *Archives of General Psychiatry, 41,* 959–967.

Neziroglu, F. (1979). A combined behavioral-pharmacotherapy approach to obsessive-compulsive disorders. In J. Oriols, C. Ballus, M. Gonzalez, & J. Prijol (Eds.), *Biological psychiatry today.* Amsterdam: Elsevier/North-Holland.

O'Sullivan, G., Noshirvani, H., Marks, I., Monteiro, W., & Lelliott, P. (1991). Six-year follow-up after exposure and clomipramine therapy for obsessive compulsive disorder. *Journal of Clinical Psychiatry, 52*(4), 150–155.

Paroxetine Study Group. (1996). Efficacy of fixed doses of paroxetine in the treatment of obsessive compulsive disorder: A randomized, double-blind, placebo-controlled trial. Unpublished manuscript, Smith Kline Beecham Co.

Pato, M. T., Zohar-Kadouch, R., Zohar, J., & Murphy, D. L. (1988). Return of symptoms after discontinuation of clomipramine in patients with obsessive-compulsive disorder. *American Journal of Psychiatry, 145*(12), 1521–1525.

Perse, T. L., Greist, J. H., Jefferson, J. W., Rosenfeld, R., & Dar, R. (1987). Fluvoxamine treatment of obsessive-compulsive disorder. *American Journal of Psychiatry, 144*(12), 1543–1548.

Pigott, T. A., Pato, M. T., Bernstein, S. E., Grover, G. N., Hill, J. L., Tolliver, T. J., & Murphy, D. L. (1990). Controlled comparisons of clomipramine and fluoxetine in the treatment of obsessive-compulsive disorder: Behavioral and biological results. *Archives of General Psychiatry, 47*(10), 926–932.

Price, L. H., Goodman, W. K., Charney, D. S., Rasmussen, S. A., & Heninger, G. R. (1987). Treatment of severe obsessive-compulsive disorder with fluvoxamine. *American Journal of Psychiatry, 144*(8), 1059–1061.

Rasmussen, S. A., & Eisen, J. L. (1989). Clinical features and phenomenology of obsessive compulsive disorder. *Psychiatric Annals, 19*(2), 67–73.

Rasmussen, S. A., & Eisen, J. L. (1990). Epidemiology of obsessive compulsive disorder. *Journal of Clinical Psychiatry, 51*(2, Suppl.), 10–13.

Rasmussen, S. A., & Tsuang, M. T. (1986). Clinical characteristics and family history in DSM–III obsessive-compulsive disorder. *American Journal of Psychiatry, 143*(3), 317–322.

Ravizza, R., Barzega, G., Bellino, S., Bogetto, F., & Maina, G. (1995). Predictors of drug treatment response in obsessive-compulsive disorder. *Journal of Clinical Psychiatry, 56,* 368–373.

Riggs, D. S., Hiss, H., & Foa, E. B. (1992). Marital distress and the treatment of obsessive-compulsive disorder. *Behavior Therapy, 23,* 585–597.

Robins, L. N., Helzer, J. E., Weissman, M. M., & Orvaschel, H. (1984). Lifetime prevalence of specific psychiatric disorders in three sites. *Archives of General Psychiatry, 41,* 949–958.

Smeraldi, E., Erzegovesi, S., Bianchi, I., Pasquali, L., Cocchi, S., & Ronchi, P. (1992). Fluvoxamine vs. clomipramine treatment in obsessive-compulsive disorder: A preliminary study. *New Trends in Experimental and Clinical Psychiatry, 2,* 63–65.

Steketee, G. (1993). Social support and treatment outcome of obsessive compulsive disorder at 9-month follow-up. *Behavioural Psychotherapy, 21*(2), 81–95.

Steketee, G. (1994). Behavioral assessment and treatment planning with obsessive compulsive disorder: A review emphasizing clinical application. *Behavior Therapy, 25*(4), 613–633.

Steketee, G., & Shapiro, L. J. (1995). Predicting behavioral treatment outcome for agoraphobia and obsessive compulsive disorder. *Clinical Psychology Review, 15*(4), 317–346.

Tamimi, R. R., Mavissakalian, M. R., Jones, B., & Olson, S. (1991). Clomipramine versus fluvoxamine in obsessive-compulsive disorder. *Annals of Clinical Psychiatry, 3,* 275–279.

Thoren, P., Asberg, M., Chronholm, B., Jornestedt, L., & Traskman, L. (1980). Chlorimipramine treatment of obsessive-compulsives. *Archives of General Psychiatry, 37,* 1281–1285.

Tollefson, G. D., Rampey, A. H., Potvin, J. H., Jenike, M. A., Rush, A. J., Dominguez, R. A., Koran, L. M., Shear, M. K., Goodman, W., & Genduso, L. A. (1994). A multicenter investigation of fixed-dose fluoxetine in the treatment of obsessive-compulsive disorder. *Archives of General Psychiatry, 51*(7), 559–567.

Turner, J. M., Jacob, R. Y., Biedel, C. D., & Himmelhoch, J. (1985). Fluoxetine treatment of obsessive-compulsive disorder. *Journal of Clinical Psychopharmacology, 5,* 207–212.

van Balkom, A. J. L. M., van Oppen, P., Vermeulen, A. W. A., van Dyck, R., Nauta, M. C. E., & Vorst, H. C. M. (1994). A meta-analysis on the treatment of obsessive compulsive disorder: A comparison of antidepressants, behavior, and cognitive therapy. *Clinical Psychology Review, 5,* 359–381.

Zohar, J., Judge, R., & OCD Paroxetine Study Investigators. (1996). Paroxetine versus clomipramine in the treatment of obsessive-compulsive disorder. *British Journal of Psychiatry, 169,* 468–474.

VII

MECHANISMS OF ACTION

The Mechanisms of Behavioral Treatment and the Problem of Therapeutic Failures

Stanley Rachman
Rosamund Shafran
University of British Columbia

The aim of this chapter is to consider the mechanisms responsible for the changes in obsessive-compulsive disorder (OCD) that are produced by behavioral therapy (BT), and to consider the relation between these mechanisms and treatment failures. This is a daunting task because of the lack of clarity about the mechanisms involved and because research findings and clinical experience do not coincide in identifying the cases that fail to respond. We are suitably daunted.

A grasp of the mechanisms should lead directly to deductions about a lack of responsiveness to treatment, so we attempt to provide an account of the explanations that have been proposed, and evaluate their present standing. The identity and causes of non-responsiveness are then considered. Overlapping explanations have been given for the effects of BT and each is discussed. However, it is essential to begin by establishing that there is indeed something that needs to be explained. Is BT an effective treatment for OCD?

REVIEWS

Analyses of the evidence accumulated on the results of BT, comprising exposure followed by response prevention, confirm that it is effective (Foa, Steketee, & Ozarow, 1985; Marks, 1987; Stanley & Turner, 1995; Steketee, 1993). On the basis of 18 studies involving 200 patients, Foa et al. (1985) concluded that 51% were left free from symptoms, 39% improved, and 10% failed to benefit. At follow-up this increased to 24% who failed to benefit. According to the comprehensive survey by Abel (1993) 70% to 92% of patients improved significantly. It appears that exposure is more effective in treating anxiety in the presence of feared stimuli and that response prevention reduces the compulsive activity, but the findings are not definitive. Resolution of this possibility may be impossible because the two main elements of treatment are interlocking; the urges must be provoked before their execution can be prevented.

There is a relation between duration of exposure and improvement, and the problem is usually alleviated to a point where the patient is able to resume a normal life. However, treatment gains do not always generalize (e.g., treatment of a hand washing condition will not necessarily lead to improvement in the checking domain). The gains are stable for the majority of patients (O'Sullivan, Noshirvani, Marks, Monteiro, & Lelliott, 1991) and those who relapse usually respond to booster treatment (Marks & O'Sullivan, 1988). A recent meta-analysis (van Balkom et al., 1994) confirmed the superiority of BT over placebo.

The original attempts to treat this disorder by BT, based on Wolpe's (1958) theory and practice, were bogged down in laborious and time-consuming attempts to desensitize seemingly endless lists of hierarchical images that provoked distress and compulsions. With minimal encouragement from clinical results there was little incentive to pursue the application of Wolpe's theory to OCD. Instead, an attempt was made to apply Mowrer's (1939, 1960) two-stage theory of fear and avoidance to the problem (see also Dollard & Miller, 1950). OCD was construed as a combination of fear and avoidance; the intense and abnormal fear was thought to be the product of a learning process ("conditioned" fear, in fact), and the compulsive behavior was regarded as an attempt to avoid, contain, or reduce this fear (Eysenck & Rachman, 1965)—views that have undergone some revision (e.g., Rachman, 1990). Influenced by Mowrer's attempt to explain the neurotic paradox (the seemingly inexplicable persistence of unadaptive abnormal behavior), it was postulated that the compulsive actions persist, and as tightly as they do, precisely because they are successful. In keeping with the dominant learning theory of the day, which stated that behavior that is followed by drive reduction will persist, Eysenck and Rachman (1965) argued that the compulsive behavior persists because it succeeds in reducing the person's anxiety drive. Indeed the anxiety-reducing effects of selected compulsive activities were demonstrated in laboratory experiments (for illustration see Rachman & Hodgson, 1980; see Fig. 26.1).

The therapeutic deductions from this Mowrerian explanation were that the conditioned fear must be unlearned, and the anxiety-reducing effects of the compulsive behavior must be blocked, broken, or replaced. Until Meyer's (1966) breakthrough, however, there was no obvious way to implement or test these deductions.

BASIS OF BEHAVIORAL TREATMENT

The basis for the main behavioral treatment of OCD, usually abbreviated as exposure and response prevention (ERP) was provided by Meyer (1966), who described the successful treatment of two severe cases by the method he called, perhaps presciently, the modification of expectations. In practice the patients were exposed to the stimuli that provoked their compulsions and were then prevented from carrying out the resulting compulsive urges, or neutralizing actions—hence the name ERP. Meyer and his colleagues followed up his initial description of the two patients with a series of cases (Meyer, Levy, & Schnurer, 1974).

Despite the encouraging clinical results, Meyer (1966; Meyer et al., 1974) did not elaborate his view that the therapy succeeded by modifying the patients' expectations. He was working in the conditioning theory ethos of the times, indeed promoting conditioning explanations, with insufficient conviction about the concept of expectations, which was in any event, suspiciously mentalistic and well before its time. For more than 20 years, nothing came of his briefly sketched theoretical notions.

Early Studies of Behavioral Therapy

Impressed by Meyer's results, Rachman and colleagues tried to incorporate into this technique Bandura's (1969) therapeutic modeling methods, which marked an important advance from a narrow conditioning explanation toward a liberalized, expanded form of learning theory. Bandura emphasized the fear-reducing power of therapeutic modeling and its value as a vehicle for conveying important (safety) information.

Encouraged by the promising results obtained in small trials (Rachman, Hodgson, & Marks, 1971; Rachman, Marks, & Hodgson, 1973), we undertook a larger study on 40 obsessional patients in which we compared BT with or without clomipramine using a 2×2 factorial design (Rachman et al., 1979). The effectiveness of treatment was assessed using behavioral, subjective, and mood measures. The behavioral treatment was followed by significant improvements on most behavioral measures. Clomipramine administration was followed by significant improvements on mood scales and some behavioral measures. There were no significant interactions between these two treatment conditions. The combination of clomipramine and BT was no more effective than BT or clomipramine used separately.

We were encouraged by these results and we also formed the opinion, not confirmable in the statistical analyses, that severe depression interfered with the progress of behavior treatment.

MECHANISMS OF CHANGE

Guided by the view that OCD comprises fear and avoidance elements, we believed that the exposure part of the treatment extinguished the fear, and the response prevention component led to the extinction of the compulsive behavior. Given that the fear was conditioned, it followed that repeated unreinforced evocations of the fear should lead to the extinction of the fear. The anxiety-reducing effects of the compulsive behavior were blocked by response prevention, and hence the compulsive behavior would be extinguished because it no longer served its function—the patients learned that whatever anxiety they experienced declined even in the absence of the compulsions, the so-called natural decay of anxiety and compulsive urges (see Figs. 26.1 and 26.2).

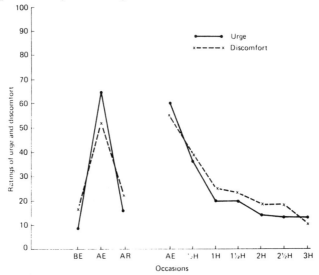

FIG. 26.1. Mean ratings for urge and discomfort across occasions (n − 11). The measurement occasions plotted on the horizontal axis are: BE = before exposure to provoking stimulus; AE = after exposure; AR = after ritual; AE = after second exposure; and half-hourly intervals up to 3 hours (Rachman & Hodgson, 1980).

The progress of the treatment appeared to resemble an extinction process and on that basis we were able to make reasonable predictions about the course of changes in compulsive behavior, but it was difficult

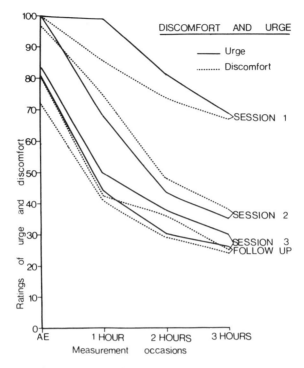

FIG. 26.2. The spontaneous decay of compulsive urges. Mean ratings of discomfort after exposure to the stimulus within and between sessions; AE = after exposure (Rachman & Hodgson, 1980).

to encompass the changes in obsessions using this explanation. It was unclear whether they should be regarded as stimuli or responses, both, or neither; in any case, no discernible extinction training was given. Moreover, there were cases in which extinction training failed to produce the expected changes in compulsive behavior and anxiety; in a clinical sense, the patients failed to benefit. They did not respond to the treatment.

An alternative explanation, given in terms of habituation processes, had the great appeal of simplicity of conception and application, plus the opportunity to connect the treatment to one of the most powerful and ubiquitous processes of adaptation—habituation itself. (*Habituation* refers to declining response amplitude as a result of repeated exposures to the same stimulus, and *extinction* refers to the decline of a learned response as a consequence of repeated, unreinforced evocations of that response.) However, it suffered from the same limitations as the extinction explanation, to which it is closely related. According to the maximal habituation model (Lader & Wing, 1966), the process of habituation is facilitated by frequent presentations of the stimulus at low levels of arousal, and it follows that behavioral treatment may be impeded if the patient is excessively aroused or anxious. Lader and Wing (1966) used their model to reinterpret desensitization effects and other BT techniques—perhaps the therapeutic mechanism was habituation. The difficulties encountered in treating extremely anxious OCD patients (e.g., Foa et al., 1985) are consistent with the habituation model. Unfortunately the model has received mixed support (e.g., Gillan & Rachman, 1974; Gumani & Vaughn, 1981; Likierman & Rachman, 1980) and the effects of habituation training tend to be situation-specific and unstable. As with Foa et al.'s (1983) cases of overvalued ideation, habituation of anxiety tends to produce within-session reductions in fear and obsessions with a strong tendency to return between sessions. The effects are not lasting. Furthermore, the value of the habituation hypothesis is weakened by the absence of an independent measure of habituation (D. M. Clark, personal communication, June, 1989) and by the elusiveness of a satisfactory explanation of habituation itself (Mackintosh, 1983).

As part of an attempt to account for the fear-reducing effects of desensitization and other behavioral methods, Lang's (1970, 1985) psychophysiological analysis of fear was used as the foundation for the model of emotional processing (Rachman, 1980). Obsessions and related indicators of abnormality were put forward as signs of incomplete emotional processing, and desensitization, exposure, and related techniques were construed as facilitators of successful emotional processing. Keeping within the Langian framework, a comparable model elaborated by Kozak and Foa (1994) has considerable value. However it is not the case that the putative fear structures must be evoked in order to be modified (e.g., cognitive BT, pharmacotherapy), and the original three-systems analysis of fear has encountered conceptual problems (Hugdahl, 1981; Rachman, 1990).

RECENT DEVELOPMENTS:
THE COGNITIVE COMPONENT

The most recent theoretical development is the introduction of a cognitive-behavioral analysis of OCD by Salkovskis (1985), a member of the Oxford group, leading contributors in the field of anxiety disorders. This fresh analysis has two advantages over the earlier discouraging attempts to introduce cognitive methods into the treatment of OCD (see Emmelkamp & Beens, 1991; Emmelkamp, Van der Helm, Van Zanten, & Plochg, 1990; Emmelkamp, Visser, & Hoekstra, 1988). Unlike the use of self-instructional training and rational emotive therapy, which were attempts by Emmelkamp and his colleagues to expand the use of existing methods into the field of OCD, the Salkovskis proposals are based on a specific, detailed, and novel cognitive analysis of OCD itself. In addition, his proposals draw strength because of their connections with the well-grounded and successful cognitive-behavioral theory and therapy of panic (Clark, 1986).

Salkovskis's basic ideas are that unwanted intrusive thoughts (which are commonly experienced; Rachman & de Silva, 1978) can become obsessive if the affected person interprets their occurrence or contents as highly significant. Obsessions are driven by negative automatic thoughts. People with OCD, it is argued, suffer from an inflated sense of responsibility. As a result they are prone to experiencing excessive guilt and are driven to neutralize the anticipated effects of their obsessions (such as harm coming to someone else). Neutralization serves to maintain and promote obsessions and compulsions because it provides short-term relief and also protects the patient's negative expectations from the possibility of disconfirmation. This analysis resembles the earlier attempts to explain the persistence of anxiety-reducing compulsions, but has a new emphasis on disconfirmation.

Broadly consistent with this approach, Freeston, Ladouceur, Thibodeau, and Gagnon (1992) found five factors in cognitive intrusions. The third factor, *evaluation*, consisted of responsibility, guilt, and disapproval and was the only significant predictor of compulsive activity scores. It was also strongly correlated with avoidance responses. It appears that an exaggerated or inflated sense of responsibility is evident in a variety of OCD phenomena, notably in compulsive checking, but also in obsessional thinking (Rachman, 1993). Affected people attach significance to and feel intensely responsible for their unacceptable sexual or other images, for their obsessional impulses to harm others, and for their blasphemous or other repugnant thoughts. The sense of inflated responsibility typically is manifested at home and at work but can spread to any situation in which people may come to harm. In many instances OCD patients appear to fuse their thoughts and actions, notably in those instances of blasphemous, sexual, or aggressive thoughts, images, or impulses, and perhaps most intensely in instances of obsessional impulses. *Fusion* refers to the phenomenon in which the patient appears to regard the obsessional activity and the forbidden action as being morally equivalent or more likely to occur precisely because they have had the thought. In their thinking, the obsession increases the probability of the feared outcome. These ideas inevitably lead to guilt and fear.

EXPERIMENTS ON RESPONSIBILITY IN OCD

In partial confirmation, recent experiments have demonstrated the connection between perceived responsibility and compulsive checking. Lopatka and Rachman (1995) carried out an experiment on 30 patients with OCD to test the hypothesis that changes in responsibility are followed by corresponding changes in the urge to check compulsively. The experimental manipulation succeeded in increasing or decreasing responsibility, as required for the experiment. Following the experimental decrease in responsibility, there was a significant decline in discomfort and the urge to carry out compulsive checking. Increased responsibility was followed by corresponding changes in discomfort and urges, but they failed to reach a statistically significant level (see Figs. 26.3 and 26.4).

Shafran (1995) conducted a similar study of 46 individuals with OCD, in which responsibility was manipulated in a different manner, but the results were similar to those of the Lopatka and Rachman (1995) study. In the high-responsibility condition, following exposure, anxiety and compulsive urges were significantly higher than in the low-responsibility condition. The effects of manipulating responsibility differed according to the type of obsessional problem. The clearest results were for those with checking compulsions, as shown in Fig. 26.5.

Additionally, Ladouceur et al. (1995) demonstrated in a group of nonclinical individuals that an experimentally induced increase in responsibility was followed by a statistically significant increase in checking behavior. The particular effects of inflated responsibility on obsessions, compulsive checking, and compulsive cleaning remain to be clarified.

The role of neutralization in producing prompt short-term relief has also been the subject of recent experimentation (Rachman & Shafran, 1995). In an experiment on a nonclinical sample of people who were selected because of their tendency to fuse unwanted thoughts and actions, it was shown that when individuals construct and write down a selected

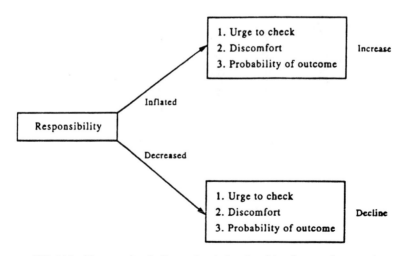

FIG. 26.3. The postulated effects of an inflated and/or decreased sense of responsibility (Lopatka & Rachman, 1995).

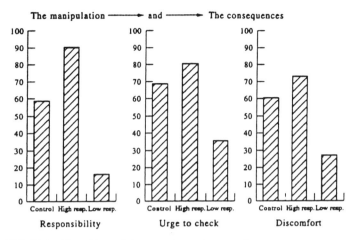

FIG. 26.4. The effects of the experimental manipulation on (a) perceived responsibility, (b) the urge to check, and (c) discomfort (Lopatka & Rachman, 1995).

Manipulating Responsibility
("Checkers" only)

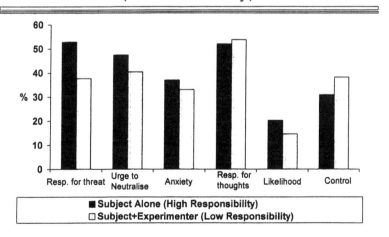

FIG. 26.5. The effects of the experimental manipulation on (a) perceived responsibility for threat, (b) the urge to check, (c) anxiety, (d) responsibility for thoughts, (d) likelihood of threat, and (e) control over threat in compulsive checkers (R. Shafran, 1995).

unwanted thought, considerable anxiety is produced and can then be relieved by carrying out a neutralizing act, such as physically destroying the written thought, or mentally taking back the unwanted thought.

COGNITIVE THERAPY

The initial results of the experimental analyses that flow from the Salkovskis theory are encouraging. Moreover, the results of the first clinical trial to employ this newer version of cognitive therapy produced significant and promising results. In a controlled study of 71 patients with OCD, both cognitive therapy and ERP led to statistically significant improvement, with a tendency for the cognitive therapy to be more effective than ERP on some measures, particularly cognitions (van Oppen et al., 1995). However, the cognitions that were assessed were general in nature and their cognitive measure could bear refinement. The value of adding cognitive therapy to traditional BT for OCD remains to be seen (James & Blackburn, 1995) as the majority of studies have been subject to methodological difficulties. Nevertheless, cognitive therapy could be used in some patients who are unwilling to undertake BT or who are perhaps resistant to it, such as those with obsessions only (discussed later). Cognitive therapy can also be used as a precursor to BT and probably will be used in conjunction with BT rather than as an alternative form of treatment. If patients are intellectually able and have good abstract thinking skills, cognitive therapy is more likely to be effective than if these skills are absent (Tallis, 1995). It is possible that cognitive therapy may be particularly useful in relapse prevention, as has been found with other psychological disorders (Cooper & Steere, 1995; Hollon, Shelton, & Davis, 1993; Wilson & Fairburn, 1993).

Cognitive BT is not without its own difficulties, however, including problems in assessing the often elusive cognitions, tracking the connections between therapeutic interventions, and cognitive shifts, the capacity of avowedly "non-cognitive" methods such as exposure to produce major changes in cognitions (see Rachman, 1994). Nevertheless, it has considerable promise and has expanded our understanding of OCD phenomena, providing the opportunity to understand the significance of the content of obsessions, a feature of OCD that early behavior therapists regarded with indifference.

Another consequence of the expansion of cognitive analyses is the fresh importance attached to guilt, which is extremely common in OCD and often more intense than anxiety itself. Phenomenologically, guilt is an important part of the disorder (Rasmussen & Eisen, 1992) although there has been relatively little research in the area. In a series of psychometric studies, trait guilt has consistently been highly associated with obsessional symptoms, even when the effects of depression have been controlled (Rachman & Shafran, 1997, unpublished data; Shafran, Watkins, & Charman, 1995; Steketee, Quay, & White, 1991). For example, in a normal sample of 291 individuals, we found a correlation of $r = .52$ between guilt and obsessive-compulsive (OC) qualities measured on the Maudsley Obsessional Compulsive Inventory (Hodgson & Rachman, 1977); in 108 obsessional patients, the correlation was $r = .49$. In the obsessional group, the correlation between guilt and OC symptoms remained at $r = .43$ even after controlling for depression and anxiety. Although the research findings are inconsistent, trait guilt has been found to be a better predictor of obsessionality than depression or anxiety (Niler & Beck, 1989; Reynolds & Salkovskis, 1991; Shafran et al., 1995). In addition, preliminary data show trait guilt to be highly associated with thought–action fusion (TAF) in terms of moral equivalence and the probability of an event occurring. Excessive guilt is regarded as a consequence of inflated responsibility, and a problem to be dealt with (Rachman, 1993). By contrast, in the early work on BT, the significance of guilt was overlooked. It was not regarded as a significant feature of OCD, and was neither assessed nor treated. It never even featured in treatment evaluation outcome studies.

Can a cognitive analysis help to explain, retrospectively, why ERP has been so effective? It is perhaps best to reconstrue the effects of ERP as a series of repeated and powerful disconfirmations that are promoted systematically in a safe, authoritative context. The broad safety implied and present in a clinical context allows the affected person to test (a) the emotional and cognitive basis of their excessive fear, and (b) the emotional and cognitive validity of the implied beliefs that carrying out the compulsive actions not only relieves anxiety but also reduces guilt and is essential and irreplaceable. For example, "If I do not wash my hands repeatedly, I will contract cancer," or "If I do not put right my repugnant obsessional thought with a neutralizing thought, my mother will be harmed," and so on.

In controlled ERP treatment, repeated contacts with the feared object or situation are never dangerous and never followed by catastrophes or harm. In programs of controlled exposure, prevention of the compulsive act (or of neutralization) is not followed by disaster but rather by a gradual decline in discomfort. These controlled, safe, systematic, repeated disconfirmations of harm lead to a decline in the catastrophic cognitions, and ultimately to a significant decrease in obsessions and compulsions. In addition, the patient's inflated sense of responsibility is implicitly reduced by the therapist's presence, advice, and therapeutic modeling. A patient's cognitive bias toward TAF, for example, the belief that a harm obsession actually increases the risk to the person featuring in the obsession, is repeatedly disconfirmed. Lack of change will be observed when the planned disconfirmatory events fail to disconfirm (e.g., as with overvalued ideation or in cases of mental pollution; Rachman, 1994). Sometimes disconfirmation is prevented because of the persistent use of avoidance or neutralization, or perhaps because the therapist is unsuccessful in helping to identify the core maladaptive beliefs. In addition to the sense of dirtiness characteristic of physical pollution, mental pollution includes feelings of moral impurity and guilt, and hence is not "soluble" in water (Rachman, 1994). Hence, repeated compulsive cleaning is rarely fully effective (e.g., Lady Macbeth). Similarly, BT exercises designed to inhibit the compulsive cleaning are off center, and likely leave the guilt unchanged. The sense of inflated responsibility is modifiable for limited periods in the laboratory but proves resistant in therapy.

Naturally, disconfirming events do take place outside of therapy, and if they are repeated or provide powerful evidential value, they can result in spontaneous remissions or at least partial relief. Our failures are the patients in whom the key cognitions are not identified, or identified but not disconfirmed. So, for example, repeated exposures that leave the patient's inflated sense of responsibility unchanged will be of little benefit in the long run. Events that increase the patient's responsibility or strengthen the key cognitions may lead to a worsening of the OCD.

Looking back to the indifferent results obtained with the specifically anti-obsessive techniques of thought-stopping and of habituation training (Likierman & Rachman, 1980; Tryon, 1979) a cognitive analysis leads to these conclusions: Insofar as these techniques eliminate the obsessions they will be effective for a substantial period, but they rarely do. If they merely reduce their frequency, and leave the perceived significance or inflated responsibility unchanged, the techniques will be valueless (Rachman, 1998).

This cognitive analysis of treatment mechanisms is testable, but has not yet been tested. Therapeutic improvements that occur in the absence of evidence of disconfirmations or of cognitive changes will damage the explanation, as will the opposite. That is, the failure of demonstrable disconfirmations or cognitive changes to produce therapeutic improvements will be equally damaging.

THERAPEUTIC FAILURES

Moving onto the failures, between 13% and 25% of suitable patients refuse treatment (Foa et al., 1983). Rather more challenging are those patients who enter treatment, are compliant, and yet fail to respond. Those cases are misleadingly termed *refractory*.

There is a discrepancy between the experience of clinicians and the research literature regarding the factors that predict poor outcome. Clinicians such as Foa, Hodgson, de Silva, Marks, Steketee, and many others have remarked that severe depression retards BT, but the statistical data do not confirm this view. One reason for this discrepancy may be traced to the strict inclusion criteria used in many of the research studies: Patients with severe depression were excluded in some studies and therefore the results show no association between outcome and this factor. In addition, few studies were designed specifically to identify prognostic indicators, and merely correlate a variety of measures with outcome. There are also conflicting signs about whether or not intense anxiety impedes treatment (e.g., Foa et al., 1985; Rachman & Hodgson, 1980).

The majority of studies have not found any relation between demographic variables such as age of onset, socio-economic status, or intelligence and the success or failure of treatment. Marital adjustment, severity, duration, symptom type, pre-morbid level of anxiety, and social support are not associated with outcome in the majority of studies. Co-morbid problems such as substance abuse, panic disorder, and social anxiety add to the complexity of treatment but are not necessarily associated with a poor outcome (Steketee & Shapiro, 1995).

Bearing in mind these limitations, the only consistent (but still sparse) findings from the research literature are that the presence of personality disorders is a poor prognostic indicator, in particular schizotypal personality disorder (Steketee & Shapiro, 1995). Inconsistent findings are that having severe depression, intense anxiety, obsessions without compulsions, and overvalued ideation are associated with a poor outcome (Foa et al., 1983; but see O'Sullivan et al., 1991; Steketee & Shapiro, 1995). Poor social functioning has been associated with treatment failure and there is some evidence of a curvilinear relation between reactivity to ERP and outcome; that is, that high or low arousal or reactivity is a poor predictor (Foa et al., 1983). Lack of motivation or failure to comply with the therapy and to practice techniques at home is also, not surprisingly, common in patients who fail to improve with treatment (Cottreaux et al., 1990; O'Sullivan et al., 1991). Patients who lack motivation, are critical of the therapist, and whose anticipatory fear of the treatment exceeds their commitment to it, are likely to drop out of therapy (Hansen, Hoogduin, Schaap, & De Haan, 1992).

Although there has been little work on the predictors of relapse, the data indicate that the greater the gains, the lower the risk of relapse (Steketee, 1993). Expressed emotion of the family may also be important in predicting relapse (Steketee, 1993). Given that relapse is lower with cognitive therapy than with other therapy for a variety of disorders such as depression (see Hollon et al., 1993) and eating disorders (see Cooper & Steere, 1995; Wilson & Fairburn, 1993), it is probable that the greatest benefit of cognitive therapy will be to enable treatment gains to be maintained.

To conclude, one is reminded of Bandura's (1969) remark about the curious relation between behavioral treatments and cognitive theory—the value of behavioral treatments is repeatedly confirmed but our explanations turn increasingly cognitive. This analysis of the mechanisms of treatment is a progress report rather than a definitive account.

REFERENCES

Abel, J. L. (1993). Exposure with response prevention and serotonergic antidepressants in the treatment of obsessive compulsive disorder: A review and implications for interdisciplinary treatment. *Behavior Research and Therapy, 31*, 463–478.

Bandura, A. (1969). *The principles of behavior modification.* New York: Holt, Rinehart, & Winston.

Clark, D. M. (1986). A cognitive approach to panic. *Behavior Research and Therapy, 24*, 461–470.

Cooper, P. J., & Steere, J. (1995). A comparison of two psychological treatments for bulimia nervosa: Implications for models of maintenance. *Behavior Research and Therapy, 33*, 875–886.

Cottreaux, J., Mollard, E., Bouvard, M., Marks, I., Sluys, M., Nury, A. M., Douge, R., & Cialdella, P. (1990). A controlled study of fluvoxamine and exposure in obsessive compulsive disorder. *International Clinical Psychopharmacology, 5*, 17–30.

Dollard, J., & Miller, N. (1950). *Personality and psychotherapy.* New York: McGraw-Hill.

Emmelkamp, P. M. G., & Beens, H. (1991). Cognitive therapy with obsessive-compulsive patients: A comparative evaluation. *Behavior Research and Therapy, 29*, 293–300.

Emmelkamp, P. M. G., Van der Helm, M., Van Zanten, B., & Plochg, I. (1990). Contributions of self-instructional training to the effectiveness of exposure in vivo: A comparison with obsessive-compulsive patients. *Behavior Research and Therapy, 18*, 61–66.

Emmelkamp, P. M. G., Visser, S., & Hoekstra, R. J. (1988). Cognitive therapy vs. exposure in vivo in the treatment of obsessive-compulsives. *Cognitive Therapy and Research, 12*, 103–114.

Eysenck, H. J., & Rachman, S. (1965). *The causes and cures of neurosis.* London: Routledge & Kegan Paul.

Foa, E. B., Grayson, J. B., Steketee, G. S., Doppelt, H. G., Turner, R. M., & Latimer, P. R. (1983). Success and failure in the behavioral treatment of obsessive-compulsives. *Journal of Consulting and Clinical Psychology, 51*, 287–297.

Foa, E. B., Steketee, G. S., & Ozarow, B. J. (1985). Behavior therapy with obsessive-compulsives: From theory to treatment. In M. Mavissakalian, S. M. Turner, & L. Michelson (Eds.), *Obsessive-compulsive disorder: Psychological and pharamacological treatment* (pp. 150–162). New York: Plenum.

Freeston, M. H., Ladouceur, R., Thibodeau, N., & Gagnon, F. (1992). Cognitive intrusions in a non-clinical population: I. Response style, subjective experience and appraisal. *Behavior Research and Therapy, 29,* 585–597.

Gillan, P., & Rachman, S. (1974). An experimental investigation of desensitization in phobic patients. *British Journal of Psychiatry, 124,* 392–401.

Gumani, P. D., & Vaughn, M. (1981). Changes in frequency and distress during prolonged repetition of obsessional thoughts. *British Journal of Clinical Psychology, 20,* 79–81.

Hansen, A. M. D., Hoogduin, C. A. L., Schaap, C., & de Haan, E. (1992). Do drop-outs differ from successfully treated obsessive-compulsives? *Behavior Research and Therapy, 30,* 547–550.

Hodgson, R., & Rachman, S. (1997). Obsessional compulsive complaints. *Behaviour Research and Therapy, 15,* 389–395.

Hollon, S.-D., Shelton, R. C., & Davis, D. D. (1993). Cognitive therapy for depression: Conceptual issues and clinical efficacy. *Journal of Consulting and Clinical Psychology, 61,* 270–275.

Hugdahl, K. (1981). The three-systems-model of fear and emotion—A critical examination. *Behavior Research and Therapy, 19,* 75–85.

James, I. A., & Blackburn, I. M. (1995). Cognitive therapy with obsessive compulsive disorder. *British Journal of Psychiatry, 166,* 444–450.

Kozak, M. J., & Foa, E. B. (1994). Obsessions, over-valued ideas and delusions in obsessive-compulsive disorder. *Behavior Research and Therapy, 32,* 343–353.

Lader, M., & Wing, L. (1966). *Physiological measures, sedative drugs and morbid anxiety.* London: Oxford University Press.

Ladouceur, R., Rheaume, J., Freeston, M. H., Aublet, F., Jean, K., Lachance, S., Langlois, F., & de Pokomandy-Morin, K. (1995). Experimental manipulations of responsibility: An analogue test for models of obsessive-compulsive disorder. *Behavior Research and Therapy, 33,* 937–946.

Lang, P. J. (1970). Stimulus control, response control and desensitization of fear. In D. Levis (Ed.), *Learning approaches to therapeutic behavior change* (pp. 84–97). Chicago: Aldine.

Lang, P. J. (1985). The cognitive psychophysiology of emotion: fear and anxiety. In A. H. Tuma & J. D. Maser (Eds.), *Anxiety and anxiety disorders* (pp. 118–142). Hillsdale, NJ: Lawrence Erlbaum Associates.

Likierman, H., & Rachman, S. J. (1980). Spontaneous decay of compulsive urges: Cumulative effects. *Behavior Research and Therapy, 18,* 387–394.

Lopatka, C., & Rachman, S. (1995). Perceived responsibility and compulsive checking: An experimental analysis. *Behavior Research and Therapy, 33,* 673–684.

Mackintosh, N. (1983). *Conditioning and associative learning.* New York: Oxford University Press.

Marks, I. (1987). *Fears, phobias, and rituals: Panic, anxiety and their disorders.* Oxford, UK: Oxford University Press.

Marks, I. M., & O'Sullivan, G. (1988). Drugs and psychological treatments for agoraphobia/panic and obsessive-compulsive disorders: A review. *British Journal of Psychiatry, 153,* 650–658.

Meyer, V. (1966). Modification of expectations in cases with obsessional rituals. *Behavior Research and Therapy, 4,* 273–280.

Meyer, V., Levy, R., & Schnurer, A. (1974). The behavioral treatment of obsessive-compulsive disorders. In H. R. Beech (Ed.), *Obsessional states* (pp. 263–274). London: Methuen.

Mowrer, O. H. (1939). Stimulus response theory of anxiety. *Psychological Review, 46,* 553–565.

Mowrer, O. H. (1960). *Leading theory and behavior.* New York: Wiley.

Niler, E. R., & Beck, S. J. (1989). The relationship among guilt, dysphoria, anxiety and obsessions in a normal population. *Behavior Research and Therapy, 27,* 213–220.

O'Sullivan, G., Noshirvani, H., Marks, I., Monteiro, W., & Lelliott, P. (1991). Six-year follow-up after exposure and clomipramine therapy for obsessive compulsive disorder. *Journal of Clinical Psychiatry, 52,* 150–155.

Rachman, S. (1980). Emotional processing. *Behavior Research and Therapy, 18,* 51–60.

Rachman, S. (1990). *Fear and courage.* New York: Freeman.

Rachman, S. (1993). Obsessions, responsibility and guilt. *Behavior Research and Therapy, 31,* 149–154.

Rachman, S. (1994). Pollution of the mind. *Behavior Research and Therapy, 32,* 311–314.

Rachman, S. (1998). A cognitive theory of obsessions. *Behaviour Research & Therapy, 35,* 793–802.

Rachman, S., Cobb, J., Grey, B., McDonald, B., Mawson, D., Sartory, G., & Stern, R. (1979). The behavioral treatment of obsessional-compulsive disorders, with and without clomipramine. *Behavior Research and Therapy, 17,* 467–478.

Rachman, S., & de Silva, P. (1978). Normal and abnormal obsessions. *Behavior Research and Therapy, 16,* 233–248.

Rachman, S., & Hodgson, R. J. (1980). *Obsessions and compulsions.* Englewood Cliffs, NJ: Prentice-Hall.

Rachman, S., Hodgson, R., & Marks, I. M. (1971). Treatment of chronic obsessive-compulsive neurosis. *Behavior Research and Therapy, 9,* 237–247.

Rachman, S., Marks, I. M., & Hodgson, R. (1973). The treatment of obsessive-compulsive neurotics by modelling and flooding in vivo. *Behavior Research and Therapy, 11,* 463–471.

Rachman, S., Shafran, R., Mitchell, D., Traut, J., & Teachman, B. (1986). How to remain neutral. *Behaviour Research & Therapy, 34,* 889–898.

Rasmussen, S., & Eisen, J. (1992). The epidemiology and clinical features of obsessive compulsive disorder. *The Psychiatric Clinics of North America, 15,* 743–758.

Reynolds, M., & Salkovskis, P. M. (1991). The relationship among guilt, dysphoria, anxiety and obsessions in a normal population: An attempted replication. *Behavior Research and Therapy, 29,* 259–265.

Salkovskis, P. M. (1985). Obsessional compulsive problems: A cognitive-behavioral analysis. *Behavior Research and Therapy, 23,* 571–583.

Shafran, R. (1995, August). *The manipulation of responsibility in obsessive compulsive disorder.* Paper presented at the World Congress of Cognitive and Behavioral Psychotherapies, Copenhagen, Denmark.

Shafran, R., Watkins, E., & Charman, T. (1995). *Guilt in obsessive-compulsive disorder.* Manuscript submitted for publication.

Stanley, M. A., & Turner, S. M. (1995). Current status of pharmacological and behavioral treatment of obsessive-compulsive disorder. *Behavior Therapy, 26,* 163–186.

Steketee, G. S. (1993). *Treatment of obsessive compulsive disorder.* London: Guilford.

Steketee, G. S., Quay, S., & White, K. (1991). Religion and guilt in OCD patients. *Journal of Anxiety Disorders, 5,* 359–367.

Steketee, G. S., & Shapiro, L. J. (1995). Predicting behavioral treatment outcome for agoraphobia and obsessive compulsive disorder. *Clinical Psychology Review, 15,* 317–346.

Tallis, F. (1995). *Obsessive compulsive disorder: Cognition and cognitive neuropsychology.* Chichester, UK: Wiley.

Tryon, G. S. (1979). A review and critique of thought stopping research. *Journal of Behavior Therapy and Experimental Psychology, 10,* 189–192.

van Balkom, A. J. L. M., van Oppen, P., Vermeulen, A. W. A., van Dyck, R., Nauta, M. C. E., & Vorst, H. C. M. (1994). A meta-analysis on the treatment of obsessive compulsive disorder: A comparison of antidepressants, behavior and cognitive therapy. *Clinical Psychology Review, 14,* 359–382.

van Oppen, P., de Haan, E., van Balkom, A. J. L. M., Spinhoven, P., Hoogduin, K., & van Dyck, R. (1995). Cognitive therapy and exposure in vivo in the treatment of obsessive compulsive disorder. *Behavior Research and Therapy, 33,* 379–390.

Wilson, G. T., & Fairburn, C. G. (1993). Cognitive treatments for eating disorders. *Journal of Consulting and Clinical Psychology, 61,* 270–275.

Wolpe, J. (1958). *Psychotherapy by reciprocal inhibition.* Stanford, CA: Stanford University Press.

27

Understanding the Mechanism of Action of Serotonin Reuptake Inhibitors in Obsessive-Compulsive Disorder: A Step Toward More Effective Treatments?

Pierre Blier
Richard Bergeron
Graciela Piñeyro
Mostafa El Mansari
McGill University

Selective serotonin (5-HT) reuptake inhibitors (SSRIs) and the tricyclic antidepressant drug clomipramine are the only agents thus far demonstrated to be effective in the treatment of obsessive-compulsive disorder (OCD; Fineberg, Bullock, Montgomery, & Montgomery, 1992). Because most of these medications belong to different chemical families and the only common property they share is their capacity to potently block the 5-HT transporter (Hyttel, 1994), it is undisputable that they exert their therapeutic effect in OCD via the 5-HT system. However, SSRIs are also effective antidepressant agents. Consequently, they must also exert their antidepressant effect via the 5-HT system. Because not all antidepressant drugs are effective in OCD but most of these have been shown to increase 5-HT neurotransmission (Blier & de Montigny, 1994), then the obvious question is what specific progressive modification of the 5-HT system do SSRIs induce that accounts for their apparently unique anti-OCD effect. If this peculiar property of SSRIs were known, an alternative treatment strategy could mimic this action by administering a pharmacological agent that would produce the same net effect on the 5-HT system (Fig. 27.1).

The occurence of the therapeutic response would thus theoretically depend only on the penetration of the agent into the brain in a sufficient

5-HT NEURON   **POSTSYNAPTIC NEURON**

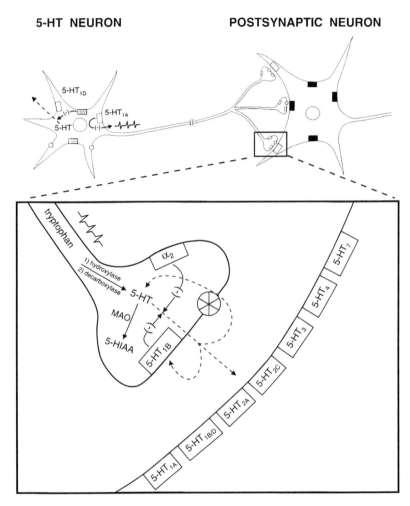

FIG. 27.1. Presynaptic and postsynaptic factors regulating the efficacy of
5-HT neurotransmission. Only the 5-HT receptors for which an electrophysiological response has been identified in unitary recording studies are
depicted. All 5-HT receptors and the α_2-adrenoceptor located on 5-HT
neurons exert a negative feedback influence on 5-HT release, or neuronal
firing in the case of the 5-HT$_{1A}$ autoreceptor, as indicated by the (–) sign.

concentration. Such a drug should then produce the same anti-OCD effect
as an SSRI but within a few days in comparison to the 12 or so weeks
generally required to obtain their maximal therapeutic effect in OCD. It
is also possible that such a strategy would lead to a more efficacious
treatment of OCD as it could produce a more pronounced effect than
SSRIs on this specific factor that modulates 5-HT neurotransmission.

TABLE 27.1
Effects of Long-Term Administration of
Antidepressant Treatments on 5-HT Neurotransmission

	Responsiveness of somatodendritic 5-HT$_{1A}$ autoreceptors	Function of terminal 5-HT$_{1B/D}$ autoreceptors	Responsiveness of postsynaptic 5-HT receptors	Net effect on 5-HT neurotransmission
TCA	0	0	↑	↑
ECT	0	0	↑	↑
SSRI	↓	↓	0	↑
MAOI	↓	0	0 or ↓	↑
5-HT$_{1A}$ agonists	↓	0	0	↑

Note. These results were obtained using electrophysiological techniques in anesthetized rats treated for at least 14 days. The net effect on overall 5-HT neurotransmission is determined from the firing activity of 5-HT neurons and the effectiveness of the electrical stimulation of the ascending 5-HT pathway on the firing activity of postsynaptic CA3 pyramidal neurons in the hippocampus. In the case of the 5-HT$_{1A}$ agonists the enhanced net effect results from an enhanced tonic activation of postsynaptic 5-HT$_{1A}$ receptors resulting from a normal amount of synaptic 5-HT (normalized 5-HT neuronal firing) and the presence of the exogenous 5-HT$_{1A}$ receptor agonist. O = no change.

EFFECTS OF ANTIDEPRESSANT TREATMENTS ON 5-HT NEUROTRANSMISSION

Extensive electrophysiological investigations carried out in our laboratory have documented that several types of antidepressant treatments enhance 5-HT neurotransmission in the rat hippocampus (for a review, see Blier & de Montigny, 1994). This net effect, common to the major types of antidepressant treatments, is, however, mediated via different mechanisms (see Table 27.1). Tricyclic antidepressant drugs, independent of their capacity to inhibit the reuptake of 5-HT or norepinephrine, enhance the responsiveness of postsynaptic 5-HT$_{1A}$ receptors[1] in the hippocampus

---

[1]When 5-HT binds to receptor sites, it may trigger various physiological responses depending on its concentration. Some of these effects can be selectively blocked by certain drugs. These observations initially led to the classification of different 5-HT receptor subtypes (initially 5-HT$_1$ and 5-HT$_2$ receptors) based on such pharmacological properties. With the advent of molecular biology, it was confirmed that the amino acid sequences encoding for the structure of these receptors could be traced back to the genetic code. There are now more than 15 5-HT receptor subtypes identified (see Boess & Martin, 1994).

with a time course that is consistent with the delayed onset of action of these drugs in major depression (de Montigny & Aghajanian, 1978). It has also been demonstrated by our group and other laboratories that this enhanced responsiveness to 5-HT also occurs in other, but not all, brain regions and that 5-HT receptor subtypes other than the 5-HT$_{1A}$ receptors are implicated. Repeated but not single electroconvulsive shock administration also induces this sensitization to 5-HT in the hippocampus (de Montigny, 1984). Monoamine oxidase inhibitors (MAOIs), SSRIs, and 5-HT$_{1A}$ agonists all induce an initial attenuation of the firing activity of 5-HT neurons on treatment initiation (Blier & de Montigny, 1983, 1985, 1990). However, this attenuation is followed by a gradual recovery to normal firing activity of 5-HT neurons with prolongation of the treatment for 2 to 3 weeks. At this point in time, MAOIs enhance 5-HT transmission by increasing the amount of 5-HT released per action potential as a result of a greater concentration of 5-HT in the terminals (Blier, de Montigny, & Azzaro, 1986). SSRIs have the same effect not by augmenting the releasable pool of 5-HT as MAOIs do, but rather by desensitizing the terminal 5-HT autoreceptor that exerts a major influence on the amount of 5-HT that is released per impulse (Chaput, de Montigny, & Blier, 1986). 5-HT$_{1A}$ agonists would produce an enhanced tonic activation of postsynaptic 5-HT$_{1A}$ receptors as a result of a normalized firing activity of 5-HT neurons, and of 5-HT release as well, in the presence of the exogenous 5-HT$_{1A}$ agonist acting on normosensitive postsynaptic 5-HT$_{1A}$ receptors (Blier & de Montigny, 1990).

DESENSITIZATION OF THE TERMINAL 5-HT AUTORECEPTOR AS AN EFFECT SPECIFIC TO LONG-TERM ADMINISTRATION OF SSRIS

The peculiar characteristic of SSRIs on the 5-HT system is their capacity to desensitize terminal 5-HT autoreceptors. Such results were obtained in the rat hippocampus and, subsequently, in the rat hypothalamus after 2- to 3-week treatments (Chaput et al., 1986; Moret & Briley, 1990). It is, however, difficult to extrapolate such results to the treatment of OCD with SSRIs for three reasons. First, the terminal 5-HT autoreceptor in the rat brain is of the 5-HT$_{1B}$ subtype, whereas in the human brain it is of the 5-HT$_{1D}$ subtype (Galzin et al., 1992; Hoyer & Middlemiss, 1989; Maura, Thellung, Andrioli, Ruelle, & Raiteri, 1993). Second, the therapeutic effect of SSRIs generally requires a much longer delay before being maximal in OCD than in depression (Fineberg et al., 1992). Third, positron emission tomography scanning studies in humans have clearly delineated the orbito-frontal cortex—head of the caudate nucleus—thalamus neuronal circuitry as being involved in mediating OCD symptomatology, and not the hippocampus or the hypothalamus (Baxter, Phelps, Mazziotta, Guze, & Schwartz, 1987; Baxter et al., 1992; for a review, see Insel, 1992).

To overcome these caveats, the following experiments were undertaken. Serotonin release and terminal 5-HT autoreceptor sensitivity were assessed in guinea pigs, as their terminal 5-HT autoreceptors are of the 5-HT_{1D} subtype. The treatment period was extended to 8 weeks in an attempt to approach the time necessary to obtain a near maximal anti-OCD effect. Finally, 5-HT release and terminal autoreceptor responsiveness were examined in the frontal cortex and in its orbito-frontal subdivision, as well as in the head of the caudate nucleus (El Mansari, Bouchard, & Blier, 1995).

The SSRIs were administered using osmotic minipumps, implanted subcutaneously, so as to obtain a constant infusion of the drugs and mimic as much as possible the plasma levels achieved in humans. Indeed, SSRIs are metabolized much more rapidly by rodents than by humans. Consequently, administering such agents even on a twice-daily basis to laboratory animals does not produce the sustained plasma levels obtained in humans with oral administration, making it difficult to extrapolate the animal data to human therapeutics. The minipumps were removed at least 2 days before carrying out the experiments to study the modifications of 5-HT release and 5-HT autoreceptor sensitivity produced by long-term SSRI administration in the absence of 5-HT reuptake blockade, which can interfere with such assays.

In brain slices preloaded with [^{3}H]5-HT and then continuously superfused, the electrically evoked release of [^{3}H]5-HT was significantly enhanced in the frontal cortex, but not in the orbito-frontal cortex or in the head of the caudate nucleus after a 3-week paroxetine treatment (Fig. 27.2). We had previously reported on this small but significant enhancement of 5-HT release in the frontal cortex after a 3-week paroxetine treatment. Unlike the hypothalamus and the hippocampus, where the increase in [^{3}H]5-HT release observed following a 3-week paroxetine treatment can be explained in part by an attenuated function or desensitization of the terminal 5-HT autoreceptor, in the frontal cortex, the enhanced [^{3}H]5-HT release is entirely attributable to a desensitization of the 5-HT transporter (Blier & Bouchard, 1994).

After an 8-week treatment, however, the evoked release of [^{3}H]5-HT was significantly enhanced in the orbito-frontal cortex to a greater extent than in the rest of the frontal cortex of the same animals: 55% versus 29%, respectively (Fig. 27.3). The concentration-effect curve using the 5-HT autoreceptor agonist 5-methoxytryptamine was shifted to the right in orbito-frontal, but not in frontal, cortex slices prepared from the same guinea pigs treated for 8 weeks with the SSRI paroxetine. These results indicate that the enhanced 5-HT release observed in the orbito-frontal

A - SEROTONIN RELEASE

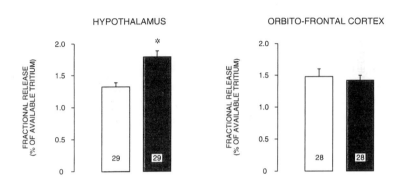

HYPOTHALAMUS

ORBITO-FRONTAL CORTEX

B - 5-HT AUTORECEPTOR SENSITIVITY

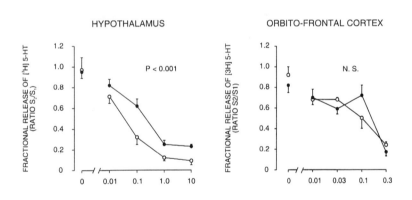

HYPOTHALAMUS

ORBITO-FRONTAL CORTEX

5-METHOXYTRYPTAMINE (μM)

FIG. 27.2. Effect of a 3-week treatment with the selective 5-HT reuptake inhibitor paroxetine (10 mg/kg/day, subcutaneously delivered using an osmotic minipump) on the electrically evoked release of [^{3}H]5-HT from preloaded guinea pig brain slices in A, and on the sensitivity of the terminal 5-HT$_{1D}$ autoreceptor. The experiments were carried out 48 hours after removing the minipumps to allow elimination of the drug. The asterisk indicates a statistically significant difference ($p < 0.05$) when compared to the mean value in the control group, using the two-tailed Student's t test. The concentration effect curves were compared using two-way analysis of variance. NS = not significant.

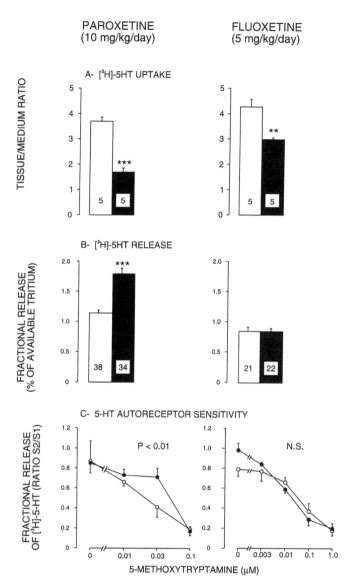

FIG. 27.3. Effect of two selective 5-HT reuptake inhibitors administered at different regimens for 8 weeks on the electrically evoked release of [³H]5-HT from preloaded guinea pig brain slices as well as on the sensitivity of the terminal 5-HT$_{1D}$ autoreceptor. The experiments were carried out 48 hours after removing the minipumps in the case of paroxetine and 96 hours in the case of fluoxetine to allow elimnation of the drugs. The [³H]5-HT uptake experiments were carried out after 7 days of treatment to ensure that steady state concentrations were achieved and the animals were sacrificed with the osmotic minipump on board. **p < .01, ***p < .001 using the two-tailed Student's *t* test. The concentration-effect curves were compared using two-way analysis of variance. *NS* = not significant.

cortex could be attributed to a desensitization of the terminal 5-HT autoreceptor in that particular brain region. Interestingly, 5-HT release and autoreceptor sensitivity were still unaltered when compared to controls in the head of the caudate nucleus after an 8-week paroxetine treatment.

The same experiments were carried out using another SSRI, fluoxetine, but at a lower regimen. Both in the orbito-frontal cortex and in the head of the caudate nucleus, the evoked release of [^{3}H]5-HT and terminal 5-HT autoreceptor sensitivity were unaltered after 3- and 8-week treatments. This outcome suggests that a marked degree of reuptake inhibition is important to induce an attenuation of the sensitivity of terminal 5-HT autoreceptors, at least in some brain regions. To verify this contention, we assessed the degree of [^{3}H]5-HT uptake inhibition induced by the 10 mg/kg/day regimen of paroxetine versus that produced by the 5 mg/kg/day regimen of fluoxetine. The paroxetine treatment produced a 56% inhibition of [^{3}H]5-HT uptake, whereas the fluoxetine treatment inhibited uptake by only 29% (Fig. 27.3). We have recently completed identical experiments using a 10 mg/kg/day regimen of fluoxetine and found that the terminal 5-HT autoreceptor was also desensitized in the orbito-frontal cortex after an 8-week treatment with this SSRI (Bergqvist, Bouchard, & Blier, 1999).

Taken together, these data indicate that the enhanced 5-HT release in the orbito-frontal cortex, manifesting itself after a prolonged SSRI treatment, is fully consistent with the delayed onset of these drugs in OCD, suggesting that such a phenomenon could be the neurobiological substratum of the therapeutic effect of 5-HT reuptake inhibition in this disorder. A greater degree of reuptake inhibition also appears essential to obtain these modifications of the function of 5-HT terminals. These findings are consistent with the common clinical observation that high doses of SSRIs are sometimes necessary to obtain an anti-OCD effect, and the results of some fixed-dose double-blind trials showing a dose-dependent therapeutic effect of SSRIs (Montgomery et al., 1993; Greist et al., 1995; Tollefson et al., 1994).

On a more theoretical note, the changes induced by SSRIs, or lack thereof, in different brain regions clearly put into evidence the distinct properties of 5-HT terminals projecting to the different regions (El Mansari et al., 1995; Piñeyro, Blier, Dennis, & de Montigny, 1994). This was also documented in our studies assessing the function of the 5-HT transporter after the previously mentioned SSRI treatment for 3 and 8 weeks. After a 3- and an 8-week treatment with paroxetine the 5-HT transporter was desensitized in the frontal cortex but not in the orbito-frontal cortex, as indicated by the loss of the capacity of paroxetine, when introduced in the superfusion medium, to enhance the electrically evoked overflow of [^{3}H]5-HT in slices prepared from the former but not the latter brain region. We had also documented that this attenuated function of 5-HT transporters is attributable to a decreased number of such sites hippocampus and frontal cortex (Piñeyro et al., 1994). The differences raise the question as to why the terminal 5-HT aut........ptors and the 5-HT transporters exhibit such differential changes during sustained and prolonged administration of SSRIs. The mechanisms underlying the differential desensitization of terminal 5-HT autoreceptors are presently under study in our laboratory and the possibilities being investigated are different G-proteins, second messenger, and ion-channel coupling. Should differences be identified, then the way could be opened for the use of selective pharmacological agents acting directly on transducing mechanisms that would produce the same functional changes as SSRIs do, but much more rapidly. Obtaining a more robust anti-OCD effect is also a possibility. This is eagerly awaited, as SSRIs in the vast majority of patients produce only a partial remission, notwithstanding the important proportion of patients not responding at all to SSRIs.

CLINICAL EVIDENCE FOR AN IMPORTANT ROLE OF 5-HT NEUROTRANSMISSION IN THE ANTI-OCD RESPONSE

Recently, it was reported that acute tryptophan depletion, which decreases brain 5-HT availability, does not induce a recurrence of OCD symptomatology in patients improved by an SSRI, in contrast to the effectiveness of this challenge paradigm in depressed patients in remission obtained by the same type of drugs (Barr et al., 1994; Delgado et al. 1990). This lack of relapse could be taken as an argument against the notion that enhanced 5-HT neurotransmission is somehow responsible for the anti-OCD effect of SSRIs. However, several factors have to be taken into account in the interpretation of these results. For instance, anomalies of the 5-HT system, such as hyposensitivity of 5-HT$_{1A}$ receptors mediating hypothermia and prolactin secretion, have consistently been documented in depressed patients, but not in OCD patients (Gross-Isseroff et al., 1994). Consequently, the status of the 5-HT system in these two groups of patients, even after the same SSRI treatment, may not be identical, at least in different brain regions. It is then conceivable that the tryptophan depletion paradigm does not produce the same changes in 5-HT transmission in depressed and OCD patients. It is instructive that in this study, the OCD patients that had depressive symptomatology prior to their SSRI treatment had a relapse of depression. This observation supports the assumption that the antidepressant and the anti-OCD effects are controlled by different brain regions. The effectiveness of lithium addition in SSRI-resistant depressed but not in OCD patients supports this possibility as well (de Montigny, 1994; McDougle, Price, Goodman, Charney, & Heninger, 1991). Lithium has been shown to increase 5-HT release in the hypothalamus, hippocampus, and spinal cord but not in the cerebral cortex or in the striatum (for a review, see Blier & de Montigny, 1992), the latter two structures being more specifically involved in OCD than in depression. Finally, because 5-HT transporters do not desensitize in the orbito-frontal cortex after prolonged SSRI administration, it is conceivable that a relapse could have occurred in these OCD patients in the acute tryptophan-depleted state had the SSRI been discontinued a few days prior to this procedure (Barr et al., 1994; El Mansari et al., 1995). This approach could be justified by the observation that the majority of OCD patients generally do not relapse immediately on cessation of their medication, but rather after at least a week or two (Pato, Zohar-Kadouch, Zohar, & Murphy, 1988).

In contrast to these negative results, the administration of the nonselective 5-HT antagonist metergoline was reported to produce a significant deterioration of OCD symptoms in patients improved by the potent 5-HT reuptake inhibitor clomipramine (Benkelfat et al., 1989). This reversal of improvement was also replicated by the same group using an SSRI (Greenberg et al., 1998). The reversal effect of metergoline occured not within the first day, but in subsequent days following its administration. Whatever the mechanism involved in this delayed effect of metergoline, this manipulation of the 5-HT system is again consistent with the longer delays necessary to obtain an improvement of OCD.

Given the possibility of obtaining at least a partial relapse with a 5-HT antagonist in OCD patients in remission, we attempted to obtain a therapeutic effect in SSRI-resistant OCD patients using pharmacological strategies aimed at enhancing the efficacy of 5-HT neurotransmission. At least two such strategies, lithium and buspirone addition, had been tested before and shown to be ineffective in double-blind trials (Grady et al., 1993; McDougle et al., 1993; McDougle et al., 1991). We therefore examined other approaches. In a first attempt, we added the 5-HT$_{1A}$ antagonist pindolol to the SSRI regimen of 13 SSRI-resistant OCD patients (Blier & Bergeron, 1996). This drug combination was reported to be effective in depressed patients treated with, but not responding to, an SSRI (Artigas, Perez, & Alvarez, 1994; Blier & Bergeron, 1995). Pindolol presumably acts by blocking selectively the cell body 5-HT$_{1A}$ autoreceptor, thus allowing 5-HT neurons to resume their normal firing activity. This drug combination produced a marked and rapid improvement of depressive symptomatology in the 11 patients who had at least mild depressive symptomatology (i.e., a Montgomery–Asberg Depression Rating Scale score of 12 or more; Montgomery & Asberg, 1979). However, there was no significant group effect of the 28-day addition of pindolol as measured by mean Yale–Brown

Obsessive Compulsive Scale scores (Y–BOCS; Fig. 27.4; Goodman, Price, Rasmussen, Mazure, Delgado, et al., 1989; Goodman, Price, Rasmussen, Mazure, Fleischmann, et al., 1989). It is noteworthy that a marked improvement was obtained in four patients (decreases in Y–BOCS scores of 7–12 points), but three of these patients also met the criteria for major depression before pindolol addition. Therefore, this strategy, by itself, remains to be further explored as an augmentation strategy in the treatment of SSRI-resistant OCD patients without concomitant depression.

Given that nine of these OCD patients still had a Y–BOCS score of 19 or more, we then attempted to potentiate 5-HT transmission by adding L-tryptophan (TRYPTAN) to the SSRI–pindolol regimen. By increasing the availability of the amino acid precursor for 5-HT, L-tryptophan, it was hoped that 5-HT release could be enhanced in these patients who had their 5-HT transporters blocked by the SSRI and their 5-HT$_{1A}$ autoreceptors on the cell body blocked by pindolol (see Fig. 27.1). Pindolol was not removed at this point so as not to destabilize the patient at least with respect to depressive symptomatology. Two weeks after the addition of 1 g of tryptophan twice daily, there was no significant improvement. The tryptophan regimen was increased to 2 g twice daily and 2 weeks later a significant improvement was noted. After another 2 weeks, some pa-

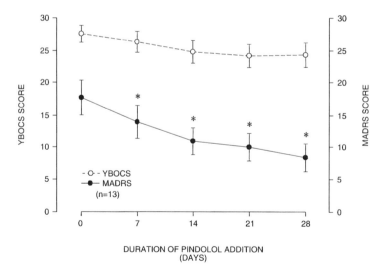

FIG. 27.4. Severity of OCD on the Yale–Brown Obsessive Compulsive Scale (Y–BOCS) and of depression on the Montgomery–Asberg Depression Rating Scale (MADRS) in patients with OCD who did not respond to a serotonin reuptake inhibitor. Pindolol was given orally three times daily at a dose of 2.5 mg while maintaining the serotonin reuptake inhibitor regimen. *p < .05, using one-way analysis of variance, when compared to the baseline (Day 0) value.

tients having received 3 g twice daily, there was a further improvement. At this point in time, there was a 35% decrease of the mean Y–BOCS score with a marked improvement in all but one patient (Fig. 27.5). Most patients improved by a few more points on the Y–BOCS when treatment was prolonged beyond 6 weeks of tryptophan administration.

Although the risk of inducing a 5-HT syndrome is always present when using more than one proserotonergic drug, we observed no manifestation of such a complication in these patients. The 5-HT syndrome occurs when there is an overactivation of 5-HT receptors that results in fever, tachy-cardia, tremors, myoclonus, agitation, confusion, and potentially death when long-acting drugs are used (Sternbach, 1991). It is possible that pindolol could have exerted a protective effect because this drug can block

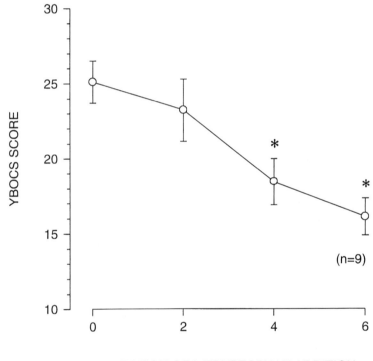

DURATION OF L-TRYPTOPHAN ADDITION
(WEEKS)

FIG. 27.5. Severity of OCD on the Yale–Brown Obsessive Compulsive Scale (Y–BOCS) in patients unresponsive to a serotonin reuptake inhibitor plus pindolol who subsequently received L-tryptophan. Tryptophan was given at a regimen of 1 g twice a day for the first 2 weeks and 2 g twice a day for the next 2 weeks. The dose was increased to 3 g twice a day from Week 4 onward in seven patients. *$p < .05$, using one-way analysis of variance, when compared to the baseline (Day 0) value.

the 5-HT syndrome induced by the 5-HT$_{1A}$ agonist 8-OH-DPAT, as well as some other effects mediated by postsynaptic 5-HT$_{1A}$ receptors (Aulakh et al., 1988; Seletti et al., 1995; Tricklebank, Forler, & Fozard, 1984). There was also no significant modification of heart rate or blood pressure by pindolol. Taken together, the apparent lack of anti-OCD effect of pindolol addition and the putative therapeutic effect of tryptophan in OCD support our hypothesis that, for a drug strategy to be effective in OCD, its main effect should be on 5-HT terminals in a brain region involved in mediating OCD symptoms. The results of this pilot trial have now been verified under double-blind conditions.

In five patients, the addition of the 5-HT$_{1A}$ agonist buspirone was attempted. Our hope was that, in the presence of pindolol, this drug could produce a beneficial effect that would not necessarily have manifested itself in the presence of the SSRI alone. Doses of 30 to 50 mg per day for 3 to 5 weeks did not produce any significant improvement. In a last attempt to further potentiate 5-HT neurotransmission, the immediate precursor of 5-HT, 5-hydroxytryptophan (5-HTP), was added to the SSRI–pindolol regimen in five patients. Because this compound is metabolized into 5-HT by a nonspecific decarboxylase enzyme that is not saturated in the brain, it was hoped that perhaps 5-HT availability could be enhanced more than by giving tryptophan (see Fig. 27.1). An oral dose of 400 mg per day of 5-HTP did not bring about any significant improvement in OCD nor did it produce any marked side effects. When the inhibitor of the decarboxylase enzyme carbidopa was added to the SSRI–pindolol–5-HTP regimen to prevent the peripheral transformation of 5-HTP and increase its brain availability, the three female patients had severe nausea and this strategy was abandoned. The two male patients tolerated this combination well. One patient failed to improve but the other had a 7-point drop in his Y–BOCS score. In fact, he was the patient who had not responded to tryptophan addition or to any other strategy, including behavioral psychotherapy. He developed diarrhea and nevertheless decided to continue this drug combination, but only for 3 weeks, as the gastrointestinal problem did not subside.

These observations on a small number of patients with buspirone support the notion that the postsynaptic 5-HT$_{1A}$ receptors are not likely to be important in the anti-OCD response. In addition, 5-HTP does not produce a therapeutic effect in SSRI-resistant OCD patients in the absence of important side effects. Nevertheless, these clinical observations suggest that if the efficacy of the 5-HT system is enhanced sufficiently by the proper strategy, some beneficial effect can be expected. Although some approaches require several pills three times a day, such as adding 4 to 6 g per day of tryptophan to an SSRI and pindolol regimen, or as much as tolerable as in the case of 5-HTP, they at least suggest that further research should be carried out in an attempt to find more effective and practical ways to enhance 5-HT transmission. It is noteworthy that no cases of intoxication (the eosinophilic myalgia syndrome) were ever encountered with the form of L-tryptophan available on prescription in Canada (L-Tryptan).

5-HT$_{1D}$ AUTORECEPTORS AS A NOVEL TARGET FOR ANTI-OCD DRUGS

The results of the experiments already described point to the terminal 5-HT autoreceptors as potentially playing a major role in the anti-OCD effect of SSRIs. A novel target for the development of a new anti-OCD medication would be the development of a selective 5-HT$_{1D}$ antagonist that would prevent the negative feedback these autoreceptors exert normally on 5-HT release. The administration of such a drug would then lead to enhanced 5-HT release and hopefully to a rapid onset of action in the OCD patient. There are, however, several factors to consider before accepting this possibility.

First, assuming that such a drug could be synthesized, one wonders if, in the human brain, there is indeed a tonic activation of terminal 5-HT autoreceptors by endogenous 5-HT. This is a sine qua non condition for an antagonist to modify the function of a receptor on which it binds. Indeed, blocking a receptor that is not activated by its endogenous ligand under basal conditions will not produce any effect. There are now three studies demonstrating that the 5-HT antagonist methiothepin enhances the electrically evoked overflow of [^{3}H]5-HT in fresh human neocortex slices (Galzin et al., 1992; Maura et al., 1993; Schlicker, Brandt, Classen, & Göthert, 1985). Because the frequency of the stimulations in all three studies was within the normal frequency of firing activity of 5-HT neurons in freely moving animals (i.e., 3 per second), and because such in vitro superfusion experiments have consistently yielded results similar to those obtained in in vivo electrophysiological and microdialysis studies in laboratory animals, we conclude that it is possible to enhance 5-HT release by interfering with the terminal 5-HT autoreceptor. It was, however, recently postulated that methiothepin could act as an inverse agonist at terminal 5-HT autoreceptors (Moret & Briley, 1993). An inverse agonist is a compound that binds to a receptor, but exerts the opposite physiological effect of an agonist. This mechanism might thus account for the observation that methiothepin is the only 5-HT receptor ligand that is actually able to markedly enhance 5-HT release by itself. Whether this is a likely possibility is beyond the scope of this chapter. Suffice to mention, there are arguments both against and in favor of this possibility (Baumann & Waldmeier, 1981; Jones, Burton, Middlemiss, Price, & Roberts, 1995). Whatever the type of interaction methiothepin exerts on terminal 5-HT autoreceptors, the mere observation that it can enhance 5-HT release by itself validates this novel therapeutic stategy: If an inverse agonist is necessary to obtain this physiological effect, then such a drug can be synthesized because methiothepin in fact does enhance 5-HT release. Methiothepin itself cannot be used for this purpose in humans as it acts on several other receptors: serotonergic, adrenergic, and dopaminergic.

Second, like 5-HT_{1A} receptors, 5-HT_{1D} receptors are located both on 5-HT neurons and on postsynaptic neurons (Waeber, Schoeffter, Palacios, & Hoyer, 1989). Consequently, if a selective 5-HT_{1D} antagonist was developed, the concomitant blockade of the pre- and postsynaptic population of 5-HT_{1D} receptors could be a major drawback if the postsynaptic 5-HT_{1D} receptors play a role in the anti-OCD response. This is a likely possibility given that 5-HT_{1D} binding sites are present in high density on postsynaptic neurons in the basal ganglia (Heuring & Peroutka, 1987), a brain region that has been implicated in OCD. To develop a 5-HT_{1D} antagonist selective for the presynaptic receptors, one must assume that these are pharmacologically different from the postsynaptic 5-HT_{1D} receptors; that is, one of these populations of receptors should present a greater binding affinity by at least two and preferably three orders of magnitude for a given compound. There is evidence for such distinct properties of pre- and postjunctional 5-HT_{1D} receptors. The experimental compound CP 122,288, which is an analogue of the 5-HT_{1D} agonist sumatriptan, is more than three orders of magnitude more potent at pre- versus postjunctional 5-HT_{1D} receptors (Beattie & Connor, 1995; Gupta et al., 1995). This observation clearly indicates that, at the very least, 5-HT_{1D} receptors are not all alike and they can be differentiated pharmacologically. It is noteworthy that molecular biology techniques had already identified two subtypes of 5-HT_{1D} receptors, namely $5\text{-HT}_{1D\alpha}$ and $5\text{-HT}_{1D\beta}$, with an amino acid homology of only about 65% (Weinshank, Zgmobick, Macchi, Branchek, & Hartig, 1992). Surprisingly, these could not be differentiated with classical 5-HT ligands. It has been proposed that the terminal 5-HT autoreceptor in the human brain is of the $5\text{-HT}_{1D\beta}$ subtype (Maura et al., 1993). This proposal, however, is now largely based on the lack of effect of the 5-HT antagonist ketanserin, which has a lesser affinity for $5\text{-HT}_{1D\beta}$ than for $5\text{-HT}_{1D\alpha}$ sites on 5-HT release on human brain slices. This proposal is also based on the fact that the terminal 5-HT autoreceptor in the mouse and rat brain is of the 5-HT_{1B} subtype, a receptor with more than 90% homology with the human $5\text{-HT}_{1D\beta}$ receptor (Boess & Martin, 1994; Maura et al., 1993).

The selectivity factor for a 5-HT_{1D} antagonist is further complicated by recent studies carried out in our laboratory indicating the presence of a 5-HT_{1D} receptor in the dorsal raphe, the nucleus containing the largest number of 5-HT neurons (El Mansari & Blier, 1996; Piñeyro & Blier, 1996; Piñeyro, de Montigny, & Blier, 1993, 1995). The dorsal raphe nucleus gives rise to a major proportion of the 5-HT innervation of the forebrain. This receptor is actually an autoreceptor because we have shown that it is located on 5-HT neurons themselves and exerts a negative feedback influence on 5-HT released from the cell body and dendrites of 5-HT neurons (Fig. 27.1). Its role is clearly distinct from that of the well-known 5-HT_{1A} autoreceptor that inhibits the firing activity of 5-HT neurons. Indeed, it is possible to inhibit 5-HT release in the dorsal raphe nucleus of anesthetized rats using a 5-HT agonist that does not alter the basal firing activity of 5-HT neurons (Piñeyro, de Montigny, & Blier, 1996). The presence of this 5-HT_{1D} autoreceptor in the raphe implies that on systemic administration of a 5-HT_{1D} antagonist acting both on autoreceptors located at the cell body and terminal levels, an increase in 5-HT release in the forebrain may not be obtained. This would occur because the blockade of the former would enhance 5-HT release in the raphe, thereby decreasing 5-HT neuronal firing activity via an increased activation of 5-HT_{1A} autoreceptors. Consequently, with the impulse flow being attenuated, the antagonism of terminal 5-HT_{1D} autoreceptors would not lead to enhanced 5-HT release. Preliminary evidence was reported supporting this hypothesis. Price et al. (1994) observed an attenuation of cortical 5-HT release in guinea pigs following the systemic administration of the 5-HT_{1D} antagonist GR 127,935 contrary to what would have been expected if the drug had antagonized only the 5-HT_{1D} autoreceptor on 5-HT terminals. In contrast, GR 127,935 markedly enhanced 5-HT release following the injection of the selective 5-HT_{1A} antagonist WAY 100,635, so as to prevent the shutting off of 5-HT neuronal firing mediated by the cell body 5-HT_{1A} autoreceptors. These results indicate that for a 5-HT_{1D} antagonist to enhance 5-HT release in the forebrain it should act solely on the terminal 5-HT_{1D} autoreceptor. Again, this possibility must rely on the notion that these 5-HT autoreceptors are different, at least pharmacologically. We have accumulated evidence in favor of this possibility. Among several obsevations, we can cite evidence that in rats the cell body 5-HT autoreceptor controlling release is of the 5-HT_{1D} subtype, whereas on terminals it is of the 5-HT_{1B} subtype (Hoyer & Middlemiss, 1989; Piñeyro et al., 1995). In conclusion, it should be possible to develop a 5-HT_{1D} antagonist selective for the terminal 5-HT_{1D} autoreceptor.

POSTSYNAPTIC 5-HT RECEPTORS AS POTENTIAL TARGETS FOR THE DEVELOPMENT OF NEW THERAPEUTIC AGENTS

Because long-term administration of SSRI apparently leads to enhanced release of 5-HT in the orbito-frontal cortex, it appears essential to determine which 5-HT receptor subtype mediates the effect of 5-HT in that particular brain region. Moreover, because 5-HT neurons also innervate other structures of the neuronal circuitry implicated in mediating OCD symptoms, the identification of these postsynaptic 5-HT receptor sub-type(s) could also provide important leads for the development of new therapeutic agents for OCD. In particular, it was previously shown that 5-HT$_2$ receptors mediate the inhibitory effect of 5-HT on the firing activity of rat caudate nucleus neurons (El Mansari et al., 1994). Preliminary results from our laboratory indicate that this is also the case in the head of the caudate nucleus in guinea pigs. The capacity to produce an exacerbation of OCD symptoms in SSRI-treated patients by the nonselective antagonist metergoline, as well as that of the more selective 5-HT$_2$ antagonist ritan-serin, would support the possibility that the therapeutic effect of SSRI could be mediated, at least in part, by this subtype of receptors. A selective 5-HT$_2$ agonist on the basis of these fundamental and clinical observations could be of use in the treatment of OCD. It is, however, well known that this receptor family is comprised of at least three subclasses: the 5-HT$_{2A}$, 5-HT$_{2B}$, and 5-HT$_{2C}$ receptors (Boess & Martin, 1994). It is presently not known which 5-HT$_2$ receptor subtype is involved in mediating the effect of 5-HT in these specific brain regions.

POTENTIAL THERAPEUTIC PHARMACOLOGICAL TARGETS OTHER THAN 5-HT RECEPTORS

Results from our laboratory have shown that 5-HT release is enhanced in the orbito-frontal cortex of guinea pigs after a 2-month treatment with an SSRI but not in the head of the caudate nucleus. Because the former structure projects to the latter and both have been implicated in the mediation of the OCD symptomatology, it is likely that an alteration of 5-HT transmission even in only one component of this orbito-frontal cortex-basal ganglia neuronal circuitry will have a repercussion on the activity of the whole circuitry. Therefore, altering transmission between any of these structures by acting on a chemospecific system linking these structures could have a profound physiological impact on this neuronal circuitry, and hopefully, on OCD symptomatology.

In conclusion, a first attempt at elucidating the possible mechanism of action of SSRIs in the treatment of OCD has yielded important information as to the possible 5-HT receptor subtype(s) involved in this therapeutic effect. A preliminary clinical trial has produced encouraging results for the treatment of SSRI-resistant OCD patients. Better comprehension of the effects of SSRIs in OCD will lead to further pharmacological strategies that could improve the rate and degree of improvement that we have obtained in the treatment of this severe and persistent disorder.

REFERENCES

Artigas, F., Perez, V., & Alvarez, E. (1994). Pindolol induces a rapid improvement of depressed patients treated with serotonin uptake inhibitors. *Archives of General Psychiatry, 51*, 248–251.

Aulakh, C. S., Wozniak, K. M., Haas, M., Hill, J. L., Zohar, J., & Murphy, D. L. (1988). Food intake, neuroendocrine and temperature effects of 8-OH-DPAT in the rat. *European Journal of Pharmacology, 146*, 253–259.

Barr, L. C., Goodman, W. K., McDougle, C., Delgado, P. L., Heninger, G. R., Charney, D., & Price, L. H. (1994). Tryptophan depletion in patients with obsessive-compulsive disorder who respond to serotonin reuptake inhibitors. *Archives of General Psychiatry, 51*, 309–317.

Baumann, P. A., & Waldmeier, P. C. (1981). Further evidence for negative feedback control of 5-HT release in the central nervous system. *Naunyn-Schmiedeberg's Archives of Pharmacology, 317*, 36–43.

Baxter, L. R., Jr., Phelps, J. M., Mazziotta, J. C., Guze, B. H., & Schwartz, J. M. (1987). Local cerebral glucose metabolic rates in obsessive-compulsive disorder: A comparison with rates in unipolar depression and normal controls. *Archives of General Psychiatry, 44*, 211–218.

Baxter, L. K., Schurtz, J. M., Bergman, K. S., Szuba, M. P., Guze, B. H., Mazziotta, J. C., Alazraki, A., Selin, C. E., Fern, M.-K., Munford, P., & Phelps, M. E. (1992). Caudate glucose metabolic rate changes with both drug and behavioral therapy for obsessive-compulsive disorder. *Archives of General Psychiatry, 49*, 681–689.

Beattie, D. T., & Connor, H. E. (1995). The pre- and postjunctional activity of CP-122,288, a conformationally restricted analogue of sumatriptan. *European Journal of Pharmacology, 276*, 271–276.

Benkelfat, C., Murphy, D. L., Zohar, J., Hill, J. L., Grover, G., & Insel, T. R. (1989). Clomipramine in obsessive-compulsive disorder: Further evidence for a serotonergic mechanism of action. *Archives of General Psychiatry, 46*, 23–28.

Bergqvist, P. B. F., Bouchard, C., & Blier, P. (1999). Effect of long-term administration of antidepressant treatments on serotonin release in brain regions involved in obsessive compulsive disorder. *Biological Psychiatry, 45*, 164–174.

Blier, P., & Bergeron, R. (1995). Effectiveness of pindolol with selected antidepressant drugs in the treatment of major depression. *Journal of Clinical Psychopharmacology, 15*, 217–222.

Blier, P., & Bergeron, R. (1996). Sequential administration of augmentation strategies in treatment-resistant obsessive-compulsive disorder: Preliminary findings. *International Clinical Psychopharmacology, 11*, 37–44.

Blier, P., & Bouchard, C. (1994). Modulation of serotonin release in the guinea pig brain following long-term administration of antidepressant drugs. *British Journal of Pharmacology, 113*, 485–495.

Blier, P., & de Montigny, C. (1983). Electrophysiological studies on the effect of repeated zimelidine administration on serotonergic neurotransmission in the rat. *Journal of Neuroscience, 3*, 1270–1278.

Blier, P., & de Montigny, C. (1985). Serotonergic but not noradrenergic neurons in rat CNS adapt to long-term treatment with monoamine oxidase inhibitors. *Neuroscience, 16*, 949–955.

Blier, P., & de Montigny, C. (1990). Differential effect of gepirone on pre- and postsynaptic serotonin receptors: Single-cell recording studies. *Journal of Clinical Psychopharmacology, 10*(Suppl.), 13–20.

Blier, P., & de Montigny C. (1992). Lack of efficacy of lithium augmentation in obsessive-compulsive disorder: The perspective of different regional effects of lithium on serotonin release in the central nervous system. *Journal of Clinical Psychopharmacology, 12*, 65–66.

Blier, P., & de Montigny, C. (1994). Current advances and trends in the treatment of depression. *Trends in Pharmacological Science, 15,* 220–226.

Blier, P., de Montigny, C., & Azzaro, A. J. (1986). Modification of serotonergic and noradrenergic neurotransmission by repeated administration of monoamine oxidase inhibitors: Electrophysiological studies in the rat CNS. *Journal of Pharmacology and Experimental Therapeutics, 237,* 987–994.

Boess, F. G., & Martin, I. L. (1994). Molecular biology of 5-HT receptors. *Neuropharmacology, 33,* 275–317.

Chaput, Y., de Montigny, C., & Blier, P. (1986). Effects of a selective 5-HT reuptake blocker, citalopram, on the sensitivity of 5-HT autoreceptors: Electrophysiological studies in the rat. *Naunyn-Schmiedeberg's Archives of Pharmacology, 333,* 342–348.

Delgado, P. L., Charney, D. S., Price, L. H., Aghajanian, G. K., Landis, H., & Heninger, G. R. (1990). Serotonin function and the mechanism of antidepressant action: Reversal of antidepressant-induced remission by rapid depletion of plasma tryptophan. *Archives of General Psychiatry, 47,* 411–418.

de Montigny, C. (1984). Electroconvulsive treatments enhance responsiveness of forebrain neurons to serotonin. *Journal of Pharmacology & Experimental Therapeutics, 228,* 230–234.

de Montigny, C. (1994). Lithium addition in treatment-resistant depression. *International Clinical Psychopharmacology, 9*(2, Suppl.), 31–35.

de Montigny, C., & Aghajanian, G. K. (1978). Tricyclic antidepressants: Long-term treatment increases responsivity of rat forebrain neurons to serotonin. *Science, 202,* 1303–1306.

El Mansari, M., & Blier, P. (1996). Functional characterization of 5-HT$_{1D}$ autoreceptors on the modulation of 5-HT release in guinea-pig mesencephalic raphe, hippocampus and frontal cortex. *British Journal of Pharmacology, 118,* 681–689.

El Mansari, M., Bouchard, C., & Blier, P. (1995). Alteration of serotonin release by selective serotonin reuptake inhibitors in the guinea pig orbitofrontal cortex: Relevance to the treatment of obsessive-compulsive disorder. *Neuropsychopharmacology, 13,* 117–127.

El Mansari, M., Radja, F., Ferron, A., Reader, T. A., Molina-Holgado, E., & Descarries, L. (1994). Hypersensitivity to serotonin and its agonists in serotonin-hyperinnervated neostriatum after neonatal dopamine denervation. *European Journal of Pharmacology, 261,* 171–178.

Fineberg, N. A., Bullock, T., Montgomery, D. B., & Montgomery, S. A. (1992). Serotonin reuptake inhibitors are the treatment of choice in obsessive compulsive disorder. *International Clinical Psychopharmacology, 7*(1, Suppl.), 43–47.

Galzin, A. M., Poirier, M. F., Lista, A., Chodkiewicz, J. P., Blier, P., Ramdine, R., Loo, H., Roux, F. X., Redondo, A., & Langer, S. Z. (1992). Characterization of the 5-hydroxytryptamine autoreceptor modulating the release of [^{3}H]5-hydroxytryptamine in slices of human neocortex. *Journal of Neurochemistry, 59,* 1293–1301.

Goodman, W. K., Price, L. H., Rasmussen, S. A., Mazure, C., Delgado, P., Heninger, G. R., & Charney, D. S. (1989). The Yale–Brown Obsessive-Compulsive Scale (Y–BOCS): Part 2. Validity. *Archives of General Psychiatry, 46,* 1012–1016.

Goodman, W. K., Price, L. H., Rasmussen, S. A., Mazure, C., Fleischmann, R. L., Hill, C. L., Henninger, G. R., & Charney, D. S. (1989). The Yale–Brown Obsessive Compulsive Scale (Y–BOCS): Part 1. Development, use, and validity. *Archives of General Psychiatry, 46,* 1006–1011.

Grady, T. A., Pigott, T. A., L'Heureux, F., Hill, J. L., Bernstein, S. E., & Murphy, D. L. (1993). Double-blind study of adjuvant buspirone for fluoxetine-treated patients with obsessive-compulsive disorder. *American Journal of Psychiatry, 150,* 819–821.

Greenberg, B. D., Benjamin, J., Martin, J. D., Keuler, D., Huang, S.-J., Altemus, M., & Murphy, D. L. (1998). Delayed obsessive-compulsive disorder system exacerbation after a single dose of a serotonin antagonist in fluoxetine-treated but not untreated patients. *Psychopharmacology, 140,* 434–444.

Greist, J., Chouinard, G., DuBoff, E., Halaris, A., Won Kim, S., Koran, L., Liebowitz, M., Lydiard, R. B., Rasmussen, S., White, K., & Sikes, C. (1995). Double-blind parallel comparison of three dosages of sertraline and placebo in outpatients with obsessive-compulsive disorder. *Archives of General Psychiatry, 52,* 289–295.

Gross-Isserof, R., Kindler, S., Kotler, M., Sasson, Y., Dolberg, O., Hendler, T., & Zohar, J. (1994). Pharmacological challenges. In E. Hollander, J. Zohar, D. Marazzati, & B. Olivier (Eds.), *Current insights in obsessive compulsive disorder* (pp. 137–147). New York: Wiley.

Gupta, P., Brown, D., Butler, P., Ellis, P., Grayson, K. L., Land, G. C., Macor, J. E., Robson, S. F., Whythes, M. J., & Shepperson, N. B. (1995). The in vivo pharmacological profile of a 5-HT$_1$ receptor agonist, CP-122,288, a selective inhibitor of neurogenic inflammation. *British Journal of Pharmacology, 116,* 2385–2390.

Heuring, R. E., & Peroutka, S. J. (1987). Characterization of a novel ^{3}H-5-hydroxytryptamine binding site subtype in bovine brain membranes. *Journal of Neuroscience, 7,* 894–903.

Hoyer, D., & Middlemiss, D. K. (1989). The pharmacology of terminal 5-HT autoreceptors in mammalian brain: Evidence for species differences. *Trends in Pharmacological Science, 10,* 130–132.

Hyttel, J. (1994). Pharmacological characterization of selective serotonin reuptake inhibitors (SSRIs). *International Clinical Psychopharmacology, 9*(1, Suppl.), 19–26.

Insel, T. R. (1992). Toward a neuroanatomy of obsessive-compulsive disorder. *Archives of General Psychiatry, 49,* 739–744.

Jones, B. J., Burton, M., Middlemiss, D. K., Price, G. W., & Roberts, C. (1995). Are the contrasting effects of GR 127,935 and methiothepin on recombinant 5-HT$_{1D}$ receptor systems physiologically relevant? *European Journal of Neuropsychopharmacology, 5*(3, Suppl.), 413–414.

Maura, G., Thellung, S., Andrioli, G. C., Ruelle, A., & Raiteri, M. (1993). Release-regulating serotonin 5-HT$_{1D}$ autoreceptors in human cerebral cortex. *Journal of Neurochemistry, 60,* 1179–1182.

McDougle, C. J., Goodman, W. K., Leckman, J. F., Holzer, J. C., Barr, L. C., McCance-Katz, E., Heninger, G. R., & Price, L. H. (1993). Limited therapeutic effect of addition of buspirone in fluvoxamine-refractory obsessive-compulsive disorder. *American Journal of Psychiatry, 150,* 647–649.

McDougle, C. J., Price, L. H., Goodman, W. K., Charney, D. S., & Heninger, G. R. (1991). A controlled trial of lithium augmentation in fluvoxamine-refractory obsessive-compulsive disorder: Lack of efficacy. *Journal of Clinical Psychopharmacology, 11,* 175–184.

Montgomery, S. A., & Asberg, M. (1979). A new depression scale designed to be sensitive to change. *British Journal of Psychiatry, 134,* 382–389.

Montgomery, S. A., McIntyre, A., Osterheider, M., Sarteschi, P., Zitterl, W., Zohar, J., Birkett, M., & Wood, A. J. (1993). A double-blind, placebo-controlled study of fluoxetine in patients with DSM–III–R obsessive-compulsive disorder. *European Journal of Neuropsychopharmacology, 3,* 143–152.

Moret, C., & Briley, M. (1990). Serotonin autoreceptor subsensitivity and antidepressant activity. *European Journal of Pharmacology, 180,* 351–356.

Moret, C., & Briley, M. (1993). The unique effect of methiothepin on the terminal serotonin autoreceptor in the rat hypothalamus could be an example of inverse agonism. *Journal of Psychopharmacology, 7,* 331–337.

Pato, M. T., Zohar-Kadouch, R., Zohar, J., & Murphy, D. L. (1988). Return of symptoms after discontinuation of clomipramine in patients with obsessive compulsive disorder. *American Journal of Psychiatry, 145,* 1521–1525.

Piñeyro, G., & Blier, P. (1996). Regulation of [^{3}H]5-HT release from rat midbrain raphe nuclei by 5-HT$_{1D}$ receptors: Effect of tetrodotoxin, G protein inactivation and long-term antidepressant administration. *Journal of Pharmacology and Experimental Therapeutics, 276,* 697–707.

Piñeyro, G., Blier, P., Dennis, T., & de Montigny, C. (1994). Desensitization of the neuronal 5-HT carrier following its long-term blockade. *Journal of Neuroscience, 14,* 3036–3047.

Piñeyro, G., de Montigny, C., & Blier, P. (1993). Regulation of somatodendritic release of 5-HT in the rat dorsal raphe by 5-HT$_{1D}$ receptors. *Society for Neuroscience Abstracts, 19,* 93.4.

Piñeyro, G., de Montigny, C., & Blier, P. (1995). 5-HT$_{1D}$ receptors regulate 5-HT release in the rat raphe nuclei: In vivo voltammetry and in vitro superfusion studies. *Neuropsychopharmacology, 13,* 249–260.

Piñeyro, G., de Montigny, C., & Blier, P. (1996). Autoregulatory properties of dorsal raphe 5-HT neurons: Possible role of electrotonic coupling and 5-HT$_{1D}$ receptors in the rat brain. *Synapse, 22,* 54–62.

Price, G. W., Roberts, C., Watson, J., Burton, M., Middlemiss, D. N., & Jones, B. J. (1994). Effects of the selective 5-HT$_{1D}$ receptor antagonist GR 127935, on in vitro and in vivo 5-HT release from guinea pig cerebral cortex. *IUPHAR Satellite Meeting on Serotonin, 3,* 107.

Schlicker, E., Brandt, F., Classen, K., & Göthert, M. (1985). Serotonin release in human cerebral cortex and its modulation via serotonin receptors. *Brain Research, 331,* 337–347.

Seletti, B., Benkelfat, C., Blier, P., Annable, L., Gilbert, F., & de Montigny, C. (1995). Serotonin$_{1A}$ receptor activation in humans by flesinoxan: Body temperature and neuroendocrine response. *Neuropsychopharmacology, 13,* 93–104.

Sternbach, H. (1991). The serotonin syndrome. *American Journal of Psychiatry, 148,* 705–713.

Tollefson, G. D., Rampey, A. H., Potvin, J. H., Jenike, M. A., Rush, A. J., Dominguez, R. A., Koran, L. M., Shear, M. K., Goodman, W., & Genduso, L. A. (1994). A multicenter investigation of fixed-dose fluoxetine in the treatment of obsessive-compulsive disorder. *Archives of General Psychiatry, 51,* 559–567.

Tricklebank, M. D., Forler, C., & Fozard, J. R. (1984). The involvement of subtypes of the 5-HT$_1$ receptor and of catecholaminergic systems in the behavioural response to 8-hydroxy-2-(di-n-propylamino)tetralin in the rat. *European Journal of Pharmacology, 106,* 271–282.

Waeber, C., Schoeffter, P., Palacios, J., & Hoyer, D. (1989). 5-HT$_{1D}$ receptors in guinea-pig and pigeon brain: Radioligand binding and biochemical studies. *Naunyn-Schmiedeberg's Archives of Pharmacology, 340,* 479–485.

Weinschank, R. L., Zgmobick, J. M., Macchi, M., Branchek, T. A., & Hartig, P. R. (1992). Human serotonin 1D receptor is encoded by a subfamily of two distinct genes: 5-HT$_{1D\alpha}$ and 5-HT$_{1D\beta}$. *Proceedings of the National Academy of Science USA, 89,* 3630–3634.

28

Specific Brain System Mediation of Obsessive-Compulsive Disorder Responsive to Either Medication or Behavior Therapy

Lewis R. Baxter, Jr.
*University of Alabama at Birmingham
and University of California, Los Angeles*

Robert F. Ackermann
University of Alabama at Birmingham

Neal R. Swerdlow
University of California, San Diego

Arthur Brody
Sanjaya Saxena
Jeffrey M. Schwartz
University of California, Los Angeles

Jane M. Gregoritch
University of Alabama at Birmingham

Paula Stoessel
Michael E. Phelps
University of California, Los Angeles

To date, the development of effective treatments for major psychiatric disorders has far exceeded our understanding of the neuropathophysiology underlying their symptomatic expression. Nevertheless, it is a firmly held tenet of modern medicine that a clear understanding of a disease's physiological mediation will result in the most rapid advances in treatment. It is for this reason that we and several colleagues at a number of universities have been studying brain function in obsessive-compulsive disorder (OCD) and related conditions for many years.

573

In this chapter we summarize literature that we feel bears most cogently on this problem, and present new data from several studies that allow us to refine ideas expressed previously. There is now ample evidence to support a detailed theory of how a specific brain system mediates OCD symptoms in patients who respond well to available OCD treatments. On the other hand, data also suggest that patients who respond poorly to such treatments may have symptoms mediated by different neuroanatomical pathways.

A BRAIN SYSTEM MEDIATING OCD SYMPTOMS— A DISCLAIMER

Why focus on a single brain system in OCD's mediation? Any neuronal system that excludes other brain regions is in all probability incomplete, given the interconnectivity of all brain regions, and the complexity of OCD's experiential and behavioral elements. Seeing the parts more coherently than the whole may reflect how the brain itself works—major systems influenced dimly by other systems on which they depend. Be that as it may, these conceptualizations are intended for use only as hypothesis generators, not as faithful representations of reality.

BRIEF REVIEW OF PRIOR FINDINGS

Many neuroimaging studies using ^{18}F-fluoro-2-deoxyglucose (FDG) and positron emission tomography (PET) to measure localized cerebral metabolic rates for glucose (LCMRGlc) have associated abnormally high orbito-frontal and head of caudate nucleus LCMRGlc with the presence of OCD (Baxter et al., 1996, for in-depth review). These same two brain regions, together with the thalamus, show increased LCMRGlc when OCD behaviors are provoked (Rauch et al., 1994). Further, increased orbital and caudate LCMRGlc decline toward normal control values when OCD patients are treated effectively with either serotonin reuptake inhibitors (SRIs), or behavioral treatments that employ the techniques of exposure and response prevention (ERP; Baxter et al., 1996; Baxter et al., 1992; Benkelfat et al., 1990; Schwartz, Stoessel, Baxter, Martin, & Phelps, 1996, for review). Finally, there are significant correlations of LCMRGlc among the orbital cortex, head of caudate, and thalamus in untreated OCD patients who eventually respond to treatments that are not present in either normal controls or depressed individuals (Baxter, 1992; Baxter et al., 1992). With effective treatment with either SRI or behavior therapy activity these three brain structures no longer show such correlations, and these correlation changes are statistically significant (Baxter et al., 1992; Schwartz et al., 1996).

Given the PET studies just mentioned and the high association of basal ganglia pathology with disorders of mood and anxiety, several teams of investigators have proposed pathological hyperfunction in a specific brain circuit involving the orbital cortex, basal ganglia, and thalamus in the mediation of OCD symptoms (Insel, 1988; Modell, Mountz, Curtis, & Greden, 1989; Rapoport & Wise, 1988; Swerdlow, 1995). Stimulated by these ideas, we have extended these conceptualizations, but have been careful to apply them only to patients who respond well to treatment with either SRI or ERP supplemented with cognitive aids (Baxter et al., 1996; Baxter et al., 1992; Schwartz et al., 1996).

CORTICO-BASAL GANGLIONIC-THALAMIC CIRCUITS

A brief, simplified overview of the organization of cortico-basal gangli-onic-thalamic system circuits is provided to aid readers in understanding the rationale for theories of OCD mediation presented and for the animal experiments reported later. Greater detail may be found in excellent, up-to-date reviews of these brain systems by Parent and colleagues (Parent, Cote, & Lavoie, 1995; Parent & Hazrati, 1995a, 1995b).

Cortical and limbic structures project direct, stimulatory (glutamatergic) efferents to the corpus striatum (consisting of the caudate nucleus, putamen, nucleus accumbens, and olfactory tubercle in primates; see Fig. 28.1). From the corpus striatum projections traverse other substriatal basal ganglia structures on their way to various thalamic nuclei. These thalamic nuclei themselves project back to the same limbic and cortical regions (Alexander & Crutcher, 1989; Alexander, DeLong, & Strick, 1986; Iversen, 1984; Nauta & Domesick, 1984). There is also substantial neuronal traffic to and from the striatum to the pontine-cerebellar system, and between that system and the thalamus. In most general terms the cerebellar system is thought to be involved in the temporal (and possibly spatial) coordination of motor behaviors (Raymond, Lisberger, & Mauk, 1996) and our belief is that its role will prove substantial.

Integration of activity in this system for final macrobehavioral output (Baxter et al., 1996) probably occurs via cross-talk among subchannels in the cortex or thalamus, and to a lesser degree in the basal ganglia (Alexander & Crutcher, 1989; Gerfen, 1992; Joel & Weinger, 1994; Parent et al., 1995; Parent & Hazrati, 1995a, 1995b). Thus, rather than being conceptualized as fully insulated from each other, these cortico-basal ganglionic-thalamic channels might best be pictured somewhat like irrigation ditches,

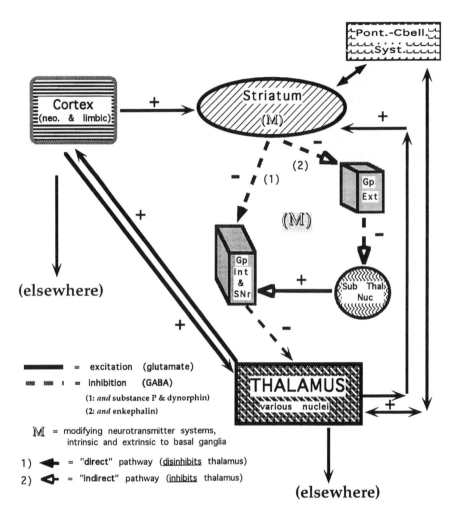

FIG. 28.1. Classic conception of cortico-basal ganglionic-thalamic circuitry. Gp = globus pallidus; Int = interna; Ext = externa; Sub Thal Nuc = subthalamic nucleus; Snr = substantia nigra, pars reticulata; Pont.-Cbell. Syst. = pontine-cerebellar system; + = excitatory output; − = inhibitory output. (Adapted from Baxter et al., 1996)

in which much of the water flows in the channels, but there is substantial cross-seepage through the mud.

Substriatal basal ganglia structures are conceptualized in the "classic model" (Albin, Young, & Penney, 1989; Alexander et al., 1986) as organized to provide a direct and an indirect route from the striatum to the thalamus (Fig. 28.1). In primates, the direct pathway projects from cortex to, striatum to, internal segment of the globus pallidus interna and substantia nigra, pars reticulata complex to, thalamus, and then back to cortex. The indirect pathway is similar from cortex to striatum, but then projects to the external segment of the globus pallidus then to subthalamic nucleus, before returning to, the internal segment of the globus pallidus and substantia nigra, there joining the common pathway from these basal ganglia outflow structures to the thalamus.

Functional Significance of Balanced Tone in Cortico-Basal Ganglionic-Thalamic Loops

In this basal ganglia system, excitatory inputs are preponderantly glutamatergic, whereas the inhibitory ones are mainly GABAergic.[1] Several minority transmitters (e.g., dynophin, substance P, enkephalin) also play important roles, however, they are expressed differentially in the direct and indirect pathways. For instance, in the direct pathway substance P and dynorphin are associated with striatal GABA efferents, whereas those going to the indirect structures coexpress enkephalin. Many other terminal neurotransmitters, from cell bodies both intrinsic and extrinsic to basal ganglia nuclei (i.e., dopamine, serotonin, somatostatin, acetylcholine) modify the activity of afferents and efferents to and from various basal ganglia structures (Parent et al., 1995; Parent & Hazrati, 1995a, 1995b, for review).

Given the nature of the predominant neurotransmitter systems in these classical basal ganglia loops, one sees (Fig. 28.1) that impulses transmitted via the direct pathway would tend to activate the system, resulting in the release of behaviors, as opposed to transmissions via the indirect pathway, which would tend to suppress their release. Such reciprocal actions may be involved in the initiation and cessation of behaviors, as necessary for adaptive function (i.e., direct pathway activation may be important for initiating and sustaining, and indirect pathway activation for halting a given basal ganglia-related behavioral routine), but details of mechanisms underlying such starting and stopping are unknown at present. Nevertheless, it is thought that in the normally functioning animal, neural tone in these two counteracting basal ganglia pathways must be in proper dynamic balance; this balance allows neural transmissions from cortical or limbic regions to the basal ganglia to result ultimately in the appropriate expression or repression of specific behaviors. If this balance is perturbed through disorders in the basal ganglia or other connecting elements of these systems, however, neurological disorders of higher behavior may result (Albin et al., 1989; Alexander et al., 1986; Graybiel, Aosaki, Flaherty,

---

[1]That is, neurons containing the compound Gamma Amino Buteric Acid (GABA), released as a neurotransmitter.

& Kimura, 1994; Swerdlow, 1995). For example, the behavioral syndromes seen in Huntington's disease have been conceptualized as the result of too much tone in the direct pathway relative to that in the indirect and behaviors seen in Parkinson's disease would be the result of less direct than indirect pathway tone (Albin et al., 1989; Swerdlow, 1995).

Similarly, based on results of the functional brain imaging studies previously cited, we have presented a model of OCD in which neural tone is greater in direct than indirect OCD-relevant basal ganglia subcircuits. In Fig. 28.2, we conceptualize the function of cortico-basal ganglionic-thalamic systems as the implementation of behavioral *macros*. Macros are complex sets of interrelated behaviors choreographed for specific situations only. They are executed in a semiautomatic way only in appropriate situations, not in others. As such macros often involve territorial

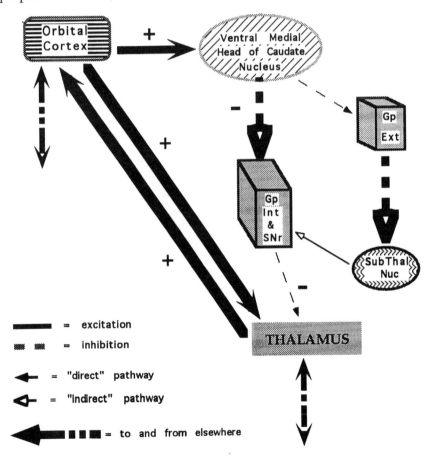

FIG. 28.2. Simple model of brain mediation of OCD symptoms. (Adapted from Baxter et al., 1996)

and social behaviors (MacLean, 1990), we believe OCD may be the result of macros and fragments of macros relating to territorial and social concerns—centering around themes of violence, hygiene (including habitat) and sexuality—that are released or continued in excess of true environmental needs.

In this model, overactivity in the direct pathway (relative to that in the indirect) results in a disinhibited thalamus ("Run macro!"), which is then susceptible to mutual impulse generation between itself and the orbital cortex, leading to a progressive amplification of the process (Fig. 28.2). The result is a self-perpetuating loop capture or lock that rivets behavior to a particular sensorimotor set and is difficult to interrupt (Baxter et al., 1996). There is insufficient neural tone in the indirect pathway ("Hold macro") to counter this drive along the direct pathway.

Support for this model comes from two studies (Baxter et al., 1992) in which good responders to OCD treatment (Yale–Brown Obsessive Compulsive Scale [Y–BOCS] Item 18 [improvement] rated ≥ 5) had significant correlations of LCMRGlc between the orbital cortex and the head of the caudate nucleus, and between the orbital cortex and the thalamus before treatment, but not after. These correlations were not obtained in either normal or depressed controls (Baxter, 1992).

We now have a sufficient sample of subjects from these two studies to demonstrate that these pre- to posttreatment correlational relations occur in separate groups treated with fluoxetine alone versus behavior therapy alone (see Table 28.1). Thus, the model shown in Fig. 28.2 applies both to subjects who respond to SRIs and those who respond to behavior therapy.

TABLE 28.1
Rank-Order Correlations (*tau*) Before and After Treatment,
Good Responders Only (Y–BOCS Item 18, ≥ 5)

	Behavior Tx (n = 13)		Drug (Fluoxetine) Rx (n = 7)	
	Pre-Rx	*Post-Rx*	*Pre-Rx*	*Post-Rx*
L Orb to L Cd	.48	.12	.88	−.33[a]
	(.03)	(.58)	(.006)	(.29)
R Orb to R Cd	.58	.18[a]	.68	−.33[a]
	(.01)	(.41)	(.03)	(.29)
L Orb to L Thal	.21	−.09	.00	−.24
	(.33)	(.68)	(.99)	(.45)
R Orb to R Thal	.61	.15[a]	.24	−.52[a]
	(.005)	(.49)	(.45)	(.09)

Note. Numbers in parentheses are p values. Tx = Treatment; Rx = Mediation treatment; L Orb = Left orbital cortex; L Cd = Left caudate nucleus; R Orb = Right orbital cortex; R Cd = Right caudate nucleus; L Thal = Left thalamus; R Thal = Right thalamus.
[a]Significant change ($p < .05$) pre- to posttreatment.

NEW DATA ON CORTICO-BASAL
GANGLIONIC-THALAMIC CIRCUITS IN PATIENTS
WHO RESPOND POORLY VERSUS THOSE WHO
RESPOND WELL TO PRESENT OCD TREATMENTS

When subjects who respond well to treatments ($n = 19$) are compared with eight people from the same studies who respond poorly (Y–BOCS item 18 < 5)—not only to treatment during those studies, but also to subsequent combined drug and behavior treatment as well—we observe that the poor treatment responders have significantly weaker correlations between these brain regions than do good responders. Table 28.2, presents clinical characteristics of these groups, and Table 28.3 presents pre- and posttreatment correlations. To illustrate, Figs. 28.3 a, b, and c display the

TABLE 28.2
Patient Characteristics: Participants With
Good Versus Poor Treatment Response

	Good Responders (Y–BOCS Item 18 ≥ 5) (n = 20)		Poor Responders (Y–BOCS Item 18 < 5) (n = 7)	
Age				
M	34.0		30.4	
SD	9.2		8.1	
Range	22–53		18–43	
Sex (M:F)	13:7		4:3	
2° Diagnoses:				
TS (mild)	0		1	
Cyclothymic	1		0	
Social phobia	1		0	
Acrophobia	1		0	
Panic	1		0	
Treatment				
Beh:Drug	13:7		5:2	
Y–BOCS	Pre-Tx	Post-Tx Δ	Pre-Tx	Post-Tx Δ
Y–B Tot				
M	24.4	44.8%	26.1	24.5%
SD	4.1	10.1	5.4	9.4
Y–B O				
M	12.4	40.7%	13.7	24.7%
SD	2.6	20.1	3.3	14.7
Y–B C				
M	12.0	46.4%	12.4	23.7%
SD	2.3	12.4	2.8	13.7

Note. Y–BOCS = Yale–Brown Obsessive Compulsive Scale; Beh = behavioral; Tx = treatment; Y–B Tot = total Y–BOCS Score; Y–O = Y–BOCS obsession items; Y–B C = Y–BOCS compulsion items.

TABLE 28.3
Patients With Good Versus Poor Response: Rank-Order
Correlations (*tau*) Before and After Treatment

	Good Responders (n = 20)			Poor Responders (n = 7)	
	Pre-Tx	*Post-Tx*		*Pre-Tx*	*Post-Tx*
L Orb to L Cd	.53	−.04		−.05	−.33
	(.001)	(.82)		(.88)	(.29)
R Orb to R Cd	.51	.02	a	.05	.14
	(.002)	(.92)		(.88)	(.65)
L Orb to L Thal	.23	−.22		.20	c
	(.17)	(.20)		(.57)	
R Orb to R Thal	.45	−.05	b	.00	c
	(.007)	(.75)		(.99)	

Note. Numbers in parentheses are *p* values. Tx = Treatment; L Orb = Left orbital cortex; L Cd = Left caudate nucleus; R Orb = Right orbital cortex; R Cd = Right caudate nucleus; L Thal = Left thalamus; R Thal = Right thalamus.
[a]Significant ($p < .05$) differences in good responders pre- to posttreatment, with poor responders pretreatment, and change pre- to posttreatment. [b]Significant ($p < .05$) differences in good responders pre- to posttreatment, and with poor responders pretreatment. [c]Thalamus local cerebral metabolic rates for glucose data posttreatment for poor responders not available.

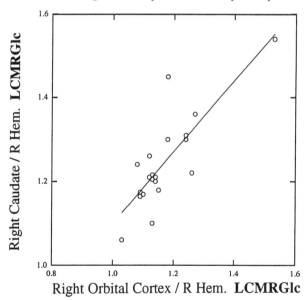

Right Orbital Cortex / R Hem. **LCMRGlc**

FIG. 28.3. Correlation of right head of caudate nucleus to right orbital cortex LCMRGlc in OCD patients with good versus poor response to treatment. (a) Good responders, before treatment. (b) Good responders after fluoxetine or behavior therapy. Dotted regression line is from 3a, for comparison. (c) Poor responders, pre- (open circles) and posttreatment (closed circles). TS = one patient with comorbid Tourette's syndrome. Dotted regression line is from 1a, for comparison.

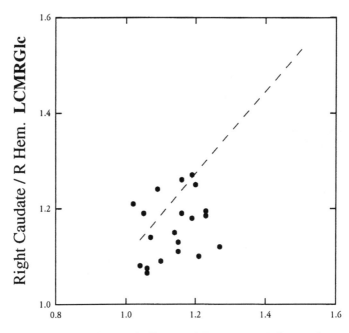

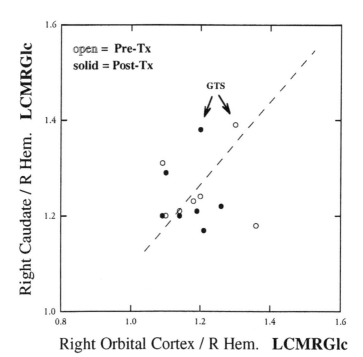

FIG. 28.3. *(Continued)*

nature of correlations between right orbital cortex and right head of caudate nucleus for both groups before and after treatment.

From these data we conclude that patients who respond poorly to these treatments constitute a different OCD group. At present, there are no other obvious differences between good responders and poor responders, and obviously more study is needed. Clearly, however, we must restrict subsequent discussion of cortico-basal ganglionic-thalamic circuits in OCD to those patients who respond well to drug or behavior therapy.

BASAL GANGLIA PATHWAYS—A CONCEPT IN NEED OF REVISION

Recent evidence (Parent & Hazrati, 1995b) suggests that the indirect pathway (which includes several nuclei in addition to those shown in Fig. 28.1) is much more complex than envisioned in the classic model, shown in Fig. 28.1. In fact, the indirect basal ganglia elements do not even form a unidirectional pathway, but are arranged as a complex regulatory system, interacting in a multitude of ways with the direct pathway. Nevertheless, authorities maintain that activity from the striatum directly to basal ganglia output structures (direct pathway) tends to disinhibit the thalamus, whereas activity routed to the globus pallidus externa (indirect system) will tend to dampen, or moderate activity in the thalamus (Parent et al., 1995; Parent & Hazrati, 1995a, 1995b). As mentioned previously, indirect system activity may be critical to turning off a behavioral macro initiated through the direct pathway once its appropriate time and situation have passed.

Because functional anatomical relations among the basal ganglia elements are very complex (Parent et al., 1995; Parent & Hazrati, 1995a, 1995b), we illustrate the general effect of striatal efferents passing to the direct pathway as disinhibiting the thalamus, whereas those routed to the indirect system (globus pallidus externa in primates, globus pallidus in rodents) are illustrated as moderating activity in the thalamus. This conceptualization is depicted in Fig. 28.4.

PROJECTION OF CORTICAL AND LIMBIC REGIONS TO DIFFERENT BASAL GANGLIA TERRITORIES

As mentioned earlier, neural activity from various cortical and limbic regions tends to course through the basal ganglia to the thalamus via different subcompartments or channels. This path leads to a topographic organization of the basal ganglia elements relative to cortex. In this regard,

Effect of Direct Pathway vs. Indirect System Domination on Basal Ganglia Out-put

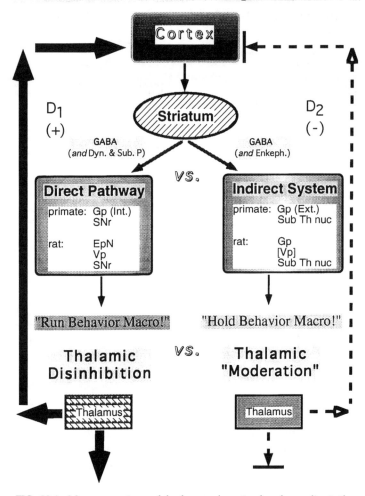

FIG. 28.4. More accurate model of normal cortico-basal ganglionic-tha-lamic interactions. Dyn = dynorphin; Sub P = substance P; Enkeph = enkephalin; EpN = endopeduncular nucleus; Vp = ventral pallidum.

the lateral prefrontal association neocortex (LPFC) projects largely to the dorsolateral aspect of the head of the caudate nucleus, whereas the orbital prefrontal paralimbic isocortex projects predominantly to the ventrome-dial region of the same structure (Mega & Cummings, 1994; Parent et al., 1995). Figure 28.5 illustrates the termination of frontal cortex afferents to the striatum in both primates and rodents. Circuits through the basal ganglia from various cortical and limbic structures are postulated to run

Cortical/Limbic Striatal In-puts

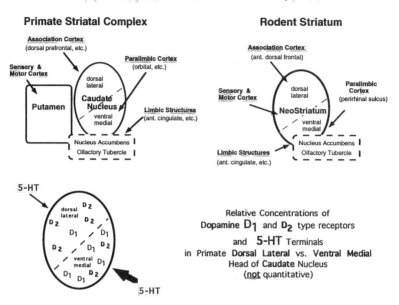

FIG. 28.5. Localization of cortical and limbic efferents to primate and rodent striatum, along with relative densities of dopamine receptor subtypes and densities of serotonin terminals. 5-HT = serotonin afferents; D_1 & D_2 = dopamine type-1 family and type-2 family receptors.

in parallel channels, segregating the mediation of behaviors and information processing specifically relevant to these different brain regions (Alexander & Crutcher, 1989; Alexander et al., 1986). This may be facilitated by the fact that the head of the caudate nucleus, like the rest of the striatum, has marked dorsolateral to ventromedial gradients in the concentrations of many neurotransmitters and their receptors, as do the corresponding sites of projection of these striatal regions in the other basal ganglia elements (Parent et al., 1995). Thus, effects on one class of receptor may have differential effects on one cortical region's subchannel through the basal ganglia, relative to other basal ganglia subchannels, emanating from other cortical regions.

Thus, we have postulated that cortical-basal ganglia system pathology along such dorsolateral to ventromedial gradients might account for the variety of symptoms seen in the OCD and Tourette's syndrome (TS) spectrum (Baxter & Guze, 1993; Baxter, Schwartz, & Guze, 1991; Baxter, Schwartz, Guze, Bergman, & Szuba, 1990). It may also account for the superimposition of major depression (Baxter et al., 1987; Baxter et al., 1989). The facts that orbital cortex projects to the ventromedial head of the caudate nucleus and that SRI medications have their highest binding density in the ventral striatum (Insel, 1992; Parent et al., 1995), support the conclusion that this striatal subregion lies along the route of OCD's brain mediation (Baxter, 1995; Baxter et al., 1996; Baxter et al., 1990; Swerdlow, 1995). There is now direct FDG-PET evidence from human and primate studies concerning the involvement of ventral medial striatum in OCD (Baxter, 1995; Baxter et al., 1996). In TS, on the other hand, motor tics are most common in the upper trunk, neck, and face. The part of the putamen that receives sensorimotor strip input from cortex involved in control of the shoulders, neck, and face is the ventral region. Further, the ventral putamen is that part in which dopamine D_2 receptors are most dense, perhaps relating directly to the effectiveness of D_2 blockers in the treatment of motor tics (Baxter et al., 1990). Thus, the relative degree of OCD versus TS symptomatology shown by a given patient, and the degree of response to SRIs or D_2 blockers, may depend on the degree of pathology in an element common to (e.g., GABA neurons) the ventral medial caudate versus ventral caudate (Baxter et al., 1996; Baxter et al., 1990). Topographical organization in the basal ganglia might also provide clues as to why in families in which OCD and TS seem to sort as a single autosomal dominant gene, but with variable expessivity (Pauls & Leckman, 1986), individuals vary on the degree and types of motor and mental symptoms (Baxter, 1995; Baxter et al., 1996; Baxter et al., 1990; Swerdlow, 1995).

AN EXPERIMENT TO ADDRESS A PROBLEM FOR THE MODEL

The model for the brain mediation of OCD's symptoms already presented depends heavily on assumed functional responses in substriatal basal ganglia structures to various prefrontal cortex inputs. To date, however, FDG-PET lacks sufficient resolution to provide reliable data from such relatively small brain regions. Thus, this model suffers from a lack of empirical support. To add details, and thereby improve the model, investigations that inform us about the role of these substriatal basal ganglia structures are critical. This was the purpose of an investigation in the rat conducted and described in the following.

Problem and Hypotheses

We sought to test predictions derived from our model by performing ^{14}C-2-deoxyglucose (2-DG) autoradiographic measurements of LCMRGlcs in rats undergoing either anterior dorsofrontal (DF) neocortex electrical stimulation or ventrofrontal (VF) paralimbic cortex stimulation in the region of the rhinal sulcus, which is thought to correspond to primate orbital cortex (Eichenbaum, Clegg, & Feeley, 1983; Uylings & van Eden, 1990). We predicted that:

1. DF stimulation would result in increased dorsolateral striatal LCMRGlc, whereas VF stimulation would result in increased ventral medial striatal LCMRGlc.

2. Both DF and VF stimulation would activate dorsal medial and other thalamic nuclei (either via the basal ganglia or directly via cortico-thalamic projections).

3. We made no specific hypothesis about the direction of effects on elements of the direct and indirect basal ganglia systems, other than that activation patterns observed in these structures might be informative. Thus, we also examined the effects of DF versus VF stimulation in the rat on LCMRGlc in globus pallidus (considered equivalent to the globus pallidus interna in primates), substantia nigra pars reticulata/endopeduncular nucleus complex (globus pallidus interna/substantia nigra pars reticulata in primates), and the subthalamic nucleus.

Methods and Materials

Young adult male Sprague–Dawley rats were maintained under anesthesia with ketamine and phenobarbital, then placed in a Kopf stereotactic device. Stainless steel 0.25 mm bipolar electrodes were then placed in the VF or DF cortex. Rats were then allowed to recover from surgery for 2 weeks before testing.

For one rat in each group, femoral artery and venous catheters were inserted under light halothane anesthesia. After recovery, 2-DG was injected and sequential blood samples were obtained. Because initial experimental results were visually striking, the subsequent rats were simply injected subcutaneously with the same amount of 2-DG without prior anesthesia, catheter insertion, or blood sampling.

Two minutes after injection with 2-DG, electrical stimulation was started, 1 second on, 3 seconds off. Current intensity was adjusted starting at 25 µA and then titrated upward (400µA maximum) until behavioral reactions (see Results section) were induced (final stimulation intensities were 200–400 µA). Forty minutes later, the rat was sacrificed with an overdose of pentobarbital and the brain removed and sectioned at 23 µm on a Leica Jung Frigicut 2800E cryostat, collecting every third section on slides. Sections were then placed against Kodak EctaScan EC-1 photographic film for 2 to 4 weeks, then developed. Tissues were stained with a standard cresyl violet Nissl stain to confirm structure identification for the corresponding 2-DG images.

Three rats were successfully implanted on the right, and two on the left for both the VF and DF placements. Controls were five rats that underwent the same procedures, but it was discovered at sacrifice that the electrodes were not in the brain (either through the brain, or deflected toward the skull). In four of these control animals the attempted stimulation was DF and in one it was VF. In all five control cases, lack of brain stimulation had been suspected because the animals did not show an obvious behavioral response with application of the current.

Image analysis was done by capturing the photographic images using a Gordon S66dx® uniform light table and a Leica Wild M3Z® isochromatic, flat-plane microscope set at 6x, coupled to an Hitachi HV-C11 CCD® color video camera. Images were displayed on a MacIntosh® computer using VideoSpigot® in a 161 × 121 pixel matrix with a 20" SuperMatch 20-T® color monitor.

Visually obvious categorical results were analyzed using Fisher's Exact Test. For parametric measurements of LCMRGlc activity in one brain region normalized to another, digitalized images were analyzed by defining the regions of interest in the section visually using Explorer 2.0 (UCLA Crump Institute for Biological Imaging, Los Angeles), which displays photographic optical densities on a 256-shade, linear white-to-black grayscale, and recording the average optical density per pixel in that region of interest. Dividing values so obtained for one structure by another produced dimensionless ratios that were used for statistical analyses. Although variances obtained from these data sets met criteria for analyses by parametric analysis of variance (ANOVA) because sample sizes were very small, confirmatory analyses were also done using the Kruskal–Wallis Rank Order ANOVA.

Results

Behavior During Stimulation. During VF stimulation rats would stop, sit back on their hind limbs, and perform activities with their front paws that resembled vigorous whisker grooming; they resumed ambulation or other nonspecific activities whenever the current was off. In contrast, when the DF animals were stimulated they stopped all gross motor activity, or displayed dystonic head twisting, then seemed to wander aimlessly when the current was off. Control rats showed no obvious reaction to electrical stimulation.

Brain Glucose Metabolic Rate Patterns. As predicted, all DF-stimulated animals showed striking 2-DG activation, ipsilateral > contralateral, at the stimulation site, the dorsolateral striatum, and dorsomedial regions of the thalamus. All VF animals showed similarly striking activation at the stimulation site, the ventromedial striatum, and dorsomedial thalamic regions (Fig. 28.6). Further, animals receiving VF stimulation showed activation of ipsilateral, and to a lesser extent contralateral, amygdaloid structures (not illustrated), and the olfactory tubercle (Fig. 28.6), whereas those receiving DF did not. Activation of the cingulate cortex or the hippocampus was not apparent with either group. The cerebellum and brain stem were not examined.

Differential results in substriatal basal ganglia structures were striking. Both DF and VF stimulation activated the substantia nigra pars reticulata, but DF stimulation strongly activated the dorsal aspect of the globus pallidus and appeared to deactivate ventral pallidum (Fig. 28.7). Conversely, VF stimulation activated the ventral pallidum (extending into the substantia innominata; Heimer, Alheid, & Zaborsky, 1985; Parent et al., 1995), but diffusely deactivated the entire globus pallidus. In control animals no such effects were apparent.

The consistency of this reciprocal effect of DF versus VF stimulation is demonstrated clearly for the globus pallidus in Fig. 28.8, which illustrates sections through that structure for all animals studied (statistical analysis for categorical judgment of activation vs. nonactivation [in fact deactivation]: globus pallidus DF = 5/5, VF = 0/5, Fisher's Exact Test p =

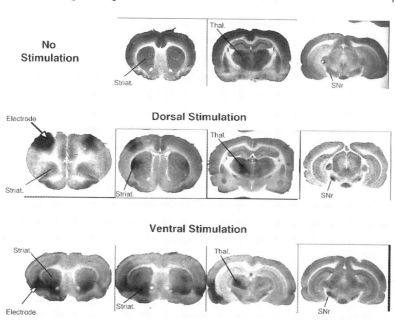

FIG. 28.6. Rat ^{14}C-2-DG autoradiographs showing effects of dorsal versus ventral frontal cortex stimulation. Striat. = striatum; Thal. = thalamus; SNr = substantia nigra, pars reticulata.

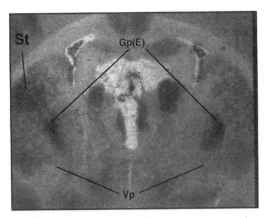

Right

Dorsal Frontal
Cortex
Stimulation

1

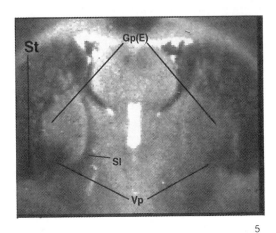

Right

Ventral Frontal
Cortex
Stimulation

5

FIG. 28.7. Effects of dorsal versus ventral frontal stimulation on rat substriatal basal ganglia elements (^{14}C-2-DG autoradiographs)—Close-up views. St = striatum; SI = substantia innominata; other abbreviations, as before.

.008, two-tailed; likewise for ventral pallidum, VF = 5/5, DF = 0/5). Although apparent bilaterally, these effects were clearly more intense in the hemisphere receiving stimulation than in the contralateral hemisphere (see Fig. 28.8).

A better estimate of the magnitude of these effects in the globus pallidus, optical density of the globus pallidus on the side of stimulation was divided by that of a similar sized region in the ipsilateral extreme dorsal striatum (right above the globus pallidus), where there was no apparent activation. Values for this ratio in VF stimulation animals were $M = 0.94$ ($SD = 0.04$; maximum = 0.98, minimum = 0.89) and corresponding DF stimulation values were $M = 1.31$ ($SD = 0.11$; maximum = 1.43,

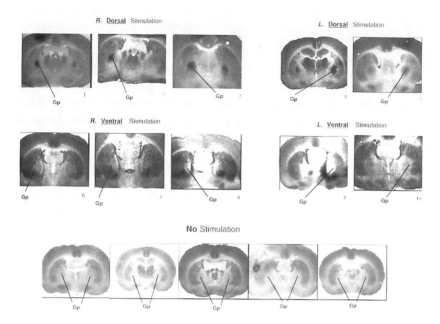

FIG. 28.8. Effects of dorsal versus ventral frontal stimulation on substriatal basal ganglia elements (^{14}C-2-DG autoradiographs) in all rats studied.

minimum = 1.16). Control animal values, calculated as the average of values for left and right hemisphere, were $M = 1.17$ ($SD = .07$; maximum = 1.27, minimum = 1.11). Differences among groups, and between all pairings were highly significant, $F(2,14) = 29.4$, $p = .0000$ (all pairings $p < .05$ by least squares difference post hoc multiple range test; Kruskal–Wallis test statistic = 11.18, $df = 2,14$, $p = .004$).

Neither the endopeduncular nucleus nor the subthalamic nucleus were visualized consistently in either the DF- or the VF-stimulated animals. These small structures may have been missed on sectioning, especially because not all tissue sections were satisfactory for mounting.

Discussion of Rat Experiment Results

Patterns of striatal and thalamic activation observed here with DF versus VF stimulation were as predicted. The rat VF stimulation pattern closely resembled that found previously with FDG-PET in a monkey undergoing left posterior medial orbital cortex electrical stimulation (Baxter et al., 1996). Likewise, amygdala activation (but not cingulate or hippocampal activation) was observed in this same monkey given orbital frontal stimulation (Baxter et al., 1996).

Under nonstarvation conditions, glucose is the predominant energy source of the brain and it is necessary for all cerebral activity (Ackermann,

Finch, Babb, & Engel, 1984; Phelps, Mazziotta, & Schelbert, 1986). Nevertheless, metabolic activity in a given brain structure tends to reflect activity at axonal terminals, in turn reflecting the energy requirements of ion pumping needed for neural transmission. This is true whether the neurotransmitters in question are excitatory or inhibitory postsynaptically (Ackermann et al., 1984). Because the vast majority of such terminals in the globus pallidus and ventral pallidum are GABA efferents from the striatum (Parent et al., 1995; Parent & Hazrati, 1995a) we assume that our observations in these structures reflect activity at GABA synapses (Fig. 28.1). Similarly, afferents to the striatum from the cortex (and other brain regions) are largely glutamatergic (Parent et al., 1995; Parent & Hazrati, 1995a, 1995b), and the regional striatal activation observed here with cortical stimulation probably reflects firing of these excitatory neuron terminals. Input to the thalamus, however, is both glutamatergic and GABAergic (Parent et al., 1995; Parent & Hazrati, 1995a, 1995b; Fig. 28.1), and effects of both probably contribute significantly to the LCMRGlc pattern observed there.

The most striking and provocative findings of this investigation, however, were in substriatal basal ganglia structures: DF stimulation activated the globus pallidus (globus pallidus externa in primates; an indirect basal ganglia system structure) and VF stimulation deactivated it. VF stimulation activated the ventral pallidum (*predominantly* a direct pathway nucleus) and DF stimulation appeared to deactivate this brain region. It is possible that the effects observed with VF stimulation in these substriatal basal ganglia structures are related to this cortical region's paralimbic properties, in that we have observed a similar effect with amygdala stimulation, albeit in only two animals to date.

Although we are unaware of any other 2-DG study that maps the basal ganglia effects of DF and VF stimulation in these specific cortical regions, Brutus et al. (1984) did report the effects of stimulating the dorsal medial nucleus of the thalamus, a specific projection site from prefrontal cortical regions, and a way station in the frontal cortico-basal ganglionic-thalamic system discussed here (see Fig. 28.1). The pattern of LCMRGlc activation they observed was remarkably similar to what we obtained with our rhinal sulcal VF stimulation, in that there was activation of the sulcal region, as well as the amygdala, the ventromedial striatum, the nucleus accumbens, and the olfactory tubercle. Although it is difficult to discern, it also appears that the globus pallidus was deactivated and ventral pallidum activated with dorsomedial thalamic electrical stimulation, just as we observed in this study with VF stimulation. Thus, it appears that driving a thalamic region with which the VF communicates can drive the specific direct basal ganglia subcircuit relevant to the VF in a way similar to stimulating the VF itself. This fits our model nicely (Fig. 28.2).

Our findings in the rat ventral pallidum are more difficult to interpret than those in the rat globus pallidus. The ventral pallidum is often described as a basal ganglia output structure, and thus part of the direct pathway. However, unlike the rat globus pallidus, which is clearly part of the indirect system only, the ventral pallidum receives GABAergic neurons that express at least some enkephalin as well as much substance P in both the primate and rodent (Heimer et al., 1985; Parent & Hazrati, 1995a); thus, ventral pallidum probably has some indirect system function, as well as a direct basal ganglia system role. Nevertheless, our observations in the ventral pallidum aside, the differential effects we observed in the rat globus pallidus by themselves suggest that DF stimulation increases striatal output via the indirect basal ganglia system, whereas VF cortex stimulation decreases it. This effect alone would result in VF stimulation shifting the balance between the direct and indirect basal ganglia systems in favor of the direct, and thus thalamic disinhibition, whereas DF stimulation would have the opposite effect (Fig. 28.9). If our observations in ventral pallidum with VF versus DF stimulation do, in fact, reflect differential direct pathway activation effects, the effects illustrated in Fig. 28.9 would be even more robust.

It should be noted here that our observation of substantia nigra pars reticulata activation with both DF and VF stimulation is not at odds with our conclusions about the differential effects of activity in DF versus VF on subchannels of direct versus indirect basal ganglia systems. Although both the globus pallidus interna (endopeduncular nucleus in rat) and substantia nigra pars reticulata are direct pathway structures, each receives separate afferents from the striatum, in contradistinction to what was once thought (Parent, 1986). Thus, although DF stimulation may activate one direct pathway channel (to the substantia nigra pars reticulata), it seems to deactivate the channel to ventral pallidum. Clearly, however, valid data for what happens in the endopeduncular (and the subthalamic) nucleus with VF versus DF stimulation are needed to help confirm or disconfirm details of our model.

IMPLICATIONS FOR THIS THEORY OF HOW THE BRAIN MEDIATES TREATMENT-RESPONSIVE OCD

Regional Neurochemical Implications

Although both globus pallidus and ventral pallidum also receive some input from other brain regions, the predominant input (GABAergic) is from the striatum (Parent & Hazrati, 1995a). This pattern of reciprocal activation and deactivation in the globus pallidus and ventral pallidum

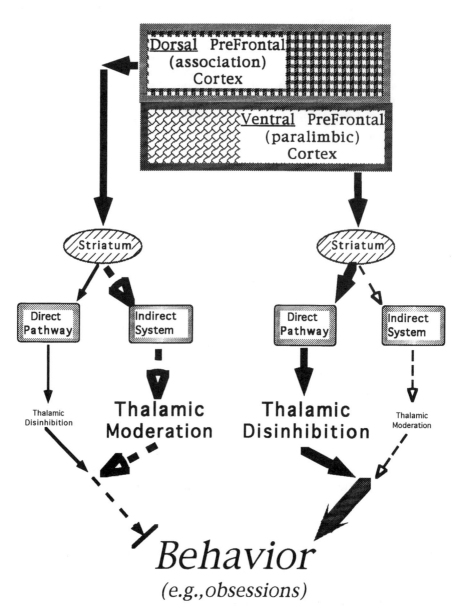

FIG. 28.9. Effects of dorsal neocortical or ventral paralimbic frontal cortex activation on direct and indirect basal ganglia systems, and consequent effects on behavior.

suggests an "either–or (but not both equally) Y-pathway, zero-sum-balance" scheme, in which direction of signal from the striatum down one path results in less signal availability for the other. We are unaware of any similar observations that would bear directly on this concept, but if true, we suggest that this effect is a consequence of the intrinsic organization of the striatum. How this either direct or indirect pathway effect would be mediated is unclear.

On a microstructure level, the striatum is organized into fairly discrete islands or striasomes surrounded by a matrix. Striasomes and the matrix have different patterns of functional neurochemical control, and interactions between these two striatal compartments appear to mediate the turning on and off of complex behaviors (Graybiel et al., 1994; Parent et al., 1995). Not only are striasomes more numerous in the region of striatum to which VF projects than in that to which DF projects, but unlike all other cortical regions, inferior prefrontal cortex, along with the cingulate cortex, sends most of its projections directly into the striasomes, and not into the matrix, as is the case for association prefrontal neocortex (Eblen & Graybiel, 1992, 1995). Furthermore, projections from posterior orbital cortex in the primate innervate only those striasomes located in the ventral medial striatum, not the dorsal lateral (Eblen & Graybiel, 1995). These differences in striasome and matrix innervation by the ventral paralimbic orbital cortex and the neocortical LPFC may be related to the neurochemical mechanisms determining that orbital efferents preferentially activate the direct pathway, whereas LPFC efferents preferentially activate the indirect pathway. This balance may determine whether a behavior macro is to be run or suppressed, or once initiated, is sustained or halted (see the following section for further mechanistic hypotheses).

Relevance to OCD Symptom Mediation

If physiological activation of orbital cortex in humans does activate the direct more than the indirect basal ganglia system (as seen here in the rat with VF electrical stimulation), and if, likewise, LPFC activates the indirect pathway relative to the indirect system, then enhanced orbital cortex activity might lead to thalamic disinhibition and impulsive actions, whereas activation of LPFC activity would result in thalamic moderation, and would thus tend to reduce impulsivity. Baxter and colleagues (Baxter et al., 1996; Baxter et al., 1992) suggested that in the OCD sufferer there is a response bias toward stimuli involving territorial concerns, and that this response bias is mediated by a pathological dominance of direct over indirect basal ganglia pathway tone, emanating from orbital cortex efferents (also see Swerdlow, 1995; Fig. 28.10). Given our findings here, overactivity in the orbital cortex, relative to that in the LPFC, could account for this dominance of direct over indirect basal ganglia system tone by itself.

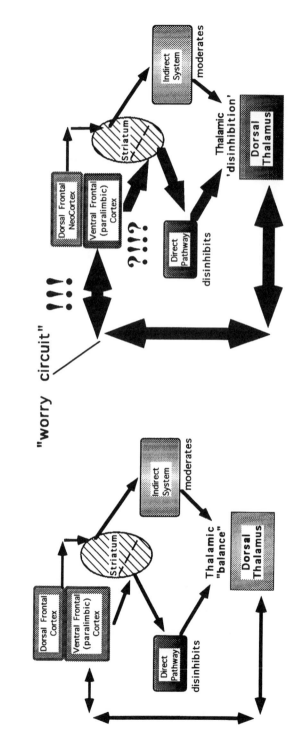

FIG. 28.10. Expanded model for cortico-basal ganglionic-thalamic system mediation of OCD through direct and indirect basal ganglia systems.

LPFC is highly implicated in many judgment and "conscious will" (e.g., "Don't just react; stop and think!") functions with regard to future consequences versus past conditions (Fuster, 1989). The feeling that it is time to stop an ongoing action may be implemented normally via an increase in indirect, relative to direct, basal ganglia pathway activity (Baxter et al., 1996). However, if relative hypertone in the direct basal ganglia pathways from the orbital cortex overwhelms relatively inadequate indirect system tone from the LPFC, this might account for the difficulty OCD patients have in countering the emotional force of obsessions, despite their rational appreciation that these thoughts are absurd or excessive. These ideas bear similarity to Janet's belief (Janet & Raymond, 1903) that in OCD a *psychasthenic will* (inadequate function in dorsal prefrontal cortex?) is overcome by relatively strong emotional impulses (hyperfunction in the ventral paralimbic orbital cortex?), leading to neurotic behavior.

Psychasthenia and Suppression

Many OCD patients can and do suppress OCD behavioral responses temporarily, but they find such holding back extraordinarily difficult, as with other disorders involving the basal ganglia. We believe this holding back is a conscious function mediated by LPFC, and is unduly difficult because of our hypothesized direct > indirect pathway neural tone imbalance.

If the OCD sufferer has insufficient ability to suppress impulsive OCD behavior responses to evocative stimuli even for a short while, behavior deconditioning via ERP will not be successful (Baer & Minichiello, 1990). One reason for such failure may be that, despite conscious effort (will), the patient's LPFC is not able to increase indirect basal ganglia system tone sufficiently to counterbalance the overdrive in the direct system, which is generated by emotional orbital cortex activity. Thus, Janet's term *psychasthenia* seems apt, at least in this relative sense.

Consideration of Depression in OCD

The psychasthenia phenomena of depression were also addressed by Janet (Janet & Raymond, 1903). Secondary major depression is commonly, although periodically, seen in association with OCD, and is usually accompanied by an increase in the severity of the primary OCD symptoms. When major depression is superimposed on OCD (secondary depression), LPFC LCMRGlc is reduced from normal values and orbital cortex rates remain abnormally elevated (Baxter et al., 1987; Baxter et al., 1989). When the depression is treated, LPFC LCMRGlc increases in proportion to the degree of symptomatic improvement (Baxter et al., 1987; Baxter et al., 1989).

In fact, many FDG-PET studies report associated decreased LPFC and head of caudate LCMRGlc when several types and varying levels of severity of primary as well as secondary major depression are present (George, Ketter, & Post, 1994, for review). When these primary depressions are treated, not only does LPFC LCMRGlc increase, but so does that in the head of the caudate nucleus (Baxter et al., 1985; Baxter et al., 1989; George et al., 1994, for reviews).[2] Because LPFC activity is significantly decreased when major depression is superimposed on OCD (Baxter et al., 1989), the resulting further decrease in neural tone through the indirect basal ganglia system (efferent from the LPFC) would account for the worsening of OCD symptoms that these patients regularly describe when secondary major depression is superimposed on their OCD. It would also account for their noted difficulty in participating effectively in behavior therapy when depressed, despite conscious desire (Baer & Minichiello, 1990; see Fig. 28.11).

Figure 28.12 (a and b) presents our current hypotheses as to where in this brain system SRI medications and behavioral deconditioning techniques exert their effects in patients with treatment-responsive OCD. Figure 28.12 is presented as a hypotheses generator, not as established theory.

BRAIN LOCALIZATION OF SPECIFIC NEUROCHEMICAL PROCESSES IN THE PATHOGENESIS AND DRUG TREATMENT OF OCD

Serotonin

At this time the only medications with established efficacy in OCD are the SRIs. Serotonin and its receptors are common in cortex, limbic structures,

---

[2]A seeming exception to the findings of decreased LPFC LCMRGlc in depression is an important study by Drevets et al. (1992). In contrast to others, this research team found increased lateral orbital LCMRGlc in patients with familial unipolar depression compared to normal controls. Although this finding may seem similar to the orbital cortex findings in OCD, and quite different from LPFC hypometabolism, it should be noted that findings of high LCMRGlc in OCD were in medial orbital cortex, not lateral (Baxter et al., 1996), and that Drevets et al. did observe an inverse correlation between LPFC LCMRGlc and depression severity. Differences in depressive symptoms in patients studied by research teams may account for why we have found decreased LPFC LCMRGlc in depression (Baxter et al., 1985, Baxter et al., 1989), whereas Drevets et al. found increased lateral orbital LCMRGlc: In our studies, patients with bipolar and unipolar depression tended to be psychomotor retarded, whereas those of Drevets et al. were agitated and highly ruminative (W. Drevets, personal communication, December 1995). Ruminations have some similarity to obsessions (but obsessions are ego-alien and ruminations are not), and high lateral orbital rates, along with an inverse correlation of LPFC LCMRGlc with depression severity, remind us of our reports of high medial orbital LCMRGlc and low LPFC LCMRGlcs that also give an inverse correlation with depression severity in OCD patients with secondary major depression (Baxter et al., 1987; Baxter et al., 1989). Drevets et al.'s familial depression may be a kind of unipolar depression related to OCD.

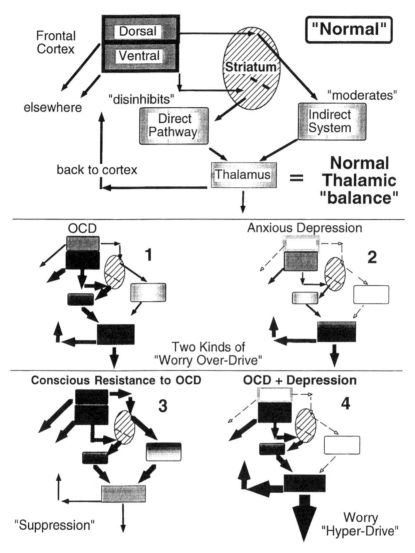

FIG. 28.11. Proposed prefrontal cortex and direct and indirect basal ganglia system involvement in depression comorbid with OCD, and when OCD patient tries conscious resistance to OCD impulses.

all basal ganglia structures, and the thalamus (Parent et al., 1995, for extensive review relative to basal ganglia). We have suggested that SRIs may exert their treatment effects in both OCD and depression by decreasing neural tone in the direct pathway relative to that in the indirect basal ganglia system (Baxter et al., 1996). How this might occur is seen in Fig. 28.13 (a and b).

Effects of OCD Psychotherapies I

OCD without Depression

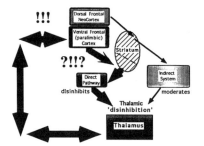

Successful SRI Rx

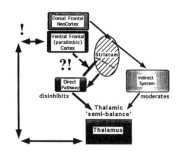

Effects of OCD Psychotherapies II

Active, Conscious Resistance

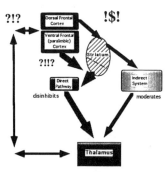

"quasi-balance"

Long-term Cognitive/Behavioral Tx

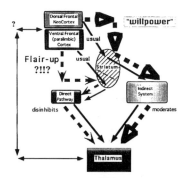

"regulation"

FIG. 28.12. Proposed prefrontal cortex and direct and indirect basal ganglia system involvement in response to SRI and behavior treatments: (a) Effect of SRI medication is envisioned as shifting more neural tone balance from direct to indirect basal ganglia systems. This is viewed as a relative shift; it is not known at this time whether the direct, indirect, or both systems change in absolute terms (see Fig. 28.14). (b) Effect of behavior therapy is envisioned as coming from increased or more efficient output from association dorsal prefrontal cortex that puts more "reason and will" through the indirect basal ganglia system, as needed (*prn*) to counter emotional "flair-ups" through the ventral paralimbic-direct basal ganglia system. This keeps the self-reinforcing drive of OCD (Figs. 28.2, 28.10, 28.11) from taking off. If OCD patients do not counter OCD urges effectively with resistance, the OCD soon takes off again and the patient is in relapse.

OCD and 5-HT: <u>Pre</u>-Rx

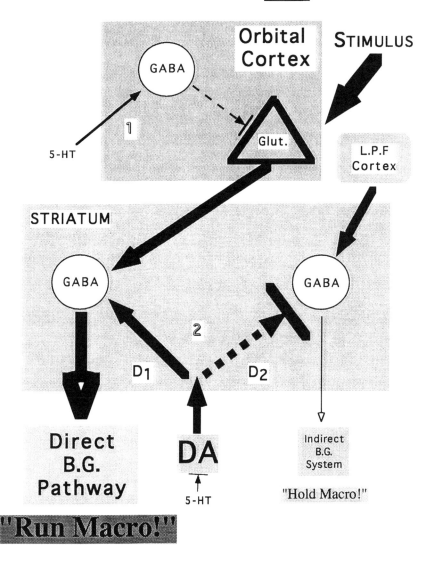

FIG. 28.13. Proposed sites of neurochemical effects in OCD treatment with SRI medications.

OCD and 5-HT: 2 Months of SRI

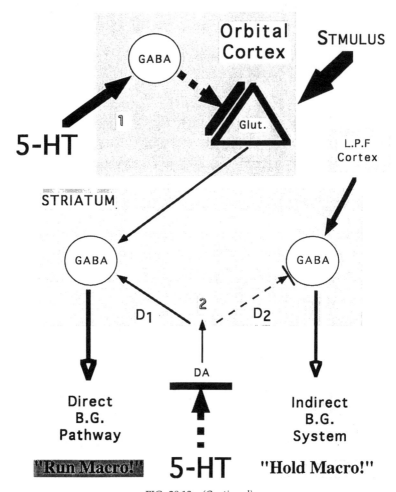

FIG. 28.13. *(Continued)*

It has been postulated that the locus of SRI therapeutic effects may be the cortex (El Mansari, Bouchard, & Blier, 1995). There are stimulatory serotonin 5-HT$_{2A}$ receptors on GABA-containing interneurons, and these same GABAergic neurons inhibit glutamatergic output neurons to the striatum and elsewhere (Parent et al., 1995; Parent & Hazrati, 1995a). Thus, stimulating these 5-HT$_{2A}$ receptors would tend to decrease activity in glutamatergic efferents from the orbital cortex to the striatum, breaking up the driven circuit. This effect would account for decreased activity in the head of caudate LCMRGlc with effective treatment of OCD with SRIs (Baxter et al., 1996; Baxter et al., 1992; Benkelfat et al., 1990), as these glutamatergic afferents account for the majority of axon terminals in the striatum (Parent et al., 1995; Parent & Hazrati, 1995a), and LCMRGlc is influenced largely by the energy requirements of afferent terminals.

On first consideration, however, it would seem that these effects of SRI medication on cortical efferents to the striatum would apply equally to LPFC and orbital cortex GABA neurons. Therefore, the overall balance between direct and indirect basal ganglia system tone might be unaffected (Fig. 28.9). Evidence suggests, however, that there are significant differences in the effects of SRI agents on orbital cortex versus LPFC. In this regard El Mansari et al. (1995) reported that when guinea pigs were given SRI agents, 5-HT_{1D} orbital serotonin autoreceptors showed desensitization, whereas those in dorsal frontal cortex did not. Further, the presynaptic serotonin transporter downregulated in dorsal frontal cortex, but not in orbital cortex. The overall effect was a significant increase in 5-HT output in ex vivo brain slice stimulation at 3 weeks (typical time for depression response to SRIs) in dorsal frontal cortex, but not in orbital. After 8 weeks (typical time for OCD response to SRIs), not only did orbital cortex show a significant augmentation of 5-HT release from baseline, but this release was, by then, significantly greater than that from dorsal frontal cortex (55% vs. 29%). In our scheme, this orbital greather than LPFC 5-HT activity would yield a greater decrease in orbital than LPFC glutamatergic output to the striatum by the typical time of OCD response to SRIs.

As they noted, these findings of El Mansari et al. (1995) are particularly provocative in that the timing of these effects fit the time that SRI drugs typically take to induce improvement in depression and OCD—3 weeks and 8 weeks, respectively. Although there are few systematic data available, it is a frequent clinical observation that OCD symptoms seem to worsen during the first few weeks of SRI administration before reversing course and getting robustly better after approximately 2 months of medication. The findings of El Mansari et al. suggest that early in the course of SRI treatment glutamatergic output from the LPFC, and thus indirect basal ganglia tone, might be decreased and only later would there be a corresponding larger decrease in 5-HT-modulated orbital output that would swing the balance between the direct and indirect systems in favor of the indirect system, and consequently to the inhibition of OCD behaviors.

Although at this time there is more evidence to support a mechanism of OCD treatment by SRI medication that has its locus in cortex, the therapeutic effects of SRIs might also depend on mediation within the basal ganglia themselves. Serotonin appears to have specific effects on striatal output through the direct pathway. Destruction of serotonergic cells in the dorsal raphe nucleus has been shown to change levels of striatal preprodynorphin messenger ribonucleic acid (Morris, Reiner, Hollt, & Herz, 1988), which is a selective marker for neurons efferent from the striatal elements to the direct pathway. Effects of 5-HT on other basal ganglia neurotransmitters might also be important (Amalric, Farin, Dormont, & Schmied, 1994).

A Serotonin-Stimulatory Neurotoxin Relation

Changes in 5-HT dynamics also offer hints about a mechanism that might contribute to OCD's pathogenesis. Swerdlow (1995) pointed out that quinolinic acid (QA), a metabolite of tryptophan via the kynurenine pathway, is a potent neurotoxin that acts at glutamate receptors on GABA neurons in the striatum. Natural endogenous concentrations of QA may cause tissue damage, but, at lower concentrations QA has a stimulatory effect on glutamate receptors, such as those found on GABA projection neurons in striatum. Although QA might increase simply when less tryptophan is converted to 5-HT, and decrease whenever 5-HT turnover increased, of greater interest is that cytokines, such as the alpha and gamma interferons, induce production of the enzyme indolamine-2,3-dioxygenase, the rate-limiting step in QA synthesis (Goodman & Frerman, 1995; Heyes, 1987). These and other cytokines are themselves induced during infections and other inflammatory responses. OCD has been linked to Sydenham's chorea (Swedo et al., 1989), an inflammatory, rheumatic illness associated with antineuronal antibodies. OCD without overt chorea is highly associated with an overabundance of D8/17 lymphocytes, a marker for rheumatic fever susceptibility (Goodman, Ward, Kablinger, & Murphy, chap. 18, this volume; S. Swedo, personal communication, June 1993). Blood serum from Sydenham's chorea patients seems to bind to striatal neurons that have the morphological characteristics of GABA efferents (S. Swedo, personal communication, July 1995). Taken together, these facts raise the possibility that QA increased by either a low turnover of 5-HT or by local inflammation may be stimulating (and possibly eventually damaging) populations of direct versus indirect GABA output neurons differentially.

Dopamine

Goodman, McDougle, and Price (1990) suggested a possible role for interactions between serotonin and dopamine in OCD's response to SRIs. Serotonin has highly significant, although complicated effects on dopaminergic projections from the substantia nigra pars compacta to the striatum (Roth & Meltzer, 1995). Although effects are complex, 5-HT inhibits dopaminergic transmission in many brain regions (Stahl & Kunovac, 1995; Yamaguchi, Mabeshima, & Kameyama, 1986). The importance of this observation is the related demonstration that dopamine stimulation at the D_1 receptor activates the direct pathway preferentially. In complementary fashion, stimulation at the D_2-type receptor deactivates the indirect pathway (Gerfen et al., 1990). Significantly, drug stimulation of D_1 receptors with the relatively selective agonist SKF 38393 evokes nonstereotypic species-typical grooming activity in the rodent (Murray & Waddington, 1989). This same D_1 agonist is reported to selectively activate LCMRGlc in the substantia nigra and endopeduncular nucleus (part of the direct basal ganglia pathway), compared to a D_2 agonist that does not (Trugman & Wooten, 1987).

Repetitive grooming and other hygienic behaviors are commonly seen in OCD patients. D_1 receptors are most dense in the ventral anterior caudate and D_2 receptors may be more dense in the dorsolateral striatal elements (Hall et al., 1994). Both, but especially D_1 receptors, are expressed on the dendrites of striatal medium-sized spiny neurons that are typical of the GABA output neurons in the brain. As shown in Figs. 28.4 and 28.12, orbital cortex and LPFC project differentially into these caudate nucleus territories. Dopamine acting on different regions of the striatum will have opposing effects on direct and indirect pathway balance.

It has been reported that dopamine D_2 blocking drugs are particularly helpful when added to SRIs in OCD patients with comorbid TS (McDougle et al., 1994). We have proposed that TS might preferentially involve the dorsal lateral striatum and ventral putamen, where D_2 receptors are abundant (Baxter et al., 1990). Given our model (Figs. 28.5 and 28.12), we predict that OCD, uncomplicated by TS, would show improved response when low doses of selective D_1 dopamine blockers are added to SRIs. Few selective (and otherwise safe) D_1 blockers exist at present, however.

Given the many possibilities for the cortical and basal ganglia sites of 5-HT dynamic changes that might mediate the response of OCD symptoms to SRI treatment, further work is clearly indicated. Based on findings in more simple animal systems, we have also suggested that changes in 5-HT system dynamics might also be involved in the response of OCD to behavioral deconditioning treatments using ERP methods (Baxter et al., 1992).

Future comparison studies of the effects of both SRIs and behavior modification on glutamatergic, GABAergic, and serotonergic dynamics within the orbital versus LPCF cortico-basal ganglionic-thalamic subchannels seem likely to provide important treatment insights for OCD, TS, and related major depressions. Animal and human PET studies, with tomographs having sufficient resolution to distinguish the globus pallidus interna from the globus pallidus externa, might be undertaken using these strategies.

ACKNOWLEDGMENTS

This research was supported, in part, by grants from the U.S. Department of Energy, the National Institute of Mental Health, the W. M. Keck Foundation, the Charles Dana Foundation, the National Alliance for Research on Schizophrenia and Affective Disorders, CTI, Inc., donations from Mr. and Mrs. Brian Harvey, Mr. Albert Levenson, Ms. Jennifer Jones Simon, and the Judson Braun Chair of Psychiatry at UCLA, and the Kathy Ireland Chair for Psychiatric Research at UAB.

This work was presented in part, at the American College of Neuropsychopharmacology, Annual Meeting, San Juan, PR, December 1995, and the Society of Biological Psychiatry Annual Meeting, New York, May 1996, as well as the conference related to this volume.

Technical assistance was provided by Mr. Wrother Meredith for electrode implantations and tissue sectioning, and Mr. Vaughn Davis for tissue sectioning.

We are indebted to many colleagues, but especially to Ms. Karron Martin-Maidment for critical involvement in the many UCLA PET studies cited. Drs. Judith Rapoport, Susan Swedo, Thomas Insel, Chalki Benkelfat, Jeffrey Cummings, D. Frank Benson, and Joaquin Fuster gave critical, formative comments over many years while we were developing these ideas.

We would especially like to acknowledge the late Dr. Daniel X. Freedman, whose constant encouragement and tough, constructive criticism contributed greatly to the implementation of the studies, and development of the theoretical ideas, presented here.

REFERENCES

Ackermann, R. F., Finch, D. M., Babb, T. L., & Engel, J. (1984). Increased glucose metabolism during long-duration recurrent inhibition of hippocampal pyramidal cells. *Journal of Neuroscience, 4,* 251–264.

Albin, R. L., Young, A. B., & Penney, J. B. (1989). The functional anatomy of basal ganglia disorders. *Trends in Neuroscience, 12,* 366–375.

Alexander, G. E., & Crutcher, M. D. (1989). Functional architecture of basal ganglia circuits: Neuronal substrates of parallel processing. *Trends in Neuroscience, 12,* 266–271.

Alexander, G. E., DeLong, M. R., & Strick, P. L. (1986). Parallel organization of functionally segregated circuits linking basal ganglia and cortex. *Annual Review of Neuroscience,* 357–381.

Amalric, M., Farin, D., Dormont, J. F., & Schmied, A. (1994). GABA-receptor activation in the globus pallidus and endopeduncular nucleus: Opposite effects on reaction time performance in the cat. *Experimental Brain Research, 102,* 244–258.

Baer, L., & Minichiello, W. E. (1990). Behavior therapy for obsessive compulsive disorder. In M. A. Jenike, L. Baer, & W. E. Minichiello (Eds.), *Obsessive-compulsive disorders: Theory and management* (2nd ed., pp. 203–232). Chicago: Year Book.

Baxter, L. R. (1992). Neuroimaging studies of obsessive-compulsive disorder. *Psychiatric Clinics of North America, 15*, 871–884.

Baxter, L. R. (1995). Neuroimaging studies of human anxiety disorders: Cutting paths of knowledge through the field of neurotic phenomena. In F. Bloom & D. Kupfer (Eds.), *Neuropsychopharmacology: The 4th generation of progress* (pp. 1287–1299). New York: Raven.

Baxter, L. R., & Guze, B. H. (1993). Neuroimaging in Tourette's and related disorders. In R. Kurland (Ed.), *Handbook of Tourette's syndrome and related tic and behavioral disorders* (pp. 289–304). Paris: Marcel Dekker.

Baxter, L. R., Phelps, M. E., Mazziotta, J. C., Guze, B. H., Schwartz, J. M., & Selin, C. E. (1987). Local cerebral glucose metabolic rates in obsessive-compulsive disorder: A comparison with rates in unipolar depression and normal controls. *Archives of General Psychiatry, 44*, 211–218.

Baxter, L. R., Phelps, M. E., Mazziotta, J. C., Schwartz, J. M., Gerner, R. H., Selin, C. E., & Sumida, R. M. (1985). Cerebral metabolic rates for glucose in mood disorder studies with positron emission tomography and fluorodeoxyglucose F-18. *Archives of General Psychiatry, 42*, 441–447.

Baxter, L. R., Saxena, S., Brody, A. L., Ackermann, R. F., Colgan, M., Schwartz, J. M., Allen-Martinez, Z., Fuster, J. M., & Phelps, M. E. (1996). Brain mediation of obsessive-compulsive disorder symptoms: Evidence from functional brain imaging studies in the human and non-human primate. *Seminars in Clinical Neuropsychiatry, 1*, 32–47.

Baxter, L. R., Schwartz, J. M., Bergman, K. S., Szuba, M. P., Guze, B. H., Mazziotta, J. C., Alazraki, A., Selin, C. E., Ferng, H.-K., Munford, P., & Phelps, M. E. (1992). Caudate glucose metabolic rate changes with both drug and behavior therapy for obsessive-compulsive disorder. *Archives of General Psychiatry, 49*, 681–689.

Baxter, L. R., Schwartz, J. M., & Guze, B. H. (1991). Brain imaging: Toward a functional neuroanatomy of OCD. In J. Zohar, T. Insel, & S. Rasmussen (Eds.), *The psychobiology of obsessive-compulsive disorder.* New York: Springer.

Baxter, L. R., Schwartz, J. M., Guze, B. H., Bergman, K., & Szuba, M. P. (1990). Neuroimaging in obsessive-compulsive disorders: Seeking the mediating neuroanatomy. In M. A. Jenike, L. Baer, & W. E. Minichiello (Eds.), *Obsessive-compulsive disorders: Theory and management* (2nd ed., pp. 167–188). Chicago: Year Book.

Baxter, L. R., Schwartz, J. M., Phelps, M. E., Mazziotta, J. C., Guze, B. H., Selin, C. E., Gerner, R. H., & Sumida, R. M. (1989). Reduction of prefrontal cortex glucose metabolism common to three types of depression. *Archives of General Psychiatry, 46*, 243–250.

Benkelfat, C., Nordahl, T. E., Semple, W. E., King, C., Murphy, D. L., & Cohen, R. M. (1990). Local cerebral glucose metabolic rates in obsessive-compulsive disorder: Patients treated with clomipramine. *Archives of General Psychiatry, 47*, 840–848.

Brutus, M., Watson, R. E., Shaikh, M. B., Siegel, H. E., Weiner, S., & Siegel, A. (1984). A [^{14}C]2-deoxyglucose analysis of the functional neuronal pathways of the limbic forebrain in the rat: IV. A pathway from the prefrontal cortical-medial thalamic system to the hypothalamus. *Brain Research, 310*, 279–293.

Drevets, W. C., Videen, T. O., Price, J. L., Preskorn, S. H., Carmichael, T., & Raichle, M. E. (1992). A functional anatomical study of unipolar depression. *Journal of Neuroscience, 12*, 3628–3641.

Eblen, F., & Graybiel, A. M. (1992). Striosome/matrix affiliations of prefronto-striatal projections in the monkey. *Society for Neuroscience Abstracts, 18*, 390.

Eblen, F., & Graybiel, A. M. (1995). Highly restricted origin of prefrontal cortical inputs to striosomes in the macaque monkey. *Journal of Neuroscience, 15*, 5999–6013.

Eichenbaum, H., Clegg, R. A., & Feeley, A. (1983). Reexamination of functional subdivisions of the rodent prefrontal cortex. *Experimental Neurology, 79*, 434–451.

El Mansari, M., Bouchard, C., & Blier, P. (1995). Alteration of serotonin release in the guinea pig orbito-frontal cortex by selective serotonin reuptake inhibitors. *Neuropsychopharmacology, 13*, 117–127.

Fuster, J. M. (1989). *The prefrontal cortex* (2nd ed.). New York: Raven.

George, M. S., Ketter, T. A., & Post, R. M. (1994). Prefrontal cortex dysfunction in clinical depression. *Depression, 2,* 59–72.

Gerfen, C. R. (1992). The neostriatal mosaic: Multiple levels of compartmental organization in the basal ganglia. *Annual Review of Neuroscience, 15,* 285–320.

Gerfen, C. R., Engber, T. M., Mahan, L. C., Susel, Z., Chase, T. N., Nonsama, F. J., & Sibley, D. R. (1990). D1 and D2 dopamine receptor-regulated gene expression of striatonigral and striatopallidal neurons. *Science, 250,* 1429–1432.

Goodman, S. I., & Frerman, F. E. (1995). Organic acidemias due to defects in lysine oxidation: 2-ketoadipic acidemia and glutaric acidemia. In C. R. Scruver, A. L. Beaudet, W. S. Sly, & D. Valle (Eds.), *The metabolic and molecular bases of inherited disease* (7th ed., pp. 1451–1460). New York: McGraw-Hill.

Goodman, W. K., McDougle, C. J., & Price, L. H. (1990). Beyond the serotonin hypothesis: A role for dopamine in some forms of obsessive-compulsive disorder? *Journal of Clinical Psychiatry, 51*(Suppl.), 36–43, 55–58.

Graybiel, A. M., Aosaki, T., Flaherty, A. W., & Kimura, M. (1994). The basal ganglia and adaptive motor control. *Science, 265,* 1826–1831.

Hall, H., Sedvall, G., Magnusson, O., Kopp, J., Halldin, C., & Farde, L. (1994). Distribution of D_1 and D_2-dopamine receptors, and dopamine and its metabolites in the human brain. *Neuropsychopharmacology, 11,* 245–256.

Heimer, L., Alheid, G. F., & Zaborsky, L. (1985). The basal ganglia. In G. Paxinos (Ed.), *The rat nervous system* (Vol. 1, pp. 37–86). Sydney: Academic Press.

Heyes, M. P. (1987). Hypothesis: A role for quinolinic acid in the neuropathology of glutaric aciduria type I. *Canadian Journal of Neurology Science, 14,* 441.

Insel, T. R. (1988). Obsessive-compulsive disorder: A neuroethological perspective. *Psychopharmacological Bulletin, 24,* 365–369.

Insel, T. R. (1992). Toward a neuroanatomy of obsessive-compulsive disorder. *Archives of General Psychiatry, 49,* 739–744.

Iversen, S. D. (1984). Behavioral aspects of cortico-subcortical interaction with special reference to frontostriatal relations. In G. Reinoso-Suarez & C. Ajmone-Marsan (Eds.), *Cortical integration.* New York: Raven.

Janet, P., & Raymond, F. (1903). *Les obsessions et la psychasthenie.* Paris: Felix Alcan.

Joel, D., & Weinger, J. (1994). The organization of the basal ganglia thalamocortical circuits: Open interconnected rather than closed segregated. *Neuroscience, 63,* 363–379.

MacLean, P. D. (1990). *The triune brain in evolution.* New York: Plenum.

McDougle, C. J., Goodman, W. K., Leckman, J. F., Lee, N. C., Heninger, G. R., & Price, L. H. (1994). Haloperidol addition in fluvoxamine-refractory obsessive-compulsive disorder. *Archives of General Psychiatry, 51,* 302–308.

Mega, M., & Cummings, J. L. (1994). Frontal-subcortical circuits and neuropsychiatric disorders. *Journal of Neuropsychiatry and Clinical Neuroscience, 6,* 358–370.

Modell, J. G., Mountz, J. M., Curtis, G. C., & Greden, J. F. (1989). Neurophysiologic dysfunction in basal ganglia/limbic striatial and thalamo-cortical circuits as a pathogenetic mechanism of obsessive-compulsive disorder. *Journal of Neuropsychiatry, 1,* 27–36.

Morris, B. J., Reiner, S., Hollt, V., & Herz, A. (1988). Regulation of striatal prodynorphin mRNA levels by the raphe-striatal pathway. *Molecular Brain Research, 4,* 15–22.

Murray, A. M., & Waddington, J. L. (1989). The induction of grooming and vacuous chewing by a series of selective D-1 dopamine receptor agonists: Two directions of D-1:D-2 interaction. *European Journal of Pharmacology, 160,* 377–384.

Nauta, W. J. H., & Domesick, V. B. (1984). Afferent and efferent relationships of the basal ganglia. In *Functions of the basal ganglia: CIBA foundation symposium (No. 107,* pp. 3–29). London: Pitman.

Parent, A. (1986). *Comparative neurobiology of the basal ganglia.* New York: Wiley.

Parent, A., Cote, P.-Y., & Lavoie, B. (1995). Chemical anatomy of primate basal ganglia. *Progress in Neurobiology, 46,* 131–197.

Parent, A., & Hazrati, L.-N. (1995a). Functional anatomy of the basal ganglia: I. The cortico-basal ganglia-thalamo-cortico loop. *Brain Research Reviews, 20,* 91–127.

Parent, A., & Hazrati, L.-N. (1995b). Functional anatomy of the basal ganglia: II. The place of subthalamic nucleus and external pallidum in basal ganglia circuitry. *Brain Research Reviews, 20,* 128–154.

Pauls, D. L., & Leckman, J. F. (1986). The inheritance of Gilles de la Tourette's syndrome and associated behaviors: Evidence for autosomal dominant transmission. *New England Journal of Medicine, 315,* 993–997.

Phelps, M. E., Mazziotta, J. C., & Schelbert, H. R. (1986). *Positron emission tomography and autoradiography.* New York: Raven.

Rapoport, J. L., & Wise, S. P. (1988). Obsessive-compulsive disorder: Is it a basal ganglia dysfunction? *Psychopharmacology Bulletin, 24,* 380–384.

Rauch, S. L., Jenike, M. A., Alpert, N. A., Baer, L., Breiter, H. C. R., & Fischman, A. J. (1994). Regional cerebral blood flow measured during symptom provocation in obsessive-compulsive disorder using 15O-labeled CO_2 and positron emission tomography. *Archives of General Psychiatry, 51,* 62–70.

Raymond, J. L., Lisberger, S. G., & Mauk, M. D. (1996). The cerebellum: A neuronal learning machine. *Science, 272,* 1126–1131.

Roth, B. L., & Meltzer, H. Y. (1995). The role of serotonin in schizophrenia. In F. E. Bloom & D. J. Kupfer (Eds.), *Psychopharmacology: The fourth generation of progress* (pp. 1215–1227). New York: Raven Press.

Schwartz, J. M., Stoessel, P. W., Baxter, L. R., Martin, K. M., & Phelps, M. E. (1996). Systematic cerebral glucose metabolic rate changes after successful behavior modification treatment of obsessive-compulsive disorder. *Archives of General Psychiatry, 53,* 109–113.

Stahl, S. M., & Kunovac, J. L. (1995). Neurotransmitter systems in obsessive-compulsive disorder. *Psychiatry, 95,* 349–378.

Swedo, S. E., Rapoport, J. L., Cheslow, D. L., Leonard, H. L., Ayoub, E. M., Hosier, D. M., & Wald, E. R. (1989). High prevalence of obsessive-compulsive symptoms in patients with Sydenham's chorea. *American Journal of Psychiatry, 146,* 246–249.

Swerdlow, N. R. (1995). Serotonin, obsessive compulsive disorder and the basal ganglia. *International Review of Psychiatry, 7,* 115–129.

Trugman, J. M., & Wooten, G. F. (1987). Selective D_1 and D_2 dopamine agonists differentially alter basal ganglia glucose utilization in rats with unilateral 6-hydroxydopamine substantia nigra lesions. *Journal of Neuroscience, 7,* 2927–2935.

Uylings, H. B. M., & van Eden, C. G. (1990). Qualitative and quantitative comparison of the prefrontal cortex in rat and in primates, including humans. *Progress in Brain Research, 85,* 31–62.

Yamaguchi, K., Mabeshima, T., & Kameyama, T. (1986). Potentiation of phencyclidine-induced dopamine-dependent behaviors in rats after pretreatments with serotonin-depleters. *Journal of Pharmacokinetics and Biodynamics, 9,* 479–489.

About The Editors

Wayne K. Goodman is Professor and Chairman of the Department of Psychiatry at the University of Florida College of Medicine in Gainesville, Florida. In 1985, after completing his psychiatry training at Yale University School of Medicine, Dr. Goodman established the Yale Obsessive-Compulsive Disorder (OCD) Clinic. Dr. Goodman served as a faculty member at Yale until he relocated in 1993 to the University of Florida, where he conducts research on the neurobiology and treatment of OCD, Tourette's Syndrome, and related disorders. He is the principal developer of the Yale–Brown Obsessive-Compulsive Scale (Y–BOCS), author of over 100 articles and chapters, and past Chairman of the Scientific Advisory Board to the national Obsessive-Compulsive Foundation, Inc., of which he was co-founder.

Jack D. Maser is Professor of Psychiatry at the University of California, San Diego, formerly Chief of the Clinical Review Branch at the National Institute of Mental Health (NIMH). He has pioneered the emergence of comorbidity as an important issue in diagnosis and classification, and is now working with a group of clinical investigators at the University of Pisa, Italy, on spectrum concepts in psychiatric diagnosis. He has been the NIMH coordinator of the five-site NIMH Collaborative Depression Study. His career spans teaching, basic and clinical research, and research administration. His clinical publications include edited books and papers on the classification of mental illness, anxiety, depression, and personality disorders.

Matthew V. Rudorfer is Assistant Chief of the Clinical Treatment Research Branch at the National Institute of Mental Health. A psychiatrist and psychopharmacologist, Dr. Rudorfer's research has focused on the psychobiology and somatic treatment of mood, anxiety, and related disorders. Much of his work has dealt with the development of new psychotropic medications, and the relation of the mechanisms of action of pharmacological and other biological treatments to the pathophysiology of mental disorders. An expert in drug metabolism, Dr. Rudorfer's publications and presentations on antidepressant pharmacokinetics in Asian volunteers have been at the forefront of the modern study of pharmacogenetics in psychopharmacology. He leads the Institute's research program in electroconvulsive therapy and is Editor-in-Chief of the *Psychopharmacology Bulletin*.

Author Index

619

635

Subject Index

A

Adaptive functioning, 54–55
Adrenergic antidepressants, 306–308
Age at onset, 29, 88–91, 354
Alprazolam, 411–412
Anticonvulsive agents, 353
Antidepressants, 31, 32, *see also specific drugs and drug classes*
   serotonergic *vs.* adrenergic, 306–308
   switching, 337–339
Anxiety, 405
   need to alleviate, 4
Anxiety-based OC spectrum disorders, 4–5
Anxiety disorders
   benzodiazepines for, 406
   cognitive biases in, 106
   cognitive mechanisms of, 119–121
   comorbid, 257–259
      and treatment outcome, 189–191, 265–266, 269
   panic disorder, 304, 338, 411
Anxiety Disorders Interview Schedule (ADIS), 158–159
Anxiety symptoms, 189–191
   assessment, 158–159, 189–190
Arginine vasopressin (AVP), 57
Assessment, 157–158, 176–177
   of anxiety symptoms, 158–159, 189–190
   behavioral observation, 174–176
   clinical interviews, 158–164
   of depressive symptoms, 191–192
   diagnostic interviews, 158–160, 193–194

and drug treatment outcome, 189–195
   Likert scales, 172–174
   of outcome in drug trials, 183–189, 194–195
   rating scales, 172–174, 189–194
   self-report instruments, 164–172
Association circuits, 56
Assumptions, 211–212, *see also* Beliefs; Cognitions
Attention
   dysfunctional, 108–109, 113–114
   selective, 120
Attentional bias, 106–108, 113–114, 120
Autism, clomipramine for, 327–328
Autoimmune process, infection-triggered, 354

B

Basal ganglia, 472
Basal ganglia out-put, 583, 584
Basal ganglia systems, 575–586, 593–596
   comorbid depression and, 598, 599
Behavioral assessment, 174–176
Behavioral Avoidance Test (BAT), 174–176
Behavioral models, 204–205
Behavioral monitoring, 176
Behavioral treatment, 9, 10, 117, 237–238, 257–258, 533–535, 544–546, *see also* Cognitive-behavioral therapy; Exposure
   for body dysmorphic disorder, 240–241
   combined drug therapy and, 490–496, 507–509, 522–525

653